Pits and Boots

Pits and Boots

Excavation of medieval and post-medieval backlands under the Bon Accord Centre, Aberdeen

Michael Roy

Archaeopress Archaeology

ARCHAEOPRESS PUBLISHING LTD
Summertown Pavilion
18-24 Middle Way
Summertown
Oxford OX2 7LG

www.archaeopress.com

ISBN 978-1-78969-487-1
ISBN 978-1-78969-488-8 (e-Pdf)

Front cover: Boxwood knife handle SF3134A, decorated with a monocerus, a mythical beast, a hybrid of several animals in particular a rhinoceros and a unicorn.

Back cover: Gordon of Rothiemay's map of Aberdeen, 1661 (Reproduced with the permission of the National Library of Scotland and under Creative Commons (CC BY 4.0) https://creativecommons.org/licenses/by/4.0/)

This publication is made available in Open Access through funding by AOC Archaeology Group

This book is available direct from Archaeopress or from our website www.archaeopress.com

Contents

List of Figures iii

Acknowledgements x

List of Contributors xi

Preface xii

1 Introduction 1
    1.1 Background to the archaeological works 1
    1.2 The site and its setting 1
    1.3 The archaeological works of 2007–08 1
    1.4 Previous archaeological investigations around Gallowgate and Upperkirkgate 3
    1.5 Dating and the chronology of the site 5
    1.6 Structure of the monograph 9
    1.7 The ceramic assemblage 10

2 Summary of Archaeological Remains by Phase 11
    2.1 Introduction 11
    2.2 Phase 1 – mid-to-late 12th century (figure 2.3) 11
    2.3 Phase 2 – late 12th to mid 13th century (figure 2.14) 17
    2.4 Phase 3 – mid-to-late 13th century(figure 2.41) 24
    2.5 Phase 4 (early) – late 13th to 14th century (figure 2.53) 31
    2.6 Phase 4 (late) – 14th to early 15th century (figure 2.62) 33
    2.7 Phase 5 (early) – 15th to 16th century (figure 2.66) 38
    2.8 Phase 5 (mid) – 15th to 16th century (figure 2.68) 40
    2.9 Phase 5 (late) – 15th/16th to mid-to-late 18th century (figure 2.74) 43
    2.10 Phase 6 – mid-to-late 18th to 20th century (figure 2.78) 48

3 Presentation of Artefactual and Ecofactual Evidence by Phase and Feature 52
    3.1 Introduction 52
    3.2 Phase 1 (mid-to-late 12th century) (figure 2.3) 52
    3.3 Phase 2 (late 12th to mid 13th century) (figure 2.14) 62
    3.4 Phase 3 (mid-to-late 13th century) (figure 2.41) 76
    3.5 Phase 4 (early) (late 13th to 14th century) (figure 2.53) 82
    3.6 Phase 4 (late) (14th to early 15th century) (figure 2.63 & Table 3.4) 84
    3.7 Phase 5 (early) (15th to 16th century) (figure 2.66) 87
    3.8 Phase 5 (mid) (15th to 16th century) (figure 2.68 & Table 3.5) 90
    3.9 Phase 5 (late) (15th/16th to mid-to-late 18th century) (figure 2.74 & Table 3.5) 94

4 Specialist Reports – Summaries of the Evidence 96
    4.1 Dating evidence 96
        4.1.1 Dendrochronology 96
    4.2 Organic artefacts 100
        4.2.1 Wooden artefacts 100
        4.2.2 Leatherwork 130
        4.2.3 Textiles 144
        4.2.4 Animal pelts and fibres 146
        4.2.5 Cordage 148
    4.3 Inorganic artefacts 149
        4.3.1 Metal artefacts 149
        4.3.2 Worked stone 177
        4.3.3 Lithics 183
        4.3.4 Vessel glass 185
        4.3.5 Crucibles 187
        4.3.6 Clay mould fragments 188

4.3.7 Industrial residues..192
4.3.8 Miscellaneous finds...195
4.3.9 Clay tobacco pipes 201
4.4 Structural materials...201
4.4.1 Structural timber...201
4.4.2 Ceramic building material 205
4.4.3 Window glass...206
4.4.4 Socketed stone 207
4.5 Ecofact analyses...208
4.5.1 Macroplant remains..208
4.5.2 Mammal bone..214
4.5.3 Bird bone..221
4.5.4 Fish bone..222
4.5.5 Insects...238
4.5.6 Soil micromorphology...239

5 Discussion: The Site in Its Context...242
5.1 The origins of Upperkirkgate and Gallowgate (phases 1 to 3) 242
5.2 Industrial activity in the medieval gallowgate (phases 1 to 4) 245
5.2.1 Leatherworking and associated processes 246
5.2.2 Other industrial processes 248
5.3 Late medieval and early post-medieval properties (phase 4 to mid phase 5) 250
5.4 Later post-medieval occupation: the gardens of aberdeen (mid-to-late phase 5)........................252
5.5 Later post-medieval occupation: houses of the gentry (late phase 5) 254
5.6 The late 18th century onwards: expansion of commerce and industry (phase 6)..........................256
5.7 Late 19th and 20th century development 257

6 Conclusions 260

References...264

Appendices...276
1 Radiocarbon dating programme 276
2 Ceramic building materials...279
3 Macroplant remains 285
4 Fish bone 311
5 Ceramics 330

List of Figures

1 Introduction

Figure 1.1 Location of Bon Accord Centre archaeological works, and previous archaeological works in the Gallowgate/Upperkirkgate area 2

Figure 1.2 Excavation area, showing evaluation trenches and location of long sections 3

Figure 1.3 Schematic reconstruction of putative early plot layout at Upperkirkgate/Gallowgate corner (reproduced with the permission of the National Library of Scotland and under Creative Commons (CC BY 4.0) https://creativecommons.org/licenses/by/4.0/) 4

2 Summary of Archaeological Remains by Phase

Figure 2.1 Working behind Gallowgate frontage from the south-west 11

Figure 2.2 Working in heavily truncated area behind Upperkirkgate frontage 11

Figure 2.3 Plan of Phase 1 features 12

Figure 2.4 Sections across Phase 1 features in east of site: 13

Figure 2.5 North-facing section of Pits C004; C005; C006 and C007 14

Figure 2.6 North-facing section of Pit C006 14

Figure 2.7 Pit C007 from west, showing Stakes C001 14

Figure 2.8 Gully C001 from north 15

Figure 2.9 Detail of horse skull with articulated vertebrae in Pit C015 15

Figure 2.10 Sections across Phase 1 features in west of site: 16

Figure 2.11 Pit A030, half-sectioned, from west. Platter SF3743 can be seen protruding from the section 16

Figure 2.12 Detail of possible remnant lining of Pit A026 from east 16

Figure 2.13 Stone line, Wall B001, from east 17

Figure 2.14 Plan of Phase 2 features 18

Figure 2.15 West-south-west-facing section of Stakes C002 18

Figure 2.16 Stakes C003 from east 18

Figure 2.17 Sections across Phase 2 features in east of site 19

Figure 2.18 Base of Wall C001 from north 20

Figure 2.19 Post-excavation view of Pit C018 from north-east 20

Figure 2.20 North-facing section of Pit C019 20

Figure 2.21 East-facing section of Pit C034 20

Figure 2.22 Plan and south-east-facing section of Pit C025 showing hurdle screen (SF3100) 21

Figure 2.23 Pit C025 during excavation, from south 21

Figure 2.24 Fragment of wooden platter in Pit C025 22

Figure 2.25 Wooden paddle in fill of Pit C025 22

Figure 2.26 Hurdle screen in Pit C025 from east 22

Figure 2.27 Structural timbers under hurdle screen in Pit C025 22

Figure 2.28 Sections across Phase 2 features in north-east of site 23

Figure 2.29 Detail of possible lining remnant in Pit C031 23

Figure 2.30 Sections across Phase 2 features to the west of Wall C001 23

Figure 2.31 Pit C026, half-sectioned, from north 24

Figure 2.32 North-facing section of Pit C037 24

Figure 2.33 East-facing section of Pit C027 and Gully C004 24

Figure 2.34 Pit C027, following excavation, from east 24

Figure 2.35 Plan and east-facing section of Well C001 25

Figure 2.36 Sections across Phase 2 features in west of site...25

Figure 2.37 Barrel of Well C001 from west 26

Figure 2.38 Half-section of barrel of Well C001 from west 26

Figure 2.39 South-facing section through stone superstructure of Well C001 26

Figure 2.40 Top of barrel, lined with stone, of Well C001 from south 26

Figure 2.41 Plan of Phase 3 features 27

Figure 2.42 Sections across Phase 3 features 28

Figure 2.43 East-facing section of Pit C042 29

Figure 2.44 Surface C002 from south 29

Figure 2.45 West-facing section of Hearth C001...29

Figure 2.46 North-facing section of Hearth C001...29

Figure 2.47 Plan and north-facing section of Hearth C002...30

Figure 2.48 Capping of Hearth C001 from south-east 30

Figure 2.49 Hearth C002 from west 30

Figure 2.50 Articulated fish vertebrae within fill of Pit C069...31

Figure 2.51 Plan, south-facing section and east-facing elevation of Well A002 32

Figure 2.52 Well A002 from south 33

Figure 2.53 Plan of early Phase 4 features 34

Figure 2.54 East-facing section behind Gallowgate 35

Figure 2.55 Central south-facing section behind Gallowgate 35

Figure 2.56 Central north-facing section behind Gallowgate 36

Figure 2.57 Plan of Oven C002 36

Figure 2.58 Oven C002 from west...37

Figure 2.59 Plan of Oven C001 37

Figure 2.60 Oven C001 from north...37

Figure 2.61 South-facing section of west of site...38

Figure 2.62 Plan of late Phase 4 features 39

Figure 2.63 Composite south-facing section at south of site, showing Pit C063B and Pit C064..................40

Figure 2.64 Post-excavation view of Pit C064 from east 40

Figure 2.65 South-facing section of Pit A024 and Well A001 41

Figure 2.66 Plan of early Phase 5 features...42

Figure 2.67 Structure C001 with capping removed from south 43

Figure 2.68 Plan of mid Phase 5 features...44

Figure 2.69 Drainage Structure C006 from east...45

Figure 2.70 West-facing section of Pit C070 45

Figure 2.71 Smithing waste, Spread C021/C022, from east 46

Figure 2.72 Well A001 from north-east...46

Figure 2.73 Surface A002 from west 46

Figure 2.74 Plan of late Phase 5 features 47

Figure 2.75 Surface C012 from north 48

Figure 2.76 Pit C080 from north-east 48

Figure 2.77 Structure A019 from north 49

Figure 2.78 Plan of Phase 6 features 50

Figure 2.79 Well C002 from south 51

4 Specialist Reports – Summaries of the Evidence

Figure 4.1 Bar diagram showing the chronological relationships between the dated oak timbers from Bon Accord 98

Figure 4.2 Turned wooden bowls; SF3884; SF3935; SF3085; SF3681; SF4294 102

Figure 4.3 Turned wooden bowls; SF3567; SF3567 base; SF4012; SF1546A 103

Figure 4.4 Turned wooden platters; SF3061; SF3743; SF2842; SF3840 105

Figure 4.5 Spindle-turned objects; SF3185; SF4584 106

Figure 4.6 Stave-built objects: casks and tub elements; C001-Stave 10; SF3562; SF3737; SF3564; SF3745 106

Figure 4.7 Stave-built objects: tankards; SF3324; SF2931 107

Figure 4.8 Tools: shovel blades; SF3359; SF3361; SF3693 109

Figure 4.9 Tools: distinct blades; SF3417; SF3630; SF3210; SF3713; SF3911C 111

Figure 4.10 Tools: scrapers/ rakes and handles; SF3911B; SF4099, SF3084B; SF3134B 112

Figure 4.11 Tools: handles and shaft of grinding mechanism; SF2583 113

Figure 4.12 Miscellaneous wooden artefacts; SF3337; SF3558; SF3631 114

Figure 4.13 Miscellaneous wooden artefacts; SF3825; SF3010 (with lead object SF3011 attached) 115

Figure 4.14 Miscellaneous wooden artefacts; SF3421A; SF3350A; SF3421B; SF3292; SF3476; SF3073; SF1546B; SF1513A 116

Figure 4.15 Decorated wooden handle; SF3134A 128

Figure 4.16 Upper: The reverse of a St John the Baptist pilgrim badge from Amiens Cathedral, bearing an equal-armed cross with expanded terminals against a cross-hatched background. Courtesy Perth Museum & Art Gallery; 129

Figure 4.17 Shoe soles; SF4196; SF3709A; SF2952; SF4176A; SF3500; SF3151A; SF3868 131

Figure 4.18 Shoe uppers; reconstructions of SF4178 (two variations of lacing are shown) & SF2875 133

Figure 4.19 Shoe uppers; reconstructions of SF2755 & SF4733 134

Figure 4.20 Scabbard SF4057 135

Figure 4.21 Sheaths, straps & decorated leather; knife sheath SF4793A; straps SF1430A; SF4793B; SF14A, B & C; decorated fragment SF1430B 136

Figure 4.22 Clothing; sleeve SF4159 137

Figure 4.23 Textile (SF4056) from Pit C032 showing remains of stitching and circular holes, where decorative metal studs may have been attached 145

Figure 4.24 Upper; hairmoss plait SF3286A; fibre bundles protrude mid-way along the plait and at the lefthand end where it curves back on itself. Note the plaited string that has been threaded through the plait 148

Figure 4.25 Miscellaneous iron objects; SF1917; SF1598B; SF1607; SF2328; SF2648; SF1628A; SF1075; SF2356 151

Figure 4.26 Tools and knives; SF1394; SF2077; SF3525C; SF4207A; SF4280; SF3525B; SF2179B 153

Figure 4.27 Padlocks and keys; SF361; SF4794 and isometric reconstruction 158

Figure 4.28 Copper alloy brooches and pins; SF3463; SF1133; SF2736; SF2988 165

Figure 4.29 Miscellaneous copper alloy objects; SF3301; SF2222; SF1780 ('locking buckle fragment); SF1600; SF549; SF172 167

Figure 4.30 The copper alloy spur SF659. The letters A, B and C refer to detailing shown in Figure 4.32 168

Figure 4.31 Detailing on the copper alloy spur SF659 168

Figure 4.32 The copper alloy trivet foot, SF6003 170

Figure 4.33 Lead objects; SF762, SF492, SF2286 175

Figure 4.34 Whetstones; SF4281; SF3083; SF3584; SF963 178

Figure 4.35 Spindle whorls; SF3849; SF3640; SF2845; SF2217 178

Figure 4.36 Grinding stones; SF2583; SF329 179

Figure 4.37 SF2583 as found, with handles and wedges in situ 179

Figure 4.38 Purbeck Limestone mortar 180

Figure 4.39 A Scottish mortar fragment; SF2393..181

Figure 4.40 Possible mortar fragment; SF2207 181

Figure 4.41 Lithics; SF4408; SF2085A; SF3014; SF2285A 184

Figure 4.42 Vessel glass; SF338; SF374A; SF374B; SF348 186

Figure 4.43 Two crucible sherds; left – SF1515, a base with plum coloured zinc enriched surface; right – SF3076.1, an almost complete profile showing its quartz rich fabric and interior surface............................187

Figure 4.44 Clay mould fragments; SF1221, SF3089, SF1168B and SF1168A, with positive view of design on SF1168B 189

Figure 4.45 Glass beads; top row from left – SF1861, SF6002, SF6016. Bottom row from left – SF6017 and SF6019 . 197

Figure 4.46 Upper; SF2781 – peg from possible dog tibia (Pit C018) 197

Figure 4.47 SF2977 – composite animal bone and leather artefact (Pit C004)...197

Figure 4.48 Ceramic spindle whorls; from left – SF2889X, SF3288 and SF1311X 198

Figure 4.49 Ceramic counters; top row from left – SF6028, SF4543X and SF3223X; bottom row from left – SF1407, SF2362 and SF6027 198

Figure 4.50 Species represented in the *in situ* structural timber assemblages..201

Figure 4.51 Re-used planking; SF3688 – plank with groove down one side and cutmarks on one face (Pit C025 fill C025D); SF3391 – plank shaped to tip at one end (Pit C025 fill C025D) 202

Figure 4.52 SF3671– plank with pinned holes down both sides (Pit C025 fill C025D) 203

Figure 4.53 Carpentry; plank SF3336 (Pit C037 fill C025D); timber SF3698 (Pit C025 fill C025D) 203

Figure 4.54 Carpentry; timber SF3976 (Pit C025 fill C025D) 204

Figure 4.55 205

Figure 4.56 SF1606; only the upper part of the stone which was recovered is illustrated here................................207

Figure 4.57 Upper; cereals recovered from Phases 1–5 by feature...209

Figure 4.58 Upper; vegetable remains recovered from Phases 1–5 by feature 210

Figure 4.59 Fishbone butchery marks (scale 1cm)...230

5 Discussion: the site in its context...**243**

Figure 5.1 Extract from Gordon of Rothiemay's map of Aberdeen, 1661 (Reproduced with the permission of the National Library of Scotland and under Creative Commons (CC BY 4.0) https://creativecommons.org/licenses/by/4.0/)..243

Figure 5.2 Extract from Alexander Milne's map, 1789 (Reproduced with the permission of the National Library of Scotland and under Creative Commons (CC BY 4.0) https://creativecommons.org/licenses/by/4.0/)..254

Figure 5.3 Extract from John Wood's map, 1828 (Reproduced with the permission of the National Library of Scotland and under Creative Commons (CC BY 4.0) https://creativecommons.org/licenses/by/4.0/)..255

Figure 5.4 Extract from Keith & Gibb's map, 1862 (Reproduced with the permission of the National Library of Scotland and under Creative Commons (CC BY 4.0) https://creativecommons.org/licenses/by/4.0/)..256

Figure 5.5 Extract from Ordnance Survey map, 1871 (Reproduced with the permission of the National Library of Scotland and under Creative Commons (CC BY 4.0) https://creativecommons.org/licenses/by/4.0/)..257

Figure 5.6 Extract from Ordnance Survey map, 1902 (Reproduced with the permission of the National Library of Scotland and under Creative Commons (CC BY 4.0) https://creativecommons.org/licenses/by/4.0/)..258

Appendices

Figure A.1.1 Oxcal graph showing distribution of radiocarbon dates from Bon Accord..278

Figure A.4.1 Cod size histograms, based on regression formulas applied to selected measurements 311

Figure A.4.2 Cod and ling minimum number of elements (MNE) for Phases 1 and 2, hand collected data only, taking into account fragmentation and number of elements in the body (lighter bars indicate the range of MNE for vertebrae, because there is natural variation in the numbers of vertebrae in cod and ling) 312

Figure A.5.1 Phase 1; 1–7 Local Redware 330

Figure A.5.2 Phase 1; 8–14 Scottish White Gritty Ware..331

Figure A.5.3 Phase 1; 15-19, 21 Stamford Ware; 22–27 Yorkshire Ware...332

Figure A.5.4.Phase 1; 28 North French redware? 29 Normandy Gritty? 30 Pingsdorf Ware. 31 Paffrath ladle. 32 Late Saxon/early medieval socketed bowl..333

Figure A5.5 Phase 2; 33–43 Local Redware 334

Figure A.5.6 Phase 2 & 2/3; 44–46 Local Redware. 47–55 Scottish White Gritty Ware. 56 Stamford Ware 335

Figure A.5.7 Phase 2; 57–64 Yorkshire Ware. 65–68 Scarborough Ware 1 336

Figure A.5.8 Phase 2; 69–70 Scarborough Ware 2. 71–77 East Anglian. 78 Paffrath cooking pot. 79 North French jug. 80 French Saintonge jug. 81 skillet unknown..337

Figure A.5.9 Phase 3 & 3/4; 82–91 Local Redware 338

Figure A.5.10 Phase 3 & 3/4; 92–94 Local Redware 339

Figure A.5.11 Phase 3 & 3/4; 95–98 Local Redware 340

Figure A.5.12 Phase 3 & 3/4; 99–103 Scottish White Gritty Ware. 104–110 Yorkshire Ware 341

Figure A.5.13 Phase 3 & 3/4; 111 – 113 Yorkshire ware. 114 -117 Scarborough Wares 1 & 2. 118 Low Countries Greyware. 119 French Gritty Ware. 120 jug unknown...342

Figure A.5.14 Phase 4; 121–131 Local Redware 343

Figure A.5.15 Phase 4; 132–138 Local Redware 344

Figure A.5.16 Phase 4 & 4/5; 139–142 Local Redware. 143–144 Scottish White Gritty Ware. 145–152 Yorkshire Ware...345

Figure A.5.17 Phase 4; 153–161 Scarborough Ware 1 & 2 346

Figure A.5.18 Phase 4 & 4/5; 162–163 North French. 164 French Rouen. 165–166 Low Countries Highly Decorated Ware. 167–168 Low Countries Greyware. 169–170 Low Countries Redware. 171 Siegburg Stoneware. 172 Langerwehe Stoneware. 173 East Anglian. 174 London Sandy. 175–176 unknown 347

Figure A.5.19 Phase 5; 177–187 Local Redware 348

Figure A.5.20 Phase 5 & 5/6; 188–191 Local Redware. 192 Scottish White Gritty Ware. 193 Yorkshire Whiteware. 194 Yorkshire Redware. 195 Yorkshire Sandy. 196–198 Scarborough Ware 1 & 2. 199 French Gritty Normandy? 200 North French. 201 French Beauvais 349

Figure A.5.21 Phase 5; 202 Martincamp. 203 French Rouen. 204 Siegburg Stoneware. 205–207 Raeren Stoneware. 208–209 Iberian Redware. 210–212 Valencian Lustreware. 213 Low Countries Greyware. 214–215 Low Countries Highly Decorated Ware. 216 Italian Scraffitto............................350

Figure A.5.22 Phases 5 & 6; 217–219 unknown. 220–221 Local Redware. 222–223 Scottish White Gritty Ware. 224 Scarborough Ware 1. 225–228 Low Countries Greyware. 229 Scottish Post-Medieval Oxidised Ware. 230 Siegburg Stoneware 351

Figure A.5.23 Modern; 231 Scottish White Gritty Ware. 232-235 Local Redware. 236 Cologne Stoneware. 238 Ball - bank? Unknown. 352

List of Tables

1 Introduction

Table 1.1 Phases 1-6; key dating evidence..6

3 Presentation of Artefactual and Ecofactual Evidence by Phase and Feature

Table 3.1 Phase 1; the artefact assemblages for key contexts and features (where quantified numbers of items are presented) 53

Table 3.2 Phase 2; the artefact assemblages for key contexts and features (where quantified numbers of items are presented) 63

Table 3.3 Phase 3; the artefact assemblages for key contexts and features (where quantified numbers of items are presented) 76

Table 3.4 Phase 4; the artefact assemblages for key contexts and features (where quantified numbers of items are presented) 83

Table 3.5 Phase 5; the artefact assemblages for key contexts and features (where quantified numbers of items are presented) 88

4 Specialist Reports – Summaries of the Evidence

Table 4.1 Dendrochronological data (arranged in order of date of feature). Key: B=bark edge; Bs= spring-felled; Bw=winter-felled; h/s=heartwood/sapwood boundary; sap= sapwood; unm= unmeasured rings 96

Table 4.2 Statistical correlations between BONACC38 and other chronologies....................................99

Table 4.3 Leather; offcuts by phase 138

Table 4.4 Leather; offcuts by feature and phase 138

Table 4.5 Textiles from Phases 1-4...144

Table 4.6 Animal fibres from Area C...147

Table 4.7 Summary of major non-modern iron artefacts 154

Table 4.8 Nail categories with dimensions..160

Table 4.9 Summary of major non-modern copper alloy artefacts 164

Table 4.10 Summary of major lead artefacts 174

Table 4.11 Crucible fragments identified during pottery assessment..187

Table 4.12 Total quantities of ferrous slag and other residues (weight g) 193

Table 4.13 Total quantities of slag amalgams (weight g) 193

Table 4.14 Total quantities of plano-convex slag cakes (weight g) 193

Table 4.15: Total quantities of unclassified slag (weight g)..193

Table 4.16 Mean dimensions of plano-convex slag cakes (weight g)..193

Table 4.17 Total quantities of slag microresidues (weight g)...194

Table 4.18 Summary of miscellaneous finds..196

Table 4.19 Dates for clay tobacco pipe fragments..200

Table 4.20 Number of identifiable specimens (NISP) count for mammals by phase...............................215

Table 4.21 Number of identifiable specimens (NISP) for bird bones by phase 221

Table 4.22 Fish bone; summary of bone counts per phase 223

Table 4.23 Fish bone; summary for major phases by taxa, hand collected and >2mm sieved 224

Table 4.24 Fish bone; butchery summary by taxa and element 229

Table 4.25 Fish pathology summary by phase and feature 233

Table 4.26 Fish bone; summary of comparative material from Castle Street, 16-18 Netherkirkgate, 30-46 Upperkirkgate, Gallowgate Middle School and 45-75 Gallowgate (Cameron and Stones 2001).......................237

Appendices

Table A1.1: Radiocarbon dating 277

Table A.2.1 Daub assemblage 279

Table A3.1 Phase 1 macroplant remains..285

Table A3.2 Phase 2 macroplant remains..291

Table A3.3 Phase 3 macroplant remains..297

Table A3.4 Phase 4 macroplant remains..302

Table A3.5 Phase 5 macroplant remains..306

Table A3.6: Moss species. 310

Table A.4.1 Summary of fish bone assemblage Phase 1, Pit C015...313

Table A.4.2: Summary of fish bone assemblance Phase 2, Layers C003 and C014.............................315

Table A.4.3 Taphonomic summary for all hand collected fish bone...318

Table A.4.4 Taphonomic summary for all sieved fish bone...319

Table A.4.5 Summary of hand collection by area, phase and taxa..320

Table A.4.6 Summary >2mm sieving by area, phase and taxa...321

Table A.4.7 Summary by minor phase group and taxa, hand collected and >2mm sieved 322

Table A.4.8 Summary of hand collected fish sizes, for major taxa and phases 323

Table A.4.9 Summary sieved fish sizes, for major taxa and phases..324

Table A.4.10 Fish element counts for major taxa...325

Table A.4.11 Fish element counts for minor taxa 328

Acknowledgements

The fieldwork and post-excavation programme, including this publication, was funded by The Scottish Retail Property Limited Partnership. The works were facilitated by them and their agents, Land Securities and SMC Jenkins & Marr Ltd. Essential help was also received by Adams Consulting and by Mansell, in particular Ian Bell, Project Manager at Mansell, who provided important advice on the construction programme and health and safety issues.

Helpful advice was received from Judith Stones, the former Keeper of Archaeology at Aberdeen City Council. Thanks are also due to the members of the excavation team, which came from the field section of AOC Archaeology Group, managed by Murray Cook and John Gooder, and the Aberdeen City Council Archaeology Unit under Alison Cameron. Particular thanks are due to the AOC supervisors: Stephen Keigthley, James Knowles, Gemma Midlane, Uyum Vehit and Krystof Kiniatkowski. Vicky Clements, senior supervisor, helped run the excavations, and undertook significant work on the upkeep of stratigraphic and other records; her input into the original data structure report was essential for the completion of this publication. Assistance was also gladly received from Lindsay Dunbar and Martin Cook, of AOC Archaeology.

Anne Crone and Ciara Clarke managed the post-excavation programme and a large team, from within AOC Archaeology and externally, were involved in bringing it to completion; the author would like to thank them all for their contributions.

Advice on the marine reservoir effect on radiocarbon samples was received from Dr Gordon Cook, of the Scottish Universities Environmental Research Centre in East Kilbride. Jackaline Robertson would like to thank Dr Allan Hall who provided advice on the assessment of the macroplant assemblage and Dr Phil Mills of the University of Leicester for advice on the ceramic building material (CBM) assemblage.

This publication has been ably edited by Dr Anne Crone. The manuscript was reviewed by Charles and Hilary Murray and its final shape owes much to their input.

List of Contributors

Michael Roy AOC Archaeology, Edgefield Road Industrial Estate, Loanhead, Midlothian, EH20 9SY
    Michael.Roy@aocarchaeology.com
Anne Crone AOC Archaeology, Edgefield Road Industrial Estate, Loanhead, Midlothian, EH20 9SY
    Anne.Crone@aocarchaeology.com
Rob Engl AOC Archaeology, Edgefield Road Industrial Estate, Loanhead, Midlothian, EH20 9SY
    Rob.Engl@aocarchaeology.com
Dennis Gallagher 4 Sylvan Place, Edinburgh, EH9 1LH
    dbgallagher100@gmail.com
George Haggarty High Bonnyton, Bonnyton Rd, Auchterhouse, Angus, DD3 OQT haggartyg@aol.com
Jennifer Harland Archaeology Institute, University of the Highlands and Islands, Orkney College UHI, East Road,
    Kirkwall, Orkney, KW15 1LX
    Jen.Harland@uhi.ac.uk
Andrew Heald AOC Archaeology, Edgefield Road Industrial Estate, Loanhead, Midlothian, EH20 9SY
    Andy.Heald@aocarchaeology.com
Dawn McLaren AOC Archaeology, Edgefield Road Industrial Estate, Loanhead, Midlothian, EH20 9SY Dawn.
    McLaren@aocarchaeology.com
Jackaline Robertson AOC Archaeology, Edgefield Road Industrial Estate, Loanhead, Midlothian, EH20 9SY Jackaline.
    Robertson@aocarchaeology.com
Clare Thomas, Stillness, Weem, Aberfeldy, Perthshire, PH15 2LD
    stillnessthomasiota10@hotmail.co.uk
Jennifer Thoms 43 Eskview Terrace, Musselburgh, EH21 6LT
    j.thoms@archaeologyscotland.org.uk
Penelope Walton Rogers The Anglo-Saxon Laboratory, Bootham House, 61 Bootham, York YO30 7BT
    penrogers@aslab.co.uk
Hugh Wilmott Department of Archaeology, University of Sheffield, Minalloy House, 10-16 Regent Street, Sheffield,
    S1 3NJ h.
    willmott@sheffield.ac.uk

Preface

The excavation took place in 2007-08, in advance of an extension to the Bon Accord Centre in Aberdeen, and uncovered the backlands of an area that would have formed part of the industrial quarter of the medieval town. The site is well-dated by dendrochronology, augmented by artefactual evidence, and indicates activity from the late 12th century AD into the early modern period, with a particularly intensive period in the 13th century. Structural evidence consists primarily of the backland boundaries, hearth/ovens, several wood-lined wells and many large pits. It is the contents of these pits and wells which forms the core of this monograph.

The waterlogged conditions within the pits and wells has meant that a remarkable assemblage of organic remains, including leather, wooden artefacts, textiles, animal pelts, fibres and cordage, has survived. The leather assemblage is the largest ever to be found in Scotland and has revealed a range of activities associated with the use of animal hides, from hide processing to tanning and shoemaking. The wood assemblage is also extensive and includes bowls, platters, coopered vessels and tools. Metalwork, crucibles, clay mould fragments and ceramics all testify to the industrial nature of the area, while the large quantities of animal and fishbone demonstrate that butchery on an industrial scale took place there.

The excavation charts the changing nature of this once-peripheral area of Aberdeen, from an industrial zone in the medieval period, to horticultural and domestic spaces in post-medieval times, and has thus greatly enhanced our knowledge of Scottish urban development.

1 Introduction

The archaeological works at the Bon Accord Centre, Aberdeen, have identified the changing nature of this area of the medieval and post-medieval city at the junction of the two major thoroughfares of Upperkirkgate and Gallowgate. In the earliest centuries of the medieval burgh's existence, the site formed part of an industrial quarter, peripheral to the core of the medieval town, where odoriferous activities such as tanning, shoemaking and dyeing were undertaken behind the Upperkirkgate. One of the most significant assemblages of leather and leatherworking waste from a European urban medieval site was recovered, consolidating the evidence for such activity in this part of the burgh.

Also identified was evidence for non-ferrous metalworking, while in the later medieval period, there is evidence for continued industrial activity, including smithing. In the early post-medieval period, the area largely formed relatively open gardens associated with properties on the Gallowgate and Upperkirkgate, including those of provosts of the city. By the 19th century the area was again associated largely with commercial and industrial activity, culminating in the construction of the offices and printworks of Aberdeen University Press.

1.1 Background to the archaeological works

in advance of the extension of the existing Bon Accord Centre in Aberdeen, archaeological works were undertaken by AOC Archaeology Group on this retail development site in the heart of medieval Aberdeen. The archaeological programme was commissioned and sponsored by Land Securities, and its extent was determined by the then Keeper of Archaeology for Aberdeen City Council, Judith Stones.

1.2 The site and its setting

the development area, centred at NGR: NJ 941 064, was located at the corner of Gallowgate and Upperkirkgate. It was bounded to the east by Gallowgate, to the north by St Paul Street and the Portland Club, to the west by the service yard of the Bon Accord Centre, and to the south by the Marischal Bar and other premises along the Upperkirkgate. Apart from the north-west of the excavation area, the site had previously been occupied by 20th century buildings. The site is referred to in the text as 'Bon Accord', as the greater part of the area of archaeological works was contained within service areas associated with the shopping centre.

The excavation area sloped down gently from the north and east, where the existing surface height was c. 20.2–20.7m above O.D. and towards the west and south, c. 19.5m above O.D. The location and extent of the site is shown in Figure 1.1.

The medieval settlement stood on fluvioglacial sand and gravel deposits over stony glacial till and Old Red Sandstone Conglomerates. There were estuarine clay deposits along the Dee and Don rivers, to the south and north of Bon Accord. The present site lies on the west side of a sand and gravel ridge running northwards along the Gallowgate and the Spital, connecting the historic centres of New Aberdeen and Old Aberdeen. To the north-west of Bon Accord formerly lay one of the major sources of fresh water for the medieval and early post-medieval town, the Loch of New Aberdeen, with an original extent of c. 100 acres (Dennison and Stones 1997: 5–6).

1.3 The archaeological works of 2007–08

in tandem with a watching brief on the removal of foundations, evaluation works were undertaken in 2007 over the zones of the development area most likely to be disturbed by ground works, which covered c. 2000m². Over most of this area, this involved the opening of trial trenches by machine to provide an initial 10% sample. It was, however, possible to characterise the extent of archaeological deposits near the Gallowgate frontage with a smaller proportion of evaluation. A total of 16 trenches, with a total area of 192m² was therefore excavated (Figure 1.2). Additionally, a series of five test pits were excavated in the service yard of the existing Bon Accord Centre, which identified only very limited archaeological deposits, and thus no further evaluation was undertaken in this area.

The trial trenches revealed significant archaeological remains towards the Gallowgate and in the north of the development area and limited remains to the south, where buildings of the Aberdeen University Press formerly stood. This led to the archaeological excavation of those areas of the site that would be disturbed by development.

The archaeological excavation lay to the immediate west of the Gallowgate, and followed the demolition of buildings associated with the Student Union (covering 19–29 Gallowgate) and the Aberdeen University Press (behind 6–8 Upperkirkgate). During the archaeological works the area was divided into different zones, which

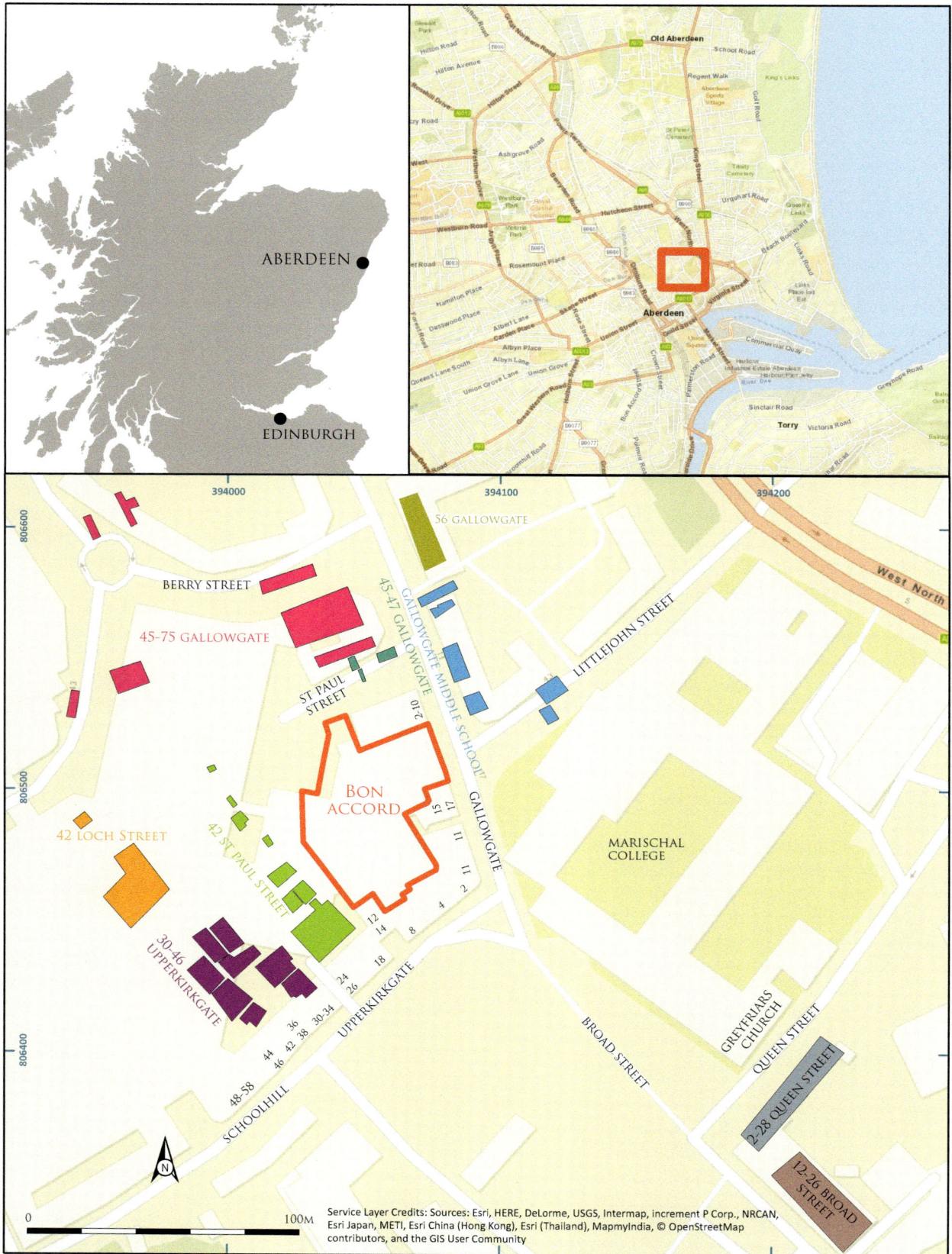

Figure 1.1 Location of Bon Accord Centre archaeological works, and previous archaeological works in the Gallowgate/Upperkirkgate area

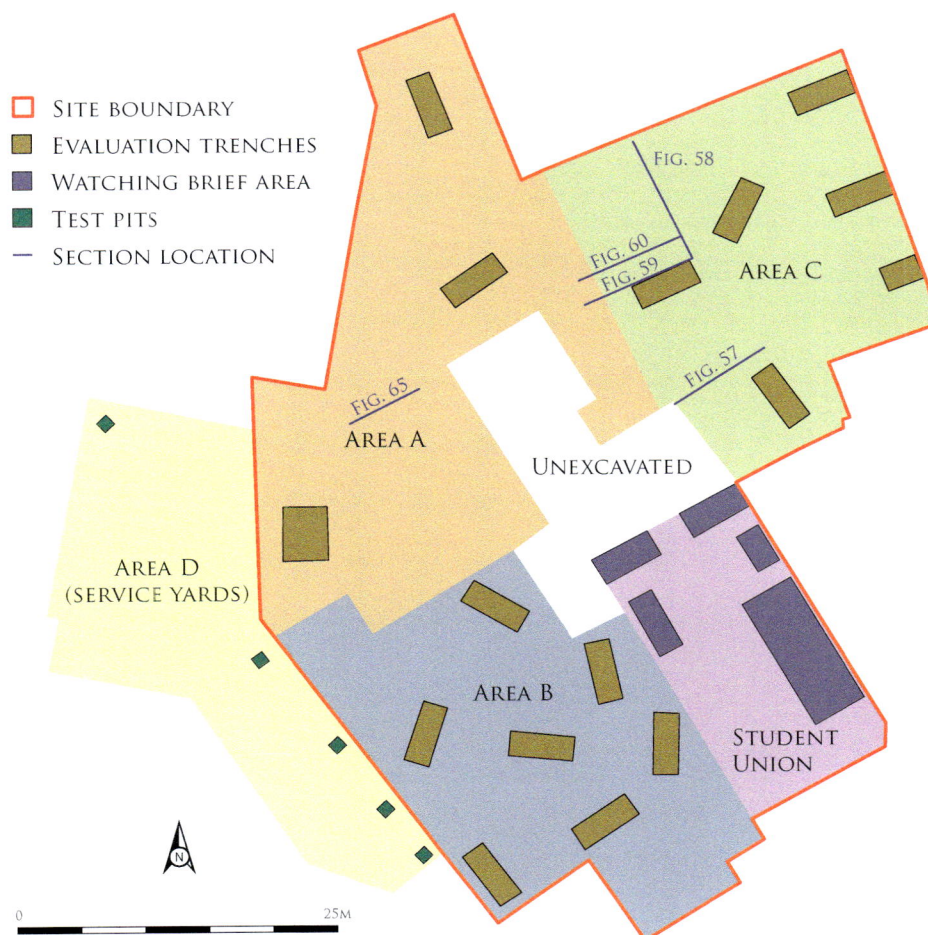

SITE BOUNDARY
EVALUATION TRENCHES
WATCHING BRIEF AREA
TEST PITS
SECTION LOCATION

FIG. 58

FIG. 60
FIG. 59

AREA C

FIG. 65

AREA A

FIG. 57

UNEXCAVATED

AREA D
(SERVICE YARDS)

AREA B

STUDENT
UNION

0   25M

Figure 1.2 Excavation area, showing evaluation trenches and location of long sections

is reflected in the labelling of archaeological features and deposits. There were three main areas: Area A covered approximately 500m² to the north-west, and comprised an open yard area adjacent to the Portland Club; Area B (c. 190m²) lay under the former 'works' building to the north of 6 Upperkirkgate, formerly part of Aberdeen University Press; Area C (c. 750m²) was adjacent the Gallowgate, and had formerly been covered by 19–29 Gallowgate and a building associated with Aberdeen University Student Union. The Bon Accord Centre Service Yard, where a watching brief was undertaken, was labelled Area D. Contamination from a modern diesel tank limited excavation in a large part of the development site, in particular between Areas A and C.

Watching briefs were also undertaken at various stages in the development process, including the clearance of existing building foundations prior to evaluation and excavation; the opening of five trenches on the ground floor of the former Aberdeen University Student Union and excavation of an area to the west of the Portland Club, following foundation consolidation works. While works within the Student Union identified only made

ground, the works adjacent the Portland Club recorded a late medieval timber-lined well.

1.4 Previous archaeological investigations around Gallowgate and Upperkirkgate

Previous archaeological investigations cover a wide area of the medieval burgh, including sites in close proximity to Bon Accord (Figure 1.1) on Gallowgate (Cameron 2001: 73–77, 80), Broad Street (Dent 1982: 26–29, 33); Queen Street (Greig 1982: 20–25) and Upperkirkgate (Stones and Cameron 2001: 60–61, 70). These have produced evidence for occupation from the late 12th century, including the laying out of burgage plot boundaries around the mid 12th century on the Upperkirkgate (Dennison and Stones 1997: 15) (Figure 1.3). Work on the eastern side of the Gallowgate suggests that the thoroughfare was widened in the 20th century and that the original east frontage lies under the present road surface (ibid 36).

The area around the Loch near the Gallowgate appears likely to have been a zone of craft concentration in the 13th and 14th centuries. Evidence for such industrial

Figure 1.3 Schematic reconstruction of putative early plot layout at Upperkirkgate/Gallowgate corner (reproduced with the permission of the National Library of Scotland and under Creative Commons (CC BY 4.0) https://creativecommons.org/licenses/by/4.0/)

activity was identified by Evans (2001) at 45–75 Gallowgate, to the north-west of the present works. The mid 13th century saw that site used for gravel quarrying, while in the later 14th century a short-lived tannery or skin yard was present, evidenced by a complex of pits to the north and a yard surface with ovens to the south (*ibid* 83, 90–94). The tanning and skinning industries were foul-smelling activities and were generally undertaken at a distance from town centres (Spearman 1988: 139). Evidence for shoemaking, cobbling and textile working, in the form of leatherworking waste, including shoe soles and offcuts, and a scutching knife associated with the processing of flax, was located within late 12th to

early 13th century pit and midden deposits recorded during excavations in 1991, on the east side of the Gallowgate at the Gallowgate Middle School Site. At the Middle School site there was evidence for wooden and, later, stone structures from the 12th century onwards (Cameron 2001: 73, 75–77, 80–81).

The 45–47 Gallowgate excavation, to the north of the present works, revealed evidence for the medieval frontage. An episode of dumping around the early 13th century was followed by construction of a building with a grooved sill-beam on a stone foundation (Murray 1984: 305–06). Murray remarks on the lack of frontage buildings in the late 12th century, and notes that until the early 14th century, although there were frontage buildings, occupation was at a relatively low density (in comparison with the Upperkirkgate), with yards and even cess pits extending to the frontage (*ibid* 311). This period was associated with industrial activity, evidenced by the presence of leather-working waste, cattle hair from preparation of hides and fragments of clay moulds. Property boundaries were defined by ditches, latterly wattle-lined. In the 14th century the frontage was still not fully developed, with open yards on either side of a wattle fence acting as a property boundary (*ibid* 306–10).

Evidence for medieval frontage structures was also identified during the excavations at 12–26 Broad Street, formerly the southern end of the medieval Gallowgate, to the south-east of the present works. Wooden buildings representing five phases of occupation from the late 12th to 14th centuries were recorded, alongside evidence of plot division (Dennison and Stones 1997: 66). A rise in ground level in the 13th and early 14th centuries was associated with changes in boundaries. The boundaries became fixed with the stabilisation of ground levels in the 14th century, interpreted by Dent as related to improvements in the removal of rubbish around buildings (Dent 1982: 33). Behind the Broad Street frontage, at the Queen Street Midden site, evidence for early 13th century domestic settlement was recorded, including an unkerbed hearth. The backland of the Broad Street area was used for waste disposal in the later 13th century and early 14th century, suggesting the existence of formal frontage properties at that time (Greig 1982: 20, 25). The process of greater efficiency in rubbish disposal is also evidenced, though perhaps at a later date (around 1400) at the 45–75 Gallowgate site, where the cessation of disposal of refuse on yard surfaces would have been associated with periodic clearing of refuse off site (Cameron 2001: 94).

Evidence for the eastern edge of the Loch, located to the north-west of the present site, was encountered during archaeological works at 45–75 Gallowgate site (Evans 2001: 85; Dennison and Stones 1997: 43).

Archaeological evidence for medieval burgage plot divisions, with a series of changes from the early 13th century to the present day, has also been recorded to the west of Bon Accord in a backland area off the Upperkirkgate, at 42 St Paul Street (Murray 1982: 77–81). Properties were laid out at right angles to the Upperkirkgate from around AD 1200. Initially the properties were irregular in size but in the early 14th century the boundaries were reorganised to create more regular rigs. Between the 15th and 17th centuries a large stone building was constructed on two adjacent properties but, in general, boundaries were not altered after the 15th century (Dennison and Stones 1997: 43).

Evidence for an oven, probably a bread oven, was found during the excavations at the 42 St Paul Street site. This feature was of fairly large capacity and situated in the open air away from frontage buildings, to reduce the risk of fire. Murray interprets the feature as belonging to a burgess family living on the frontage, rather than that of a baker (Murray 1982: 53, 55, 81).

A large excavation of a backland area at 30-46 Upperkirkgate revealed that this area appeared to have developed later or less intensively than the 42 St Paul Street to its east, which might be indicative of the medieval settlement developing gradually downhill and westwards from the Broad Street/Castle Street centre (Dennison and Stones 1997: 44). At this site, further evidence for burgage plot division was encountered, in the form of parallel ditches, aligned north-west/south-east, giving a plot width of *c.* 4.5m. These probably represented the remains of 13th to 14th century boundaries (Stones and Cameron 2001: 71). Murray (1984: 309), discussing the site of 45–47 Gallowgate, suggests that the width of rigs was generally between 5m and 6m.

Water for medieval and early post-medieval properties would have been derived from wells or barrels used to collect rainwater (Stell 2002: 107–08). Such features have been encountered nearby: an unlined 17th century well was recorded at 45–75 Gallowgate (Evans 2001: 95) and a late 14th/early 15th century barrel well or water-butt was found at Gallowgate Middle School (Cameron 2001: 77).

1.5 Dating and the chronology of the site

activity on the site has been divided into six main phases (1–6), from the late 12th century to the late 19th/early 20th century (Table 1.1). However, it became clear during excavation, and subsequently following works on the artefact assemblages, that the phasing of the site was more straightforward in some areas than in others. The eastern part of the site, close to the Gallowgate frontage, had seen substantial activity during Phases 1 to 3 (later 12th to 13th centuries), with the laying down of occupation deposits with clear boundaries, and a recognisable sequence of cut features (though with some difficulties in discerning where features were recut or replaced), so that the three initial phases could thus be clearly identified in this area. However, at a distance from the frontage the identification of three separate phases during the 12th and 13th centuries was more problematic and some of the deposits and features from this period cannot be confidently placed within a particular phase. In addition, the truncation of large parts of the site, whether by post-medieval frontage structures or by later construction, also rendered the understanding of the later stratigraphic sequence difficult, in particular those deposits identified in the

Table 1.1 Phases 1-6; key dating evidence

Phase 1 (mid-to-late 12th century)	
Dendrochronology	/
Ceramics	Layer A001/C001; 12th–13th century date (Aberdeen Fabric 8, Scottish White Gritty Ware, Stamford Ware, Yorkshire-type Ware, East Anglian Ware & London Sandy Ware)
	Pits A027 & A030; 12th–13th century date (Local Redware, Scottish White Gritty Ware, Stamford Ware, Yorkshire-type Ware & London Sandy Ware)
	Pits C001, C003, C004, C005, C006, C007, C008 and C009; second quarter 12th century (i.e. Scottish White Gritty Ware & London Sandy Ware)
Other artefacts	Pits C004 and C009; shoe components & leather working waste dating to 12th–13th centuries
Phase 2 (late 12th to mid 13th century)	
Dendrochronology	Gully C001 SF3602; discarded oak timber, felled *tpq* AD 1184. Gully probably out of use by mid-13th century at earliest
	Pit C025; discarded oak timbers, felled winter/spring AD 1209/10. Pit probably backfilled sometime in first half of the 13th century at the earliest
	Pit C027; two discarded oak timbers felled *tpq* AD 1133 and AD 1149. Pit probably backfilled around the turn of the 12th/13th century at the earliest
	Pit C033; SF3201 felled winter/spring AD 1200/01. SF3719 & SF3717 felled *tpq* AD 1226 and AD 1233 respectively. If discarded, it is unlikely that the pit began to be backfilled until the later 13th century at the earliest
	Pit C099; oak timber felled sometime between AD 1152–AD 1190.Pit would have been backfilled around the turn of the 12th/13th century at the earliest.
	Ph C018; *in situ* oak post felled sometime between AD 1204–AD 1240, so the structure probably erected sometime first half of 13th century
	Stakeline Stakes C002; oak stake felled *c.* AD 1197
	Wall C001; SF4260 felled *tpq* AD 1221. Wall was probably built around the middle of 13th century
Ceramics	Spreads A018 and A019; 12th or 13th century date (Local Redware)
Other artefacts	Layer A002; SF2391, silver halfpenny dated between AD 1205 & AD 1207
	Pit C025; leather shoe sole of mainly 13th century date
	Pit C036; SF3490, fragment of late medieval plain window glass
Phase 3 (mid-to-late 13th century)	
Dendrochronology	Well A002; felling dates of AD 1242, AD 1243 & AD 1246. The range of felling dates suggests either stockpiling or re-use of old timber, although there was no visible evidence of re-use
	Pit C069; SF2378 felled in the winter/spring of AD 1281/2. Pit probably backfilled around the turn of the 13th/14th century at the earliest
	Posthole C011; post probably felled sometime between AD 1262–AD 1294 so the associated structure was probably constructed in the latter half of the 13th century
Ceramics	/
Other artefacts	Pit C044 and Pit C048 (both Phase 3 or 4); leather shoe parts with forms predominantly of 13th century date
Early Phase 4 (late 13th to 14th century)	

Dendrochronology	Layer C075; SF4239 probably felled sometime between AD 1245–AD 1260; the layer probably accumulated in the latter half of the 13th century at the earliest
Ceramics	Layer A003; 14th century (Local Redware, Aberdeen Fabric 8, Scottish White Gritty Ware, Scarborough-type Ware, Stamford Ware, Yorkshire-type Ware, London Sandy Ware, Low Countries Greyware & North French-type Ware).
	Spread A027; 14th century (Local Redware, Scarborough-type Ware Fabric 1 & Low Countries Greyware).
Other artefacts	/
Late Phase 4 (14th to early 15th century)	
Dendrochronology	A single oak timber discarded in a fill of Pit C064, SF3753, was probably felled sometime between AD 1266 and AD 1302; the pit could have been backfilled as early as late 13th century
Ceramics	Layer C020; likely 15th century (and perhaps later) date (Local Redware, Aberdeen Fabric 8, Scarborough-type Ware, Yorkshire-type Ware, Low Countries Redware, Low Countries Greyware, Rouen-type Ware, Siegburg Stoneware & Raeren Stoneware.
	Pit A024; 14th century date (Local Redware, Scarborough-type Ware & Langerwehe-type Stoneware)
	Pit C085; 14th century (Local Redware, Scottish White Gritty Ware, Scarborough-type Ware Fabric 1, Yorkshire-type Ware, Normandy Gritty Ware & Low Countries Greyware)
Other artefacts	/
Early Phase 5 (15th to 16th century)	
Dendrochronology	/
Ceramics	Layer A005; 15th century or later date (Low Countries Greyware, North French-type Ware, Siegburg Stoneware, Langerwehe-type Stoneware & Raeren Stoneware)
	Layers A033, A034 & C034; 15th century or later pottery (Valencian Lustreware, Siegburg Stoneware, Langerwehe-type Stoneware & Raeren Stoneware)
	Spreads A020 & C058; 15th century or later pottery (Local Redware, Langerwehe-type Stoneware & Raeren Stoneware)
Other artefacts	/
Mid Phase 5 (15th to 16th century)	
Dendrochronology	Well A001; barrel constructed *tpq* AD 1365. Allowing for long working life the well could have been constructed at any time from the early 15th century onwards
Ceramics	Layer A006, Spreads C021/C022 & C149, & Pit C070; Scottish Post-Medieval Oxidised Ware
	Layer A013; 15th century or later date (Low Countries Greyware, Iberian Redware, Langerwehe-type Stoneware & Raeren Stoneware)
	Layer A025; 15th century or later (Langerwehe-type Stoneware & Raeren Stoneware)
	Layer C009/C010/C031; 15th/16th century (Saintonge Ware, Siegburg Stoneware, Langerwehe-type Stoneware & Raeren Stoneware)
	Spread A013; Raeren Stoneware
	Surface C009; Raeren Stoneware

	Well A001; 15th century or later (Langerwehe-type Stoneware & Raeren Stoneware)
Other artefacts	Spread A013; SF1888, copper farthing of James III
	Spread C021/C022; SF1090, fragment of 15th-early 17th century window glass
Late Phase 5 (15th/16th century to mid-to-late 18th century)	
Dendrochronology	/
Ceramics	Layer A007/A008; Scottish Post-Medieval Oxidised Ware
	Layer A010/A011; 15th century or later (Iberian Redware, Siegburg Stoneware, Langerwehe-type Stoneware, Raeren Stoneware & Frechen Stoneware)
	Layer C039; 15th century or later (Raeren Stoneware)
	Pits C028 & C101; 15th century or later (Local Redware, Raeren Stoneware & Scottish Post-Medieval Oxidised Ware)
	Pit C080; 15th century or later (Local Redware and Frechen Stoneware)
Other artefacts	Layer A007/A008; SF837B, James III copper farthing, 17th century clay tobacco pipe fragments including fragment of a Dutch pipe dated to between 1660 and 1680
	Layer C052; clay tobacco pipe of possible 17th century date
	Pit B001; fragment of mid-17th century Dutch clay tobacco pipe
	Pit C080; SF402, fragment of 15th to early 17th century window glass
Phase 6 (mid-to-late 18th century to 20th century)	
Dendrochronology	/
Ceramics	Layer C011; mixed pottery assemblage including porcelain
	Pit C078; modern earthenware and porcelain
	Surface C017; modern earthenware
	Well C002; Joggled Redware, modern earthenware, White Salt Glaze Ware & porcelain
Other artefacts	Layer C011; clay tobacco pipe fragments, predominantly of likely 19th century date
	Layer C028; fragments of 19th century clay tobacco pipe
	Pit C078; SF 2122D, copper penny AD 1806 – AD 1860. SF 2122C, bronze farthing AD 1865. SF 2118, late 18th to mid 19th century wine or cordial glass & a machine-produced spoon. Clay tobacco pipe fragments from the 17th to the 19th century
	Pit C081; SF 374B, G rim of a wine glass of possible 18th century date. SF 348, fragments of a mid-late 18th century wide-flanged glass bowl. Clay tobacco pipe fragments of 19th century date. Riveted leather sole – construction dates to the mid 19th century to the early 20th century
	Structure C012; SF 2433A, late 19th-century press-moulded boat-shaped glass salt. SF 2433B, late 19th-century press-moulded octagonal tumbler. SF 2433C, late 19th century oil lamp globe
	Well C002; fragments of 19th century clay tobacco pipe

text as belonging to Phase 4 (late 13th/14th century to early 15th century) onwards.

The surface revealed by the initial watching brief had undergone significant disturbance and truncation, and much of the site had undergone processes such as the excavation of service trenches and piling, which will have moved material through the site stratigraphy; in expansive deposits and features such as Pit C025, excavation work had to be undertaken around substantial concrete piles. There were also areas on the edge of the site that could not be fully investigated due to the danger of disturbing or undermining walls of buildings that stood to the north and south on the Gallowgate frontage. This led to the cut for Well A002 being excavated in two separate exercises; indeed, it was not identified as the construction cut for a well until a watching brief after the main excavation had ceased. Elsewhere, some cut features and the surrounding features could not be fully excavated, and their stratigraphic interpretation and place in the site chronology remains problematic. For example, Pit C085, which on excavation appeared to belong to either Phase 5 or 6 (i.e. 15th century or later) contained an assemblage of pottery including 14th century material that pointed to a Phase 4 origin. The chronology of such features remains enigmatic.

As described above the stratigraphic relationships of Phase 1 to 3 deposits and features were reasonably clearly visible, at least in the east of the site, while Phase 6 (later post-medieval) and modern deposits and features could also be reasonably defined, with Phase 6 comprising structural elements of buildings, floor surfaces and drainage features behind the Upperkirkgate and Gallowgate frontages, and stratigraphically associated features and deposits. However, the sequence of intervening Phase 4 to 5 deposits and associated features was difficult to discern, with deposits being separated by truncation by walls, service trenches and construction disturbance. Here, it was the sequence of occupation deposits and garden soils in the west of the site that was most clearly discernible. While Phases 4 and 5 have been subdivided stratigraphically, the sequence from early Phase 4 to late Phase 5 is therefore clearest in this part of the site, with deposits further east representing a patchwork of remains.

There were changes in the artefact, and in particular the pottery, assemblages which aided understanding of the chronological sequence of activity across the site and across the phases (Table 1.1), and this was of particular importance in understanding Phases 4 and 5, with spot dating of pottery leading, for example, to differentiation of deposits and features from around the 14th century to 15th/16th century. The common disturbance of deposits, e.g. by infilling of pits with

material containing earlier artefacts, and the potential for residual and intrusive artefacts, means that elements of this sequence are problematic, for example in Pit C085, with its 14th century (Phase 4) pottery assemblage appearing to lie in a later part of the site stratigraphy (see above). It is accepted that this feature and some other elements of the Phase 4 and 5 sequence cannot be confidently asserted as being accurately located in the site stratigraphy.

The absolute chronology of the excavated remains at Bon Accord has depended heavily on the recovery of a significant quantity of structural timbers which had survived within waterlogged medieval features and deposits. The dendrochronological analysis of 42 timbers from four large features, Well A001, Well A002, Pit C025 and Pit C033 suggests an intense period of building activity throughout the 13th century, which continued into the 14th century (Chapter 4.1). However, the absence of dendrochronological data beyond the late 13th century suggests that building activity in and around the site may have petered out during the 14th century. The only dendrochronological evidence for later activity was derived from Well A001, which suggests that the well was probably not constructed until the 15th century at the earliest.

Some radiocarbon dates were obtained, primarily to address issues relating to the ceramic assemblage (see below). Dates were obtained for pottery residues and leather offcuts from the same context (Appendix 1). While the residues produced some very anomalous early dates, the leather offcuts produced dates which accord with the phase dating (Appendix 1).

1.6 Structure of the monograph

this monograph is divided into a number of sections, leading to a summary of the significance of the excavation within the context of medieval and post-medieval Aberdeen.

Following this introduction, the excavated evidence will be presented in Chapter 2 by phase, identifying significant elements in the site stratigraphy. Deposits and features have been labelled with single letter prefixes (A, B, C and D) to indicate the separate areas in which they were located. For example, Layer A001 and Pit A001 were to be found in Area A, while Layer C001 and Pit C001 were in Area C. On occasion, a deposit or feature crossed more than one excavation area; where this is relevant it is noted in the text.

In Chapter 3 the artefactual and ecofactual evidence is presented by phase and feature. The contents of the key features and deposits, as well as those with significant assemblages, are summarised so that the full range of evidence deriving from each feature and deposit can be appreciated. This has facilitated the interpretation of the features and deposits and has helped to elucidate the various and changing activities undertaken on the site. However, only evidence derived from the medieval and early post-medieval Phases 1 to 5 is included. The artefactual and ecofactual evidence for Phase 6 (mid-to-late 18th to 20th century) is not included within this volume, for want of space, unless they are of particular interest or are relict and belong to one of the previous phases. Full cataloguing and reporting of the Phase 6 evidence can be found in the site archive.

Chapter 4 consists of assemblage-based presentations of each artefact and ecofact type, with more detailed descriptions of the data where necessary and discussion of the evidence in terms of regional/national significance, contribution to field of study, etc. Full copies of the specialist reports, including methodologies, can be found in the site archive.

The monograph concludes with a discussion of the site in its immediate context (Chapter 5) which will refer to the historical setting of the site and discuss the significance of the excavation for the understanding of medieval and post-medieval Aberdeen.

Finally, Chapter 6 examines the contribution of the Bon Accord excavation to both regional and European studies of urban medieval economies.

1.7 The ceramic assemblage

the ceramic assemblage from Bon Accord is the largest such assemblage ever retrieved from an urban excavation in Scotland, amounting to some 20,000 sherds. The assemblage was fully recorded by George Haggarty and Derek Hall, and chemical and petrographic analyses were undertaken to study source area (Jones, R 2012). A programme of radiocarbon dating, of residues on the pottery and associated organic finds, was undertaken to address questions of early local ceramic manufacture and longevity of use (Appendix 1). Fourier-transform infrared spectroscopy (FTIR) analysis was also undertaken on residues in one Redware vessel (Jones, J 2012).

Unfortunately, a comprehensive overview of the ceramic assemblage, which would have drawn together these strands of evidence, was not completed, and it has therefore not been possible to fully integrate the ceramic evidence into the narrative of the site. The primary record consists of a spreadsheet in which the fabric types have been tabulated by context and form (i.e. bowl, mug, jug etc.), and the number of sherds present in each context are recorded. As described above, the ceramic assemblage has been vital in understanding the sequence of activity across the site, in particular during Phases 4 and 5. The key chronologically diagnostic fabrics, drawn from this spreadsheet, are referred to throughout the text and key assemblages are listed in Table 1.1. Illustrations of a representative sample of the ceramics were also prepared and these are presented in Appendix 5 so that the great range of fabrics and forms found on the site can be appreciated.

The primary record, the fabric/context spreadsheet, is too unwieldy for publication but it is available in the site archive, along with the unpublished analytical reports and other documentation, for future researchers to interrogate.

2 Summary of Archaeological Remains by Phase

2.1 Introduction

The watching brief and evaluation works revealed medieval and post-medieval archaeological deposits surviving relatively undisturbed in the north and west of the development site, in both Areas A and C. However, cellarage and deep piling had damaged the eastern side of Area C (Figure 2.1), immediately adjacent to the Gallowgate, and the southern end of Area A. More limited remains were encountered in Area B, which had been damaged by deep foundations for 6 Upperkirkgate (Figure 2.2). There was also occasional survival of medieval pits in the east of the adjacent Bon Accord Centre Service Yard (Area D), though this area had largely been truncated by construction works for the Bon Accord Centre. Additionally, contamination from a modern diesel tank limited the extent of excavation in the central part of the site, in particular between Areas A and C.

The features and deposits have been divided into six phases of activity, on the basis of stratigraphy, as well as dendrochronological, radiocarbon and artefactual evidence (Table 1.1, Chapter 1). A full description of the artefacts and ecofacts recovered is presented by context in Chapter 3; in the present chapter this material is referenced where it contributes to the interpretation of particular features and deposits.

Deposits and features in the various excavation areas (A, B, C and D) have been named with single letter prefixes indicating the separate areas in which they occurred. For example, Layer A001 and Pit A001 were to be found in Area A, while Layer C001 and Pit C001 were in Area C. On occasion, it was identified that a deposit or feature occurred in more than one area; where this is apparent it is noted in the text below.

2.2 Phase 1 – mid-to-late 12th century (figure 2.3)

a range of cut features, commonly pits, were recorded from Phase 1, cut through natural deposits. The pit features in this phase were utilised for refuse disposal and for industrial processes including tanning. The fills of these pits were usually waterlogged, and therefore permitted the survival of assemblages of organic material including leather waste and wood artefacts. Boundaries broadly in line with the Upperkirkgate and Gallowgate were marked by gullies and stake lines.

The earliest phase of activity on the site was marked by features cut through natural deposits of gravel-rich

Figure 2.1 Working behind Gallowgate frontage from the south-west

Figure 2.2 Working in heavily truncated area behind Upperkirkgate frontage

11

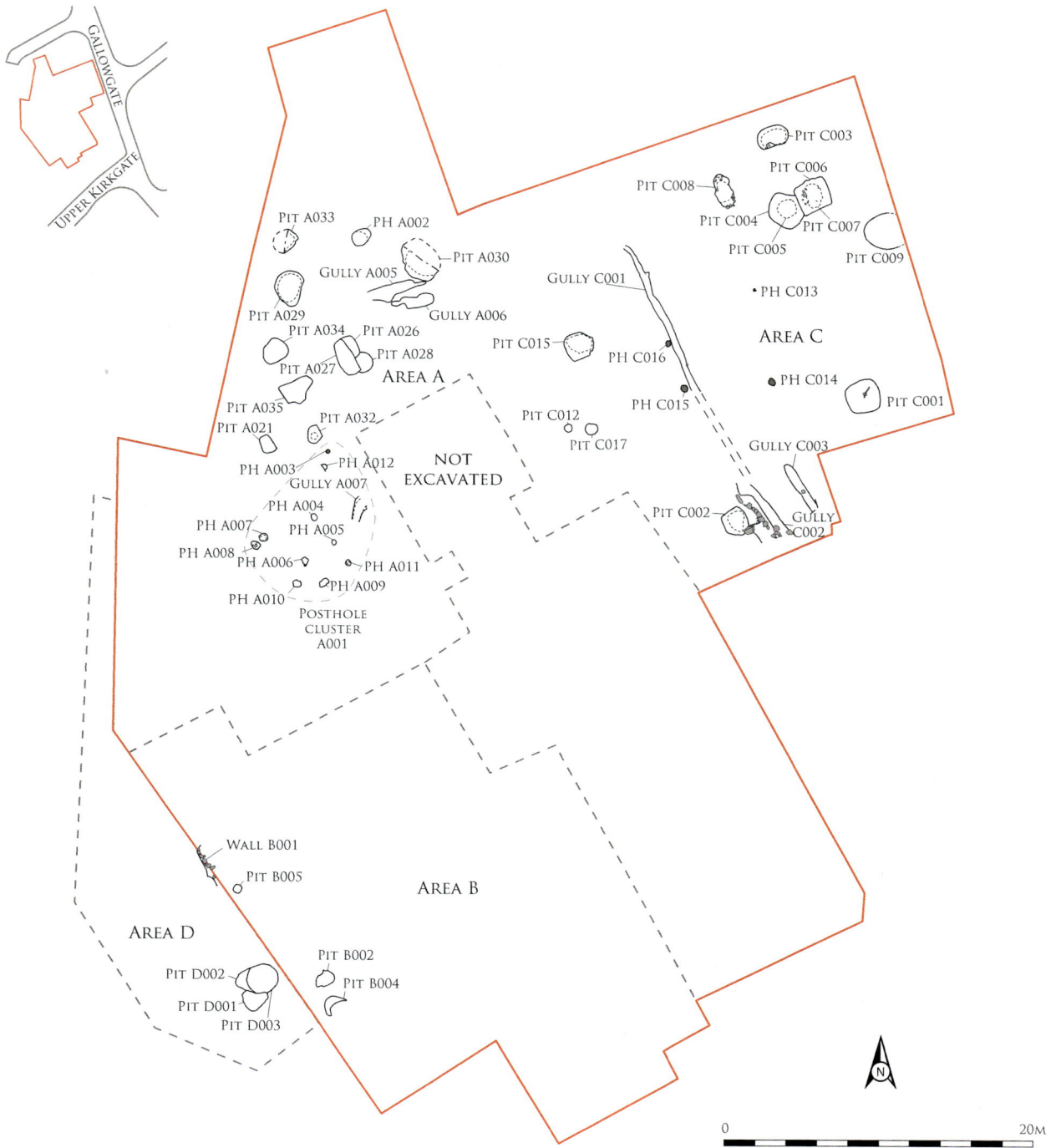

Figure 2.3 Plan of Phase 1 features

clay and sand and overlying interface deposits between the natural clay and anthropogenic deposits. There is a small quantity of worked lithic material, indicating residual prehistoric activity; it is only in the lowermost deposits, such as interface deposit Layer C001, that this material might be *in situ*.

Many of the Phase 1 features comprised pits, commonly with waterlogged, dark grey/brown clay and clay silt fills, conducive to the survival of organic material including leather and wood. As with subsequent medieval phases of activity, a large proportion of the archaeological features were recorded in Area C, near the Gallowgate frontage. Gully features indicated the existence of boundaries broadly perpendicular to the Upperkirkgate. However, there was also activity further to the west, in Area A, including an area of likely postholes that may relate to a structure, though these could not be dated more closely than between Phases 1 and 3. Several features, including Pit A028 and Pit C004

A

W   E

MODERN DISTURBANCE   CUT FOR PIPE

C001F

C001D

C001C

C001A

C001B   C001B

GRINDING MECHANISM

B

S   N

C015E

C015D

C015C   C015C

C015B

C015A

C

W   E

C017c

C017b

C017a

0   1M

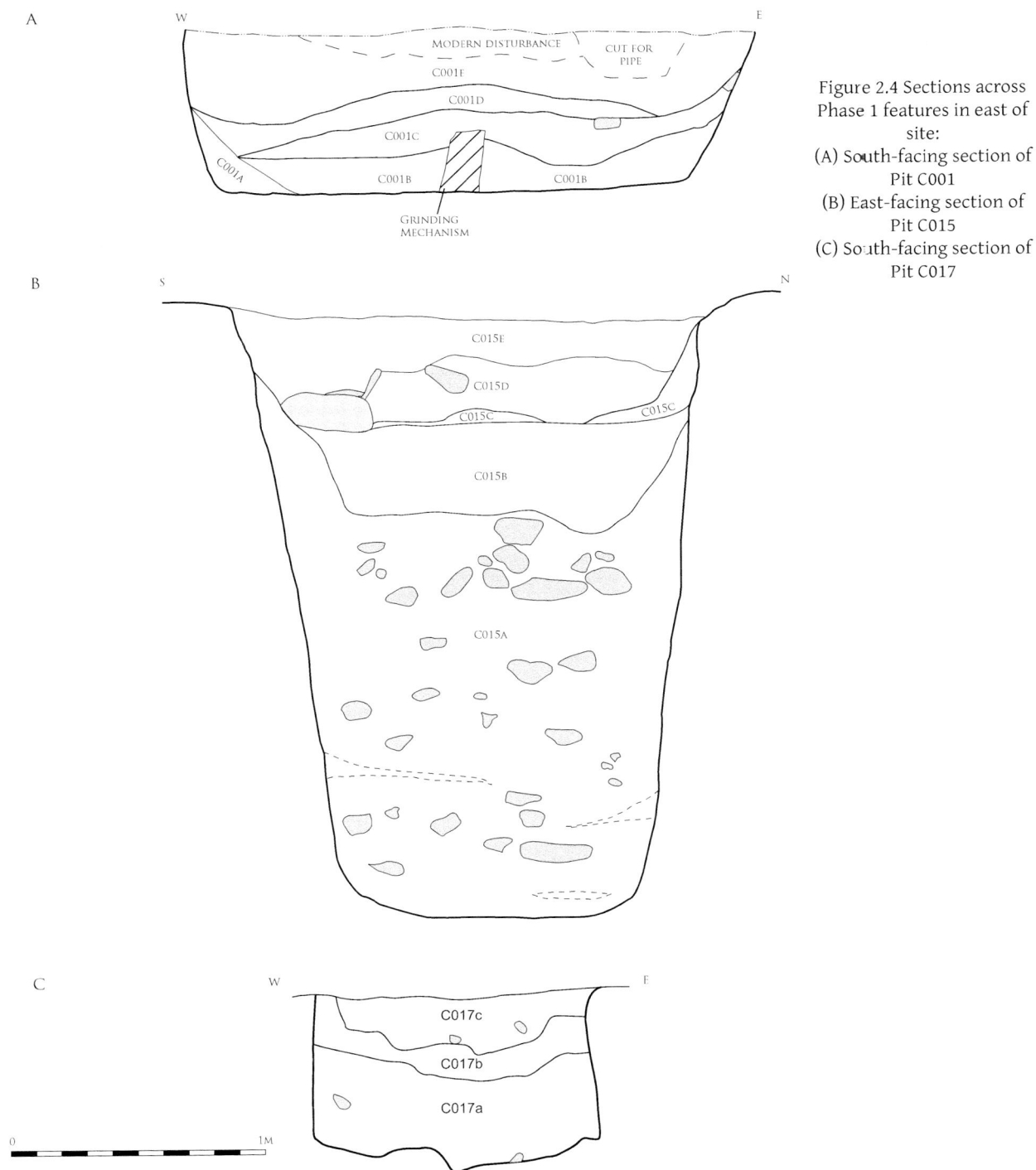

Figure 2.4 Sections across Phase 1 features in east of site:
(A) South-facing section of Pit C001
(B) East-facing section of Pit C015
(C) South-facing section of Pit C017

had either been recut or were truncated by features also of likely Phase 1 date, indicating considerable activity within this phase.

Layer A001/C001, a thin interface layer consisting of a mixture of the overlying deposits with the natural, was present over much of the site; it contained a small assemblage of chipped stone debitage. Numerous pits, utilised for refuse disposal and also in some instances

for industrial processes including tanning, were identified cut through the subsoil and interface layer.

Features cutting the natural strata in Area C, behind the existing Gallowgate frontage, included sub-square Pit C001 (Figure 2.4A); sub-circular Pits C003 and C008; Pit C009 and Ph C013 and Ph C014. The latter existed in isolation and could not be related to any other structural features.

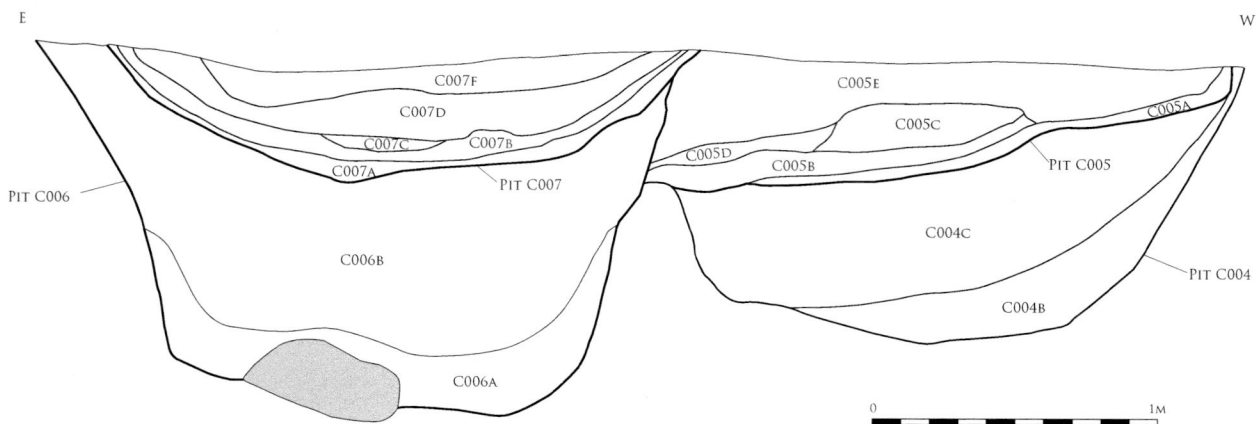

E ... W

PIT C006

C007F
C007D
C007C   C007B
C007A   PIT C007

C005E
C005C
C005A
C005D   C005B   PIT C005

C006B

C004C   PIT C004

C004B

C006A

0 ... 1M

Figure 2.5 North-facing section of Pits C004; C005; C006 and C007

In this area there was also a sequence of four pits (Figure 2.5), with waste from leatherworking activity. The 2.6m diameter circular Pit C004, had a remnant clay lining and contained a used shoe and leatherworking assemblage of 12th to 13th century date; it was recut by Pit C005 (also with a sandy clay lining), which again contained leather waste together with goat hair and possible lambskin. This had in turn been truncated to the east by sub-rectangular Pit C006 (Figure 2.6), which was recut as Pit C007 (Figure 2.7).

The clayey sand lining of Pit C007 had been truncated by 35 irregularly spaced stake holes, Stakes C001, likely a Phase 2 feature (Figure 2.14, see later), while its fill was overlain by dumped humic material, Spread C002. It is conceivable that, because of the extent of truncation by cellarage in this area, part of this sequence of pit features may be slightly later in date than Phase 1, but pottery recovered from the fills of several of these features (Pits C001, C003, C004–C007, C008 and C009) indicates that this is actually likely to represent a discrete group of relatively early date (perhaps the second quarter of the 12th century), the earliest evidence for medieval use of this area.

Crossing Area C, and broadly parallel with the existing Gallowgate thoroughfare, was a shallow 0.4m wide north/south aligned linear Gully C001 (Figure 2.8). This feature was a relatively long-lived boundary and appeared to continue in use in Phase 2, perhaps being recut; dendrochronological evidence points to its backfilling in the mid 13th century at the earliest. To the immediate west of this gully were Ph C015 and Ph C016, cut into interface Layer C001. To the south, Gully C002, which was lined with stone, was also cut into Layer C001, and formed a continuation of Gully C001; Gully C003 was a very shallow parallel feature to the east.

To the west of Gully C001, sub-circular Pit C002 was also cut into Layer C001. To the north were three further

Figure 2.6 North-facing section of Pit C006

Figure 2.7 Pit C007 from west, showing Stakes C001

pits: large sub-square Pit C015 (Figure 2.4B) cut through Layer C001, which contained common refuse material, especially animal bone in its silty clay fills and may have been recut (Figure 2.9); small sub-circular Pit C017 (Figure 2.4C), again cut through Layer C001, and 0.5m diameter circular Pit C012, which cut natural subsoil.

There were a number of thin spreads over the natural and Layer C001 that predated the build-up of a major dark grey/brown silty clay deposit, Layer C003, in Phase 2. These deposits included dark greyish brown silty clay Layer C002 to the west of Gully C001, which overlay the fills of Ph C016 and Pits C015 and C017.

To the west, in Area A, the interface deposit over natural subsoil was recorded as Layer A001. Several pit features were cut into Layer A001, many of which contained pottery and leather of between 12th and 14th century date. These included shallow sub-circular Pit A029; sub-circular Pit A030 (Figure 2.10A), with common finds including worked wood (Figure 2.11) and leather of mainly 13th–14th century date; shallow oval Pit A032; irregular Pit A033 (Figure 2.10B); shallow sub-circular Pit A034 and shallow, flat-based, sub-rectangular Pit A035 (Figure 2.10C), which lay over ash deposit Spread A050. In addition, a sequence of three large pits was uncovered: shallow sub-circular Pit A028, which was possibly lined with sandy clay, truncated by a 1.4m deep circular Pit A026 (Figure 2.12), which lay under sub-rectangular Pit A027. The last two features contained fills with quantities of twigs, bark and wood chips, which could be interpreted as the remains of organic lining material for tanning pits. Pit A026 contained a small leather assemblage including fragments of footwear of likely 12th–13th century date, while Pit A027 also contained pottery of a similar date and an assemblage of leather and leatherworking waste.

These features may represent extraction and/or refuse pits in an area peripheral to both the Gallowgate and the Upperkirkgate, though several may have functioned as tanning pits. Ph A002 was also present in this period. Several postholes in this area (Ph A003 to Ph A012) date to between Phase 1 and Phase 3 and appear to form a coherent unit (Ph Cluster A001). Given their close proximity it is possible that they relate to a single structure though truncation caused by later walls makes their interpretation as a group problematic. Ph A007 and Ph A008 appeared to form a north-western corner, while Ph A010 formed a south-western corner. Ph A004, Ph A005 and Ph A011 may have formed the eastern boundary for a small structure measuring roughly 4m east/west by 5m north/south, though, given the extent of later disturbance, such a structure may have continued to the east.

Another Phase 1 to 3 feature, cut into Layer A001, was oval Pit A021, which was truncated by a likely Phase 4 feature, south/north-aligned Gully A008 (Figure 2.53).

Several small drainage features of Phase 1 date were identified: irregular shallow Gullies A005, A006 and A007. Unlike features to the east, these did not clearly represent boundary features, though both Gullies A005 and A006 were on a broadly east/west alignment.

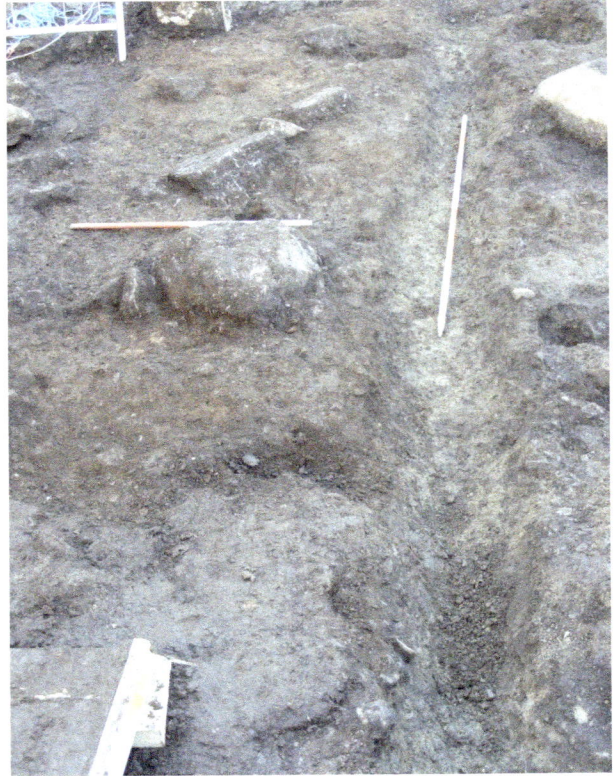

Figure 2.8 Gully C001 from north

Figure 2.9 Detail of horse skull with articulated vertebrae in Pit C015

Interpretation of the chronology of features in Areas B and D was problematic due to the extent of truncation associated with 20th century construction and demolition. However, the majority of the medieval features in this area probably originated between Phases 1 and 3, i.e. between the late 12th and late 13th centuries. In this area a small number of large pits were recorded, commonly containing dark grey organic-rich fills with dumped material. Large Pit B003 (only seen in section) and irregular Pit B004 were cut into natural.

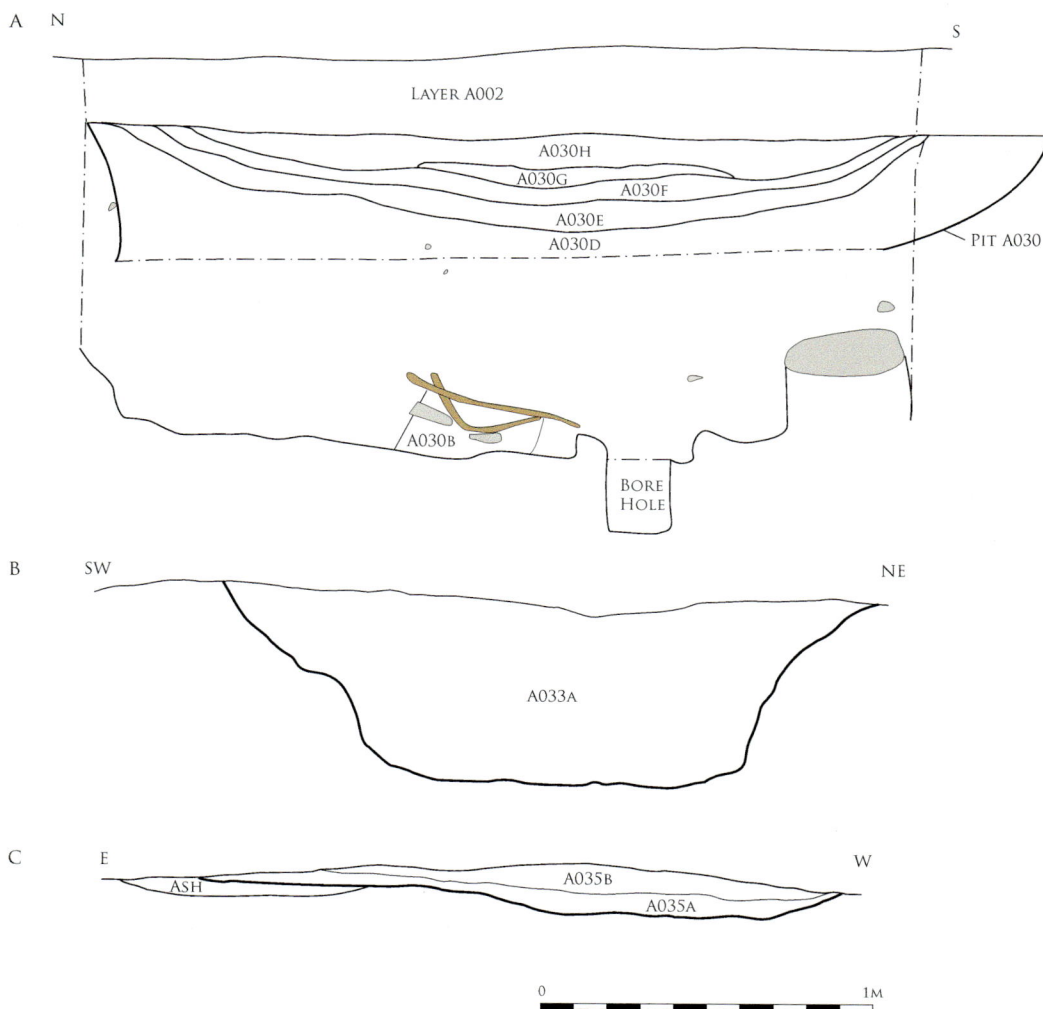

Figure 2.10 Sections across Phase 1 features in west of site:
(A) West-facing section of Pit A030
(B) South-east-facing section of Pit A033
(C) North-facing section of Pit A035

Figure 2.11 Pit A030, half-sectioned, from west. Platter SF3743 can be seen protruding from the section

Figure 2.12 Detail of possible remnant lining of Pit A026 from east

Figure 2.13 Stone line, Wall B001, from east

Small sub-circular Pit B005, also of likely medieval date, overlay a thin interface deposit over natural. Layer B001, overlying natural, was a light orange red clay with stones; it was truncated by oval Pit B002. To the west, Pits D001 and D002 over the natural subsoil were truncated by 2m diameter Pit D003. Under heavy truncation, a north/south-aligned stone line, Wall B001, measuring 2.25m in length (Figure 2.13), possibly a wall remnant, has tentatively been assigned to Phase 1 on ceramic evidence. This overlay the remnants of Layer B002, equivalent to Layer A001/C001.

Many of the Phase 1 features, such as Pits A030 and C015, contained large quantities of dumped material including animal bone, worked wooden artefacts, pottery and leather, indicating that refuse disposal was at least an element of their purpose. The great depth of Pit C015 suggests, however, that it was not a simple refuse pit. It may primarily have served a drainage or industrial function before being backfilled; potentially the upper fills represent a recut. In this earliest phase of activity leather appears in the fills of numerous pits, including Pits C001, C009 and C015, indicating that leatherworking and shoe production (cordwaining) and cobbling processes were undertaken in this area. The presence of bark and other rich organic material, commonly in basal, possible lining fills, suggests that tanning of hides was also undertaken at this early period.

2.3 Phase 2 – late 12th to mid 13th century (figure 2.14)

this phase was marked by a build-up of occupation deposits which covered the site apart from where deep truncation had taken place. Lenses of sand and gravel probably marked intentional levelling activities. Numerous linear stake and hurdle boundaries marked roughly north/south-aligned plot divisions running back from Upperkirkgate. Parallel with these, a rubble wall base and gullies probably formed further boundary features. There were many large pits, commonly of rectangular or sub-rectangular shape and often located within a single plot bounded by stake lines. These pits

were probably associated with industrial activities such as tanning, as large quantities of leather artefacts were recovered. A single piece of human bone (SF2785) was found within one of these pits. Also recovered were wooden artefacts including turned bowls and platter fragments, paddles, and structural wood. A significant feature in this phase was a well lined with a wooden barrel and with a stone-lined superstructure. To the west, at a distance from both the Gallowgate and Upperkirkgate frontages, were occupation deposits of a relatively peripheral backland area.

Layer C003/A002 was the major occupation deposit associated with this phase but there were also minor occupation deposits such as Spreads C007, C008 and C009.

Layer C003/A002 (also recorded as Layer C014 and Layer C054), consisted of a build-up of grey silty clay which covered the majority of the site, with the exception of zones of deep truncation. It contained numerous lenses of clay and sand material. Overlying this major deposit were lenses of material, often including sand and gravel derived from the local subsoil, interpreted as being derived from intentional levelling activities, such as Spread C005 and Layer C049. This gravel levelling was overlain by remnant cobble Surface C001, which stretched 2.5m north/south.

The deposits of this period were pierced by numerous groups of stake bases, associated with hurdle remnants, which formed linear boundaries. The most conspicuous stake line, Stakes C002 (Figure 2.15) formed a boundary, slightly east of and parallel with Phase 1 Gully C001, again apparently demarcating a rough north/south plot division running back from Upperkirkgate. Deposits built up around Stakes C002, including Spread C041, were interrupted by Ph C018, which contained a timber post that was probably a slightly later element of this stake line; dendrochronological analysis of this timber provides a felling range of AD 1200 to 1240. Ph C019 was also identified on this boundary line, while to the north it is possible that Pit C033 originated as a posthole. A similar arrangement of post pits forming an alignment adjacent to 14th century tannery pits has been recognised at Castlecliffe, St Andrews, where there was also evidence for stakeholes between such pits (Lewis 1996: 616–67), indicating the use of space up to the boundary line.

Further remnant north/south stake alignments, Stakes C003A/C003B (Figure 2.16) and Stakes C004, were recorded to the east and west of this boundary line. The Stakes C003A/C003B alignment was constructed using oak roundwood (except for one alder), all between 40–70mm in diameter. Birch, oak, alder and willow were used for the withies. C004 was more mixed, with oak, birch and willow roundwood stakes. The distance

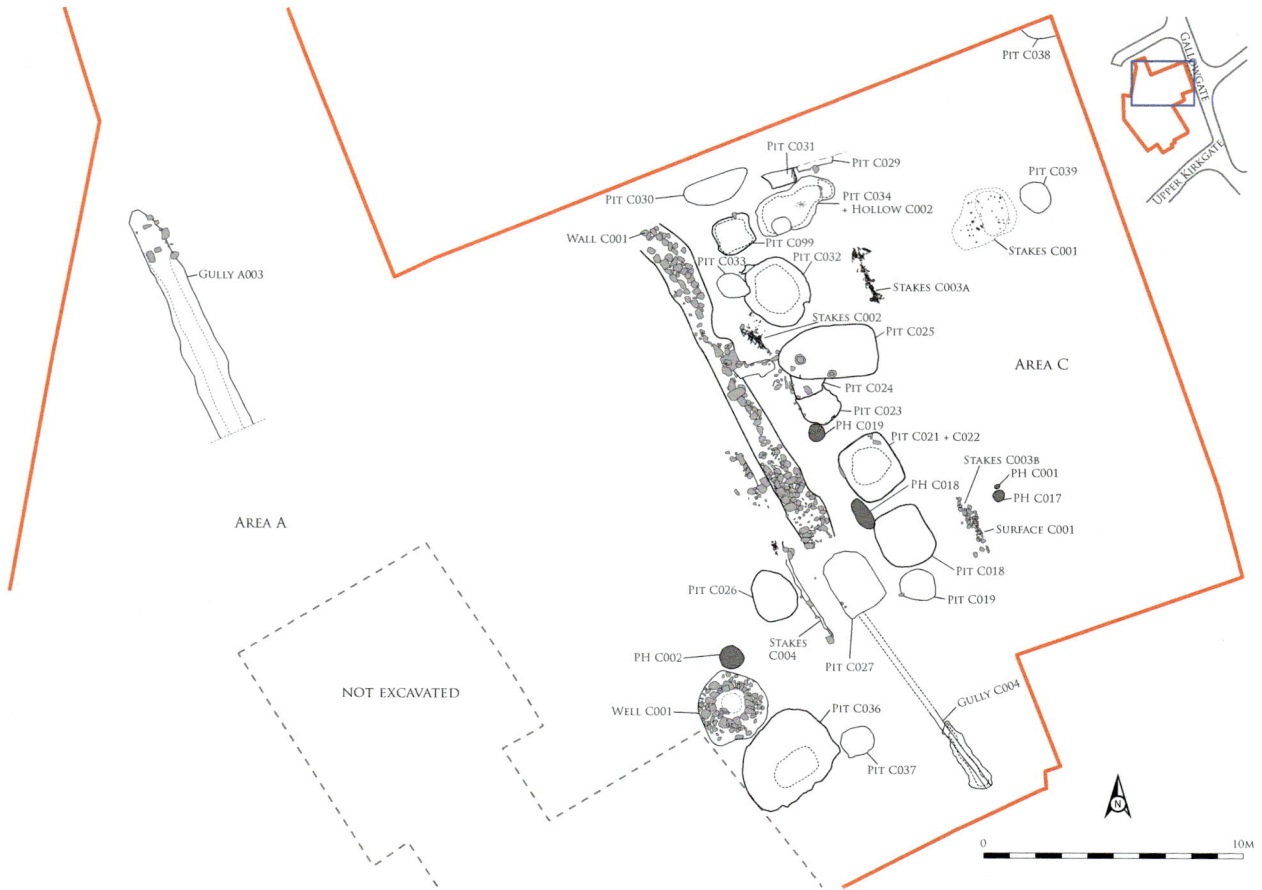

Figure 2.14 Plan of Phase 2 features

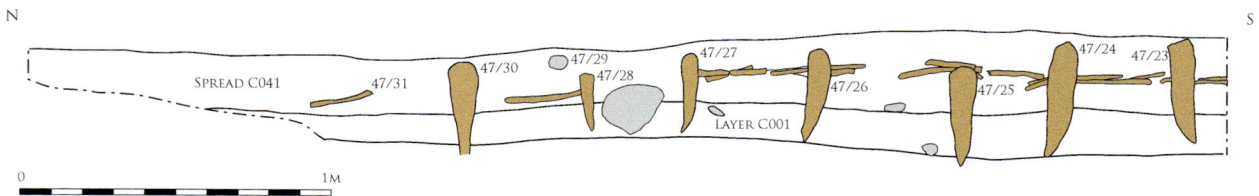

Figure 2.15 West-south-west-facing section of Stakes C002

between Stakes C002 and C003 was *c.* 5m, perhaps indicating a plot width. The distance between Stakes C002 and C004, to the west, was *c.* 3.5m. It is notable that a significant number of large pits, of possible industrial function, were located within the linear strip bounded by Stakes C002 and C004. There was evidence that these features were backfilled and subsequently either recut on roughly the same location, or truncated by other Phase 2 pits, suggesting a period of considerable activity, e.g. Pits C021 and C022 (Figure 2.17C).

A major problem for the interpretation of features in the east of Area C, close to the Gallowgate, was the truncation of medieval deposits caused by post-medieval structures in this area. This leads to a possibility that features identified as belonging to Phase 2 in this area

Figure 2.16 Stakes C003 from east

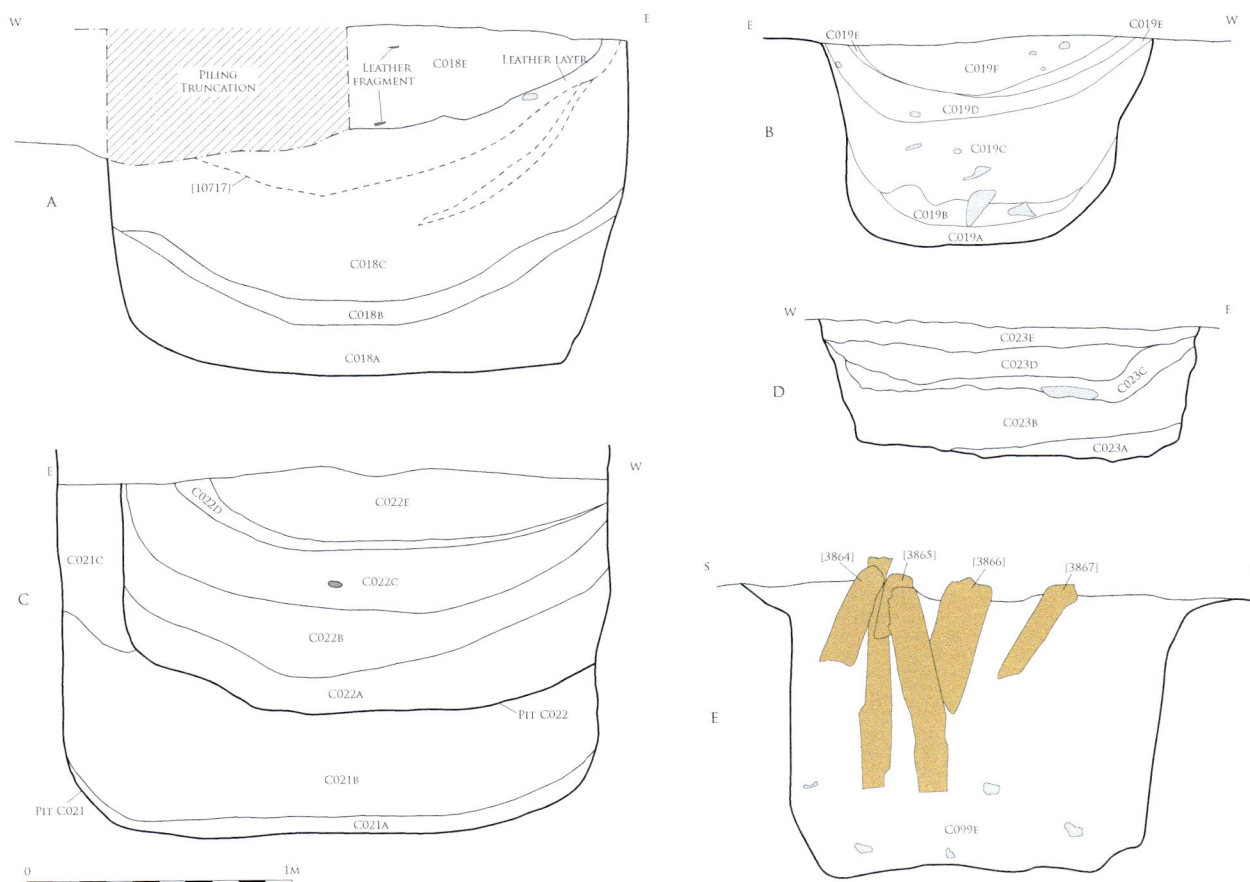

Figure 2.17 Sections across Phase 2 features in east of site
(A) South-facing section of Pit C018
(B) North-facing section of Pit C019
(C) North-facing section of Pits C021 and C022
(D) South-facing section of Pit C023
(E) East-facing section of Pit C099

may on occasion actually be of Phase 3 date. However, certain boundary features, including Stakes C002 and C004 were unequivocally of Phase 2 date, and the features delimited by them can reasonably be ascribed to this period. Also, clearly underlying Phase 3 deposits was rubble Wall C001 (Figure 2.18), which together with Gully C001 may have formed a substantial boundary feature during Phase 2. Wall C001 was the base of a rubble wall running roughly north/south, parallel with and immediately east of Stakes C004 and Gully C001.

As noted above, during this phase a number of large pits were recorded, commonly of rectangular or sub-rectangular shape and possibly associated with industrial activities such as tanning, given the presence of large quantities of leather artefacts. Furthermore, the edges of several of these features were defined by lining materials that included clay, wattle construction, reused wood, and heavily organic (often peat-like) matter. The major fills of these features generally comprised clay silts and silty clays. Many, but not all,

of these features lay in the linear north/south strip of ground between Stakes C002 and C003. These included sub-rectangular Pit C018 (Figure 2.17A & 2.19), which was truncated by sub-square Pit C019 (Figure 2.17B & 2.20) and sub-square clay-lined Pit C021, and its recut Pit C022 (Figure 2.17C), which contained branches, remnants of its lining. Uniquely, a single piece of human bone (SF2785) was found in the uppermost fill of Pit C018. This was a fragment of right ilium from an adult male of early middle age (26-35 years). Disturbance of the upper fill of the pit by 20th century piling is likely to account for the fragmentation of the remains. It is unclear whether the human bone was placed in the pit during its period of initial backfill or at a later period (Rachel Ives, *pers comm*).

Also in Area C was irregular Pit C023 (Figure 2.17D), which contained degraded timber and frequent twigs in its organic-rich fills, again possibly remnants of lining. This was cut by another irregular Pit C024, the edge of which was partially defined by wooden material. Also

Figure 2.18 Base of Wall C001 from north

Figure 2.20 North-facing section of Pit C019

Figure 2.21 East-facing section of Pit C034

Figure 2.19 Post-excavation view of Pit C018 from north-east

in this strip of ground was irregular Pit C033, which had its edge partially defined by areas of greenish grey clay – possible degraded lining – and was stratigraphically over sub-oval Pit C032. Immediately north were shallow irregular Pit C034 (Figure 2.21) and sub-square Pit C099 (Figure 2.17E). Pit C025 was an exceptionally large lined sub-rectangular pit of *c.* 4m length, lined with both a peat-like material and blueish grey clay (Figures 2.22 & 2.23), cutting Pit C024, indicating that it may have been a relatively late feature in this phase. In spite of

truncation by modern piling, a remarkable assemblage of artefacts was recovered from this feature, including turned wooden bowls and platter fragments (Figures 2.23 & 2.24), wooden paddles (Figure 2.25), redeposited structural wood and a sizeable block of hurdle screen, overlying timbers (Figures 2.26 & 2.27), perhaps used to cap the pit once it had been backfilled with rubbish. There was more hurdle-like material within the pit, possibly remnants of the pit's lining or further dumped structural material.

To the north only the southern edge of sub-circular Pit C030 (Figure 2.28A) was recorded as it lay on the limit of the excavation. Smaller features in this area included Ph C019 and Hollow C002, a feature probably derived from compaction and associated with Spread C010 and Spread C044 (not illustrated) as well as small Pit C029, associated with sandy silt Spread C043 (not illustrated), and Pit C031 (Figure 2.28B). The last two pits were also only visible in part as they lay on the edge of the site. Pit C029, the edge of which was partially defined by degraded wood, may have extended beyond the

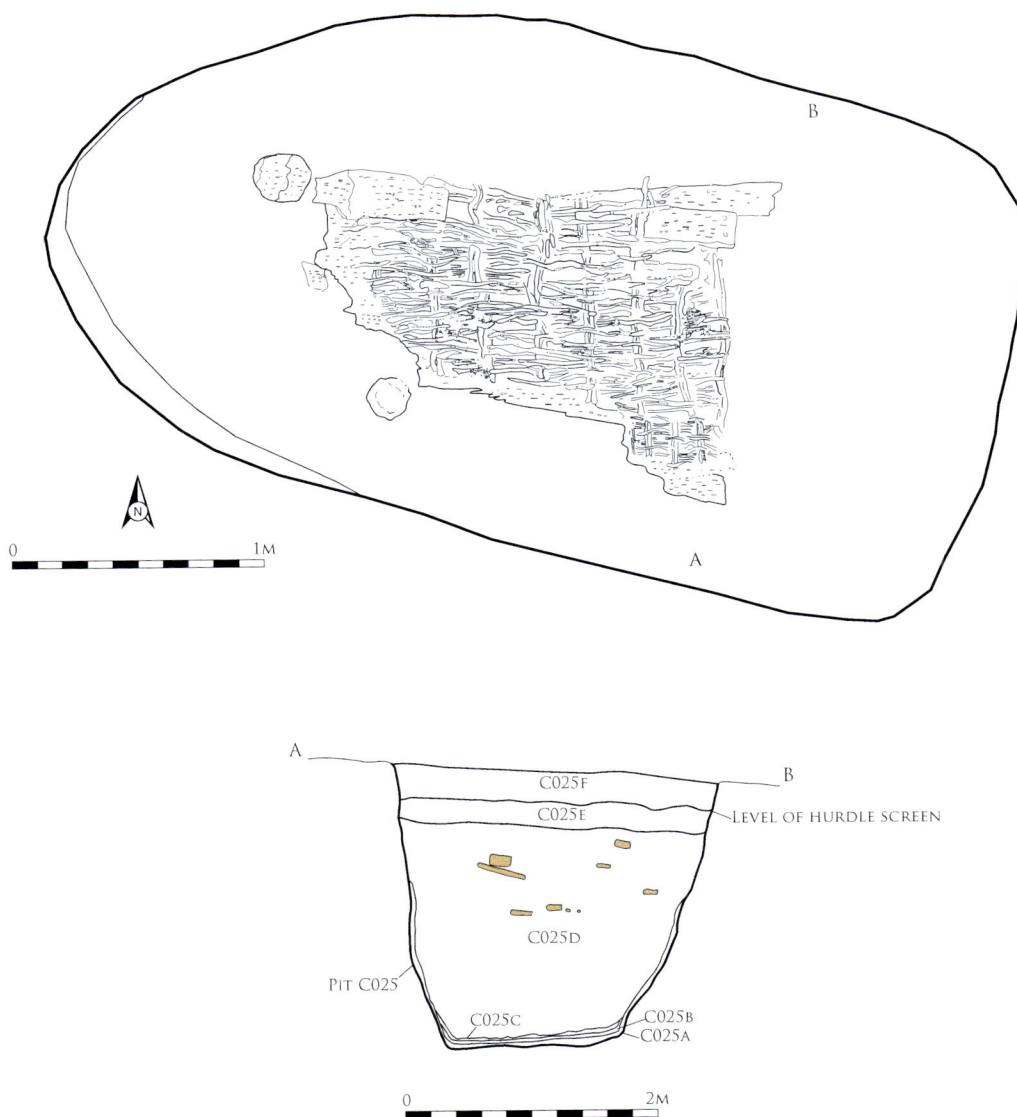

Figure 2.22 Plan and south-east-facing section of Pit C025 showing hurdle screen (SF3100)

Figure 2.23 Pit C025 during excavation, from south

boundary delineated by Stakes C003. Where visible, Pit C031 (Figure 2.29) was lined with a crude wattle construction packed with greyish brown clay and organic material, possibly including turfs.

To the west, and within *c.* 8m, of the boundary formed by Wall C001, Gully C001 and Stakes C002 there were several more significant features. These included large Pit C026 (Figure 2.30A), which contained frequent twigs and branches in its organic silty clay fills, possible remnants of lining material (Figure 2.31).

Also in this area were irregular, vertical-sided Pit C037 (Figures 2.30B & 2.32) and Ph C002 (the latter possibly a small pit).

South/north-aligned Gully C004 ran towards and may have led into sub-rectangular Pit C027 (Figure 2.33);

Figure 2.24 Fragment of wooden platter in Pit C025

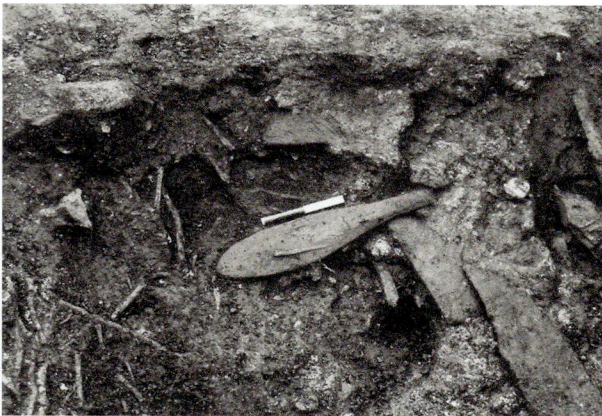

Figure 2.26 Hurdle screen in Pit C025 from east

Figure 2.25 Wooden paddle in fill of Pit C025

Figure 2.27 Structural timbers under hurdle screen in Pit C025

these last two features were cut into gravel levelling Spread C005. Pit C027 lay immediately south of the apparent termination of Wall C001 and had a blueish grey clay lining at its base and contained a mixed organic-rich fill with frequent twigs and structural wood (Figure 2.34). It is likely that Gully C004 was a continuation of the boundary line demarcated by Wall C001.

Timber-lined Well C001 (Figure 2.35) also lay to the west of the boundary lines, adjacent to large Pit C036

(Figure 2.36A). Well C001 lay within a circular cut, which was over 2m in diameter. The well structure comprised a wooden barrel lining (Figures 2.37 & 2.38) under a circular stone lining superstructure (Figures 2.39 & 2.40). The heavily organic lower fills of Pit C036 contained pieces of wood and twigs that may again have been remnants of a lining structure.

In the east of Area C, Layer C003 was cut by Pit C038, which was only partially visible as it lay on the north-

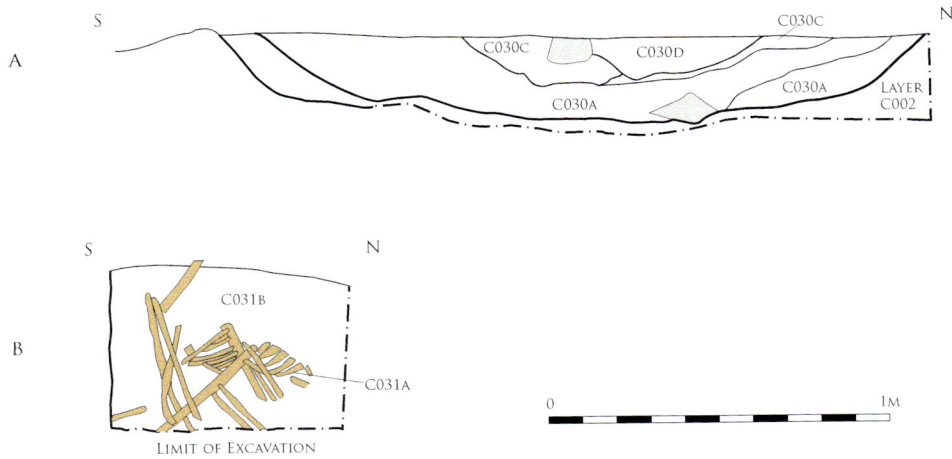

Figure 2.28 Sections across Phase 2 features in north-east of site
(A) East-facing section of Pit C030
(B) East-facing section of Pit C031

Figure 2.29 Detail of possible lining remnant in Pit C031

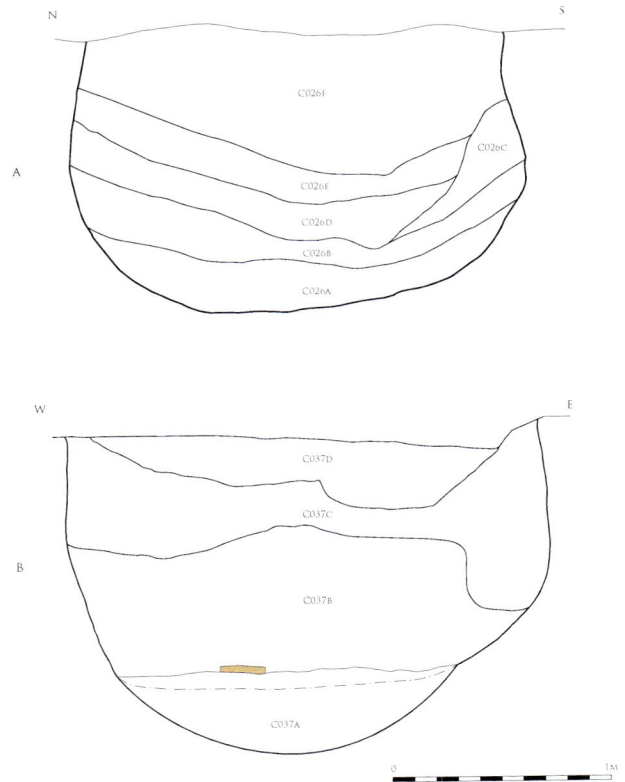

Figure 2.30 Sections across Phase 2 features to the west of
Wall C001
(A) West-facing section of Pit C026
(B) South-facing section of Pit C037

eastern corner of the site. To the south were truncated Pit C039 and two closely situated likely posthole bases, Ph C001 and Ph C017, which may have been elements of a structure. Also, a cluster of 35 irregularly spaced stake holes, Stakes C001, likely a Phase 2 feature, were located in this area. This fenceline was constructed using small undressed hazel roundwood stakes, 20–35mm in diameter.

Phase 2 in Area A, at a distance from both the Gallowgate and Upperkirkgate frontages, was marked by the deposition of a thick layer of dark grey brown clay silt, Layer A002/A012. There were several smaller dumped deposits, dated to between Phases 1 and 3, over Layer A001, including clay Spreads A019, A023 and A024 (not illustrated) and Layer A032 (not illustrated). Layer A002 lay beneath several small spreads of similar material and Phase 4 major occupation deposits such as Layer A003. The dating of features cut into Layer

A002 could commonly not be securely differentiated between Phases 2 and 3; in this relatively peripheral backland area there was apparently less activity than towards the Gallowgate frontage, where build up of occupation deposits was more rapid between Phases 1

Figure 2.31 Pit C026, half-sectioned, from north

Figure 2.33 East-facing section of Pit C027 and Gully C004

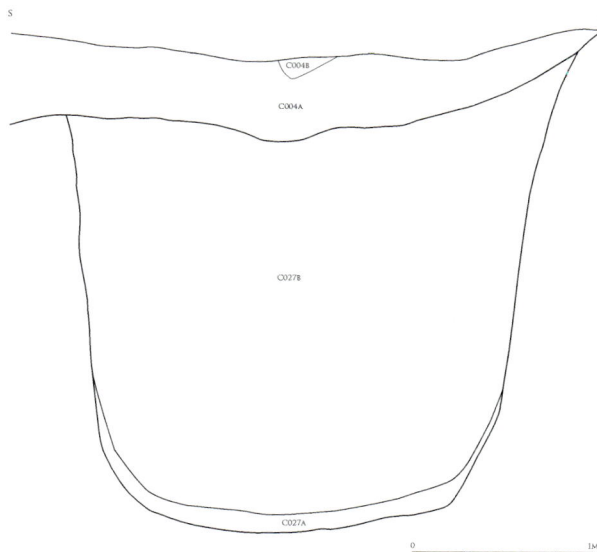

Figure 2.32 North-facing section of Pit C037

Figure 2.34 Pit C027, following excavation, from east

and 4. For example, dendrochronological analysis gives the construction of timber-lined Well A002 (Chapter 4.1), a likely mid 13th century date suggesting that it was in use during Phase 3.

A significant Phase 2 or 3 feature cut into Layer A002 was Gully A003 (Figure 2.36B), a north/south-aligned linear feature, which given its orientation, parallel with the stake lines to the east, may have formed part of an early boundary off the Upperkirkgate.

2.4 Phase 3 – mid-to-late 13th century(figure 2.41)

further occupation deposits accumulated during this phase although substantial truncation had occurred, in particular close to the Gallowgate frontage. Behind the Gallowgate, occupation deposits contained burnt bone and charred cereal grains indicative of an occupation surface or possible midden. Pits, filled with refuse material including leather, animal bone and structural timbers were excavated through the occupation deposits. Remains of stone-built structures were recorded, including two hearth features with limited evidence for a more substantial feature. Further back from the Gallowgate was a substantial timber-lined well, likely in use in the later 13th century. The well shaft contained a large quadrilateral timber structure.

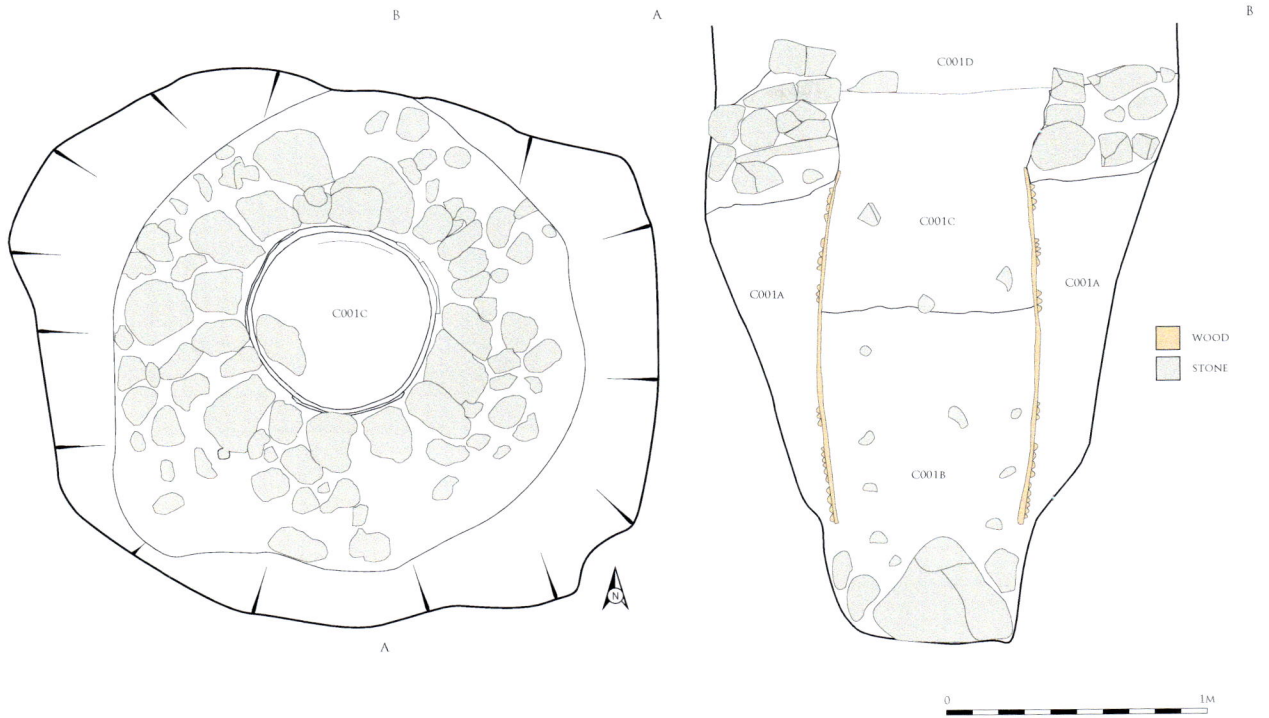

Figure 2.35 Plan and east-facing section of Well C001

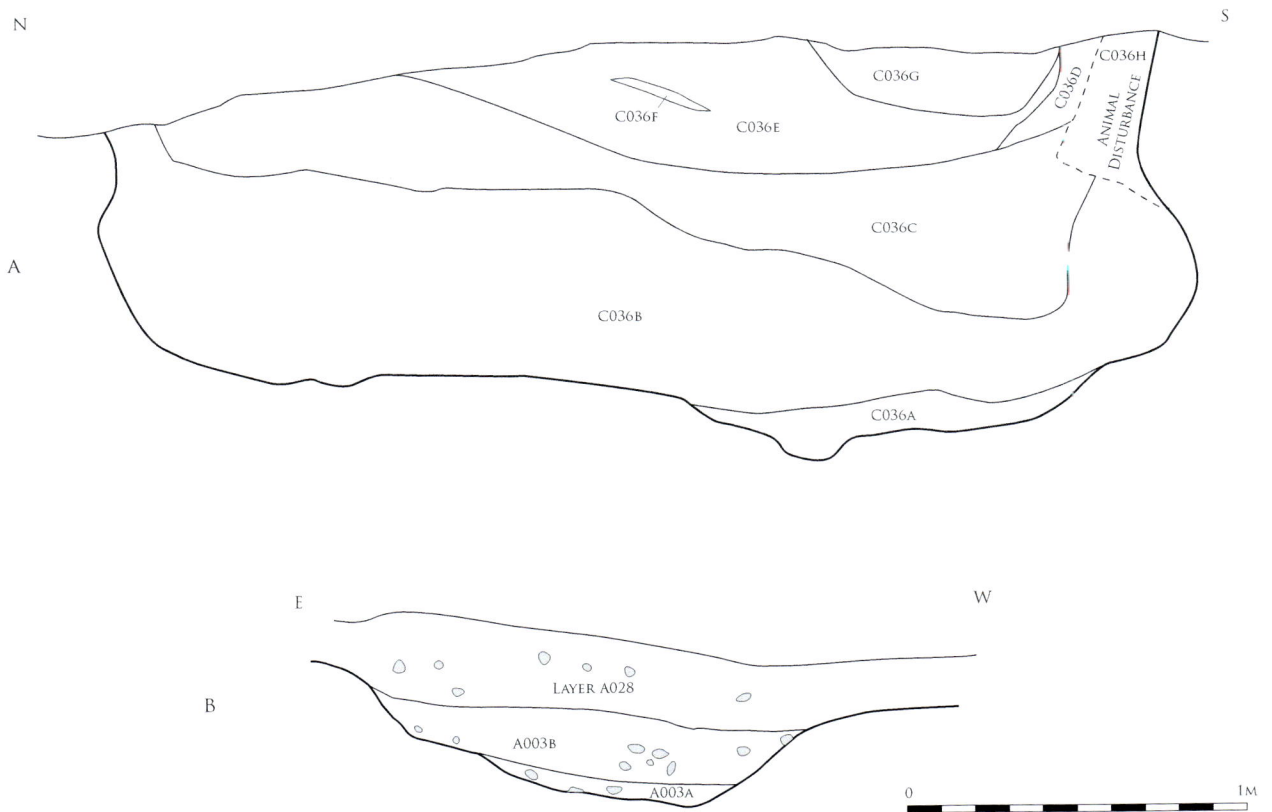

Figure 2.36 Sections across Phase 2 features in west of site
(A) South-west-facing section of Pit C036
(B) North-facing section of Gully A003

Figure 2.37 Barrel of Well C001 from west

Figure 2.38 Half-section of barrel of Well C001 from west

Figure 2.39 South-facing section through stone superstructure of Well C001

Figure 2.40 Top of barrel, lined with stone, of Well C001 from south

The third major phase of archaeological activity involved the accumulation of further dark brown/grey silty clay occupation deposits. There were relatively few features of secure Phase 3 date in Areas A, B or D; as noted above several features could not be more closely dated than between Phases 1 (or 2) and 3. Additionally, later disturbance, whether during the medieval period (as with Pit C048) or by late post-medieval and modern construction, led to difficulties in securely dating the features of this phase.

Later medieval and early post-medieval (i.e. Phase 3 to Phase 5) features and deposits in the east of Area C have been removed by later post-medieval truncation. In the south-west of Area C a likely early Phase 3 levelling deposit of clay and gravel, Layer C004 (not illustrated) was truncated by small Pit C035.

The late Phase 2/early Phase 3 deposits in Area C behind the truncated Gallowgate frontage were mostly overlain

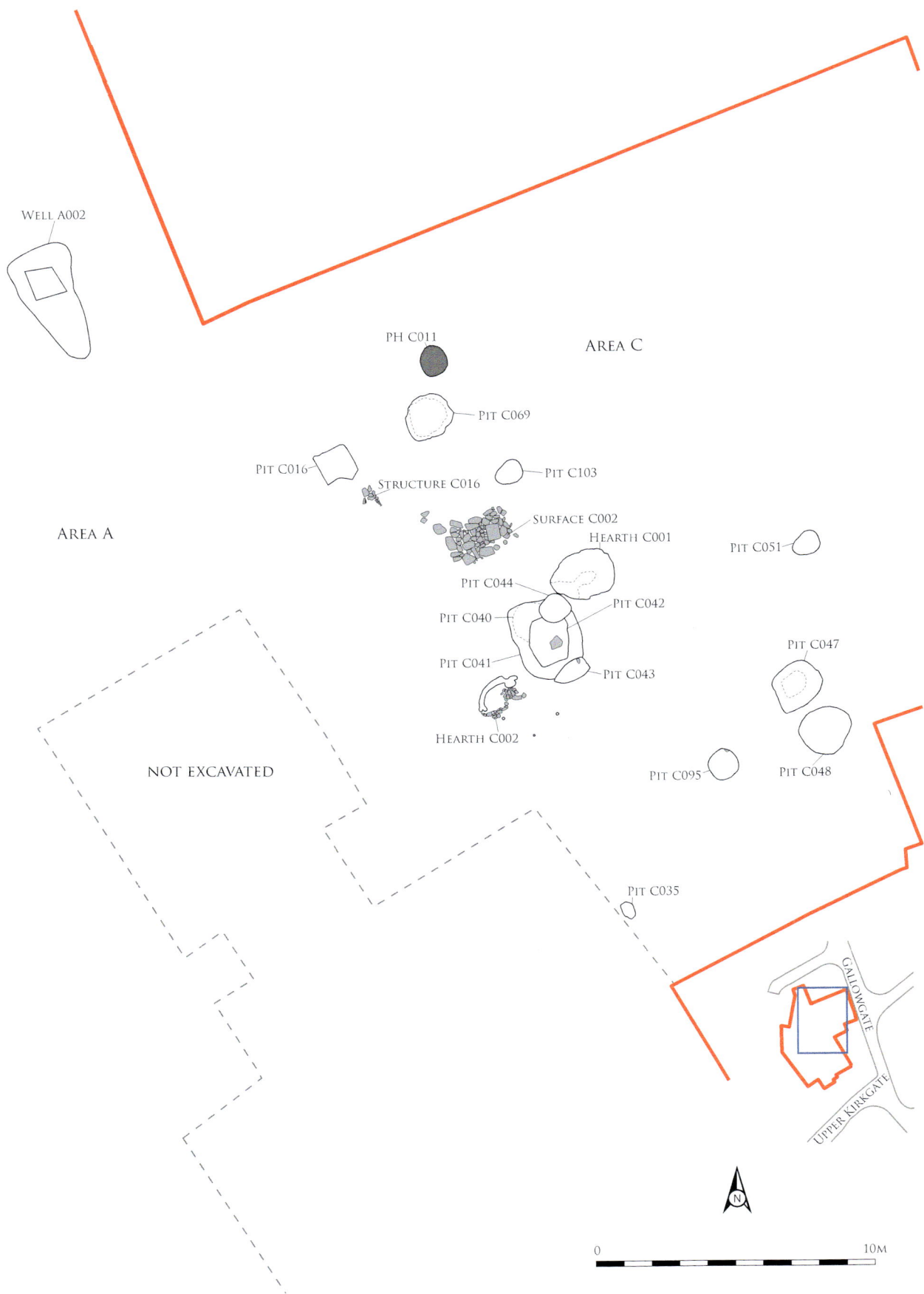

Well A002

PH C011

Area C

Pit C069

Pit C016

Structure C016

Pit C103

Surface C002

Hearth C001

Pit C051

Area A

Pit C044

Pit C042

Pit C040

Pit C047

Pit C041

Pit C043

Hearth C002

Not Excavated

Pit C095

Pit C048

Pit C035

Gallowgate

Upper Kirkgate

N

0   10m

Figure 2.41 Plan of Phase 3 features

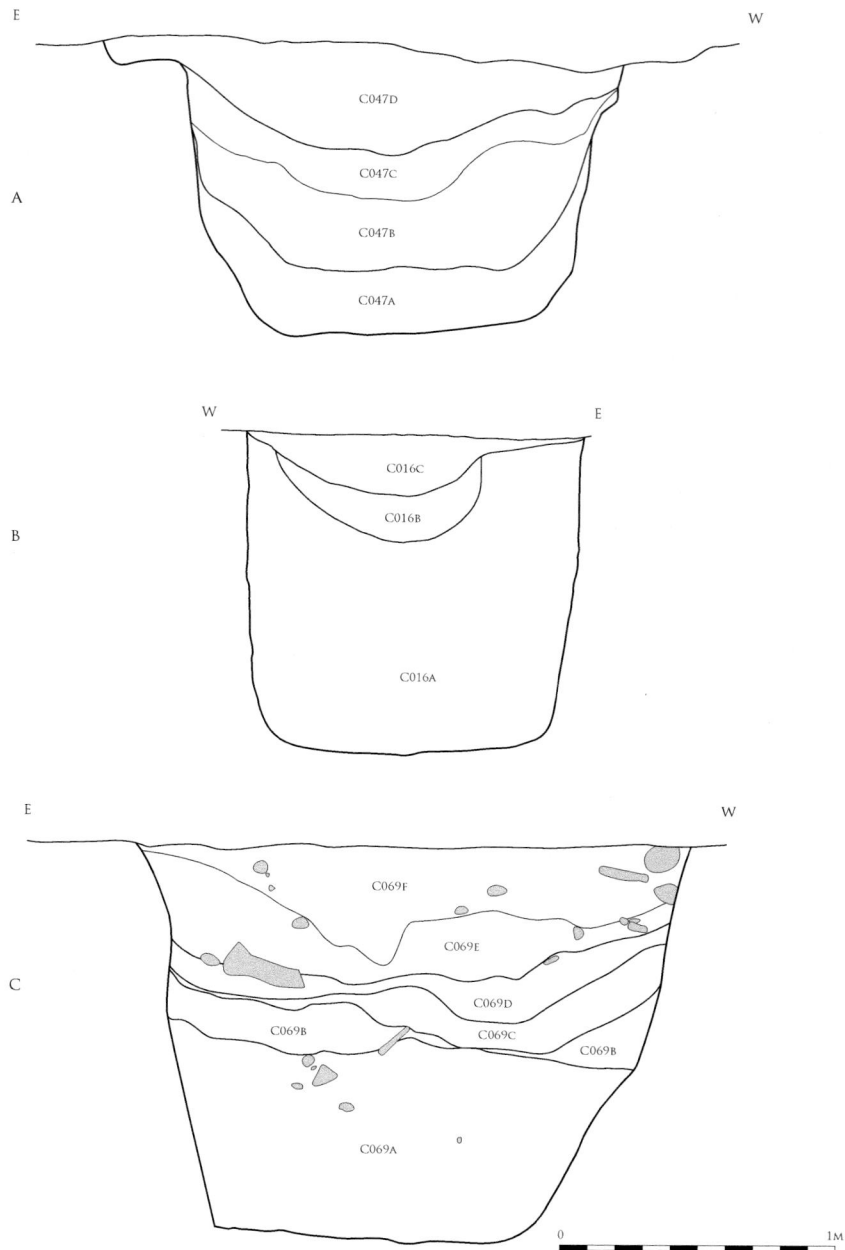

Figure 2.42 Sections across Phase 3 features
(A) North-facing section of Pit C047
(B) South-facing section of Pit C016
(C) North-facing section of Pit C069

by a silty clay Layer C005 (also recorded as Layer C050), which was a major occupation build-up layer, cut by pit and hearth features and covered by occasional dump deposits such as clay Spread C011. Numerous processes could be responsible for this deposit including periodic natural deposition of sand and silt interspersed with dumping of occupation waste or intentional infilling of an uneven floor surface with sand and silt deposits. The high organic content and diversity of material present in Layer C005 includes evidence for anthropogenic input in the form of burnt bone and charred cereal grains indicative of an occupation surface or possible midden. The presence of banded horizontally aligned plant fragments may be indicative of the intentional deposition of plant material over the occupation surface possibly as a floor covering.

Figure 2.43 East-facing section of Pit C042

Figure 2.44 Surface C002 from south

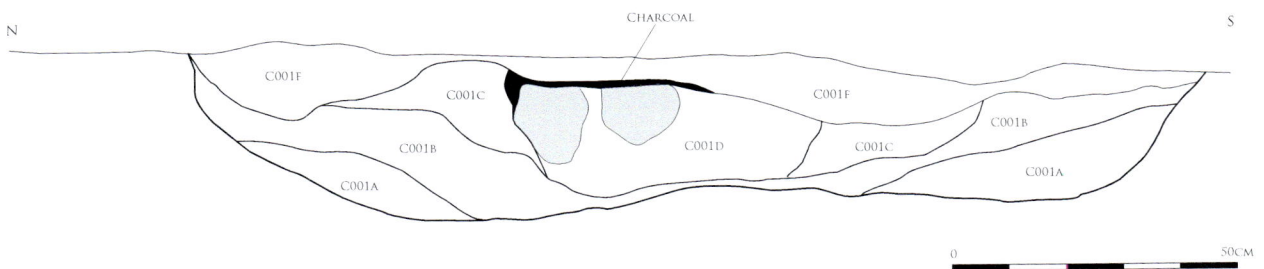

Figure 2.45 West-facing section of Hearth C001

Nearby, Phase 3 (or less likely Phase 4) clay silt Layer C019 (not illustrated) overlay Layer C005 and an area of silt levelling, Spread C154. Sub-circular Pit C048 cut through Layer C019 was likely of Phase 3 or perhaps Phase 4 date. It contained relatively early pottery, and while it had been disturbed by a shallow cut, Pit C050 (not illustrated), the preponderance of evidence suggests a Phase 3 date. Irregular Pit C047 (Figure 2.42A), which appeared to have had a clay lining, was stratigraphically earlier than Pit C048.

In the centre of Area C was a group of pits excavated through Layer C005 and filled with refuse material including quantities of leather and animal bone. Heavily truncated circular Pit C040 had been cut by wood-lined sub-circular Pit C041, which was in turn truncated by sub-circular Pits C042 and C043. Pit C042 (Figure 2.43) was itself truncated by Pit C044.

Further north was remnant stone Surface C002 (Figure 2.44) and a small spread of stones bonded with clay, Structure C016; it is possible that these stone groups represent a single, truncated structure of unknown function.

The shallow cuts for stone-built Hearths C001 (Figures 2.45 & 2.46) and C002 (Figure 2.47) were located nearby.

Figure 2.46 North-facing section of Hearth C001

Hearth C001 had apparently been capped with a large spread of redeposited clay subsoil (Figure 2.48). Hearth C002 was an oval cut filled with ashy material and lined with a clay-bonded stone structure, which was open towards the east (Figure 2.49). Apart from stone Surface C002 and Structure C016 there was no clear indication of a building associated with these hearths. Given their distance from Upperkirkgate (and Gallowgate) it is

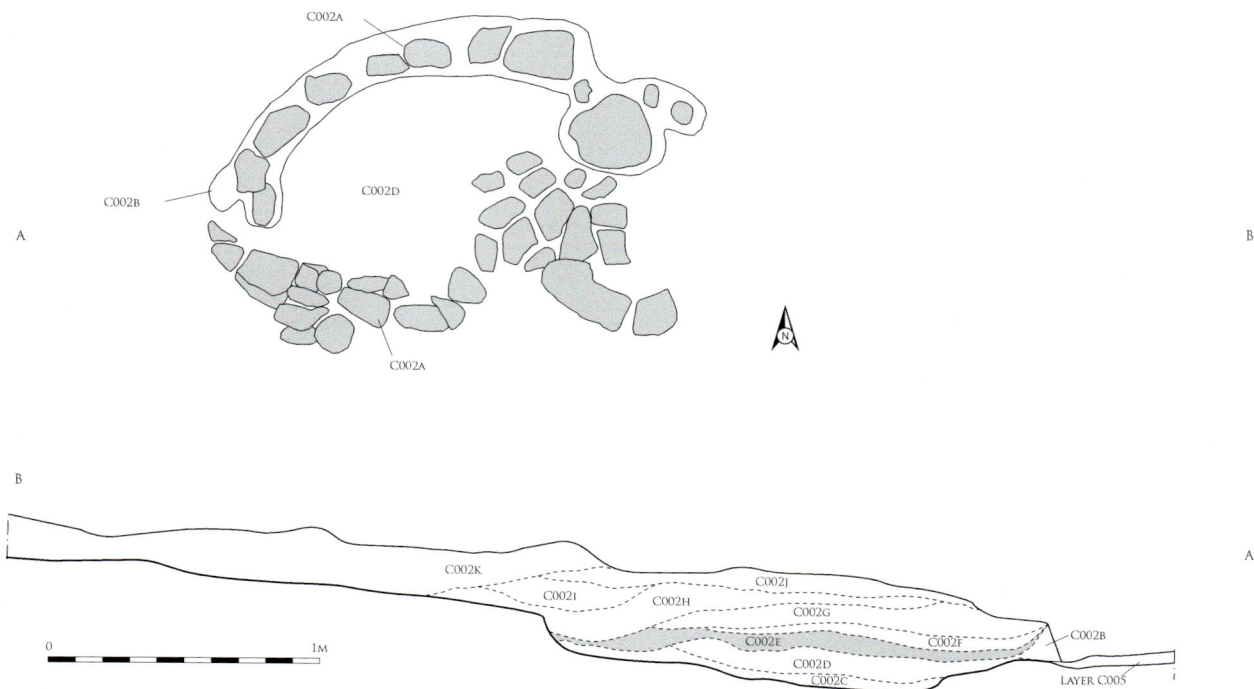

Figure 2.47 Plan and north-facing section of Hearth C002

Figure 2.48 Capping of Hearth C001 from south-east

possible that they were backland features associated with small-scale industrial activity. Thin silt dump or levelling Layers C006 and C007 overlay Layer C005 and were cut by a shallow feature, Pit C103, visible in section (Figure 2.56B, see later), likely to be a truncated pit. Also cut into Phase 3 deposits was badly truncated Pit C051, which belonged to Phase 3 or 4.

Further north, Ph C011 was an irregular feature associated with the remains of a timber post while square Pit C016 (Figure 2.42B) was heavily truncated by a post-medieval well. Pit C069 (Figure 2.42C) was a large circular pit likely dated to Phase 3 or the transition of

Figure 2.49 Hearth C002 from west

Phase 3 and 4, cut through Layer C005. It contained a sizeable assemblage of organic material including fish bone (Figure 2.50) and structural timbers, one of which produced a felling date of AD 1281; carbon residue from

Figure 2.50 Articulated fish vertebrae within fill of Pit C069

a pottery vessel within the pit fill provided a date of cal AD 1215–1300 (SUERC-26675; Appendix 1, Table A1.1).

In Areas A, B and D, Phase 2 deposit Layer A032 (not illustrated) was sealed by probable Phase 3 silty clay occupation Layer A031 (not illustrated); this is likely to be equivalent in date to nearby sandy clay occupation Layer A028 (of late Phase 2/Phase 3 date), which covered Phase 2 Gully A003. As noted above, dendrochronological analysis gives the construction of timber-lined Well A002 (Figure 2.51), cut through Layer A028, a likely mid 13th century date, indicating that it was probably in use in the late 13th century.

The well structure (Figure 2.52) lay within a large sub-rectangular cut with steep sides and a flat base, containing a deep shaft for the well to the north. The entire cut measured 5.5m north/south by up to 3.5m east/west, though the main shaft measured 2.4m by 2.4m. To the south the cut was approximately 1.6m deep with a base at c. 15.8m O.D. The shaft to the north had steep, slightly concave sides, and reached a depth of at least 15.2m O.D., before standing water prevented further excavation; probing identified a probable base at 14.68m O.D. The cut was lined with blue grey clay.

Within the well shaft was a timber structure constructed with vertical posts with square sections at four corners, which acted as retaining supports for the planks and posts that formed the sides of the well. These timbers had been laid horizontally to the west, south and east, with vertical planks to the north, supported by horizontal cross timbers. This northern side had suffered a degree of collapse in historic times. Elsewhere the sides of the well generally comprised horizontal planks laid on edge, each with a length between roughly 1.0 and 1.5m. Several of these horizontal timbers were reused posts. The structure had external dimensions of approximately 1.2m north/south by 1.2m east/west, though it was an irregular quadrilateral shape. Behind the structure, on four sides, was clay silt with a gravel

fill associated with the construction of the well. To the north of the structure, adjacent to the area of damaged timbers, there was a dark clay fill, probably derived from the partial collapse of this side of the well during its use. Given the substantial effort that went into the construction of this well, it is reasonable to believe that it was in use for a considerable length of time, before being backfilled.

2.5 Phase 4 (early) – late 13th to 14th century (figure 2.53)

deposits associated with Phase 4 survived behind the substantial truncation caused by the later buildings of the Gallowgate frontage. During this phase there was a further accumulation of occupation and dump deposits, a process that continued through the later part of the phase. The base of an east/west-aligned clay-bonded stone wall was visible for a length of 5.8m while a sequence of two large kiln or oven features, clay-bonded stone structures, was recorded. The presence of charred grain within a nearby pit may indicate that one or both of the ovens was used in the processing of food.

In the west of Area C, behind the area truncated by late post-medieval cellarage, the major deposit over the Phase 3 archaeology was a silt deposit, again derived from medieval occupation and dumping. This was recorded as Layers C008A, C026, C033, C041 and C075. Soil micromorphology indicates that the base of Layer C026 presented a sharp boundary with the underlying Layer C005. The dipping nature of the minerals in this deposit indicates that it was dumped possibly to seal the rich organic layer below.

It is likely that occupation deposits developed continuously over the site during the relatively long period of Phase 4. Due to similarities in several of the occupation deposits, which probably built up in a continuous process, through deposition, general churning through agencies such as footfall, silting in puddles, and plant growth, there was difficulty in the separation of some Phase 4 deposits, most notably the greyish brown silty occupation deposit Layers C008 and C008A where post-excavation study of the recovered pottery indicates that this deposit developed over a prolonged period and a division has been made between Layers C008A (early Phase 4) and C008 (late Phase 4).

Features cut through Layer C075 included sub-circular clay and twig-lined Pit C053 (Figures 2.53 & 2.54) in the north-east of the site, which lay under Ph C003, of likely late Phase 4 date. Remnant east/west-aligned clay-bonded stone Wall C002 stood nearby, a single layer of stones visible for a length of 5.8m over Layer C075.

Also in this area, Layer C075 was overlain by a large kiln or oven feature, Oven C002 (Figures 2.55A, 2.56B &

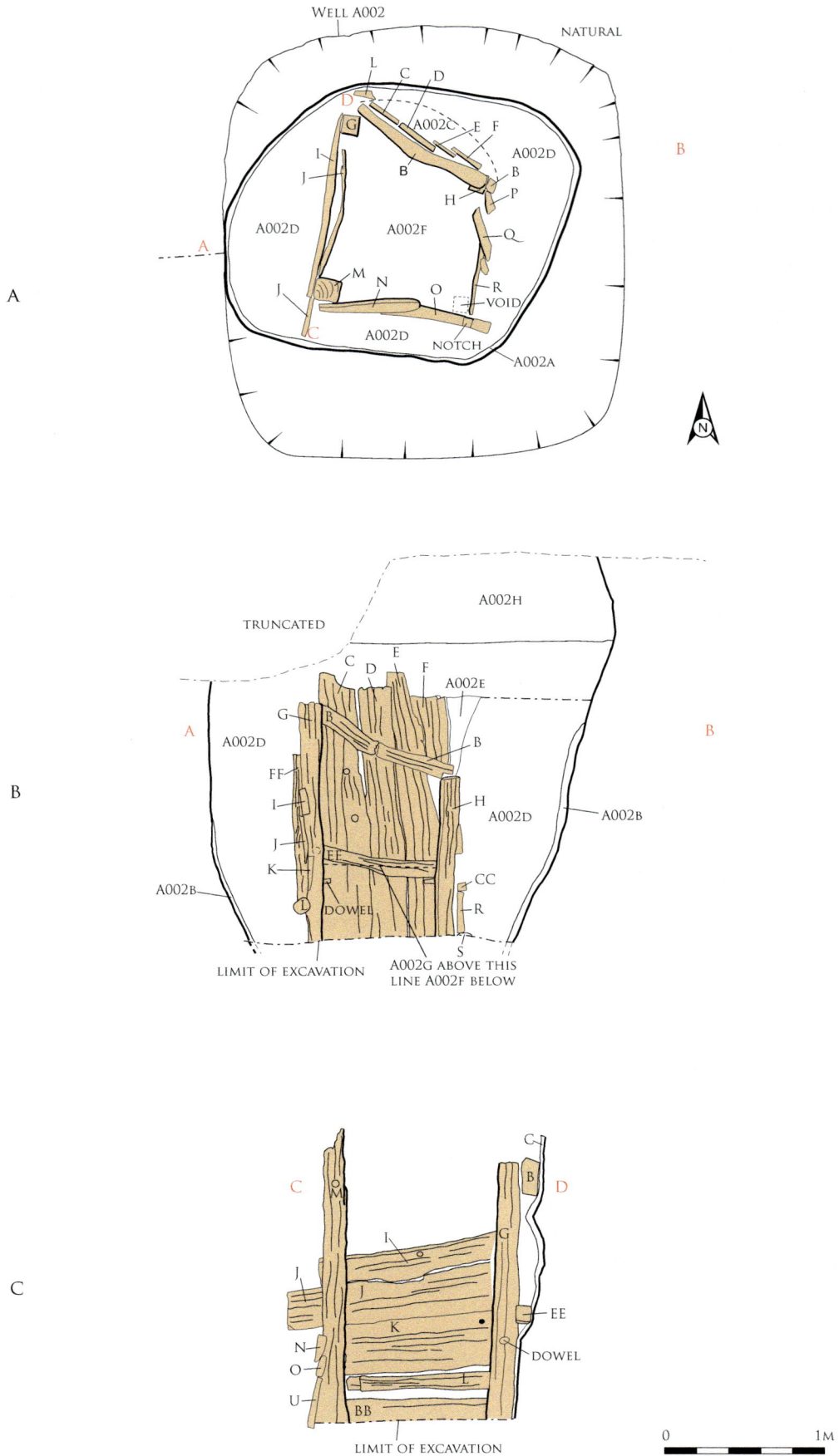

Figure 2.51 Plan, south-facing section and east-facing elevation of Well A002

Figure 2.52 Well A002 from south

2.57), which was 2.5m long east/west, and comprised a clay-bonded wall base surrounding a cobble and clay floor (Figure 2.58). Soil micromorphology indicated the presence of possible burnt animal dung in association with this feature. However, in addition to fuel residue and charred organic remains this deposit also contained frequent unburned organic material including partially decomposed plant fragments and probable coprolites indicating that this was a midden/waste deposit.

Oven C002 overlay the remains of a possible earlier version of this type of kiln/oven structure, Oven C001 (Figures 2.56B & 2.59). This oven consisted of an area of stones set in clay and was over 4m in length east/west and *c.* 0.3m deep (Figure 2.60). Sequences of similar stone-built ovens were recorded by Murray and Murray (1993: 125-26, fig. 8) in 14th and 15th century contexts at castle hill, Rattray, Aberdeenshire. Oven C001 lay under clay Surfaces C005 and C007, which may represent material deposited in preparation for the construction of Oven C002. Soil micromorphology revealed that the upper deposit of Oven C001 was laminated and contained horizontally-aligned voids and cracks, indicating that the upper part of the deposit was waterlain, perhaps representing a period of flooding or deliberate dumping of alluvial or lacustrine clay possibly to cover an underlying midden deposit. The sharp discontinuity boundaries between this deposit and those it overlies and underlies add further weight to the hypothesis that this layer was rapidly deposited.

The banded nature of the deposits associated with Oven C001 is indicative of periodic accumulation perhaps in a series of dumps or spreads. Its compaction could be interpreted as intentional tamping or ramming of earth. The nature of the voids within this deposit is also consistent with a deposit that has been trampled. It is therefore possible that it represented preparation for the construction of a building, hearth or floor.

The soil micromorphology samples from Oven C002 and Oven C001 (Chapter 4.5.6) contain high quantities of ash and other fuel residues indicative of the accumulation of fuel waste. The surrounding soil does not appear to be burned and it is likely that these deposits represented dumped fuel waste and hearth rakings as opposed to the actual combustion event(s). Unburnt inclusions indicative of human activity, including bone and plant fragments, were also present. Notably, the condition of the mineral grains was such that if the sediment was subjected to periodic heating the temperature cannot have reached above 800°C. The presence of charred grain within a fill of Pit C054, to the south, could indicate that one or both of the ovens was used in the processing of food.

To the south, Layer C026 (of which Layer 026A formed a lower element) contained Surface C003, a deposit of clay with small stones, which was probably a capping deposit over Phase 3 Hearth C002. Layer C026 also lay under small Pit C054, possibly an isolated posthole. Truncated Pit C055, possibly a posthole, was cut through Layer C033 while sub-circular Pit C059 cut Layer C008A.

In the west end of Area A, pottery evidence suggests that sub-rectangular Pit A011 (Figure 2.61), although cut through likely Phase 3 Layer A031, was an early Phase 4 feature. If Pit A011 is indeed a Phase 4 feature, then it follows that Gully A008, which fed into it from the north is also of this phase. Pit A011 lay under clay Layer A019, which was itself cut by shallow sub-circular Pit A010. Layer A019 was probably contemporary with Layer A003, which covered the backfill of timber-lined Well A002 to the north, indicating that it ceased to function by this time.

In the north-west of Area A, charcoal-rich clay dump deposits, including Layer A029 (not illustrated), overlay earlier Layer A002. Some of this material may have derived from a hearth or oven. Another possible Phase 4 deposit over Layer A002 was sandy clay with charcoal dump/occupation Spread A027, dated by pottery to the 14th century.

2.6 Phase 4 (late) – 14th to early 15th century (figure 2.62)

in the later part of Phase 4, further dump/occupation deposits accumulated. It appears, from soil

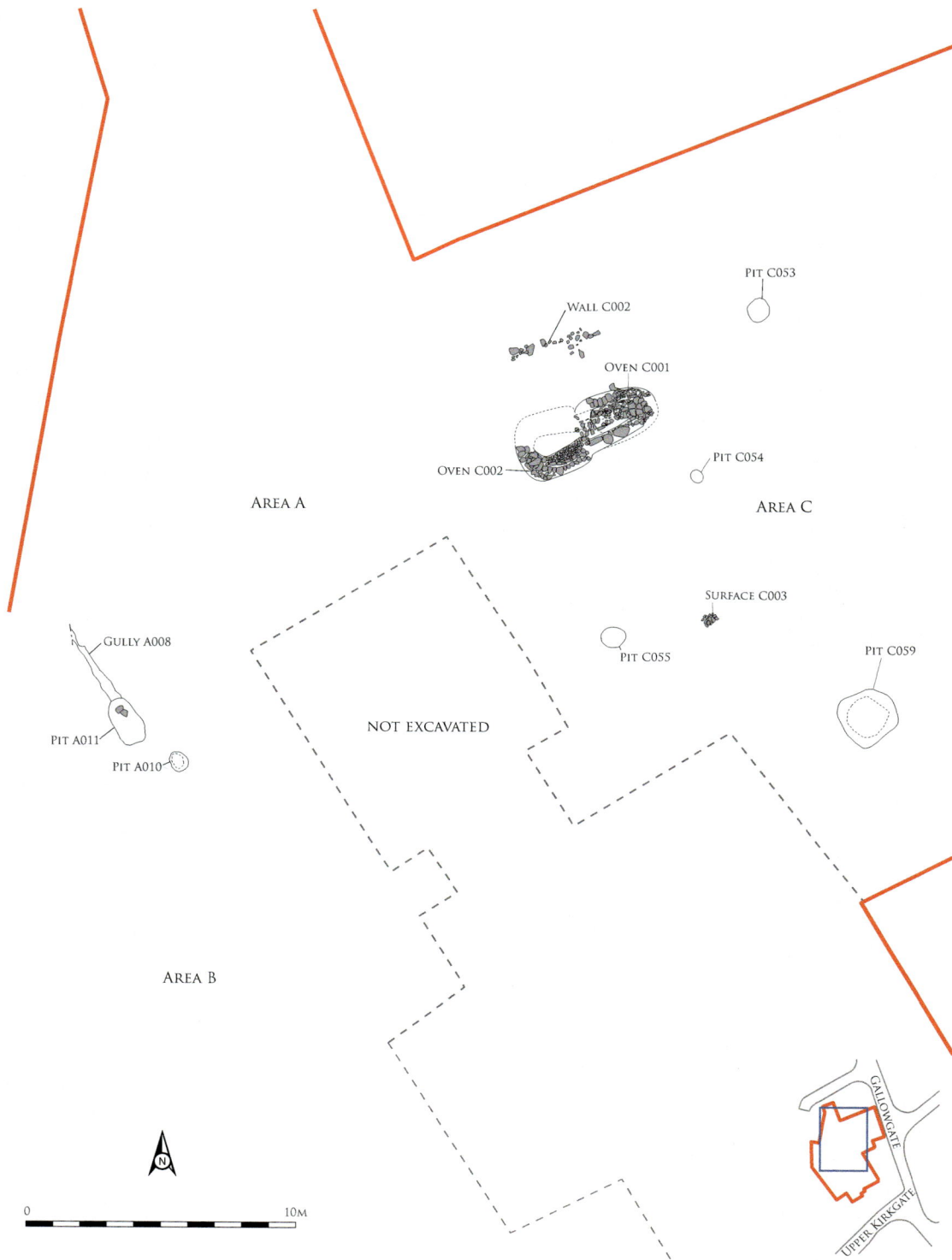

PIT C053

WALL C002

OVEN C001

PIT C054

OVEN C002

AREA A

AREA C

SURFACE C003

GULLY A008

PIT C055

PIT C059

PIT A011

PIT A010

NOT EXCAVATED

AREA B

N

GALLOWGATE

UPPER KIRKGATE

0   10M

Figure 2.53 Plan of early Phase 4 features

S

A

LAYER C075

LAYER C005

LAYER C003

WALL C001

PIT C053

C003B

C003A

PH C003

C053D

C053C

C053B

C053A

B

A

N

SPREAD C152

LAYER C075

SPREAD C013

SPREAD C009

LAYER C005

SPREAD C009

WALL C001

LAYER C003

B

0

2M

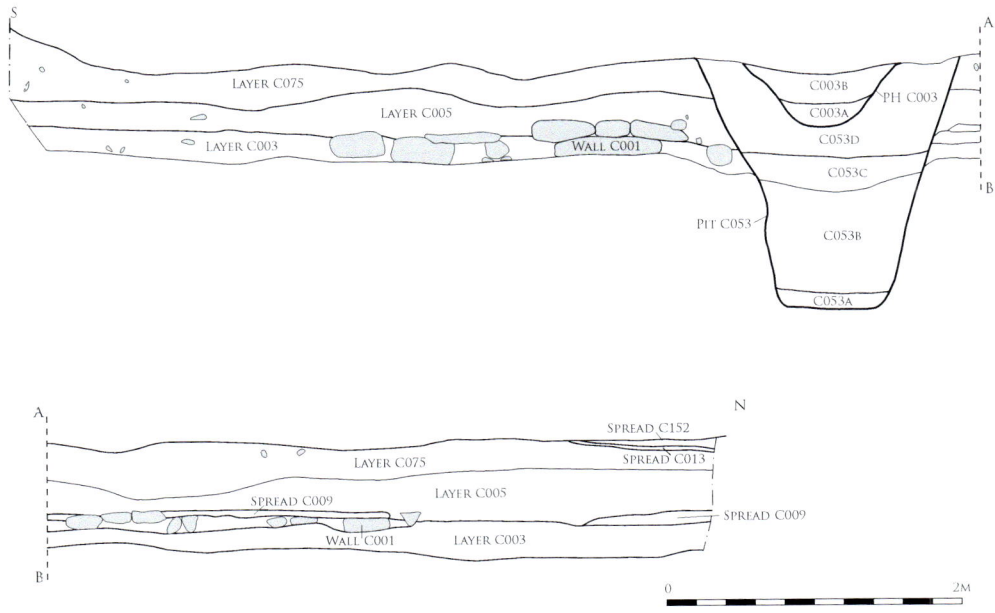

Figure 2.54 East-facing section behind Gallowgate

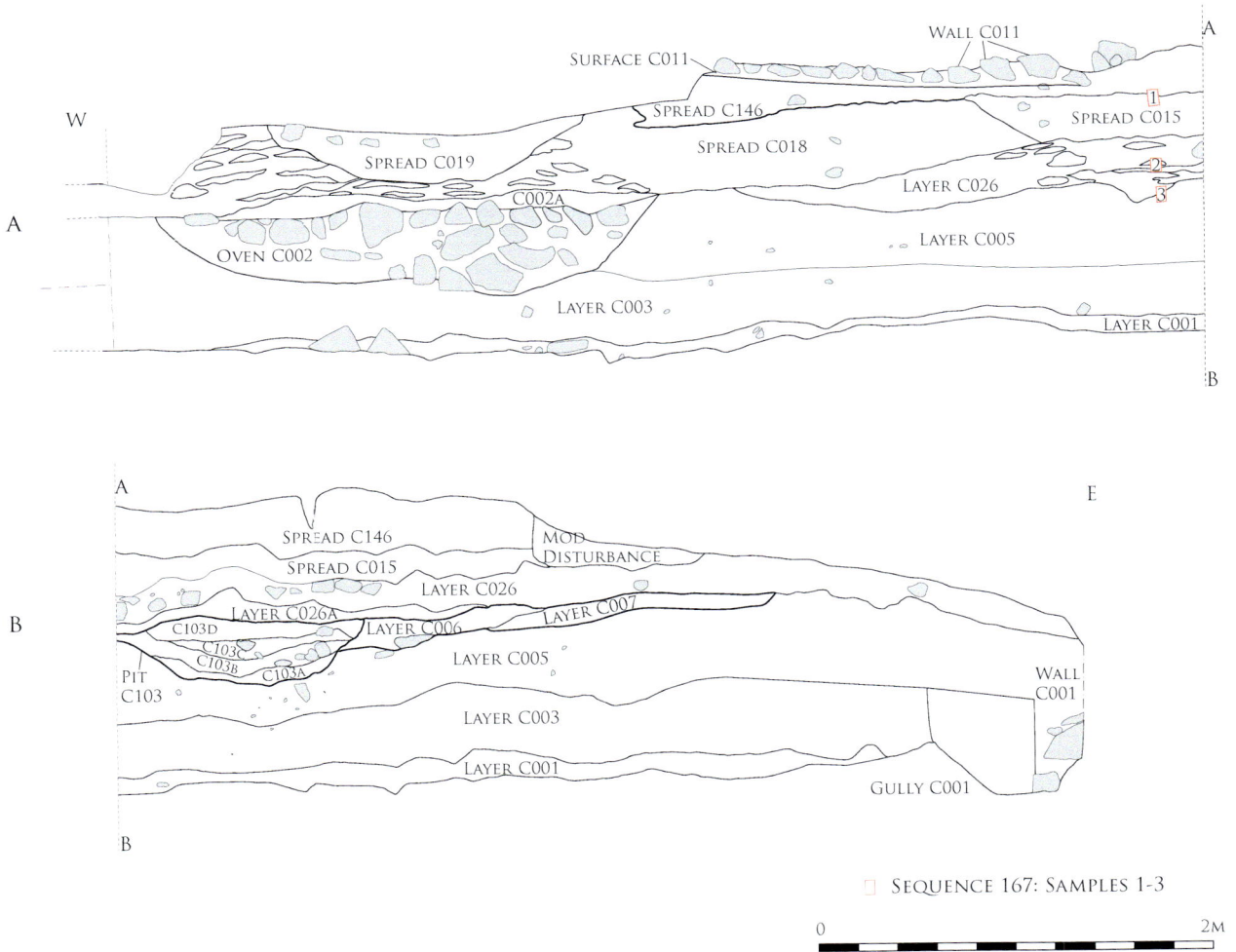

WALL C011

A

SURFACE C011

1

SPREAD C146

SPREAD C015

W

SPREAD C018

SPREAD C019

LAYER C026

2

3

A

C002A

LAYER C005

OVEN C002

LAYER C003

LAYER C001

B

A

E

SPREAD C146

MOD
DISTURBANCE

SPREAD C015

LAYER C026

B

LAYER C026A

LAYER C006

LAYER C007

C103D

C103C

LAYER C005

WALL
C001

C103B

C103A

PIT
C103

LAYER C003

LAYER C001

GULLY C001

B

☐ SEQUENCE 167: SAMPLES 1-3

0

2M

Figure 2.55 Central south-facing section behind Gallowgate
(A) West of south-facing section, showing Oven C002
(B) East of south-facing section, showing Pit C103

E
W

A

SPREAD C019
SPREAD C027
TRUNCATED
SPREAD C146
SPREAD C019
SPREAD C027
SURFACE C007
LAYER C075
LAYER C075
SPREAD
C157
LAYER C005
LAYER C075
LAYER C005
LAYER C003
WALL C001
LAYER C003
GULLY C001

B

E
W

SPREAD C146
SPREAD C019
SPREAD C027
SPREAD C018
SPREAD C157
SPREAD C166
SPREAD C027
SPREAD C164
SPREAD C159
OVEN C002
OVEN C002
LAYER C003
OVEN C001
SPREAD C157
SPREAD C159

□ SEQUENCE 164: SAMPLES 1-7
□ SEQUENCE 165: SAMPLES 4-5

0   2M

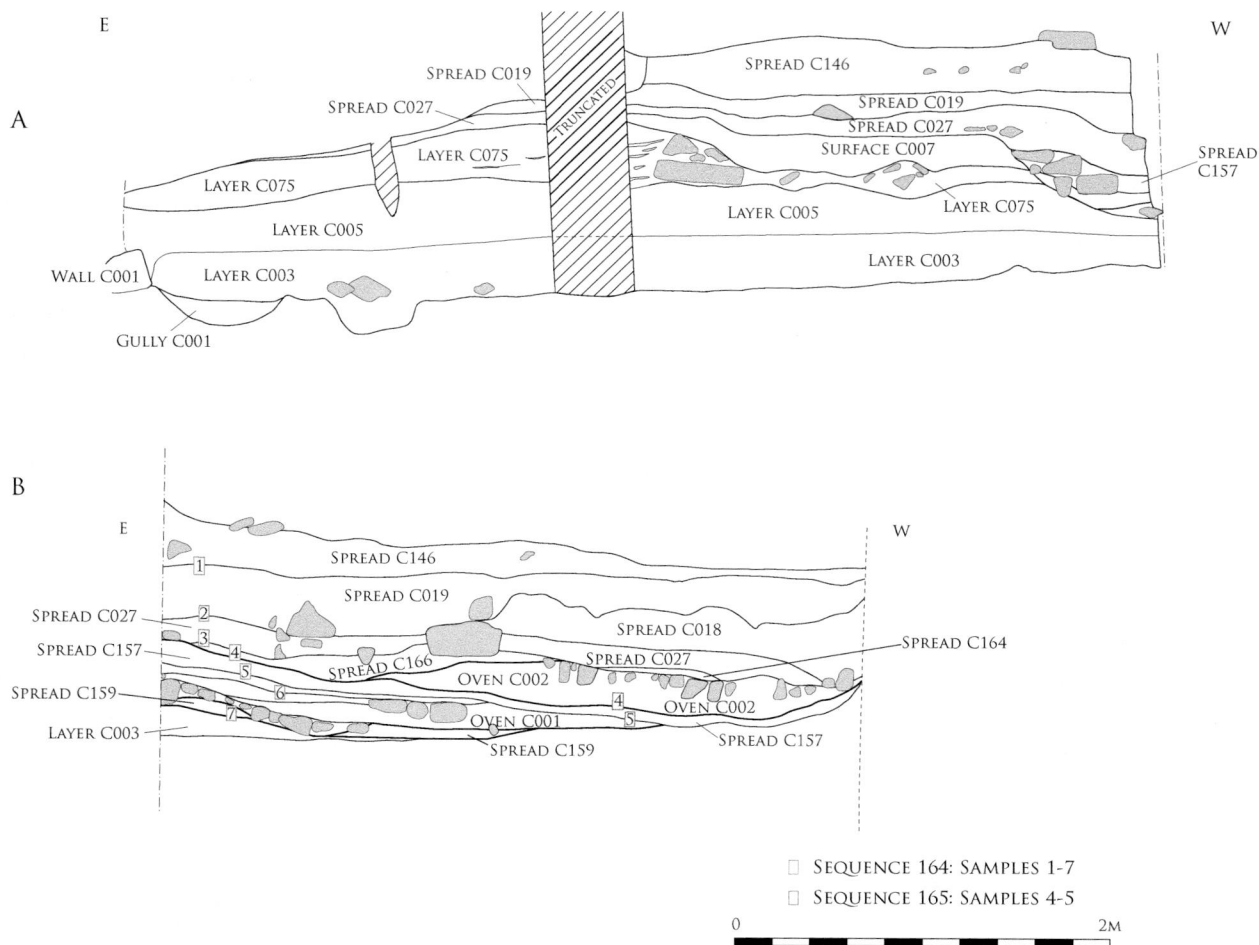

Figure 2.56 Central north-facing section behind Gallowgate
(A) East of north-facing section
(B) West of north-facing section, showing Oven C001 and Oven C002

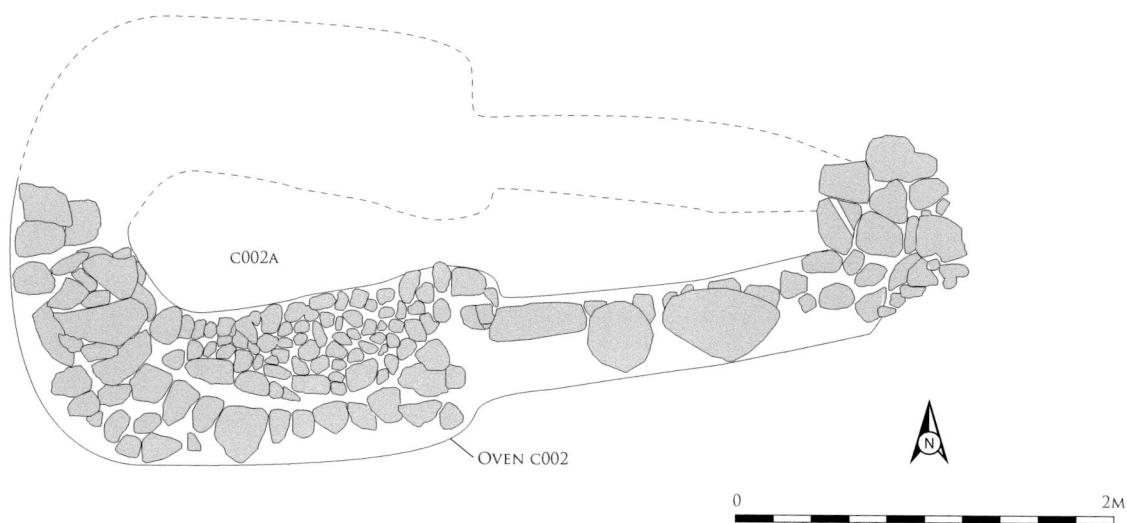

C002A

OVEN C002

N

0   2M

Figure 2.57 Plan of Oven C002

Figure 2.58 Oven C002 from west

micromorphology, that during this phase domestic and/or industrial waste was periodically spread across the site. As well as various cut features, generally likely to have functioned as refuse pits, late Phase 4 saw the construction of stone structures, including a possible stone drain and stone walls. One of these walls, a clay-bonded rubble wall, may demarcate a late medieval boundary running off the Upperkirkgate, to the west of the boundaries visible in earlier periods. In the west of

the site, thick garden soil was recorded, cut by a feature that may have been a well or cistern.

In the north-west of Area C, Layer C075 lay under deposits of sandy clay such as Spreads C012 and C013, and silty clay, including dump/occupation deposit, Layer C059, which was cut by shallow sub-circular Pit A025 (and its recut Pit C067) and lay under irregular Pit C065 (the latter perhaps a Phase 5 feature). Ph C003 was an isolated feature, of possible late Phase 4 date. Nearby, Oven C002 was overlain by numerous spreads of probable rake-out deposits and dumped material (including clay silt deposits Spread C166 and Spread C164), which likely dated to late Phase 4, when the feature was no longer in use. The soil micromorphology of Spread C166 indicates that it was mainly comprised of burned organic matter. It is probable that this material was the 'washed' remnants of grass-rich ash and it may have derived from burnt matter rich in grasses – possibly fuel, fodder, bedding or thatch. It does not appear to have been an *in situ* deposit; it is more probable that it represented the dumped remains from burning activity elsewhere, possibly ash from a hearth. Soil micromorphology suggests that in Phase 4 midden piles comprising domestic and/or industrial wastes were periodically spread across the site.

In the south of Area C, heavily truncated Pit C085 (not illustrated) was dated by ceramic evidence to the 14th century; it overlay clay silt dump Layer C025/C035.

Later Phase 4 occupation deposits in Area C also included clay Layer C020, over Layer C026. There is some pottery of likely 15th century or later date in late Phase 4 deposits including Layer C020. While this material may be intrusive, it suggests that the latest deposits within Phase 4 actually date to the early 15th century. Layer C020 was cut by shallow Pit C097. Possible stone drain Structure C002 (an east/west-aligned linear stone setting) and the sub-square area of cobble Surface C013,

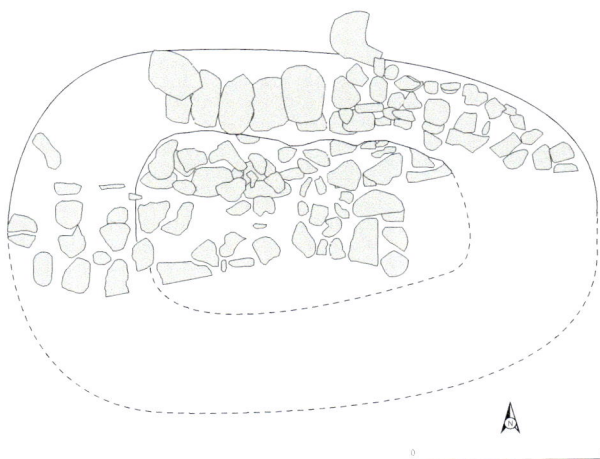

Figure 2.59 Plan of Oven C001

Figure 2.60 Oven C001 from north

measuring roughly 1.8m east/west by 1.7m north/south, possibly the remains of a demolished structure, were constructed above it. A short section of east/west-aligned stone line, Wall C010 (perhaps remnants of a feature adjacent to boundary Wall C007), also lay over Layer C020, though this may belong to early Phase 5.

Silty clay Layer C072 (also recorded as Layer C069) was a further late Phase 4 occupation deposit, which lay under the remains of north/south-aligned clay-bonded Wall C005. It was also cut by sub-circular Pit C073, which may date to Phase 5.

To the south, in Area C, silty clay Layer C008 was contemporary with Layer C072. It was cut by small oval Pit C061 and by deep vertical-sided Pit C064 (Figures 2.63 & 2.64). The fill of the latter feature contained a timber with a felling date of between AD 1261 and AD 1302. As this timber was waste material and not *in situ*, it is likely to have been in circulation for some time following its felling, and therefore a 14th century date for its deposition is likely.

Wall C007 was a clay-bonded rubble wall which, given its alignment, may demarcate a late medieval boundary running off the Upperkirkgate, to the west of boundaries visible in earlier periods (it may date to Phase 5). As noted above, the short east/west base of Wall C010 may represent an associated structure. To the north an occupation deposit, Spread C040, was at a similar point in the stratigraphy as Layer C008.

In Area A, in late Phase 4, Layer A003 was covered by Layer A004, a thick deposit of silty clay garden soil, and further spreads of material. The only feature to cut directly into Layer A004 in the west Area C was circular Pit A024 (Figure 2.65). This pit, dated by pottery to around the 14th century, had vertical sides and a flat base. It is postulated that it may represent the cut for a well or cistern, particularly as it was truncated at a later date by a shaft for barrel Well A001 (Figure 2.65), which may represent the replacement of the barrel lining.

In Area A, Layer A015 (over Layer A019), a dark clay silt garden soil, was equivalent to Layer A004. It was truncated by small sub-square Pit A008, perhaps an isolated posthole, and directly overlain by a lens of silty clay, Spread A009 (not illustrated).

Although the numerous pits of Phase 4 date were often more shallow than in earlier phases and may have mainly functioned as refuse rather than extraction or industrial features, the depth of Pit C064 suggested that it may originally have had a drainage function.

2.7 Phase 5 (early) – 15th to 16th century (figure 2.66)

the earliest part of Phase 5 was marked by the deposition of clay and clay with gravel deposits. There were also garden soil deposits in the west of the site. Segments of clay-bonded rubble wall formed the north-east corner of a putative structure. Another clay-bonded stone structure ran 7m north-west/south-east and incorporated a drain.

The Phase 5 period comprised late medieval and early post-medieval activity (dated approximately from the 15th century to the mid-to-late 18th century). Archaeological deposits and features of this phase were severely impacted by later truncation, including building foundations and services This has made interpretation of stratigraphy problematic – for example the deposits and features of early and middle parts of Phase 5 could not be more clearly defined than to the 15th and 16th centuries.

Overlying Phase 4 deposits were clay and gritty clay with gravel deposits including Spread C018 – these represented the build-up of material during late medieval (15th century) occupation. Silty clay Spread C019 was a possible sealing/levelling deposit over Phase 4 Oven C002. Soil micromorphology of Spread C019 indicates that it was consistent with a dumped deposit. It was mixed and turbated, with lighter areas

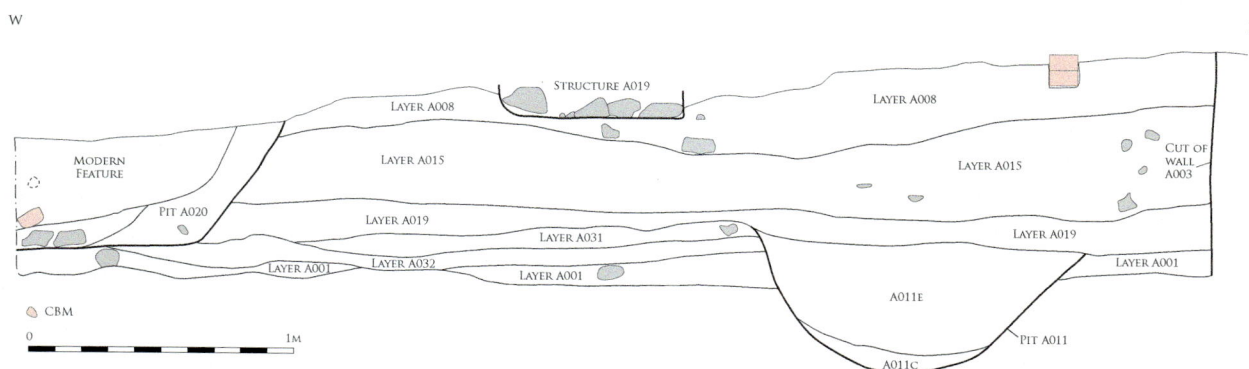

Figure 2.61 South-facing section of west of site

Pit C065

PH C003

Area C

Pit C067

Pit A024

Pit A025

Structure C002

Pit C056

Area A

Surface C013

Wall C010

Pit C097

Pit C073

Pit C064

Wall C010

Wall C007

Wall C005

NOT EXCAVATED

Pit C061

PHC004

Wall C007

Pit A008

Gallowgate

Upper Kirkgate

0   10m

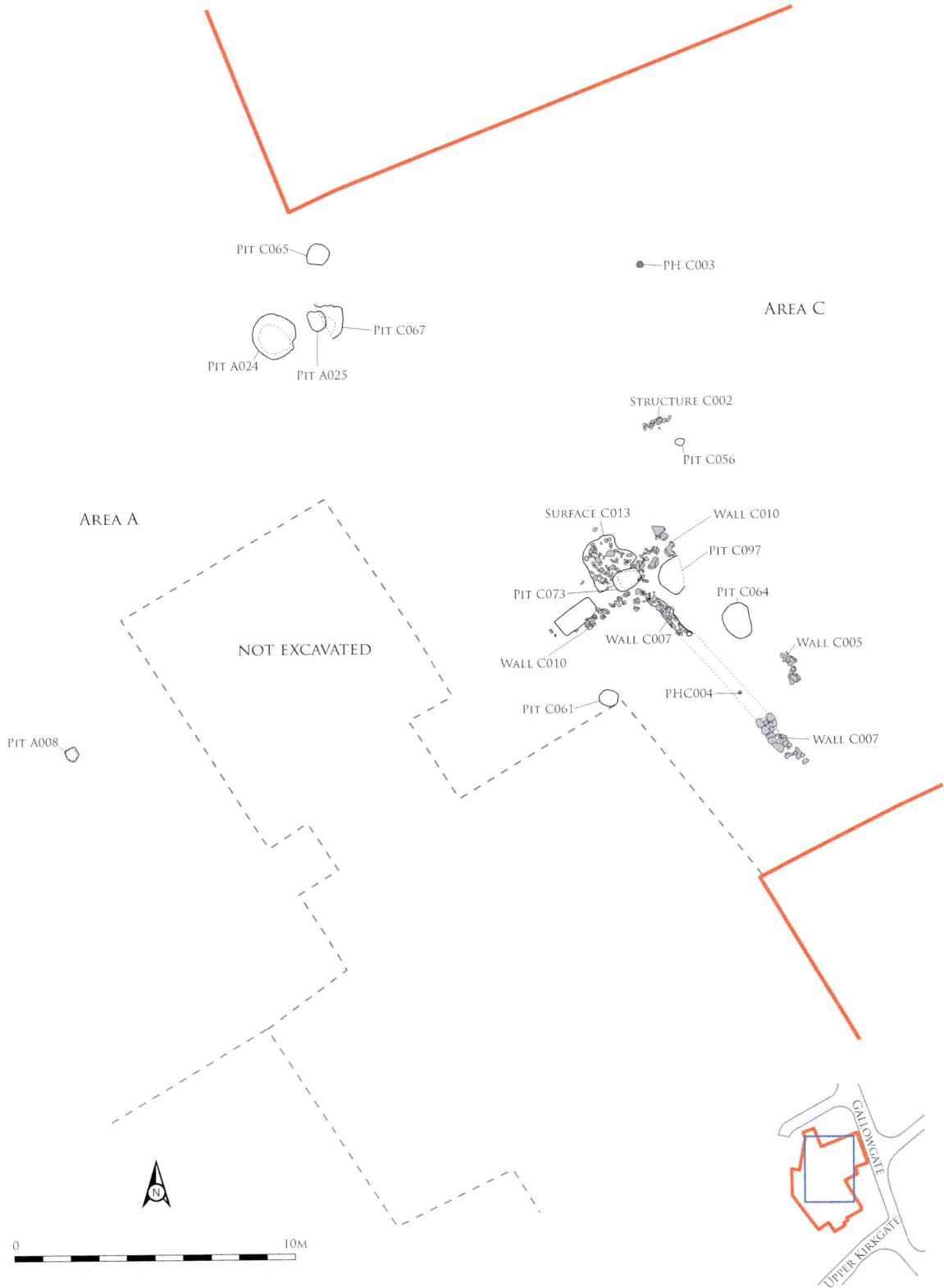

Figure 2.62 Plan of late Phase 4 features

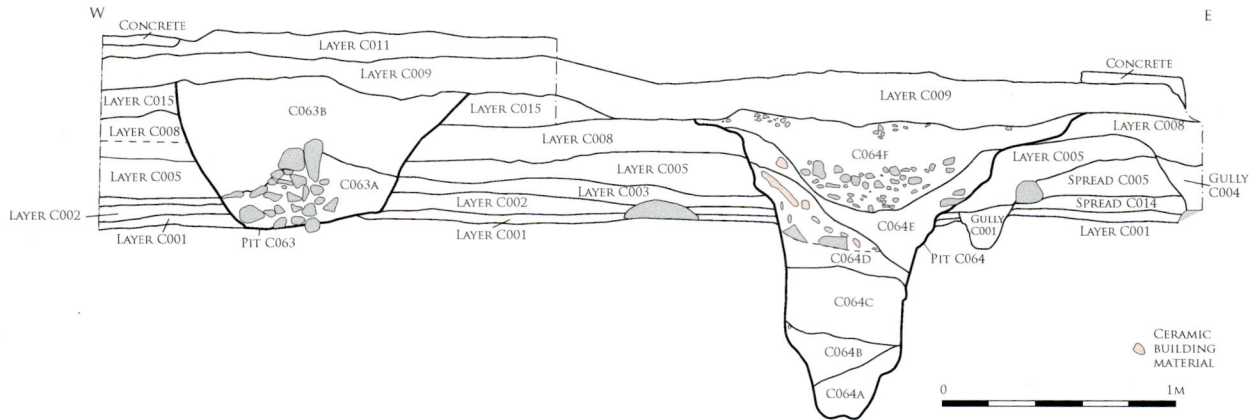

Figure 2.63 Composite south-facing section at south of site, showing Pit C063B and Pit C064

Figure 2.64 Post-excavation view of Pit C064 from east

showing a slightly higher incidence of degraded plant fragments. Textural pedofeatures consistent with physical movement and disturbance were also present.

Two segments of remnant clay-bonded rubble wall, apparently forming the north-east corner of a structure, Wall C003 and Wall C004 stood over silty clay and silt occupation deposits, Spreads C017, C058 and C059, and near Oven C002, and were of likely early Phase 5 date, as may be Pit C065 (Figure 2.62).

Nearby, in an area of heavy truncation in Area C, clay occupation deposit, Layer C016 was truncated by Ph C007.

In the south of Area C, silty clay occupation Layer C017, a likely early Phase 5 deposit, was cut by heavily truncated sub-circular Pit C079 and lay under various deposits including silt dump Spread C085 and clay occupation Layer C015. Clay-bonded stone Structure C001 (Figure 2.67) overlay Layer C015; this structure measured 7m in length and 0.54m wide; it incorporated a drain. Given its north-west/south-east alignment,

which contrasted with both earlier and later boundaries off the Upperkirkgate, it is interpreted as primarily a drainage feature.

In Area A, overlying Phase 4 Layer A004 was a variety of thin deposits, generally comprising mixed clays and clay silts. In Area A, Layer A024 (Phase 4 or 5), a large area of clay silt overlying Layer A004 was truncated by Ph A001. Deposits immediately overlying Layer A004 were also truncated by oval Pit A006, which had itself been truncated by modern activity.

Ph A001 was overlain by Layer A005, a dark clay deposit with frequent charcoal inclusions, perhaps derived from a hearth or oven. Structure A015, the remnant of an east/west-aligned stone wall, measuring 1.2m in length, overlay Layer A005. Layer A005 was covered by Layer A021, a clay silt garden soil, and broadly contemporary sandy clay Layer A022 and silty clay Layer A023. Layer A023 lay under Layer A020, a dark clay deposit.

In the north-west of Area A, overlying Phase 4 Layer A029, Layer A034 was a silty clay occupation deposit, which was truncated by irregular north/south Gully A004 and small sub-circular Pit A023 and covered by silty clay Layers A033 and A030.

2.8 Phase 5 (mid) – 15th to 16th century (figure 2.68)

deposits from the middle of Phase 5 comprised occupation deposits and, generally further west, garden soils. One of the built-up dump/occupation deposits contained significant quantities of ferrous slag, likely evidence for iron smithing in proximity to the site. Structural remains included the badly truncated remains of a clay-bonded rubble wall, which extended over 8m south/north in accord with the general line of boundaries off the Upperkirkgate. To its east, towards Gallowgate, were the remains of two

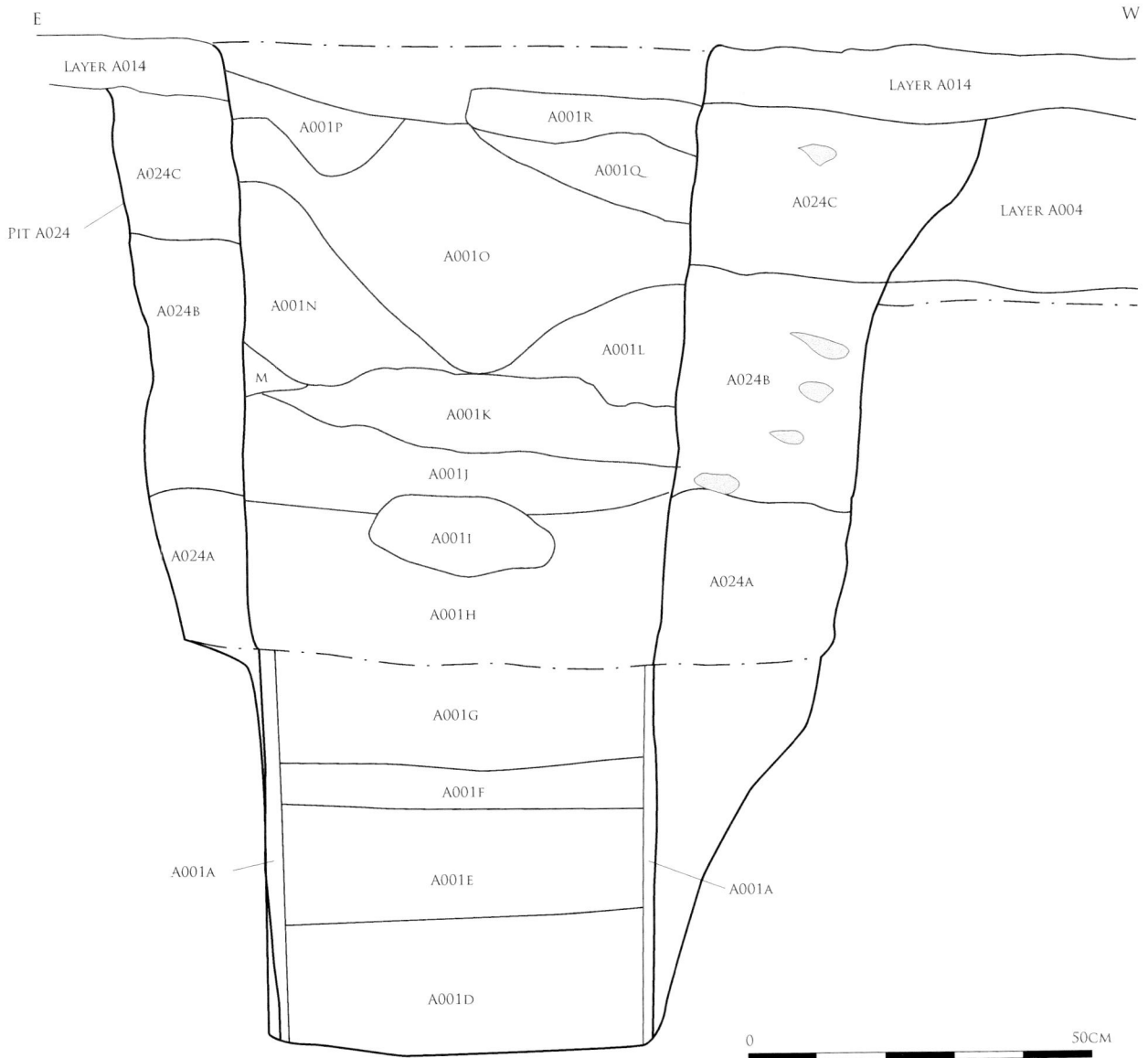

Figure 2.65 South-facing section of Pit A024 and Well A001

areas of clay-bonded rubble wall and likely associated floor surfaces. A stone-lined sub-circular pit fed by an east/west-aligned ditch may have been a cistern. To its west was the construction cut for a barrel-lined water butt or well. Its fill lay under garden soils, which in turn lay under a north/south-aligned clay-bonded stone wall, over 10m long, another major boundary feature perpendicular to Upperkirkgate.

In Area C, behind the late post-medieval cellarage, the major mid Phase 5 occupation deposits comprised Layer C009 to the south and Layer C010 to the north; this was marked by a large number of lenses, including clay material that may have derived from former constructions or surfaces. In an area much damaged by truncation by modern pits including the setting for a diesel tank, Layer C031 was contemporary with Layers C009 and C010. This deposit was cut by Ph C006 and Ph C008, perhaps elements of a single structure (perhaps a fence line). Layer C031/C010 also lay under badly truncated and largely robbed-out clay-bonded rubble Wall C019, which extended over 8m south/north before reaching Structure C006. The wall was generally c. 0.95 to 1.00m wide though it was found to be subsiding to the west due to 20th century construction works. Its north/south alignment was in accord with the general line of boundaries off the Upperkirkgate and it is possible that this wall was a predecessor to Wall A001, which formed part of a later post-medieval courtyard boundary.

To the east of Wall C019, Layer C010 was overlain by clay-bonded rubble Structure C006, which commonly

41

PIT A023

GULLY A004

STRUCTURE A015

WALL C004   WALL C003

PH C007

PIT A006

AREA A

PIT C028

AREA C

NOT EXCAVATED

PH A001

STRUCTURE C001   PIT C079

AREA B

GALLOWGATE

UPPER KIRKGATE

0   10M

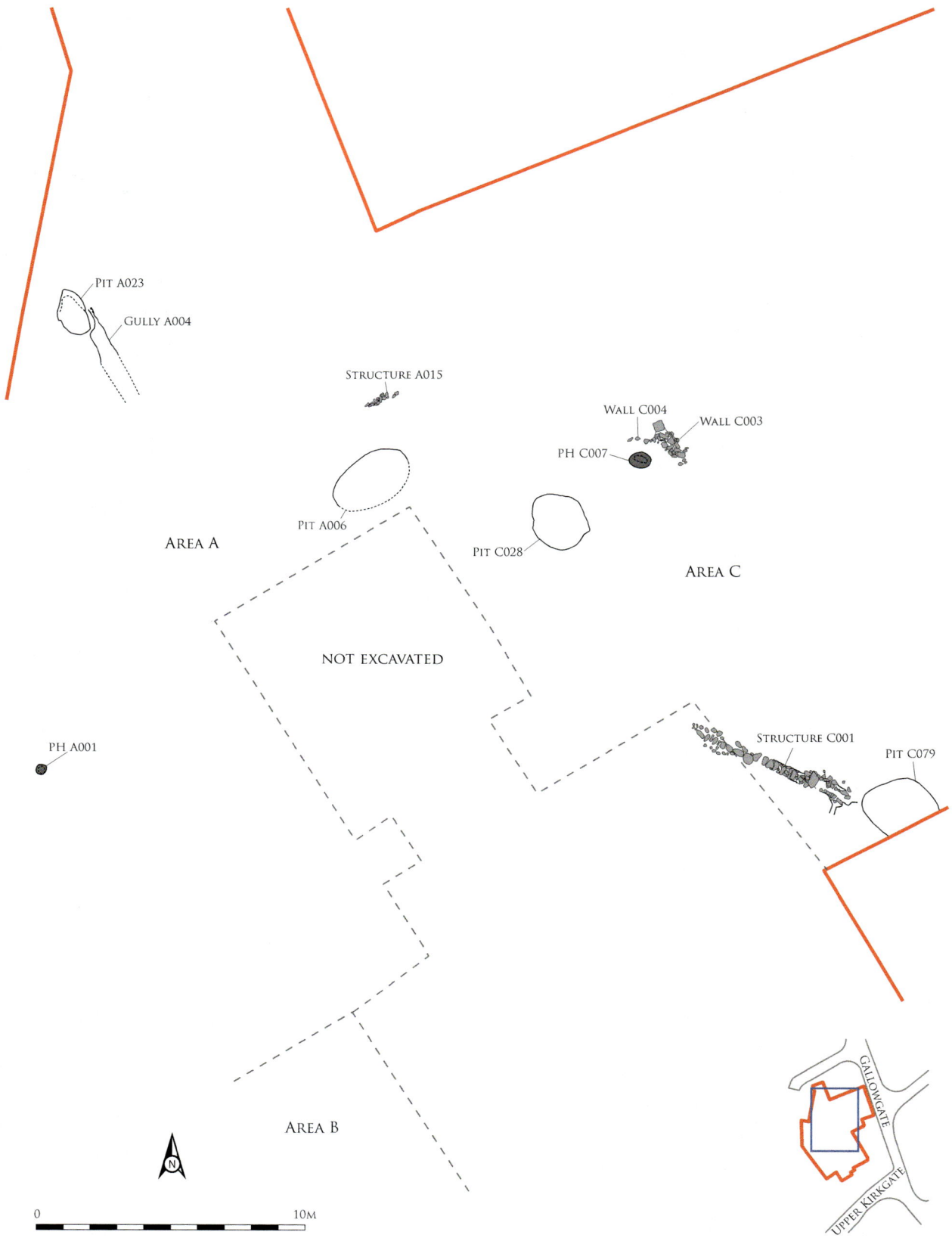

Figure 2.66 Plan of early Phase 5 features

Figure 2.67 Structure C001 with capping removed from south

survived to just a single course in height and contained a drainage element (Figure 2.69). Clay Surface C010, to the north, extended 3.6m east/west and was likely the remains of a floor associated with this wall, while similarly clay Surface C022 extended 2.8m east/west to the south of Structure C006. Given the presence of remnant clay floor Surfaces C010 and C022 to the north and south respectively of Structure C006, it is likely that this was not merely a drainage structure but marked a boundary. Other likely mid Phase 5 features above Layer C010 included Ditch C001 and stone-lined sub-circular Pit C070 (Figure 2.70) and steep-sided oval Pit C077 to the north of Structure C006. East/west-aligned Ditch C001, which was 1.65m in length, 0.72m wide and 0.15m deep, appeared to feed into Pit C070, which may have been a cistern.

Above Layer C010 was a build-up of clay dumps and occupation deposits including Spreads C028, C152, C026, C025, C024, C023 and clay Spread C021/C022, which lay stratigraphically over Pit C070. Spread C021/C022 contained significant quantities of ferrous slag, likely evidence for iron smithing in proximity to the site area (Figure 2.71). It lay adjacent to daub and charcoal Spread C099.

In the centre of Area C Layer C009 lay under circular Pit C071 and Pit C083.

Further south, Layer C009 was overlain by the remains of clay-bonded cobble Surface C009 and under truncated clay-bonded rubble Wall C009, the remnants of a structure in this area. Though badly truncated, Surface C009 appears to be contemporary with Wall C009.

In the same area, early Phase 5 Layer C015 was truncated by stone-lined Pit C063 (Figure 2.63), of early or mid Phase 5 date.

To the north-west, in Area A, Layer A014/A017 was a silty clay deposit, which was overlain by clay silt occupation deposit or garden soil, Layer A018 (which lay under similar Layer A016) and was truncated by shallow rectangular Pit A003 and Well A001, a barrel-lined water butt or well (Figure 2.72). The construction cut for this feature was circular in plan with regular vertical sides, approximately 0.67m in diameter and 1.6m deep. At a depth of 0.9m from the top of the cut was the wooden barrel, which was approximately 0.6m in interior diameter. It was constructed from 19 wooden staves, each approximately 0.10–0.12m wide and 0.01–0.02m thick, with an average length of 0.55m. The fills of the well generally consisted of thin layers of silty clay with lenses of sand.

After it fell into disuse, Well A001 was infilled; these deposits lay directly beneath Layer A013, a deep clay silt garden soil, which was truncated by irregular Pit A001, perhaps a robber trench of Wall C019, and linear feature Structure A018, the construction cut for a rubble wall identified during earlier evaluation works, the western extension of Structure C006.

Major garden soil Layer A006 covered Layer A030 and A033 and was broadly contemporary with Layer A014. Layer A006 was truncated by the construction cut for north/south-aligned sandy clay-bonded stone Wall A004, with a surviving length over 10m and a width of 1.3m. This major boundary wall, perpendicular to Upperkirkgate, was associated with Surfaces A002 (Figure 2.73) and A002A, two small areas of cobbled floor or kerbing, which were overlain by built-up clay silt deposits (Spread A013 and Layer A025).

2.9 Phase 5 (late) – 15th/16th to mid-to-late 18th century (figure 2.74)

the broad post-medieval period covered by the end of Phase 5 was again marked by dump and occupation deposits, with garden soils to the west. There was a series of cobble surfaces, perhaps the remains of a path from the Upperkirkgate, the last of which lay under a stone-lined cistern. Further north were heavily truncated remnants of mid-to-late Phase 5 clay-bonded rubble walls, associated with a possible clay floor. There was also a stone-lined pit, possibly a soakaway. To the west, a pit contained several flagstones, forming the base of a structure of unknown function, which contained clay tobacco pipe and was overlain by a sequence of post-medieval garden soil deposits prevalent in this area. A substantial stone-lined drain ran 13.2m south/north across one of these garden soils.

The end of Phase 5 is difficult to discern due to the presence of mixed artefact material, suggesting both residual and intrusive elements, but likely commenced

Figure 2.68 Plan of mid Phase 5 features

AREA C

WALL C009

SURFACE C009

PIT C063

PIT C071

SURFACE C010

SURFACE C022

STRUCTURE C006

SPREAD C099

SPREAD C021

POSTHOLE C006

PIT C083

POSTHOLE C008

DITCH C001

PIT C070

PIT C077

WALL C019

PIT A001

WELL A001

STRUCTURE A018

PIT A003

WALL A004

WALL A004

SURFACE A002

SURFACE A002A

AREA A

NOT EXCAVATED

GALLOWGATE

UPPER KIRKGATE

N

10M

0

Figure 2.69 Drainage Structure C006 from east

around the late 15th or 16th century and extended to the mid-to-late 18th century. In Area C, numerous spreads of clay and silty clay dump and occupation deposits including Layers C018, C030, C044 and C046 were present over Layer C009/C010 and overlying features. There was heavy truncation by 19th century and later activity and several of these, including Layer C030, may be of mid Phase 5 date.

Surface C009 was replaced by cobble Surfaces C009A, C011 and C012 in turn; the latter included a linear kerb or drainage feature, Structure C005, and might be of Phase 6 date. However, Surface C012 (Figure 2.75) lay stratigraphically under Pit C080 (Figure 2.76), a stone-lined possible cistern, likely to date to late Phase 5, due to the presence of post-medieval glass artefacts. It is possible that these surfaces represent the remains of a path from the Upperkirkgate.

In the north-west of Area C, behind the Gallowgate truncation, was a grey clay silt Spread C146 (equivalent to Layers C009 and C010). Soil micromorphological analysis identified evidence for post-depositional alteration of Spread C146, including bioturbation from root activity. It was overlain by the possible heavily truncated remnants of mid-to-late Phase 5 clay-bonded rubble structures, Walls C011 and C012, aligned south-east/north-west and east west respectively, which

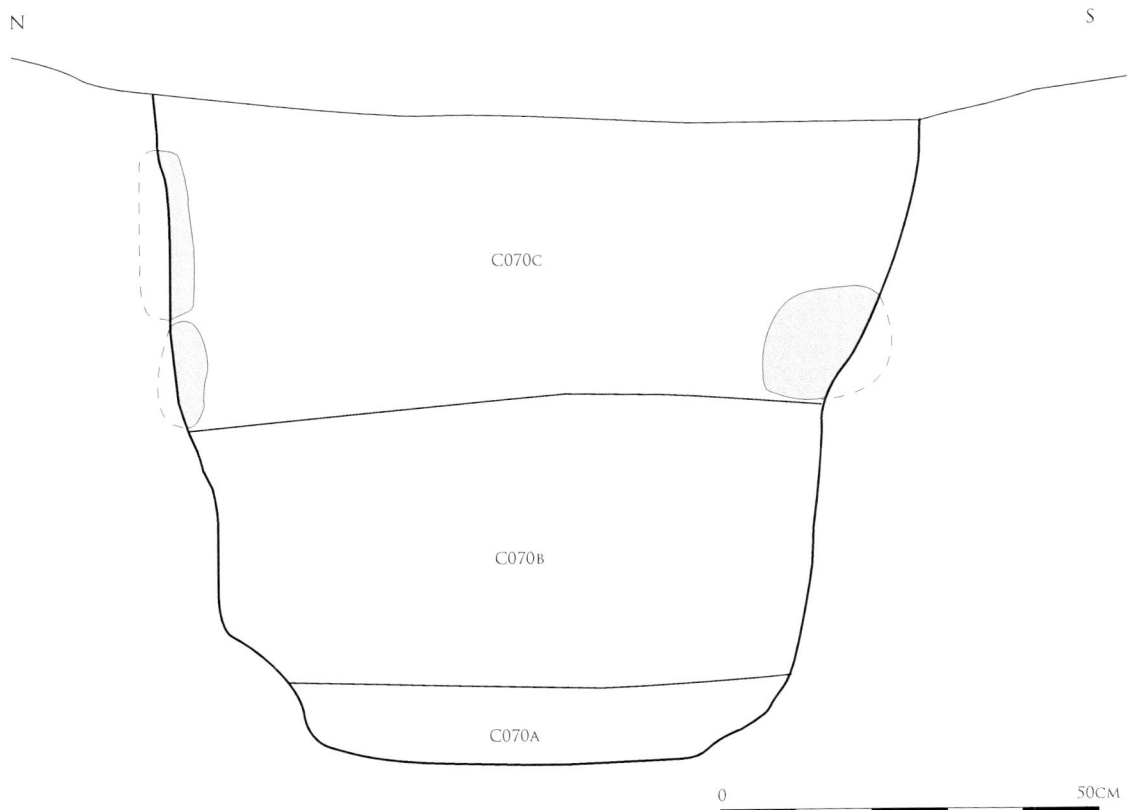

Figure 2.70 West-facing section of Pit C070

Figure 2.71 Smithing waste, Spread C021/C022, from east

Figure 2.72 Well A001 from north-east

Figure 2.73 Surface A002 from west

were associated with a possible thin clay floor deposit, Surface C014, cut by Ph C010. Nearby, circular Pit C028 and its recut, Pit C101 (not illustrated), contained clay pipe and pottery indicative of a late Phase 5 date.

Further north, stone-lined possible soakaway Pit C074 overlay Wall C019 and a remnant stone surface of mid-to-late Phase 5 date, Surface C023. This area lay under a clay occupation deposit with charcoal inclusions, Layer C052.

Silt Layer C030 overlay earlier Phase 5 deposit Layer C031 and was cut by the badly truncated remains of a possible linear drainage feature, Gully C012, and its recuts. This area lay under a dark organic clay deposit, Layer C039. Due to heavy truncation, it was difficult to phase many features, but shallow sub-circular Pit C075, sub-square Pit C076, Ph C009 and Gully C008 (a 2.6m long east-west aligned stone-filled drainage feature) cut through Layer C044 and Ph C005 through silty clay Layer C046 were likely late Phase 5, or perhaps slightly later, in date.

In the south of Area C, cobble Surfaces C009A and C011 may represent a path from the Upperkirkgate. Vertical-sided sub-circular Pit C082, stratigraphically under Surface C009A was a mid or late Phase 5 feature. Above earlier Pit C079, stone-lined Pit C104, which was at least 0.8m deep, may have been a soakaway.

In Area A, the base of a rectangular Pit A009, which was c. 0.4m deep, was lined with large flagstones up to 0.15m in depth; its fill contained 17th–19th century clay tobacco pipe and it is likely to date to late Phase 5. It was overlain by Layer A008, one of the general deposits associated with the latest activity in Phase 5 – garden soils, Layers A007 and A008, both of which contained 17th century clay pipe. Layer A007 was a dark silty clay observed to the north-east of this area over occupation or dumped deposits of mid Phase 5 date including clay silt Spread A017. Layer A008 was a similar deposit observed to the south-west.

Structure A019 (Figures 2.62 & 2.77) was a stone-lined drain that ran 13.2m south/north across the surface of Layer A008. The drain was constructed of stones laid on edge in two parallel rows forming the sides and a flat layer of stones forming a base. Further east, Pit A007 was irregularly shaped and truncated Layer A007 and dark clay occupation Layer C058, which was contemporary with Layers C009 and C010.

Pit A007

Pit C075

Pit C076

Pit C074

PH C009

Gully C008

Wall C014

Wall C011

Wall C012

Surface C023

PH C010

AREA A

Pit C028

PH C005

Pit C080

Pit C082

AREA C

Gully C012

Surface C012

Structure A019

Structure C005

Pit C104

Pit A009

NOT EXCAVATED

AREA B

Pit B001

GALLOWGATE

UPPER KIRKGATE

0   10M

Figure 2.74 Plan of late Phase 5 features

Pit A007 was overlain by Layer A010, a clay silt garden soil, which was overlain by north/south rubble wall remnant, Wall C014, possibly a replacement of Wall C019. In the west of the area, above Layer A008, Layer A011, a sandy silt deposit with fragments of brick, mortar and stone was likely equivalent in date to Layer A010. These were the latest surviving late post-medieval garden soils, and probably continued into Phase 6.

In Area B, sub-rectangular Pit B001, cut into natural, likely belongs to the later post-medieval period, and contained mid 17th century clay pipe.

2.10 Phase 6 – mid-to-late 18th to 20th century (figure 2.78)

the last phase of late post-medieval to 20th century remains was marked by the survival of structural elements of buildings, together with floor surfaces and drainage features behind the Upperkirkgate and Gallowgate frontages. On the Gallowgate frontage were remains of lime-mortar bonded cellar walls – at least some of which may be 18th century in date. These walls and patches of the cobble and brick floors of the cellars and associated yards overlay and truncated earlier deposits. Brick drainage structures were visible in the floor surfaces. Much of the area to the west of the Gallowgate cellars was covered by late post-medieval garden soil. There were various late post-medieval/ modern cut features in this open area to the west of the Gallowgate cellars including an east/west-aligned drainage gully. Further water management features included a stone-lined well. Further west, a series of lime mortar-bonded rubble walls probably defined a large open courtyard visible on late post-medieval mapping. Further mortar-bonded rubble walls defined likely 19th century structures, including two cellars which contained a network of brick drains and a large building associated with brick-lined ducts. These large, probably industrial, structures may have been associated with a printworks known to have occupied this area in the 19th century.

The final phase of archaeological activity dated from approximately the mid-to-late 18th century into the 20th century and comprised the building of a range of brick and lime mortar-bonded rubble walled structures behind Upperkirkgate in Areas B and D (Figure 1.2, Chapter 1) and frontage buildings on the Gallowgate (Area C), with surfaces, drainage and refuse disposal features in open areas behind these frontage buildings.

On the Gallowgate frontage the remains of cellars, dated to the late 18th or 19th century, were recorded. The outlines of at least two large buildings are marked on Keith and Gibbs' plan of 1862; somewhat different building outlines are visible on earlier maps such as

Figure 2.75 Surface C012 from north

Figure 2.76 Pit C080 from north-east

Milne's plan of 1789 and Wood's map of 1828, though these, especially the latter, are schematic. It is possible; however, that at least some of the lime-bonded walls on site may be 18th century in date. In particular, the west wall of Structure C008 to the south is earlier than the west and south walls of Structure C007 to the north and may be identifiable with a wall line on Milne's plan. The Ordnance Survey (OS) map of 1871 indicates that a northern structure incorporates a small courtyard

(Concert Court) and a roofed passage from the Gallowgate. Large elements of the lime-mortar bonded rubble walls of the cellars, Structure C007 to the north and Structure 008 to the south, and patches of the cobble and brick floors of the cellars and yards, Surface C018, overlay medieval deposits.

The remains of these cellars largely correspond with buildings depicted on the 1871 map. A large north/south stone wall with an opening from the east stood back *c.* 1m from the present-day Gallowgate frontage (Structure C007a), forming the east wall of Structure C007, which was also evidenced by remnant rubble walls to the south and west and brick and cobble surfaces. Structure C007 corresponds with a group of buildings surrounding Concert Court and incorporating a roofed access to the east. The OS map shows the courtyard to have been entered via a staircase from the south-west corner. Although no evidence for a staircase was encountered the surviving brick and cobble surfaces in the north-west corner of Structure C007 lay at a similar depth to the cellarage elsewhere, indicating that Concert Court lay below present street level. Several brick drainage structures were visible in these surfaces including Structures C009, C010 and C011; it is likely that Structures C009 and C010 lay within this small open courtyard. Cellar Structure C008, to the south, was evidenced by substantial mortar-bonded rubble walls on the Gallowgate frontage and to the west. Modern foundations had caused large scale disturbance to this building, though it was clearly the same as a building marked on the 1871 OS map to the south-east of Concert Court.

It is clear that Structures C007 and C008 date to at least the mid 19th century, perhaps as early as the later 18th century, and that they stand on the site of earlier frontage buildings, now wholly removed.

To the west of Structure C007, irregular rubble and brick Wall C017 formed what may have been the north-western corner of a building. It is possible that this is a small remnant of a building marked to the west of Concert Court in 1871. To the immediate west, however, sandy mortar-bonded rubble Wall C016, over Phase 5 Layer C052, abutted likely courtyard Wall A001. The location of Wall C016 correlates well with the building shown to the west of Concert Court, and therefore Wall C017 may relate to an earlier structure.

In the area depicted on post-medieval mapping as open ground to the west of the Gallowgate frontage, between Phase 5 Layer C009 and likely Phase 6 Layer C011, cobble Surface C012 may have continued in use from late Phase 5 into Phase 6, as it appeared to be associated with Pit C081, a feature dated to Phase 6 by the presence of artefacts including late post-medieval clay tobacco pipe, and Pit C082, which may date to late Phase 5.

Figure 2.77 Structure A019 from north

Much of the west of Area C, to the immediate west of the Gallowgate cellars, was covered by dark grey clay, Layer C011, the latest surviving late post-medieval garden soil, probably originating in late Phase 5 and broadly contemporary with Layers A010 and A011 in Area A; this was contemporary with silty clay dump Layer C028/Spread C034 in the south of Area C.

Probable late post-medieval wall remains to the south of Structure C008 included a group of dressed stones, Wall C018 (not illustrated), which were not *in situ* but appeared to be associated with a small area of floor, comprising stones set in sandy mortar, Surface C017 to the immediate west; these may predate Structure C008. Also in this area, probable 19th or 20th century Pit C084 was visible in section. Likely Phase 4 Pit C085 (not illustrated) was stratigraphically under stone-lined pit C078. Rectangular Pit C088 and Pit C089 to the west of Structure C008 are likely to be relatively late in date – late 19th or 20th century.

Further late post-medieval/modern cut features in the open area to the west of the Gallowgate cellars included east/west linear drainage Gully C015, which was cut through silty clay Layer C028 and disturbed Wall C018. In the north-west of Area C was brick-lined drainage feature, Structure C012, associated with cobble Surface C018, and stone-lined Well C002 (Figure 2.79). These features were in an area apparently covered by the building associated with Wall C016 in 1871, and it is

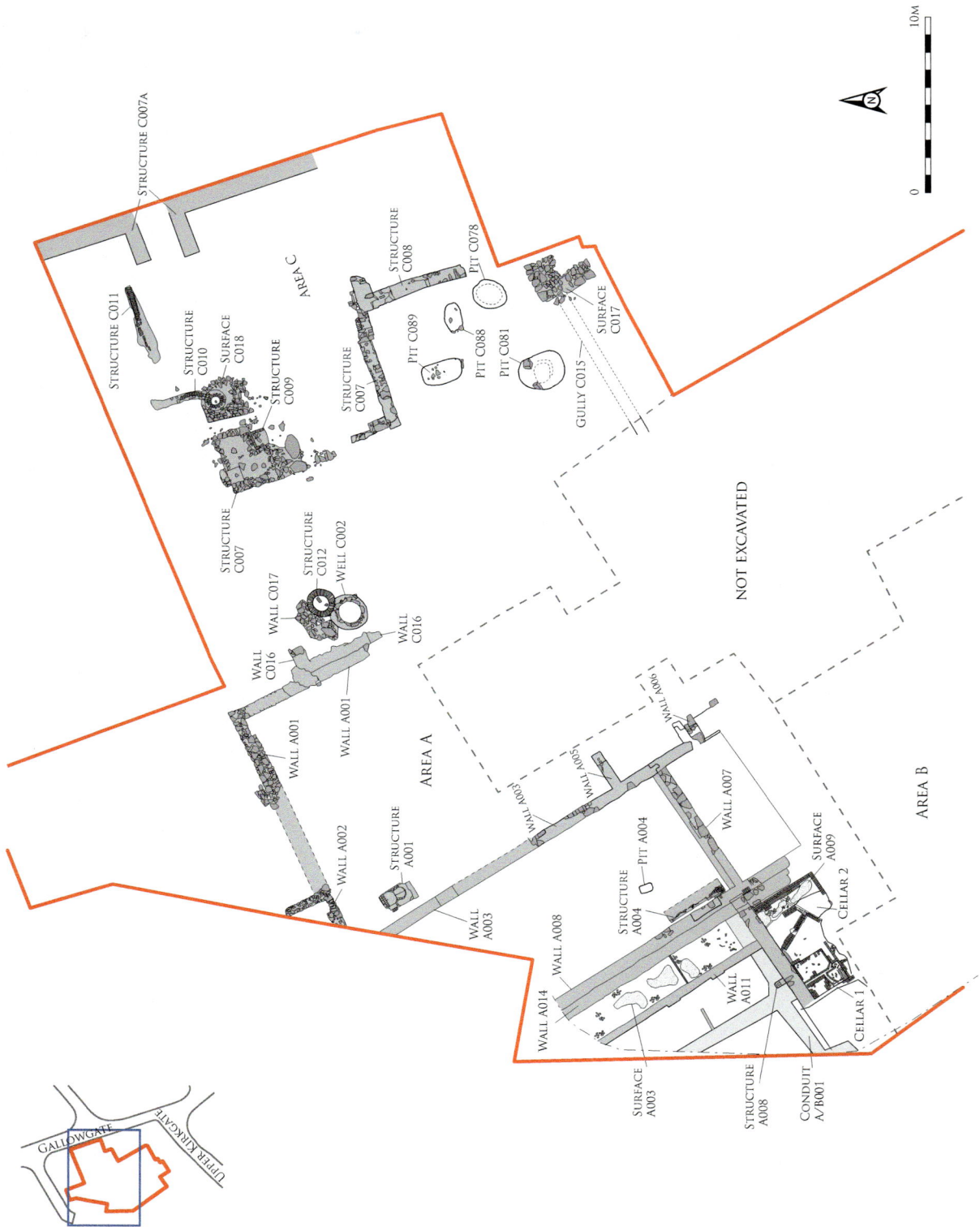

Figure 2.78 Plan of Phase 6 features

therefore theorised that although clearly late post-medieval in date they pre-date this structure.

In the north-west of Area A, sections of lime mortar-bonded rubble Wall A001 were constructed over Phase 5 Layer A010. These may have formed the north-east corner of a yard visible on late post-medieval mapping (including Milne's map of 1789) and have been interpreted as dating to around the late 18th century (though Wall A001 is associated with 17th century clay pipe and may therefore be earlier). Within this courtyard area, also bounded by likely later mortar-bonded rubble Walls A003 and A005 to the west and south, Structure A001 was a small rectangular structure of unknown function with four walls of red brick sitting on stone foundations. Beneath the flagstone floor of this structure were levelling/demolition deposits that included fragments of brick and slate over a brick surface. The construction cut for this structure truncated Layer A007. Further late 18th or 19th century cut features included sub-square Pit A004, cut into Layer A008, while Wall A002 over Later A010 formed the south-east corner of a structure that ran beyond the limit of excavation.

Parallel mortar-bonded rubble Walls A003 and A008 ran north/south in the west of Area A. Wall A007 formed a partition of the area bounded by these walls, with a concrete cellar floor to the south. These likely 19th century structures all truncated Layer A007. The area north of Wall A007 is shown as a courtyard on the OS map of 1871. Mortar-bonded rubble Walls A005 and A006 abutted Wall A003 at their western ends, while a north/south drain, Structure A004, ran east of Wall A008.

Two cellars in the south-west of Area A were recorded over Phase 5 deposits. Cellar 1 (to the west) was bounded by a major rubble wall to the north and brick partition walls to the west, south and east. Cellar 2 (to the east) was bounded by the same rubble wall to the north, another rubble wall to the east and brick walls to the west and south. Under the floor surfaces of the two cellars was a network of brick drains. The floor of Cellar 2 also covered cobble Surface A009, possibly related to Surface A003 to the north of the cellar.

The northern rubble wall of the cellars formed the southern wall of a building, apparently visible on mid

Figure 2.79 Well C002 from south

19th century maps (including the 1871 OS map; Figure 5.5, Chapter 5). Rubble Walls A011 and A014 formed a narrow corridor with a cobble floor, Surface A003. Wall A014 abutted Wall A008, noted above. A series of brick-lined ducts associated with this linear building, Conduit A/B001, which included a vertical brick flue/drain opening, Structure A008, was present on the extreme western edge of the excavated area.

The demolition infill deposits over these floors and walls provided relatively little indication of the purpose of these 19th century buildings. It is possible these were large industrial premises, perhaps associated with printworks known to have occupied this area off Upperkirkgate.

In the heavily truncated Area B, Phase 6 layers included Layer B003, a dark organic silt with lenses of sand – sherds of pottery, glass, iron and wood recovered from this layer date it to the 19th century. Layer B006 was a dark sandy silt demolition deposit.

Late Phase 6 deposits such as clay silt and stone dump Spreads C045 and clay with rubble dump Layer C021 (not illustrated) in Area C were covered by general late 20th century deposits derived from building demolition, including Layers A009, B005 and D001, equivalent to Layer C012, and hardcore deposit Layer C013.

3 Presentation of Artefactual and Ecofactual Evidence by Phase and Feature

3.1 Introduction

With large and varied artefact and ecofact assemblages there is always a danger that by reporting on them separately in discrete specialist reports the connection between their context and thus their taphonomic value is lost. In this section an attempt has been made to present the context assemblages in their entirety, to aid in the interpretation of the feature or deposit. To avoid repetition of detail, the evidence for those contexts mentioned in this chapter, from which artefact assemblages have been retrieved, has been tabulated as far as possible. In Tables 3.1–3.5 the artefact types present in each context are highlighted, together with the numbers of items present; this will guide the reader to detailed descriptions in the relevant report in Chapter 4, in either tables or catalogues. It should be noted that if a context does not appear in these tables, then no artefacts were retrieved. The leather, ceramics and industrial residues have been treated differently because these were such large assemblages that individual cataloguing was not viable. In these cases, very brief summaries of the contents are presented in this section. For the same reasons of size, the ecofact assemblages are summarised by context here rather than in Chapter 4, where the reader can find overviews of the assemblages.

Only those contexts from Phases 1 to 5 that contain either significant artefact and/or ecofact assemblages are described here. Material from Phase 6 and 'modern' deposits, of later 20th century date, are included within the site archive.

The format for Chapter 3 is as follows:

Feature Name (e.g. **Pit C038** = Pit 038 in Area C)

Short description of feature, including description of any associated structural timbers

Dating evidence (e.g. dendrochronology and C14 if any)
Leather
Ceramics
Industrial residues
Macroplant remains
Animal bone
Bird bone
Fish bone (fish lengths are quoted in cm TL and the numbers of each species of that length are given)
Interpretation

N.B: The dendrochronological dates quoted below have all been calculated using the sapwood estimates given in Table 4.1, Chapter 4. Most of the timbers that have been dendro-dated had been dumped into the pits, presumably when their useful life was over. In attempting to estimate when the pit was backfilled an allowance of up to two decades has been made for the duration of that useful life, the 'period of use' of the timbers. Although this is obviously quite an arbitrary timespan, it is based on the assumption that wood of the quality and size found at Bon Accord (Chapter 4.1) was unlikely to have been junked after only a few years of use. However, the timber could also have been in use for a lot longer than two decades so the estimated dates for backfilling are qualified by 'at the earliest'.

3.2 Phase 1 (mid-to-late 12th century) (figure 2.3)

Layer A001/C001

Thin layer of mid brown sandy clay over subsoil.

Ceramics: Aberdeen Fabric 8 (jug sherds); Scottish White Gritty Ware (jug sherds); Stamford Ware (jug sherds); Yorkshire-type Ware (jug sherds); East Anglian Ware (cooking pot sherds), and London Sandy Ware (jug sherds).

Interpretation
Interface layer, including relatively undisturbed topsoil.

Layer C002

Thin dark greyish brown silty clay occupation deposit over backfills of Ph C016 and Pits C015 and C017.

Ceramics: Local Redware (jug and cooking pot sherds); Aberdeen Fabric 8 (jug sherds); Scottish White Gritty Ware (jug sherds); Yorkshire-type Ware (jug sherds); London Sandy Ware (jug sherds); North French-type Ware (jug sherds), and Paffrath-type Ware (a sherd from a ladle).

Animal bone: Nineteen of the 41 animal bone fragments analysed were from cattle; 58% were bones of the skull and feet, low meat-producing elements of the carcass. This suggests that the bones had derived from butchery activities rather than as waste from the domestic table. Ten of the 18 (56%) sheep/goat bones were similarly from low meat yielding parts of the skeleton. Four bone fragments from this assemblage displayed butchery

Table 3.1 Phase 1; the artefact assemblages for key contexts and features (where quantified numbers of items are presented)

Context	Wood	Leather	Textiles	Animal fibres	Cordage	Metalwork	Worked stone	Lithics	Glass	Crucibles	Clay moulds	Industrial residues	Misc	Clay pipes	Ceramic building material	Window glass	Ceramic vessels
A001/C001						2	1										
Layer C002						4											
Gully C001	1	157		1		1	1	1									
Gully C002		1				1											
Pit A026	1	6											1				
Pit A027	2	197				1											
Pit A030	4	53															
Pit B002																	
Pit C001	2	317					1										
Pit C002						1		1									
Pit C003			1			1											
Pit C004		36				1							1				
Pit C005		48		2													
Pit C006	2	198	2		2												
Pit C007		19															
Pit C008		48				1											
Pit C009		421															
Pit C015	1	408				1							1				
Pit C017		1															
Ph C013																	

marks and three showed signs of having been burned. The bones were in poor condition and this may indicate that the layer had accumulated relatively slowly.

Fish bone: Of 15 fish bones six were identified as cod cranial and vertebral fragments, and four were identified as ling. Cod 80–100cm TL x3; cod >100cm TL x3; Ling >100cm TL x4.

Interpretation
Occupation deposit.

Gully C001 (Figure 2.8, Chapter 2)

Shallow 0.4m wide north/south-aligned gully with dark reddish and greyish brown clay silt fill (A) over subsoil

(Phase 1, but the dendrochronological evidence and leatherwork suggest it may have continued in use into Phase 2).

The reused fragments of two oak planks were found in the gully. SF3602 was a short plank, only 0.31m long roughly squared at one end and chopped obliquely at the other. A groove ran along its thicker edge, and a nail penetrated its thickness just behind the groove; this may have come from tongue-and-groove paneling or cladding. SF3604 had been chopped to a stake-like tip at one end.

Dating evidence: The two oak planks were selected for dendrochronological analysis (Table 4.1; Figure 4.1, Chapter 4). SF3602 provided a *terminus post quem* of AD

1184 for its felling. Allowing for missing rings and a period of use the gully was probably out of use by the middle of the 13th century at the earliest.

Leather: The assemblage comprises; shoe components x29; straps x1; offcuts, scraps & miscellanea x127. This includes a sole and an upper (Perth High Street comparanda are 13th–14th century in date).

Ceramics: Local Redware (jug and cooking pot sherds); Aberdeen Fabric 8 (jug sherds); Scottish White Gritty Ware (jug and cooking pot sherds); Stamford Ware (jug sherds); Yorkshire-type Ware (jug sherds); London Sandy Ware (jug sherds), and North French-type Ware (a jug sherd).

Industrial residues: The assemblage comprises; slag amalgams x2, 214.5g; unclassified slag x1, 6.8g.

Macroplant remains: The macroplant remains were dominated by waste ground and arable weed species such as annual nettle, redshank, common chickweed, corncockle, hemp nettle, rush, *Sphagnum* moss and leaf litter. There was a smaller quantity of food remains consisting of hazelnut shell, crab apple and cereal remains including bran. The upper part of the fill contained only small quantities of bracken and sedge.

The waste ground weed taxa were probably growing close to the gully while the food remains were either deliberately dumped into the gully or entered it via drainage. The presence of bran and corn cockle is typically indicative of human cess.

Animal bone: Almost 60% of the 73 animal bones analysed were from cattle while 26% were from sheep and goats. The other animals represented were pig (two fragments, both butchered) and red deer (one antler fragment). The cattle bone assemblage was dominated by the bones of the head and feet (60%) but fragments of high meat yielding bones were also present, two of which were butchered. In contrast the bones from the sheep and goats were from a range of elements with c. 30% coming from the skull and feet. Three horn cores from goat were present. The high proportion of 'waste' bone from the skull and feet suggests that the assemblage may derive from butchery waste while the horn cores may reflect horn-working nearby. The state of preservation of the bones suggests that they may have been moved around within the feature, perhaps by running water.

Fish bone: This feature produced 40 identifiable fish bones. Ling was represented by 22 cranial and vertebral elements; an articulating basioccipital and first vertebrae were butchered, as was an abdominal vertebra (Figure 4.59B, Chapter 4). Cod was represented by 16 bones, 15 of which were vertebrae. There were

two haddock. Ling >100cm TL x22; cod 50–80cm TL x2; cod 80–100cm TL x10; cod >100cm TL x4; haddock 30–50cm TL x1; haddock 50–80cm TL x1.

Interpretation
Drainage and boundary feature delineating property boundary behind Gallowgate and roughly perpendicular with Upperkirkgate.

Gully C002

Stone-lined north/south-aligned gully with a dark brownish grey clay silt fill (A) over Layer C001. Continuation of Gully C001.

Ceramics: Local Redware (jug and cooking pot sherds); Aberdeen Fabric 8 (jug sherds); Scottish White Gritty Ware (jug sherds); Yorkshire-type Ware (jug sherds), and London Sandy Ware (jug sherds).

Macroplant remains: The macroplant assemblage recovered from this gully was small and consisted of charred bread/club wheat, oat caryopses and pale *persicaria*. Charcoal and wood chips were also present. This material probably originated from domestic activities such as cooking and cleaning.

Animal bone: Thirty-nine bone fragments were analysed, of which 51% were cattle. One sheep and two goat horn cores were present but the other ovicaprid bones could not be distinguished between sheep and goat. Some 60% of the cattle bones derived from the feet and skulls as did 53% of the ovicaprid bones.

Fish bone: Seven cod vertebrae and a single ling fragment were present. Cod 80–100cm TL x4; cod >100cm TL x3; ling >100cm TL x1.

Interpretation
Southern element of Gully C001.

Pit A026 (Figure 2.12, Chapter 2)

Circular pit with numerous branches and twigs in (possible remnant lining) brown silty clay basal fill (A). This fill lay under dark grey clay silt (B), which was under dark grey clay silt (C). The pit was stratigraphically over Pit A028.

Leather: The assemblage comprises; shoe components x5; offcuts x1. This includes three shoe components (all uppers) which have parallels belonging predominantly to the 12th–13th centuries.

Ceramics: Local Redware (jug and cooking pot sherds) and Scottish White Gritty Ware (jug sherds).

Industrial residues: The assemblage comprises; plano-convex slag cake x1, 172.1g; unclassified slag x6, 210.7g; ferrous hammerscale microresidues <0.3g.

Macroplant remains: The only food/flavouring plant material recovered from this pit was from an upper fill (C), which contained a small quantity of raspberry. The remainder of the plant assemblage consisted of small quantities of waste ground weed taxa. A large quantity of wood chips, some of which were worked, along with a small number of bark fragments were present in lower fills (A) and (B). The presence of wood chips and bark in the lower fill suggests that this pit in its earlier existence was used for the dumping of floor debris from nearby workshops. The absence of chaff, straw, cereal and animal dung indicates that this material did not originate from animal stabling.

Animal bone: Nineteen fragments of bone from cattle, sheep and red deer were analysed. None of the bone fragments displayed evidence of butchery or burning. The pit fill contexts were probably damp and the pit may contain re-deposited material, which would account for the poor condition of the bones.

Bird bone: There was one carpometacarpus identified as bantam.

Fish bone: There were three haddock vertebrae and another vertebra from the cod family. Two bones were crushed. Haddock 15–50cm TL x3; cod 15–30cm TL x1.

Interpretation
This may be a 'layaway' pit, for the tanning of leather (Chapter 5.2).

Pit A027

Sub-circular pit containing abundant twigs in a dark brown clay silt fill (A). Over Pit A026.

Leather: The assemblage comprises; shoe components x21; straps x1; clothing x1; offcuts, scraps & miscellanea x174. This includes three shoe components (two soles and a model sole – SF3151A; Figure 4.17, Chapter 4) (Perth High Street comparanda are 12th–14th century in date, predominantly 13th century).

Ceramics: Local Redware (a cooking pot sherd); Scottish White Gritty Ware (jug sherds); Stamford Ware (a jug sherd); Yorkshire-type Ware (a jug sherd), and London Sandy Ware (a jug sherd).

Macroplant remains: The plant remains consisted of small fragments of hazelnut shell, wood chips and bark fragments.

Fish bone: Of 37 fish bone fragments two cod bones and two ling cleithra could be identified. Cod 80–100cm TL x2; ling 80–100cm TL x1; ling >100cm TL x1.

Interpretation
This may be a 'layaway' pit, for the tanning of leather (Chapter 5.2).

Pit A030 (Figure 2.10A & 2.11, Chapter 2)

Deep sub-circular pit over Layer A001. At the base was a thin deposit of light blue grey clay, disturbed subsoil (A) (not illustrated). This lay under an organic dark brown silty sand fill (B) and the main fills, a dark brown/grey silty clay (C) (not illustrated) and mid greyish brown silty clay (D). Above this were several thin layers of material including dark brown sandy silt (E) and (G); light orangeish grey silty sand (F) and mid brown clayey silt (H).

Leather: The assemblage comprises; shoe components x24; straps x1; offcuts, scraps & miscellanea x28. This includes one sole of a form with Perth High Street comparanda mainly 13th–14th century in date; a shoe component with Perth High Street parallels chiefly of 13th–15th century date, and another sole with Perth High Street comparanda from the 12th to 14th centuries.

Ceramics: Local Redware (jug sherds); Scottish White Gritty Ware (jug sherds); Yorkshire-type Ware (jug sherds), and London Sandy Ware (jug sherds).

Macroplant remains: The waterlogged assemblage was concentrated in two lower fills, in particular (B). The plant remains in these levels were dominated by arable and waste ground weed species. The food residues included cereal bran, oat chaff, raspberry and *Sphagnum* moss. The earlier fills suggest that this feature was utilised for the disposal of possible human waste with moss being used for hygiene purposes. The plant remains from an upper fill (F) consisted of a small quantity of charred cereal caryopses. This fill appears to represent abandonment, with rapid backfilling preventing the accumulation of further waste material.

Animal bone: An animal bone assemblage of 39 fragments, mainly from cattle, was analysed. Six fragments of pig bone were present and one fragment of bone identifiable as sheep. Two pieces of bone from red deer were retrieved. For all species a range of body parts are present, with no predominance of any one body part over the others. The animal remains were generally fragmented and the majority (64%) was derived from low meat-producing bones from the skull and lower legs. Although only two fragments displayed butchery marks it seems likely, from the body parts present, that this assemblage represents butchery waste. The good preservation of the bone suggests the pit was filled quickly and remained relatively free-draining.

Bird bone: There were two well preserved tibio-tarsus bones, one of domestic fowl and one of bantam.

Fish bone: Of 78 fish bones 21 were identified as cod from a variety of vertebral and cranial elements, 21 bones were ling, and a single saithe cranial bone was recovered. Two of the larger cod were butchered dentaries, cut or chopped near the central articulation. A ling parasphenoid was found in articulation with a basioccipital. Cod 80–100cm TL x6; cod >100cm TL x15; ling 80–100cm TL x2; ling >100cm TL x1; saithe >100cm TL x1.

Interpretation
Likely refuse pit, though substantial depth (2m) indicates possibility that this feature was originally used for some other process.

Pit B002

Oval pit with a dark grey silty clay fill (A) over Layer B001.

Ceramics: Local Redware (jug sherds) and Scottish White Gritty Ware (jug sherds).

Macroplant remains: The plant remains from this pit were small and were dominated by waste ground weed taxa, in particular fat hen. Trace amounts of raspberry and fig were recovered which suggests that small volumes of faecal matter may have been disposed of within this pit. There is no evidence to suggest that the fat hen was also being consumed.

Interpretation
Likely refuse pit.

Pit C001 (Figure 2.4A, Chapter 2)

Large, 0.8m deep, sub-square pit over subsoil. On the west of the pit, the lowest fill was a dark brown silty clay with sand deposit (A). This lay under the main base fill (B) a dark brown clay silt. Above this was a dark brown silty clay deposit (C) with much organic material, including straw and moss, under further dark brown silty clay (D). The uppermost surviving fill in a truncated feature was dark brown clay silt (E).

Leather: The assemblage comprises; shoe components x14; offcuts, scraps & miscellanea x303.

Ceramics: Scottish White Gritty Ware (cooking pot sherds); Stamford Ware (jug sherds), and Pingsdorf-type Ware.

Macroplant remains: The plant assemblage from this pit was not large and was dominated by the presence of large pieces of birch bark and worked wood chips that were particularly prevalent in one of the lower fills (C). The bark appeared to have been deliberately removed in large strips. There was also a large volume of birch seeds. The cultivated plants included small quantities of wheat/rye bran. The rest of the plant assemblage was dominated by weed taxa typical of disturbed ground. The only other plants recovered were small concentrations of *Sphagnum* leaves and bracken.

Bark, in particular birch bark, has previously been used to identify the presence of tanning pits on other medieval sites in Aberdeen and York (Hall *et al.* 2004: 20, 23), so this pit was perhaps used either for the tanning process or for the disposal of tanning waste. The waste ground weed taxa are typical of the local environment during the medieval period. The presence of cereal remains, moss and bracken indicate that mixed rubbish from other sources was also disposed of within this feature.

Animal bone: Thirty-four animal bones from this pit were analysed. Half were from cattle and six fragments were from sheep and goat. Two cat bones and seven pig bones were also present. Slightly fewer than half of the cattle bones were from the skull and feet of the animal (47%). The condition of the bones suggests that the pit filled relatively quickly.

The presence of cat is interesting – two bones are from a young cat, possibly the same individual. One is from the front leg (humerus) and the other from the hind leg (tibia). The absence of the remaining cat skeleton is curious and may suggest that the cat bones are intrusive. This would, however, contradict the evidence that suggests the pit filled up quickly. The assemblage from this pit is different from those retrieved from the contemporary gullies and layer. There are more species represented; fewer 'waste' bones from the skull and feet and the bones are generally in better condition.

Fish bone: Hand collection produced 53 fragments, of which 16 were cod, seven were haddock and six were ling. Sieving of a deposit identified in the field as a possible articulated fish proved to be more than one fish, and included both cod and ling. A total of 158 fragments were not identified, many of which were tiny fragments from larger cod family fish. Cod 50–80cm TL x1; cod 80–100cm TL x4; cod >100cm TL x 11; haddock 30–50cm TL x6; haddock 50–80cm TL x1; ling >100cm TL x6.

Interpretation
This may be a 'handler' pit, for the tanning of leather (Chapter 5.2).

Pit C002

Sub-circular, 0.75m deep pit containing a dark brown clay silt basal fill (A) under a dark grey sandy clay (B). Over Layer C001.

Ceramics: Local Redware (jug sherds); Scottish White Gritty Ware (jug and cooking pot sherds); Stamford Ware (a jug sherd); Yorkshire-type Ware (jug sherds), and London Sandy Ware (a jug sherd).

Macroplant remains: The plant assemblage consisted mainly of charred cereal caryopses and waterlogged cereal periderm fragments. There were a few weed taxa, including birch and buttercup, and some wood chips. This pit was probably used for the disposal of mixed rubbish.

Animal bone: Of ten bone fragments six came from cattle and one from red deer. Two bone fragments were found to have butchery marks on them. The poor condition of the bone suggests either a slow accumulation within the pit, or waterlogged conditions.

Interpretation
Possible refuse pit.

Pit C003

Sub-circular 0.55m deep pit over subsoil. The basal fill (A) was a brown organic clay silt, which lay under grey sandy clay (B). This was in turn under a dark brown/ grey sandy silt (C), which lay under a thin deposit of black sand with coal inclusions (D) and stones (E).

Ceramics: Scottish White Gritty Ware (jug and cooking pot sherds) and Yorkshire-type Ware (jug sherds).

Macroplant remains: Waste ground weed taxa, charred cereal caryopses and hazelnut shell were concentrated in the lower and upper fills (A) and (C) along with charcoal and a compact brown homogeneous peat/ midden type material. The only plant remains recovered from the middle fill (B) were a small quantity of charred cereal caryopses and sedge. The plant remains recovered from the middle fill (B) were not as abundant and varied as those identified in the lower and upper fills. This indicates that this pit was either left unused or abandoned for a short period before being reopened to allow for the deposition of further material. There is no strong evidence to suggest the disposal of stable, industrial or even human/animal waste occurred within this feature. Instead these remains represent mixed rubbish originating from several sources.

Animal bone: One hundred identifiable animal bones were analysed, of which 78 were from cattle, 11 from sheep/goat and three from pig. The remaining fragments were identified as large or medium mammal. The majority of the cattle bones (81%) were from the skull and feet while most of the other cattle bones (11) were metapodials – the low meat producing bones of the lower leg. Thus, only four fragments of cattle bone were from high meat yielding body parts. This, together with the presence of butchery marks on only one fragment of cattle bone, implies that the cattle bone in this pit is not waste from the domestic kitchen but may be the product of some industrial process.

The sheep/goat bones do not show the same pattern. Of the 15 bones retrieved, six were from the head and feet; two metapodials were also present. Six ovicaprid bone fragments from high meat-yielding parts of the body were present, five of which were evidently from young animals. This, together with the presence of butchery marks on two of the sheep/goat bones, suggests the animals may have been consumed as food. Two of the three pig bones were butchered and all three may have come from one individual foreleg. One fragment of cat femur was present, with five butchery marks. The knife marks were in the middle of the bone shaft and may have resulted from skinning. The condition of the bones suggests that the pit filled reasonably quickly, probably with the by-products of some industrial process that may have involved skinning or dismembering animals.

Fish bone: Of 69 fish bones 11 were cod, from both the cranium and vertebral column, ten were ling, both cranial and vertebral, and there was one flounder or plaice element. Cod 80–100cm TL x5; cod >100cm TL x6; ling 80–100cm TL x7; ling >100cm TL x3; flounder/ plaice 30–50cm TL x1.

Interpretation
Refuse pit including animal bone from the removal of skull and feet bones in the early preparation of hides.

Pit C004 (Figure 2.5, Chapter 2)

Large, *c.* 1.0m deep, circular pit with possible thin light-yellow clay lining (A) (not illustrated), over subsoil. The lining material lay under a mid brown sandy silt with organic inclusions (B), which was sealed by a compacted dark brown sandy silt (C).

Leather: The assemblage comprises; shoe components x24; straps x1; offcuts, scraps & miscellanea x11. This includes an upper shoe component of 12th–13th century date.

A composite bone and leather artefact (SF2977), of unknown function, was recovered from fill (C) (Figure 4.47, Chapter 4). This is the atlas of an adult cow that has had a small piece of leather tied through the left transverse foramen.

Ceramics: Scottish White Gritty Ware (jug and cooking pot sherds).

Macroplant remains: The plant assemblage was dominated by cereal, in particular large quantities of waterlogged oat and oat spikelets. The only other edible food plant recovered was strawberry. There was a large concentration of bracken and moss with background traces of waste ground weed taxa. Bark fragments and wood chips were also present, some of which appear to have been worked. The composition of the plant material remains consistent throughout the fills with no obvious changes in usage. This pit appears to have been used primarily for the disposal of stable waste along with some mixed rubbish. Some of the oat chaff formed frequent inclusions in what appeared to be decayed animal dung.

Animal bone: Forty-seven animal bone fragments were analysed from this pit, of which 29 (62%) were cattle. Eight (28%) of the cattle bones were from the head and feet of the animal and eight were fragments of metapodials. Five cattle bone fragments displayed butchery marks. The 11 sheep and goat bones included seven from the head and feet and one metapodial. Four were butchered. Two pig bones, both from the fore-leg, were retrieved; one of these was butchered. The generally good condition of the bones in this pit suggests that they were deposited rapidly and that the pit was free-draining. The assemblage differs from that retrieved from pit C003, with proportionately more bones from the high meat-yielding parts of the skeleton, suggesting that perhaps the pit was filled with domestic rubbish.

Fish bone: Of 13 fish bones two ling and two cod vertebrae were identified. Ling >100cm TL x2; cod >100cm TL x1; cod 80–100cm TL x1.

Interpretation
Likely refuse pit; presence of bark and wood chips may indicate its use in the tanning process.

Pit C005 (Figure 2.5, Chapter 2)

Recut, *c.* 0.5m deep, of Pit C004, lined with blue grey sandy clay (A). The lining lay under a dark brown sandy silt (B), which was sealed by blueish grey sandy clay (C) and light brownish red sandy clay with much wood inclusions (D). The upper fill (E) was a mid brown sandy silt.

Leather: The assemblage comprises; shoe components x8; offcuts, scraps & miscellanea x40.

Ceramics: Scottish White Gritty Ware (cooking pot sherds) and Stamford Ware (jug sherds).

Macroplant remains: The macroplant assemblage included relatively large components of waterlogged oat spikelets along with straw/grass culm fragments. There was also evidence of imported heathland/moor material in the form of bell heather, heather, birch, bracken and large quantities of moss, together with traces of wild weed taxa, wood chips and bark. This deposit is representative of mixed remains which primarily include stable clearings along with possible building material, turfs, bedding or packing material. A significant proportion of the oat remains had been embedded into compressed layers, possibly as a result of residual build up and continual trampling on stable floors. There is no evidence that any of this material such as the heather, wood, moss or bracken was used as a fuel source as no charred fragments were observed within the assemblage.

Animal bone: Seventeen animal bones were analysed from this pit with cattle, sheep, goat and ovicaprids being represented. Four bones had butchery marks, including one goat horn core, which had knife marks from the removal of the horn. 10 bones were from the skulls and feet. The condition of the bones varied between good and poor with approximately half in each category. Although this is a very small sample there are hints that the faunal remains have derived from industrial activities. The general condition of the bones implies that preservation conditions in the pit were not very good. This may be due to excessive wetness or it may reflect slow filling of the pit or the inclusion of redeposited material.

Fish bone: Sixteen fish bone fragments were recorded of which six cod, two ling and a single haddock could be identified. All fragments were from the vertebral or appendicular areas of the skeleton. Cod 50–80cm TL x1; cod 80–100cm TL x4; cod >100cm TL x1; ling 80–100cm TL x1; ling >100cm TL x1; haddock 30–50cm TL x1.

Interpretation
Likely refuse pit containing evidence of the early preparation of hides, including disposal of skull and feet bones and animal hair.

Pit C006 (Figures 2.5 & 2.6, Chapter 2)

Large, *c.* 1.2m deep, subrectangular pit truncating Pit C005. A dark greyish brown silty sand fill (A) lay under mid brown silty sand with organic inclusions (B).

Leather: The assemblage comprises; shoe components x37; straps x3; offcuts, scraps & miscellanea x158. This includes three sole shapes and two upper styles with a date range from the 12th to the 14th centuries.

Ceramics: Scottish White Gritty Ware (jug and cooking pot sherds); Stamford Ware (a jug sherd), and Normandy Gritty Ware (jug and cooking pot sherds).

Animal bone: Fifty-six identifiable bone fragments were analysed and goat, sheep, ovicaprids, cattle, pig and cat were present. No pattern in body part analysis was detected among the cattle bones. Pig bones were relatively abundant with 15 identifiable fragments being retrieved, of which 11 came from the higher meat yielding bones. At least one young pig and one mature pig were represented. The sheep bones, similarly, had a fairly high proportion of high meat-yielding bones (38%). Of the assemblage 29% displayed butchery marks. The relatively high proportions of meat-rich skeletal elements, the presence of only the main food-producing domesticates and the relatively high frequency of butchery marks suggest this pit mainly contains domestic waste from the kitchen. The condition of the bone fragments indicates the pit contexts were secure and free-draining.

Bird bone: A humerus and one ulna from a bantam came from opposite sides of the skeleton and do not represent the remains of a semi-articulated wing. A single domestic fowl bone was identified as a coracoid.

Fish bone: 130 fish bones were recorded of which there were 32 (25%) cod, 29 (22%) ling and nine haddock. A range of element types was recorded for cod and ling. One cod cleithrum was butchered and two of the ling bones bore butchery marks. Cod 80–100cm TL x14; cod >100cm TL x18; ling >100cm TL x29; haddock 50–80cm TL x9.

Interpretation
Likely domestic refuse pit.

Pit C007 (Figures 2.5 & 2.7, Chapter 2)

Recut of Pit C006, *c.* 0.4m deep, with a light yellow clayey sand lining (A). The lining lay under a mid reddish brown clayey sand with organic inclusions (B), which lay under a lens of dark greyish brown organic silt (C) and a dump of dark brown organic sandy silt (D). Above this was a thin deposit of mid greyish brown sand (E) in the east of the pit (not illustrated), which was sealed by organic mid greyish brown silty sand (F).

Leather: The assemblage comprises; shoe components x4; clothing – a possible sleeve; offcuts, scraps & miscellanea x14.

Ceramics: Scottish White Gritty Ware (jug sherds) and Yorkshire-type Ware (sherds of a jug and cooking pots).

Macroplant remains: The plant assemblage was varied and included both charred and waterlogged food remains

along with heathland/moor, arable and waste ground weed taxa. Bracken, willow leaves, moss and wood chips were also present. This is a mixed assemblage with no obvious evidence of selective disposal. This pit was probably used to dispose of waste from several sources including workshops, stabling, turfs and possibly human faecal matter. A large quantity of *Hylocomium splendens* was identified among the mosses; on other medieval sites it has been suggested that this could have been used for hygiene purposes like toilet paper (Hall *et al.* 2004: 8).

Animal bone: The animal bone assemblage included 13 cattle bone fragments, six ovicaprid bones and two fragments which could only be identified as medium (sheep-sized) mammal. Five of the ovicaprid bones were mandible fragments, representing a minimum of three elements. One bovid scapula displayed two dismembering marks. Most of the cattle bone fragments (69%) were from the head and feet. The prevalence of skull and feet bones and the presence of dismembering marks on a cattle bone hint that the pit contains butchery waste. The variable state of the bones might indicate non-uniform conditions in the pit or the inclusion of redeposited material within the pit fill. Alternatively, it may suggest that the pit filled slowly.

Bird bone: There was one domestic fowl femur.

Fish bone: Of 61 fish bones, 16 were ling, seven were cod and there were single fragments of haddock and salmon. Ling >100cm TL x16; cod 50–80cm TL x1; cod 80–100cm TL x5; cod >100cm TL x1; haddock 30–50cm TL x1.

Interpretation
Likely refuse pit containing possible evidence of the disposal of skull and feet bones in the preparation of hides.

Pit C008

Irregular sub-circular pit containing a dark brown sandy silt basal fill (A) under mid brownish green clay silt (B). Over subsoil.

Leather: The assemblage comprises; shoe components x9; offcuts, scraps & miscellanea x39. This includes a shoe sole (Perth High Street comparanda are 13th–14th century in date).

Ceramics: Scottish White Gritty Ware (jug and cooking pot sherds) and London Sandy Ware (jug sherds).

Macroplant remains: The preservation of the plant material from this pit was excellent; several heather leaf fragments still retained part of their original pigmentation. The overall composition of the assemblage was of mixed origin, including cultivated oat, oat spikelets, cereal bran, hazelnut shell, cabbage, heathland material, moss, waste ground weed taxa and worked wood chips. This assemblage appears to have originated from the disposal of both stabling waste and human faecal matter. The hazelnut shells were intact except for a single hole on the surface which is attributable to rodents extracting the fruit. The mosses identified included large quantities of those species typically used as toilet paper on other medieval sites.

Animal bone: Seventeen animal bone fragments were analysed, of which ten were from cattle, three from sheep/goat and the remainder identified as large or medium sized mammals. The majority of the cattle bones (60%) were from the heads and feet while one of the ovicaprid bones derived from these low meat-yielding body parts. Four bone fragments displayed butchery marks.

Fish bone: Of 97 fish bones, 38 (39%) were cod, from both the cranium and vertebral column, 33 (34%) were ling, both vertebrae and cranial elements, and a single salmon family vertebra was also recorded. Butchery marks were present on two cod vertebrae and a premaxilla. Cod 80–100cm TL x23; cod >100cm TL x15; ling >100cm TL x33.

Interpretation
Likely refuse pit.

Pit C009

Large pit, *c.* 3m in diameter and 0.5m deep, with a main fill comprising mid greyish brown clayey silt (A) under dark brownish grey organic clayey silt (B). Over subsoil.

Leather: The assemblage comprises; shoe components x50; straps x7 (SF14A–C; Figure 4.21, Chapter 4); offcuts, scraps & miscellanea x364. This includes ten soles and three uppers with a date range from the 12th to the 13th centuries.

Ceramics: Scottish White Gritty Ware (jug sherds).

Animal bone: Seven of the 19 animal bone fragments analysed derived from cattle, six from ovicaprids and two from cat. The remaining four fragments could only be identified as large mammal and were probably cattle. None of the cattle fragments bore any signs of butchery or other taphonomic markers. The cat bones were both from the pelvic girdle and had multiple butchery marks. The condition of the bone fragments suggests the pit was filled fairly quickly. The presence of butchered cat bones in this pit is puzzling as the marks on the two pelvises suggest that the cat had been dismembered, its hind legs removed. Such marks should not result from simple skinning of the animal (McCormick 1994).

Bird bone: Three domestic fowl bones consisted of one femur and two tarso-metatarsals. The femur from a red grouse was also present.

Fish bone: Of 169 fish bones 66 (39%) were cod, 27 (16%) were ling, six (3.5%) were haddock and there was a single turbot. The cod included a mixture of cranial and vertebral elements. One cod fragment was burnt and a cod abdominal vertebra had been butchered. A small portion of articulated ling cranium was present. Cod 50–80cm TL x2; cod 80–100cm TL x28; cod >100cm TL x36; haddock 30–50cm TL x4; haddock 50–80cm TL x2; ling 80–100cm TL x1; ling >100cm TL x26; turbot 50–80cm TL x1.

Interpretation
Likely refuse pit.

Pit C015 (Figure 2.4B, Chapter 2)

Large, 2.5m deep, sub-square pit over Layer C001, perhaps recut. The main, basal fill (A) was a brown silty clay with lenses of blue clay and black sandy silt. This lay under a possible, but uncertain recut. The deposit above (A) was a heavily compacted dark grey organic clay (B), which lay under lenses of gritty clay with stones (C) and a dark grey gritty clay (D). The uppermost fill was a dark grey/brown silty clay (E).

Leather: The assemblage comprises; shoes components x40; straps x4 (SF4793B; Figure 4.21, Chapter 4); clothing? x1; offcuts, scraps & miscellanea x363. This includes three sole shapes and two upper styles (Perth High Street comparanda are 12th–14th century in date. One of these is SF4733 (Figure 4.19), an ankle boot with side lacing. There was also a decorated fragment, probably part of knife sheath (SF4793A) (Figure 4.21).

Ceramics: Local Redware (jug and cooking pot sherds); Aberdeen Fabric 8 (jug sherds); Scottish White Gritty Ware (jug sherds); Scarborough-type Ware Fabric 2 (jug sherds); Stamford Ware (jug sherds), and Yorkshire-type Ware (jug sherds).

Macroplant remains: The preservation of the plant material within the pit fills was excellent. Small quantities of waterlogged wheat/rye bran were identified along with fragments of corn cockle. The assemblage was dominated by waste ground weed taxa, *Sphagnum* moss, bark and wood chips. Bran was recovered from two contexts, suggesting that this pit was for a short period used for the disposal of human faecal waste. The worked wood chips and cess material suggests that this pit was the receptacle for mixed remains.

Animal bone: A large assemblage of 291 identifiable animal bone fragments was analysed. The most abundant species represented was cattle, with 135 bone fragments, while 78 fragments were derived from ovicaprids and 30 from equids – probably horse but possibly donkey or mule. Twelve cat bones were present, as were 12 from dog or possibly fox. Other animals represented in the assemblage included pig, roe deer and red deer. Of the cattle bones 47% were derived from the head and feet of the animals, while the figure for ovicaprids was higher at 65%. One third of the horse bones were from the low meat-yielding bones of the feet and head (Figure 2.9, Chapter 2). Twenty-two goat horn cores were retrieved.

The wide range of species present suggests the bone does not originate from domestic waste. Cat, dog and horse remains would not be expected to be part of table waste. The presence of 22 horn cores from goat suggests horn-working was taking place nearby. The horse remains come from at least two animals, both fully grown. The dog remains may have come from one individual, a young almost fully mature animal. At least two cats are represented in the remains, at least one of which had not reached maturity. The cats and dogs may have been killed for their skins. The animal remains appear to represent the waste material from industrial activities such as horn (and possible antler) working and, perhaps, the curing of skins from dogs, cats and perhaps horse as well as other domesticates such as sheep and cattle. Cattle metapodials and skulls are abundant; this has been interpreted elsewhere (e.g. O'Connor 1984) as evidence of tanning waste. This pattern is not repeated with the ovicaprid bones as no metapodials were retrieved but the large number of goat horn cores suggests specialised use of the animals. The condition of the animal bone suggests the pit filled reasonably rapidly and was free-draining.

Bird bone: The tibio-tarsus of a domestic goose and the femur of a domestic fowl were present.

Fish bone: Some 1129 fish fragments were retrieved. This large assemblage is summarised in Appendix 4, Table A.4.1. The large number of cod vertebrae contrasts with the smaller number of cranial elements, even when considering the frequent occurrence of vertebrae with a single skeleton. The same is apparent for ling. This does not appear to be a recovery bias, as the sieved material tends towards the same pattern; thus it appears this deposit contained the remains of several fish bodies with few corresponding heads. Several vertebrae were butchered.

Interpretation
Pit including refuse from potentially several industrial processes including horn-working and curing of skins.

The large quantity of cod and ling vertebrae indicates the disposal of material from some form of fish processing/ butchery though it is unknown whether this relates to an industrial process, such as glue-making for instance. The great depth of the feature suggests the possibility that prior to its backfill the pit may have functioned as a 'layaway' pit in the tanning of hides (Chapter 5.2).

Pit C017 (Figure 2.4C, Chapter 2)

Small sub-circular pit, *c.* 0.6m deep, over Layer C001. The basal fill of this feature was a mid brown organic clay silt (A), which lay under a dark grey organic clay (B). The uppermost fill was a light-to-mid grey sandy silt (C).

Leather: The assemblage comprises; offcuts x1.

Ceramics: Yorkshire-type Ware (sherds of jugs and a cooking pot).

Macroplant remains: The lower fills of this pit were dominated by useful taxa such as oats, oat chaff and straw, some of which was embedded in what could either be decomposed faecal material or compact degraded floor matter. Other food remains were hazelnut and raspberry. Small fragments of peat and burnt peat were found in the upper fill. The rest of the assemblage was made up of local waste ground weed taxa. This material is representative of floor waste, more likely from stable clearing rather than domestic, industrial or building residue. The oats and oat chaff appear to have been animal feed/bedding. The burnt peat remains are indicative of fuel material.

Interpretation
Likely refuse pit.

Ph C013

Posthole with mixed dark brown/grey fill (A) over subsoil.

The *in situ* post (SF3958) was roughly square in cross-section and had been converted from a birch log so that the bark was still intact in places.

Ceramics: Local Redware (jug sherds); Scottish White Gritty Ware (jug sherds); Scarborough-type Ware Fabrics 1 and 2 (jug sherds); Stamford Ware (a jug sherd), and Yorkshire-type Ware (jug sherds).

Interpretation
Isolated posthole feature.

Spread C002

Black humic silt dump deposit overlying backfill of Pit C007.

Fish bone: Sieving produced 103 fish bones of which a single herring vertebra, a flounder fragment, two halibut family vertebrae, one sole family vertebra, two plaice cranial elements, a single haddock bone and three cod bones could be identified. This range of taxa and the small sizes of fish found, including the two smaller cod, contrasts strongly with the rest of the assemblage and probably indicates fishing in a different habitat. Flounder 15–20cm TL x1; plaice 15–30cm x1; plaice 30–50cm TL x1; haddock 30–50cm TL x1; cod 15–30cm TL x1; cod 30–50cm TL x1; cod >100cm TL x1.

Interpretation
Dump deposit or upper fill of Pit C007.

3.3 Phase 2 (late 12th to mid 13th century) (figure 2.14)

Layer A002/A012/C003/C014/C054

Dark greyish brown silty clay occupation deposit with clay and sand lenses.

Dating evidence: A leather offcut from Layer C003 produced a date of cal AD 990–1160 (SUERC-26673; Appendix 1, Table A1.1). This deposit also contained a silver cut halfpenny dating to the reign of King John of England (SF2391). It is a rare example of a class Vb2 coin minted by Hunfrei at Rochester and can be dated to between AD 1205 and AD 1207.

Leather: The presence of a large number of triangular offcuts and of sole fragments with seams across the waste indicates manufacture of new shoes and repair or reuse of old ones. The assemblage comprises; shoe components x131; straps x13; offcuts, scraps & miscellanea x1201. This includes 17 soles and an upper style which suggest a date range from the 12th to the 15th centuries, probably predominantly the 13th to 14th centuries, i.e. SF2952 (Figure 4.17, Chapter 4).

Industrial residues: The assemblage comprises; plano-convex slag cakes x3, 275.8g; slag amalgam x1, 214.3g; unclassified slag x1, 15.3g.

Ceramics: Local Redware (sherds from jugs, cooking pots and other vessels); Aberdeen Fabric 8 (jug sherds); Scottish White Gritty Ware (jug and cooking pot sherds); Stamford Ware (jug sherds); Yorkshire-type Ware (jug sherds); East Anglian Ware (cooking pot sherds); London Sandy Ware (jug sherds); Low Countries Redware (jug sherds), and North French-type Ware (jug sherds).

Macroplant remains: The plant assemblage was varied and consisted of food remains, moss, heathland, waste ground and arable weed taxa. The food remains included cereal bran, chaff, flax, raspberry, hazelnut shell and charred cereal caryopses. The heather remains constituted a mixture of seeds, leaves and buds, some of which had been charred. Other finds included charcoal, peat, burnt peat, wood chips and bark. This was a mixed deposit with rubbish originating from a variety of sources such as food, fuel and possible building material in the form of turves. There was no evidence that stable waste was disposed of in this layer.

Animal bone: A total of 395 animal bones were analysed. There are abundant bones from the meat-producing elements of both cattle and ovicaprids. Bones from the head, metapodials and feet of cattle were plentiful. Similarly, the ovicaprid assemblage has large quantities of bones from the high-meat elements and from the skull, with fewer metapodials and bones from the feet. One fragment of radius from sheep displayed butchery marks. These were most likely caused by the filleting of meat from the bone, rather than by the dismemberment of the carcass. Ten goat horn cores were retrieved, two of which bore knife marks resulting from the removal of the horn. Other species represented were roe deer, red deer and pig. One fragment of roe deer metacarpal was present. Six red deer bones were present, including a fragment of worked antler and four metapodials, two of which bore knife marks. Of the 24 pig bones retrieved 14 were from high meat-yielding elements, four of which had evidence of butchering.

In general, the assemblage suggests that the cattle remains reflect a mixture of different types of activity. Similarly, the abundance of high meat bones in the ovicaprid assemblage suggests butchery or domestic waste, while the goat horn cores indicate more specialised animal bone-working activities. The red deer assemblage, though small, may indicate bone and antler working and the pig bone fragments appear to represent domestic consumption of these animals. Thus, the bones in this layer derive from a number of different activities.

Fish bone: Layer C003 produced 1103 fish bones. As one of the largest assemblages taxa, elements and sizes are summarised in Appendix 4, Table A.4.2. Cod and ling dominate the assemblage, a few haddock were recovered, and trace quantities of a few other species were present. A moderate number of butchered and pathological specimens were noted. Cod cleithra appear slightly over-represented compared to other elements, but both cod heads and vertebrae were being deposited together.

Interpretation
General occupation deposit.

Table 3.2 Phase 2; the artefact assemblages for key contexts and features (where quantified numbers of items are presented)

Context	Wooden artefacts	Leather	Textiles	Animal fibres	Cordage	Metalwork	Worked stone	Lithics	Glass	Crucibles	Clay moulds	Industrial residues	Misc	Clay pipes	Ceramic building material	Window glass	Ceramic vessels
Layer A002 etc		1345		10		16	1	2			1		1				
Gully C004		132	1			2											
Hollow C002		1086															
Pit C018	1	1389		6		6				3			1				
Pit C019	1	453				3	1				1						
Pit C021	2	131															
Pit C022	3	500				2	1										
Pit C023		492															
Pit C024	3	26															
Pit C025	24	388	2		2	3							2				
Pit C026	1	10															
Pit C027		23															
Pit C029	1																
Pit C031		50															
Pit C032	2	490	1														
Pit C033	3																
Pit C034		26															
Pit C036		47														1	
Pit C037	1	38				3											
Pit C099		44				1											
Ph C018						1											
Spread C008		1															
Spread C043	1	142		3				1									
Stakes C002				1													
Wall C001		1															
Well C001	1							1									

Gully C004

South/north-aligned gully, with a width of up to 1.2m, running towards and perhaps originally feeding into, Pit C027. It contained a major dark grey clay silt fill (A) and lenses of clay and silty clay (B). Over Spread C005 and overlying Gully C002.

Leather: The assemblage included a few used shoe components and leather working waste, including waste from cutting out soles. The assemblage comprises; shoe components x5; straps x1; offcuts, scraps & miscellanea x126.

Ceramics: Local Redware (jug and cooking pot sherds); Aberdeen Fabric 8 (jug sherds); Scottish White Gritty Ware (jug and cooking pot sherds); Scarborough-type Ware Fabrics 1 and 2 (jug sherds); Stamford Ware (jug sherds); Yorkshire-type Ware (jug sherds); London Sandy Ware (jug sherds); Rouen-type Ware (a jug sherd), and North French-type Ware (jug sherds).

Macroplant remains: The plant assemblage was dominated by waste ground weed taxa with small fragments of hazelnut shell and raspberry seeds. This feature appears to have had an open water surface where material was allowed to accumulate before being backfilled.

Fish bone: Of 35 fish bones 25 were cod, from both cranial and vertebral elements. There were also three ling, a single herring vertebra and two haddock vertebrae. One cod had been butchered and the herring and haddock bones had been burnt. Cod 50–80cm TL x1; cod 80–100cm TL x14; >100cm TL x10; ling >100cm TL x3; haddock 15–30cm TL x2.

Interpretation
Drainage and boundary feature. A Phase 2 element of Gully C002 and therefore related to boundary Gully C001.

Hollow C002

Compaction feature over backfill of Pits C030 and C034. It contained a major deposit of mixed organic silty clay with sand (A) and lenses of yellowish orange silty clay (B) and blueish grey clay (C) and (D).

Leather: The assemblage comprises; shoe components x137; straps x3; offcuts, scraps & miscellanea x946. This includes 14 soles (i.e. SF4176A & SF3868; Figure 4.17, Chapter 4) and one upper (SF4178; Figure 4.18) of a style which suggest a date range from the 12th to the 15th centuries, probably predominantly the 13th to 14th centuries. There was also a fragment with stud holes, possibly from a legging or sleeve (SF4159; Figure 4.22). The large number of triangular offcuts indicates that

new soles were being cut, while the presence of soles with seams across waist or tread demonstrates that shoes were either being repaired or new shoes were being made from old ones.

Ceramics: Local Redware (jug sherds); Scottish White Gritty Ware (jug and cooking pot sherds); Stamford Ware (jug sherds), and Yorkshire-type Ware (sherds of jugs and a cooking pot).

Animal bone: Twenty-three animal bone fragments were analysed, 13 of which were from cattle and the remainder from ovicaprids. Two goat horn cores were present, along with four horn cores from cattle. Both goat horn cores and one of the cattle horn cores have dismembering marks at the base of the horn core, most probably resulting from the removal of the horn. Four other bones displayed butchery marks. This small assemblage has two noteworthy features: firstly, a high proportion (30%) of bones display butchery marks; and secondly horn cores make up a high proportion (26%) of the assemblage. This suggests the dumping of waste from specialised bone or horn-working activities.

Fish bone: Of 259 fragments of fish bone 116 (45%) were cod. Although cranial and vertebral elements were noted, 23 of these fragments were cleithra. Ling was represented by 24 fragments, from a mix of cranial and vertebral elements. There were three haddock cleithra and a single vertebra of saithe or pollack. Flatfish were also identified, including five plaice, one flounder/plaice, one turbot family vertebra and six halibut family elements. Butchery marks were identified on four cod and two ling.

Cod 30–50cm TL x1; cod 80–100cm TL x30; cod >100cm TL x85; ling 80–100cm TL x2; ling >100cm TL x22; haddock 30–50cm TL x3; saithe/pollack >100cm TL; place 30–50cm TL x3; plaice 50–80cm TL x2; flounder/plaice 50–80cm TL x1; turbot family 50–80cm TL x1; halibut family 30–50cm TL x2.

Interpretation
Dumped and compacted waste material overlying Pits C030 and C034.

Pit C018 (Figures 2.17A & 2.19, Chapter 2)

Sub-rectangular, 1.3m deep, pit with heavily organic greyish brown silt basal fill (A). This laid under a grey organic silty clay fill (B), which was sealed by the major fill, a dark greyish brown organic clayey silt containing leather and wood fragments (C) and was under a major leather dump (D). Overlying this was an organic clayey silt deposit (E), which had been truncated by 20th century piling. Over Layer C054.

Leather: The assemblage comprises; shoe components x74; straps x1; offcuts, scraps & miscellanea x1314. This includes one sole shape and one upper style, ranging in date from the 13th to the 14th centuries.

Ceramics: Scottish White Gritty Ware (jug sherds); Yorkshire-type Ware (jug sherds); Rouen-type Ware (a jug sherd), and North French-type Ware (a jug sherd).

Macroplant remains: The plant assemblage consisted of a mixture of food, flavouring and useful plants such as wheat/rye/oat bran, hazelnut shell, blackberry, meadow sweet and weld/dyers rocket. There were also large quantities of moss, arable weeds and waste ground weed taxa.

This sample contained a large quantity of decayed fibrous plant matter. The presence of spiral thickenings coupled with decayed *Isatis tinctoria* silicula fruit confirmed the identification of *Isatis tinctororia* L but no other part of the plant, such as stems or leaf matter was noted. Of all the features examined, this pit is amongst the most likely to have been used as either a dye bath or for the disposal of dyeing waste. This pit also contained a small quantity of mixed waste along with what appeared to be faecal matter.

A single piece of human bone (SF2785) was found in fill (E). This was a fragment of adult right ilium, with enough surviving features to identify it as a male of early middle age (Middle Adult A, 26–35 years) (Rachel Ives, *pers comm*).

Animal bone: There were 121 identifiable fragments of animal bone with cattle, ovicaprids, pig, red deer and cat being represented. A fragment of tibia shaft, possibly dog, which had been worked at both ends was present. The cattle, ovicaprid and pig assemblages were dominated by high meat-yielding bones, many of which were butchered. Red deer was represented by predominantly worked antler (five fragments); a mandible and another antler fragment did not appear to be worked. There were five goat horn cores, one of which had knife marks indicating the horn had been removed.

The bones in this pit were derived from horn and antler working as well as other activities. The cattle, pig and ovicaprid bones were predominantly from the main, meat-bearing body parts so they may represent household waste. However, an industrial process such as tanning, where the complete body may have been disposed of following skinning, would result in the presence of the meat-producing body parts as well as the limb extremities and the heads. Alternatively, the bones in this pit may originate from a number of sources and represent several activities or sets of activities.

Bird bone: There were three bantam bones identified as two humeri and one tarso-metatarsus. One humerus had evidence of butchery marks in the form of three cut marks along the proximal end. These remains are butchery waste. There was also one duck coracoid bone.

Fish bone: Of 163 fish bones 73 (45%) were cod. A total of 17 (10%) ling bones were identified. Both the cod and ling were represented by cranial and vertebral elements. Six haddock fragments and a single plaice were also found. Butchery marks were observed on seven cod. Cod 50–80cm TL x2; cod 80–100cm TL x38; cod >100cm TL x33; haddock 30–50cm TL x4; haddock 50–80cm TL x2; plaice 30–50cm TL x1.

Interpretation
Pit containing refuse associated with several activities, including de-hairing; hide preparation, dyeing and likely domestic waste.

Pit C019 (Figures 2.17B & 2.20, Chapter 2)

Sub-square pit, 0.8m deep, overlying Pit C018. The basal fill (A) was a mid yellowish grey silty sand, which lay under a waterlogged dark brown organic clay (B). The main fill overlying this was a dark brown sandy clayey silt (C), which was sealed by a layer of dark reddish brown sandy clay silt (D) with peat-like lumps. Over this was a thin yellow clay lens (E), which was sealed by the upper fill, a dark brown sandy silt (F).

Leather: The assemblage comprises; shoe components x39; offcuts, scraps & miscellanea x414. This includes three sole shapes suggesting a possible date range from the 12th to the 14th or 15th centuries.

Ceramics: Local Redware (jug sherds); Aberdeen Fabric 8 (jug sherds); Scottish White Gritty Ware (jug and cooking pot sherds); Stamford Ware (jug sherds), and Yorkshire-type Ware (jug sherds).

Macroplant remains: The macroplant remains from two upper fills, (C) and (D), were dominated by waste ground weed taxa. Fill (B) contained edible and useful species such as blackthorn, wild cherry, hazelnut, raspberry, flax, turnip/cabbage, apple, cereal bran and cereal chaff along with some background traces of waste ground and arable weed species. The only macroplant remains recovered from the lowest fill, (A) was a small quantity of goosefoot and wood chips. While there is a near absence of macroplant remains and other finds from the lowest fill, the overlying deposit, (B), appears to have been used for the disposal of human waste. This sequence suggests that the pit originally presented an open water surface, and that later it was deliberately used for disposal of human waste.

Animal bone: The 14 animal bones analysed were predominantly from the head and feet, mainly from cattle, with goat (horn core) and pig also represented. The assemblage suggests poor preservation conditions and, possibly, that the animal bones may be butchery waste removed in the early stages of carcass preparation.

Fish bone: Of 40 fish bones seven were cod vertebrae and nine were ling vertebrae. There was also a single haddock cranial element. Cod 80–100cm TL x2; cod >100cm TL x2; ling >100cm TL x9; haddock 30–50cm TL x1.

Interpretation

Pit of unknown original function, though latterly utilised for disposal of refuse and cess.

Pit C021 (Figure 2.17C, Chapter 2)

Sub-square pit, *c.* 1.7m deep, with many twigs/branches against its sides and a redeposited blue clay lining at the base (A), over Layer C003. The lining lay under a yellowish green organic clay fill (B), which lay under a dark grey clayey silt deposit (C).

The only structural timber of any note was SF3054, an alder log which had been shaped to a tip at one end, while at the other end it was forked, the forked branches trimmed to short stumps.

Leather: The assemblage comprises; shoe components x7; straps x1; clothing? x1; offcuts, scraps & miscellanea x122.

Ceramics: Normandy Gritty Ware (a jug sherd).

Macroplant remains: The plant assemblage consisted mainly of *Sphagnum* moss and a few weed taxa. The plant assemblage suggests that in its primary function the pit held water long enough for vegetation and litter from the nearby landscape to accumulate. There is no evidence that this pit was used for the deliberate dumping of industrial, domestic or stable refuse.

Animal bone: Twenty-two fragments of identifiable animal bone were analysed, of which 10 derived from what had probably been one complete dog. One cat tibia was also present. The remainder of the assemblage came from the common food-producing animals but was so limited that no pattern of body part representation could be detected.

Fish bone: There were nine fish bones, seven of which were cod and one was ling. One cod was butchered. Cod 80–100cm TL x6; cod >100cm TL x1; ling >100cm TL x1.

Interpretation

Pit of unknown function, though its depth and the presence of a possible twig/branch lining may indicate that it originally had an industrial function such as a 'layaway' pit in the tanning process (Chapter 5.2).

Pit C022 (Figure 2.17C, Chapter 2)

Recut, 0.95m deep, of Pit C021. The basal fill (A) was a yellowish brown clay, containing possible remnant structural branches. This was sealed by an organic dark brown clay (B). Over this was an organic black silty clay (C), which lay under a thin organic black clay silt (D), under dark greyish black sandy clay (E).

The fragmented remains of a hurdle screen, composed primarily of hazel with some willow, were recovered from this pit.

Leather: The assemblage comprises; shoe components x47; straps x4; offcuts, scraps & miscellanea x449. This includes five soles and two ankle boot uppers (SF2875; Figure 4.18; SF2755; Figure 4.19, Chapter 4) of a style indicating a possible date range from the 12th to the 15th centuries.

Ceramics: Scottish White Gritty Ware (jug and cooking pot sherds) and Stamford Ware (jug sherds).

Macroplant remains: The plant remains from the lower fills were dominated by food taxa such as cultivated oat, oat spikelets, bread/club wheat, straw/hay, cherry, sloe, blackthorn and *Sphagnum* moss. Small quantities of heath/moor/peat taxa were also recovered in a charred condition, and wild weed taxa typically associated with both waste and arable land was also present. Bark was present in all fills but only those fragments recovered from the basal fill displayed any evidence of working. This pit appears to have contained mixed rubbish in the form of food plants, refuse from animal stables, fuel and possible building material. The charred moss and peat fragments suggest that this material had been used as a fuel source before being dumped in the pit. The fragments of bark appeared to have been removed in large strips and then used to tie wood fragments/branches together. The large fragments of bark recovered from the basal fill may have been used to line the bottom of this pit. Alternatively, these bark fragments could simply have been disposed of as rubbish.

Animal bone: A total of 102 identifiable animal bone fragments were analysed, with cattle, ovicaprid, pig, goat, horse, dog and cat all present. Of the 45 fragments of cattle bone 16 came from the head and feet; eight metapodial fragments and eight fragments from meat-rich bones. Bones from throughout the skeleton were present in the ovicaprid assemblage with approximately half being from meat-rich elements. The small (nine fragments) pig assemblage was dominated by the meat-rich elements. One goat horn core was retrieved and three cat limb bones. Two fragments of horse bone were also present. The range of species present and the abundance of cattle hooves and skulls argues against this being predominantly a domestic waste dump and suggests that waste from some industrial processes is present in the pit. The condition of the bone suggests that the pit filled up quickly and was free-draining.

Bird bone: Of the 10 bird bones analysed seven were bantam, two were domestic goose and one was duck. The bantam bones consisted of two humeri, four tibio-tarsus and one tarso-metatarsus. The tarso-metatarsus had a noticeable build up of bone where the spur should be. This could have been a pathological condition but could also be damage caused to the bird during activities associated with cock fighting. The domestic goose bones were a sternum and tibio-tarsus. The duck bone was a tibio-tarsus which bore two cut marks towards the distal end of the shaft, signifying that it was butchery waste.

Fish bone: Of 98 fish bones 52 (53%) were cod, equally represented by cranial and vertebral elements. Ling were represented by 14 (14%) cranial and vertebral elements, one of which had been butchered. There were also four haddock vertebrae, two herring vertebrae and two halibut family fragments. Cod 30-50cm TL x1; cod 80–100cm TL x13; cod >100cm TL x38; ling >100cm TL x14; halibut family 30–50cm TL x1; halibut family 50–80cm TL x1; haddock 15–30cm TL x1; haddock 30–50cm TL x1.

Interpretation
Possibly a 'handler' pit associated with tanning process (Chapter 5.2). Latterly utilised for refuse disposal.

Pit C023 (Figure 2.17D, Chapter 2)

Irregular, *c.* 0.6m deep, pit. The basal fill was a mid-to-dark reddish brown silt (A), which was sealed by a dark greyish brown clayey silt (B) with frequent inclusions of degraded timber and twigs (possible remnants of lining). This lay under light brown clay silt (C), which was in turn under dark brown clayey silt (D) and sandy silt (E). Over Layer C003.

Leather: The assemblage comprises; shoe components x24; straps x1; offcuts, scraps & miscellanea x467. This includes three soles suggesting a date range from the 13th to the 15th centuries.

Ceramics: Yorkshire-type Ware (jug sherds).

Macroplant remains: The plant assemblage was spread throughout the pit fills. Food remains included hazelnut

shell, cabbage, parsnip, cereal chaff along with grass/cereal culm nodes and straw fragments. Other finds included peat, compact floor material and wood chips. Inclusions within the compact floor material were straw and chaff. This is a mixed deposit, some of which may have originated from the disposal of human waste and stable clearing.

Animal bone: The 13 animal bone fragments analysed included seven from cattle, three from pig and two ovicaprid bones. One fragment of cat pelvis was also present. This small assemblage indicates good preservation conditions and suggests reasonably rapid infilling.

Bird bone: There were two bones, one domestic fowl synsacrum and a tibio-tarsus from a bantam.

Fish bone: Of 13 fish bones five were cod and three were ling. Cod 80–100cm TL x3; cod >100cm TL x2; ling >100cm TL x3.

Interpretation
While containing a mixed assemblage of refuse material, the presence of wood chips, and twigs indicates that it is possible that this may be the base of a small 'handler' pit (Chapter 5.2).

Pit C024

Irregular, 1.2m deep, pit with edge defined in part by wooden material. The basal fill was a dark brown silty clay (A), which lay under wooden material in a light reddish brown sandy clay (B). This was sealed by a dark brown sandy silt with much organic material (C). Truncated Pit C023.

Some of the wood from this pit probably formed a lining. There were two roundwood posts, one of ash and one of alder, as well as oak stakes and two short oak planks, the ends of which were buckled from insertion into firm ground. SF3633B had been cut down from a larger plank; both ends had been neatly rounded but there were redundant pegholes some with radially-cleft oak pegs still *in situ*.

Leather: The assemblage comprises; shoe components x5; offcuts x21. This includes two soles of 13th to 14th century date.

Ceramics: Local Redware (jug sherds); Yorkshire-type Ware (jug sherds); East Anglian Ware (cooking pot sherds); London Sandy Ware (jug sherds); Normandy Gritty Ware (a jug sherd); North French-type Ware (a jug sherd), and Paffrath-type Ware (a cooking pot sherd).

Macroplant remains: A mixed macroplant assemblage contained food plants, waste ground weed taxa and potentially useful plants. These included hazelnut shell, turnip, cereal bran, flax and *Prunella vulgaris* L. (self heal). Fragments of moss and worked wood chips were also present. The moss was probably used for hygiene purposes akin to toilet paper. This assemblage represents the disposal of food residue along with human waste.

Fish bone: This pit produced a single butchered cod cleithrum (Figure 4.59F, Chapter 4) and five ling fragments, one of which was also butchered. Cod >100cm TL x1; ling >100cm TL x5.

Interpretation
Refuse pit including cess.

Pit C025 (Figures 2.22–2.27, Chapter 2)

Large sub-rectangular pit edged with interleaved humic peat-like material (B) and clay (A) and (C), containing timber building debris, over Pit C024. This possible lining/residue material lay under the main fill of the pit, a dark reddish brown organic sandy clay (D), which was under dark grey/brown clayey sandy silt (E). A hurdle screen largely sealed the latter deposit; this was covered in turn by a greyish brown silty sand deposit with clay lenses (F).

The western half of Pit C025 was covered by the remains of a hurdle screen overlying a timber frame (SF3100), which covered a large part of fill (E). SF3100 had been laid over a number of oak planks. The surviving fragment was 1.50m wide and 1.20m high and it had been constructed with double sails set roughly 0.20m apart. The sails and withies were a roughly equal mix of willow and hazel.

In the fills of the pit were large quantities of structural timbers including 18 plank fragments, seven posts, five stakes and two large beams with complex joints. The planks may have formed earlier coverings for the pit. With one exception they were all radially-split oak planks and the more complete examples displayed one squared end while the other was shaped to a point. The exception was SF3622, which had been fashioned from a log of hazel, by cleaving large chords off opposing sides. Four of the planks (SF3566; SF3655; SF3688 and SF3694) displayed narrow grooves down their wider edges and must have originally been components in tongue-and-groove panelling. One surface of SF3688 was covered in knifemarks and must have been used temporarily as a cutting block.

Some of the posts form a distinctive group: SF4602; SF4604 and SF4605 are all flat-bottomed posts trimmed from oak logs to a roughly square cross-section. They survive to substantial heights of 2.27m, 2.24m and 1.91m respectively and are very similar in cross-sectional dimensions. SF3621 may form part of the same group; although fashioned from a quarter-log of oak and with evidence, in the form of relict auger holes, that it has been cut down from a larger object, it is also flat-based and 1.63m in height. These may be related to the function of the pit, possibly forming part of a superstructure over the pit. The other posts in the pit are also flat-bottomed but have been fashioned from undressed alder logs and are generally smaller in height.

SF3976 is a complex structural timber (Figure 4.54, Chapter 4). It has been fashioned from a large oak log, some 0.23m in diameter which is forked at one end. One fork has been deliberately chopped off while the other has been left longer and has broken off. The other end has been trimmed flat. The 'upper' surface of the log has been trimmed flat and at either end of the flattened area are pairs of holes, 30mm in diameter and 60mm deep; the pegs are still *in situ* in one pair. The flattened end and the trimmed fork suggest that it was intended to be upright, perhaps with boards pegged to the flattened area. Like the posts described above, it may also have formed part of the superstructure above or around the pit.

Dating evidence: Ten oak timbers discarded in this pit were selected for dendrochronological analysis (Table 4.1; Figure 4.1, Chapter 4). These included a mixture of undressed roundwood timbers and radially-split planking, several of which had the remains of a groove at their thicker end. Eight sequences could be dated but the level of correlation between them was not so high as to suggest that they came from the same source or structure. One of the planks was felled in the winter/spring of AD 1209/10 and the other dated timbers which retain some of their outer sapwood rings were probably felled at around the same time. Thus, allowing for a period of use, the pit was probably backfilled sometime in the first half of the 13th century at the earliest.

Leather: The assemblage comprises; shoe components x32; offcuts, scraps & miscellanea x356. This includes a single sole shape with parallels from the 12th to the 14th centuries but belonged mainly to the 13th century.

Ceramics: Local Redware (jug and cooking pot sherds); Aberdeen Fabric 8 (jug sherds); Scottish White Gritty Ware (jug sherds); Stamford Ware (a jug sherd); Yorkshire-type Ware (jug sherds); East Anglian Ware (cooking pot sherds), and London Sandy Ware (jug sherds).

Macroplant remains: The macroplant remains recovered from the three upper fills are typical of rubbish commonly associated with cess pit refuse. Amongst the food plants and flavourings were blackthorn, cherry, walnut, strawberry, hazelnut, oat spikelets, cereal bran and straw. Bark and *Sphagnum* moss were also more abundant in the upper three fills. Lower fill (B) contained only a small quantity of weed taxa and hazelnut shell. This implies that the lower fill was rapidly built up, which prevented the accumulation of plant material and other environmental evidence. The plant materials recovered from the three upper fills are typical of cess/midden rubbish such as human faecal matter and stable clearing. The large quantities of bark in the three upper fills might have derived from lining of the pit to prevent seepage and the nearby soil becoming contaminated with human/animal waste. If the bark was deliberately used to line this feature then this indicates that the primary function of this pit was to act as a receptacle for faecal waste, as opposed to other features on site which appear to have been used haphazardly for dumping waste. This also implies that there may have been nearby resources such as wells, food storage or industrial activities which had to be protected from faecal contaminants spreading within the soil. The moss was probably used akin to toilet paper.

Animal bone: Cattle, ovicaprids, pig and red deer were represented among the 159 animal bones analysed. Bones from the skull and feet were most common among the cattle bone (36%) with high-meat bones comprising 30% of the cattle assemblage. In contrast over half (53%) of the ovicaprid bone fragments were from the meat-producing skeletal elements. Metapodials were not abundant in either species. There were 16 pig bones retrieved, of which 68% were metapodials but this relatively high figure is in part due to pigs having twice as many metapodials as ungulates. Indeed, all the metapodials present may have originated from just two pigs.

This bone assemblage is not dominated by hooves, skulls and metapodials and therefore does not appear to derive from carcass preparation or from tanning. However, two goat horn cores are present, so some industrial material may be included. Some 12% of the assemblage carried butchery marks. The bones were well preserved, suggesting the pit filled reasonably quickly and was free draining.

Fish bone: This pit produced 134 fish bones of which 66 (49%) were cod, 24 (18%) were ling and there were three haddock and one whiting. Both cod and ling were represented by cranial and vertebral elements. Evidence of butchery was observed on nine cod and two ling. Cod 80–100cm TL x27; cod >100cm TL x39; ling 50–80cm TL x1; ling >100cm TL x23; haddock 50–80cm TL x3; whiting 30–50cm TL x1.

Interpretation
The scale of this feature suggests that this pit may originally have been utilised for an industrial process, perhaps as a 'layaway' in tanning – evidenced by the presence of a humic peat-like lining material near the base of the feature. However, the major upper fills of this feature contain a mixture of waste material.

Pit C026 (Figures 2.30A & 2.31, Chapter 2)

Large, 1.8m deep, sub-circular pit. The basal fill (A) was a reddish brown silty clay with numerous twigs (possibly a degraded lining). This was sealed by a greenish grey silty clay fill (B). Above this, on the southern side of the pit, was a deposit of greenish grey silt with charcoal (C), which lay under mixed greenish brown silt and reddish and clayey silt (D) under dark greyish brown clayey silt (E). The major, upper, fill of the pit was a dark brownish grey silty clay with frequent charcoal and oganic inclusions (F). Over Layer C014.

Leather: The assemblage comprises; shoe components x6; straps x1; offcuts x3. This includes two sole shapes with a date range from the 12th to the 14th centuries.

Ceramics: Yorkshire-type Ware (jug sherds) and London Sandy Ware (jug sherds).

Macroplant remains: The macroplant remains recovered from this pit were dominated by weed taxa with only a smaller quantity of edible or useful plants present. *Chenopodium album* L. (fat hen) and *Persicaria lapathifolium* L. (pale persicaria) were particularly abundant in two of the lower fills (B) and (C). The food and useful taxa consisted of small quantities of heather, oat spikelets, cereal periderm fragments and a small quantity of charred cereal caryopses. This pit appears to have been used for the dumping of mixed rubbish, some of which may have originated from stable and human waste.

Fish bone: This feature produced one cod and two ling. Cod >100cm TL x1; ling >100cm TL x2.

Interpretation
Likely refuse pit.

Pit C027 (Figures 2.33 & 2.34, Chapter 2)

Very deep (2.7m) sub-rectangular pit with bluish grey clay lining (or slumping) of base (A) and common twigs and structural wood in its major dark grey organic silty clay fill (B). It was associated with Gully C004 and over Spread C005.

The structural timber included two oak planks, both of which were probably reused. SF4024 was pierced by three holes of varying diameter and bore a cluster of nailholes at one end, while SF4226 was also pierced by a single hole close to the squared end.

Dating evidence: The two oak planks produced *termini post quem* of AD 1133 and AD 1149 for their felling (Table 7; s 83). Allowing for missing rings and a period of use the pit was probably backfilled around the turn of the 12th/13th century at the earliest.

Leather: The assemblage comprises; shoe components x2; offcuts, scraps & miscellanea x21.

Ceramics: Local Redware (a cooking pot sherd); Scottish White Gritty Ware (jug sherds), and Yorkshire-type Ware (jug sherds).

Macroplant remains: A large concentration of a compact mid brown peat-like material was recovered which contained frequent inclusions of grass, straw, bracken, wood chips and chaff. This appears to be the remnants of plant litter flooring which had been compacted by trampling. There were also trace amounts of worm egg capsules and some beetle remains. The plant assemblage was not overly large and consisted mainly of local waste ground weed taxa. The only food plants recovered were a few fragments of hazelnut shell and oat chaff. The plant material does not appear to have originated from turves and is more likely to be a floor residue; probably from a stable.

Animal bone: The analysed animal bone comprised 91 identifiable bones from cattle, ovicaprid, pig, dog, cat, horse and red deer. The horse and red deer are represented by only one bone each while there are two cat bones and two dog bones present. Bones from the head and feet were the most abundant group (49%) among the cattle assemblage. Similarly, among the ovicaprid bone that could be assigned to goat, 11 out of the 12 bones were from the head and feet, with five being horn core. This skewed the ovicaprid assemblage (only 31 bone fragments in total) resulting in it resembling the cattle assemblage with 45% of the bones derived from the head and feet. The range of species present and the prevalence of skull and hoof bones reflect industrial processes, perhaps including carcass preparation for the table. The presence of goat horn core and an antler fragment suggests horn-working nearby.

Bird bone: One bantam tarso-metatarsus and one skull fragment of domestic fowl were present.

Fish bone: The assemblage contained ten cod, three ling and one saithe. One cod maxilla was butchered, an unusual element to display evidence of butchery. Cod 80–100cm TL x4; cod >100cm TL x6; ling 80–100cm TL x1; ling >100cm TL x2; saithe 80–100cm TL x1.

Interpretation
Given the depth of this pit and the presence of much organic material, it is possible that this feature originally functioned as a 'layaway' pit in the tanning process (Chapter 5.2). It latterly functioned as a refuse pit and may contain evidence for the processing of hides and the working of horn core and antler horn.

Pit C029

Small rectangular pit with edge defined in part by degraded organic material under a dark brownish grey clay fill (A). Over Layer C003.

Ceramics: Local Redware (jug sherds).

Macroplant remains: A mixed plant assemblage contained food/useful plants, arable and waste ground weed taxa. The food plants consisted of hazelnut shell, fig seeds, raspberry, cereal bran and chaff while the useful plants were flax and self heal. Arable weeds consisted of wild radish and corn cockle. Other finds included moss and wood chips. The material in this pit originated from mixed remains although it also appears to have been the receptacle for faecal matter.

Fish bone: This assemblage produced two cod, two ling and three haddock. Sieving produced one tiny vertebra that could only be identified as a cod family fish, as well as two haddock elements. One of the ling had been butchered. Cod 80–100cm TL x1; cod >100cm TL x1; ling >100cm TL x2; haddock 15–30cm TL x1; haddock 30–50cm TL x1; haddock 50–80cm TL x1.

Interpretation
This feature was used for the disposal of refuse including cess.

Pit C031 (Figures 2.28B & 2.29, Chapter 2)

Sub-square pit, only partially excavated as on edge of excavation area. Feature had a lining of wattle and clay (A) on east and south faces of pit under a main fill of dark brownish grey sandy silt clay with lenses of clay and organic material (B). Over Layer C003.

Leather: The assemblage comprises; shoe components x4; offcuts, scraps & miscellanea x46. This includes one sole shape, probably of 13th to 14th century date.

Macroplant remains: The plant remains represented a mixed deposit of worked wood chips, heathland material, food/useful plants and weed taxa. The food/useful plants consisted of hazelnut shell, oat chaff, spiklets, cereal bran, wild cherry and flax. A fairly compact turf material that had frequent inclusions of decayed straw, heather and bracken was also present. This pit represents mixed remains from activities such as stabling, possible building material, workshop waste and food residue along with what may have been faecal matter. The material initially identified as turf may in fact have been compacted plant litter flooring material. Of particular note was the condition of the hazelnut shell and wild cherry fruit stones recovered. Unlike most other deposits where hazelnut shells were recovered as fragments, these hazelnut shells were intact except for a small hole in the outer shells marked with what appeared to be rodent teeth marks. Similarly, the external surface of the wild cherry fruit stones displayed evidence of rodent damage. These foods supplies may have been damaged in storage by pests and subsequently disposed of or they may have been gnawed in the pit after disposal.

Fish bone: Of 26 fish bones there were four cod and ten ling cranial elements, and a single gurnard family vertebra. One of the ling had been butchered. Cod >100cm TL x4; ling >100cm TL x10; gurnard family 15–30cm TL x1.

Interpretation
Refuse pit, though apparent wattle, clay and turf lining material may indicate that it originally had an unknown industrial function.

Pit C032

Irregular, steep-sided sub-oval pit with highly organic mid reddish brown clay silt fill (A) with common twigs (perhaps remnants of lining material). Approximately 2m in depth. Over Layer C003.

Dating evidence: A sample from a leather shoe from the pit fill produced a date of cal AD 1020–1210 (SUERC-26664; Appendix 1, Table A1.1).

Leather: The assemblage comprises; shoe components x26; straps x1; offcuts, scraps & miscellanea x463. This includes a sole and upper style suggesting a date range from the 12th to the 14th centuries. Several fragments of a scabbard, SF4057 (Figure 4.20, Chapter 4) were also present.

Ceramics: Scottish White Gritty Ware (jug and cooking pot sherds); Stamford Ware (jug sherds), and London Sandy Ware (jug sherds).

Macroplant remains: The plant material recovered from the upper element of this mixed fill consisted of small quantities of oak buds, bark, bracken, viola, sheep's sorrel, wild grass culm nodes and moss, some of which still adhered to the surface of the bark. The lower part of the fill contained a larger quantity of waste ground weed taxa, arable weed taxa, oat chaff, grass, hay/straw and charred heather. The plant remains recovered from the upper element of the pit fill appears to have

been collected from a wooded landscape. There is also evidence of turf or peat material. The inclusion of the moss is probably unintentional and was introduced as a byproduct growing on the bark. This material may have been collected for building insulation or as a floor or pit lining. The material from the lower part of the fill may have originated from stable clearings and there is some evidence that charred heather, which formed part of a turf block, was used as a fuel source.

Animal bone: A total of 38 animal bones were analysed and cattle, ovicaprid, pig, dog and roe deer were present. There were four goat horn cores, two of which had knife marks at the base indicating where the horn had been removed from the bone. No general pattern was obvious in the body parts represented due to the relatively small size of the assemblages from each of the species present. The assemblage tells us little of the function of the pit other than that waste from horn-working was deposited. The good condition of the bone suggests that the pit filled quickly and was free-draining.

Fish bone: This pit produced 139 fish bone fragments of which 34 were cod and 29 were ling. A single haddock, saithe and saithe/pollack were also noted. Both cod and ling included cranial and vertebral elements. Cod 50–80cm TL x1; cod 80–100cm TL x5; cod >100cm TL x28; ling >100cm TL x29. Haddock 50–80cm TL x1; saithe 80–100cm TL x1; saithe/pollack 80–100cm TL x1.

Interpretation
This feature was latterly used for the disposal of refuse but may have originated as a 'layaway' pit in the tanning process (Chapter 5.2).

Pit C033

Irregular pit, 0.7m deep. The greenish grey clay basal deposit (A) may have been a clay lining. The main fill was a dark brownish grey sandy silt (B). Over Pit C032.

Amongst the structural timbers found in this pit were six oak planks, a large oak stake and an oak post base. The dating indicates that the planks came from different sources and many of them appear to have been chopped down from larger planks. For instance, SF3740 is only 0.31m long with one end neatly squared and the other deliberately curved, and with a central hole with peg *in situ*. SF3717A is similarly small, only 0.39m in length although more irregularly shaped. SF3719 displays a groove along its thicker edge and must have originally come from tongue-and-groove paneling or cladding.

SF3721 is the base of a large flat-bottomed post. Fashioned from an oak log 0.22m in diameter it is charred over the base and sides and only survives to a height of 0.10m. It may have been deliberately charred to prevent decay in the ground, although none of the other flat-bottomed posts found at Bon Accord had been treated in that way.

Dating evidence: The six oak planks were selected for dendrochronological analysis (Table 4.1; Figure 4.1, Chapter 4). These were mainly radially-split planks but also included a quarter-log. One timber (SF3201) had been felled in the winter/spring of AD 1200/01 but there was also later material in the pit (timbers SF3719 and SF3717) which provided *termini post quem* of AD 1226 and AD 1233 respectively for their felling. Allowing for missing rings and a period of use it is unlikely that the pit began to be backfilled until the late 13th century at the earliest. However, it is possible that the planks were largely *in situ*, forming part of a short-lived structure associated with the pit, accounting for their location within a late Phase 2 feature. This is supported by the clear disturbance of this feature by Phase 6 drainage Structure C009.

Ceramics: Local Redware (jug and cooking pot sherds); Scottish White Gritty Ware (jug and cooking pot sherds); Yorkshire-type Ware (jug sherds), and London Sandy Ware (jug sherds).

Macroplant remains: The small macroplant assemblage was dominated by waste ground weed taxa along with some oat spikelets, cereal bran, apple, moss, arable weeds and bracken fragments. Other finds included charcoal and wood chips. This material appears to represent mixed rubbish and contains what could be human faecal waste. Of the moss identified *Campylopus* sp has no specific use and probably grew in the near locality or was brought to site as an accidental inclusion on woodland material. The greatest concentration of moss was *Hylocomium splendens*, which is among the most commonly used mosses for hygiene purposes.

Fish bone: This pit produced 32 fish bones of which ten were cod and four were ling. One of the cod had been butchered. Cod 50–80cm TL x1; cod 80–100cm TL x7; cod >100cm TL x2; ling >100cm TL x4.

Interpretation
Pit of unknown function, though putative lining may indicate an industrial purpose. However, it may also have functioned as part of the boundary largely defined by Stakes C002.

Pit C034 (Figure 2.21, Chapter 2)

Flat-based, 0.46m deep, irregular shaped pit with heavily organic silty clay fill (A) over Layer C003 (given shallow depth it is possible that this may be the truncated base of a Phase 3 pit).

Leather: The assemblage comprises; shoe components x1; offcuts, scraps & miscellanea x25.

Ceramics: Scottish White Gritty Ware (jug sherds) and Yorkshire-type Ware (jug sherds).

Macroplant remains: The plant assemblage was dominated by small quantities of weed taxa and some cereal chaff.

Animal bone: A total of 35 animal bone fragments were analysed. Cattle, red deer, goat, sheep and pigs were represented in very small quantities. Eight out of the 16 cattle bones derived from the head and feet. One fragment of goat skull, with horn core attached, was present and bore cut marks from the removal of the horn. The red deer bone was metatarsal, rather than worked antler. Nine bone fragments displayed butchery marks. Patterns interpreted as indicators of industrial activities such as horn-working or carcass preparation in other features, namely a predominance of the low meat-producing bones of the head and feet in cattle and the presence of worked horn core, are present, suggesting that these are the remains from industrial rather than domestic waste. The good condition of the material suggests that the pit filled rapidly and has been relatively free-draining.

Bird bone: There were three bones of domestic fowl, two humeri and one tarso-metatarsus.

Fish bone: This feature produced 447 fish bones of which 152 (34%) were cod and 78 (17%) were ling. Both vertebrae and cranial elements were noted for cod and ling. The ling included two almost complete, articulated ling crania. Such pristine, large and articulated specimens from an excavation are rare. Not only does this mean that fish heads were being discarded whole, but that preservation was exceptional and disturbance minimal. There were also six haddock and single examples of halibut, saithe, ray family and gurnard family. Butchery marks were observed on 13 cod, one ling and one haddock. Cod 15–30cm TL x1; cod 80–100cm TL x50; cod >100cm TL x101; ling 80–100cm TL x1; ling >100cm TL x77; haddock 15–30cm TL x1; haddock 30–50cm TL x2; haddock 50–80cm TL x3; saithe 80–100cm TL x1;

Interpretation
Pit of unknown function, containing evidence of possible hide preparation in the form of animal skull and feet bones. Likely latterly used as a refuse pit.

Pit C036 (Figure 2.36A, Chapter 2)

Oval, steep-sided, pit with large pieces of wood and frequent twigs (possible remnants of lining) in organic-rich mixed lower fills, over Layer C003. The basal fill (A) was a brownish grey silty sand, under blueish grey sandy clay with frequent organic material (B). This lay under dark brownish grey organic sandy and clay silt (C) with many twig inclusions and lenses of clay. Over this was a disturbed deposit of brownish grey sandy silt (D) under a mixed deposit of brownish grey clay and blueish grey sandy silt (E) with a lens of greyish black and brownish orange sandy silt with frequent charcoal (F). The upper fill was a brownish grey silty sand (G). In the south side of the pit was an area of yellowish red sandy clay (H) derived from animal disturbance.

Leather: The assemblage comprises; shoe components x7; straps x3; offcuts, scraps & miscellanea x37.

Ceramics: Aberdeen Fabric 8 (jug sherds); Stamford Ware (a jug sherd); Yorkshire-type Ware (jug sherds); London Sandy Ware (jug sherds); Rouen-type Ware (a jug sherd), and North French-type Ware (a jug sherd).

Macroplant remains: The plant remains from this pit included food, potentially useful plants, moss, arable and waste ground weed taxa. The plant remains identified were wheat/rye cereal bran, cabbage, onion, apple, bird cherry, hazelnut shell, flax, weld/dyers rocket, *atriplex* sp(p) (oraches) and *Spergula arvensis* L. (corn spurrey). Other finds included moss and charcoal. This pit primarily contained human faecal matter along with some mixed rubbish from other sources. There is no evidence that any material from stabling was deposited within this feature.

Animal bone: Twenty-one animal bone fragments were analysed. Of the 16 cattle bones eight were from high meat-yielding elements and four were metapodials; all these bones could have come from a single individual. The only other bones identifiable to species were three from sheep/goat. One of these was a mandible and the others were meat-yielding bones. This small assemblage represents food waste. The material is quite discoloured and not particularly well preserved suggesting the pit may have filled up fairly slowly or may have contained redeposited material.

Fish bone: The small fish bone assemblage included two cod, one haddock and one ling.

Cod >100cm TL x2; haddock 30–50cm TL x1; ling >100cm TL x1.

Interpretation
Pit used in the disposal of refuse including cess. Given the apparent lining of the pit, and its great depth, it may potentially have originally been utilised for an industrial purpose, perhaps involving the retention of water.

Pit C037 (Figures 2.30B & 2.32, Chapter 2)

Irregular. 1.4m deep, pit containing timber and organic material in its lower fills, over Layer C003. The primary fill was a light grey clay silt (A), which lay under a mixed deposit of orange and dark brownish grey silt with charcoal flecks (B). This was sealed by a black organic clay with peat-like material (C), which was underneath dark brownish grey clay silt (D).

Leather: The assemblage comprises; shoe components x5; offcuts, scraps & miscellanea x33.

Ceramics: Local Redware (jug and cooking pot sherds); Aberdeen Fabric 8 (jug sherds); Scottish White Gritty Ware (jug sherds); Stamford Ware (jug sherds); Yorkshire-type Ware (jug and cooking pot sherds), and North French-type Ware (a jug sherd).

Macroplant remains: This pit contained a mixed plant assemblage containing weed taxa, heathland material, moss fragments and food waste. The heath and woodland material consisted of heather, violet, birch seeds and leaf litter from birch trees, some of which was charred. The food residue consisted of hazelnut shell, raspberry, cabbage, chaff, oat spikelets and charred cereal caryopses. This pit was possibly used for dumping human faecal matter, floor waste and fuel material. The plant remains recovered from fill (C) were dominated by a significant quantity of bracken, moss, peat, bark, wood chips, heather buds, flowers and leaves which had all been charred. This indicates that fuel material such as peat or grass turvess/sods was being disposed of. The weed taxa are representative of vegetation growing in the local environment.

Animal bone: Seventy animal bone fragments were analysed. The majority (64%) were from cattle, while 27% were ovicaprid. The only other species present was pig, represented by one bone. The cattle bones were primarily from the skull and feet (47%) together with nine metapodials. Eleven cattle bone fragments (24%) were from the high meat-producing parts of the skeleton. Meat-yielding bone dominated the ovicaprid remains, comprising 12 of the 19 fragments. There were four goat horn cores. The assemblage indicates that the cattle bones may derive from industrial processes, such as carcass preparation or tanning of hides, rather than from domestic table waste. The goat horn cores suggest some industrial use of ovicaprids, although the ovicaprid assemblage appears to be dominated by higher meat-yielding bones. There may, however, be an alternative explanation for the apparently higher frequency of high meat-producing bones in ovicaprid than in cattle. The condition of the bones suggests the pit filled reasonably rapidly and that the pit was fairly free-draining.

Bird bone: There was one radius from a domestic goose.

Fish bone: This assemblage consisted of 14 cod and one haddock. Two of the cod were butchered and could be articulated together, joining the butchery marks; this is a rare occurrence. Cod 80–100cm TL x13; cod >100cm TL x1; haddock 30–50cm TL x1.

Interpretation
Pit of uncertain function, though latterly used in disposal of refuse.

Pit C099 (Figure 2.17E, Chapter 2)

Sub-square pit, *c.* 1.0m deep, and containing a dark brown organic silty clay fill (A), which contained a number of timbers. Over Layer C003.

A group of planks stood upright along the west edge of this pit, suggesting that the pit had been backfilled shortly after their deposition. They were all radially-split oak planks, the lower ends of which had been roughly squared.

Dating evidence: Two of the oak planks were selected for dendrochronological analysis (Table 4.1; Figure 4.1, Chapter 4). One of the timbers was probably felled sometime between AD 1152 and AD 1190. Allowing for missing rings and a period of use the pit would have been backfilled around the turn of the 12th/13th century at the earliest.

Leather: The assemblage comprises; shoe components x4; offcuts, scraps & miscellanea x40.

Ceramics: Yorkshire-type Ware (jug sherds) and London Sandy Ware (a jug sherd).

Macroplant remains: The plant assemblage from this pit contained only a few weed taxa, charred cereal caryopses, bracken and moss fragments.

Animal bone: There were 12 animal bone fragments, with cattle, goat, roe deer and ovicaprid bones being present. Three fragments were butchered, all with dismembering marks, and one piece of cattle phalanx had been oxidised through burning. The presence of one roe deer phalanx is noteworthy as is the burnt bone.

Fish bone: Of 64 fish bones 16 were cod, 11 were ling, three were halibut family and there was a single saithe. Two of the cod and one of the ling displayed butchery marks. Cod 30–50cm TL x1; cod 80–100cm TL x6; cod >100cm TL x9. Ling 80–100cm TL x1; ling >100cm TL x10; saithe 80–100cm TL x1; halibut 30–50cm TL x1.

Interpretation
Pit of unknown function.

Ph C018

Posthole for large timber (B) associated with brown clay silt packing (A). Over Spread C041. The base of the post (B) had survived *in situ*. The post was square in cross-section and the base had been chopped flat. It had been fashioned from an oak log at least 0.2m in diameter.

Dating evidence: The oak post was selected for dendrochronological analysis (Table 4.1; Figure 4.1, Chapter 4). The timber was probably felled sometime between AD 1204 and AD 1240, so the structure of which the posthole is a part was probably erected sometime in the first half of the 13th century.

Ceramics: Yorkshire-type Ware (a jug sherd).

Interpretation
This posthole may be associated with the boundary defined by Stakes C002.

Spread C008

Dark greyish brown silty clay occupation deposit over Spread C007 (Phase 2 or 3).

Leather: The assemblage comprises; miscellanea x1.

Ceramics: Local Redware (a jug sherd); Scottish White Gritty Ware (a jug sherd) and Stamford Ware (jug sherds).

Animal bone: Thirty-three animal bone fragments were analysed. Both the cattle and ovicaprid assemblages were dominated by bones from the head and feet. Four horn cores from cattle and four from goat were retrieved. Although the assemblage is small it appears to represent material derived from industrial, rather than domestic, activities. The good condition of the bones suggests rapid deposition and covering of the material as well as free-draining conditions.

Interpretation
Dump or occupation deposit.

Spread C010

Greyish brown silt dump deposit with shell and bone over Hollow C002.

Macroplant remains: Amongst the small assemblage of plant materials from this deposit were heathland/moor taxa, *Sphagnum* moss along with background traces of waste ground weed species. The presence of heather, bracken, violets, *Sphagnum* moss and matted straw indicates that building material such as turfs, and fuel may all have been disposed of in this deposit.

Fish bone: This deposit included one salmon and trout family vertebra, an unusual find on this site and possible evidence of fishing in nearby river systems rather than marine environments. Also present were two cod vertebrae. Cod 80–100cm TL x2.

Interpretation
Dump or occupation deposit.

Spread C043

Greyish brown sandy silt occupation or dump deposit over Pit C029.

Leather: The assemblage comprises; shoe components x11; straps x2; offcuts, scraps & miscellanea x129. This includes two sole shapes with a date range from the 12th to the 14th centuries.

Ceramics: Local Redware (jug sherds); Aberdeen Fabric 8 (jug sherds); Scottish White Gritty Ware (cooking pot sherds), and Yorkshire-type Ware (jug sherds).

Animal bone: Analysis of 17 animal bones was undertaken; this included bone from cattle, ovicaprid, pig and a horse incisor. The good condition of the bone suggests that this was a free-draining and stable environment.

Fish bone: This deposit contained a total of 333 fish bones, of which 110 (33%) were ling and 86 (26%) were cod. Both cod and ling were represented by cranial and vertebral elements but cod cleithra appeared slightly more frequent than other elements. Butchery marks were observed on nine cod and one ling fragment. Ling 50–80cm Tl x1; ling >100cm TL x109; cod 80–100cm TL x24; cod >100cm TL x62; haddock 30–50cm TL x1; flounder/plaice 30–50cm TL x1.

Interpretation
Occupation or dump material.

Stakes C002 (Figure 2.15, Chapter 2)

North/south stake alignment with occasional hurdle remnants over Spread C005.

The stakes in this fenceline were a mixture of undressed alder, oak, willow, hazel and birch roundwood stems; they ranged widely in diameter from 25mm to 160mm. There were also some larger oak posts, one of which had been fashioned from recycled timber. The withies were a similar mixture of species to the stakes, with a single piece of *Pomoideae*; all were between 10 to 30mm in diameter.

Eleven undressed roundwood stake tips in Layer C003 are thought to have come from Stakes C002. Of these, six were oak, three alder and one was hazel; they varied in diameter from 40 to 90mm.

Dating evidence: Special Sample 48/2, a roundwood oak stake in this stakeline, was selected for dendrochronological analysis (Table 4.1; Figure 4.1, Chapter 4). The timber was probably felled *c.* AD 1197, the ambiguity about the specific felling date arising because of slight damage to the sapwood.

Fish bone: This feature produced 24 fish bones of which eight were an articulating sequence of ling vertebrae, butchered with chop and cut marks. There were six cod of which two had also been butchered, and a single haddock. Ling >100cm TL x1; cod 50–80cm TL x1; cod 80–100cm TL x5; haddock 50–80cm TL x1.

Interpretation
Stake alignment forming boundary roughly parallel with Gallowgate and perpendicular to Upperkirkgate.

Wall C001 (Figure 2.18, Chapter 2)

North/south-aligned unbonded rubble wall base, measuring at least 15m north/south, over Layer C003.

Dating evidence: A single oak timber associated with this wall was selected for dendrochronological analysis (Table 4.1; Figure 4.1, Chapter 4). SF4260 was felled some time after AD 1221. If the timber was originally a constituent of the wall then, allowing for missing rings the wall was probably built around the middle of the 13th century.

Leather: The assemblage comprises; offcut x1.

Interpretation
Base of stone wall, demarcating a boundary running roughly perpendicular to the Upperkirkgate,

Well C001 (Figures 2.35 & 2.37–2.40, Chapter 2)

Timber barrel and stone-lined well over Layer C003. Well C001 comprised a barrel lining under an upper circular stone structure located within a nearly vertical-sided, 2m diameter, construction cut. The fill of the construction cut was a mixed deposit comprising redeposited silty sand subsoil and greyish black clay silt (A). This lay under the stone superstructure of the well. The basal fill of the well structure comprised a waterlogged brownish black clay silt with frequent stone inclusions (B). This lay under a blueish grey waterlogged clay silt (C) with occasional peat-like inclusions and frequent stones. The upper part of the well cut was filled with a dark greyish black clay silt with frequent stones (D).

Table 3.3 Phase 3; the artefact assemblages for key contexts and features (where quantified numbers of items are presented)

Context	Wooden artefacts	Leather	Textiles	Animal fibres	Cordage	Metalwork	Worked stone	Lithics	Glass	Crucibles	Clay moulds	Industrial residues	Misc	Clay pipes	Ceramic building material	Window glass	Ceramic vessels
Layer A028						1							1				
Layer C005/050		30		1		2											
Layer C019		2401	2	5		3	1			2	2						
Hearth C001																	
Hearth C002																	
Pit C016													1				
Pit C041		6															
Pit C042		78	1										1				
Pit C044		2															
Pit C047		20	1			1											
Pit C048		537	1	2		1	2										
Pit 069		1	1			1	3										
Well A002	1	5											2				

Ceramics: Local Redware (jug sherds); Scottish White Gritty Ware (jug sherds), and Yorkshire-type Ware (jug sherds).

Macroplant remains: The plant assemblage was dominated by waste ground weed taxa with some heathland/moor material. The food plants were restricted to a small quantity of raspberry, hazelnut shell and charred cereal caryopses. There is evidence of turf material in the infilling deposits in the form of compact peat material with inclusions of crowberry, violets, buttercups and heather. The turves were clearly disposed of in the well but it is unclear whether they were disposed of after being utilised elsewhere on site. There was no evidence of charring so it is unlikely that the turves were a fuel source and were more likely used as a building material. The remainder of this assemblage probably originated from the local vegetation and nearby litter which was allowed to accumulate within this feature.

Animal bone: There were 24 animal bones including cattle, ovicaprid and pig bone.

Interpretation
Well or large water butt.

3.4 Phase 3 (mid-to-late 13th century) (figure 2.41)

Layer A028

Sandy clay occupation deposit over Gully A003 (late Phase 2/Phase 3).

Ceramics: Local Redware (jug sherds); Aberdeen Fabric 8 (jug sherds); Scottish White Gritty Ware (jug sherds); Scarborough-type Ware Fabrics 1 and 2 (jug sherds); Yorkshire-type Ware (jug sherds); London Sandy Ware (jug sherds); Low Countries Redware (a jug sherd); Low Countries Greyware (a jug sherd), and North French-type Ware (jug sherds).

Interpretation
Occupation deposit.

Layer C005/C050

Dark grey clay silt occupation deposit overlying features cut into Layer C003.

Leather: The leather assemblage comprises; shoe components x8; straps x1; offcuts, scraps & miscellanea x21.

Ceramics: Local Redware (sherds from jugs, cooking pots and other vessels); Aberdeen Fabric 8 (jug sherds); Scottish White Gritty Ware (jug and cooking pot sherds); Stamford Ware (jug sherds); Yorkshire-type Ware (jug sherds), and London Sandy Ware (a jug sherd).

Macroplant remains: The plant assemblage contained mostly waste ground weed taxa with very few useful taxa. The only edible food remains identified were hazelnut shell and charred oat. Other finds included bark fragments, wood chips and charcoal.

Animal bone: Seventy fragments of animal bone were analysed. Thirty-four fragments were cattle and 16 of those were from the head and feet. Four cattle metapodial fragments were present as were eight fragments from the high-meat producing elements of the body. There were 17 fragments of ovicaprid bone, elements from all over the body. One bone each from cat, dog and red deer was retrieved, along with four from horse. The layer probably reflects accumulation of bones from several activities.

Fish bone: This deposit produced a total of 501 fish bones, mostly retrieved by sieving. Unusually for the site, haddock was the most common taxa, with 73 fragments identified. Both cranial and vertebral elements were identified. Seven ling, four cod and one cod family were also identified. One cod had been butchered. Haddock 15–30cm TL x2; haddock 30–50cm TL x70; cod 30–50cm TL x1; cod 80–100cm TL x2; cod >100cm TL x5; ling >100cm TL x7; cod family 15–30cm TL x1.

Interpretation
Major occupation deposit.

Layer C019

Brown clay silt occupation deposit over Layer C005 and Spread C154 (Phase 3 or 4).

Leather: The leather assemblage comprises; shoe components x191; straps & thongs x10 (i.e. SF1430A; Figure 4.21, Chapter 4); offcuts, scraps & miscellanea x2200. This includes three sole shapes which range in date from the 13th to the 15th centuries. There was also a decorated triangular fragment, SF1430B (Figure 4.21).

Ceramics: Local Redware (jug and cooking pot sherds); Aberdeen Fabric 8 (jug sherds); Scottish White Gritty Ware (jug sherds); Scarborough-type Ware Fabrics 1 and 2 (jug sherds); Stamford Ware (a jug sherd); Yorkshire-type Ware (jug sherds); London Sandy Ware (jug sherds), and Paffrath-type Ware (a sherd from a ladle).

Animal bone: An assemblage of 142 animal bone fragments was analysed. Cattle, ovicaprids, red deer, horse, pig, dog and cat were represented. No particular body part dominated the cattle bone assemblage. Around 40% of the ovicaprid bone fragments were from high meat-producing skeletal elements. Two of the bones were goat horn core. All but one of the seven fragments of pig bone were from the meat-producing elements, the exception being a mandible. A proximal phalanx and three fragments of radius and ulna from horse were present as was a complete cat tibia and a fragment of dog pelvis. The faunal evidence points to a mixed assemblage and a fairly poor preservation environment with waterlogging in places. The layer is likely to have accumulated slowly and the bones are likely to reflect a range of activities and processes.

Fish bone: This feature produced a total of 52 fish bones of which 31 were cod, 12 were ling and there was a single saithe/pollack. Cod 80–100cm TL x16; cod >100cm TL x15; ling >100cm TL x12; saithe/pollack 80–100cm TL x1.

Interpretation
Occupation deposit.

Hearth C001 (Figures 2.45, 2.46 & 2.48, Chapter 2)

Circular stone-lined hearth. The sub-circular cut measured *c.* 2.4m by 1.8m. The base of the cut was lined with a brownish grey clay silt (A), which lay under black sandy silt (B). There was then a light brown sandy silt (C) which was overlain by the surviving structure of the hearth, a circular arrangement of stones set in heat-affected orange sandy silt (D), forming a surface measuring *c.* 1.2m north/south by 0.6m east/west. Above this was a thin deposit of black charcoal (E) which was sealed by a layer of light greyish brown sandy silt with charcoal and baked clay inclusions (F). Over Layer C005.

Ceramics: Local Redware (jug sherds); Aberdeen Fabric 8 (a jug sherd); Scarborough-type Ware Fabrics 1 and 2 (jug sherds), and Yorkshire-type Ware (jug sherds).

Macroplant remains: The plant assemblage contained large quantities of waste ground weed taxa with smaller amounts of edible plants, heather, *Sphagnum* moss (some of which was charred) and arable weed taxa. The food plants were hazelnut, oat, cereal bran, onion and charred cereal caryopses. Other finds included small quantities of bark, wood chips some of which were worked, charcoal and burnt peat fragments.

Evidence of burning included the occasional charred fragment of *Sphagnum* moss and peat fragments which were concentrated in deposit (C). Analysis of a sample described as a 'peat brick' consisted of compressed layers of wood chips, bracken, burnt peat, fish bone, weed taxa and cereal refuse. Given the coherent shape of this 'brick', it is more readily understood as compacted plant litter flooring material in which debris from various sources has been allowed to accumulate before being dumped in the hearth along with other refuse. There was no evidence that turves were burnt as a fuel source within this hearth, nor were there any large quantities of charred macroplant remains such as cereal caryopses which would indicate that it was used to dry grain or prepare food. If this feature was used as a hearth it was probably for industrial activities and was subsequently used for the disposal of mixed rubbish.

Interpretation
Hearth, possibly for small-scale industrial process.

Hearth C002 (Figures 2.47 & 2.49, Chapter 2)

Clay-bonded stone-lined hearth structure within shallow cut measuring *c.* 2.5m east/west, open towards east. The edge of the feature was largely defined by a border of stones set in light grey clay (A), with the west end defined by a band of heat-affected orange/yellow clay (B), which overlay two thin deposits of black (C) and orange clay (D), the latter forming the floor of the hearth. Above this was a thin deposit of white ash (E), which was sealed by a red clay layer (F), perhaps a relining of the hearth. This was in turn sealed by dark yellow/orange sand (G) and grey clay (H). Above these were deposits of dark (I), light grey (J) and black silty clay (K), all containing charcoal. Over Layer C005.

Ceramic building material; A large quantity of highly fragmented clay daub was recovered during sample processing. Some of the fragments were between 30 and 40mm in thickness and most of the daub displayed clear evidence of having been reconsolidated and built up several times. Some of the larger fragments bore the impressions of wooden laths but it was not possible to determine the size of the laths.

The daub assemblage probably represents a hearth lining which was in use for a significant period of time. The continual addition of new clay to strengthen old damaged layers suggests that this hearth was used for longer or perhaps was exposed to a higher temperature than other similar features on this site. The timber lath impressions indicate that this daub clay covered a wooden structure which would have formed part of the wall lining. There is no evidence of any surviving floor or roof material, including intercutting timber slots or wattle impressions. Instead, small fragments of curved daub were recovered which by comparison with material recovered at 45–75 Gallowgate appeared to derive from hearths that were not roofed over in the conventional sense (Cameron *et al.* 2001: 206). If the hearth was not enclosed, this could have lowered the temperature to which the daub lining would have been exposed.

Macroplant remains: A small plant assemblage consisted of cereal remains, raspberry, waste ground weed taxa and charred cereal caryopses. The combination of food with weed species (and industrial waste) suggests that mixed rubbish was being disposed of. The waste ground taxa were probably growing nearby before being accidentally deposited within these deposits.

Fish bone: This feature produced two fish bones: one from a whiting and one only identified as cod family. Both were charred.

Interpretation
Hearth, perhaps unroofed, which may have been in use for a relatively low temperature process.

Pit C016 (Figure 2.42B, Chapter 2)

Vertical-sided square pit, at least 1.2m in depth, but truncated by post-medieval structure. The main fill of black clay (A) contained much pottery. This lay under two minor fills of redeposited clay and gravel subsoil (B) and silty clay (C), perhaps representing disturbance. Over Layer C005.

Ceramics: Local Redware (sherds from jugs, cooking pots and other vessels); Aberdeen Fabric 8 (jug sherds); Scarborough-type Ware Fabrics 1 and 2 (jug sherds), and London Sandy Ware (jug sherds).

Macroplant remains: The plant assemblage was small and consisted of mixed remains. The plant species were dominated by waste ground weed taxa with smaller quantities of food plants such as raspberry and charred oat caryopses. This material represents a small mixed deposit and as such is difficult to interpret in terms of usage, but it is probably an accumulation of mixed rubbish from different sources.

Fish bone: This feature produced two fish bones, one haddock and one cod family. The latter was most likely stomach contents from a much larger fish, as it would have had little food value. Haddock 15–30cm TL x1; cod family <15cm Tl x1.

Interpretation
Pit of unknown function.

Pit C041

Heavily truncated sub-circular pit, 2.0m deep, with possible lining material of branches within dark greyish brown silty clay main fill (A). The main fill was sealed by light brownish grey silty sand (B), which lay under dark greyish brown silty clay (C). Over Pit C040.

Leather: The assemblage comprises; shoe components x2; offcuts, scraps & miscellanea x4.

Ceramics: Local Redware (jug sherds); Scottish White Gritty Ware (jug sherds); Scarborough-type Ware Fabric 1 (jug sherds); Yorkshire-type Ware (jug sherds), and London Sandy Ware (jug sherds).

Fish bone: Five ling and three cod fragments were identified. Ling >100cm TL x5; cod >100cm TL x3.

Interpretation
Pit of unknown function, though potential lining may indicate an industrial function.

Pit C042 (Figure 2.43, Chapter 2)

Roughly 2.1m diameter sub-circular pit, with depth of *c.* 1.5m. The main fill was a dark greyish brown organic silty clay (A). Above this was a shallow fill of dark brown silty clay (B) under light brownish grey silty clay (C). Over Pit C041.

Leather: The assemblage comprises; shoe components x9; offcuts, scraps & miscellanea x69.

Ceramics: Local Redware (jug sherds); Aberdeen Fabric 8 (jug sherds); Scottish White Gritty Ware (jug sherds); Stamford Ware (jug sherds); Yorkshire-type Ware (jug sherds); London Sandy Ware (a jug sherd), and Newcastle Ware (jug sherds).

Macroplant remains: This assemblage was dominated by a poorly preserved peat-like material with obvious inclusions of *Sphagnum* leaves. The remainder of this assemblage was dominated by waste ground taxa that included arable weeds such as wild radish. The only cultivated plant remains were oat spikelets. This material appears to have originated from different sources, possibly from a floor surface such as stable clearing.

Animal bone: Forty-three identifiable animal bone fragments were analysed. Cattle, ovicaprids, dog, horse and pig were present, with the latter two being represented by only one bone each. The cattle assemblage, though small, was dominated by bones from the head and feet. One dog was represented in the assemblage, with ten bones present. The animal had had a broken fore-leg early in life, which had healed, leaving the bone quite bent and distorted. One sheep or goat tibia had a circular hole drilled through its distal end. The generally good condition of the assemblage suggests that the pit filled quickly.

Fish bone: A total of 24 fish fragments were found of which ten were cod, three were ling and there was a single flounder/plaice. Cod 80–100cm TL x6; cod >100cm TL x4; ling 80–100cm TL x1; ling >100cm TL x2; flounder/plaice 30–50cm TL x1.

Interpretation
Pit of uncertain function, though perhaps for refuse disposal.

Pit C044

Small pit or posthole, with diameter of 0.45m and depth of 0.34m, containing dark brown sandy clay silt (A). Over Pit C042.

Leather: The assemblage comprises; shoe components x2. These are both components with a date range of 12th–14th century but are mainly 13th century.

Ceramics: Yorkshire-type Ware (jug sherds).

Macroplant remains: The only plant remains recovered were a small quantity of waste ground weed taxa and *Cenococcum* sclerotia. This pit appears to have presented an open water surface that was left open long enough for vegetation growing in the local environment to accumulate.

Interpretation
Isolated posthole or small pit.

Pit C047 (Figure 2.42A, Chapter 2)

Irregular, 1.1m deep, pit with a dark yellowish brown organic clay basal fill (A) under light brown silty sand (B). Above this was a dark brown silt with lenses of clay (C), and the feature was sealed by a mixed organic deposit of brownish grey silty clay and light brown and grey clay (D). Over Surface C001.

Leather: This assemblage comprises; shoe components x7; offcuts, scraps & miscellanea x13. This includea a sole of 13th–14th century date.

Ceramics: Scottish White Gritty Ware (cooking pot sherds) and Yorkshire-type Ware (jug sherds).

Macroplant remains: The only plant material recovered from fill (C) was a very small concentration of weed taxa. The macroplant remains were concentrated in the lower fill (A). The assemblage was dominated by a large quantity of wheat/rye bran and cabbage. The only arable weed seed recovered was corn cockle. There were also background traces of bracken and waste ground weed seeds. Moss fragments were the only other major component of the plant assemblage. The limited recovery of plant material from upper fill (C) indicates that the pit was abandoned and then rapidly built up, preventing either the deposition of human waste or seeds from waste ground plants growing nearby. The high quantity of plant remains recovered from the lower deposits suggests that this pit was abandoned for a time before being reused. The large quantity of bran and moss, in particular *Hylocomium splendens*, typically used as a form of toilet paper, suggests the presence of human faecal waste.

Fish bone: A total of 175 fish bones were found of which 106 (60%) were cod and 49 (28%) were ling. Most cod fragments were vertebrae, rather than cranial elements. Two elements had been butchered. Almost all the ling were also vertebrae. There were also five saithe. Cod 50–80cm TL x4; cod 80–100cm TL x43; cod >100cm TL x59; ling >100cm TL x49; saithe 50–80cm TL x3; saithe 80–100cm TL x2.

Interpretation
Pit of unknown function, utilised at least latterly for refuse disposal.

Pit C048

Sub-circular pit, 1.5m deep, with much organic material in mixed basal fill of yellowish green clay and dark brown silt (A). The upper fill (B) was a dark brown clay silt. Over Layer C019 and truncating Pit C047 (Phase 3 or 4).

In this pit there was a group of roundwood stakes, a mixture of oak, birch, alder and hazel. They all had facetted tips and were between 35 and 45mm in diameter so they may have come from the same structure, possibly a hurdle screen.

Dating evidence: A sample of leather from the pit fill produced a date of cal AD 890–1150 (SUERC-26669; Appendix 1, Table A1.1).

Leather: This assemblage comprises; shoe components x26; offcuts, scraps & miscellanea x511. This includes a sole of 12th–14th century, but mainly 13th century date.

Ceramics: Local Redware (jug sherds); Aberdeen Fabric 8 (jug sherds); Scottish White Gritty Ware (jug and cooking pot sherds); Scarborough-type Ware Fabrics 1 and 2 (jug sherds); Yorkshire-type Ware (jug and cooking pot sherds); Grimston Ware (jug sherds); London Sandy Ware (jug sherds); Normandy Gritty Ware (sherds of jugs and a cooking pot); North French-type Ware (a jug sherd), and Newcastle Ware (jug sherds).

Macroplant remains: The plant assemblage was concentrated in the lower fill and contained small quantities of heathland/moor taxa, waste ground weed taxa and a small quantity of food remains. Other finds included charcoal and wood chips. This was a mixed deposit with what appears to be rubbish from different sources.

Animal bone: An assemblage of 113 bone fragments was analysed. The 35 cattle bones were mainly from the heads and feet of the animals, while the ovicaprid bone fragments were primarily the high meat-yielding elements. Two metatarsals from red deer were present as well as seven pig bones. The bones suggest several activities led to the deposition of the faunal remains. Their relatively poor condition suggests the pit may have filled up slowly and that it was not free-draining.

Bird bone: There were two domestic fowl bones, a humerus and femur, as well as the carpometacarpus of a domestic goose.

Fish bone: A total of 151 fish bones were identified, of which there were 52 (34%) cod and 46 (30%) ling. Both cranial and vertebral elements were represented for cod and ling. There was evidence of butchery on two cod and two ling elements. Two haddock, a cod family element, and a single halibut family were also found. Sieving produced a small sea scorpion family fish. Cod 30–50cm TL x1; cod 80–100cm TL x16; cod >100cm TL x35; cod family 80–100cm TL x1; ling 80–100cm TL x2; ling >100cm TL x44; haddock 30–50cm TL x1; haddock 50–80cm TL x1; halibut 30–50cm TL x1.

Interpretation
Pit used for a variety of refuse including animal fibres and bones indicative of hide preparation. This feature may have had another purpose, such as a 'layaway' pit prior to use for refuse, although there was no clear evidence for this beyond its significant depth.

Pit C069 (Figures 2.42C & 2.50, Chapter 2)

Large, 1m deep, roughly circular pit (Phase 3 to 4).

The major, basal, fill of this feature was a mixture of grey clay and dark grey organic silt (A). Overlying this was a mid brown sandy silt (B), which was sealed by mid grey silty clay (C). This was overlain by brown organic clay (D), which was under reddish grey sandy clay (E). The pit was sealed by orangeish brown sandy silt (F). Cut through Layer C005.

Dating evidence: Carbon residue from a pottery vessel within the pit fill provided a date of cal AD 1215–1300 (SUERC-26675; Appendix 1, Table A1.1).

Three oak timbers discarded in this pit were selected for dendrochronological analysis, all of them radially-split planks (Table 4.1; Figure 4.1, Chapter 4). SF2378 from fill C069E was felled in the winter/spring of AD 1281/2; allowing for a period of use for the plank, the pit was probably backfilled around the turn of the 13th/14th century at the earliest.

Leather: The assemblage comprises; shoe components x1.

Ceramic building material: A large quantity of daub was recovered, none of the fragments exceeding 40mm in thickness. Impressions of wooden laths survived on three fragments. The daub had been exposed to extremely high temperatures as some of the fragments displayed evidence of vitrification and extensive charring. There was evidence that some of the fragments had been repeatedly repaired while in use. The daub probably represents a hearth lining which was subjected to extreme heat and had to be repaired frequently.

Ceramics: Local Redware (jug sherds); Scarborough-type Ware Fabrics 1 and 2 (jug sherds); Yorkshire-type Ware; Low Countries Greyware (a jug sherd), and Rouen-type Ware (jug sherds).

Macroplant remains: There was no significant change in the composition of the macroplant assemblage throughout this pit, which included plant material from both cultivated and disturbed ground. Edible charred and waterlogged cereal caryopses, chaff, fig seeds, hazelnut shell and raspberry were present, although they were concentrated in fill (A). There were also large quantities of common chickweed and knotgrass, spread throughout the pit fills with smaller quantities of thistle and nettles. Corn cockle, a common contaminant of cultivated cereals in the medieval period, was also recovered. Other useful plants identified included self heal and *Sphagnum* moss. There was also evidence of possible faecal matter in fill (A).

The nature of the assemblage indicates that this pit was perhaps used primarily as a dump for human faecal and stable waste which was allowed to accumulate for an extended period of time. The presence of agricultural weed taxa such as corn cockle suggests that this material was disposed of at the same time as the cereal remains. This could be residue from cereal processing such as winnowing and threshing or, given the small volume recovered, it is more likely to be waste animal feed cleared from stable floorings. The large volume of waste ground weed taxa present reinforces the argument that this pit remained open for extended periods of time enabling nearby weed taxa to become trapped within the deposits as they formed. If this was a midden/cess deposit the nitrogen-rich soil would be an excellent environment to encourage the growth of certain weed taxa such as nettles. The presence of *Sphagnum* moss appears to have been a deliberate inclusion and may have been used as a medieval substitute for toilet paper.

Fish bone: This feature produced 158 fish bones, 73 of which were identified. A wide range of taxa was noted.

There were 19 haddock, 17 cod, 12 saithe, 14 which could only be identified as cod, saithe or pollack, four saithe/pollack, two cod family and single examples of ray family, gurnard family and whiting. Two cod fragments had been butchered. This feature was unusual in that no ling bones were identified. Haddock 15–30cm TL x2; haddock 30–50cm TL x5; haddock 50–80cm TL x12; cod 50–80cm TL x2; cod 80–100cm TL x15; saithe 50–80cm TL x10; saithe 80–100cm TL x2; cod/saithe/pollack 80–100cm TL x1; cod/saithe/pollack 50–80cm TL x12; saithe/pollack 50–80cm TL x4; cod family 30–50cm TL x1; cod family 50–80cm TL x1; gurnard family 30–50cm TL x1; whiting 15–30cm TL x1.

Interpretation
Refuse pit.

Ph C011

Posthole, containing remains of timber post, with a mid grey silty sand with stones basal fill (A) under reddish brown gritty sand (B). Over Layer C005.

The post had survived *in situ* to a height of 0.52m. It was rectangular in cross-section, 0.30 x 0.14m, and had been fashioned from an oak log. The base had been chopped roughly flat.

Dating evidence: The post was selected for dendrochronological analysis (Table 4.1; Figure 4.1, Chapter 4). SF1879 was probably felled sometime between AD 1262 and AD 1294 so the structure of which the posthole is a part was probably constructed in the latter half of the 13th century.

Macroplant remains: The plant assemblage from this feature consisted of a small quantity of waste ground weed taxa and some moss fragments.

Interpretation
Isolated posthole feature.

Well A002 (Figures 2.51 & 2.52, Chapter 2)

Timber-lined well over Layer A028 (late Phase 2/Phase 3).

A large sub-rectangular construction cut with steep sides contained a deep well shaft to its north. The entire cut measured 5.5m north/south by up to 3.5m east/west, with the main shaft measuring 2.4m by 2.4m in plan. The well shaft had steep, slightly concave sides and reached a depth of at least 15.2m O.D., before standing water prevented further excavation; probing identified a probable base at 14.68m O.D. The cut was lined with a light bluish grey clay (A) and contained a roughly square timber structure (B) with four vertical corner posts, which retained planks and posts that formed the sides of the well. Several of the timbers were reused. The structure had external dimensions of approximately 1.2m by 1.2m. To the south a basal construction fill (C) of dark reddish brown clay was overlain by the main construction fill, external to the structure, of dark greyish brown clay silt (D). To the north there was an area of disturbed construction fill (E), representing the partial collapse of the structure, perhaps during use. The lower fill of the well was a waterlogged mid reddish brown organic clay (F), which lay under dark reddish brow silty clay (G). The top of the well shaft was sealed by dark brown silty clay (H).

The south-east corner of this pit was damaged by machine during the watching brief and most of the south side had been removed so it was not clear how this side of the timber lining had been constructed. Posts G, H and M, and possibly SF5009, had been set at each corner and behind these a lining of radially split planks had been set. On the north, east and possibly the south sides the planks had been set vertically into the ground, whereas on the west side the planks had been set horizontally. Small horizontal beams, B and EE, the ends of which were secured behind the corner posts, held the vertical planks in position on the north side and the same arrangement may have held on the south side; a horizontal beam, O, one end of which was tucked behind corner post M, may have performed the same function on this side.

The west side may be a later repair, hence the difference in construction. There were two posts in the north-west corner; FF lay inside G and appeared to hold the horizontal, B, in place. G had been inserted in front of the post and the horizontal, possibly after the collapse of the west side. However, this difference could simply relate to how the lining was constructed.

The corner posts and the horizontal beams were generally trapezoidal or rectangular in cross-section. The corner posts all had lap joints at each end into which the horizontal beams holding the planks in position were pegged. The horizontal beams were similarly jointed to lap against the uprights. Oak pegs were used to secure all the joints.

Radially-split planks lined the walls of the pit. The upper ends of each plank had been roughly squared while the lower end, which was inserted into the ground, had been chopped to an often irregular and shallow point. They varied greatly in length; E, a plank on the north side, was 2.33m long, while R, in the east wall, was only 0.95m long. Many of the planks displayed single pegholes and two had nailholes, all of which appeared to be redundant within the construction of the pit.

Two of the corner posts also displayed apparently redundant features. M had two pegholes penetrating one face and two nails on another face, while G had a lap joint with peg *in situ* which was not securing anything in its current position.

Dating evidence: Thirteen oak timbers used in the construction of this pit were selected for dendrochronological analysis, 11 from the *in situ* lining and two from the fill (Table 4.1; Figure 4.1, Chapter 4). All 13 sequences correlated well together, and this suggests that the two planks found in the fill of the pit also originally formed part of the lining; indeed correlations between one of the lining planks and one of the planks in the fill was so high as to indicate that they had come from the same tree. One of the corner posts, SF5056, was felled in the spring/summer of AD 1242, two of the planks were felled in AD 1243 while another of the corner posts, Post G, was felled in the spring/ summer of AD 1246. The range of felling dates present suggests that either there was some stockpiling of large timbers over a few years until there was sufficient for a large construction project, or that old timbers were reused in the construction of the pit, although there was no visible evidence of reuse (Chapter 4.1).

Leather: This assemblage comprises; shoe components x3; offcuts, scraps & miscellanea x2.

Ceramics: Local Redware (sherds from jugs, a cooking pot and another vessel); Scarborough-type Ware Fabrics 1 and 2 (jug sherds), and Yorkshire-type Ware (jug sherds).

Macroplant remains: The plant assemblage included worked wood chips, food remains and weed taxa. The food remains included fig seeds, parsnip and cabbage/ turnip. A large quantity of self heal was recovered, the largest concentration recovered from the site. The majority of the plant remains consisted of waste ground weed taxa. This feature appears to have been used for the dumping of mixed remains including workshop waste and faecal matter. There is no evidence that stabling waste was disposed of within this pit.

Interpretation
Well, perhaps in use for a considerable period of time.

3.5 Phase 4 (early) (late 13th to 14th century) (figure 2.53)

Layer A003/A019

Dark brown clay silt/silty clay occupation deposit over Layer A002 and backfill of Well A002.

Ceramics: Local Redware (sherds from jugs and cooking pots); Aberdeen Fabric 8 (jug sherds); Scottish White

Table 3.4 Phase 4; the artefact assemblages for key contexts and features (where quantified numbers of items are presented)

Context	Wooden artefacts	Leather	Textiles	Animal fibres	Cordage	Metalwork	Worked stone	Lithics	Glass	Crucibles	Clay moulds	Industrial residues	Misc	Clay pipes	Ceramic building material	Window glass	Ceramic vessels
Layer A003/A019						2											
Layer C008A etc.		45		1		5	2				1						
Pit C053										1							
Spread A027						1											
Layer A004						1	1										
Layer A015						2	1									1	
Layer C008						3							1				
Layer C020						2						2	1				
Layer C025/C035																	
Layer C069/C072		2				1											
Pit A024																	
Pit C064	1																
Pit C085						1											
Ph C003		69											1				
Spread C040		2															
Wall C007						1	1										

Gritty Ware (jug and cooking pot sherds); Scarborough-type Ware Fabrics 1 and 2 (jug sherds); Stamford Ware (jug sherds); Yorkshire-type Ware (jug sherds); London Sandy Ware (jug sherds); Low Countries Greyware (jug sherds), and North French-type Ware (jug sherds).

Macroplant remains: The plant assemblage recovered from this deposit consisted of a small quantity of charred cereal remains.

Interpretation
Occupation deposit.

Layer C008A/C026/C033/C041/C075

Mid to dark greyish brown silt occupation deposit over features cut into Layer C005.

Dating evidence: A discarded oak timber was selected for dendrochronological analysis (Table 4.1; Figure 4.1, Chapter 4). SF4239 was a radially-split plank which was probably felled sometime between AD 1245 and AD 1260; allowing for a period of use the layer probably accumulated in the latter half of the 13th century at the earliest.

Leather: This assemblage comprises; shoe components x8; offcuts, scraps & miscellanea x37. This includes a sole of 12th–13th century date.

Ceramics: Local Redware (jug and cooking pot sherds); Aberdeen Fabric 8 (jug sherds); Scottish White Gritty Ware (jug and cooking pot sherds); Scarborough-type Ware Fabrics 1 and 2 (jug sherds); Stamford Ware (jug sherds); Yorkshire-type Ware (jug sherds); East Anglian Ware (cooking pot sherds); London Sandy Ware (jug sherds); Low Countries Highly Decorated Ware (jug sherds); North French-type Ware (a jug sherd), and Valencian Lustreware (a bowl/dish sherd).

Industrial residues: The assemblage comprises; slag amalgam x1, 290.1g; plano-convex slag cakes x2, 461.3g; unclassified slag x2, 56.5g; vitrified clay x1, possibly kiln lining material, 236.1g; fuel ash slag, 44.0g; hammerscale microresidues c. 0.1g.

Animal bone: A total of 148 animal bone fragments were analysed. The 73 cattle bones included 21 bone fragments from the head and feet and 19 from the higher meat-producing body parts. Similarly, the ovicaprid remains showed no strong bias towards one body part. The bones probably come from both food waste and industrial activity. Their condition suggests that they accumulated reasonably quickly and were buried in a free-draining environment.

Fish bone: Of 98 fish bones 47 (48%) were ling, 39 (40%) were cod, and there was a single saithe/pollack. Ling and cod were both represented by cranial and vertebral elements. Ling 80–100cm TL x1; ling >100cm TL x46; cod 80–100cm TL x26; cod >100cm TL x13; saithe/pollack 80–100cm TL x1.

Interpretation
Occupation deposit.

Pit C053

Sub-circular pit, 1.8m deep. The basal fill (A) was a thin deposit of blueish grey silty clay, which lay under a major deposit of blueish grey clay with decomposed wood fragments (B), possibly representing a lining of the pit. Above this was blueish grey clayey silt (C) and grey heavily organic silty clay (D). Over Layer C075.

Ceramics: Local Redware (jug sherds).

Macroplant remains: The plant remains included traces of waste ground taxa, heathland/moor taxa and moss fragments. The heathland/moor material consisted of heather, buttercup, violet and festuca grass. The only edible plant remains were hazelnut shell and raspberry. There is no evidence that this feature was used for the disposal of human and/or stabling waste.

Interpretation
This may be an industrial feature, such as a 'layaway' pit, for the tanning of leather (Chapter 5.2).

Pit C054

Small, 0.17m deep, irregular pit containing grey/brown sandy silt with baked clay (A). Over Layer C026.

Macroplant remains: The plant remains included a small quantity of charred cereal caryopses, chaff and weed taxa. Barley, bread wheat, wheat/rye, rye and oat were present. The barley caryopses had begun to germinate prior to charring. This can indicate brewing but given the small quantity present it is more likely that they had been probably stored in damp/unsuitable conditions. The cereal remains are of mixed species and may be refuse from a drying kiln.

Interpretation
Small pit or isolated posthole. The presence of charred cereal might indicate that drying of grain was undertaken in Oven C001 and/or Oven C002 to the north.

Spread A027

Sandy clay with charcoal inclusions over Layer A002 (Phase 4).

Ceramics: Local Redware (jug and cooking pot sherds); Scarborough-type Ware Fabric 1 (jug sherds), and Low Countries Greyware (a jug sherd).

Fish bone: A single haddock vertebra was recovered.

Interpretation
Dump or occupation deposit.

3.6 Phase 4 (late) (14th to early 15th century) (figure 2.63 & Table 3.4)

Layer A004

Dark brown silty clay garden soil over Layer A003.

Ceramic building material: Twenty-three fragments of daub were recovered three of which displayed at least one flat surface, along with impressions of timber laths. The daub did not appear to have been fully baked, nor did it display any evidence of burning so it is unlikely that it was used to line a hearth. Instead, it is more probable that it was used as a wall lining.

Ceramics: Local Redware (sherds from jugs); Scottish White Gritty Ware (jug sherds); Scarborough-type Ware Fabrics 1 and 2 (jug sherds); Stamford Ware (jug sherds); Yorkshire-type Ware (jug sherds); Low Countries Greyware (jug sherds), and Raeren Stoneware (sherds from a mug and another vessel).

Macroplant remains: Plant remains comprised a small quantity of charred barley and oat caryopses. The only other find was a small quantity of *Cenococcum* sclerotia.

Interpretation
Garden soil.

Layer A015

Dark greyish brown clay silt garden soil over Layer A019 and contemporary with Layer A004.

Ceramics: Local Redware (sherds from jugs, cooking pots and other vessels); Aberdeen Fabric 8 (jug sherds); Scottish White Gritty Ware (jug sherds); Scarborough-type Ware Fabrics 1 and 2 (jug sherds); Stamford Ware (jug sherds); Yorkshire-type Ware (sherds from jugs and a cooking pot); London Sandy Ware (jug sherds); Low Countries Greyware (a jug sherd); Rouen-type Ware (a jug sherd); North French-type Ware (jug sherds); Paffrath-type Ware (a sherd from a ladle), and Langerwehe-type Stoneware (jug sherds).

Animal bone: More than half (57%) of the 74 animal bone fragments analysed were from cattle with sheep, pig, dog, horse and roe deer also present. One bone, a cattle phalanx, had been chopped through with a large blade. Bones from the meat-rich parts of the skeleton were most abundant (43%) in the cattle assemblage with bones from the head and feet (low meat) making up 26%. In the ovicaprid bone assemblage, the meat-rich elements were also most abundant (47%) with metapodials being the next most common element (16%). The bone assemblage may have derived from a number of different activities. The preservation of the bone suggests the layer accumulated slowly but was relatively free-draining.

Fish bone: Of five fish bones one was identified as haddock and one as cod. Haddock 50–80cm TL x1; cod >100cm TL x1.

Interpretation
Garden soil.

Layer C008

Greyish brown silty clay occupation deposit over features cut into Layer C075 and contemporary with Layer C072.

Ceramics: Local Redware (sherds from jugs and cooking pots); Aberdeen Fabric 8 (jug sherds); Scottish White Gritty Ware (jug sherds); Scarborough-type Ware Fabrics 1 and 2 (jug sherds); Stamford Ware (jug sherds); Yorkshire-type ware (jug sherds); London Sandy Ware (jug sherds); Low Countries Highly Decorated Ware (jug sherds); Low Countries Greyware (jug sherds); Rouen-type Ware (jug sherds); North French-type Ware (jug sherds); Saintonge Ware (a jug sherd); Paffrath-type Ware (a sherd from a ladle); Newcastle Ware, and Beverley Ware.

Industrial residues: The assemblage comprises; iron bloom fragment x1, 807.8g; slag amalgam x1, 121.6g; plano-convex slag cake x1, 74.5g; unclassified slag x13, 1017.1g; ferrous microresidues, possibly hammerscale, 1.3g; fuel ash slag, 84.7g; coal, 1.0g.

Macroplant remains: The macroplant remains were minimal and consisted of fat hen, raspberry, charred barley and oats.

Animal bone: Twenty-two fragments of identifiable animal bone were analysed. Cattle and ovicaprid were represented by small assemblages, neither of which was large enough to demonstrate any pattern in the body parts represented. One fragment of cat tibia was also present.

Fish bone: A single cod fragment was identified.

Interpretation
Occupation deposit.

Layer C020

Brown/grey clay occupation deposit over features overlying Layer C026.

Ceramics: Local Redware (jug and cooking pot sherds); Aberdeen Fabric 8 (jug sherds); Scarborough-type Ware Fabrics 1 and 2 (jug sherds); Yorkshire-type Ware (jug sherds); Low Countries Redware (jug sherds); Low Countries Greyware (jug sherds); Rouen-type Ware (a jug sherd); Siegburg Stoneware (jug sherds), and Raeren Stoneware (sherds from mugs and other vessels).

Fish bone: Ten fragments of fish were noted. These included four cod, a single haddock and a single ling. Cod 80–100cm TL x2; cod >100cm TL x2; haddock 50–80cm TL x1; ling >100cm TL x1.

Interpretation
Occupation deposit.

Layer C025/C035

Brown clay silt dump deposit over Layer C005 (Phase 4).

Ceramics: Local Redware (jug sherds); Scottish White Gritty Ware (jug sherds); Scarborough-type Ware Fabric 1 (jug sherds), and Yorkshire-type Ware (jug sherds).

Industrial residues: The assemblage comprises; unclassified slag x57, 432.9g; slag spheres, 0.5g; hammerscale (or possibly metal filing) microresidues, 19.8g.

Interpretation
Dump deposit.

Layer C069/C072

Dark reddish or greyish brown clay silt occupation deposit over Layer C008A.

Leather: This assemblage comprises; shoe components x1; offcuts x1.

Ceramics: Local Redware (sherds from jugs, cooking pots and other vessels); Aberdeen Fabric 8 (jug sherds); Scottish White Gritty Ware (jug sherds); Scarborough-type Ware Fabrics 1 and 2 (jug sherds); Yorkshire-type Ware (jug sherds); London Sandy Ware (a jug sherd); Low Countries Greyware (a jug sherd); Rouen-type Ware (a jug sherd), and North French-type Ware (jug sherds).

Fish bone: Of 12 fish bone one was identified as a flatfish and one as cod. Cod 15–30cm TL x1.

Interpretation
Occupation deposit.

Pit A024 (*Figure 2.65, Chapter 2*)

Circular pit, 1.5m deep, with near vertical sides and a flat base. It contained a dark brownish grey silty clay lower fill (A), under mid brownish grey silty clay (B). The upper fill was a dark brownish grey clayey silt (C). Over Layer A004.

Ceramics: Local Redware (jug sherds); Scarborough-type Ware Fabric 1 (a jug sherd), and Langerwehe-type Stoneware (a jug sherd).

Animal bone: Nineteen fragments of animal bone were analysed. Almost half were proximal phalanges (foot bones) from cattle; a patella and a fragment of skull were also present representing other low meat-producing bones. All but four of the bone fragments came from cattle or probable cattle (cattle-sized animals). The remaining four fragments were classified as ovicaprid or medium-sized mammals and are most likely from sheep or goat. Two of the bone fragments bore large chop marks most likely caused by dismembering the carcass using a large blade such as a cleaver. The animal bones are probably butchery waste left after the preparation of carcasses for the domestic table. They are in reasonably good condition suggesting rapid deposition and perhaps implying the pit was filled deliberately.

Interpretation
This probably represents an original cut for a well or cistern; it was truncated at a later date by barrel-lined Well A001.

Pit C064 (*Figure 2.64, Chapter 2*)

Vertical-sided, 2.6m deep, pit. The basal fill (A) was a waterlogged silty clay, which was sealed by a dark brownish grey sandy clay with irregular stones (B). This was in turn sealed by fill (C), which comprised compact black clay with daub fragments. The overlying fill (D) lay against the west side of the pit and was extremely rich in daub. It was sealed by fill (E), a dark silty clay, which lay under a grey silty clay fill (F) that was rich in cobbles. Over Layer C008.

Dating evidence: A single oak timber discarded in fill (C) of the pit was selected for dendrochronological analysis (Table 4.1; Figure 4.1, Chapter 4). SF3753 was a large radially-split plank which was probably felled sometime between AD 1266 and AD 1302; allowing for a period of use, the pit could have been backfilled as early as the late 13th century.

Ceramic building material: A total of 214 daub fragments were retrieved, ranging in thickness from 25mm to 110mm. There were two distinct types present suggesting different sources. The larger fragments, which ranged from 70mm to 110mm across had no obvious organic and inorganic inclusions, and there was no evidence of timber lath impressions or of burning. These fragments did, however, have curved faces which suggest that they may have formed part of a lining which had been moulded around the walls and base of a small pit.

In contrast the smaller fragments, between 25mm and 60mm across, have extensive organic and inorganic inclusions along with timber lath impressions. Much of it was burnt but there is no evidence that it was exposed extensively at a high temperature. This daub is likely to have been the lining of a hearth which was not fully enclosed or roofed over, which may have affected the level of heat intensity it experienced. Several of the smaller fragments had also been built up with new daub layers, probably as the original layer became friable due to exposure to heat and other factors.

None of the daub from this pit was *in situ*. The material was worn and abraded suggesting that it had been broken up before being deposited within this pit.

Ceramics: Local Redware (jug sherds); Scarborough-type Ware Fabric 1 (jug sherds); Yorkshire-type Ware (jug sherds), and Rouen-type Ware (jug sherds).

Macroplant remains: Amongst the plant assemblage recovered were food plants, other useful plants and waste ground weed taxa. The food plants consisted of fig, hazelnut shell, strawberry, cabbage and charred cereal caryopses. A small quantity of weld/dyers rocket, moss and bracken was also recovered. The charred cereal remains were concentrated in the upper fill, (F), while the remainder of the waterlogged assemblage was spread throughout the lower deposits. It appears that human waste was disposed of in the lower deposits and then the upper fill was built up rapidly. The weld/dyers rocket seeds identified in this pit were the largest quantity recovered from the site. However, the absence of any other part of the plant (such as the roots) or other material typically needed to produce dye means that the evidence for this particular activity being undertaken during this period on this part of the site is not strong.

Animal bone: Twenty-five animal bones were analysed. Approximately half of the assemblage was made up of cattle bones. In this pit there was only one ovicaprid bone – a fragment of metatarsal from sheep. There were six teeth and one metacarpal fragment from horse present as well as two red deer bones, one antler fragment and one fragment of scapula. A piece of cat humerus was also present. The range of species suggests it may represent the waste products from industrial bone-working. The good condition of the bones suggests that the pit filled quickly and remained a stable, free-draining environment.

Interpretation
Pit of unknown original function, though depth suggests that it may have been utilised for water retention and presence of woad remains may indicate dyeing. Latterly used for disposal of waste material, including industrial debris.

Pit C085

Heavily truncated pit, 0.6m deep. Contained dark brown clay with lighter lenses (A) under dark grey clay with brick fragments (B). Over Layer C025 (Phase 4 or later).

Ceramics: Local Redware (jug sherds); Scottish White Gritty Ware (jug and cooking pot sherds); Scarborough-type Ware Fabric 1 (jug sherds); Yorkshire-type Ware (jug sherds); Normandy Gritty Ware (a jug sherd), and Low Countries Greyware (jug sherds).

Interpretation
Pit of unknown function.

Ph C003

Posthole, 0.4m in depth, containing a timber post. The lower fill (A) was a dark brownish grey silty clay, which was sealed by light greyish brown sandy clay (B). The base of the post, an undressed log of alder, had survived *in situ.* Truncated Pit C053 (Phase 4).

Leather: This assemblage comprises; shoe components x2; offcuts, scraps & miscellanea x67.

Ceramics: Scottish White Gritty Ware (jug sherds) and Yorkshire-type Ware (sherds of jugs and a cooking pot).

Macroplant remains: The plant assemblage was small and dominated by weed taxa, specifically common chickweed. The only edible plants recovered were a single charred oat caryopsis and some hazelnut shell.

The small size of the assemblage suggests that this is probably redeposited material.

Fish bone: Of 225 fish bones from this feature 61 were cod, 50 were ling and there were single examples of a flatfish, pollack, the ray family and gurnard family. Butchery marks were observed on six cod (Figure 4.59C, Chapter 4) and three ling. Cod 80–100cm TL x18; cod >100cm TL x42; ling >100cm TL x50; flatfish 30–50cm TL x1; pollack 80–100cm TL x1.

Interpretation
Isolated posthole.

Spread C040

Greyish brown silt occupation deposit, broadly contemporary with Layer C008.

Leather: This assemblage comprises; shoe components x2. This includes SF4196 (Figure 4.17, Chapter 4) a component of 13th–14th century date.

Ceramics: Local Redware (jug and cooking pot sherds); Aberdeen Fabric 8 (jug sherds); Scottish White Gritty Ware (jug sherds); Scarborough-type Ware Fabrics 1 and 2 (jug sherds); Stamford Ware (a jug sherd); Yorkshire-type Ware (jug sherds), and Humberware.

Interpretation
Occupation deposit.

Wall C007

Roughly north/south-aligned clay-bonded rubble wall, measuring at least 8m long south/north, but truncated, and up to 0.5m wide and surviving to 0.5m high (2–3 courses). Stood over Layer C008 (late Phase 4 or early Phase 5).

Ceramics: Local Redware (jug sherds); Scarborough-type Ware Fabrics 1 and 2 (jug sherds); Yorkshire-type Ware (jug sherds), and North French-type Ware (a jug sherd).

Interpretation
Remnant wall, possibly forming boundary running roughly perpendicular to Upperkirkgate.

3.7 Phase 5 (early) (15th to 16th century) (figure 2.66)

Layer A005

Dark grey clay garden soil with charcoal inclusions over backfill of Ph A001.

Ceramics: Local Redware (jug sherds); Aberdeen Fabric 8 (jug sherds); Scottish White Gritty Ware (jug sherds);

Table 3.5 Phase 5; the artefact assemblages for key contexts and features (where quantified numbers of items are presented)

Note: ■ denotes a shaded cell (presence indicated, not quantified).

Context	Wooden artefacts	Leather	Textiles	Animal fibres	Cordage	Metalwork	Worked stone	Lithics	Glass	Crucibles	Clay moulds	Industrial residues	Misc	Clay pipes	Ceramic building material	Window glass	Ceramic vessels
Layer A005						1											■
Layer A033																	■
Layer A034						1											■
Layer C015						3											■
Layer C017																	■
Layer C034						2											■
Spread C017																	■
Spread C058						1						■					■
Spread C059												■					■
Spread C065						1											■
Spread C085																	■
Layer A006																	■
Layer A013						1	1										■
Layer A014/A017						4						■				2	■
Layer A016																	■
Layer A025																	■
Layer C009 etc		1				3	2	1				■		1	■		■
Pit C063		2															■
Pit C070																	■
Pit C071		1										■					■
Pit C077											1						■
Spread A013						1											■
Spread C021/C022												■				1	■
Spread C023		2				1						■					■
Wall C009						2									■		■
Well A001	2	2				2	1					■					■
Layer A007/A008						10						■	1	2			■
Layer A010/A011						1						■					■
Gully C012												■					■
Pit C028												■					■
Pit C080						1	1									1	■

Scarborough-type Ware Fabric 1 (a jug sherd); Low Countries Greyware (jug sherds); North French-type Ware (jug sherds); Siegburg Stoneware (a jug sherd); Langerwehe-type Stoneware (jug sherds), and Raeren Stoneware (sherds from mugs and other vessels).

Macroplant remains: The plant assemblage contained a small quantity of charred cereal caryopses.

Interpretation
Garden soil.

Layer A033

Light brown silty clay garden soil/occupation deposit over backfill of Pit A023 (early to mid Phase 5).

Ceramics: Local Redware (sherds from jugs and another vessel); Scottish White Gritty Ware (a jug sherd); Low Countries Redware (jug sherds); Valencian Lustreware (a sherd from a bowl/dish); Siegburg Stoneware (jug sherds); Langerwehe-type Stoneware (jug sherds), and Raeren Stoneware (mug sherds).

Macroplant remains: The only plant remains were a small quantity of poorly preserved charred cereal caryopses.

Fish bone: A single ling vertebra and seven whiting vertebrae were found; the latter were all burnt. Ling >100cm TL x1; whiting 15–30cm TL x7.

Interpretation
Garden soil/occupation deposit.

Layer A034

Light brown silty clay occupation deposit/garden soil over Layer A029.

Ceramics: Local Redware (jug sherds); Yorkshire-type Ware (jug sherds); London Sandy Ware (a jug sherd); Siegburg Stoneware (a jug sherd), and Raeren Stoneware (mug sherds).

Macroplant remains: The plant material from this deposit consisted of a small quantity of weed taxa, raspberry and charred cereal caryopses.

Interpretation
Garden soil/occupation deposit.

Layer C015

Grey clay occupation deposit over Layer C017 (early to mid Phase 5).

Ceramics: Local Redware (jug and cooking pot sherds); Aberdeen Fabric 8 (jug sherds); Scottish White Gritty

Ware (jug sherds); Scarborough-type Ware Fabrics 1 and 2 (jug sherds); Yorkshire-type Ware (jug sherds); Low Countries Greyware (jug sherds); North French-type Ware (jug sherds), and Iberian Redware.

Macroplant remains: The plant assemblage consisted of small quantities charred cereal caryopses.

Interpretation
Occupation deposit.

Layer C017

Dark grey silty clay occupation deposit over backfill of Pit C035 (Early Phase 5 or Late Phase 4).

Ceramics: Local Redware (jug sherds); Scottish White Gritty Ware (jug sherds); Scarborough-type Ware Fabrics 1 and 2 (jug sherds); Low Countries Redware (a jug sherd); Rouen-type Ware (a jug sherd); North French-type Ware (a jug sherd), and Raeren Stoneware.

Macroplant remains: The only plant remains recovered comprised a small quantity of poorly preserved charred cereal caryopses, sedge and *Cenococcum* sclerotia.

Fish bone: Three fish bones were identified, two cod and one ling. Cod 80–100cm TL x2; ling >100cm TL x1.

Interpretation
Occupation deposit.

Layer C034

Mid brown grey clay occupation deposit over Layer C016 (early to mid Phase 5).

Ceramics: Local Redware (jug sherds); Yorkshire-type Ware (a jug sherd); Low Countries Redware (jug sherds); Low Countries Greyware (jug sherds), and Raeren Stoneware.

Interpretation
Occupation deposit.

Gully A004

Irregular, 0.2m deep, north/south gully with dark brown clay fill (A). Over Layer A034 (early to mid Phase 5).

Fish bone: This sieved feature produced a haddock vertebra, a cod family vertebra and, unusually, a single carp family vertebra. The latter indicates some small degree of freshwater fishing. Haddock 15–30cm TL x1; cod family 15–30cm TL x1.

Interpretation
Drainage feature.

Spread C017

Mid greyish brown sandy silt over Spread C059.

Ceramics: Local Redware (jug sherds).

Macroplant remains: Amongst the small plant assemblage were food and potentially useful dye plants in the form of cabbage, raspberry, charred cereal caryopses, cereal chaff and weld/dyers rocket. The remainder consisted of waste ground weed taxa which were not particularly well preserved. The assemblage represents domestic waste and faecal matter that was allowed to accumulate. The single seed of weld/dyers rocket that was recovered may represent dyeing and/or the disposal of dyeing waste.

Interpretation
Occupation deposit/dump.

Spread C058

Dark brown silty clay dump over Layer C026.

Ceramics: Local Redware (jug and cooking pot sherds); Scottish White Gritty Ware (jug sherds); Yorkshire-type Ware (jug sherds); East Anglian Ware (jug sherds), and Langerwehe-type Stoneware (a jug sherd).

Industrial residues: The assemblage comprises; plano-convex slag cake x2, 534.6g; slag amalgam x1, 75.1g; unclassified slag x3, 78.0g; hammerscale microresidues, 0.3g.

Interpretation
Dump/occupation deposit.

Spread C059

Dark greyish brown silt occupation deposit over Layer C026.

Ceramics: Local Redware (jug sherds) and Scarborough-type Ware Fabric 1 (jug sherds).

Industrial residues: The assemblage comprises; plano-convex slag cake x1, 312g; unclassified slag x1, 2.3g; hammerscale microresidues, 0.5g.

Macroplant remains: The plant assemblage was dominated by food plants such as fig, raspberry, strawberry, cabbage and charred cereal caryopses including rye, oat and barley. The only weed seeds recovered were fat hen and sedge.

This deposit appears to have been covered over quickly as very few common waste ground weed taxa were recovered. There were also very few insect remains or other evidence of decomposers typically associated with human faecal matter. This could represent floor clearings or a small concentration of human faecal waste that was disposed of and quickly covered over.

Interpretation
Dump/occupation deposit.

Spread C065

Reddish brown clay silt deposit over Layer C019 (Phase 4 or 5).

Ceramics: Local Redware (jug sherds); Scarborough-type Ware Fabric 1 (a jug sherd), and Yorkshire-type Ware (a jug sherd).

Interpretation
Dump/occupation deposit.

Spread C085

Dark grey silt dump over Layer C017 (Phase 5).

Ceramics: Local Redware (jug and cooking pot sherds); Aberdeen Fabric 8 (jug sherds); Scottish White Gritty Ware (jug sherds); Scarborough-type Ware Fabrics 1 and 2 (jug sherds), and Yorkshire-type Ware (a jug sherd and a cooking pot sherd).

Fish bone: Three cod bones were identified. Cod 80–100cm TL x1; cod >100cm TL x2.

Interpretation
Dump deposit.

3.8 Phase 5 (mid) (15th to 16th century) (figure 2.68 & Table 3.5)

Layer A006

Mid brown sandy silt garden soil layer over Layers A030 and A033 (early to mid Phase 5).

Ceramics: Local Redware (jug sherds); Yorkshire-type Ware (a jug sherd); London Sandy Ware (a jug sherd); Low Countries Greyware (jug sherds); Valencian Lustreware (bowl/dish sherd); Siegburg Stoneware (jug sherds); Raeren Stoneware, and Scottish Post-Medieval Oxidised Ware (sherds fom a jug and other vessels).

Macroplant remains: The only plant remains recovered was a small quantity of charred cereal caryopses, as well as *Cenococcum* sclerotia.

Interpretation
Garden soil.

Layer A013

Mid brown clay silt garden soil over backfill of Well A001.

Ceramics: Local Redware (sherds from cooking pots and another vessel); Low Countries Redware (a jug sherd); Low Countries Greyware (jug sherds); Iberian Redware; Langerwehe-type Stoneware (jug sherds), and Raeren Stoneware (mug sherds).

Interpretation
Garden soil.

Layer A014/A017

Mid to dark brown silty clay garden soil (early to mid Phase 5).

Ceramics: Local Redware (sherds from jugs and another vessel); Scottish White Gritty Ware (jug sherds); Scarborough-type Ware Fabric 1 (jug sherds); Low Countries Redware (jug sherds); Low Countries Greyware (jug sherds); Siegburg Stoneware (jug sherds); Langerwehe-type Stoneware (jug sherds), and Raeren Stoneware (sherds from mugs and another vessel).

Industrial residues: The assemblage comprises; unclassified slag x3, 48.8g; run slag x1, 24.0g; fuel ash slag, 149.8g; hammerscale microresidues, 0.6g.

Interpretation
Garden soil.

Layer A016

Dark brown clay silt occupation/garden soil over Layer A018 (mid to late Phase 5).

Ceramics: Local Redware (jug sherds) and Langerwehe-type Stoneware (jug sherds).

Fish bone: A single ray family bone was recovered.

Interpretation
Garden soil/occupation deposit.

Layer A025

Dark brown clay silt spread over Surface A002A (mid to late Phase 5).

Ceramics: Local Redware (jug sherds); Scarborough-type Ware Fabric 1 (a jug sherd); Yorkshire-type Ware (jug

sherds); Langerwehe-type Stoneware (a jug sherd), and Raeren Stoneware (mug sherds).

Macroplant remains: Amongst the plant remains was a small quantity of poorly preserved charred cereal caryopses and *Cenococcum* sclerotia.

Interpretation
Dump/occupation deposit.

Layer C009/C010/C031

Greyish brown clay occupation deposit over Layer C008.

Industrial residues: The assemblage comprises; plano-convex slag cake x1, 284.9g; slag amalgam x1, 149.4g; unclassified slag x13, 169.5g; fuel ash slag, 155.8g; hammerscale microresidues, 0.7 g.

Ceramic building material: Nine large fragments of daub were collected from Layer C010. It was very abraded but five had flat surfaces; they were between 40mm and 80mm in thickness. There were impressions of timber laths on some of the fragments; the laths were 25mm wide and where the wood had survived it was identified as oak. There was evidence of burning and there were patches of oxidisation/reduction along the external flat faces. However, the burn marks were not extensive and there was no evidence of vitrification or of exposure to intense heat over an extended period of time. One piece of burnt daub displayed evidence that extra clay had been added to its initial structure over time as there was a variance in the daub colour and the concentration of inclusions used to strengthen the material.

The thickness of the daub fragments together with the evidence for a framework of oak laths suggests that this material was used as a lining which needed to be strengthened. It seems more likely that it was used in an industrial/commercial setting rather than in a domestic structure. However, it is unlikely that this material was originally used in heavy industry such as metalworking as the evidence of burning is limited and not extensive. It is more probable that it was used to line a feature which would experience regular low temperatures only, particularly if the feature was not fully enclosed.

Ceramics: Local Redware (sherds from jugs and cooking pots); Aberdeen Fabric 8 (jug sherds); Scottish White Gritty Ware (jug sherds); Scarborough-type Ware Fabrics 1 and 2 (jug sherds); Stamford Ware (jug sherds); Yorkshire-type Ware (jug sherds); London Sandy Ware (jug sherds); Low Countries Redware (including a jug sherd); Rouen-type Ware (a jug sherd); North French-type Ware (jug sherds); Saintonge Ware (jug sherds); Siegburg Stoneware (jug sherds); Langerwehe-type

Stoneware (jug sherds) and Raeren Stoneware (mug sherds).

Macroplant remains: The only plant material recovered was a small quantity of weed taxa, poorly preserved charred cereal caryopses and compact inclusions of a poorly preserved brown peat-like midden material. The waterlogged weed taxa were only recovered from a lower element of this deposit. The plant remains in the uppermost deposits consisted only of poorly preserved charred cereal caryopses. This suggests that the upper material was rapidly built up, preventing the deposition of large quantities of plant remains.

Fish bone: A single cod fragment was identified.

Interpretation
Occupation deposit.

Pit C063

Rectangular pit, 1.2m deep, lined with disturbed stones set in grey clay (A), and containing mid brown silty sand with rubble infill (B), over Layer C015 (early or mid Phase 5).

Leather: The assemblage comprises; offcuts x2.

Ceramics: Local Redware (sherds of jugs, a cooking pot and another vessel); Aberdeen Fabric 8 (jug sherds); Scottish White Gritty Ware (jug sherds); Scarborough-type Ware Fabric 1 (jug sherds); Yorkshire-type Ware (jug sherds); Low Countries Greyware (a jug sherd), and Langerwehe-type Stoneware (jug sherds).

Animal bone: 39 animal bone fragments were analysed, and cattle, ovicaprids and red deer were represented. The red deer was represented entirely by antler and six of the eight fragments showed obvious signs of having been worked. Similarly, a piece of horn core from cattle had two cut marks at the base, probably resulting from the removal of the horn. There was no sign of any particular body part dominating the assemblage in the case of the cattle or the ovicaprids. This pit contains evidence of horn and antler working and a total of 36% of the assemblage is marked by knives or cleavers. The condition of the bones indicates they have been within a stable environment and that the pit most probably was filled relatively quickly.

Bird bone: A tibio-tarsus from a bantam and a sternum from a domestic fowl were present.

Fish bone: Of ten fish bones there was four ling, three cod and a single haddock. Ling >100cm TL x4; cod 80–100cm TL x3; haddock 50–80cm TL x1.

Interpretation
Possible soakaway feature.

Pit C070 (Figure 2.70, Chapter 2)

Stone-lined sub-circular pit, 1.2m deep. A thin basal deposit of dark grey silty clay (A) lay under a mid grey silty clay (B). The feature was sealed by similar deposit (C). Over Layer C009, possibly associated with Ditch C001.

Ceramics: Local Redware (jug and cooking pot sherds); Scarborough-type Ware Fabric 2 (a jug sherd); Yorkshire-type Ware (jug sherds); Low Countries Redware (a jug sherd); Low Countries Greyware (jug sherds); Iberian Redware; Valencian Lustreware (a bowl/dish sherd); Siegburg Stoneware (jug sherds); Raeren Stoneware (sherds of a mug and other vessels), and Scottish Post-Medieval Oxidised Ware (jug sherds).

Animal bone: Thirty-three bone fragments were analysed, of which 61% could be identified as cattle and 18% as ovicaprid. The cattle bone assemblage was dominated by low meat-yielding bones. No other species were present, but seven bone fragments could be identified only as large or medium sized mammal, probably from cattle and ovicaprid respectively. The assemblage hints at its being the product of industrial rather than domestic waste. The condition of the bone suggests it accumulated quickly and then remained in a free-draining and stable environment.

Interpretation
Possible drainage feature.

Pit C071

Circular pit, *c.* 0.9m deep. The lowest fill, a dark brownish grey silt (A) lay under a light greyish brown clay silt (B). Both of these contained substantial quantities of slag. Above these fills was a dark grey sandy silt (C), which was sealed by a greyish brown clayey silt (D). Over Layer C009.

Leather: The assemblage comprises; offcut x1.

Ceramics: Local Redware (jug sherds) and Rouen-type Ware (a jug sherd).

Industrial residues: The assemblage comprises; unclassified slag x71, 497.4g; fuel ash slag, 428.2g; burnt fuel, 2.1g; hammerscale microresidues, 0.4g.

Macroplant remains: A modest plant assemblage contained a relatively large collection of fig seeds as well as cereal bran, raspberry and charred cereal caryopses. There was also a small quantity of waste ground weed taxa, wood chips and small inclusions of moss fragments. The presence of bran, fruit seeds and moss tend to suggest that this pit was the receptacle for human waste as opposed to the dumping of stable or workshop/industrial debris.

Interpretation
Refuse pit.

Pit C077

Steep-sided oval pit, 0.8m deep. The basal fill was a black silty clay (A), which was under a dark grey organic silt (B). The upper fill was a mixed light grey and light brown clay with ash (C). Over Layer C010.

Ceramics: Local Redware (sherds of jugs and a cooking pot); Yorkshire-type Ware (jug sherds); London Sandy Ware (a jug sherd), and Low Countries Greyware (a jug sherd).

Fish bone: A single burnt cod family vertebra was recovered.

Interpretation
Pit of unknown function.

Spread A013

Dark brown clay silt spread, built up over Surface A002 (mid to late Phase 5).

Dating evidence: This deposit contained a copper farthing of James III (SF1888), dating to the late 15th century.

Ceramics: Local Redware (jug sherds) and Raeren Stoneware (a mug sherd).

Fish bone: A single haddock fragment was identified.

Interpretation
Occupation deposit.

Spread C021/C022 (Figure 2.71, Chapter 2)

Black clay dump with significant quantities of slag over backfill of Pit C070.

Ceramics: Local Redware (jug sherds); Scarborough-type Ware Fabrics 1 (a jug sherd), and Scottish Post-Medieval Oxidised Ware (a jug sherd).

Industrial residues: The assemblage comprises; plano-convex slag cakes x4, 923.5g; slag amalgams x12, 3924.7g; unclassified slag x1000+, 8673.4g; microresidues including small quantities of slag spheres, 1053.5g; burnt fuel, 86g.

This deposit accounted for 29.8% (14.66 kg) of all industrial residues recovered from the site. It also contained occasional heavily corroded iron objects.

Interpretation
A discrete deposit of ironworking waste.

Spread C023

Dark brown clay dump with charcoal inclusions over Spread C025.

Leather: The assemblage comprises; offcuts x2.

Ceramics: Local Redware (jug and cooking pot sherds); Scarborough-type Ware Fabrics 1 and 2 (jug sherds); Low Countries Redware (sherds of jugs and other vessels); Siegburg Stoneware (a jug sherd), and Raeren Stoneware.

Industrial residues: The assemblage comprises; slag amalgam x1, 309.5g; unclassified slag x2, 119.1g; hammerscale microresidues, 4.2g.

Interpretation
Dump deposit.

Wall C009

Clay-bonded rubble wall remnant, which was truncated and extensively disturbed by robbing-out. Extended at least 4m west/east. Likely to be contemporary with Surface C009 to north. Over Layer C009 (mid to late Phase 5).

Ceramic building material: Thirty fragments of daub were recovered, no more than 20mm thick. Two fragments were burnt in the centre and along the surface. This material does not appear to have been used as a lining for metalworking or in a high temperature hearth. Instead it was probably used as a lining which was exposed to low temperatures.

Ceramics: Local Redware (jug sherds).

Interpretation
Wall remnant.

Well A001 (Figures 2.65 & 2.72, Chapter 2)

Barrel-lined pit. The construction cut was circular in plan with near vertical sides, approximately 0.67m in diameter and 1.6m deep. The well structure (A) comprised a wooden barrel constructed from 19 wooden staves, which was approximately 0.6m in interior diameter. To the south-west construction fills were apparent (perhaps actually related to an earlier feature, Pit A024), comprising a grey organic silty clay

(B) under grey brown silt (C). There were numerous fills within the barrel of Well A001, including minor lenses. At the base a dark grey clay with sand (D) lay under mixed deposits of brown sand and organic grey clay (E) and (F), which were under a dark blue grey silty clay (G). Overlying this deposit were deposits of small stones (H) and organic material (I). Above this was a layer of mid grey silty clay (J), which lay under dark grey clay silt (K). This was overlain by lenses of dark grey silty clay (L), mid yellowish grey sandy silt (M) and brownish grey silty clay (N). These were sealed by dark grey clay silt (O), which in turn lay under lenses of mid grey sandy clay (P), mid brownish yellow clayey sand (Q) and mid orangeish grey sandy silt (R). Over Layer A014 (early to mid Phase 5).

Dating evidence: Some eight staves from the barrel lining this well were selected for dendrochronological analysis (Table 4.1; Figure 4.1, Chapter 4). The outermost ring of the barrel master chronology is dated to AD 1350, providing a *terminus post quem* of AD 1365 for the construction of the barrel. Allowing for missing rings the barrel is likely to have been constructed in the latter half of the 14th century and it then probably had a long working life before being used to line the well. Thus, we can say no more than that the well could have been constructed at any time from the early 15th century onwards.

Leather: The assemblage comprises; miscellanea x2.

Ceramics: Local Redware (jug and cooking pot sherds); Scottish White Gritty Ware (jug sherds); Scarborough-type Ware Fabrics 1 and 2 (jug sherds); Yorkshire-type Ware (jug sherds); London Sandy Ware (jug sherds); Low Countries Greyware (jug sherds); Langerwehe-type Stoneware (a jug sherd), and Raeren Stoneware (sherds from mugs and other vessels).

Industrial residues: The assemblage comprises; plano-convex slag cakes x2, 71.3g; slag amalgams x7, 672.7g; unclassified slag x58, 957.4g; hammerscale microresidues, 4.0g.

Macroplant remains: A large plant assemblage contained food plants, useful plants, arable weed taxa, waste ground taxa and a small quantity of heathland/moor material. The food plants consisted of hazelnut shell, fig, cabbage, blackberry, raspberry, apple, wheat/rye bran and charred cereal caryopses. The economically useful plant remains consisted of self heal, weld/dyers rocket and moss fragments. The heathland/moor material was made up only of small fragments of heather, charred heather, buttercup and violets. Other finds included worked wood chips, charcoal and insect remains.

The plant assemblage (and insect remains) was concentrated in three lower fills (B), (E) and (F) with only trace amounts of food plants and weed taxa recovered from the upper deposits. This suggests that the upper fills of the well were built up rapidly while the lower fills (B), (E) and (F) appear to have been deliberately used for the disposal of human waste.

Animal bone: There were 35 fragments of animal bone, of which nine were cattle bones, five from the head and feet, three metapodials and one astragalus. This prevalence of the low meat-yielding bones of the body periphery suggests that the cattle remains represent the waste products from butchery or from an industrial process such as tanning. Seventeen cat bones came from all parts of the body including the skull, suggesting the presence of one complete cat. One cat humerus bore two tiny marks that may have been cut marks on the distal half of the bone. Five fragments of bone from sheep and ovicaprid were also retrieved, one of which was butchered. One fragment of goat humerus was retrieved. This small collection of six ovicaprid bones contains three bone fragments from the high meat-yielding body parts, one fragment from the skull and two metapodial fragments. As with cattle, this hints at the presence of what may be butchery and table waste. A fragment of pig scapula, displaying no taphonomic features, was also present.

The faunal remains suggest the presence of mixed waste in the well fills. The bones from the common domesticates, sheep and cattle may have derived from butchery activities or industrial activities such as tanning. The pig and ovicaprid bones may have come from household waste from the domestic table. The cat may have been drowned in the well or alternatively, a skinned carcass may have been disposed of. The state of preservation of the bones indicates a stable environment and rapid deposition.

Fish bone: The fish bone assemblage included a single cod, four sand eel family, a single charred cod family, a haddock and a whiting. Cod >100cm TL x1; cod family 15–30cm TL x1; haddock 15–30cm TL x1; whiting 15–30cm TL x1.

Interpretation
Barrel-lined water butt or well.

3.9 Phase 5 (late) (15th/16th to mid-to-late 18th century) (figure 2.74 & Table 3.5)

Layer A007/A008

Dark greyish brown silty clay garden soil over Spreads A008 and A017 and Wall C019.

Ceramics: Local Redware (jug sherds); Scottish White Gritty Ware (jug sherds); Scarborough-type Ware Fabrics 1 and 2 (jug sherds); Low Countries Redware; Low Countries Greyware; Martincamp-type flask (sherd from a flask); Paffrath-type Ware (cooking pot sherd); Siegburg Stoneware (jug sherds); Langerwehe-type Stoneware (jug sherds); Raeren Stoneware (sherds from mugs and other vessels), and Scottish Post-Medieval Oxidised Ware (a jug sherd).

Industrial residues: The assemblage comprises; unclassified slag x32, 776.4g; slag spheres, 0.1g; fuel ash slag, 63.6g; hammerscale microresidues, 0.9g.

Macroplant remains: The plant assemblage was minimal and contained background traces of weed taxa, charred barley and cereal caryopses.

Animal bone: Almost half of the 82 animal bone fragments analysed derived from cattle. Half of the bone fragments were from the higher meat-producing elements of the skeleton, with the bones from the heads and feet being relatively under-represented. Sheep, pig, roe deer and dog were also represented. In the sheep assemblage the meatier elements were also most prevalent (76%). A range of elements were present, from both low- and high-meat yielding body parts. Four fragments displayed butchery marks. The assemblage represents domestic waste rather than the product of industrial activities such as carcass preparation or tanning. The condition of the bone fragments suggests they accumulated slowly, with perhaps some redeposition.

Fish bone: This feature produced four cod and three ling. Cod 80–100cm TL x2; cod >100cm TL x2; ling >100cm TL x3.

Interpretation
Garden soil.

Layer A010/A011

Dark brown clayey/sandy silt garden soil over Layer A007/A008.

Ceramics: Local Redware (jug and cooking pot sherds); Scottish White Gritty Ware (jug sherds); Scarborough-type Ware Fabrics 1 and 2 (jug sherds); Yorkshire-type Ware (jug sherds); London Sandy Ware (a jug sherd); Low Countries Highly Decorated Ware (a jug sherd); Low Countries Redware; Low Countries Greyware (jug sherds); North French-type Ware (jug sherds); Beauvais Earthenware (a jug sherd); Iberian Redware; Siegburg Stoneware (jug sherds); Langerwehe-type Stoneware (jug sherds); Raeren Stoneware (sherds from a mug and other vessels), and Frechen Stoneware (a jug sherd).

Industrial residues: The assemblage comprises; slag amalgams x2, 319.0g; run slag x1, 49.2g.

Bird bone: Two ulnas from a bantam and one femur from a domestic fowl were present.

Interpretation
Garden soil.

Gully C012

Heavily truncated feature, possibly originally a drainage gully. Contained a yellowish brown clay silt basal fill (A) under waterlogged clay silt (B), which lay under a dark brown silty clay deposit with slag (C). Over Layer C030.

Ceramics: Local Redware (jug sherds).

Industrial residues: The assemblage comprises; plano-convex slag cake x1, 38.81g; slag amalgams x7, 1059.4g; unclassified slag x68, 1111.9g; fuel ash slag, 35.8g; burnt fuel residues, 71.5g; coal, 33.0g; hammerscale, 12.0g; slag spheres, 0.5g.

Interpretation
Possible drainage feature.

Pit C028

Truncated circular pit, *c.* 3m in depth, with a blueish grey clay basal fill (A) under a dark grey organic silty clay fill (B). Over Layer C003 (likely Phase 5).

Ceramics: Local Redware (jug sherds); Yorkshire-type ware (jug sherds); Low Countries Redware (jug sherds); Raeren Stoneware, and Scottish Post-Medieval Oxidised Ware.

Industrial residues: The assemblage comprises; run slag x1, 16.5g; unclassified slag x2, 9.3g; burnt coal, 13.6g; hammerscale microresidues, 0.4g.

Interpretation
Pit potentially used for drainage function.

Pit C080 (Figure 2.76, Chapter 2)

Sub-oval pit, at least 2m in depth, lined with crudely coursed clay-bonded rubble. The waterlogged basal fill (A) contained blueish grey sandy silt and humic clay. This lay under a deposit of rubble in a silty sand matrix (B), which was covered by a backfill of dark brown clay silt (C). Over Structure C005 (late Phase 5 or Phase 6).

Ceramics: Local Redware (jug sherds) and Frechen Stoneware (a jug sherd).

4 Specialist Reports – Summaries of the Evidence

4.1 Dating evidence

4.1.1 Dendrochronology
Anne Crone

The dendrochronological study of the Bon Accord wood assemblage has consisted of the analysis of 42 individual timbers from 12 contexts, plus eight staves from the barrel lining of Well A001 (Table 4.1). The barrel staves apart, the bulk of the dendrochronological samples came from three large features: Well A002 (13 samples); Pit C025 (ten samples) and Pit C033 (six samples).

Of the 42 individual timbers 38 have been dendro-dated, as has the barrel chronology (Figure 4.1). Some of the timbers have produced exact felling dates of AD 1200/01,

Table 4.1 Dendrochronological data (arranged in order of date of feature). Key: B=bark edge; Bs= spring-felled; Bw=winter-felled; h/s=heartwood/sapwood boundary; sap= sapwood; unm= unmeasured rings

Feature	Finds No.	Description	Redundant features	No. rings	Beginning date	End date	End rings	Interpretation
Well A001	various	x8 barrel staves		149	1202	1350	0	tpq 1365
Pit C069	2378	plank		258	1024	1281	13 B	felled w/s 1281/2
Pit C069	2377	plank		126	949	1074	0	tpq 1084
Pit C069	4386	plank		78	-	-	16 sap	undated
Pit C064	3753	plank		228	1034	1261	5 sap	felled 1266–1302
Ph C011	1879	post		152	1111	1262	14 sap	felled 1262–1294
Layer C075	4239	plank		285	961	1245	31 sap	felled 1245–1260
Well A002	G	beam	peghole	129	1117	1245	23 Bs	felled s/s 1246
Well A002	I	plank	peghole	267	977	1243	27 B	felled 1243
Well A002	C	plank	peghole	362	881	1242	38 Bs	felled s/s 1243
Well A002	H	post		138	1104	1241	19 Bs	felled s/s 1242
Well A002	M	beam	nails	121	1121	1241	19 sap	felled 1241–1268
Well A002	J	plank	peg/nail	239	1001	1239	15 sap	felled 1239–1270
Well A002	U	plank		181	1059	1239	7 sap	felled 1239–1278
Well A002	X	plank		134	1100	1233	4 sap	felled 1233–1275
Well A002	D	plank	nail?	325	898	1222	h/s?	tpq 1232
Well A002	E	plank	nails	184	1025	1208	0	tpq 1218
Well A002	5008	plank		227	920	1146	h/s?	tpq 1156
Well A002	P	plank		131	969	1099	0	tpq 1109
Well A002	5035	plank		92	964	1055	0	tpq 1065
Pit C033	3717	plank		193	1031	1223	0	tpq 1233
Pit C033	3201	plank	peghole	151	1050	1200	17 Bw	felled w/s 1200/01
Pit C033	3719	plank	groove	245	950	1194	0 + 22 unm	tpq 1226

Feature	Finds No.	Description	Redundant features	No. rings	Beginning date	End date	End rings	Interpretation
Pit C033	3199	stake?	peghole	306	867	1172	0 + 8 unm	tpq 1190
Pit C033	3738	plank		156	-	-	6 sap	undated
Pit C033	3740	plank	peghole	122	-	-	14 sap	undated
Pit C025	3391	plank		313	897	1209	26 Bw	felled w/s 1209/10
Pit C025	3976	post		157	1016	1172	3 sap	felled 1172–1215
Pit C025	3284	plank	pin	137	1033	1169	6 sap	felled 1169-1209
Pit C025	4605	post		146	1024	1169	h/s?	tpq 1179
Pit C025	3911a	plank		96	1061	1156	0	tpq 1166
Pit C025	3694	plank	groove	235	918	1152	0	tpq 1162
Pit C025	3655	plank	groove	154	991	1144	0	tpq 1154
Pit C025	3446	plank		160	978	1137	0	tpq 1147
Pit C025	3566	plank	groove	163	-	-	0	undated
Pit C025	4602	post		125	-	-	13 B	undated
Wall C001	4260	plank		185	1027	1211	0	tpq 1221
Ph C018	S28	post		113	1088	1200	6 sap	felled 1204–1240
Stakes C002	S48/2	stake		108	1078	1185	8 sap + 12 unm	felled c. 1197
Gully C001	3602	plank	groove	180	995	1174	0	tpq 1184
Gully C001	3604	plank		112	-	-	0	undated
Pit C099	3864	plank		156	989	1144	h/s?	felled 1152–1190
Pit C099	3866	plank		127	959	1085	0	tpq 1095
Pit C027	4024	plank	pegholes	158	982	1139	0	tpq 1149
Pit C027	4226	plank	peghole	100	1024	1123	0	tpq 1133

AD 1209/10, AD 1243, AD 1246 and AD 1281/2, indicating an intense period of building activity throughout the 13th century. Although the interpretation of the *termini post quem* felling dates and estimated felling ranges for the other timbers is more ambivalent, they also tend to support a floruit of activity on the site throughout the 13th century. This pit-digging activity continued into the 14th century but the absence of any dendrochronological data beyond the late 13th century tends to suggest that building activity in and around the site petered out during the 14th century. The only dendrochronological evidence for later activity on the site is the barrel chronology from Well A001 which suggests that the well was probably not constructed until the 15th century at the earliest.

With the exception of the barrel staves, all the dendro-dated oak from Bon Accord is native-grown. This is not unexpected for timber of this date but it is perhaps

worth stating, partly because of the dominance of imported timber in the Scottish dendrochronological record in later centuries (Crone & Mills 2012), but also because Aberdeen had been developing trading links with the Continent from the 12th century, following its establishment as a royal burgh (Cameron & Stones 2001: 307). Although the physical evidence for this early trade is mainly ceramic (*ibid* 308) it is not inconceivable that timber was also imported. That being said, the earliest dendrochronological evidence for imported timber in Scotland is the 14th century structural timbers from Queen Mary's House, St Andrews which are eastern Baltic in origin (Baillie 1995: 132).

Most of the existing native Scottish chronologies are listed in Table 4.2; apart from the structural timbers from Darnaway Castle and the Chapel Royal, Stirling Palace, all of the data has been retrieved from archaeological excavations. The Bon Accord

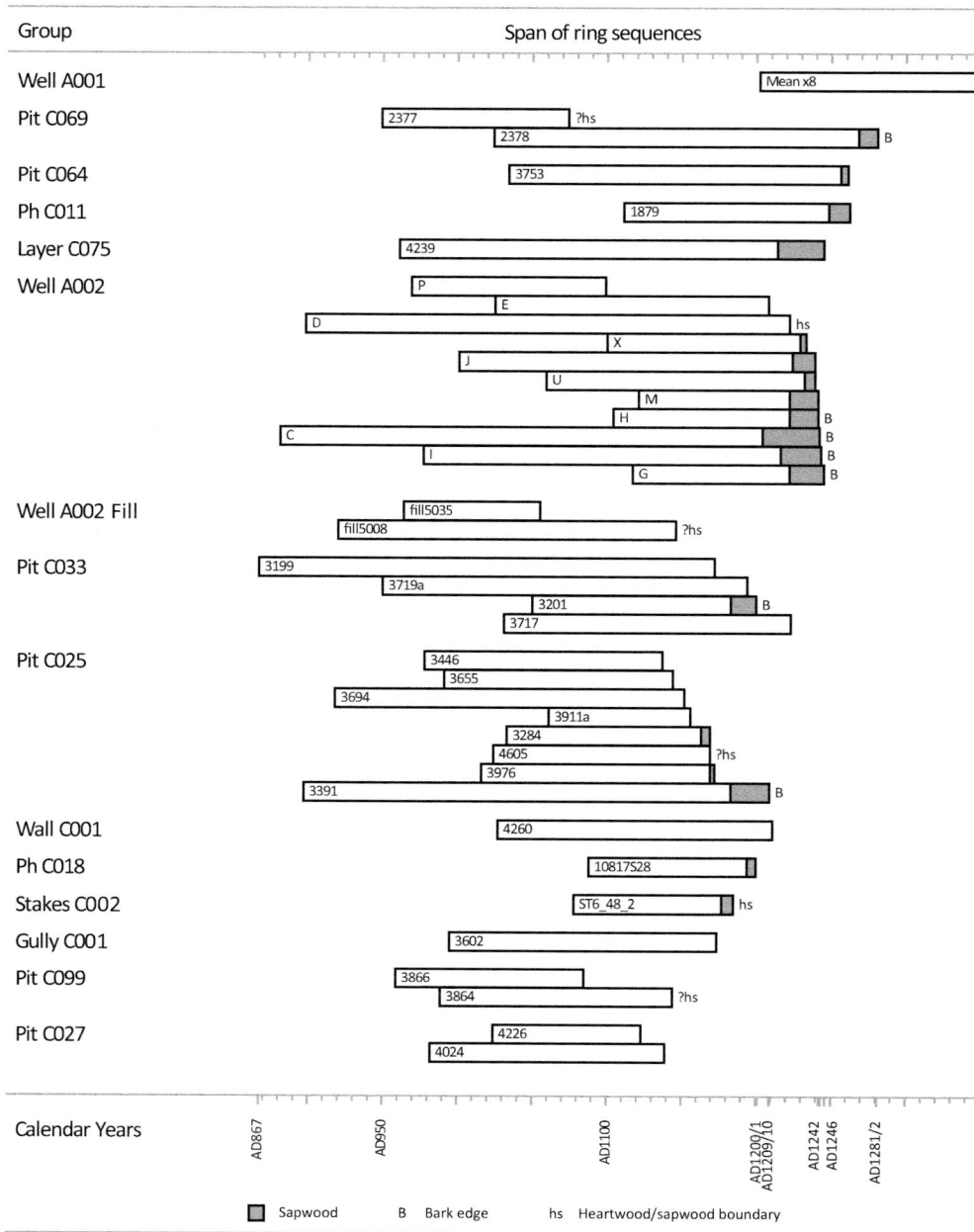

Figure 4.1 Bar diagram showing the chronological relationships between the dated oak timbers from Bon Accord

dendrochronological assemblage is the largest from any urban medieval site in Scotland. Apart from Perth High Street (Crone & Baillie 2010) and the exceptionally well-preserved timber linings of the wells in Elgin (Murray *et al.* 2009), most urban sites have produced only a handful of suitable samples (Crone 2000b). The site at 45–75 Gallowgate produced only five timbers suitable for dendrochronological analysis, for example (*ibid* 203). One of these timbers produced a felling date of AD 1184/5 testifying to late 12th century building activity in the vicinity just before the floruit of activity on the Bon Accord site.

All of the dated native oak timbers from Bon Accord have been averaged together to produce a site chronology, BONACC38, which is 415 years in length, and covers the period AD 867 to AD 1281. This new site chronology has strengthened regional coverage and has undoubtedly improved our ability to date medieval timber in Scotland. The robustness of the site chronology is reflected in the strength of the correlations with other native Scottish chronologies (Table 4.2); as is to be expected the correlations are highest with those sites which are geographically closest, i.e. Gallowgate, Elgin and Darnaway, the strength of the correlations tailing off

Table 4.2 Statistical correlations between BONACC38 and other chronologies

	BONACC38 AD 867–1281	P002x13 AD 881–1245	P033x2 AD 867–1223	P025x4p AD 897–1209
Native Scottish site chronologies				
GALGATE (AD 929–1191) Gallowgate, Aberdeen	11.88	8.69	8.73	7.48
ELGINW1&2 (AD 908–1290) Wells 1 & 2, High St, Elgin	11.76	9.96	8.73	7.48
ELGINW3 (AD 886–1301) Well 3, High St, Elgin	10.38	8.70	5.15	7.78
DARNAWAY (AD 946–1387) Darnaway Castle, Moray	8.60	6.85	6.52	5.02
SCOTLANDMN (AD 946–1975) south-central Scotland master	6.88	5.88	4.81	5.39
PERTHx9 (AD 949–1204) High St, Perth	6.32	5.82	4.08	3.55
CHAPELRO (AD 1055–1406) Chapel Royal, Stirling Castle	6.14	4.62	4.61	–
SPYNMEAN (AD 1074–1236) Spynie Castle, Moray	4.87	3.99	4.61	–
PERTHx3 (AD 1033–1150) High St, Perth	4.71	4.73	–	–
INVMAS2 (AD 933–1169) Castle St, Inverness	4.91	–	3.62	5.17
RKELVIN (AD 1056–1334) River Kelvin, Glasgow	4.43	3.79	–	–
GLASGHST (AD 983–1190) High St, Glasgow	3.54	–	–	–
Northern English site chronologies				
BEVLY_M2 (AD 1002–1324) Hall Garth, Beverley, Yorkshire	6.83			
CARL_MED (AD 893–1600) Carlisle, Cumbria	6.50			
WASDALE (AD 995–1214) Wasdale Beck logboat, Windermere	6.20			
LANES _IM (AD 917–1193) The Lanes, Carlisle, Cumbria	5.45			
Danish regional chronologies				
9M456784 (109 BC–AD 1986) West Denmark	6.10			
JUTLAND 6 (AD 846–1793) Jutland	5.11			
Swedish regional chronologies				
SM000002 (AD 578–1293) Skaane & Blekinge	5.87			
SM000001 (AD 651–1496) SW Skaane	5.33			

further south. However, it has also produced significant correlations with chronologies from northern England and, more remarkably, with some regional chronologies from Denmark and Sweden (Table 4.2); this is the first time that a chronology of native-grown oak has correlated with both native chronologies and foreign chronologies, and again reflects the strength of the climatic signal embedded within the site chronology.

The dendrochronological study at Bon Accord has focused on the end-dates of the timber to provide a chronological framework for the site, but the birth-dates of the trees are also worth consideration. Most of the dated timbers are radially split planks and consequently, the innermost rings have often not survived. Nonetheless, it is clear that the longest-lived timber present on the site started growth in the latter half of the 9th century (Figure 4.1; Table 4.1). The earliest growth-rings on the four longest sequences found at Bon Accord are dated to AD 867, AD 881, AD 897 and AD 898; the longest-lived of these timbers is at least 362 years old so it is unlikely many more inner rings have been lost. With the exception of single timbers from Glasgow Cathedral (AD 896) and Elgin Well 3 (AD 886), there is no medieval assemblage from Scotland which extends back in time beyond the mid 10th century AD (Crone 2006) so the Bon Accord assemblage represents a real extension to regional coverage back into the 9th century AD. The non-random clustering of birthdates around the mid 10th century AD seen in many of the other Scottish assemblages may reflect a socio-economic 'event' which allowed woodlands to begin to regenerate at this time, such as the abandonment of land, or more likely through resource control by major landowners (ibid). This 'event' cannot be detected in the Bon Accord assemblage, so it may not have affected the woodlands around Aberdeen.

Apart from the lining of Well A001 and the post in Posthole C011, all the timbers which have been dendro-dated are ex situ; they mostly represent debris which has been used to backfill the pits and could therefore have come from any variety of structures and woodlands. The mixed quality of the timber reflects this variety, with planks split from very long-lived, slow-grown trunks, as well as young, fast-grown roundwood, much of which was not viable for dendrochronological analysis. On the whole, though, the burghers of Aberdeen appear to have had access to good quality timber, some of it coming from mature woodland where trees over 362 years old were still growing. Oak of this age and quality was used to construct the wells in the backland properties behind the High Street, Elgin in the early 14th century (Crone 2000b: 213; Murray et al. 2009: 222) and the roof of Darnaway Castle in the late 14th century (Stell and Baillie 1993) so north-east Scotland must have been well-supplied with tracts of mature woodland during this period. Such woodlands may not have lain

far outside the burgh; a royal 'Forest of Aberdeen' is mentioned in the *Liber de Calchou* in AD 1163 and was large enough to require four foresters (Anderson 1967: 121). In AD 1313 Robert I granted to the burgesses and city of Aberdeen 'the care and custody' of his Forest of Stocket, which lay adjacent to the burgh and which Anderson (*ibid* 122) notes may once have formed part of the Forest of Aberdeen. Perhaps the demands of the burgh during the 13th century had reduced the once-great Forest of Aberdeen to smaller, discrete pockets of woodland such as the Forest of Stocket by the 14th century.

The barrel from Bon Accord is the fourth such barrel to be dated in Scotland, all of them reused as well linings and all from foreign sources. The barrel lining Well A001 was probably constructed in the 14th century, possibly somewhere along the river Meuse and its tributaries in Belgium or northeastern France (Marta Dominguez Delmas, *pers comm*). The 12th century barrel from the High Street, Perth also came from northeastern France and, given this provenance it was probably imported carrying wine (Crone 2005). Another barrel, also dendro-dated to the 14th century was found in a well on the Middle School site on Gallowgate but this barrel came from the eastern Baltic (Crone *et al.* 2001: 222); it may have arrived from there carrying a commodity such as honey or ale, but it could also have been made in Aberdeen with ready-made staves which were being imported from that region. This may also be true of the late 16th century barrel found at St Patrick's Church in the Cowgate, Edinburgh but in this case the pre-prepared staves were imported from Scandinavia (Crone 2008b). It is interesting that all the dendro-dated barrels in Scotland have so far proved to be imports; we have yet to identify locally-made barrels although there must have been an active coopering industry in most Scottish towns, particularly the ports.

4.2 Organic artefacts

4.2.1 Wooden artefacts
Anne Crone

Introduction

In all, 77 wooden artefacts were retrieved from 26 features, mainly pits or wells. These range from the barrels lining Wells C001 and A001 which are treated as single artefacts, as is the shaft from the rotary grindstone and its associated wedges, to simple wedges and trenails. The richest context was Pit C025, from which 25 wooden artefacts were retrieved, but on the whole most contexts produced only one or two artefacts at most. The bulk of the wooden artefacts come from Phases 1 and 2 but a small number were found in Phases 3, 4 and 5 contexts, including the barrel lining Well A001.

This is not a large assemblage when compared with that from Perth High Street, where over 700 finds were recorded (although this figure also includes stakes and other *ex situ* structural material; Curteis *et al.* 2012). However, it is the richest yet to have been found in Aberdeen (Crone *et al.* 2001; Murray 1984a; Stones 1982b) and is one of a relatively small number of assemblages of medieval wooden artefacts from Scotland. Other urban excavations in Scotland have produced pockets of waterlogged deposits in which small caches of wooden artefacts have survived, such as the wells at Elgin (Murray *et al.* 2009: 221) and St Andrews (Crone 2001), but the only other significant assemblages are those from castle excavations, at Threave (Barber 1981) and Caerlaverock (MacIvor and Gallagher 1999: 227–33), which are probably more representative of single high status households.

Despite its relatively small size, the assemblage from Bon Accord is extremely varied and its character has provided valuable insights into the nature of the activities taking place in the backlands and their environs. The assemblage is discussed below by general category.

Turned and carved vessels

Morris (2000: 2165) cautions against the use of specific terminology in describing the range of vessels manufactured and used during the medieval period. Certainly, the variety of size and profile present amongst the Bon Accord vessels (Figures 4.2–4.4) testifies to a range of very different functions which such terminology might obscure. Morris (*ibid* 2176) defines all those vessels with height:diameter ratios of between 1:2 and 1:6 as bowls. At Bon Accord the height:diameter ratio varies from 1:3 to 1:7, though it could not be calculated for some of the larger, more fragmented vessels. On the assumption that the diameter of the vessel implies some qualitative difference in function the assemblage has been divided into two very general categories, bowls (diameter under 250mm) and platters (diameter over 250mm).

Bowls

There are eight examples which fall into this general category (SF1546A, SF3085, SF3567, SF3681, SF3884, SF3935, SF4012 & SF4294) (Figures 4.2 & 4.3). There are three of alder, three of ash, one of willow and one of field maple, and they range in diameter from 127mm to 220mm and in height from 32mm to 70mm. SF1546A, SF3085, SF3884, SF3935 and SF4294 are simple forms, open rounded bowls with rounded rims (vessel profile 2/rim profile g – see Morris 2000: fig. 1017), and plain bases, concave, convex and flat respectively. SF4012 is a slightly more sophisticated variant of this simple form,

with a squared, upright rim (rim profile l – see Morris 2000: fig. 1017) and a distinct turned base.

The other two bowls in the assemblage are much less utilitarian; they are both very finely made, with thin walls and distinctive, unusual shapes, suggestive of a source in a wealthy household. SF3681 is the smallest of the vessels in the assemblage; it has a relatively wide, flat rim (rim profile f – see Morris 2000: fig. 1017) around a small bowl only 91mm in diameter. The sharpness of the gouge marks in the base of the bowl and the turning marks suggest that this vessel may not have been used.

SF3567 also has a wide flat rim but what marks it as unusual is the central container, the walls of which project up from the surface of the rim. This is a very rare style, not seen in any of the much larger published assemblages of turned vessels from York, Southampton or Waterford. The closest comparison is a single example found in 13th century deposits in Novgorod (Kolchin 1989: Vol 1, 62; Vol 2, 302). Kolchin (*ibid*) described this unique vessel as a dish for serving *kissel*, a Russian dessert of stewed fruit thickened with starch; the *kissel* would have been placed in the central container, while cake or bread would have been laid on the wide rim. Although the Novgorod example has a more pronounced foot and is twice as large, SF3567 could have been used in the same way and may have originated in the same cultural milieu. It was made of field maple and was therefore almost certainly an import into Aberdeen.

SF3567 is also unusual amongst the Bon Accord assemblage in that its surfaces have been burnished or polished, and there are owner's or maker's marks on the base (Figure 4.3). Owner's or maker's marks are frequently found in other assemblages, most often as incised or burnt marks on the bases of vessels (cf. Hurley and McCutcheon 1997: 562; Platt and Coleman-Smith 1975: 229). Several of the wooden bowls from Threave Castle have heart-shaped motifs burnt onto their bases, identifying them as belonging to the Douglas family (Barber 1981: 117–19).

A pentacle has been incised on the base of SF1546A (Figure 4.3) – a similar mark was found on a lid from medieval deposits in Exeter (Allan and Morris 1984: 16). Morris (2000: 2261) has suggested that such marks may be symbolic, designed to protect the contents of the vessels.

The upper surfaces of both SF3567 and SF4012 bear many fine knifemarks, presumably relating to their use (Figure 4.3). There are similar knifemarks on the base of SF3884, suggesting that it was also used as a chopping board (Figure 4.2). Nearly all the bowls from Perth High Street displayed cutmarks on their bases (Curteis *et al.*

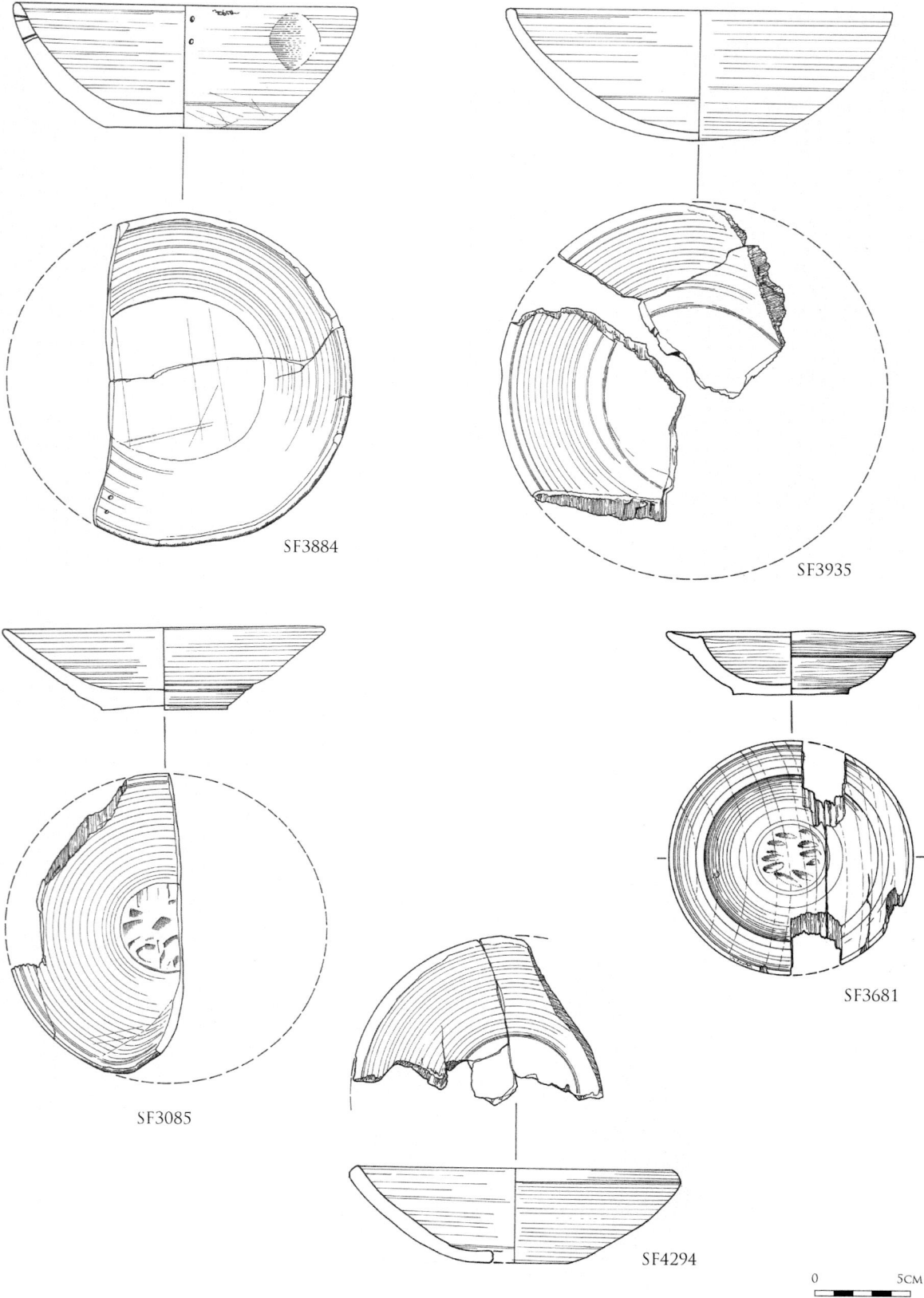

Figure 4.2 Turned wooden bowls; SF3884; SF3935; SF3085; SF3681; SF4294

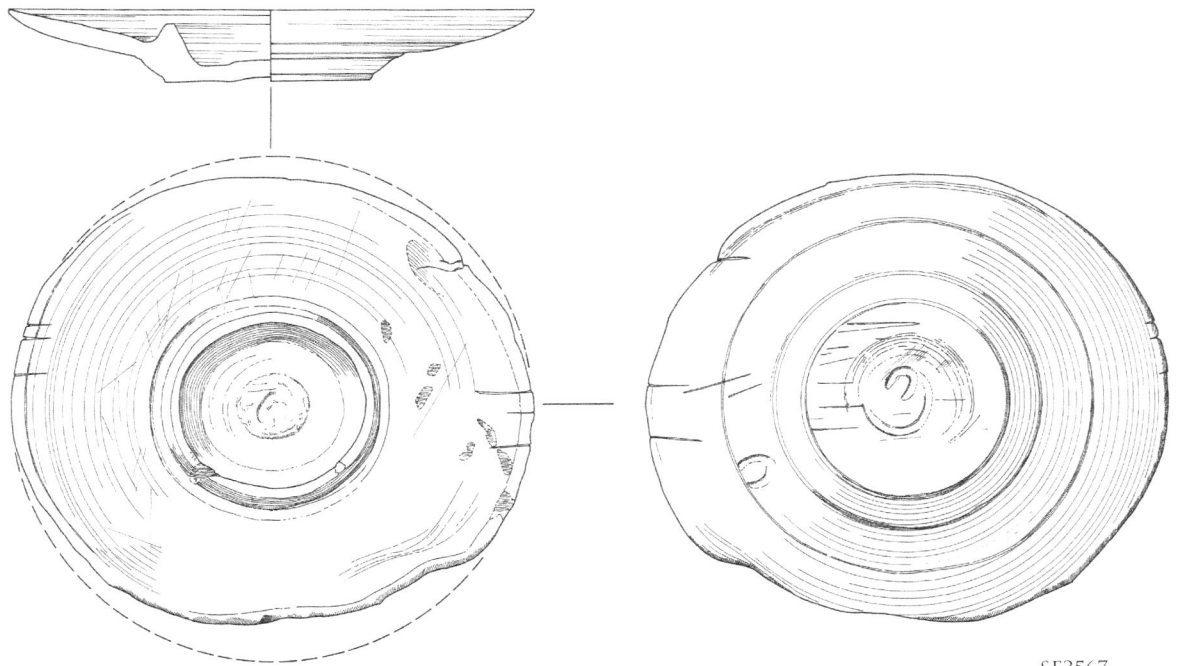

SF3567

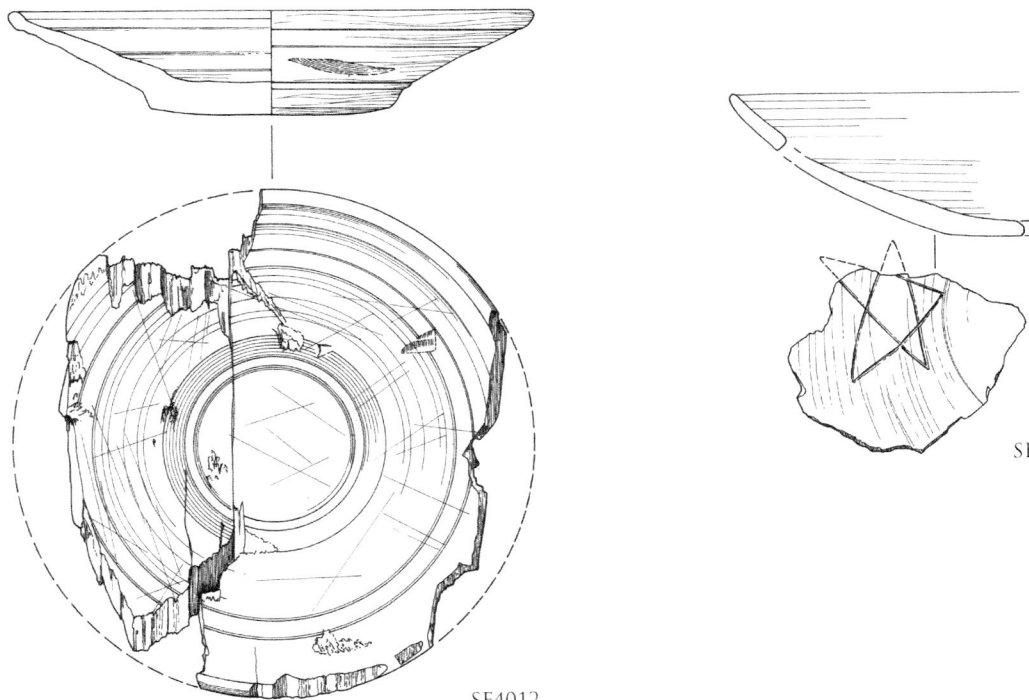

SF4012

SF1546A

0   5CM

Figure 4.3 Turned wooden bowls; SF3567; SF3567 base; SF4012; SF1546A

2012: 255) indicating that this must have been common practice.

Platters

There are six vessels in the assemblage that can be categorised as platters because of the shallowness of the angle between base and wall (SF2842, SF3061, SF3710, SF3743, SF3840 & SF3767) (Figure 4.4). Although SF3840 has a height:diameter ratio of 1:5 and thus falls into the bowl category, its large diameter (c. 600mm) indicates a distinct difference in function and so it is included in this category.

All the platters have been made from ash. Most are extremely fragmentary so estimates of size are necessarily tentative. SF3710 has thin walls, 9mm thick, but the larger platters have walls and bases between 12mm and 21mm thick. SF3743 is the most complete of this group and is approximately 370mm in diameter. SF3061 is also at least 375mm in diameter but there are examples in this group which are significantly larger – SF2842 and SF3840 have estimated diameters of 630mm and 600mm, respectively. This size of wooden vessel is exceptional amongst medieval assemblages; of a sample of 338 turned vessels from contexts dating from AD 400 to AD 1500 only 5% were greater than 300mm, and these were all medieval in date (Morris 2000: 2178–79). Morris (ibid) describes these vessels as heavy and thick-walled, usually with squared rims (as is the case with SF2842 and SF3840), and used as dairy bowls for butter and cream. Several of the platters are charred in patches – SF2842 on the upper surface and SF3840 on the under surface. This could be post-depositional but it may also relate to use and function.

The two largest platters, SF2842 and SF3840, display turning marks but the concave facets over the undersurface of SF3743 (Figure 4.4) indicate that it had been carved. The surfaces of the other platters are either smooth or decayed so their means of fabrication cannot be determined. However, the thin walls of SF3710 and the slightly projecting rim on the external surface of SF3061 (Figure 4.4) suggest that these were also turned. Carved vessels are rarely found in medieval contexts (Morris 2000: 2116). Of more than 120 vessels found in York, only one was carved (ibid 2276). Large carved platters may have been more common in Scotland; an ash platter, very similar in appearance to SF3743 and possibly hewn, was found in 13th–14th century deposits at the Netherkirkgate (Crone et al. 2001: 213–14), while at Perth High Street three large hewn platters, all over 400mm across and thick-walled, were recovered from 11th, 12th and 13th century deposits (Curteis et al. 2012: 259).

Spindle-turned items

Apart from the carved vessel, SF3743, the bowls and platters described above were all face-turned, i.e. the grain of the wood lay perpendicular to the axis of rotation of the pole-lathe (Morris 2000: 2122). This was the standard method by which most medieval vessels were fashioned but smaller vessels and other objects could also be spindle-turned, the grain of the wood lying parallel to the axis of rotation of the pole-lathe (ibid).

There are only two objects from Bon Accord which have been spindle-turned. The alder lid, SF3185 (Figure 4.5), is a finely made object with a flanged, recessed rim and decorative knob-like handle, which would have fit snugly over a wooden or ceramic vessel. A near-identical lid of alder was found at Coppergate, York though from 10th century AD deposits (Morris 2000: 2186–88). Morris (ibid) suggested that the hollow design of these lids, as opposed to the more common flat-bottomed lids, probably reflected a functional difference. Perth High St has also produced a group of spindle turned lids, two of which had similarly recessed rims while another two had knob-like handles (Curteis et al. 2012: 258).

SF4584 (Figure 4.5), a disc of alder of uncertain function with concave upper and lower surfaces, has also been spindle-turned. It is possible that it is turning waste from the manufacture of a lid like SF3185; it has a pronounced ridge around the perimeter which mirrors the groove visible on the hollow roof of SF3185. If it were the waste from within the hollow lid, then the parent lid would have been larger, with an internal rim diameter of c. 170mm. However, as there is no other evidence that lathe-turned wooden vessels were manufactured on the site, this object may have served some other purpose.

Repairs

Two of the vessels described above have been repaired. The small platter, SF3743, had cracked in half and been repaired with metal rivets inserted into narrow slots on either side of the crack (Figure 4.4). The two small holes along the broken edge of SF3884 (Figure 4.2) suggest that this bowl had been repaired using wire thread rather than staples. Repaired vessels are occasionally, though not frequently, found on other sites and both staples and wire thread have been employed (cf. Hurley and McCutcheon 1997: 562; Morris 2000: 2189). Wooden vessels were probably repaired because, despite being ubiquitous, their manufacture may well have been a seasonal occupation, and townsfolk would have been dependent on the visits of itinerant turners to replenish their supplies (Morris 2000: 2189). A copper alloy rivet

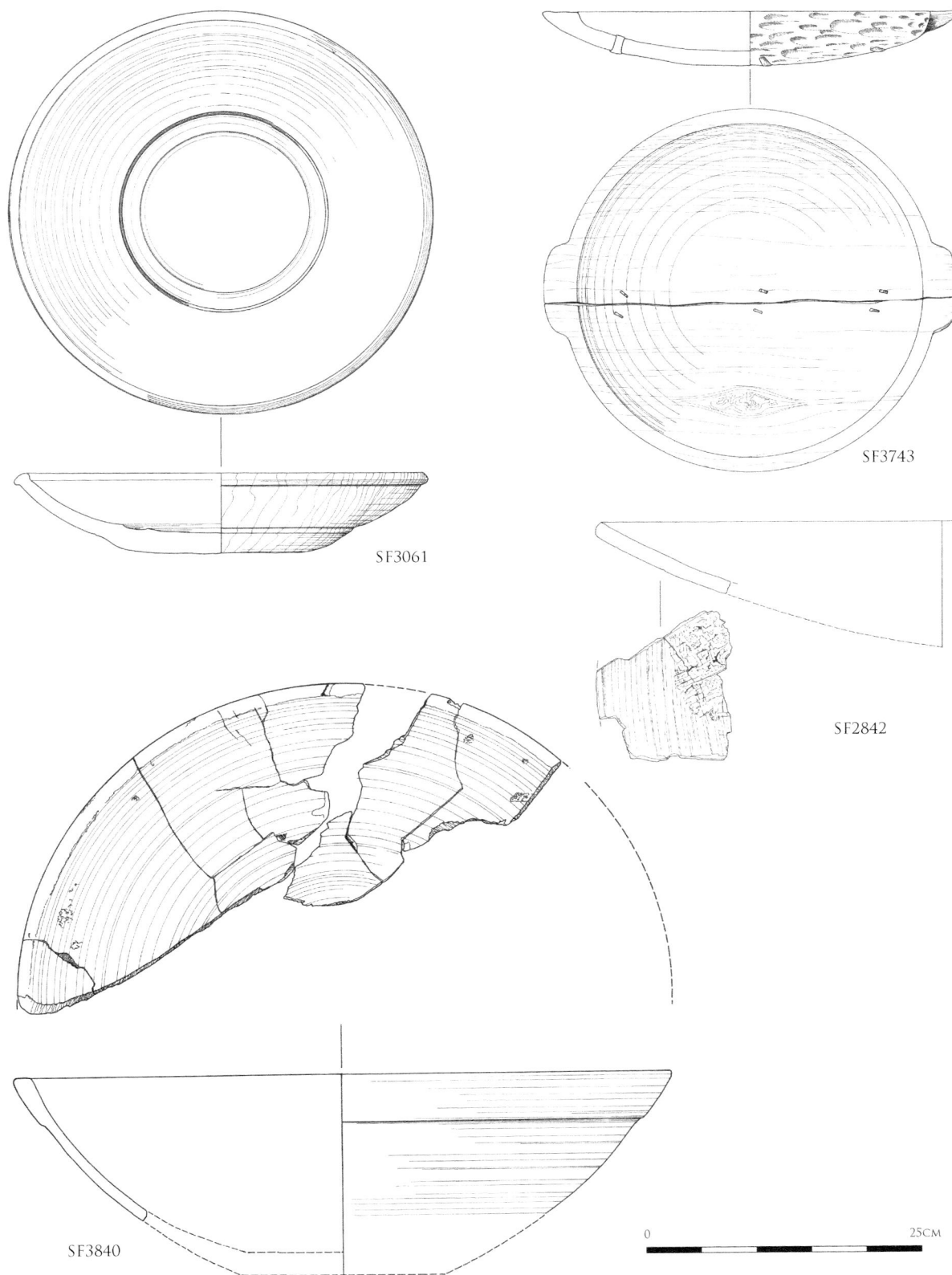

Figure 4.4 Turned wooden platters; SF3061; SF3743; SF2842; SF3840

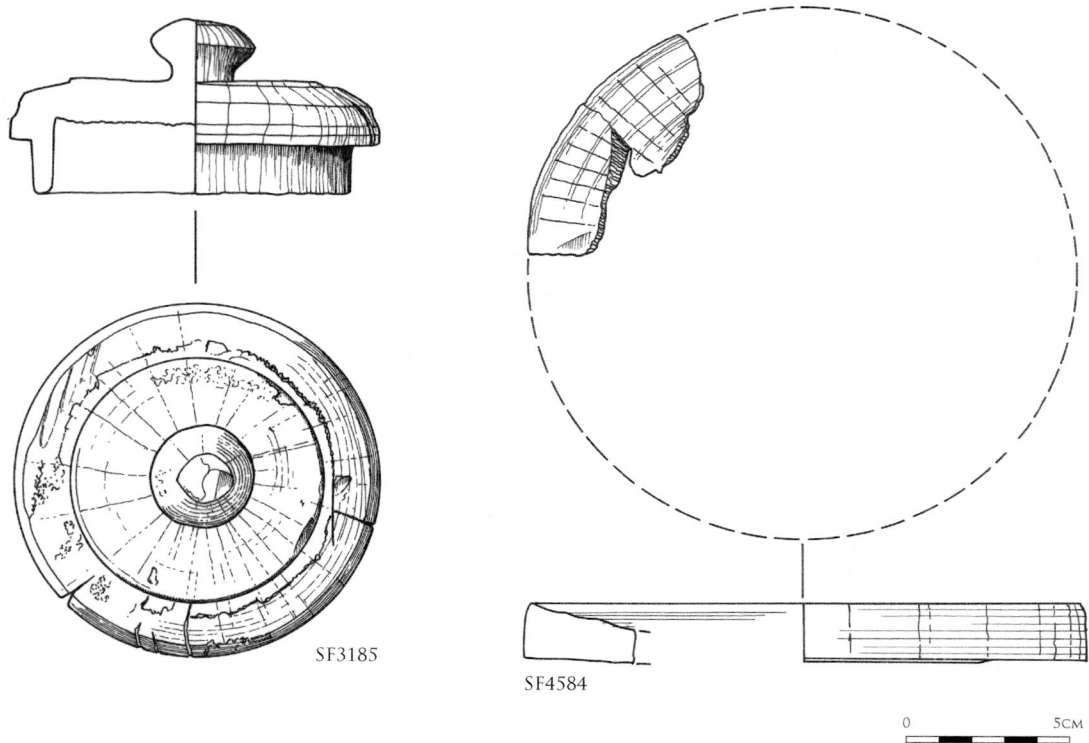

Figure 4.5 Spindle-turned objects; SF3185; SF4584

(SF1678) which would have been used in the repair of wooden vessels was also found in the Phase 2 Pit C019 (Section 4.3.1).

Stave-built vessels

Casks and tubs

The evidence for coopered vessels at Bon Accord includes the casks used as linings in Well C001 and Well A001, nine individual vertical staves and four cant staves (the curved stave forming the outer edge of a cask lid), all of them fashioned from radially-split oak. All the staves probably came from casks, which are closed at both ends, as opposed to tubs, which are open-topped. A range of vessel sizes is present. The most complete cask, C001, stands to a height of 1.4m (Figure 4.6) and has a basal diameter of 0.82m. The basal diameter of A001 was only 0.67m but it may have been as tall as C001; although it had only survived to a height of 0.64m the cut of the well was 1.6m deep so it may have been a tall, thin barrel. The most complete of the individual staves, SF3745 (Figure 4.6), came from a cask *c.* 0.53m in height, nearly a third of the size of C001; this difference in size must relate to function and contents.

The estimated diameters of the four cant staves are comparable to that of C001, ranging from 0.76m to 0.90m and therefore, if they came from casks, they were

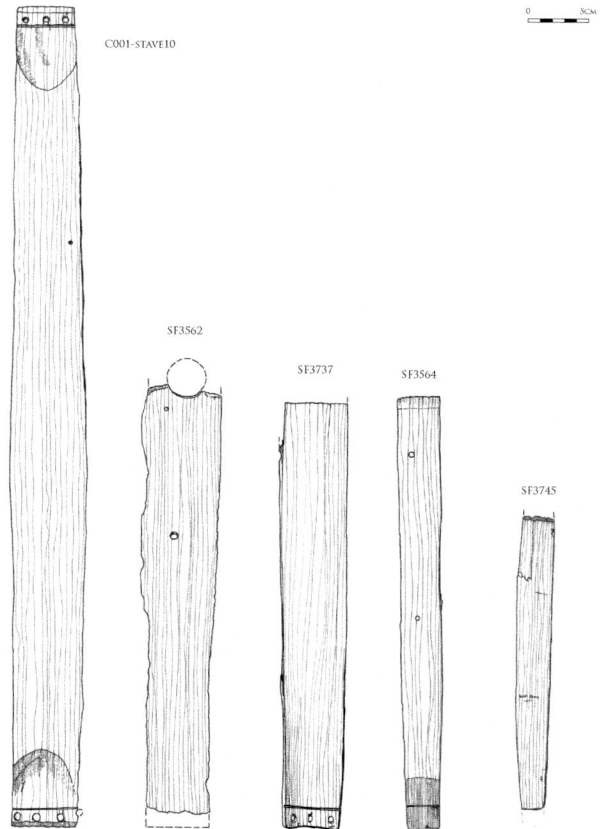

Figure 4.6 Stave-built objects: casks and tub elements; C001-Stave 10; SF3562; SF3737; SF3564; SF3745

106

probably of similar height. However, it is impossible to determine whether the staves came from casks or tubs. Of the other individual staves, three had also come from casks of roughly similar dimensions to C001 but had been chopped in half. SF3562 (Figure 4.6), SF3633, SF3737 (Figure 4.6) and SF3739 had been cut down to heights of *c.* 0.75m, 0.73m, 0.72m and 0.73m respectively (thus with roughly complete heights of between 1.44m and 1.5m) by obliquely angled chops across their midpoint. The similarity in height suggests that they had all been roughly cut down with the same purpose in mind, possibly to form a lining for a pit. Another stave, SF3564, probably belongs to this group of cut-down cask staves; it is also 0.73m in height but the upper end is more neatly squared and chamfered so it could be a tub stave (Figure 4.6).

The casks used as linings for Wells C001 and A001 are all punctured by numerous holes of varying diameter, as are SF3562 and SF3564. Some of these are likely to have been the bungholes and ventholes necessary if the cask were carrying fermented liquors, such as wine. The lines of holes drilled into the ends of diametrically opposed staves on the casks of Wells C001 (Figure 4.6) and A001 were probably to secure strengthening battens across the head and base of the cask (see Allen 1995: illus 1). Several barrels from Anglo-Scandinavian contexts at Coppergate, York display multiple pegholes in similar positions (Morris 2000: 2249) as does a 12th/13th century cask from Exeter (Allan and Morris 1984). A number of medieval illustrations show casks in use with battens in place across the headpiece (Morris 2000: 2249). Morris (*ibid*) comments that, as most of these illustrations appear to be of wine casks resting horizontally, the battens may have been used to reinforce the heads of casks used in this position.

Many of these casks may have been imported into Aberdeen carrying wine or other commodities. All the barrels from Scottish contexts which have been dendrochronologically dated have come from foreign sources. The 14th century cask in Well A001 probably came from the area covering modern-day Belgium and northeastern France (Section 4.1), so it was conceivably imported containing wine. The cask from the Gallowgate Middle School site which, like A001 was also 14th century in date and was reused as a well lining in the early 15th century, had come from the eastern Baltic; it arrived either as ready-made staves which were subsequently coopered or containing foodstuffs such as honey and ale (Crone 2001: 222).

Once they arrived in Aberdeen, the casks were put to a long and useful life. At Bon Accord they were used whole to line wells, or chopped in half, possibly for use as tubs or as linings for troughs and pits. The surface of the cant stave, SF3377, is covered in chopmarks, presumably because it was subsequently used as a chopping board, a common fate for coopered vessel lids (Morris 2000: 2257).

Tankard

SF3324 (Figure 4.7) is very different from the cask components described above. It is a small stave of Scots pine, probably from a little mug or tankard which stood some 133mm high. The stave is not tapered and so the vessel was probably straight-sided, with an estimated diameter of *c.* 110–120mm. The closest comparanda for

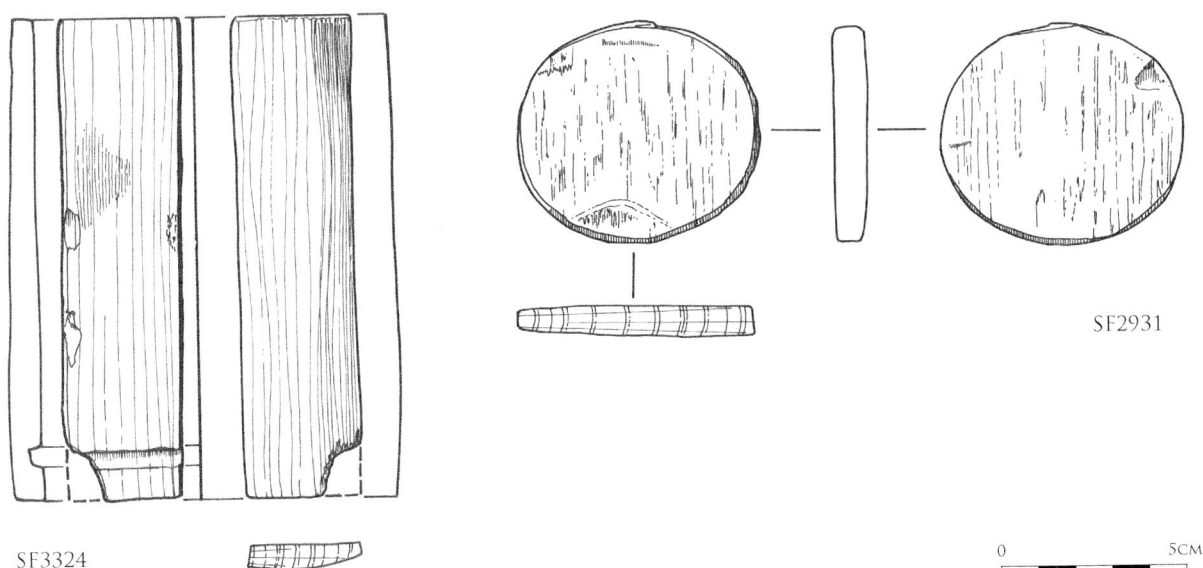

SF3324

SF2931

0   5CM

Figure 4.7 Stave-built objects: tankards; SF3324; SF2931

the Bon Accord stave in terms of size and profile are the small stave-built vessels commonly found in Anglo-Saxon graves of 5th–7th century date throughout England, a handful of which were made of pine (Cook 2004). Setting aside the remote possibility that the mug was an heirloom, the use of pine in the manufacture of artefacts is relatively unusual in mainland Britain until the early modern period and therefore it is likely the tankard was brought to Aberdeen, either as a trade commodity or as a personal possession.

Pine was regularly used for the construction of stave-built vessels in the Scandinavian countries and those around the Baltic, where it was commonly available. Several examples will suffice to demonstrate this. Pine was used in the manufacture of nearly 60% of the stave-built containers found in 13th to 16th century contexts excavated around the Vilnius Lower Castle, Lithuania, almost exclusively for straight-sided containers rather than casks (Pukiene and Baubaite 2011: 156). In medieval Novgorod both spruce and pine were used extensively in the probably local manufacture of casks, kegs and other stave-built vessels; pine was preferred for open-topped vessels (Comey 2007). Pine was the third most common species found in the stave-built vessels of Hiberno-Norse Dublin and as it no longer grew in Ireland by that period many of the vessels must have been imported into Dublin from Scandinavia (although there was some manufacture of pine vessels in Dublin, probably from recycled wood; Comey 2010: 103–04). This trade is likely to have been the source of the only pine stave found in York, in a 10th century AD context, although Morris (2000: 2226–27) observes that the pine could have been obtained and worked locally. Although described as a bucket stave because it had a lug handle, this stave was from a straight-sided vessel remarkably similar in height and diameter to SF3324.

Pine tankard staves have been found elsewhere in Scotland. Perth High Street has produced one of the largest assemblages of tankard staves in the UK, several of which have been provisionally identified as of 'imported softwood timber' (Curteis *et al.* 2012: 226). However, they differ from SF3324 in that they are smaller in height and are also slightly tapered in profile, one flaring out towards the rim, and one tapered towards the rim. An unfinished straight-sided pine stave for a small vessel was recovered from 8th–9th century deposits in the ditch around the settlement cemetery at The Carrick, Midross, Loch Lomond (Crone, *forthcoming*), and a straight-sided stave of pine of very similar height to SF3324 was retrieved from post-medieval deposits at the Biggings, Papa Stour, in Shetland (Morris 1999: 185–86). Although not comparable in date to the Bon Accord stave these latter examples serve to demonstrate the likely Scandinavian affinities of these stave-built pine vessels.

The oak disc, SF2931 (Figure 4.7) could conceivably be the base for a small stave-built vessel such as a tankard or bowl. It is very similar in size to an object identified as such from Perth High Street, but whereas the example from Perth has a chamfered edge to slot into the croze groove cut into the staves, SF2931 simply tapers in thickness towards the perimeter.

Tools

All the tools described below were found in Phase 2 pits and all but three came from Pit C025. A wide range of tools is present but the function of some is more obvious than others and it is thus difficult to categorise the assemblage. There are few obvious comparanda for many of the tools but wherever possible general functions have been ascribed on the basis of overall morphology.

Shovel blades

Amongst the more obvious tools are three composite or separate-bladed shovel blades, all fashioned from radial-split oak. There is a large corpus of separate-bladed shovel blades from medieval sites in Britain, Ireland and the Continent, mostly from 10th to 14th century contexts, although the earliest known comes from an 8th/9th century Irish crannog and post-medieval examples are known (Morris 2000: 2313–14).

Although there is some variety in shape amongst the Bon Accord examples, they all display the distinguishing features of this type of implement: sloping shoulders, a broad flat blade and a large central socket for the handle (Figure 4.8). The handle was slotted into the socket through the upper surface and the upper and lower edges of the socket were sloped so that the handle lay at a very shallow angle to the blade (for reconstruction see Morris 1980: fig. 4). The handle was usually fixed to the blade with pegs inserted into holes just above the socket; this area of the blade is damaged on SF3359 but on SF3361 there are two holes for this purpose, one above the other, while on SF3693 there are the remains of a single hole. Several of the shovel blades from York have diamond-shaped necks, while other examples have notched shoulders, and Morris (*ibid*) has suggested that this was in order that rope could be bound around the blade and handle to secure the junction more thoroughly. There is no evidence to suggest that the Bon Accord shovels had been doubly secured. Their composite design allowed broken blades to be easily replaced and Morris (*ibid*) notes that most blades are broken or split; all the examples from Bon Accord have been split in two and on SF3693 and SF3359 the neck above the handle socket has also been damaged.

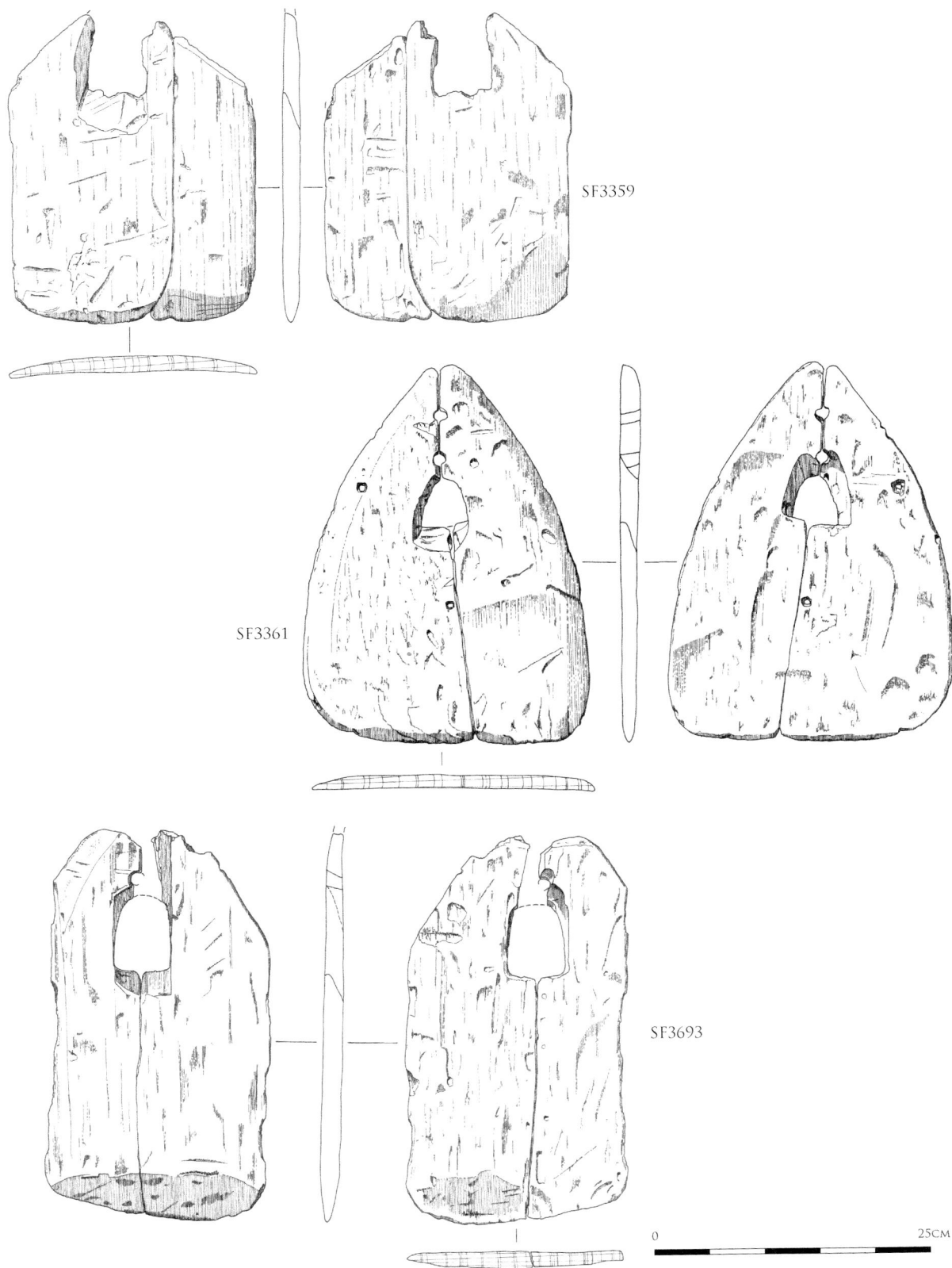

Figure 4.8 Tools: shovel blades; SF3359; SF3361; SF3693

The shallow angle between handle and blade, and the relative weakness of the junction between them means that these implements would have functioned best as shovels for shifting, 'soft, loose materials such as earth, mortar, grain, dung and mud' (Morris 2000: 2315). Contemporary illustrations show a similar implement being used to clear mud from a watercourse and to mix mortar (Morris 1980; 210). The variety in shape displayed by the Bon Accord shovel blades is seen throughout the known corpus (Morris 1980: fig. 2; Morris 2000: 2314; Curteis *et al.* 2012: 280) and may reflect different applications. Two of the blades from Bon Accord are rectangular while the third is teardrop-shaped, and all three are contemporary (they were all found in Pit C025), which makes it more likely that the differences in shape relate to a difference in application rather than styles changing over time. All three had neatly bevelled edges, hinting at their use with fragile materials.

Tools with distinct blades

There are four implements from the site which, although there are marked differences in shape and overall morphology, all display a distinct blade and handle, are of roughly the same length, and could have been used for stirring, beating or crushing. The only complete example in this group is SF3630 (Figure 4.9) which most resembles either a weaving sword or a scutching knife (used in flax processing). However, the hole towards the tip of the blade suggests that the tip was fixed in place while the handle and blade moved freely, so it could be the knife used in a breaker, an implement used during flax processing to crush the outer layer of flax stems. The breaker consisted of a horizontal bar with a groove down the centre, within which the wooden knife was fixed at one end so that the blade could be brought down on the flax stems lying across the breaker. SF3210 (Figure 4.9) is a small paddle-like implement of pine which could have been used for stirring; axemarks are still visible on the blade, suggesting that the faces were not worn, and there is charring around the tip on one face. SF3417 (Figure 4.9) is a heavy implement of hazel, shaped like a cricket bat, which would have needed two hands to use; the surfaces of the blade are pitted and rough, suggesting that it had been used for beating or pounding. Finally, SF3713 (Figure 4.9) is a similar bat-like implement of oak but without a distinct handle, although the tapered end can be easily grasped. It displays few wear marks so may have been used for stirring and lifting.

SF3911C (Figure 4.9) is the tip of a small blade of oak which could have been a knife in itself, or could have been part of an implement such as a weaving sword, or even the tip of a shuttle (cf. Kublo 2007: fig 9.11).

Scrapers/ rakes?

SF3911B (Figure 4.10) is a flat, wide implement which consists only of a blade with a tapered working edge. It can be held neatly in the hand and the two holes may have secured a leather strap behind which the hand slotted. If held in this manner the implement could have functioned as a scraper or perhaps as a hand shovel. Although much less substantial and without the central hole for the handle, SF3911B does resemble in shape the solid rakes found in York and other English towns (Morris 2000: 2319). Their contexts suggest that they could have been used for raking ashes out of ovens, salt in brine pans and tan in a tannery (*ibid*).

SF4099 (Figure 4.10) is morphologically quite similar to SF3911B, in that it is a thin, flat implement consisting only of the blade which widens to a working edge. There are two holes at the top of the implement which might have secured a strap or handle and a line of holes along the working edge. It is very similar in size and shape to a strainer from PerthHigh Street (Curteis *et al.* 2012: 264–65) but does not have the multiple holes necessary for such an implement. It might have functioned, like SF3911B, as a scraper but it is difficult to envisage a role for the holes along the edge.

Tool handles

There are three handles (Figure 4.10) from the site. SF3084B and SF3134B are handles for whittle tang knives, although the blade is no longer *in situ* in either. SF3134B was broken at the 'working' end and as there was no socket visible, just a single nail hammered into one face, it is unclear what tool it was attached to. SF3084B and SF3134B have been simply fashioned by trimming lengths of roundwood, and fine striae around the handles suggest that they had probably been bound, possibly with leather strips or cord.

SF3134A (Figure 4.15) is an altogether more exotic item, distinguished by both its unusual decoration (Section 4.2.1.1) and by the use of an exotic species, boxwood, for its manufacture. Boxwood would have been selected for the handle because its dense, smooth grain made it ideal for engraving and also because its light yellow colour could be polished up to look like ivory (Morris 2000 2311). In archaeological contexts it is found to have been used mainly in the manufacture of combs (cf. Smirnova 2007) but also for handles. For instance, of the 61 wooden handles from contexts dating from the 12th century to the early 15th century found in London before 1987 43% had been made from boxwood (Cowgill *et al.* 1987: 24–25). The only boxwood handle found in York was elaborately carved in the Scandinavian Ringerike style and Morris (2000: 2284) has suggested that it was craftsman-made rather than homemade.

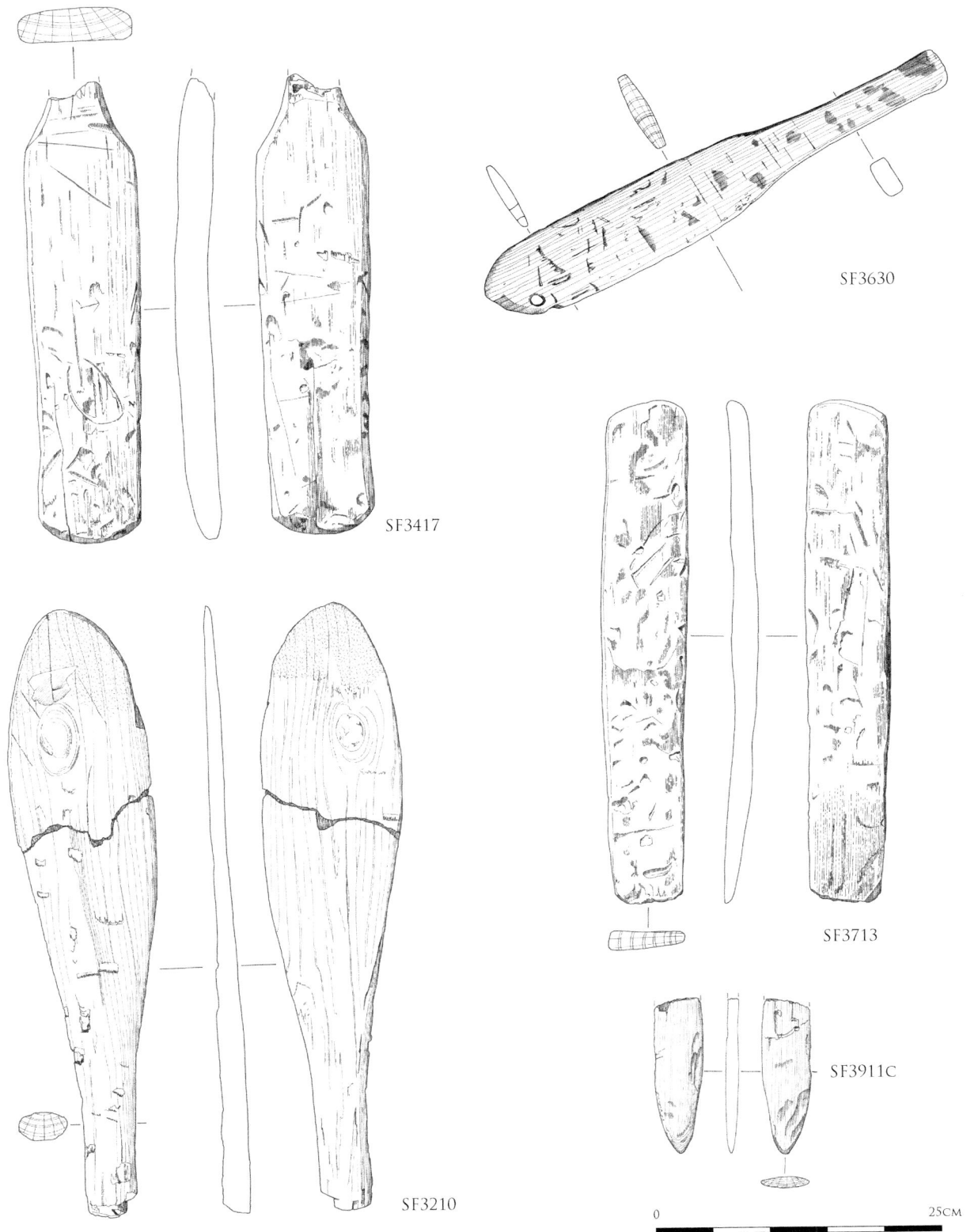

Figure 4.9 Tools: distinct blades; SF3417; SF3630; SF3210; SF3713; SF3911C

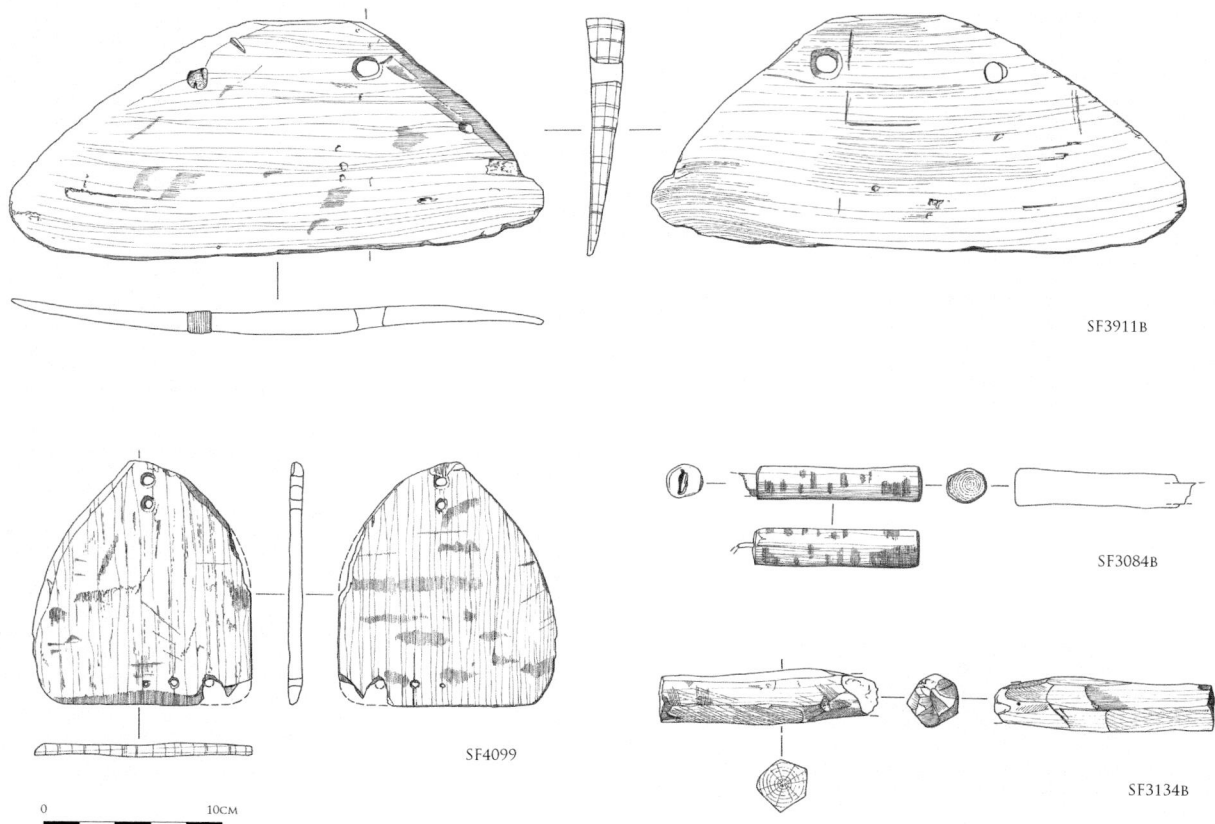

Figure 4.10 Tools: scrapers/ rakes and handles; SF3911B; SF4099, SF3084B; SF3134B

Aspects of the decoration on SF3134A hint at more homely manufacture but there is nothing in the style and content of the decoration to indicate where this might have happened and it could as easily have been made in Aberdeen as abroad (Section 4.2.1.1).

The grinding mechanism

The recovery of a rotary grindstone together with its wooden shaft, SF2583 (Figure 4.11), still in position is a very rare find and raises questions as to how it was operated. The grindstone alone is usually all that survives and consequently little thought has been given to the means by which they were actually mounted and powered. In discussing the large assemblage of rotary grindstones from 16–22 Coppergate, York (Mainman and Rogers 2000: 2479–84) the authors state that they '... would have been mounted on a horizontal axle...' which is certainly true, but how was the axle supported and how was it rotated? There are a few early illustrations of rotary grindstones in use; the earliest is that in the early 9th century AD Utrecht Psalter (White 1962: 110) and there is another in the mid 14th century AD Luttrell Psalter (*ibid* 111). Both depict the grindstone mounted on a shaft with crank handles on either side. In the Luttrell Psalter two men are operating the crank

handles on either side of the stone, which is mounted in a box.

Indeed, the way in which small grindstones were mounted and turned may not have changed much over the centuries; in 1864 Charles Holtzapffel wrote, '...*when the stone does not exceed about one foot in diameter, it is commonly mounted on the upper edges of the little wooden box or trough, which serves both to support the pivots of the axis on which the stone revolves, and to contain the water with which it is moistened. The one extremity of the spindle is squared for the winch-handle, the central part is squared for the convenience of wedging on the stone with wooden wedges, and there are cylindrical necks or pivots on the axis, the bearings for which are sometimes of hard wood such as lignum vitae, or far better of metal. In the most common form, two iron staples which surround the pivots are simply driven into the top edges of the wood trough; in the best form the trough and bearings are both of metal...*(Holtzapffel 1864: 1105)'.

None of the grindstones from Bon Accord exceed one foot (i.e. 300mm) in diameter (SF329 is 170mm and SF2583 is 230mm – Section 4.3.2) so they could have been mounted within a box or trough as described above. However, there was no wear at the ends of the

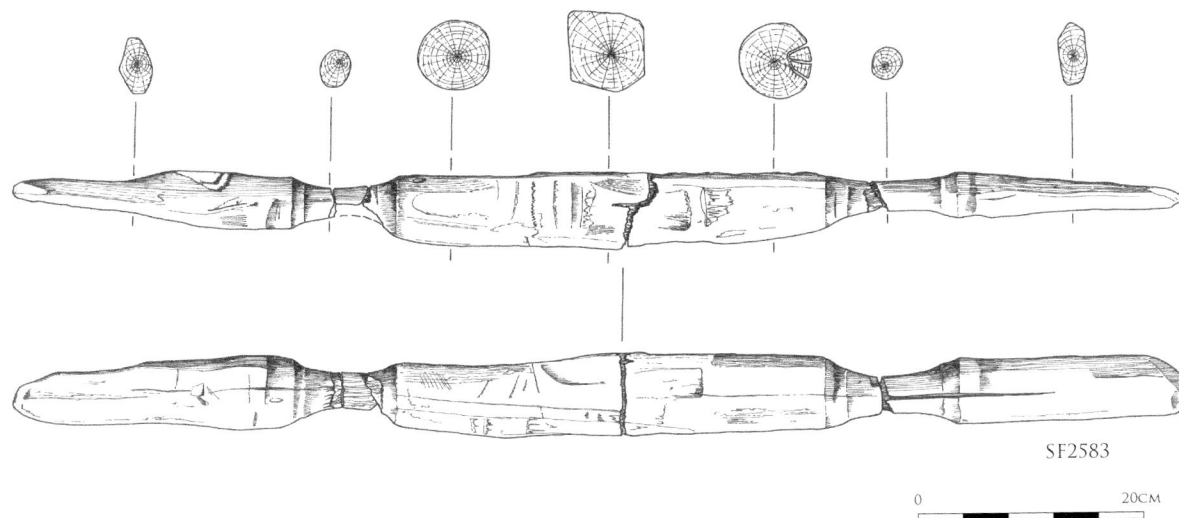

Figure 4.11 Tools: handles and shaft of grinding mechanism; SF2583

paddle-like handles to suggest that they had been inserted into crank handles like those depicted in the Psalters, nor would their shape have been conducive to insertion. Rather, it seems more probable, given the design of the handles, that the grinding mechanism was suspended from a frame, with ropes coiled around the grooves between the shaft and handles which were then attached to a foot pedal. The grinding mechanism would have been operated in much the same way as a pole lathe, sharpening taking place on the downward reciprocal motion.

At least seven other oak wedges, of rough and ready manufacture, were retrieved from across the site and these were probably put to the same sort of use as those used in wedging the handle firmly within the grindstone. Indeed, they may have been used with the other grindstones found on the site.

Miscellaneous

As with any archaeological wood assemblage there are many objects which have clearly been deliberately designed but whose function is no longer apparent (see for example Perth High Street; Curteis *et al.* 2012: 302–16). Indeed, some of them might as easily belong in the structural category. These include SF3337, a rectangular board with handle-like projections at either end (Figure 4.12); SF3558, a panel that has been shaped to an expanding curve (Figure 4.12), and SF3825, a small oak lath with tiny holes drilled along each edge (Figure 4.13). There is also SF3631 whose size, finish and complex joints suggest a loom or furniture component (Figure 4.12), and SF3010, an oak board to which a sheet of lead (SF3011) has been attached with nails (Figure 4.13). The lead sheet is decorative (Section 4.3.1) but it

would have made the object heavier and it may have been intended to weight it down while in water.

Summarised below are objects which, although having more identifiable functions, do not fit neatly into the major categories described above.

Container handle

SF1513A (Figure 4.14) is a finely made curved handle of yew which was originally attached to the lid of a container such as a box. A similar type of handle, also made of yew, was found in late 14th century deposits in York (Morris 2000: 2290–92, 2414). This example is slightly smaller and is rectangular in profile, with a zoomorphic terminal to the foot. SF1513A would have been pinned to the lid whereas the York example would probably have been glued. Differences apart, they both represent a valuable personal item, a relatively small and dainty container, possibly made entirely of yew, a species which in mainland Britain is generally reserved for small carved objects, such as the locket from 16–18 Netherkirkgate (Crone *et al.* 2001: 217–19).

Perforated disc

SF1546B (Figure 4.14) is a perforated oak disc which could have one of many functions. The most obvious use is as a spindle whorl, although at 7mm in diameter the central hole could only have held a small spindle suitable for the spinning of light thread, which is at odds with the use of oak and the thickness of the object. A perforated oak disc of very similar dimensions from York was dismissed as a whorl, possibly because the perforation was only 5mm (Morris 2000: 2386–87). Alternatively, it could be a float for a light fishing net;

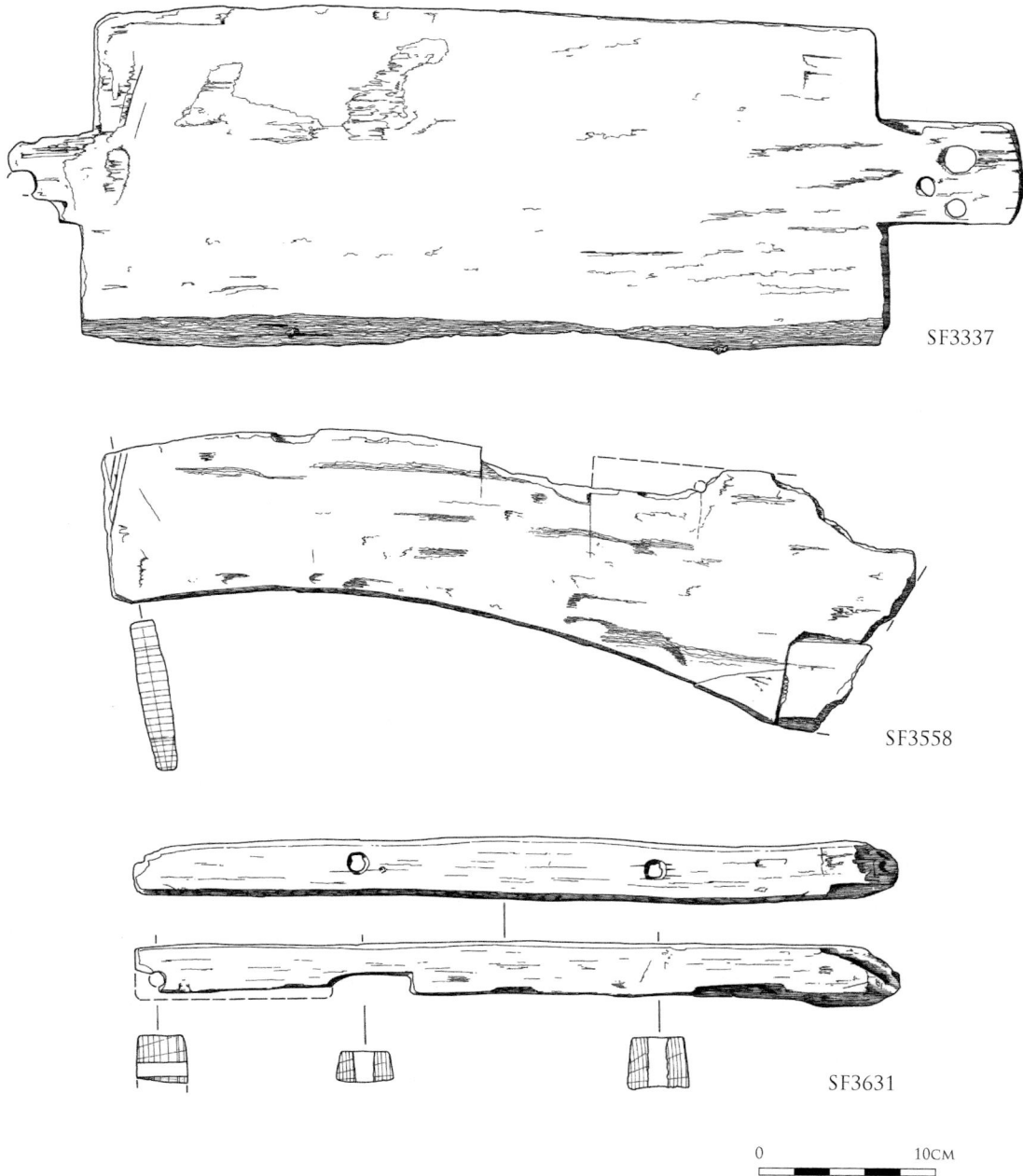

Figure 4.12 Miscellaneous wooden artefacts; SF3337; SF3558; SF3631

small perforated wooden discs have been identified as such at Novgorod (Rybina 2007: 127).

Toggle

SF3073 (Figure 4.14) is a small toggle made from a length of hazel roundwood. It looks exactly like the toggles found on modern duffel coats, although slightly larger. In Roman contexts toggles with more bulbous ends have been described as tent fasteners (Polzer 2008) but those with the most similar morphology to SF3073 tend to be found in nautical contexts (*ibid*). The assemblage from the 9th century AD Oseberg ship burial illustrates

the range of toggle sizes used in the rigging of the ship; these include examples similar in size to SF3073 (Brøgger and Shetelig 1971: 66). At Novgorod toggles were divided on the basis of size; those 60–160mm in length were identified as sail rigging equipment, and were referred to as 'gags' (Kolchin 1989: Vol 1, 102–03; Vol 2, 351), while those 30–50mm in length were identified as buttons (Kolchin 1989, Vol 1, 139–40; Vol 2, 382). On this basis SF3073 would originally have had a nautical function. A single wooden toggle was found at Perth High Street, identical in size to SF3073 (Curteis *et al.* 2012: 281–82).

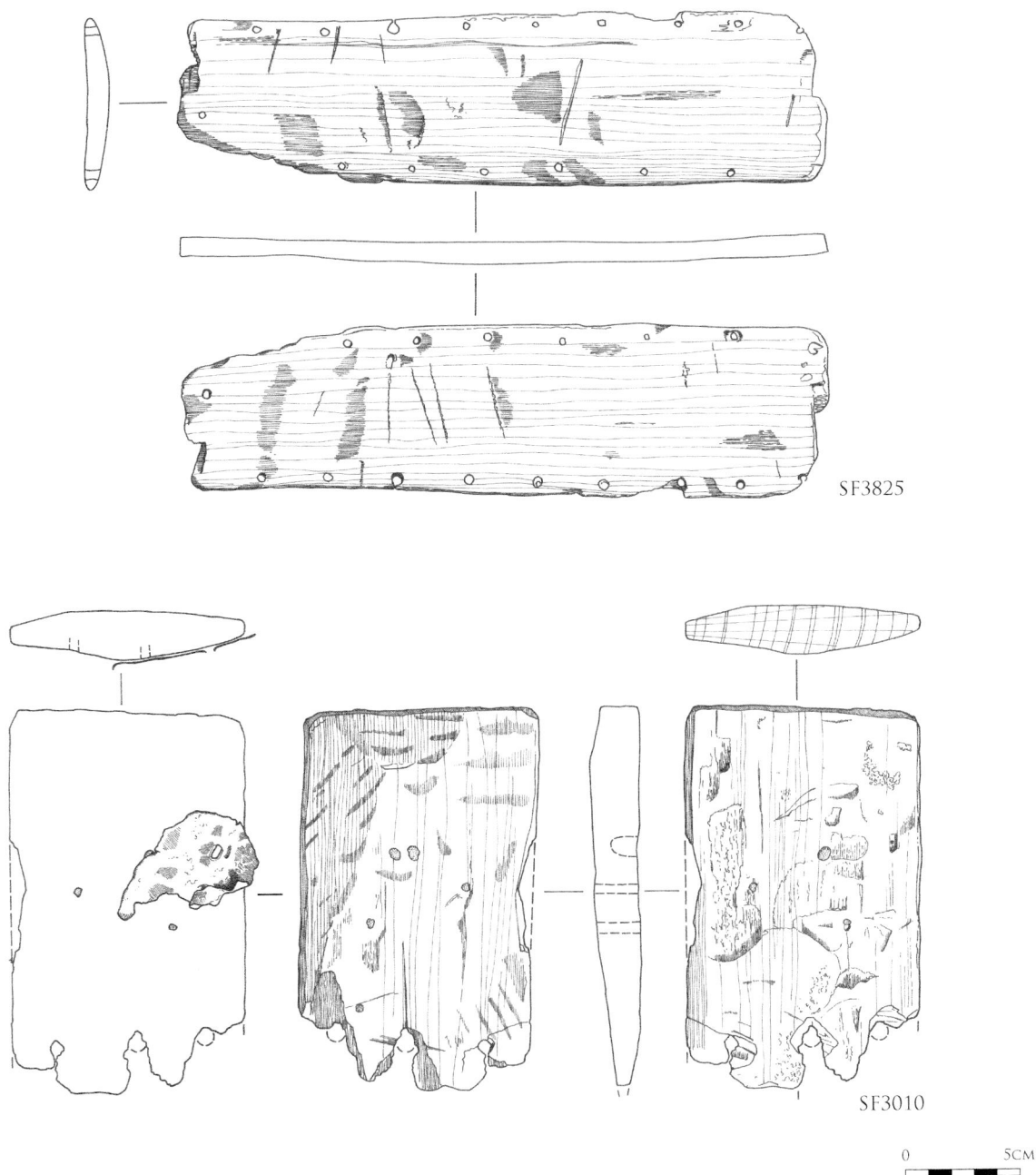

Figure 4.13 Miscellaneous wooden artefacts; SF3825; SF3010 (with lead object SF3011 attached)

Complex wedges?

There are three objects in the assemblage, all from Pit C025, which are wedge-like in appearance but differ markedly from the roughly and rapidly manufactured oak wedges mentioned above. SF3350A, SF3421A and SF3421B (Figure 4.14) have been fashioned much more deliberately, with neatly flattened, rectangular tops tapering to a chisel edge. However, none of them bears any clue as to their function; their tops have not been hammered and there are none of the compression marks that one might expect from insertion between hard surfaces. SF3421A has been made from holly, a heavy, hard wood, and this may have a bearing on its function.

Bung or stopper

SF3476 (Figure 4.14) is a bung or stopper of willow which could have been used in the spout of a ceramic pitcher or the neck of a bottle. Numerous bungs or stoppers have been found at Perth High Street, although none

115

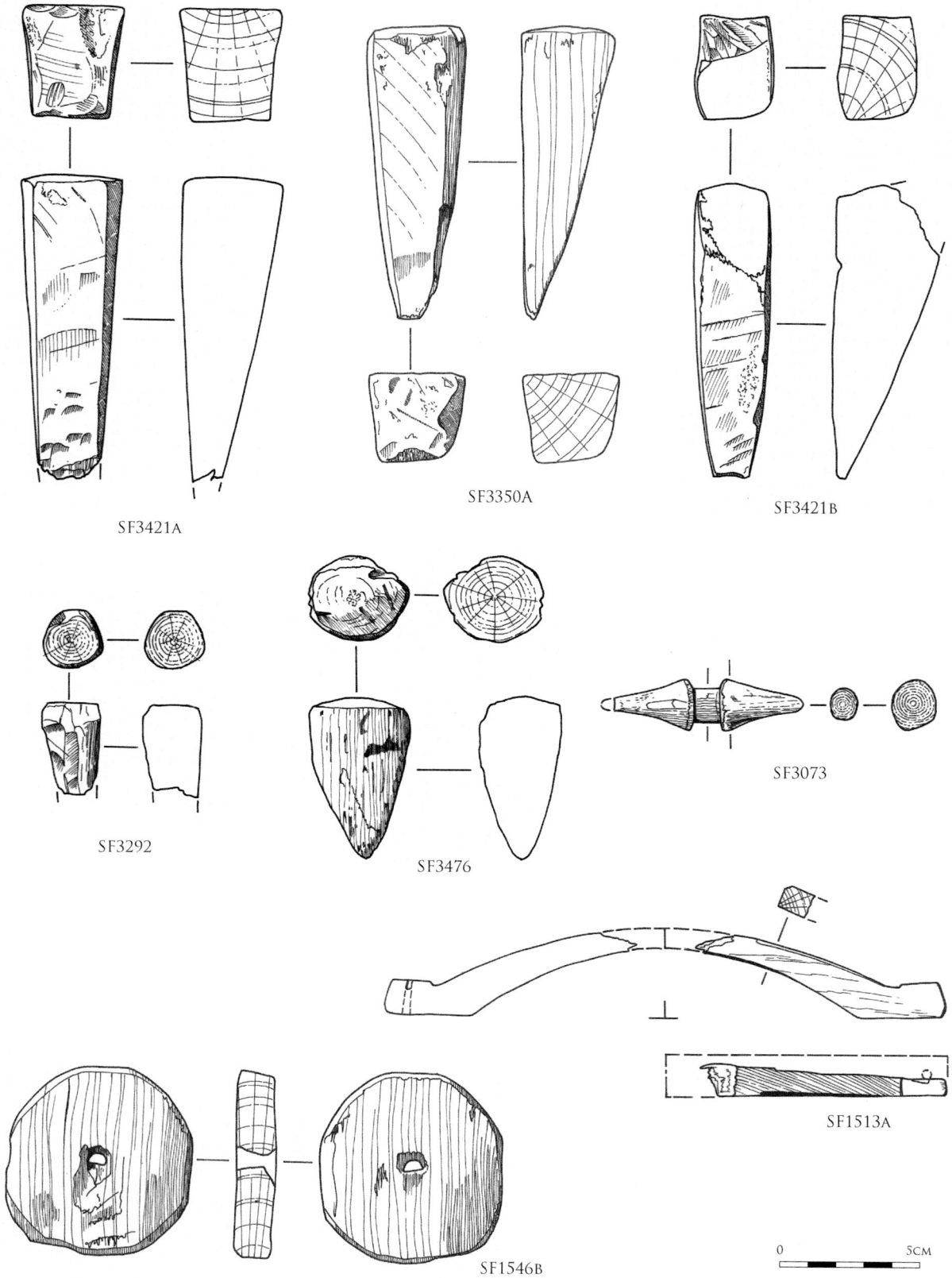

Figure 4.14 Miscellaneous wooden artefacts; SF3421A; SF3350A; SF3421B; SF3292; SF3476; SF3073; SF1546B; SF1513A

of them have the distinct head which SF3476 displays (Curteis *et al.* 2012: 246). A stopper of similar dimensions and morphology comes from York and Morris (2000: 2266) comments that the head would have enabled the stopper to be easily gripped and twisted out.

Pins, pegs, dowels or trenails?

There is a class of small artefact, ubiquitous in most medieval wood assemblages, which defies simple categorisation; although morphology and dimensions are often very similar, these artefacts could have fulfilled a variety of functions. These are the lengths of whittled roundwood which are variously described as pins, pegs, dowels or trenails. All the whittled roundwood objects from Bon Accord are incomplete, making categorisation more difficult. The majority are hazel but there are also examples of oak and willow, and they include examples which are both round and roughly rectangular in cross-section. The two largest objects in terms of diameter also have distinct heads, SF3292 (Figure 4.14) and SF3758A; they could be stoppers like SF3476 (see above) but their shafts do not taper so abruptly and they could equally be trenails. The remainder of the assemblage vary from 6mm to 20mm in width but are mostly around 15mm across, and the longest surviving length is 119mm. Bale pins, which were used to secure sacks of raw wool, have been found in great numbers in many medieval port sites (see for example Perth High Street; Curteis *et al.* 2012: 265–72) and other trading centres but, although there is a great variation in length even on the same site, they are generally less than 10mm across and are usually fashioned from radially-split billets of roundwood (Morris 2000: 2328–29). Only one of the whittled roundwood objects from Bon Accord fits this description; SF3758 is a radial-split pin of willow, 6mm across. Only one other example of a bale pin has been recovered from all the excavated sites in Aberdeen, at 16–18 Netherkirkgate (Crone *et al.* 2001: 213).

Discussion

Wood species

Most of the artefacts found at Bon Accord have been made from native species – oak, ash, alder, willow or hazel – all of which would have been readily available in the environs of Aberdeen. It is clear that particular species were selected for specific functions. Oak accounts for nearly half of the objects, being used in the manufacture of all the cask and tub components and almost all of the tools, and wedges; strength was paramount for all these objects, hence the use of oak. Ash was used exclusively in the manufacture of bowls and platters; of the 14 examples found at Bon Accord nine had been turned from ash. Ash was by far the most common species used for face-turned vessels in the

British Isles throughout the medieval period (Morris 2000: 2196–98), possibly because when turned the grain makes decorative swirls on the surface of the vessel. Most of the other vessels had been turned from alder, including the two spindle-turned objects. Again, this reflects national patterns, alder being the second most popular species for turning (*ibid*); it is easy to turn and does not retain flavours.

Apart from the turned vessels alder was also used to make the handles of the grindstone and the two complex wedges. One of the turned vessels had been made from willow but mostly this species was used to make small objects like the bung, the bale pin, a trenail and a handle. Similarly, hazel was mainly employed to make small pins and pegs, as well as the toggle and a handle. Most of the willow and hazel objects had been simply whittled from lengths of roundwood, the only exception being the bat-like tool, SF3417, which had been fashioned from a chord cleft off a hazel log.

Two artefacts were manufactured from species which would have been exotic to Aberdeen and its environs: the engraved boxwood handle, SF3134A, and the maple bowl, SF3567. Box does grow naturally in the chalk downlands of southern England (Perring and Walters 1990: 98) but more extensive stands are found in a band across southern Europe and into Asia Minor (Smirnova 2007: 299) and these provided the main sources of the boxwood used in the manufacture of combs and handles throughout the medieval and post-medieval periods in Europe. Boxwood was imported into the British Isles as a raw material and Hall (Section 4.2.1.1) has argued that the handle could have been manufactured in Aberdeen by a local craftsman.

Field maple is found throughout southern England and much of Europe (Perring and Walters 1990: 173), but is not native to Scotland and therefore the bowl must have been brought readymade to Aberdeen; the unprocessed wood is unlikely to have been imported as turning in the medieval period was mainly done on green wood (Morris 2000: 2125). The unusual style of the bowl, possibly unique and at the very least rare amongst British assemblages, also suggests a foreign origin.

The other unusual species present at Bon Accord are yew, pine and holly, although all of them would have been available in the hinterland of Aberdeen, as indeed elsewhere in mainland Britain. However, their rarity in archaeological assemblages suggests that cultural choice may have been as much a factor in their selection as availability. On mainland Britain yew was generally reserved for small carved objects, as typified by the handle from Bon Accord and the locket from 16–18 Netherkirkgate. Virtually all the artefacts of yew found in Anglo-Scandinavian York fall into this category, i.e. a cup, spoons, spatulae, tool handles, a spindle and a bobbin. In contrast, in Dublin during the same period yew was the favoured species of the native cooper, used in the manufacture of small-to-medium-sized vessels and accounting for 33% of all stave-built vessel components found there (Comey 2010: 127, 167). Oak was available and also used in coopering, so cultural factors must have influenced the choice of yew.

Holly is rarely used for the manufacture of artefacts, possibly because it warps badly if not fully seasoned. The author knows of only one other object made of holly, a handled tool with serrated teeth from the 7th century AD crannog at Buiston, Ayrshire (Crone 2000a: 120).

Despite its ubiquity in the Scottish landscape very little pine wood has been found on archaeological sites, either as artefacts or even as fuel (Crone 2008a: 285–86), and it may be that it was reserved for specialised uses, such as 'fir candles', the splinters of pine which were used for lighting in rural Scottish homes into very recent times (Grant 1961: 184). Apart from the 'softwood' staves from Perth High Street mentioned above (unfortunately, species identification of the Perth assemblage was not undertaken and so it is uncertain how much, if any, pine was present), the only other significant artefact of pine from a medieval context in Scotland is the toy sword from Caerlaverock (MacIvor and Gallagher 1999: 229). With this in mind it seems most probable, as argued above, that the small pine tankard represented by stave SF3324 was imported into Aberdeen from Scandinavia or northern Europe, particularly as pine was commonly used in the manufacture of stave-built vessels and many other types of artefact in these areas. On the same grounds, the only other pine artefact from Bon Accord, the paddle-like tool, SF3210, may also have been imported, although equally this prosaic functional item could have been fashioned from recycled timber which had entered Aberdeen in some other guise.

Thus, the boxwood handle, the maple bowl and the pine tankard stave provide firm evidence of trading links. Other items in the assemblage may also have been imported; the dendrochronological analysis of one of the barrels demonstrated that it had come from northern France (Section 4.1).

Industrial and domestic activity

Apart from the barrels used to line some of the wells, all the wooden artefacts had been discarded as debris in the contexts from which they have been retrieved, the wells and pits of the backland properties, and presumably relate to activities taking place locally. The assemblage divides very generally into domestic and industrial artefacts and can thus tell us something of the nature of the activities in the backlands.

All the wooden implements were retrieved from the Phase 2 pits and include shovels, scrapers, and paddle and bat-like tools suitable for beating, pounding and stirring. It is likely that the preparation of animal skins, and their subsequent tanning, and possibly dyeing (Section 4.5.1), took place on the site and all of these implements could have been employed in those industries. The shovels would have been ideal for shifting the ash, dung and oak bark used in the tanning process, while the scrapers and the bat-like tools might have been used for pounding and scouring the hides to remove the hair and flesh. The paddle-like tools could have been used for moving and lifting the leather in the tanning pits.

There is no evidence in the assemblage for equipment associated with more domestic activities, such as spinning and weaving, apart from a possible spindle whorl. One of the tools, SF3630, may have originally been used in flax processing, though there is no other evidence for this activity on the site, and it may have been reused.

One of the significant features of the assemblage is the presence of several very large platters. Whilst they could have had a domestic function (see above), these relatively unusual vessels may relate to particular activities taking place on the site; in the context of the tanning industry they could have been used, for example, for mixing dyes. The other turned vessels in the assemblage are small bowls and platters, more at home in a domestic context. However, there are none of the other items that one might anticipate in a medieval domestic assemblage – spoons and cups for instance. Some of the more simple bowls may represent the personal possessions of labourers working in the backlands, but there are items in the assemblage which must originally have been the possessions of more wealthy individuals. These include the unusual maple bowl which was intact when discarded, and the container represented by the yew handle; these may have come from wealthy households nearby.

A far greater range of coopered vessels, such as that retrieved from Perth High Street, might be expected in a domestic assemblage. Apart from the small tankard, all the coopered vessels represented at Bon Accord are large casks that have been subsequently cut down, possibly for use as water butts or well/cistern linings.

Overall, the assemblage appears to be more industrial than domestic in character, particularly in Phase 2. The more domestic elements of the assemblage could have arrived on the site as personal possessions or as debris from nearby households.

Summary

The wooden artefacts from Bon Accord constitute the second largest medieval assemblage to be found in Scotland. Much of it is utilitarian material, of forms commonly recorded in excavations of contemporary Scottish and European settlements, but it has also brought some rare and unusual items into the repertoire, namely the group of exceptionally large platters; the uniquely carved boxwood handle; the maple bowl and the composite shaft and handles of the grindstone.

Catalogue of wooden artefacts

SF   1513A (Figure 4.14)
Phase/Feature   Phase 2/Pit C019
Description: container handle
Species: Yew (*Taxus baccata*)
This is a splinter off a D-shaped handle which has probably broken off the lid of a container such as a box. The surviving fragment is 88mm long, but it would probably originally have been *c.* 200mm long, and 32mm high permitting the fingers of the hand to fit comfortably under the handle. The handle curves upwards from a foot that is 31mm long, delicately shaped at the end and notched at its junction with the curve. The upper and lower surfaces and one face survive, the other face having cleft off. The scar left by a very fine pin is visible in the cleft surface; it penetrates the foot and must have secured the handle to the box. The handle is 13mm thick at the foot tapering to 9mm at its highest point. The fragment is 12mm wide but if it is assumed that the pin was inserted centrally within the foot and that the handle broke off around the pin, then the handle would have been *c.* 24mm wide. It is very finely made, with very faint striae from knifemarks only visible under the microscope. The edge between the lower surface and face has been finely bevelled.

SF   1513B
Phase/Feature   Phase 2/Pit C019
Description: vessel stave?
Species: Oak (*Quercus* sp.)
Radially-split lath, 67mm long, 50mm wide and 6mm thick, regular in cross-section. One end has been chopped across at an angle, the other is broken.

SF   1546A   (Figure 4.3)
Phase/Feature   Phase 1/Pit C006
Description: bowl fragments
Species: Ash (*Fraxinus excelsior*)
Both fragments are ash and of similar appearance but they do not join. a) is a rim fragment with a simple, rounded profile, tapering from a wall thickness of 7mm to 3mm at the rim. It is from a vessel with an estimated diameter, at the rim of *c.* 250mm. b) is a large fragment, 100mm x 80mm across, from the base of a vessel. This fragment is 10mm thick at the junction between base and wall, tapering to 5mm in the centre of the base, and 6mm at the wall. On the base of b), just on the junction with the wall, a pentangle has been incised into the wood. Another, rather shaky line appears to curve around the pentangle, but this does not look so deliberate. The inner surface of the vessel is charred. Assuming that the two fragments belong to the same vessel, reconstruction suggests that it might have been approximately 60mm high.

SF   1546B (Figure 4.14)
Phase/Feature   Phase 1/Pit C006
Description: perforated disc
Species: Oak (*Quercus* sp.)
A circular disc 66mm in diameter and 12mm thick, fashioned from a radially-split lath. The edges parallel with the grain have not been curved but on the curved edges knife cuts are visible. It has a central perforation 7mm in diameter, which has been cut out from both faces.

SF   2583 (Figure 4.11)
Phase/Feature   Phase 1/Pit C001
Description: shaft and handles from grinding wheel
Species: Alder (*Alnus glutinosa*)
The shaft and attached handles have been shaped from a single length of alder roundwood, 1.03m in length. The shaft is 380mm long. The central portion, about 150mm wide, which fitted inside the grindstone, is roughly rectangular in cross-section, 63mm x 70mm; axemarks from shaping are visible on some of the faces and the bark edge has survived at one corner. The shaft reduces to a rounded cross-section 63mm in diameter at either end. Between the shaft and the handles is a section 90mm long and 37mm in diameter which bears wear grooves. Although both handles are roughly paddle-shaped, they differ in size and overall morphology. One is 250mm long, 63mm x 50mm at the thickest point, tapering to 33mm at its tip, which is damaged; this handle is more bulbous in cross-section than the other. The other handle is only 220mm long, 56mm x 40mm at the thickest point, tapering to 18mm at the tip, which is roughly squared off. Facets from shaping are visible along the edge of this handle.
The shaft and handles were found with a grindstone (also SF2583 – Section 4.3.2) still *in situ* around the shaft. The wooden shaft was roughly rectangular but it sat within a circular hole in the grindstone, which was also significantly larger than the shaft. The shaft therefore had to be secured firmly within the grindstone and this was done using oak wedges, also found *in situ*. Single wedges had been inserted down three faces on either

side of the grindstone; in two instances double wedges had been used. The wedges were very roughly fashioned from radially-split oak and varied in thickness from 7mm to 15mm.

SF   2623
Phase/Feature   Phase 1/Pit C001
Description: tip of pin
Species: Hazel (*Corylus avellana*)

Facetted tip, 37mm long, roughly rectangular in cross-section, 9mm x 6mm across. Converted from a larger roundwood stem.

SF   2842 (Figure 4.4)
Phase/Feature   Phase 2/Pit C022
Description: platter fragments
Species: Ash (*Fraxinus excelsior*)

The two fragments join and are part of a large, flat platter. The larger of the fragments retains part of the rim. There are turning marks on the upper and lower surfaces of the platter and, on the basis of their curvature and distance from the rim, it is estimated that the diameter of the platter would have been *c.* 630mm. The platter is 13mm thick. The rim is squared and is defined by a raised ridge 6mm below the rim on the upper surface. The upper surface is charred towards the centre of the platter.

SF   2931 (Figure 4.7)
Phase/Feature   Phase 2/Pit C022
Description: disc
Species: Oak (*Quercus* sp.)

A finely-made disc, cut from a radially-split lath, slightly oval, 60mm x 65mm. It is thicker in the middle, along the grain, tapering from 9mm at midpoint to 6mm at each side. It is too large to be a gaming counter, such as that found at 16–18 Netherkirkgate (Crone *et al.* 2001: 219; SF516). It is of similar size to the perforated disc, SF1546B, but it lacks the central hole and is more finely made. This could be the base for a small stave-built vessel.

SF   3010 (Figure 4.13)
Phase/Feature   Phase 2/Well C001
Description: board with lead sheet (SF3011) attached
Species   Oak (*Quercus* sp.)

Rectangular board, 172mm long and 103mm wide, fashioned from a radially-split plank. Although regular in width along its length, it bulges in thickness along its length from 15mm at one end to 22mm, then tapering to 8mm at the other end. Similarly it bulges in thickness across its width, from 7mm along the edge to 21mm in the middle. The thicker end has been deliberately shaped square but it is less clear whether the thinner end has also been deliberately shaped because it is fragmented and decayed. At the thinner end there are two, or possibly three, holes, at least 6mm in diameter.

There appears to be a circular depression on one face around the central hole. Five nails have been driven into one face, presumably to attach the lead sheet (SF3011), and on the other face is a nailhole which does not penetrate the thickness of the board.

SF   3061 (Figure 4.4)
Phase/Feature   Phase 1/Pit A026
Description: platter fragments
Species: Ash (*Fraxinus excelsior*)

The fragments are in poor condition and there are no clear joins. Nonetheless, it is possible to assemble the fragments to form a shallow platter that is *c.* 375mm in diameter. The vessel looks slightly oval but this may have been caused by shrinkage across the grain; there are traces of turning marks at the junction between wall and base so it is unlikely to have been deliberately oval.

The base is defined on two of the larger fragments by a shallow curved depression, and the rim survives on one fragment. The wall of the platter is 21mm thick at the junction between wall and base, narrowing to 19mm on the base and 11mm along the wall. It thickens to 14mm at the rim, which is rounded in profile with a projecting lip on the underside.

SF   3073 (Figure 4.14)
Phase/Feature   Phase 2/Pit C018
Description: toggle
Species: Hazel (*Corylus avellana*)

This object is complete, except for the very tip of one end. It is now 68mm in length but was probably originally 71mm long. It has been fashioned from a small roundwood stem and is oval in cross-section, 15mm x 20mm across at the widest point. The central shaft is 10mm long and 12mm in diameter. Each end is cone-shaped, tapering from 15mm x 20mm at the base to a fine point. Facets are visible on the tips but the surface is generally quite worn.

SF   3084B (Figure 4.10)
Phase/Feature   Phase 2/Pit C022
Description: socketed handle
Species: Hazel (*Corylus avellana*)

The handle has been fashioned from a length of roundwood and is complete. It is 92mm long and oval in cross-section, 19mm x 21mm. Knife facets are visible along the length of the handle and it flares out slightly at the end, which is bevelled. Along the edges of some of the facets, fine compression marks less than 1mm thick are visible, suggesting that the handle was once bound with leather or twine. At the other end is an eye-shaped socket, 5mm x 12mm and 45mm deep. A piece of fishbone was found protruding from the socket; x-rays have shown that it does not fill the socket and may have ended up there serendipitously.

SF 3085 (Figure 4.2)
Phase/Feature Phase 2/Pit C021
Description: turned bowl
Species: Alder (*Alnus glutinosa*)

Only half of the bowl survives. It is 66mm in diameter at the base, expanding to 169mm in diameter at the rim and stands 44mm high. The rim is a simple, rounded form, and the walls thicken from 3mm at that point to 13mm at the junction between wall and base. The undersurface of the base is slightly concave and faint chisel marks are visible from the removal of the turning waste. The inner surface of the bowl is covered in fine turning marks, while the exterior surface is decorated by a single groove just above the junction with the base, and a pair of grooves, 2mm apart, and some 12mm above the base.

SF 3113
Phase/Feature Phase 5/Well A001
Description: cant stave
Species: Oak (*Quercus* sp.)

The cant stave is the curved outermost stave from a lid/ base for a stave-built vessel, fashioned from a radially-split board. The lid/base is 25mm thick and would have been 790mm in diameter. The curved edge has an asymmetric bevel. Along the straight, inner edge are two pegholes 10mm in diameter, with oak dowels still *in situ*; these would have secured the stave to the adjoining stave.

SF No: 3134A (Figure 4.15)
Phase/Feature Phase 1/Pit A027
Description: socketed handle
Species: Box (*Buxus sempervirens*)

The handle has been fashioned out of a length of roundwood; the pith lies to one side on the end of the handle. The handle is complete; it is 101mm long and rectangular in cross-section, 16mm x 30mm across at each end. The handle is 'bone-shaped', tapering in from each end towards the middle where it is only 27mm wide; the corners are rounded and it sits very comfortably in the hand. The tang socket is 11mm wide, 3mm thick and 53mm deep.

The surfaces on the lower half of the handle are eroded but the wide faces towards the socketed end are covered in finely-incised decoration (Section 4.2.1.1).

SF No: 3134B (Figure 4.10)
Phase/Feature Phase 1/Pit A027
Description: handle?
Species: Willow (*Salix* sp.)

This possible handle has been fashioned from a short length of roundwood, which has been pared vigorously down its length, creating six large facets and making the handle hexagonal in cross-section. The handle is now 120mm in length but the 'working' end is broken and incomplete; it is 28mm x 33mm across. The end of the handle has been shaped flat and knifemark facets are still visible on that surface. The handle tapers from the end towards the middle, then expands out before tapering again towards the working end. It fits comfortably in the hand. There are narrow striae across the edge of one of the facets which may have been caused by a binding around the handle. A small nail had been inserted radially near the 'working' end of the handle.

SF 3135A
Phase/Feature Phase 2/Pit C021
Description: pin/peg
Species: Hazel (*Corylus avellana*)

This pin has been fashioned from a quarter stem of roundwood. It is 117mm long but both ends are broken. It is rectangular in cross-section at one end, 8mm x 13mm, tapering to a more rounded point, 7mm across. There are facets along its length.

SF 3185 (Figure 4.5)
Phase/Feature Phase 2/Pit C025
Description: lid with handle
Species: Alder (*Alnus glutinosa*)

The lid, or cover, is complete. It has been spindle-turned from a slice cut across a small branch or stem, in such a way that the pith lies at the centre of the lid; as a consequence the lid has cracked radially along the rays. The lid is 112mm in diameter and 55mm in height. It is domed in profile, with a centrally-placed circular handle 32mm in diameter and 20mm high. There are decorative grooves around the perimeter of the lid and mid-way across the surface. The lid has a hollow interior and a flanged rim which would have sat within the walls of a vessel with an interior diameter of 96mm.

SF 3210 (Figure 4.9)
Phase/Feature Phase 2/Pit C025
Description: paddle-shaped tool
Species: Scots pine (*Pinus sylvestris*)

This paddle-shaped tool has been fashioned from a chord cleft off the trunk of a tree. In cross-section it is flat on one side and convex on the other, tapering from 13mm thick in the centre to 7mm at each edge. As the growth rings curve away from the convex surface and do not lie concentric with it this shape must be a deliberate part of the design. Shallow axe facets are visible on the convex face. The tool is 550mm long overall and consists of an oval blade 410mm long which tapers to a handle, oval in cross-section, 42mm x 25mm. The handle is broken and only a stump 140mm long survives. The lower half of the convex face and the very tip of the flat face are charred.

SF 3292 (Figure 4.14)
Phase/Feature Phase 2/Pit C025
Description: trenail, or bung
Species: Hazel (*Corylus avellana*)

This object has been whittled from a length of roundwood; the bark is still *in situ* around the head. It has a flat head that is 9mm deep and below this the shaft tapers towards the tip, which is missing. It is 20mm in diameter at the head but at the tip is more oval in cross-section, 15mm across.

SF   3324 (Figure 4.7)
Phase/Feature   Phase 2/Pit C033
Description: vessel stave
Species: Scots pine (*Pinus sylvestris*)

The stave is complete except for some damage to one corner at its base. It is 133mm long and 31mm wide, regular in width down its length. It varies in thickness from 4mm to 6mm across its width. Some 9mm above the base is a groove, 4mm wide and 4mm deep, for the base of the vessel. On the basis of a curvature at the base it is estimated that the parent vessel may have been between 110mm and 120mm in diameter. There is no evidence of the compression bands indicative of binding on the external surface of the stave.

SF   3337 (Figure 4.12)
Phase/Feature   Phase 2/Pit C037
Description: board with handles
Species: Oak (*Quercus* sp.)

This object has been fashioned from a radially-split board 15mm thick. The surfaces have not been dressed and still bear the ridges caused by cleaving. It is rectangular in shape, 190mm wide and 440mm long, with rectangular 'handles' projecting out from each end. The most complete handle is 80mm long and 60mm wide and is perforated by three holes, two 9mm in diameter and one 16mm in diameter, which are laid out in irregular fashion. The other handle is broken, but the chord of a hole, at least 15mm in diameter is visible. The function of this object is unknown.

SF   3350A (Figure 4.14)
Phase/Feature   Phase 2/Pit C025
Description: wedge
Species: Alder (*Alnus glutinosa*)

A complete wedge, fashioned from a quarter-stem. It is 117mm in length and is square in cross-section, tapering from 32mm x 32mm to a chisel point 8mm across. The top is squared flat and there is possible wear damage down one edge.

SF   3359 (Figure 4.8)
Phase/Feature   Phase 2/Pit C025
Description: composite shovel blade
Species: Oak (*Quercus* sp.)

This composite shovel blade has been fashioned from a radially-split board. It is 288mm in length overall, 220mm wide and 15mm thick. The blade is straight-sided with rounded corners at the base, while the shoulders taper towards the handle socket, the upper edge of which is missing. One face is completely flat

while on the other face the edges are all bevelled. The handle socket is roughly square, *c.* 55mm wide and up to 50mm deep. The socket is angled downwards towards the bevelled face, which would suggest that the flat face was the working face, the shaft of the handle supporting the blade from behind. The socket lies asymmetric to the centre line of the shovel; this may be deliberate (although see design of other shovels, e.g. SF3361) or it might be that a splinter of wood has broken off along one edge and has simply been repaired by bevelling the broken edge.

SF   3361 (Figure 4.8)
Phase/Feature   Phase 2/Pit C025
Description: composite shovel blade
Species: Oak (*Quercus* sp.)

This composite blade has been fashioned from a radially-split board and is complete, although now in two pieces. It is 356mm long, 258mm at its widest point, and it tapers in thickness from 18mm at the top to 11mm at the bottom of the blade. It is roughly teardrop-shaped with a flattened base to the blade. One face is completely flat while on the other face all the edges are bevelled. The handle socket lies some 110mm below the top of the spade; it is 70mm deep and tapers in width from 50mm at the base to a rounded top, some 19mm across. Like SF3359 the socket is angled downwards towards the bevelled face, which would suggest that the flat face was the working face, the shaft of the handle supporting the blade from behind. Along the centre line of the shovel are three pegholes, two above the handle socket and one below, presumably for fixing the handle in place. From top to bottom the diameters of the holes are 10mm, 12mm and 6mm. The two uppermost holes are angled down towards the flat face of the spade. A possibly unfinished hole, 8mm in diameter, lies along one edge of the spade.

SF   3377
Phase/Feature   Phase 5/Well A001
Description: cant stave
Species: Oak (*Quercus* sp.)

The curved outer stave from a lid/base, fashioned from a radially-split board, very decayed around the outer edge. The lid/base is 20mm thick and would have been about 800mm in diameter. The curved edge has an asymmetric bevel which is variable in width along the edge. Along the straight, inner edge are two pegholes, with oak dowels, 8mm in diameter, still *in situ*. The lid may latterly have been used as a work surface, either on or off the vessel; the flat unbevelled face bears multiple cutmarks.

SF   3417 (Figure 4.9)
Phase/Feature   Phase 2/Pit C025
Description: bat-like tool
Species: Hazel (*Corylus avellana*)

This tool has been fashioned from a chord cleft off a trunk and is shaped like a cricket bat. It is 420mm in length but the handle has broken off. The blade of the tool is roughly 360mm long and the shoulders taper, slightly asymmetrically, to a rectangular handle 50mm wide and 20mm thick. The blade is a very regular 28mm in thickness from shoulders to tip but tapers very slightly in width from 100mm just below the shoulder to 90mm at the tip. All the edges of the tool are rounded, and there is a very slight curvature along the length, although this could be post-depositional. The surface around the handle and shoulders is smooth but over the rest of the blade it is pitted and rough, presumably reflecting use wear.

SF   3421A (Figure 4.14)
Phase/Feature   Phase 2/Pit C025
Description: wedge?
Species: Holly (*Ilex aquifolium*)

This object looks like a wedge but is more carefully made than other wedges from the site. It is rectangular in cross-section, 25mm x 40mm across, the sides curving down towards a chisel edge which runs across the width of the object. It is 109mm long and has been fashioned from a quarter-stem; the 'back' is cleft but the other three sides have been neatly curved. The top has been pared roughly flat; knife facets are visible.

SF   3421B (Figure 4.14)
Phase/Feature   Phase 2/Pit C025
Description: wedge?
Species: Alder (*Alnus glutinosa*)

This wedge is 113mm long and has been fashioned from a half-stem. It is incomplete, the chisel edge having broken off. It tapers from a roughly rectangular cross-section at the top, which measures 41mm x 36mm x 28mm, to a chisel edge which lies parallel with one of the short sides. The top has been squared off.

SF   3444
Phase/Feature   Phase 2/Pit C025
Description: cant stave
Species: Oak (*Quercus* sp.)

The curved outer stave from a lid/base, fashioned from a radially-split board. The lid/base is 27mm thick and would have been about 760mm in diameter. The curved edge is bevelled on one face. There are no pegholes along the inner edge.

SF   3476 (Figure 4.14)
Phase/Feature   Phase 2/Pit C025
Description: bung?
Species: Willow (*Salix* sp.)

A bung, fashioned from a length of roundwood, and complete. It is 60mm long and slightly oval in cross-section, 32mm x 35mm. The head is 21mm deep and below this it tapers symmetrically to a centrally positioned point. The top of the head is slightly domed;

radial knifemarks are visible around a tuft in the centre where it was severed from the stem. The outer surface of the head is charred; as the charring is limited to this area this suggests that the bung was burnt while still *in situ* in a vessel.

SF   3558 (Figure 4.12)
Phase/Feature   Phase 2/Pit C025
Description: curved panel
Species: Oak (*Quercus* sp.)

This object has been fashioned from a radially-split board 15mm thick; it is regular in thickness along its entire length. It is at least 455mm long but is broken at one end. The complete end is neatly squared and 90mm wide. The object expands to 132mm at the broken end and is curved along both edges. A small hole, 6mm in diameter, perforates the board and lies some 10mm in from the curved 'outer' edge. The function of this object is unknown but it could be a panel from a larger composite object.

SF   3562 (Figure 4.6)
Phase/Feature   Phase 2/Pit C025
Description: vessel stave
Species: Oak (*Quercus* sp.)

A vessel stave, broken off at the croze groove at one end, and chopped off at a slight angle at the other. The remaining length is 720mm and it tapers from 130mm at one end to 104mm at the other. A hole, 45mm in diameter, has been chopped in half at the wider end suggesting that although there is no sign of a belly it probably came from a cut-down barrel rather than a tub. A bung hole was often positioned at the pitch or belly to allow air into the cask as liquid was decanted. Some 230mm below the chopped end is another hole, 11mm in diameter, and to one side of the large hole is a small hole, 6mm in diameter, with a peg of hazel roundwood still *in situ*.

SF   3564 (Figure 4.6)
Phase/Feature   Phase 2/Pit C025
Description: vessel stave
Species: Oak (*Quercus* sp.)

A stave, 730mm in length and tapering very slightly in width from 68mm at the top to 55mm at the bottom. The upper end is neatly squared and chamfered and, as there is no evidence of a belly, this may have come from a tub. However, it remains possible that it has come from a cut-down barrel. The croze groove lies some 40mm above the base and the inner surface of the upper end is chamfered, possibly for the insertion of a lid. There are two holes; 90mm below the upper end and close to one edge is a hole, 7mm in diameter, with a peg still *in situ*, while halfway down and in the middle of the stave is the second hole, 6mm in diameter.

SF   3567 (Figure 4.3)
Phase/Feature   Phase 2/Pit C025

Description: turned bowl
Species: Field maple (*Acer campestre*)
This is a footed dish with a central cup, which measures 193mm by 220mm at the rim. Its slightly oval shape may be the result of using green, i.e. unseasoned, wood for turning, the bowl distorting along the grain as the wood dried out (Morris 2000: 2125). It varies in height from 30mm to 42mm but it is buckled and distorted as a result of post-depositional pressures and its original height was probably about 32mm. The dish rises from the foot, 84mm in diameter and 10mm high. Within the centre of the dish is a cup-shaped depression which has been hollowed out of the body of the foot. This cup is 77mm x 70mm and it has a raised rim 4mm wide and which stands 8mm above the upper surface of the dish; the cup is 18mm deep from rim to base. In the centre of the base of the cup is a rough raised circular patch where the turning core has been cut out. The walls of the dish are 8mm thick but taper to a simple rounded rim 2–3mm thick. There is a decorative groove on the upper surface of the dish some 5mm inside the rim but otherwise the upper surface is remarkably smooth and free of turning marks. The surfaces of the dish may have been polished or burnished but there are also fine cutmarks, presumably from use, over the upper surface. Turning marks are visible on the undersurface of the dish and there are also deeper grooves 35mm in from the rim and around the base and top of the foot. The base of the foot is slightly concave and in the centre of the foot is an impression that resembles a horseshoe, 14mm across. An identical impression is visible on the underside of the dish. This may be an owner's or maker's mark.

SF   3618
Phase/Feature   Phase 1–2/Gully C001
Description: vessel stave?
Species: Oak (*Quercus* sp.)
This is a length of radially-split lath, both ends of which are broken; the surviving length is 145mm. It is regular in width (48mm) and thickness (6mm) and could be a stave from a small vessel.

SF No: 3630 (Figure 4.9)
Phase/Feature   Phase 2/Pit C024
Description: scutching knife?
Species: Oak (*Quercus* sp.)
This tool has been fashioned from a radially-split board and is complete. It is 450mm long and consists of a knife-shaped blade 270mm long and 76mm at its widest, extending from an offset handle. The blade is 9mm thick at the tip and increases in thickness towards the junction with the handle, where it is 16mm thick. The handle is rectangular in cross-section, 34mm by 16–20mm; it expands slightly to form a bulbous end. The edges of the blade are squared; there are no knife-edges. Knife-cuts from shaping are visible on both faces of the blade and both faces are also slightly charred. A

hole, 11mm in diameter, lies close to the curved 'lower' edge of the blade; beyond this the tip is damaged.

SF   3631 (Figure 4.12)
Phase/Feature   Phase 2/Pit C024
Description: furniture component?
Species: Oak (*Quercus* sp.)
This is a small square beam fashioned from a radially-split piece. It may have broken off a larger timber; three of the faces have been dressed but one face is cleft and there is an incomplete hole, 9mm in diameter at one end. It is now 430mm long and 35mm by 30mm square. One end is broken while the other has been squared. The cleft face is pierced by two holes, both 9mm in diameter, neither of which fully pierce the thickness of the beam. One of the holes lies to one side of a shallow notch which is 11mm deep with a sloping base. The incomplete hole penetrates the beam at right angles to the other holes. The direction of the holes suggests joints at right angles to the beam and this, together with the small dimensions of the beam suggest that it might be a component of furniture or loom.

SF   3633C
Phase/Feature   Phase 2/Pit C024
Description: vessel stave
Species: Oak (*Quercus* sp.)
A vessel stave, 590mm long and 130mm wide, in very poor condition. The croze groove is just visible at the base. The surviving length of the stave suggests that it may have come from a cut-down barrel but the upper end is too decayed for this to be certain.

SF   3633D
Phase/Feature   Phase 2/Pit C024
Description: vessel stave
Species: Oak (*Quercus* sp.)
A vessel stave, 730mm long and tapering in width from 135mm at the top to 12mm at the base. The croze groove lies 35mm above the base and the upper end has been chopped off at an oblique angle. This probably came from a cut-down barrel.

SF   3672
Phase/Feature   Phase 2/Pit C025
Description: vessel stave
Species: Oak (*Quercus* sp.)
An incomplete vessel stave, damaged down one edge and broken at both ends. It is 130mm wide and 14mm thick. One side of the croze groove survives at one end, the end of the stave having broken off at this point. There are three holes in a row down the length of the stave, all 10mm in diameter. A peg is still *in situ* in one hole.

SF   3681 (Figure 4.2)
Phase/Feature   Phase 2/Pit C025
Description: turned bowl

Species: Alder (*Alnus glutinosa*)

A finely-made bowl in two parts which join, although fragments are missing. It is 127mm in diameter at the outer rim and stands 34mm high. It rises from a base 60mm in diameter which has a tiny pedestal, 2mm high. The walls are 8mm thick, narrowing to 2mm at the outer rim. The rim itself is thin and flat and projects out from the walls for 20mm; it is decorated by two pronounced ridges 2mm wide, one defining the outer edge and one defining the inner edge. Fine turning marks are visible on all the uppermost surfaces, but in the bottom of the bowl is a roughly circular area within which there are tiny gouge marks, 2–3mm wide, from where the turning waste has been removed. The base is more roughly finished but the exterior walls of the bowl are also finely finished. The sharpness of the gouge marks and turning marks suggests that this bowl may not have been used.

SF   3693 (Figure 4.8)
Phase/Feature   Phase 2/Pit C025
Description: composite shovel blade
Species: Oak (*Quercus* sp.)

A composite shovel blade in two fragments, damaged above the handle socket and along one edge. The shovel is rectangular in shape and at least 360mm long and some 200mm wide. The blade is 18mm thick, tapering to 14mm at the top, and unlike the other examples (3359b/3361b and 3359a/3361a) its edges are chamfered both front and back. The shape of the handle socket mimics the shape of the blade; it is 52mm wide and 65mm deep. A single hole, 12mm in diameter penetrates the thickness of the spade just above the handle socket; it is angled in the same direction as the socket.

SF   3710A
Phase/Feature   Phase 2/Spread C043
Description: platter fragment
Species: Ash (*Fraxinus excelsior*)

A small fragment of vessel only 114mm long and 45mm wide, from the junction between base and wall. The base is 5mm thick while the wall is 9mm thick. The shallow angle between base and wall suggests a plate. The curvature of the junction indicates a diameter of 160mm at the base and, as the wall extends some 35mm beyond the junction, the plate must have been at least 230mm in diameter at the rim.

SF   3713
Phase/Feature   Phase 2/Pit C029
Description: bat-like tool?
Species: Oak (*Quercus* sp.)

Fashioned from a radially-split board, the object is 455mm long and tapers towards one end in both width (from 71mm to 63mm) and thickness (from 23mm to 8mm). There is no handle but the narrower end can be easily grasped. All the edges are rounded.

SF   3737 (Figure 4.6)
Phase/Feature   Phase 2/Pit C033
Description: vessel stave
Species: Oak (*Quercus* sp.)

A vessel stave, 720mm long, tapering from 116mm in width at one end to 90mm at the base. The croze groove sits 40mm above the base and below the groove are three holes drilled downwards from exterior to interior. A possible peg, fashioned from a quarter-stem of hazel (*Corylus avellana*) was found in one of the holes. As these holes probably secured strengthening battens across the head of the vessel, this was probably a stave from a cut-down barrel rather than a tub. The interior surface at the upper end is slightly chamfered.

SF   3739
Phase/Feature   Phase 2/Pit C033
Description: vessel stave
Species: Oak (*Quercus* sp.)

A vessel stave of heavy dimensions. It is 730mm long, tapers from 136mm to 118mm in width and from 22mm to 15mm in thickness. The croze groove lies 35mm above the base. The upper end has been chopped off at an angle so it may have come from a cut-down barrel rather than a tub, although there is no evidence of a belly on the surviving length.

SF   3743 (Figure 4.4)
Phase/Feature   Phase 1/Pit A030
Description: platter fragments
Species: Ash (*Fraxinus excelsior*)

This vessel has dried out and distorted since its retrieval. Photographs of it *in situ* (Figure 2.11) show a shallow platter with thick walls. It is approximately 370mm in diameter at the rim and is at least 50mm high. The walls are up to 14mm thick and end in a flat rim. The rim projects out to form small flat handles on either side. Small concave facets from an axe or knife are visible over the undersurface suggesting that the vessel was carved rather than turned. The vessel had cracked in half during its lifetime and it had been repaired; three sets of paired slots span the crack, the corrosion products of the metal staples visible around the slots, which are 9mm wide.

SF   3745 (Figure 4.6)
Phase/Feature   Phase 1/Pit A030
Description: barrel stave
Species: Oak (*Quercus* sp.)

This is a stave from a small barrel. The surviving length of the stave is 490mm but it has broken off at the croze groove at each end; assuming that the groove sat *c.* 20mm above each end, the original height of the barrel may have been *c.* 530mm. The stave is a very regular 10mm in thickness and is 52mm wide at the belly, tapering to 40mm at each end.

SF   3758A
Phase/Feature   Phase 1/Pit A030
Description: trenail, or bung
Species: Willow (*Salix* sp.)

The trenail, or bung, has been fashioned from a radially-split lath and is 90mm long. The head has been pared to an oval cross-section, 21mm x 30mm across, and the top has been shaped flat; knifemarks are also visible on the upper surface. The head is 20mm deep and below that the shaft tapers to a more rounded point, 16mm in diameter.

SF   3758C
Phase/Feature   Phase 1/Pit A030
Description: bale pin?
Species: Willow (*Salix* sp.)

A small pin or peg, the upper part of which is broken off, leaving a surviving length of 52mm. It has been radially split from a small length of roundwood and is triangular in cross-section, 6mm across, tapering to a fine point.

SF   3767
Phase/Feature   Phase 2/Pit C026
Description: platter fragments
Species: Ash (*Fraxinus excelsior*)

There are eight eroded fragments of a vessel, six of which join together to form a piece 90mm by 160mm. The fragments are 14mm thick, suggesting a large vessel but there is nothing in the curvature of the assembled fragments to suggest whether it is a bowl or platter.

SF   3825 (Figure 4.13)
Phase/Feature   Phase 2/Pit C025
Description: pierced lath
Species: Oak (*Quercus* sp.)

This object has been fashioned from a radially-split lath. Both ends are damaged but the surviving length is 282mm. It is 78mm wide and maintains a regular width down its length. In cross-section it is flat on one face while the edges are bevelled on the other. Along each edge are drilled holes set in approximately 5mm from the edge. Along the more complete edge there are nine holes, with six holes on the other. These do not lie symmetrically across from each other; there is no obvious patterning to their positioning. Most of the holes are 2.5–3mm in diameter but one is 4.5mm. Wooden pins are still *in situ* in nine of the holes. There is no evidence of any compression around or between the holes.

SF   3840 (Figure 4.4)
Phase/Feature   Phase 2/Pit C025
Description: platter fragments
Species: Ash (*Fraxinus excelsior*)

Nine fragments join together to form part of the wall of a large platter with an estimated diameter of 600mm. The vessel was at least 130mm high and possibly as much

as 187mm. It has a flat, square rim (17mm thick) below which is a collar, 47mm deep. Below this collar the walls of the vessel are 9 to 10mm thick. Crude turning marks are visible on the inner surface and there are patches of charring on the exterior.

SF   3884 (Figure 4.2)
Phase/Feature   Phase 2/Pit C025
Description: turned bowl
Species: Ash (*Fraxinus excelsior*)

About a third of this turned bowl is missing and there is some distortion to its shape. It is 180mm in diameter at the rim and narrows to 83mm in diameter at the base, and stands some 66mm in height. It is quite regular in thickness, being 9mm at the centre of the base, expanding to 11mm up the walls and finally tapering to 5mm at the simple, rounded rim. A groove 4mm below the rim is the only decorative feature. The base is slightly convex and bears fine knifemarks, suggesting the bowl had been turned upside down and used as a chopping board. A shallow, plectrum-shaped facet on the exterior surface is probably from the initial axe-dressing to shape the roughout (Morris 2000: 2133).

The bowl has probably been repaired during its life; along the broken edge are two small holes, 1.5–2mm in diameter and 11mm apart. However, there is no evidence of wear or compression around the holes, as one might expect had there been rivets through them.

SF   3911B (Figure 4.10)
Phase/Feature   Phase 2/Pit C025
Description: Scraper tool?
Species: Oak (*Quercus* sp.)

This tool has been fashioned from a radially-split board and appears to be complete. In shape it is a trapezium, the parallel edges forming the handle and blade of the tool. The tool is 65mm wide along the handle edge and expands to 300mm along the blade edge; it also tapers in thickness from 20mm at the handle to 3mm at the blade. The shoulders of the tool are also tapered along the edges. Just below and at either end of the handle are two drilled holes, one 11mm in diameter and the other tapering from 15mm to 11mm; the smaller hole has an oak peg *in situ*. The holes lie 95mm apart. The tool fits snugly between palm and thumb, and the pegs may have been used to secure a leather strap behind which the hand slotted.

SF   3911C (Figure 4.9)
Phase/Feature   Phase 2/Pit C025
Description: knife-like tool/scraper?
Species: Oak (*Quercus* sp.)

This tool has been fashioned from a chord, possibly split off a larger radially-split board. It is 140mm long but is broken at one end. It is 40mm wide at the broken end but expands slightly to a maximum width of 42mm. It is knife-shaped, the 'upper' edge flatter than the 'lower', which curves upwards to meet at a rounded point. In cross-section it is flat on one face while the other is convex, tapering towards either edge from a maximum thickness of 9mm at midpoint.

SF   3935 (Figure 4.2)
Phase/Feature   Phase 2/Pit C025
Description: turned bowl fragments
Species: Ash (*Fraxinus excelsior*)

Of the five surviving fragments of this turned bowl, four fit together. The fifth fragment is the largest and includes a complete profile from rim to base. The bowl has an estimated diameter of 202mm at the rim, flaring up from a rounded base, approximately 90mm in diameter. It stands 70mm high. The walls are 9mm at their thickest point, tapering to 4mm on the base and 4mm at the rim. The rim has a simple, rounded profile, defined by a groove on the interior, some 6mm below the rim.

SF   4012 (Figure 4.3)
Phase/Feature   Phase 2/Pit C032
Description: turned bowl
Species: Alder (*Alnus glutinosa*)

This is a footed bowl with a distinct carination at the junction between base and wall. It survives in two pieces. It is 220mm in diameter at the rim, and 102mm at the base. The base is a raised foot, 6mm high and the overall height of the bowl is 45mm. Within the centre of the bowl is a depression which sits over the foot and is 90mm in diameter and 3mm deep. The walls of the bowl are 10mm thick at the junction with the base, narrowing to 6mm at the rim, which is distinguished from the walls by a raised ridge 6mm deep. There are fine cutmarks all over the upper surface of the bowl, possibly use wear. A single axemark is visible on the undersurface, possibly from the initial shaping of the roughout (Morris 2000: 2133).

SF   4099 (Figure 4.10)
Phase/Feature   Phase 2/Pit C032
Description: scraper tool?
Species: Oak (*Quercus* sp.)

This tool has been fashioned from a radially-split board. It is a rough triangular shape, with a flat 'working' edge between two curved sides which meet at a point. It is 142mm long, from point to flat edge, and 121mm at its widest between the two curved sides. It is 7mm thick and all the edges are bevelled on one face, while the other face is flat to the edge. Just below the pointed end are two holes, one immediately above the other. The upper is 6mm in diameter, the lower is 4mm; there are possible compression marks leading from the upper hole to one edge, possibly formed by a strap or handle. Above the flat edge are two small holes, 2mm and 4mm in diameter which also pierce the tool and lie 11mm apart. There may be a third hole on the same alignment but this part of the tool is damaged.

SF   4294 (Figure 4.2)
Phase/Feature   Phase 4/Pit C064
Description: turned bowl fragments
Species: Willow (*Salix* sp.)

All that remains of this bowl are 11 major fragments, of which three fit together and include both rim and base. Another five fragments, including a rim, join together but this composite piece has been distorted. The bowl has an open, rounded profile expanding from a diameter of 54mm at the base to 173mm in diameter at the rim. The vessel stands 51mm high. The walls are 8mm thick at the rim and thicken to 9mm. Little survives of the base but it appears to be flat and is 7mm thick. The figuring of the grain is very pronounced.

SF   4584 (Figure 4.5)
Phase/Feature   Phase 1/Pit C015
Description: turning waste?
Species: Alder (*Alnus glutinosa*)

These two conjoining fragments are from a disc which would have been *c.* 170mm in diameter. The disc is 17mm high around the circumference and 11mm towards the centre; both faces are concave, although one is deeper than the other. There is a distinct ridge, 2mm wide, around the edge of the disc on the most concave face. The pith of the branch would have lain at the centre of the disc, the growth-rings lying concentric with the edge, as one might expect with lathe-turning waste. However, there is no evidence of turning marks or gouge marks where it was separated from the finished vessel.

SF No: 5034
Phase/Feature   Phase 2–3/Well A002
Description: cant stave
Species: Oak (*Quercus* sp.)

The curved outer stave from a lid/base, fashioned from a radially-split board. The lid/base is 18mm thick and would have been about 900mm in diameter. The curved edge is bevelled on both faces. There are no pegholes along the inner edge of the stave.

Well C001 (Phase 2); barrel (Figures 2.35 & 2.37–2.40, Chapter 2)
Phase/Feature   Phase 2/Well C001
Description: barrel
Species: Oak (*Quercus* sp.)

This complete barrel is 1.4m high, with a diameter of 0.93m at the belly and of 0.82m at either end. It is made from 23 radially-split oak staves, bound top and bottom by 24 hoops of split withies organised in groups of five, four and three above the pitch and three, four and five below. The hoops are mainly hazel with some willow; where they overlap they have been bound with thin strips of willow, the bindings extending for up to 300mm along the hoops. The staves are about 10mm thick but are variable in width, maximum width at the pitch varying from 85mm to 180mm. Several of the

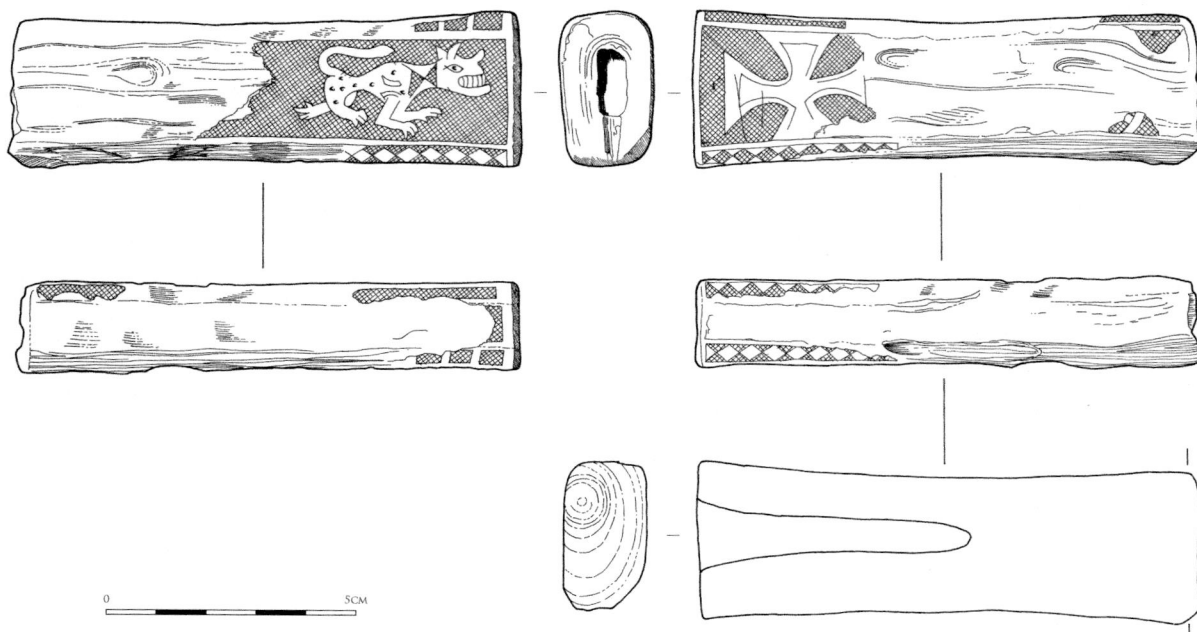

Figure 4.15 Decorated wooden handle; SF3134A

staves have small holes, 6mm to 9mm in diameter, at about the level of the pitch with pegs still *in situ*. There are much larger holes in two staves on opposite sides of the barrel, one 24mm and the other 45mm in diameter. These were probably bung holes to allow air into the barrel as liquid was decanted out through a vent hole in one head.

The croze groove lies 35mm in from each end of the barrel. Just below the groove, at each end, are groups of six pegholes spread across adjoining pairs of staves which lie diametrically across from each other (Figure 4.6). These pegholes were 10mm in diameter and angled down towards the interior of the barrel. These holes probably secured strengthening battens across the head of the barrel.

Well A001 (Phase 5); barrel (Figure 2.65, Chapter 2)
Phase/Feature   Phase 5/Well A001
Description: barrel
Species: Oak (*Quercus* sp.)
The upper ends of the staves of this vessel are decayed and they only survive to a maximum height of 0.64m; it is not immediately evident whether this is a barrel that has been cut in half to line the well or whether a tub has been used. The vessel consists of 19 staves and has a diameter at the base of 0.67m and of 0.76m at the top; if it is a cut-down barrel then it has been cut off below the belly. The staves vary little in width, from 120mm to 136mm at the top, and in thickness from 8mm to 15m. The vessel is bound by 11 hoops of split withies organised in groups of four, three and four. A mixture of species has been used for the hoops, primarily hazel

and willow but an oak and an alder hoop are also present. The hoops have been bound with thin strips of willow, the bindings extending up to 300mm along the hoops and positioned at exactly the same point on the circumference of the vessel. One stave bears three holes, 6mm to 8mm in diameter, two with pegs still *in situ*, while another stave has one hole with an oak peg also *in situ*.

The croze groove lies 35mm in from the end of the barrel, and on pairs of adjoining staves there are rows of 12 pegholes just below the groove. The paired staves bearing these holes lie diametrically across from each other. As these holes probably secured strengthening battens across the head of the vessel, it suggests that this was a cut-down barrel rather than a tub.

4.2.1.1 Decorated wooden handle
Mark Hall

The decoration on this handle (SF3134A) is both fascinating and unique (Figure 4.15). Unfortunately, it is incomplete. It survives best at the bottom end of the handle, i.e. the blade-end. It comprises two main elements – a Maltese style cross and a monstrous-looking hybrid, quadruped creature on the opposing broad faces. It seems likely that the worn part of the upper and middle handle may have carried related motifs. These motifs are set against a background pattern that survives on much of the handle; when new it would have covered the whole handle. It consists of a carefully executed cross-hatch pattern, which on the narrow faces is worked into contrasting chevron patterns and on one narrow face a hint of a pattern of squares with blank separators. The cross-hatching is very typical of that which is commonly seen on a range of widely-available metalwork, generally lead alloy/pewter pilgrimage souvenirs and secular badges (for example Spencer 1998; Van Beuningen and Koldeweij 1993; Van Beuningen *et al.* 2001). At one point the cross-hatching has gone awry, as two linked, triangular cells of the pattern have been incised on the beast's neck. The cross-hatching and the presumed error may support the idea that the handle was decorated by a junior craftsman, perhaps one proficient across more than one craft operation. The end of the handle is roughly finished and may suggest it terminated in a metalwork end-cap.

The uniqueness of the handle lies in the style of its decoration and the choice of motifs it exhibits. Boxwood knife handles tend to be either very plain (e.g. Cowgill *et al.* 1987: cat. 103, 115 & 133) or highly decorative, such as a late 15th–early 16th century English example depicting the Tree of Jesse (Robinson 2008: 122–23). This latter example demonstrates how boxwood lends itself to detailed carving, as does a 14th century English gittern in the British Museum (Cherry 1991b: 7–11) and the range of devotional items (including pomanders, rosary beads and miniature altars) made in the Low Countries and Germany (Russell 1999). The decoration of the Bon Accord handle occupies a middle ground between these two approaches in being detailed and all-over but incised rather than carved in deep relief.

With regard to its two main motifs, the choice of a Maltese cross is not unusual; it occurs widely in medieval art, part of the range of cross images that were used to reinforce other images and add an amuletic quality deriving from the perceived power of the rood, the most ubiquitous of Christian cults (Hall 2007: 77–83, and see Figure 4.16 for a more elaborate version of the cross against a cross-hatched background on the reverse of a St John the Baptist pilgrimage badge). The deployment of a cross on a knife handle, however, is not particularly common and neither is the curious hybrid creature on the opposite face.

The overall body-shape, legs and tail (especially its swish) of the beast reflect those of a lion or panther (though the tail could also be attributed to a horse or unicorn), whilst the heavy-set head, with its single, short horn reflects a rhinoceros. The spots on the body could relate to either animal. Isidore of Seville and the later bestiary tradition cite both lions/lionesses and panthers as being spotted (Barney *et al.* 2006: 251–52; Baxter 1998: 49–50). The tough hide of the rhinoceros is not so much spotted as dimpled, a feature well captured in Dürer's famous engraving made in 1515 (Hahn 2003: 52), and on other contemporary drawings (Bedini 1997: 122 fig. 26). Rhinoceroses were no strangers to the

Figure 4.16 Upper: The reverse of a St John the Baptist pilgrim badge from Amiens Cathedral, bearing an equal-armed cross with expanded terminals against a cross-hatched background. Courtesy Perth Museum & Art Gallery; Lower: A monstrous monocerus from the pages of the *Bestaire of Philippe de Thaon* (Merton College Library MS. 249, Folio 3r), a 13th century work produced in England. Copyright - The Warden and Fellows of Merton College, Oxford.

menageries of Roman emperors (*ibid,* 115) but they were rare indeed in medieval European menageries, which is why the Indian example presented as a gift first to the king of Portugal and then to Pope Leo X in the early 16th century excited such interest across Europe (*ibid,* 111–36). Nonetheless, stories (and classical images) of rhinoceroses, if not the beasts themselves, did circulate and in bestiaries these became the monocerus (in some bestiaries the monocerus and the unicorn were treated as the same, following the earlier accounts of both Pliny the Elder and Isidore of Seville, who gives rhinoceros as a Greek word meaning 'with horn in nose'; Figure 4.16 and see other unicorn and monocerus entries in the *Medieval Bestiary* on line). In the bestiaries the monocerus was a hybrid having the head of a stag, the body of a horse, the feet of an elephant, the tail of a boar and a single, very long, black horn growing from the forehead. This description does not really accord with the beast on the Aberdeen handle but it is not hard to credit that verbal accounts of such a creature, rather than even a first-hand glimpse of a bestiary depiction or description, would have influenced the Aberdeen version. The seeming singularity of the depiction and its stylistic attributes do not link it to any particular production centre (boxwood was carved across northern Europe as well as in Mediterranean and Near Eastern lands where it grew best) and they do not preclude the handle being carved by a craftsman in Aberdeen as a local commission. Excavations at the Carmelite Friary, Linlithgow, in 1983 and 1984, recovered a group of scale-tang knives including an example with part of its decorated wooden handle surviving (Stones *et al.* 1989: 162 & illus. 104, 247L). The wood is not identified but the decoration is incised and is thematically related to the Bon Accord handle. Two elements survive. The first is a two legged hybrid with a human head wearing a liripipe hood. Such hybrid creatures are familiar as marginalia in illuminated manuscripts and carved in wood and stone. The second element is the head of an animal, probably another hybrid. The monstrous hybridity makes it a good match for the Aberdeen handle. The excavators do not rule out the knife handle having been made in Scotland. The art-historical and archaeological dating converge on the late 13th–early 14th century, which also puts the Linlithgow knife in the same time frame as the Aberdeen handle.

Whittle-tang knives are consistent with a 12th–15th century date, when this was the commonest form of knife, scale-tang knives not being introduced, according to the London evidence, until the 14th century (Cowgill *et al.* 1987: 25–26). The decoration of the Bon Accord handle is more typical of the 13th and 14th centuries but as this is probably a one-off, individual piece, this in itself is not a tight guide to its dating. It certainly does not gainsay the Phase 2 dating (late 12th to mid 13th century) of the pit from which it was excavated. It may lack the accomplishment of execution but its vitality and uniqueness (like that of the Linlithgow example) permit comparison with the relief-carved ivory knife handle depicting a Maying celebrant from Perth (Hall 2001) and reminds us that Scotland's medieval burghs had a dynamic craft base fully in tune with European sensibilities.

4.2.2 Leatherwork
Clare Thomas
(written 2015)

Introduction

The assemblage consists of 12,414 separate items, or 13,668 separate fragments, of leather, comprising shoes, straps, sheaths or scabbards, miscellaneous items such as clothing, and waste material. Waste material, with 10,425 offcuts and 646 scraps, forms the largest category (89%). Shoe components at 1084 (9%) make up

a smaller but significant group, with several different sole and upper types. Other important items include a possible sleeve and a scabbard. The material has parallels in assemblages from other sites in Aberdeen and from elsewhere in Scotland, notably Perth, as well as from England and abroad.

Many items, especially uppers, straps and the scabbard, comprise several different pieces, especially where delamination has occurred. Hence, there is a difference between the number of items and the number of fragments recorded. A full report, with methodology, tables, and catalogue of the leather assemblage can be found in the site archive.

Animal species

The species of a sub-sample of the leatherwork was identified. Most of it, 76%, proved to be cattlehide. The remainder consisted almost entirely of deerskin (20%), with only a small amount of goat or sheepskin (5%). The proportions of animal species were broadly similar in both Phases 1 and 2. The items made of deerskin comprised shoe parts, miscellaneous objects and waste material. The proportions of animal species in the leatherwork are in contrast to those identified in the animal pelts, where sheep or lamb was most common, followed by goat, and then cattle (Section 4.2.4). Deerskin did not feature at all.

At York, cattlehide predominated from the late 9th to mid 11th centuries; goatskin/sheepskin then became more common, with cattlehide and goatskin/sheepskin roughly equal from the late 11th to early 13th centuries. Thereafter, cattlehide became more common (Mould *et al.* 2003: 3267). A similar pattern was observed in London (Grew and de Neergaard 1988: 44–46). A fragment of an unknown item of late 12th century date from Coppergate, York, was recognised as deerskin (Mould *et al.* 2003: 3267). The London report states that 'some of those described as sheep/goat may have been deer, but we are not yet certain of the diagnostic pattern of the latter' (Grew and de Neergaard 1988: 44).

Shoes

The shoe leather comprises 62 complete or nearly complete soles and 28 substantial parts of uppers, as well as many more sole and upper fragments, repair clump soles and stitching channels.

Construction

All of the shoes are of turnshoe construction; that is, they are made inside out, with the flesh side outwards, by sewing the lasting margin of the upper to the edge of a single sole. The shoe was then turned the right way round, with the grain side of the leather on the outside, and the sole/upper seams on the inside.

The soles all have edge-flesh stitching channels, with stitch lengths mostly of 5–8mm. The uppers have lasting margins with grain-flesh stitching channels, with stitch lengths mostly of 5–8mm. Fragments of upper were usually joined together with butted edge-flesh seams, with a stitch length of 2.5–4.5mm. Occasionally, the grain surface has been folded slightly, to form an edge. The sole-upper seam was usually strengthened and made more waterproof by the insertion of a rand, a wedge-shaped strip of leather.

Soles were normally made in one piece; however, the assemblage includes 26 examples of two-part soles, usually joined at the waist, e.g. SF4196, Spread C040 (Figure 4.17). These include 11 foreparts and 12 seats sewn across the waist, as well as two foreparts and one toe sewn across the tread. Such soles were probably structurally weak and are probably a reflection of repair or reuse. Many examples of similar two-part soles were found at Perth High Street (Thomas and Bogdan 2012: 175–77).

Three examples of thread have been noticed; although not analysed these are probably linen. No signs of woollen or silk thread have been recognised.

Soles

The soles have been divided into groups, depending on their alignment, their toe shape, and the extent of indentation at the waist. Where appropriate, reference has been made to types identified at Perth High Street (PHS), which give broad dating ranges.

(i) Straight aligned with rounded toe (PHS Type 1): Fifteen soles have a straight alignment and a rounded toe; six of these have only a slight narrowing at the waist, while three have none. This group includes a child's sole. Six were from Phase 1, six from Phase 2, with one from Phase 4, and two unstratified. Dated parallels range between the 12th and 13th centuries. This was the commonest type at 42 St Paul Street, Aberdeen, and the second most numerous at Perth High Street (Stones 1982a: 191–97; Thomas and Bogdan 2012: 164).

(ii) Straight aligned with oval toe (PHS Type 2): The 26 soles in this group are similar to those in Group (i) but have oval toes. The majority (12) have an obvious narrowing at the waist, while seven have only a slight narrowing. Eleven were from Phase 1, with another 12 from Phase 2, and three from Phase 3. Parallels, mainly of 12th to 14th century date, include 27 previous examples from Aberdeen (Stones 1982a: 191–97; Thomas 2001: 243) This was the third most common shape at Perth High Street,

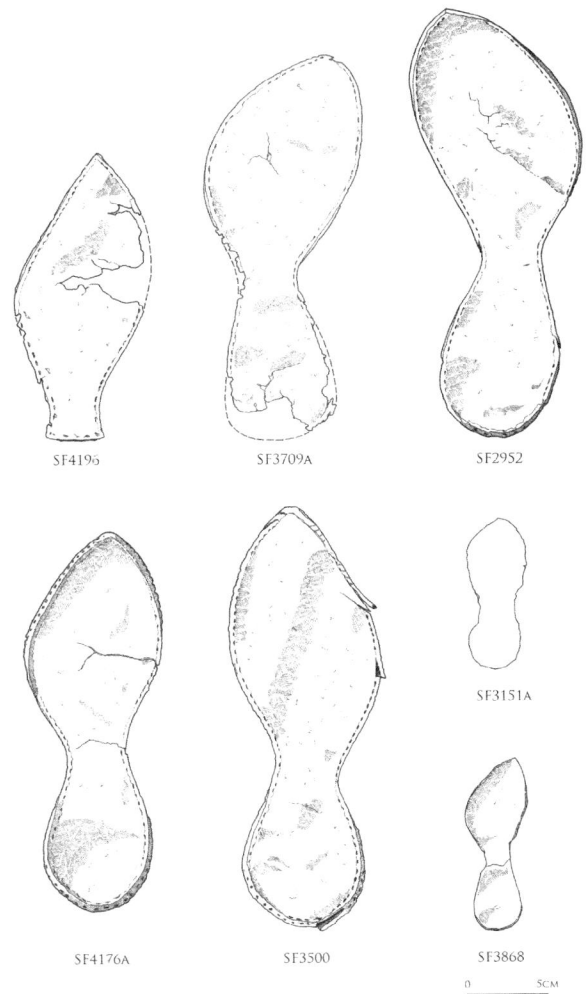

Figure 4.17 Shoe soles; SF4196; SF3709A; SF2952; SF4176A; SF3500; SF3151A; SF3868

where it was mainly of 13th century date (Thomas and Bogdan 2012: 164, 170).

(iii) Straight aligned with broad pointed toe: Four soles are similar to those in Groups (i) and (ii) but end in pointed toes. Two were from Phase 1, two from Phase 2. They are in some respects similar to those of PHS Type 5 but lack the latter's pronounced waists and bulging rear foreparts. It is possible that they are a variant of PHS Type 6 soles, which were wide with out-turned pointed toes. However, the latter usually had little or no waist. PHS Type 6 soles were of 12th century date. Parallels from London were of late 11th century date (Vince 1991: 230–35).

(iv) Inclined inwards with oval toe (PHS Type 3): The 29 soles in this group have a more natural foot shape, mostly with narrow or very narrow waists, and foreparts which are inclined inwards, ending in oval toes, e.g. SF3709A, Spread C043 (Figure 4.17); one example has

a rounded toe. Six were from Phase 1, 20 from Phase 2, with two from Phase 3 and one unstratified. It was the commonest shape at Perth High Street, with 63 examples. It ranged in date from the 12th to the 14th centuries, but belonged predominantly to the second half of the 13th century. It was also the principal type at Kirk Close, Perth, where it was of 13th to 14th century date (Thomas and Bogdan 2012: 170; Thomas 1988: 175–76).

(v) Inclined inwards with pointed toe (PHS Type 5): Fourteen soles resemble those of PHS Type 5, with narrow or very narrow waists, and foreparts inclined inwards to a usually broad pointed toe e.g. SF2952 Layer C003 (Figure 4.17). Two were from Phase 1, ten from Phase 2, with one from Phase 3 and one unstratified. At Perth High Street, they dated to *c.* 1250–1350 (Thomas and Bogdan 2012: 170–72). Other examples of 13th to 15th century date include London (early 13th century, mid-late 14th century) (Grew and de Neergaard 1988: 57–66, fig 90, 98, 100) and Sandwell Priory (15th century) (Thomas 1991: 104, nos 14, 15).

(vi) Slender with pointed toe (PHS Type 4): Six soles are quite slender, ending in a pointed toe, e.g. SF4176A Hollow C002 (Figure 4.17) and SF3500 Pit C023 (Figure 4.17). The first was made of deerskin. One was from Phase 1, three from Phase 2, one from Phase 3 and another from Phase 4 or 5. Parallels for this elegant shape, chiefly of 13th to 14th century date, include Threave Castle, Galloway (late 14th–early 15th century) and Perth High Street (late 12th to mid 14th centuries, mainly 14th) (Thomas 1981: 123–26; Thomas and Bogdan 2012:, 172).

(vii) Model soles: Two exceptionally small soles have no stitching, only cut edges. One has been cut on a straight alignment, with an oval toe (SF3151A, Pit A027) (Figure 4.17), while the other is slender, with a narrow waist and generously curved forepart inclined inwards to a pointed toe (SF3868, Hollow C002) (Figure 4.17).

Very small children's shoes have been found at several sites, including Perth High Street. (Thomas and Bogdan 2012: 177–79) However, these are even smaller. This fact, together with the absence of stitching, suggests that they were style models, representing soles similar to those of PHS Types 2 and 4.

Uppers

The 181 fragments of uppers include 18 substantial or nearly complete examples, as well as 30 vamps, 13 quarters and nine side or leg pieces. They were mostly of one-piece wrap-around design, with additional inserts, side-pieces, leg-flaps and heel stiffeners.

Two vamps (SF3008, Layer C003; SF4176B, Hollow C002) and two quarters (SF4177, Hollow C002; SF4223,

Pit C009) had seams on either side, showing that they were from shoes with separate vamps and quarters. This is not a common feature of medieval uppers, which usually had one fragment comprising both vamp and quarters. It is sometimes explained by a high leg, as on one example from Perth High Street (Type H). Otherwise it may reflect repair or reuse (Thomas and Bogdan 2012: 221–25).

Fastening methods

Evidence was found for three different fastening methods.

(i) Horizontal thongs (PHS Type B(i)): Three uppers had horizontal wrap-around thongs; one example, of deerskin, had a pair of slits forming a slot or tunnel hole for a horizontal thong on either side of the quarters (SF2875 Pit C022) (Figure 4.18), while one such slot survives on another upper (SF4221A, Pit C009). The latter also had the vertical edge of the quarters folded inwards to form a 5–15mm wide hem. The third upper was a child's, with a surviving bit of thong threaded through a hole on the closed side of the vamp wing, and a single thong hole at the vamp throat (SF2008A, Layer C003). One was from Phase 1, with two from Phase 2. Two small upper fragments also had evidence for horizontal thonging (SF4756, Pit C099; SF4793C, Pit C015).

Three uppers of this type were recorded from Gallowgate Middle School, Aberdeen, one of which (579) had a similar but more elaborate hem (Thomas 2001: 243). Two other examples of vertical hems were found at Perth High Street, where this type of fastening ranged in date from the early 12th to the mid 13th century, but was predominantly of 12th date (Thomas and Bogdan 2012: 201).

(ii) Vertical thongs (PHS Type B(iii): (SF2936A, Pit C006; SF2976, Pit C004; SF4221B, Pit C009; SF3251, Pit A026; SF4178, Hollow C002; SF4221C, Pit C009).

Five uppers and one small fragment had vertical thongs which had been used to secure horizontal thongs. The thongs were threaded through slots on either side of the quarters; on one example, (SF4178) (Figure 4.18), the thong overlapped onto the vamp wing. This upper has clear marks from two horizontal thongs, while another (SF2936A) has a surviving stretch of horizontal thong. Five were from Phase 1, one from Phase 2.

This type of boot appears to belong predominantly to the 12th–13th centuries, as, for example, at Perth High Street, where 16 such boots were of mid 12th to early 13th century date (Thomas and Bogdan 2012: 207–10).

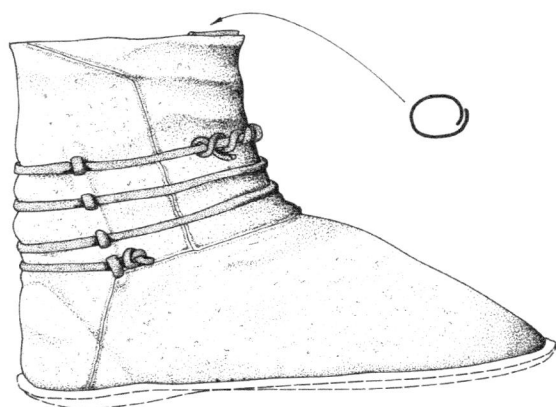

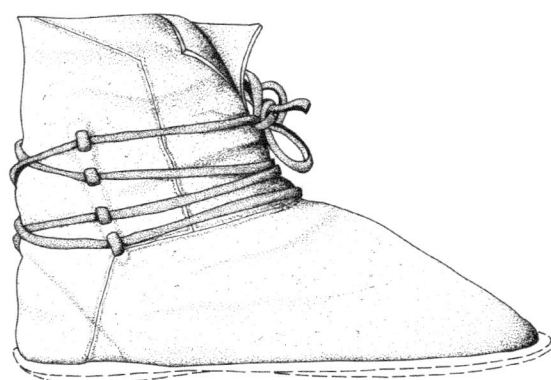

SF4178

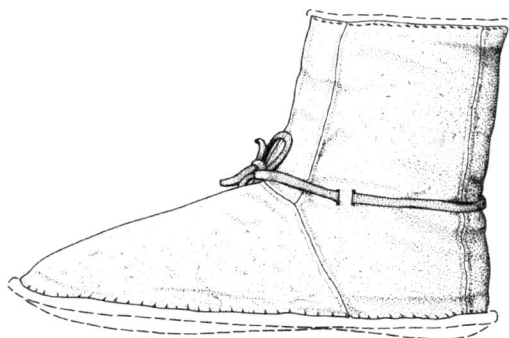

SF2875

0   5CM

Figure 4.18 Shoe uppers; reconstructions of SF4178 (two variations of lacing are shown) & SF2875

(iii) Side-lacing (PHS Type C or D): (SF4308, Gully C001; SF3774, Pit C033; SF3129, Pit C018; SF2755, Pit C022; SF4733, Pit C015 (Figure 4.19); SF2936B, Pit C006; SF4266, Pit C032)

Five uppers and three small fragments had vertical rows of thong holes for side-lacing. Five examples (SF4308, SF3129, SF2755, SF4733 & SF4266) had tunnel stitching on the flesh side to secure tie-hole facings. One (SF2755, Pit C022) was from a boot, and is therefore comparable to PHS Type C. The other examples are too fragmentary to determine whether they were from boots or shoes. Three were from Phase 1 and five from Phase 2.

At Perth High Street Type C boots ranged in date from the second half of the 12th century to the early 14th century but were mainly of mid 13th to early 14th century. Type D, which consisted of low shoes, belonged to the mid to later 13th century (Thomas and Bogdan 2012: 210–18).

Repairs and reuse

All the shoe fragments were worn, with cracks and tears in both soles and uppers. Evidence for repair existed in the form of 27 clump soles, and in tunnel stitching for their attachment on twenty soles. This is normal for medieval turnshoes, as the single sole would have worn through very quickly. Most of this evidence was from Phases 1 and 2. Five uppers had signs of repair. On the first, (SF3985, Pit C018) a worn lasting margin had been replaced with a stitching channel with a closer stitch length; furthermore, a grain-flesh stitching channel, with the grain bent to form an edge, had been substituted for an edge-flesh stitching channel. More unusually, a second upper (SF2960, Layer C003) had a patch added.

Further evidence for repair survives in soles with seams across the waist, tread or even diagonally across the seam. As mentioned above, two-part soles would have been weak at the join, and are unlikely to be an original feature. Reuse is another possible explanation. Most of such soles were from Phase 2.

Other evidence for reuse exists in the presence of four shoes where the vamp was separate from the quarters, as mentioned above. This is probably the result of either repair or reuse. One of these had then had the lasting margin neatly cut away, suggesting that the remaining part of the upper was intended to be reused in some way, possibly for patching (Hollow C002). Most of the evidence for repair or reuse of uppers comes from Phase 2.

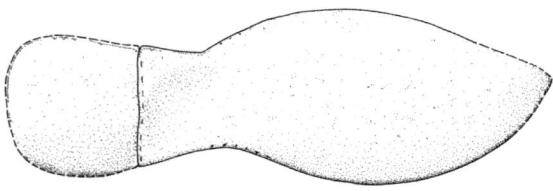

SF2755

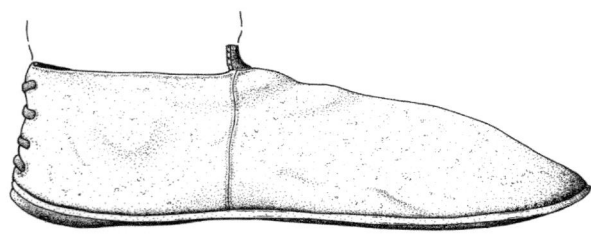

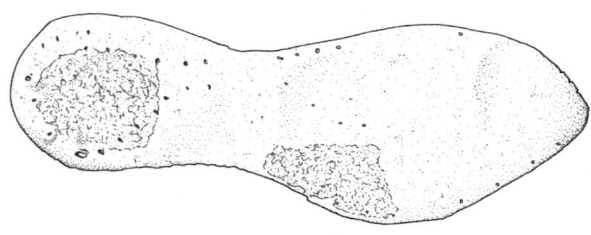

SF4733

Figure 4.19 Shoe uppers; reconstructions of SF2755 & SF4733

Bunions

One sole (SF2008B, Layer C003) has been distorted by a bunion (*hallux valgus*). In this foot condition, the great toe is pushed outwards and the joint becomes swollen. This results in a bulge in the vamp. As medieval turnshoes were dished, they also became distorted, with the stitching channel pushed outwards and a hole under the area of the big toe joint (Swallow 1973: 29). Five examples of damage caused by bunions were recorded at Perth High Street, with one complete shoe,

four soles and an upper affected (Thomas and Bogdan 2012: 249–50).

Sheaths and scabbards

At least eight fragments appear to form part of a long, narrow scabbard, formed of a large piece of leather folded twice and stitched up the centre with a butted edge-flesh seam (SF4057; Phase 2 Pit C032) (Figure 4.20). The scabbard has been strengthened by the addition of extra strips, attached by thonging. It is also possible that the thonging enabled the attachment of smaller, subsidiary sheaths. Fragment (4057b) probably forms the narrow, bottom end. The presence of this narrow stitched end indicates that this was a scabbard and not a belt.

As none of the fragments appear to join together, it is hard to determine the size of the scabbard. It has a minimum length of approximately 600mm. The width of the base of the scabbard may have been about 30mm, while its maximum surviving width is 78mm.

The nearest parallel is a long plain sheath of late 12th century date from Perth High Street; however, it did not have any thonging (Thomas and Bogdan 2012: 271) Other plain scabbards, again without thonging, were found at Waterford, Ireland (12th century)(Hurley 1997: 736–42) and Gloucester (Goudge 1979: 193–66). A plain one from London is described as a lining (Cowgill, de Neergaard and Griffiths 1987: 160). Decorated sword scabbards include one from London which had two smaller sheaths attached to it, and a late 11th–early 12th century example from Waterford (Cowgill *et al.* 1987: 168; Hurley 1997: 736–42).

A small decorated fragment is probably part of a knife sheath (SF4793A – Phase 1 Pit C015) (Figure 4.21). The decoration consists of engraved horizontal and vertical lines, enclosing diagonal bands forming triangles and lozenges. It has been engraved with a blunt tool on wet leather.

Decorated knife sheaths were common, when most people carried their own knife. The use of conventionalised heraldic devices such as shields, lozenges or fleur-de-lys does not imply that their owners were entitled to wear such emblems but rather that they wished to imitate the nobility (Richardson 1959: 106).

Straps

The 66 straps include straps of both single and double thickness, as well as a few thongs and a toggle.

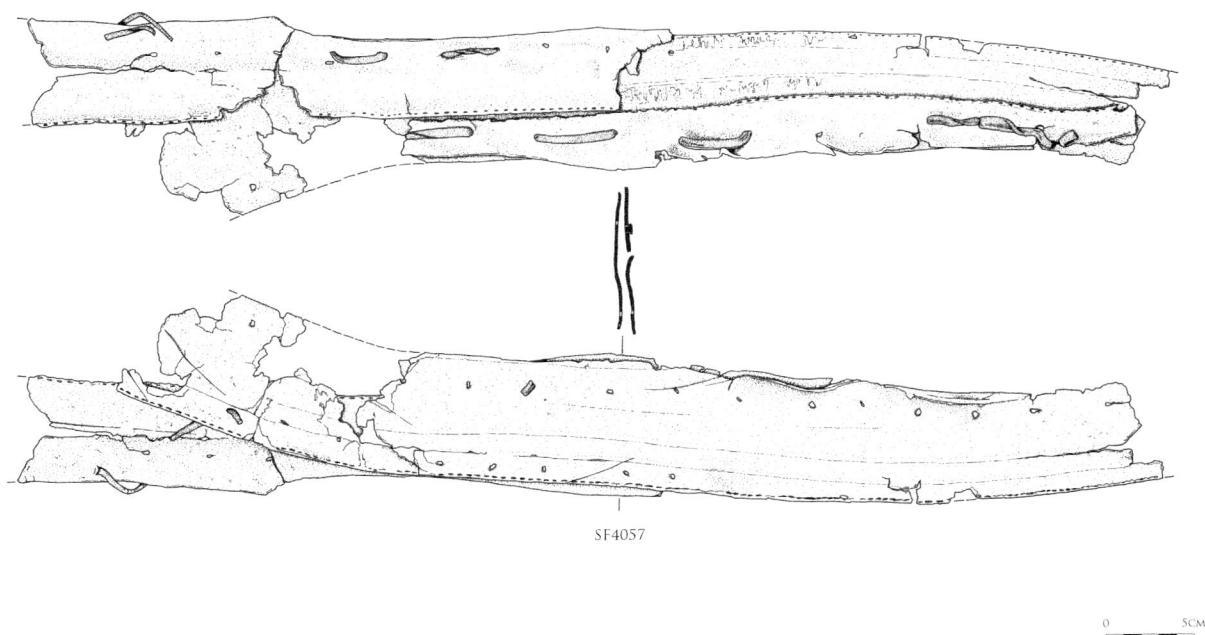

SF4057

Figure 4.20 Scabbard SF4057

Straps of single thickness

Straps of single thickness have cut edges, usually with a row of grain-flesh slits parallel to each long edge. Some of the 28 examples in this assemblage have holes for the pin of a buckle, for instance: SF3458, Pit C036; others, such as SF1430A, Layer C019 (Figure 4.21), have holes possibly from the attachment of the buckle itself. Most of these straps came from Phases 1 and 2.

Straps folded once

This category includes 24 straps where a strip of leather has been folded once along its length and stitched where the two edges meet; it does not include very narrow strips which are probably top bands or bindings. The best preserved of these, SF4793B from Pit C015 (Figure 4.21), has been folded 40mm from cut end; an oblong hole on the fold and round holes, for studs or rivets, on either side of fold, show where a buckle has been attached. Another strap, SF14A from Pit C009 (Figure 4.21), has a row of round or oval holes along a central line. These straps were found in contexts from Phases 1, 2 and 3.

Straps folded twice

Two straps, SF14B and SF14C, Pit C009 (Figure 4.21), have been formed by folding a strip of leather twice along its length, and stitching the two edges together with a butted edge-grain seam. Both have been perforated along an approximately central line by irregularly spaced round or oval holes, penetrating through both layers and parts of the seam. The round holes bear an impression of studs. Both these straps came from Phase 1.

Such straps would have had a wide variety of uses, including clothes fastenings, attachments on bags and utensils, horse tack and harness. Egan and Pritchard (1991: 35), for example, describe how long straps of single thickness were joined together to form floor length girdles.

Miscellaneous items

Miscellaneous items include eight possible pieces of clothing and three decorated fragments.

Clothing

Identification of possible items of clothing is hampered by the irregular nature of the fragments involved. The significant features are size, indications of seams, especially along edges, and impressions of studs.

One piece, SF4159 from Hollow C002 (Figure 4.22), has possibly been a sleeve reinforced with studs. It is slightly tapered, with grain-flesh stitching along two opposing long sides. The two short ends appear to have a row of studs parallel to a cut edge. The main body of the fragment is perforated by five full length parallel vertical rows of stud holes and two parallel horizontal rows. These horizontal rows are each crossed by four short vertical rows, in the space between the full length vertical rows.

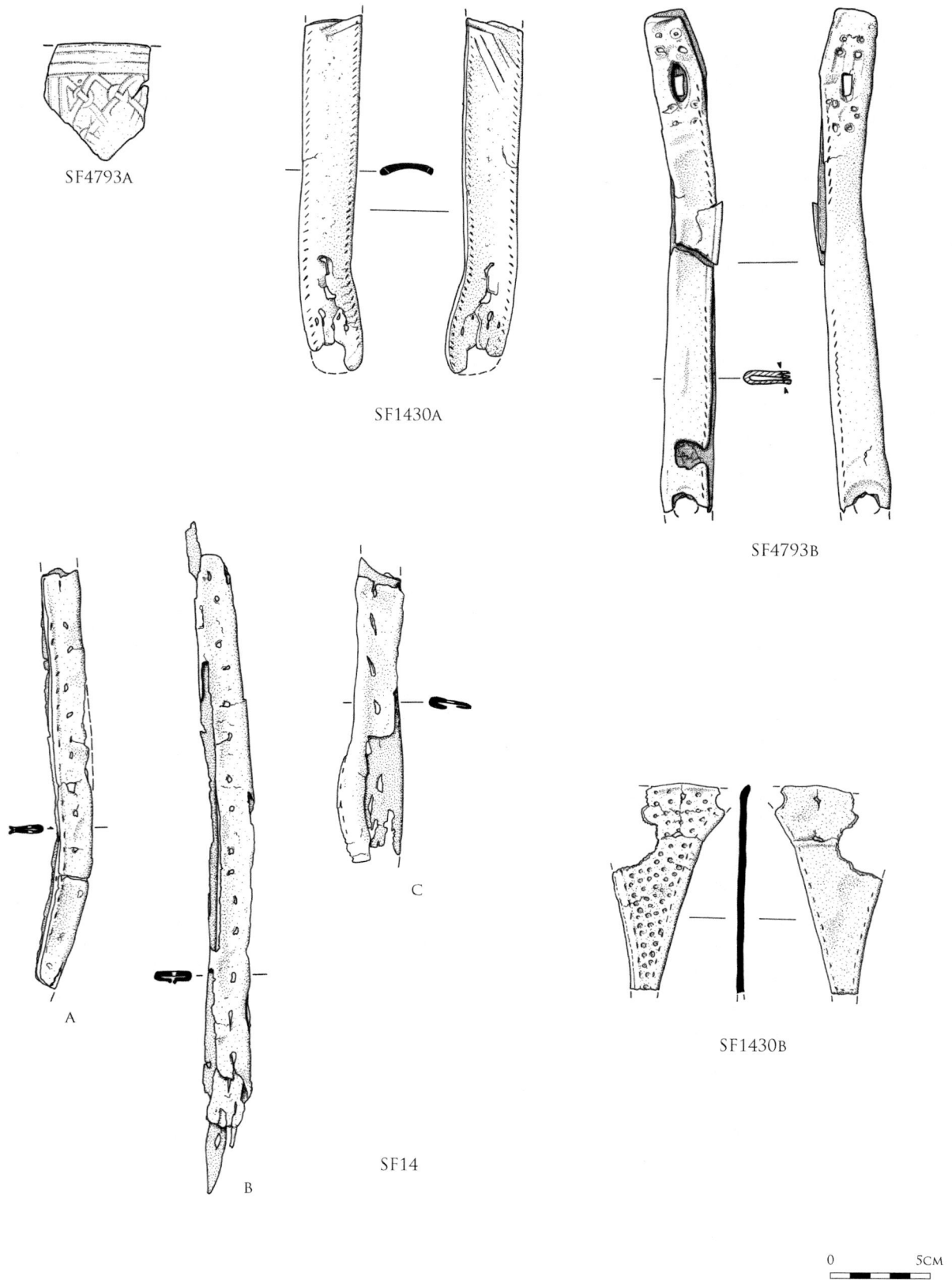

Figure 4.21 Sheaths, straps & decorated leather; knife sheath SF4793A; straps SF1430A; SF4793B; SF14A, B & C; decorated fragment SF1430B

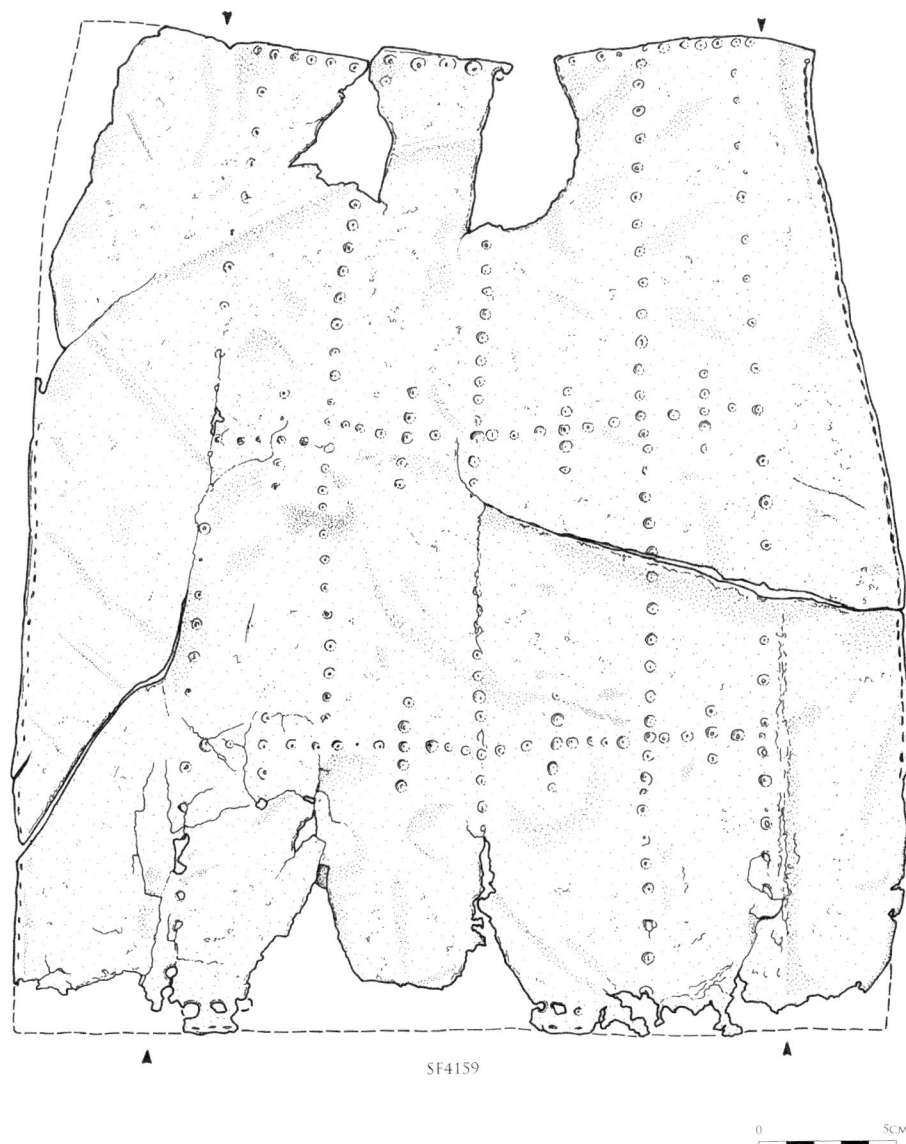

Figure 4.22 Clothing; sleeve SF4159

The two stitched edges appear to match, indicating that they were stitched together, thus making a tapered tube, such as a legging or sleeve. The measurements suggest that, unless the leather has shrunk significantly or it was intended for a child or small adult, it would be tight as a legging. Accordingly, a sleeve might be more appropriate. This item came from Phase 2.

Impressions of studs were also found on two other fragments: SF2462, Pit C007 and SF2875B, Pit C002. Twelve fragments with marks from rivets or studs were found at 45–75 Gallowgate, Aberdeen (Thomas 2001: 251).

Another possible item of clothing, SF3151b from Pit A027, has two loosely oversewn edges and, parallel to

one of these, four pairs of lace holes, as well as a single lace hole. There are also two groups of three grain-flesh stitch holes. The grain side has two horizontal lines as if rubbed by thongs; one of these runs past a single thong hole.

This could be part of an upper of a boot with side or central lacing. However, a number of features suggest that it is not footwear: the loosely oversewn nature of the top edge; the positioning of the lace holes in pairs; the presence of the two groups of three stitch holes; the absence of other seams, including lasting margin and edge-flesh stitching channels. It is more likely to be part of an item of clothing.

Table 4.3 Leather; offcuts by phase

Phase	1	2	3	4	5	6	Unstratified	Total	% of total assemblage
Triangular offcuts	384	1807	581	27	5	2	26	2832	22.8
Broad strip offcuts	18	61	22		2		1	104	0.8
Narrow strip offcuts	470	2028	1334	21	7	2	12	3874	31.2
Trapezoidal offcuts	68	328	99	9			2	506	4.1
Irregular offcuts	556	1815	668	38	11	3	18	3109	25.0
Total	1496	6039	2704	95	25	7	59	10,425	84.0
Scraps	80	359	196	6	1		4	646	5.2

Decorated items

Two approximately triangular items have been decorated with punched dots. The first, SF1430B, Layer C019 (Figure 4.21), has its edges defined by a plain band, marked by a row of grain-flesh slits. The triangular space enclosed by the band has been filled with punched dots.

A second, smaller item, made of deerskin, SF3977 from Spread C099, has oversewn, slightly curved edges, forming an approximately triangular shape filled with punched dots. This is possibly a panel from something bigger.

A third fragment, SF2616 from Layer C003, again approximately triangular in shape, has six irregularly spaced round grain-flesh holes.

One of these items was from Phase 2, one from Phase 3 and the third from Phase 5.

Two similar items from Perth High Street had also been decorated with punched dots; 481 came from a late 12th century deposit, while 2272 dated to the third quarter of the 13th century (Thomas and Bogdan 2012: 279, 284, fig. 158).

Waste material

The assemblage includes 10,425 offcuts and 646 scraps. The offcuts consist of 2832 (27%) triangles, 104 (0.1 %) broad strips, 3874 (37%) narrow strips, 506 (5%) trapezoidal and 3109 (30%) irregularly shaped items. The triangular offcuts mostly had slightly curved edges; these are typical waste from cutting out new soles. Most

of the offcuts were not worn, indicating that they are from the manufacture of new shoes, not from cobbling or reuse. The irregular offcuts included fragments from the original trimming of hides.

Phase 2 produced the most offcuts (6039 or 58% of all offcuts), then Phase 3 (2704 or 26% (Tables 4.3 & 4.4). The sheer quantity of offcuts – 84% of the total number of items, or 76% of the total number of separate

Table 4.4 Leather; offcuts by feature and phase

Phase	1	2	3/4
Pit C001	284		
Pit C009	351		
Pit C015	344		
Hollow C002		879	
Layer C003		1088	
Pit C018		1247	
Pit C019		385	
Pit C022		449	
Pit C023		549	
Pit C025		312	
Pit C032		447	
Layer C019			2038
Pit C048			456

fragments, combined with the large numbers of offcuts from certain contexts, indicates that leather working, and in particular shoe making, was taking place on or near the site.

Conclusion

This assemblage is, in terms of number of items, the biggest ever found in Scotland, with 12,414 items or 13,668 fragments. The largest category comprises waste material. Shoe material, though much smaller, is well represented, with six sole shapes and three upper styles. Possibly the most interesting items, however, are the scabbard and the items with studs or traces of studs, especially the sleeve.

The concentration of waste material at Bon Accord is significant, as it is very clear evidence for leather working on or near the site. The relative paucity of shoe and other material suggests that, although there is evidence for repair and reuse, most of the activity comprised production of new items from new leather. The scarcity of large pieces of uppers, especially as compared to the earlier phases of Perth High Street, may also imply that worn-out shoes were being to a large extent reused before being discarded. Furthermore, the nature of the assemblage, with a great preponderance of waste material and relatively few shoe components, suggests that this is industrial, not domestic, waste.

Evidence from elsewhere indicates that leather working activity may have been carried out elsewhere, although nearby, with the waste material dumped at the Bon Accord site. At Bristol Bridge, for instance, leather waste was dumped in a river revetment structure (Thomas, archive report).

This assemblage is also significant for the use of deerskin for both shoes and miscellaneous items, and for the paucity of evidence for goatskin.

The evidence from the shoes suggests that the assemblage is of approximately 12th to 14th century date, possibly 12th to 13th century. Previous leather finds from Aberdeen include the assemblages from Broad Street, Queen Street, 42 St Paul Street, 16–18 Netherkirkgate, 30–46 Upperkirkgate, Gallowgate Middle School and 45–75 Gallowgate (Stones 1982a: 191–97; Thomas 2001: 241–58). The Bon Accord assemblage is much bigger than any of these, but otherwise is broadly similar in the range of leather objects represented.

This assemblage is twice as big as that from Perth High Street, which comprised approximately 6000 items. However, at Bon Accord, offcuts and scraps form 89% of the assemblage, whereas at Perth, they only comprised about 50%. Shoe components, miscellanea and sheaths

played a bigger role, not just in terms of number of items, but also as regards variety.

The shoe material from Bon Accord includes several sole shapes, but only a few upper styles. It is particularly noticeable that there are no examples of PHS upper styles K or L. Type K, with front latchets fastened with thongs and toggles, dated to the 13th and 14th centuries; it was very well represented at both Perth High Street and at Kirk Close, Perth (Thomas and Bogdan 2012: 225–29; Thomas 1988: 179). Type L uppers have a central opening down the vamp, with one or two lace holes. It was the only upper style at Threave Castle, Galloway, where it dated to the 14th and early 15th centuries (Thomas 1981: 123–26). An example from 45–75 Gallowgate, Aberdeen, came from a 17th century context (Thomas 2001: 249, 256). Another shoe feature not represented in the Bon Accord assemblage is the upturned triangular seat, which is characteristic of 10th–11th century shoes in both England and the Continent, as, for instance, in London (Vince, 1991: 213–35) and Schleswig (Schnack 1992: 38, 39,169). On the other hand, the shoe construction methods and styles represented in the Bon Accord assemblage, with their parallels elsewhere in Scotland, England and the Continent, clearly indicate that the leatherworkers of Aberdeen were following the traditions and using the skills of a pan-European craft.

In several instances comparisons with the Perth High Street leather assemblage provide a later date than the putative date of the medieval features themselves. For example, Pit A030 which is dated to the 12th century Phase 1, contains shoe components that resemble PHS forms variously of 13th–14th century, 13th–15th century and 12th–14th century form. It is unclear whether this derives from the longevity of some shoe forms or represents actual variation in assemblages between Perth and Aberdeen.

Catalogue of illustrated leather
(L = length; W = width; Th = thickness; D = diameter)

SF   4196 (Figure 4.17)
Phase/Feature   Phase 4/Spread C040
Description: left forepart sewn across waist
Slender left forepart, sewn across rear of waist; narrow waist, pointed toe. Edge-flesh stitching channel, stitch L 6mm. Very worn, with holes and cracks.
L 182mm; W at rear of waist 35mm; W at waist 30mm; max W of forepart 79mm; Th 3mm.

SF   3709A (Figure 4.17)
Phase/Feature   Phase 2/Spread C043
Description: left sole
Fragment of left sole, with slender seat, torn near rear, very narrow waist, and forepart markedly inclined

inwards, ending in oval toe. Edge-flesh stitching channel, stitch L 4mm. Worn and delaminated, stitching channel incomplete at toe and outer waist; rear of seat missing. Possibly stitching for seat clump.

Surviving L 239mm; surviving W of seat 60mm; W of waist 34mm; max W of forepart 93mm.

SF 2952 (Figure 4.17)
Phase/Feature Phase 2/Layer C003
Description: right sole

Complete right sole with long broad seat, very narrow waist and broad forepart, inclined markedly inwards, ending in broad pointed toe. Edge-flesh stitching channel, stitch L 4.5–5mm. Worn, with a small slit in seat, and with slight cracks in stitching channel at outer seat, on both sides of waist and towards rear of outer forepart.

L 270mm; max W of seat 71mm; W of waist 37mm; max W of forepart 98mm; Th c. 4mm

SF 4176A (Figure 4.17)
Phase/Feature Phase 2/Hollow C002
Description: left sole

Complete left sole, with long seat, very narrow waist and slender forepart, ending in a pointed toe. Edge-flesh stitching channel, stitch L 6mm. Worn, with two cracks in forepart.

L 245mm; max W of seat 68mm; W of waist 36mm; max W of forepart 84mm; Th 2mm.

SF 3500 (Figure 4.17)
Phase/Feature Phase 2/Pit C023
Description: right sole

Slender complete right sole with narrow waist, gently curved straight-aligned forepart ending in pointed toe. Edge-flesh stitching channel, stitch L 4mm.

L 269mm, max W of seat 75mm, W of waist 40mm, max W of forepart 90mm.

Worn, with two very small holes in front forepart, one in seat. Slight delamination at rear of seat. Short slit at outer edge of forepart. Grain side of rear of seat and of area near split in forepart worn.

SF 3151A (Figure 4.17)
Phase/Feature Phase 1/Pit A027 fill (A)
Description: model sole

Very small left sole, with rounded seat, narrowing at waist and straight aligned forepart, ending in an almost central oval toe. Cut edges, no stitching. Delaminated into separate grain and flesh layers; flesh layer is longer.

L 85mm (grain), 94mm (flesh); max W of seat 30mm; W of waist 19mm; max W of forepart 35mm.

This is almost certainly a model sole.

SF SF3868 (Figure 4.17)
Phase/Feature Phase 2/Hollow C002
Description: model sole

Very small slender sole, with no stitching channels, just cut edges, grain side up. Long seat, narrow waist, forepart inclined inwards to pointed toe. Partially torn at rear of waist.

L 110mm; max W of seat 28mm; W of waist 14mm; max W of forepart 38mm.

The absence of stitching and the tiny proportions suggest that this is a model or an example of a particular style, rather than a child's sole.

SF 4178 (Figure 4.18)
Phase/Feature Phase 2/Hollow C002
Description: upper with vertical thonging

Three joining fragments of upper, originally one, with vertical thonging.

a. Vamp, with vamp wing and throat; lasting margin with grain-flesh stitching channel, stitch L 5–6mm. Edge-flesh stitching channels on vamp wing and throat, stitch L 3.5mm. All other edges torn. Small bit of thong threaded through slit near corner of vamp wing and throat; thong on grain side is 6mm W and 6.5mm L. On flesh side, thong forms a small tab, 6mm x 14mm. Worn, with several cracks and tears.
Length from toe to throat approximately 122mm.

b. Small, approximately triangular fragment, fitting onto vamp wing, with lasting margin and edge-flesh stitching channel as above; third edge torn.
Dimensions 20mm x 55mm.

c. Quarters, with leg flap, part of vamp throat and two vertical thongs. Lasting margin as above. Edge-flesh stitching channel, as above, on vamp throat, and on vertical and diagonal edges of quarters. Top edge and vertical edge of leg flap cut. Two vertical thongs, threaded through slits, with four stretches of thong on grain side, on each side of quarters; one of these thongs joins that which emerges from vamp wing. Above the other thong, small oval thong hole. On grain side, mark made by two horizontal thongs between the two lowest stretches of vertical thong. On flesh side, stitching for triangular heel-stiffener. This fragment joins vamp on tear near vamp throat. Diagonal and horizontal edges on other side of quarters match vamp wing and vamp throat. Worn, with several tears and cracks.
Height from lasting margin to top of quarters approximately 160mm.

Upper of boot with at least two layers of horizontal thongs held in place by two vertical thongs; missing second leg flap and stiffener.

SF 2875 (Figure 4.18)
Phase/Feature Phase 2/Pit C022 fill (E)
Description: upper of ankle boot with slots for horizontal thong

Three matching fragments of almost complete upper of one-piece design, missing only heel stiffener.

- a. Large piece comprising vamp with vamp throat and vamp wing and quarters. Lasting margin with grain-flesh stitching channel, stitch L 5mm; very neat round holes, diameter 1.5mm. Edge-flesh stitching channel, stitch L 3.5mm on vamp wing and throat and on vertical edge of quarters. Top edge and open vertical edge of quarters oversewn. Pair of slits forming slot for horizontal thong on closed side of quarters. Stitching on flesh side for heel stiffener.
- b. Side piece, fitting between vamp wing and quarters. Lasting margin as above; edge-flesh stitching channel, as above, on two vertical and one diagonal edges; top edge oversewn. Two slits forming slot for horizontal thong. Stitching on flesh side for corner of heel stiffener.
- c. Small rectangular insert, fitting next to side-piece, above vamp throat, with two edge-flesh stitching channels, as above, and two oversewn edges.
  This is an ankle-boot of one-piece design, with two extra pieces, and with slots for a horizontal thong.

Approximate L of boot 215mm.

SF	2755 (Figure 4.19)
Phase/Feature	Phase 2/Pit C022 fill (E)
Description:	sole and upper of ankle boot with side lacing sole sewn across front of seat

Sole fragment, consisting of straight-aligned forepart and waist, sewn across front of seat; missing toe. Edge-flesh stitching channel, stitch L 6–7mm. Tunnel stitching for forepart clump for missing area. Worn.
L 188mm; surviving W of seat 60mm; W of waist 47mm; max W of forepart 88mm; Th 3mm.

Three fragments of upper of ankle boot with side lacing

- a. Largest fragment consists of vamp and quarters, including vamp wing and vamp throat. No lasting margin survives. Edge-flesh stitching channels on vamp wing, vamp throat and on vertical edge of quarters above vamp throat; stitch L 3mm. Top edge and vertical edge of quarters oversewn. Parallel to oversewn vertical edge, eight round thong holes, D 2.5mm; holes are spaced 13–15mm apart. Worn and torn, partially delaminated.
- b. Approximately square fragment, with four thong holes, as above, parallel to oversewn edge. Two other edges with edge-flesh stitching channels, stitch L 3mm; fourth edge oversewn. On flesh side, tunnel stitching for thong hole strengthener or facing.
  Dimensions 59mm x 64mm x 1.5mm.

Fits opposite top of quarters, above vamp throat.

- c. Short strip with three thong holes, as above, next to an oversewn edge. Two edge-flesh stitching channels, stitch L 3mm. Fourth edge torn. Dimensions 42mm x 7–11mm x 1.5mm. This is either an insert, or a thong hole strengthener or facing. It is very small for an insert; however, a facing should have oversewn edges, not edge-flesh stitching channels.

SF	4733 (Figure 4.19)
Phase/Feature	Phase 1/Pit C015 fill (A)
Description:	left sole, clump sole, rand, upper of ankle boot with side lacing

- a. Complete left sole, with narrowing at waist, forepart inclined inwards to oval toe. Edge-flesh stitching channel, stitch L 5–7mm. Tunnel stitch holes for surviving forepart clump and for seat clump, which is missing.
  Worn, especially at rear of seat and at tread; hole in rear of seat and small hole in front of forepart, probably caused by stitching for clump.
  L 285mm; max W of seat 80mm; W of waist 59mm; max W of forepart 99mm; Th 4mm.
- b. Forepart clump sole, crudely cut, possibly from old sole, with projection at inner rear towards waist. Tunnel stitching for attachment to sole. Worn, especially at front.
  L 150mm; max W 95mm; Th 3mm.
- c. Five fragments of rand, stitch L 5–7mm. One fragment also has tunnel stitch holes for attachment of clump sole.
- d. Almost complete upper of one-piece design, with thong holes for side lacing, consisting of large fragment with vamp and quarters, side piece with thong holes, small insert, stiffener and possible top band. Missing small leg flap and thong hole facings.
- i. Large fragment of upper, comprising vamp with broad oval toe and quarters with four thong holes for side lacing. Small leg flap, 47mm x 10mm, at vamp throat; missing second leg flap. Lasting margin with grain-flesh stitching channel, stitch L 5–7mm. Edge-flesh stitching channel on vamp wing and vamp throat and on diagonal edge of quarters, beneath thong holes, stitch L 3mm. Top edge of quarters and of leg flap oversewn, probably for attachment of top band. Stitching for attachment of thong hole strengthener or facing, now missing, on adjacent edge and on flesh side. Tunnel stitching on inside of quarters for stiffener, which survives. Thong holes measure 5mm x 3mm, 5mm x 2.5mm, 3.5mm x 2.5mm and 3.5mm x 2mm and are set 15mm, 13mm and 12mm apart. Worn, especially at outer vamp. Probable height of quarters above sole c. 60mm.

ii. Approximately trapezoidal fragment of upper, consisting of side-piece, fitting between vamp wing and quarters, with four thong holes matching those on quarters. Lasting margin matches that on main upper piece, as does edge-flesh stitching channel below thong holes and on the other long vertical edge. Edge adjacent to thong holes and top edge oversewn. Tunnel stitching on flesh side for attachment of thong hole strengthener or facing, which is now missing. Thong holes measure 7mm x 2.5mm, 4mm x 3mm, 4mm x 3mm, 4mm x 2mm and are 12mm, 12mm and 14mm apart. H 99mm, W 40mm.

iii. Very small triangular insert, with lasting margin and two edge-flesh stitching channels, matching those on large fragment. Insert fits between vertical edge of quarters and side-piece.

iv. Approximately triangular heel-stiffener, with lasting margin and with tunnel stitching for attachment to quarters, matching that on inside of quarters. Stiffener extends beyond quarters to include insert and side-piece. Dimensions 26mm x 14mm.

v. Possible top band consists of thin strip, 260mm x 3mm x 2mm, with one oversewn edge and one cut edge.

SF 4057 (Figure 4.20)
Phase/Feature Phase 2/Pit C032 fill (A)
Description: scabbard
At least eight fragments of scabbard.

a. Largest fragment, 460mm x 60–78mm x 1mm, with one long butted edge-flesh stitching channel, stitch L 5–6mm. Other long edge appears to have been either cut or split. Both short ends torn. Adjacent to butted stitching channel, and 7–8mm from it, seven oval thong holes, 4.5mm x 2mm, 5mm x 2.5mm, 4mm x 1.5mm, 5mm x 1.5mm, 2.5mm x 3.5mm, 5mm x 2mm, last one torn. Holes are spaced 31mm, 32mm, 47mm, 30mm, 97mm and 35mm apart. Holes are set in a band approximately 28mm wide which appears to have been worn smooth. Two small round holes, diameter 1.5mm, next to inner edge of this band.
Other long edge has a strip, 28–32mm wide, arranged lengthways, with a thong threaded through oval holes. Four stretches of thong survive on grain side; these are 40mm, 41mm, 41mm, 29mm and 40mm long, 5–6mm wide and 1mm thick. Position of a fifth piece of thong is marked by two oval holes. Inner edge of strip has a butted edge-flesh stitching channel, stitch L 4mm. Grain surface of larger fragment underneath this strip worn smooth, which

suggests that the other worn area has had a strip on top of it.

b. (b) Strip, 156mm x 57–60mm x 1.5mm, with butted edge-flesh stitching channel, stitch L 4.5mm, along one long edge. Very faint trace of stitching on other long edge. Central split at one end of fragment, now torn, but probably an original feature. Faint trace of stitching at this end, suggesting item may have been folded and ends stitched together.
Other short end torn. Stretch of thong survives on both grain and flesh sides, 3mm wide, 1mm thick, 34mm long on grain side, 50mm on flesh side, slotted through oval hole, 3mm x 1mm. Three other oval thong holes survive, 3.5mm x 1mm, 4mm x 1mm and 5mm x 2mm.

c. (c) Strip, 223mm x 47–49mm, with one butted edge-flesh stitching channel on one long edge, stitch L 5.5mm. Other long edge cut. Both short ends torn. Adjacent to cut edge, two stretches of thong, 4.5–6mm wide and 1mm thick, each 32mm long, have been threaded through oval holes, 4mm x 1.5mm.

d. (d) Strip, 220mm x 80mm, delaminated, with one butted edge-flesh stitching channel, stitch L 4mm, along one long edge. Part of other long edge cut, rest torn, including short edges. Adjacent to cut edge, traces of two thong holes, plus suggestion of more along torn edge. Crease and three oval thong holes adjacent to stitched edge suggest that this has been folded.

e. (e) Strip, 203mm x 42mm, delaminated, with one butted edge-flesh stitching channel, stitch L 5.5mm along one long edge. Other long edge probably cut, other edges torn.

f. (f) Approximately oblong fragment, 85mm x 80mm, delaminated, with one butted edge-flesh stitching channel, stitch L 5mm and one cut edge, rest torn. Stretch of thong, 40mm x 4mm x 1mm, threaded through oval hole, near stitched edge. One oval thong hole near cut edge.

g. (g) Irregularly shaped fragment, 105mm x 50mm, delaminated, with one butted edge-flesh stitching channel, stitch L 5mm along one edge. All other edges torn. Three oval thong holes, approximately 30mm and 35mm apart.

h. (h) Small strip, 70mm x 25mm x 1.5mm, with one butted edge-flesh stitching channel, stitch L 5mm along one long edge; other long edge cut. Short edges torn. Short length of thong, approximately 30mm x 5mm x 1mm, threaded through oval thong hole.
These are most probably parts of a scabbard or sheath, formed of one large piece of leather folded twice and stitched up the centre with a butted edge-flesh seam. The scabbard has been

strengthened by the addition of extra strips, attached by thonging.

Fragment (b) probably forms the narrow, bottom end. The presence of this narrow stitched end suggests that this was a scabbard and not a belt.

SF 4793A (Figure 4.21)
Phase/Feature Phase 1/Pit C015 fill (A)
Description: decorated fragment, probably part of knife sheath

Small fragment with linear decoration, probably made using a blunt tool on wet leather. Top edge cut, all other edges torn.

Decoration: Three horizontal lines at top, 5.5mm apart. Below this, on left, two vertical lines form a band 4.5mm wide. To the right of this band, pairs of diagonal lines form 3mm wide interlocking bands enclosing triangular and diamond shapes. On right hand side of fragment, lines become slightly curved.

Fragment is very worn, especially the lower part, where the decoration is obscured; partially delaminated.

Surviving W 48mm; surviving L 60mm.

SF 1430A (Figure 4.21)
Phase/Feature Phase 3 or 4/Layer C019
Description: strap of single thickness

Strap of single thickness of leather, both long edges cut, both short edges torn. Parallel to both long edges, strap is perforated by row of diagonal slits, 2.5mm x 1mm, and approximately 3mm to 3.5mm apart. Up to 60mm from one end, strap is perforated by at least six oval holes, now enlarged and torn. Possibly remains of attachment of buckle. Near other short end, small oval hole, 3mm x 5mm, on grain side, c. 0.25mm deep. Worn, especially at end with holes.

L 186mm; W 29–31mm; Th 4mm.

SF 4793B (Figure 4.21)
Phase/Feature Phase 1/Pit C015 fill (A)
Description: strap folded once with holes for buckle

Strap formed of strip folded once lengthways. Row of slits, 3mm x 0.25mm and 5mm apart (centre to centre), parallel to long cut edges, suggests that these have been stitched together. One short end torn, the other cut. The strap has been folded 40mm from cut end; an oblong hole, 13mm x 5mm, sits on the fold. On end side of fold, four round holes, diameter 2mm for studs or rivets; on other side of fold, six holes, diameter 2–4mm. At torn end of strap, suggestion of hole, plus one very small one, 2.5mm x 1mm, 30mm from end.

Surviving L 260mm; W 26mm (folded); Th 4mm (single). Holes near cut end show that buckle has been attached here.

SF 14A (Figure 4.21)
Phase/Feature Phase 1/Pit C009 fill (A)
Description: strap folded once

Strap formed by folding tapered single strip of leather once; stitched together where edges meet with grain-flesh seam, stitch L 7mm. Perforated along an approximately central line by round (diameter 2mm) or oval (1.5mm x 3.5mm) holes which penetrate through both layers; holes are 13–18mm apart. Worn and completely delaminated into separate grain and flesh layers, so that there appear to be two different thicknesses. Both ends torn.

Surviving L 220mm; W 10–20mm (as folded).

SF 14B (Figure 4.21)
Phase/Feature Phase 1/Pit C009 fill (A)
Description: strap folded twice

Strap formed by folding strip of leather twice; stitched together with butted edge-grain stitching channel, stitch L 8mm. Perforated along an approximately central line by irregularly spaced and irregularly shaped oval holes. Exceedingly worn and completely delaminated into two separate layers. Both ends torn.

Surviving L 160mm; W 22mm (as folded).

SF 14C (Figure 4.21)
Phase/Feature Phase 1/Pit C009 fill (A)
Description: strap folded twice

Strap formed by folding strip of leather twice; stitched together with butted edge-grain stitching channel, stitch L 9mm. Perforated along an approximately central line by irregularly spaced round or oval holes, penetrating through both layers. Round holes have a diameter of 2.5mm and bear impression of studs. Oval holes measure approximately 2mm x 3mm. Holes have been made after item has been stitched, as holes penetrate through parts of the seam. Exceedingly worn and delaminated. Torn at both ends.

Surviving L 355mm; W 20mm (folded)

It is possible that straps 14B and 14C are part of the same item; however, no joins are visible.

SF 1430B (Figure 4.21)
Phase/Feature Phase 3 or 4/Layer C019
Description: decorated triangular fragment

Approximately triangular fragment, edges defined by plain band 5mm wide, edge marked by grain-flesh slits 7mm apart. Space within area defined by bands filled with plain dots, diameter 2mm and 5mm apart (centre to centre). Dots have been stamped with a hollow punch.

Worn, one end truncated, other end partially torn.

L 115mm; surviving W 14–38mm; Th 3.5mm.

SF 4159 (Figure 4.22)
Phase/Feature Phase 2/Hollow C002
Description: fragment with stud holes – legging or sleeve?

Large, slightly tapered fragment with two grain-flesh stitching channels, stitch L 6mm, on long opposite sides of fragment. One short side cut, with adjacent row of stud holes; the other short edge is mostly torn, but has a few stud holes. Fragment is perforated by five full length parallel vertical rows of stud holes. Two parallel horizontal rows run between the two outermost vertical rows; these horizontal rows are each crossed by four short vertical rows, in the space between the full length vertical rows.

Dimensions 242–320mm x 374mm x 1mm.

The two stitched edges appear to match, indicating that they were stitched together, thus making a tapered tube, such as a legging or sleeve. The measurements suggest that, unless the leather has shrunk significantly or it was intended for a child or small adult, it would be tight as a legging. Accordingly, a sleeve might be more appropriate.

4.2.3 Textiles
Penelope Walton Rogers (The Anglo-Saxon Laboratory)
(written 2009)

Introduction

Textiles were recovered in relatively small numbers from Area C, from levels attributed to Phases 1 to 6. All appear to be clothing fabrics and they divide naturally into two groups. Those deposited in the mid-to-late 12th to 13th centuries, Phases 1–3, are the kinds of wool twills which are likely to have been worn by artisans and the poorer social strata, while the second group, from the late medieval, post-medieval and early modern occupation of the site, Phases 5–6, represents a greater range of fabric-type, including some good quality wool textiles, linen and silk. Material from Phases 1 to 5 is discussed below; details of Phase 6 textiles can be found in the site archive.

Table 4.5 Textiles from Phases 1-4

Context/Find	Fibre	Weave	Threads per cm/ spin direction	Notes
Phase 1				
Pit C003/SF2737	Wool	2/1 twill	8–9/Z x 7/S	?Yellow/brown dye
Pit C006/SF1549	Wool (light & dark fibres)	Yarns	S-spun, 2mm thick	Yarn from a coarse textile
Pit C006/SF2794	Wool (light & dark fibres)	2/2 twill	7/Z x 5–6/S	Felted from wear
Phase 2				
Pit C032/SF4056	Wool	2/2 twill	15/Z x 12/S	Seam/hem and weaving fault
Pit C025/SF3912A	Wool	2/1 twill	13/Z x 10/S	-
Gully C004/SF3339	Wool (light & dark fibres)	2/1 twill	11/Z x 12/Z	Weaving fault
Spread C041/SF4089	Wool (light & dark fibres)	2/1 twill	9/Z x 11/S	Seam/hem
Pit C025/SF3358	Wool	2/1 twill	10/Z x 10/S	Seam
Phase 3				
Pit C042/SF4210	Wool	2/1 twill	11/Z,S x 9/S	Occasional S in Z-system; no dye detected
Pit C047/SF3022	Wool	2/2 twill	11–12/Z x 11–13/Z	-
Phase 3 or 4				
Layer C019/SF1330A	Wool	2/2 twill	13–14/Z x 10–11/S	-
Layer C019/SF1330B	Wool	2/1 twill	16–18/Z x 15/Z	?Yellow/brown dye
Pit C069/SF2139	Linen	2/1 twill	9/Z x 12–14/Z	-
Pit C048/SF1462	Wool (light & dark fibres)	2/2 twill	11/Z x 11/S	-

Figure 4.23 Textile (SF4056) from Pit C032 showing remains of stitching and circular holes, where decorative metal studs may have been attached

Phases 1–3 (Table 4.5)

The earliest fragment, SF2737, came from Pit C003, Phase 1, but it is similar in character to the textiles from pits, gullies and occupation layers of Phases 2 and 3, and to textile SF2794 from Pit C006, so that these 11 textiles can be treated as a single group. All pieces are ragged and some of them have patches of uneven felting, which suggests extensive wear. Several of them have remains of seams in the form of folded edges, curving cut edges and rows of stitch holes, which indicates that they originated in clothing. One piece, SF4056, from Pit C032, has one cut edge rolled inwards, with remains of stitching, probably hemming, carried out with a thick pair of Z-spun yarns; a second cut edge folded inwards to a depth of 8mm; and two regular circular holes, 3mm diameter, which may represent where decorative metal studs were attached (Figure 4.23). Riveted metal studs have often been recorded on leather goods of this period, but there is evidence from 14th century London that they could also be mounted on textile (Egan and Pritchard 1991: 162, 179).

Although the 11 textiles have a similar appearance, seven have been woven in 2/1 twill and four in 2/2 twill (Table 4.5). They are medium-weight fabrics with thread-counts (number of threads per cm) ranging from 8 x 7 to 16–18 x 15. Two textiles, one 2/2 and the other

2/1 twill, have Z-spun yarn in warp and weft (ZZ) and the others have Z-spun yarn in one direction, probably the warp, and S-spun in the other (ZS). One of these last, SF4210 from Pit C042, has an occasional S-spun yarn in the Z-spun system, arranged in the order, 1S, 18Z, 1S, 19Z, 1S, 6(+)Z, which may represent the remains of a pattern. It can be compared with a 2/1 twill from medieval Fishergate, York, which had single threads in a contrasting colour (Walton Rogers 2002: 2880–81), although no dye could be detected in SF4210.

Apart from this possible attempt at patterning, there is little evidence for the kinds of process that give extra value to the cloth. There has been no soft-finishing in the form of fulling or teaselling and the only evidence for dyeing was a yellow-brown extract of uncertain origin in SF2737 and SF1330A. At least three of the textiles have been made from naturally pigmented wools, grey in the case of SF3339 and SF4089 and brown or black in the Z-spun yarn of SF1462. In addition, two textiles, SF3339 and SF4056, have a weaving fault: in the former a line of the weave has been omitted, and in the latter loose threads miss their binding points and float over the surface of the fabric. These would have made noticeable flaws in the cloth and suggest that these textiles, though functional, were not particularly valuable.

Medieval textiles from sites in Aberdeen have been reviewed by Gabra-Sanders (2001). She has shown that the 2/1 twill structure was the most common in Aberdeen in the 13th and 14th centuries, as it was in other towns of northwest Europe before it receded in the late 14th and 15th century. However, 72% of the 162 textiles from Aberdeen were felted or fulled, some so heavily that the weave could not be identified (Gabra-Sanders 2001, 223–24) and it is generally agreed that by the 13th century most urban-made wool textiles other than fine 'worsteds' were soft-finished (Crowfoot et al. 1992: 35–36). The absence of finish in the Bon Accord group therefore sets them apart from the general run of urban textiles of the period.

2/2 twill occurs much less frequently in late medieval sites, although there were four pieces with ZS spin from 16–18 Netherkirkgate (Gabra-Sanders 2001: 224) and occasional examples, sometimes ZZ, sometimes ZS, in similar qualities to the Bon Accord pieces, from 13th century Newcastle-upon-Tyne (Walton 1988: 91), late 13th century Southampton (Crowfoot 1975: 338–39), 13th/14th century Perth (Bennett 1987: 165), 13th to 15th century Coventry (Walton unpublished) and 14th century London (Crowfoot et al. 1992: 27, 36–40). In contrast, 2/2 twills, often made from pigmented wools, were in use in the Scottish islands from the Norse occupation to the 20th century, where they were supplemented by small amounts of 2/1 twill (Walton Rogers 1999: 195–97). Textiles made from brown, grey or black wools were known at the time as 'russets' and were regarded as the proper clothing for country people (Strutt 1842: II, 105ff). It is possible, then, that the textiles from Phases 1–3 are mainly cheap rural fabrics, in contrast with the soft-finished urban products more commonly identified in other 13th and 14th century sites in Aberdeen.

Phase 3–4

Textile SF2139 from Pit C069, Phase 3 or 4, represents an unusual example of a linen woven in 2/1 twill. Textiles made of plant fibres (linens in the broadest sense) do not survive well in either aerated or acidic soils, and no linens were recorded in Gabra-Sanders' survey. In this instance, however, the textile appears to have been charred before burial, which has allowed it to survive in altered form (Walton 1989a: 300, 312). The fibre was identified by microscopy as a partially processed plant fibre from the diameter range of 10–14microns and 37–50microns, and by the smooth fibre profiles with occasional bulges and constrictions. Most surviving examples of medieval linens are simple fabrics in tabby weave and only one other example in 2/1 twill, with a comparable thread-count of 10/Z x 8/Z, has been recorded, at 14th century Crown Court, Quayside, Newcastle upon Tyne (Walton 1989b: 174).

Phase 5

Textile SF735 from Spread C058 is another example of wool 2/1 twill, but this time it has been soft-finished, probably by fulling. It has also been dyed. Dyes are usually characterised analytically by their absorption spectra and by chromatographic separation, but in this instance the dye showed only poorly defined absorption in the region where yellow and brown colorants occur (Walton and Taylor 1991). However, during testing, each sample of SF735 gave off the strong, pleasant aroma of the crottle dyes. The crottles are classified as BWM (boiling water method) lichens (Bolton 1991: 19–27; Casselman 1996: 10), and they are a traditional dyestuff of the Scottish highlands and islands (Grierson 1986: 185–87). The lichens mostly used in these areas were dark crottle, *Parmelia omphalodes*, and light crottle, *P.saxatalis*, which were gathered from rocks and trees and used for rich shades of orange and brown (Grierson *ibid*). They are long-lasting dyes, which are very difficult to extract and characterise by chemical means, but their distinctive perfume when heated in liquids can be taken as a strong indicator of their presence. The same lichens were used in the perfume industry and the smell of the fabric is still employed to authenticate the use of crottle in traditional Harris tweeds (Casselman 1996: 11–12).

4.2.4 Animal pelts and fibres
Penelope Walton Rogers (The Anglo-Saxon Laboratory)
(written 2009)

Introduction

Substantial quantities of animal fibre were recovered from the site, from Phases 1–6 (Table 4.6). Some were disaggregated fibres mixed with other organic debris, but most were still in 'staples', the locks of fibre that form naturally in an animal's coat. Some of the latter clearly represented the remains of animal pelts: at the proximal end of the staple there were fibre roots and black decayed remains of skin. Most of the pelts can be attributed to Phases 2–4, when the site was almost certainly used for the processing of animal skins. The remains from other phases are more likely to represent domestic and other more general occupation debris.

The animal species can be identified by microscopy of the fibre. The diagnostic features are the range of fibre diameters, the nature of the cuticular scale pattern, the distribution of pigment, the presence or absence of medullas (central air channel), and the shape of the cross-section (Appleyard 1978; Wildman 1954). The results for individual specimens have been recorded in detail and are summarised in the archive report and Table 4.6.

Results

From Phase 1, there was a tuft of hair, SF4310, from horse or cattle recovered from Gully C001 and the remains of lambskin and some brown-black goat hair, SF2383, from Pit C005. In the medieval period lambskin, sometimes traded under the name of 'budge', was used for the linings of winter garments and shoes (Veale 1966: 14–18). The other items were represented by small amounts of fibre and do not point to any particular industrial activity.

Much larger amounts of fibre were recovered from between Phase 2 and early Phase 4. The most extensive remains, from sub-rectangular Pit C018, appear to represent a single brown-black goatskin killed in summer. The coat of goat changes through the year and this example lacked the fine underwool of autumn-winter growth (Ryder 1987: 8). There were also remains of cattle hide, calfskin (the coat of young cattle is different from that of adults: Wildman 1954: 135–58), brown and white sheepskins, white goatskin and further examples of brown-black goatskin, from Layers C003, C019 and C050, Spread C043 and Pit C048. It seems likely that some of the pits in this area were used for the de-hairing of skins, probably by soaking them in an alkaline liquor prepared from wood ash or lime (Cherry 1991a: 296). Medieval records such as those from Northampton show that there was a distinction

Table 4.6 Animal fibres from Area C

Phase 1			
Gully C001/SF4310	50–55mm	?Hide	Uncertain: brown cattle or horse
Pit C005/SF2383A	>25mm	-	Brown-black goat hair
Pit C005/SF2383B	15–20mm	Skin	Light brown possibly lambskin
Phase 2			
Layer C003/SF1228	30–35mm	?Hide	Brown cattle hair
Layer C003/SF1379A	-	-	Brown, probably coarse calf hair
Layer C003/SF1379B	-	-	White, sheep's wool
Layer C003/SF1420	-	-	Brown-black goat hair
Layer C003/SF1427	30–35mm	-	Not identified
Layer C003/SF1951	-	-	Not identified
Layer C003/SF1186	-	-	Brown sheep's wool
Layer C003/SF1195	45mm	Skin	White sheepskin
Layer C003/SF1238	45mm	Skin	Brown sheep's wool, similar to 1186
Layer C003/SF3578	50mm	Skin	Brown sheepskin, HM fleece type
Pit C018/SF2321	-	-	Same as 3126 and 4127
Pit C018/SF2790	-	-	Same as 3126 and 4127
Pit C018/SF3069	35mm	-	Same as 3126 and 4127
Pit C018/SF3126	35–55mm	Skin	Brown-black goatskin, summer coat
Pit C018/SF4127	50mm	?Skin	Brown-black goatskin, summer coat
Pit C018/SF4290	-	-	Same as 3126 and 4127
Stakes C002/SF3729	-	-	White, possibly sheep's wool
Spread C043/SF3425	70mm	-	Light brown: ?cattle or ?horse
Spread C043/SF3429	-	-	White goat
Spread C043/SF3847	25–40mm	-	Pale, probably cattle
Phase 3			
Layer C050/SF3897	30–35mm	?Skin	Probably off-white lambskin
Phase 3 or 4			
Layer C019/SF777	-	-	White, probably sheep's wool
Layer C019/SF1173	-	-	Pale calf hair
Layer C019/SF1438	30–40mm	?Skin	Brown cattle hair
Layer C019/SF2277	40–50mm	-	Possibly black goat
Layer C019/SF3942	-	-	Not identified
Pit C048/SF3916	35mm	?Skin	Brown cattle hair
Pit C048/SF3590	40–65mm	Skin	Dark brown/black goatskin
Phase 4			
Layer C041/SF2791	50mm	?Skin	White sheepskin, GM fleece type
Phase 5			
Spread C099/SF3467	60–70mm	Skin	White sheepskin, HM fleece type
Phase 6			
Structure C012/SF1301	-	-	Loose fibres of sheep's wool

between the tanners who vegetable-tanned adult cattle hides, and the whittawyers who treated the skins of sheep, goat, deer, horse and dog (and calf can be added to the list) with alum and oil (Cherry 1991a: 299). Both would require preliminary de-hairing, and it would appear that at Bon Accord both heavy and light skins were being processed on the same site, between Phase 2 and early Phase 4.

The animal fibres from later levels of the site are derived only from sheep, a white sheepskin, SF2791, from Layer C041 (Phase 4), another, SF3467, from Spread C099 (Phase 5) and some loose fibres of white wool, SF1301, from Structure C012 (Phase 6). The skins may represent remains of clothing or furnishings and the loose wool the raw material for spinning. There is therefore no evidence for skin preparation later than early Phase 4.

4.2.5 Cordage
Anne Crone

Four lengths of plaited hair moss (*Polytrichum commune*) rope and a length of plaited hair moss string were found in Phase 1 Pit C006 and Phase 2 Pit C025. In each length the fibres have been combed out, removing all but the occasional leaf. The ropes have all been fashioned by plaiting bundles of fibres, new bundles being added in to increase length; the point at which one bundle of fibres ends and the next one begins is visible mid-way along SF1555 and on several points on SF3286A (Figure 4.24). The two lengths found in Pit C006 (SF1555 and SF2940) could be part of the same original rope, SF2940 representing an unravelled fragment. However, the two lengths found in Pit C025 are more likely to represent two separate ropes, as SF3286B does not have the string that is threaded through the plait of SF3286A (Figure 4.24). The string may have been a means of strengthening the rope although it does not appear to be frayed along the surviving length.

Hair moss grows in open woodland and acid mires and can grow to lengths of about 0.4m (Dickson 1973). The usefulness of the long, tough, pliable stems has been recognised since at least the Bronze Age. Twist ropes of hair moss were used to tie the joints between the planking of one of the North Ferriby boats (Wright and Churchill 1965) and it is even reported to have been used as a kind of shroud in a Bronze Age grave at Ferniegair, Hamilton (Miller 1947). A flattened circle of woven hair moss with a fringe of long strands, retrieved from the bottom of the ditch at the Roman fort of Newstead, was interpreted by the excavator as an unfinished basket (Curle 1911: 108; Henshall 1950: 152), but a very similar object from the Roman fort at Vindolanda has been interpreted as a hat with a fringe (Wild 1994). A short length of a 3-strand plait and four bundles of hair moss in various stages of preparation were found on the Early Historic crannog at Buiston, Ayrshire (Crone 2000c:

Figure 4.24 Upper; hairmoss plait SF3286A; fibre bundles protrude mid-way along the plait and at the lefthand end where it curves back on itself. Note the plaited string that has been threaded through the plait.
Lower; Hairmoss plait SF3286B

133–34), and at Lochlee, another Early Historic crannog close to Buiston, a 4-strand plait and four fringed plaits of hair moss were also found (Munro 1882: 95, 136).

There are numerous examples of hair moss ropes from urban medieval deposits in the British Isles (Shrewsbury – Barker 1961; Trig Lane, London – Rhodes 1982; Coppergate, York – Hall 1989: 393–97; Perth – Ford and Robinson 1987) and Europe (for example, Aachen and Bergen – reported in Walton Rogers and Hall 2001). The finds are invariably 3-strand plaited ropes and most are short fragments, although some extraordinary lengths have been found, such as the 2.89m length from Trig Lane, London and the 10m length, from a 13th century latrine pit, in Aachen (reported in Hall 1989). Lengths of hair moss rope have also been recovered from other Aberdeen sites (Walton Rogers and Hall 2001); the length from Gallowgate Middle School was a twisted 2-ply rope knotted at one end, while the example from 45–75 Gallowgate was the more standard 3-strand plait.

The plaited lengths of hair moss have been described as ropes but Henshall (1950: 154), when discussing the hair moss from Lochlee crannog, suggested that the moss was plaited simply to keep it tidy and manageable for later use, as is done with raffia. Hair moss was used to make soft besoms, or brooms, for the dusting of beds, curtains, carpets and hangings in the 18th century (Hall 1989), while Curle (1911: 358) reported that baskets, hassocks and brooms made of hair moss had been presented to Kew Museum in the 19th century. This material is still used to make basketry today. As plaited rope it would have had myriad uses on a semi-industrial site like Bon Accord.

Catalogue of cordage

SF   1555
Phase/Feature   Phase 1/Pit C006 fill (B)
Description: plait
SF1555 is a length of 3-strand hair moss plait, 560mm long when straightened out. The plait has loosened and is now 45mm wide by 26mm thick at its best-preserved point. Midway along its length is the junction where new bundles of fibres have been worked into the plait. Both ends are frayed and unfinished.

SF   2940
Phase/Feature   Phase 1/Pit C006 fill (B)
Description: plait
SF2940 is a length of hair moss plait, 310mm long. It has unravelled and only two strands survive loosely twisted at one point. At this point it is 30mm wide and 20mm thick.

SF   3286A (Figure 4.24)
Phase/Feature   Phase 2/Pit C025 fill (D)
Description: plait
SF3286A is a length of 3-strand hair moss plait which is now bent back on itself but when straightened out is 450mm long. The plait has loosened and is now 36mm wide and 12mm thick. There are two points at which the ends of fibre-bundles protrude, suggesting that lengths of hair moss c. 170–180mm long were being used. Both ends are frayed and unfinished. A tightly plaited length of hair moss string, 3mm wide and 1mm thick, has been threaded through the plait up through the outer loops on one side. There are knots at two points along its length and one end is finished by a knot to tie off the fibres. The other end is unfinished. It is 620mm long and protrudes from each end of the bigger plait by 110mm at the finished end and 60mm at the other.

SF   3286B (Figure 4.24)
Phase/Feature   Phase 2/Pit C025 fill (D)
Description: plait
SF3286B is a tightly woven length of 3-strand plait, 200mm long and 30mm wide by 8mm thick. Both ends are frayed and unfinished.

4.3 Inorganic artefacts

4.3.1 Metal artefacts
Dawn McLaren with contributions by K. Paton, A. Sibley and N. Holmes

Overview

A total of 1389 metal objects were recovered. This includes 1241 iron and 148 non-ferrous metal objects (122 copper-based alloy and silver objects, and 26 lead-based alloys) which range in date from the late 11th/12th century AD to the recent past. Metal finds were recovered from all phases, with the vast majority, particularly that of iron, deriving from the later medieval, post-medieval and modern contexts. Most of the objects were in a broken or damaged state and in some instances were too fragmentary to allow identification of form or date. Many metal objects, particularly those made of iron, are long-lived types making comment on specific chronology problematic.

Most of the finds recovered are fragments of fittings relating to structures and internal fixtures but also present are small numbers of household items including candlesticks and vessel fragments; horse equipment; dress accessories such as buckles, brooches, lace chapes and a strap-end; barrel padlock fragments and other security equipment as well as tool fragments. Significant items present include a highly decorated late 11th/12th century spur and a probable medieval lead alloy gemstone bezel.

Metal finds were individually examined macroscopically, where necessary utilising a binocular microscope and 10x hand-lens. X-radiography aided the analysis; identification of iron objects relied heavily on x-radiography and measurements taken from x-rays. Non-ferrous metals have been described here under three broad groups: copper alloy, silver and lead but it should be noted that no compositional analysis (e.g. ED-XRF) was undertaken to refine these broad alloy groups.

Due to the large quantities of metal finds from later, late medieval, post-medieval and modern contexts (Phases 5 and 6) the following report will explicitly focus on objects from Phases 1 to 4, relating to activity dating from the 12th to 15th centuries, but with specific comments on diagnostic artefacts from all phases. Detailed catalogue descriptions are presented only on illustrated objects but the assemblage is discussed by alloy type and functional group. A full methodology and catalogue of all metal objects (Phases 1 to 6) is contained in the site archive.

Iron

A total of 1242 iron objects, nails and miscellaneous spalls are present amongst the metal assemblage. The ironwork is severely corroded and identification could only be undertaken with the aid of x-radiographs. From a typological point of view much of the material is undiagnostic of a particular period: for example, square-sectioned nails were in use from the Iron Age through to the post-medieval period.

The following discussion focuses on objects from Phases 1 to 4 where identification of function and/or date has been possible. Objects from Phases 5 and 6 will not be discussed in detail unless they are diagnostic types and/or suggestive of an early, possibly medieval, date.

Weaponry

A single arrowhead (SF2356; Figure 4.25) was recovered from a layer of late post-medieval or modern disturbance within Area C. It has a small triangular blade which has a diamond cross-section and short rounded barbs with a short square-sectioned shoulder. No socket survives but it is assumed that a narrow conical ferrule would once have extended from the square-sectioned shoulder. It conforms broadly to Jessop's type MP1 arrowhead, a general purpose form in use over a long period, from the 11th to the 15th century (Jessop 1996: 196, fig 1). This type of arrowhead is a common find on urban sites and could have been employed in either hunting or warfare (LMMC, 1940). Similar, contemporary, examples have been found on other Scottish sites, including Rattray, Aberdeen (Goodall in Murray & Murray 1993: 188, fig 39, 177), Perth (Caldwell and Bogden 2012: 193, illus 153; Ford 1987b: 130, 132, illus 65, no 62) and Urquhart Castle (Samson 1982: 468–69, nos 16 & 17).

Horse equipment

Horse-related equipment was present in the form of horseshoe nails, fragmentary horseshoes and a star rowel. The condition of most of these items and the contexts of recovery imply that they were casual losses during use. The nails, in particular, were found in fairly small numbers considering the duration of occupation on site and most show signs of use in the form of damage to the head or shank and the loss of the tip.

The function and history of horseshoes have been discussed by Clark (1995: 75–84), leading to an established typology, at least for medieval London. Six horseshoe fragments are present amongst the assemblage but only three shoes were sufficiently intact to enable comparison with Clark's scheme. Detailed examination confirms the presence of at least one medieval Type 2b shoe (*ibid*, 86–87, fig 62) and two later medieval examples (Type 4; *ibid*, 88–89, fig

69). The remaining three shoes recovered from Spread A036 (Phase 3) and Layers A014 and C058 (Mid Phase 5) were severely fractured and/or degraded precluding identification of type. A similar variety of horseshoe types are known from a range of Scottish medieval sites including: Tantallon Castle, East Lothian (Caldwell 1991: illus 4, nos 32); Perth (Cox 1996: 773–74, illus 21, no 297; Ford 1987b: 137;), Edinburgh Castle (Clark 1997b: 161–62, illus 133, no 84) and Aberdeen (Goodall 1982b: 188–89, no 83).

A total of 12 horseshoe nails are present and have been described following Clark's (1995) typochronological classification scheme. It is likely that further incomplete examples are present amongst the incomplete nails discussed under structural fittings. Four (SF1354, SF1157, SF2328, SF2992A) come from medieval contexts in Area A, with a further three nails (SF1015, SF4207B, SF6015) coming from early phases in Area C. The remaining five nails come from post-medieval contexts.

Three of Clark's (1995) four types of medieval/early post-medieval horseshoe nail are present at Bon Accord including type 2 'fiddle key' nails, type 3 nails with expanded head and ears and type 4 nails with rectangular heads. Of the types represented at Bon Accord, 'fiddle key' nails represent the earliest form, as defined by Clark – a type which saw a long duration of production and use with examples known from 11th century through to 15th century contexts in London (*ibid*, 86–87) and saw use in conjunction with both type 2 and type 3 styles of horseshoe. Only one example of this form of nail was identified at Bon Accord (SF429) and was found in a late medieval/early post-medieval context (Layer C009). The most common form of horseshoe nail on site was Clark's type 3 nail represented by ten examples recovered from Phase 1–6 contexts. This includes a substantially complete nail (SF2328; Figure 4.25) which came from layer A002 which is now damaged but shows no obvious signs of use or wear. Type 4 nails are represented by a single example (SF2522) which was recovered from the fill of a late medieval/post-medieval well (A001). The low number of horseshoe nails recognised amongst the assemblage and their wide distribution both spatially and chronologically argues that most of these represent casual loses during use.

The most significant item amongst this group is a well-preserved star-shaped iron spur rowel (SF2648; Figure 4.25) which was recovered from Layer A015, a Phase 4 deposit likely of 14th to 15th century date. It shows signs of wear, implying casual loss during use rather than purposeful discard. Rowel spurs were introduced in the 13th century as an alternative to prick spurs and quickly replaced them becoming the typical spur fitting in production and use from the late 13th century (Ellis 1995: 127–29; Egan 1995). Simple star-shaped rowels

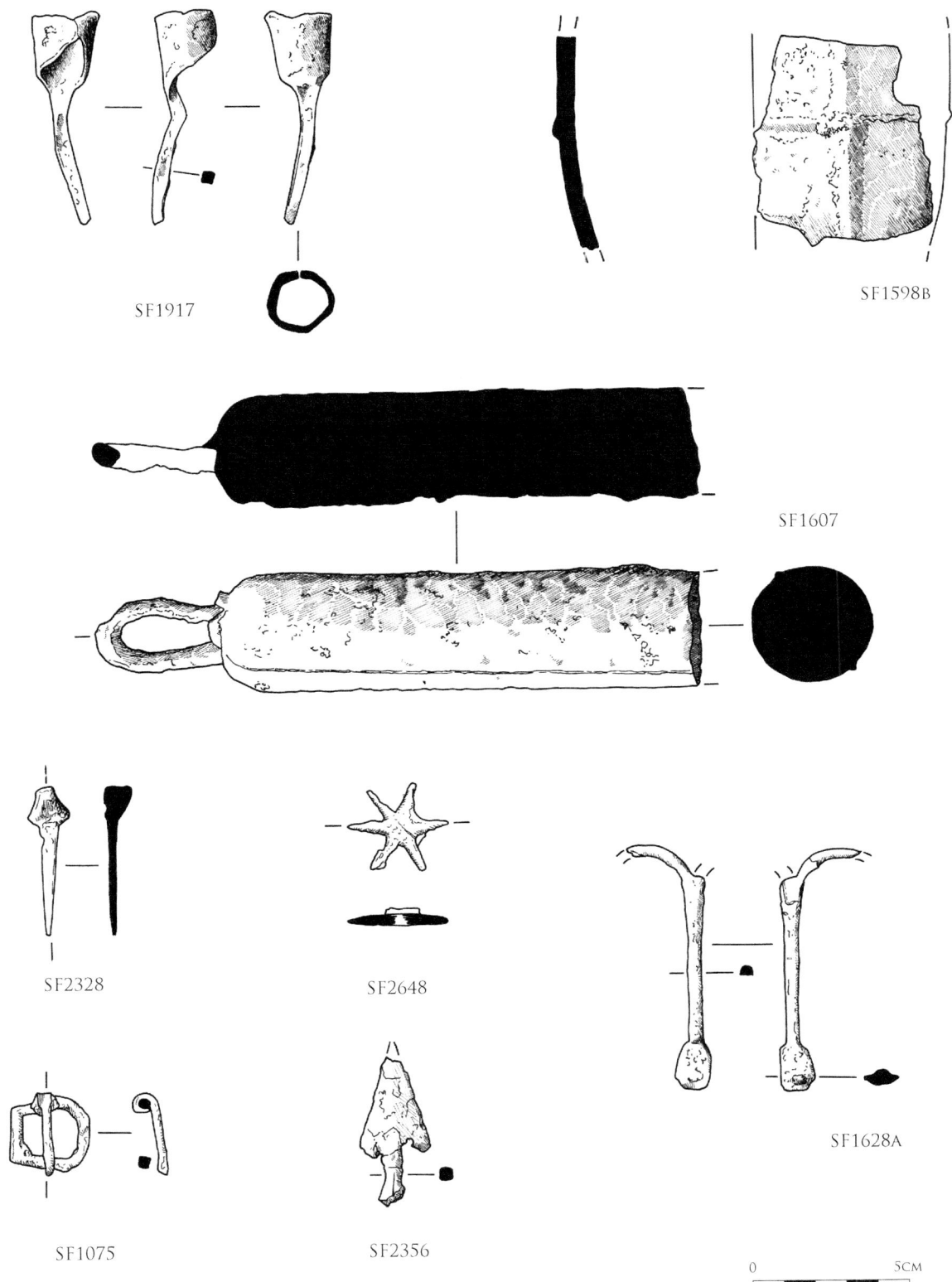

Figure 4.25 Miscellaneous iron objects; SF1917; SF1598B; SF1607; SF2328; SF2648; SF1628A; SF1075; SF2356

with a varying number of points saw use from the inception of rowel spur use until modern times, making typological dating of detached rowels problematic (*ibid*, 147). The example from Bon Accord is very similar in form, size and finish to a 13th century example from London (*ibid*, 147: fig 106, no.358), while a similar small star-shaped rowel of 15th century date is present on an iron spur at Tantallon Castle attesting to the long-lived currency of this horse-related fitting (Caldwell 1991: 340–42, illus 4, no 31).

Dress accessories

Two simple D-shaped iron buckle frames (SF1075, Figure 4.25; SF1390) were recovered from late medieval/ early post-medieval layers (A007 & A017). Such simple buckles had a long currency of use from the 13th to 15th centuries and could have been used for a variety of purposes, the most common of which was as a fastening for items of personal dress (Egan and Pritchard 1991: 53). Although iron buckles are known from 13th century contexts they tend to be less common than their copper alloy counterparts and are more typical of later use, consistent with the 15th to mid 18th century date of the contexts of recovery at Bon Accord.

Similar D-shaped buckles are known from a range of Scottish medieval sites including: Springwood Park, Kelso (Ford 1998: 710, illus 19, no 3), Jedburgh Abbey, Scottish Borders (Caldwell 1995b: 91, illus 81), Threave Castle, Galloway (Caldwell 1981: 116, fig 12, no 117), Tantallon Castle, East Lothian (Caldwell 1991: illus 4, no 30), Perth (Ford 1987b: 131–32, illus 65 no 66; Franklin and Goodall 2012: 124–25, illus 125, nos 1–4) and Edinburgh Castle (Clark 1997b: 154–56, illus 130, no 26).

In addition to the two iron buckles mentioned is a brooch or buckle pin which comes from Spread A015 dating to Phase 6 (SF6013). It cannot be closely dated but would be consistent with brooch pins in use from the medieval to late post-medieval periods.

Tools

Iron tools are well represented amongst the Bon Accord metal assemblage (28) including many long-lived tool types (such as knives, chisels and punches). The wide range of tools present include knives of various forms, small shears and scissor fragments, a spoon-type auger bit, an axe-hammer or wedge, a serrated blade probably from a hand-held saw, file fragments and currier's knife. These tools represent a suite of craft and industrial activities such as stone masonry, carpentry, leather and textile working as well as metalworking although in the case of the knives, assigning a specific function to the blades has not generally been attempted as these are best considered general purpose tools that could have fulfilled multiple functions in both a domestic

and industrial setting. The majority of these tools came from Phase 5 and 6 deposits, suggesting a post-medieval (or perhaps late medieval) date for their production, use and discard.

Chisels: One robust chisel (SF2706) came from spread A039 (Phase 6). The recovery of this item from a late post-medieval context indicates recent use and discard but tools such as this have known from medieval contexts in Britain and is readily paralleled with an example from Winchester, Hampshire (Goodall 2011: 52 fig 4.3, C32) dating to the mid 12th to early 13th century. The Bon Accord example is short and robust, consistent with stout stonemason's chisels (*ibid*, 45). In contrast, SF3525B is a carpenter's tool (Figure 4.26). It was recovered from the fill of a late post-medieval well (C002).

Auger bit: One auger bit (SF1806), for use in woodworking, came from Wall A003 (Phase 6). It is similar to examples listed and illustrated by Goodall (1981: 52–53, fig 51, no 11; 2011: 24, fig 3.6, 3.7). They were used for drilling holes into items of wood including structural timbers, furniture, panelling and vessels. Auger bits such as this example are a long-lived type and cannot be closely dated on form alone. The size and style are consistent with medieval examples but could equally be post-medieval in date as examples from Perth (Ford 1987b: 134–35, illus 67, no 95; Franklin and Goodall 2012: 146, illus 133, no. 195) and Urquhart Castle (Samson 1982: 469–71, fig 4, nos 45 to 47) attest. Medieval examples are known from Threave Castle, Galloway (Caldwell 1981: 112, fig 11, no 77).

Knives: These common tools (14) were used for a variety of purposes in daily life and the range of types and of size and shape is considerable. No distinctive early medieval knife forms were recognised amongst this group and the majority of examples derive from post-medieval contexts. With the exception of one handle from a folding knife from a Phase 6 deposit (SF1637), all of the knives from Bon Accord were of whittle tang variety. Only three knives (SF1394 (Figure 4.26), SF2259 & SF4207A (Figure 4.26)) were recovered from Phase 1 to 4 contexts and have been individually catalogued and classified, where possible, in accordance with established typochronological schemes (e.g. Cowgill *et al.* 1987; Goodall 2011). In addition, two possible knife tang fragments were present in Phase 2/3 and Phase 4 contexts (SF2076, SF2147A). Those from Phases 5 to 6 are summarised in Table 4.7 and include robust blades or files (SF2153A–C) and a possible currier's knife (SF2153D).

Similar examples are common occurrences amongst excavated Scottish medieval site assemblages including those from Perth (Cox 1996: 773, 775–76, illus 21, nos 332, 333, 340; Ford 1987b: 131–32, illus 65, nos 74–77,

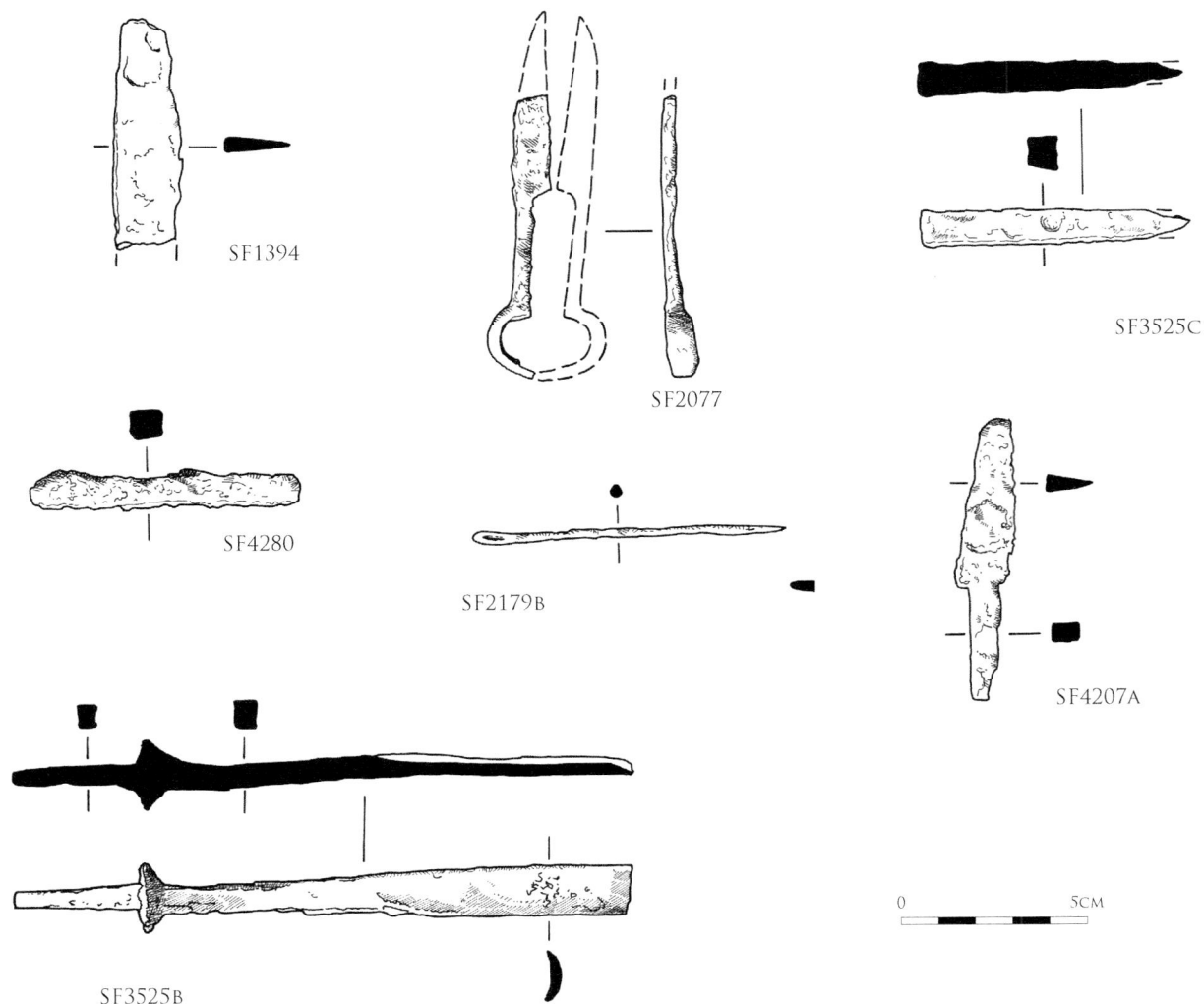

Figure 4.26 Tools and knives; SF1394; SF2077; SF3525C; SF4207A; SF4280; SF3525B; SF2179B

80–83), Edinburgh Castle (Clark 1997b: 154–55, illus 130, nos1, 10, 11) and Aberdeen (Goodall 1982b: 188–89, no 87).

Shears and scissors: Shears were introduced into Europe in the 6th or 7th centuries but only came into widespread use in the late 13th or 14th century. Although scissors are known from medieval contexts, shears were in more widespread use than often represented by surviving archaeological finds (see Goodall 1981: 58–59). At Bon Accord, both shears and scissors are represented amongst the iron assemblage. A small set of shears, missing the blade and handle on one side (SF2077; Figure 4.26) came from early Phase 5 deposits (Layer A005). These are consistent with Goodall's type 2A shears which range in length 95–328mm and typically have curved or slanted junctions between the handle and blade (Goodall 2011: 111–12) with the broad date

range 11th to 15th century. A possible arm fragment from a set of pivoting scissors or shears was unstratified.

While small shears were used for domestic purposes, scissors may have been preferred by tradesmen such as hatters, glovers, tailors and barbers (Cox 1996: 781). Scottish examples include those from Perth (Cox 1996: 780–81, illus 24, no 415; Franklin and Goodall 2012: 133).

Punches: A possible punch (SF4280), likely to have been used in sheet metalworking, was recovered from the fill of Gully C001 associated with Phase 1 and 2 activity (Figure 4.26). The form of the punch, with square-section and slight burring of the head through use, is suggestive of use as a metalworking tool (Goodall 2011: 10). Punches were also commonly used for wood and stone working but more commonly have circular-sectioned shanks and generally lack significant damage

Table 4.7 Summary of major non-modern iron artefacts

Area A	Wire/bar/sheet/strip	Weaponry	Horse equipment	Dress accessories	Household equipment	Tools	Fittings	Other
Phase 1			SF1354 horseshoe nail			SF1394 knife blade	SF3279 bar or fitting fragment	
Phase 1 or 2						SF4280 possible punch		
Phase 2	SF3097 rod with spherical head		SF1157 horseshoe nail; SF2328 horseshoe nail; SF2992A horseshoe nail		SF1146 small rotary key		SF2922B timber dog fragment (tenter hook?); SF3220 holdfast	
Phase 2 or 3						SF2076 knife tang or tapering tool tip		SF2351B unidentified object fragment
Phase 3			SF2299 incomplete horseshoe					
Phase 4	SF1178 bar or off-cut		SF2293 incomplete horseshoe; SF2648 star rowel				SF2538 U-shaped fitting; SF2836 distorted ring	
Phase 4 or 5							SF1982 timber dog (tenter hook?)	
Phase 5	SF1628A tapering strip; SF1702A & B rod fragments; SF1716A-C rod fragments; SF1730 bar fragment; SF1916C perforated strip fragment; SF2003 perforated sheet fragment; SF2012 strip; SF2025 rod fragment; SF2094 strip fragment		SF1916A horseshoe nail; SF1916B incomplete horseshoe; SF2522 horseshoe nail	SF1075 D-shaped buckle; SF1390 D-shaped buckle frame	SF1917 cupped candlestick; SF2179B needle; SF2179A door bolt fragment	SF2077 small shears; SF2161 knife blade tip	SF1075 hooked fitting; SF1109 key-shaped fitting; SF1702C staple-like fitting; SF1716D composite sheet metal fitting; SF1716 sheet metal fitting fragments; SF1916D possible hinge fragment; SF2016 hooked fitting fragment; SF2502 U-shaped loop fitting, possibly from a weight; SF2534A perforated binding strip fragment; SF2534 structural bracket fragment or machine part	SF1850 sheet fragment with decorative rivets; SF2571 curving iron strip
Phase 6	SF1660B sheet metal fragments; SF2660 strip fragment; SF ** fine wire fragment			SF6013 brooch or buckle pin		SF1806 spoon-type auger bit; SF2153 knife blade fragment; SF2706 chisel; SF2713 rowel-tipped tool; SF2713G axe-hammer or wedge	SF1660A sheet metal frame or fitting; SF2658 perforated binding strip; SF2669 timber dog	
Modern						SF733 possible punch		

Area B	Wire/bar/sheet/strip	Weaponry	Horse equipment	Dress accessories	Household equipment	Tools	Fittings	Other
Phase 6	SF1598 strip fragment; SF1608 distorted strip fragment; SF1637A bar fragment				SF1598B possible ribbed vessel fragment	SF1637 handle from a folding knife	SF1564 strap fragment; SF1637B-D strap fragments	SF1607 weight
Modern						SF1972 punch?		

Area A	Wire/bar/sheet/strip	Weaponry	Horse equipment	Dress accessories	Household equipment	Tools	Fittings	Other
Area C	Wire/bar/sheet/strip	Weaponry	Horse equipment	Dress accessories	Household equipment	Tools	Fittings	Other
Phase 1	SF418A-C wire loop fragments; SF418D bar fragment		SF1015 horseshoe nail		SF4794 barrel padlock and bolt		SF418E robust cast collar (?modern)	
Phase 1 or 2						SF4280 possible punch		
Phase 2	SF3183A tapering strip; SF3183B wire fragment; SF4183B bar fragment		SF1416 horseshoe fragment			SF1735A saw blade fragment	SF620 U-shaped staple; SF2637 bar-shaped fitting, damaged; SF3094 square sectioned bar with decorative terminal; SF1735B staple or fitting	SF1537 cylindrical ferrule fragment; SF4183A ferrule fragment; SF 2447 fragmentary composite object
Phase 4	SF555 bar fragment; SF1742 rectangular bar		SF4207B horseshoe nail; SF6015 horseshoe nail		SF4397 twisted handle	SF2147A knife tang; SF2559 knife; SF4207A knife	SF574 Substantial iron bar with nail in situ at one end	SF 2997 ferrule fragments;
Phase 4 or 5					SF361 padlock key; SF3498 latch rest or door bolt; SF4303 barrel padlock fragments			SF2497 ferrule fragment
Phase 5	SF582A square-sectioned bar fragment; SF582B sheet metal fragments; SF669 bar fragment; SF851 rod fragment		SF429 horseshoe nail; SF2569A horseshoe nail; SF2804 horseshoe fragment				SF1752 rove; SF2246 hasp	
Phase 5 or 6	SF976B & C curving sheet fragments; SF976D strip fragment		SF223B horseshoe fragment				SF223A angle bracket; SF976A angle bracket	
Phase 6	SF80 sheet fragment; SF116 rod fragment; SF135 rod fragment; SF197 bar fragment; SF263A wire fragment; SF244 sheet fragment; SF351 strip fragment; SF709A strip fragment; SF864A & B ?modern wire hoop fragments; SF2355 tapering rod fragment	SF2356 arrowhead	SF207 horseshoe nail		SF392 pricket candlestick; SF709B rim fragment of iron cauldron	SF709C file fragment; SF709D tool handle; SF722A knifeblade; SF2153A knife or file fragment; SF2153B knife blade and handle; SF2153C knife or file; SF2153D curry knife; SF3525B curving chisel or gouge; SF3525C punch	SF87 rove with nail in situ; SF182 strap fitting; SF182B staple or fitting; SF263B strap fitting; SF292A notched bar fitting; SF292B holdfast; SF343 small hook fragment; SF3525A sheet metal fitting	SF2424A & B, F & G steelyard weights
Modern							SF2353A L-shaped wall anchor; SF2353B decorative domed cap; SF2793 binding strip or fitting	

	Wire/bar/sheet/strip	Weaponry	Horse equipment	Dress accessories	Household equipment	Tools	Fittings	Other
Area A								
Unstratified	SF741 bar fragment; SF741F & G sheet metal fragments; SF1618 rod fragment				SF741D rim fragment from sheet metal vessel; SF1205 possible arm from small scissors/shears	SF741C knife blade	SF741B incomplete strip fitting; SF741E perforated binding strap fragments; SF1025B modern fitting; SF4785 possible binding strip	SF2823 Jew's harp; SF4066 ferrule fragment

to the head as that seen on metalworking examples. A slightly larger but similar punch comes from Inchaffray Abbey, Perth & Kinross (Ford 1996: 503, illus 18, no 28). A further three possible punches (SF733, SF1972, SF3525C, Figure 4.26) come from late post-medieval and modern contexts at Bon Accord (Table 4.7).

Saw blade: A single short fragment of a fine serrated blade or saw with straight back and parallel cutting edge (SF1735A) came from the fill of Pit C037, dated to the late 12th to 13th century. Morris (2000) suggests that there is little evidence of saws in Britain until the late medieval period. Few actual medieval saw blades survive (Goodall 2011: 25) but the production techniques observed in some finished objects and contemporary medieval pictorial representations demonstrate they were far more commonly used than their archaeological survival attests (Goodman 1964: 125).

The form of the Bon Accord saw blade indicates that this is a hand-held saw of a type typically used in carpentry (Goodall 2011: 26). Yet the wealth of evidence for animal carcass processing on site means that it is entirely possible that metal saws of this form were employed at Bon Accord as butchery implements. In form, the Bon Accord saw blade is similar, although smaller than, a 13th century example from Windcliff, Isle of Wight (Dunning 1939: 135–37, fig 3; Goodall 2011: 38, fig 3.8, no B95). A similar fragment comes from a mid 14th to early 15th century context at Bedern, York (Ottaway and Rogers 2002: 2728).

Files: Whittle-tanged hand-held files for use in metalworking and woodworking are known to have been in use throughout the medieval period (see discussions in Goodall 2011: 11; Ottaway and Rogers 2002, 2722). At least one whittle-tanged file is present amongst the Bon Accord assemblage (SF709C), retrieved from the fill of a post-medieval well (C002) and further examples may be present (e.g. SF2153A & C; Table 4.7). The rounded profile of the blade and the form of the teeth of SF709C is suggestive of a post-medieval date.

Wedge: A single probable woodworking wedge was identified at Bon Accord (SF2713G), recovered from Spread A039 associated with post-medieval clay tobacco pipe. Simple iron wedges were used throughout the medieval period to split timber trunks (Ottaway and Rogers 2002: 2728). Wood cleaving wedges are still in use today, their form having changed very little since medieval times (Goodall 2011: 27). The example from Bon Accord consists of a robust square-sectioned bar tapering in width and thickness from mid-length at one end terminating in a blunt squared blade. It is consistent in shape and size for an axe-hammer blade but there is no obvious perforation or socket to facilitate hafting.

Musical instruments

Small metal instruments known as Jew's harps are folk instruments with a wide geographical distribution (Egan 2010: 284). They are typically produced in iron and are known from both medieval and post-medieval contexts in London and beyond. Egan (2010: 284, fig 217) defines three basic forms of metal Jew's harps known from London but due to the friable and fragmentary condition of the Bon Accord example, it has not been possible to align this example with established typochronological schemes. At Bon Accord, a Jew's harp (SF2823) was unstratified but based on its size, it is consistent with medieval examples from London and an early date for its production cannot be ruled out.

Ferrules

This group consists of a wide variety of iron conical or cylindrical collar-like fittings in a range of sizes and shapes. Five examples come from Phases 2, 4, 4/5 and unstratified but due to their poor condition, the purpose of these objects is not clear. They could have performed a range of functions including chapes (e.g. SF2497), socketed tool fittings (e.g. SF2997) or collar-type reinforcements for composite objects (e.g. SF4066).

Security equipment

At least two padlocks, a padlock key, a rotary key and door bolts are present amongst the assemblage. It is likely that further fragments of similar objects are present amongst the sheet and bar fragments but the incomplete condition precludes precise identification.

Padlocks: 'Barrel' or cylindrical sheet metal padlocks were the most common type of medieval padlock and were typically used to lock chests, gates and doors (Ford 1998: 713; Goodall 2011: 231). Goodall's study of medieval barrel padlocks has identified five major types (2011: 231–34). Two incomplete examples were identified (SF4303 & SF4794, Figure 4.27) at Bon Accord, one from the infill of Phase 1 Pit C015 and the other from the fill of a well or soakaway (Late Phase 5). The poor condition of both examples precludes confident identification in line with Goodall's typological scheme but the fragments that survive are suggestive of Type A or B locks which are distinguished by the form of tube associated with the sheet metal case. In Type A examples, the tube is directly attached whereas in Type B locks, the case and tube are separated by a rectangular or trapezoidal fin. Figure 4.27 shows a tentative reconstruction of SF4794 as a Type A padlock but the damage to the upper surface and loss of the tube means that the object could equally be of Type B form. The presence of longitudinal rods between the end plates of the barrel-shaped body of SF4794 would be consistent with Goodall's Type B1 locks which are

known from medieval contexts up to the 14th century (2011: 231–32, 244, Fig 10.6, I11–19). Unusually, SF4794 has a small loop fastening adjacent to the end plate on one of the ribs, which would have allowed a fine chain to be attached to the stem of the bolt. Barrel padlocks and associated fragments have been found at Rattray, Aberdeenshire (Goodall in Murray & Murray 1993: 180–2, fig 35), Aberdeen (Goodall 1982, 188, illl 108), Lochmaben Castle, Dumfriesshire (MacDonald and Laing 1975: 148) and Perth (Franklin and Goodall 2012: 151–56).

In addition to the padlock fragments from Bon Accord, at least two lock bolts (SF2179A & SF3498) from fairly large plate- or stock-locks were also recognised, both from Phase 5 (Spread C149 and Layer A008). Lock bolts functioned as the sliding bolt within a composite fixed lock mechanism, which were opened with a rotary key (Goodall 2011: 235). The sizes of the lock bolts from Bon Accord are both suggestive of use on a wooden door to a building rather than on a smaller item of furniture.

Keys: A padlock key (SF361, Figure 4.27) is a type used with barrel padlocks and is consistent with Goodall's Type 4a keys which have laterally set bits with radiating wards and looped terminals (2011: 237, 239, fig 10.3). Keys of this form are found throughout the medieval period but most are 11th to 13th century in date indicating that the Bon Accord key is medieval despite its late medieval/early post-medieval context of recovery (Layer C034). This type of key could have been pushed over the barbed bolts of barrel padlocks with keyholes in the end plate or drawn along those with T-shaped keyholes (*ibid*, 237 & 239). The circular looped terminal would have acted both as a handle and for suspension, perhaps on a belt, and is similar to examples from Threave Castle, Galloway (Caldwell 1981: 116, fig 12, no 121) and the medieval settlement at Springwood, Kelso (Ford 1998: 713, illus 20, no. 22).

The small rotary key (SF1146), which comes from a Phase 2 layer (A002), is difficult to categorise with confidence due to its poor condition. When compared with Goodall's typological scheme of medieval rotary keys, the Bon Accord example is most consistent with Type E keys which have solid stems and tips which end in line with the end of the bit. Keys of this type were introduced in the 13th century and continued in use throughout the medieval period (2011: 241, fig 10.4). The small size of this key suggests use on a casket.

Keys and padlocks are known from a range of Scottish medieval sites including: Tantallon Castle, East Lothian (Caldwell 1991: illus 4, nos 37–38); Edinburgh Castle (Clark 1997b: 160–1, illus 133, nos 78, 81) and Aberdeen (Goodall 1982a: 188–89, no 73). A minimum of 42 barrel padlocks were represented amongst the iron objects from excavations in Perth (Franklin and

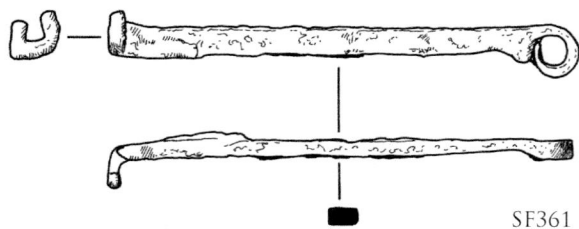

SF361

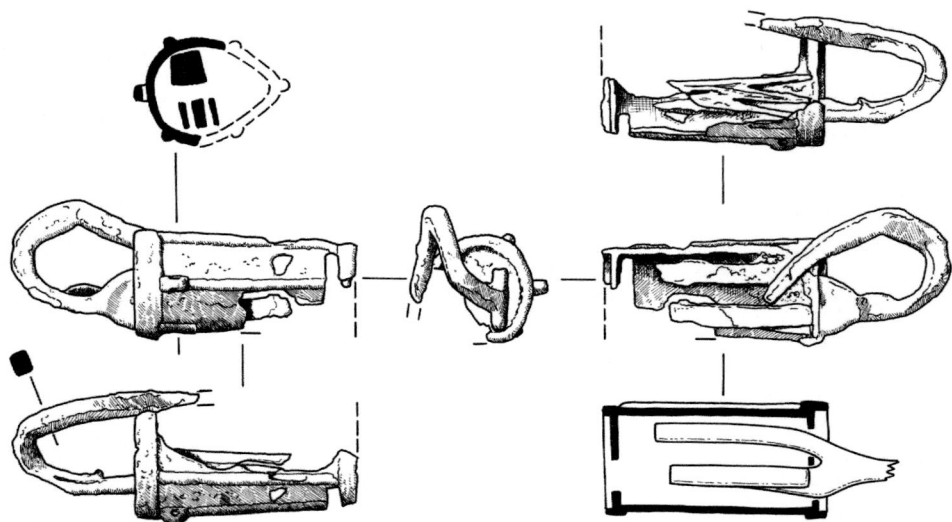

SF4794

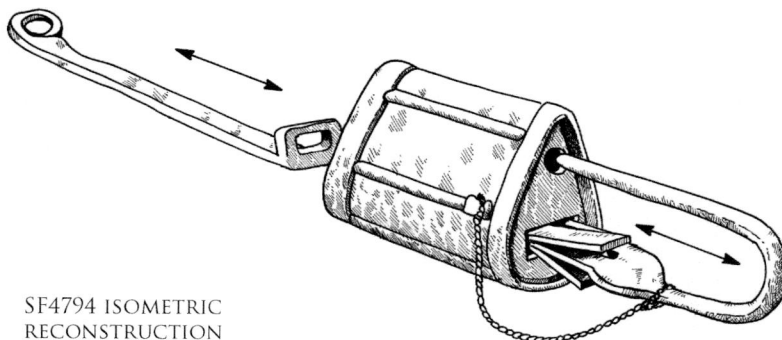

SF4794 ISOMETRIC
RECONSTRUCTION
NOT TO SCALE

0   5CM

Figure 4.27 Padlocks and keys; SF361; SF4794 and isometric reconstruction

Goodall 2012: 151–56, illus 136–39) and over 50 padlock slide keys were also identified (*ibid*, 156–57, illus 140–42). The large number of items of security equipment from medieval urban contexts at Perth implies that their rarity amongst the Bon Accord assemblage is a reflection of their poor archaeological survival and subsequent difficulties with recognition rather than reflecting a genuine absence during the medieval and post-medieval periods. Many of the unidentified sheet fragments noted amongst the assemblage could well derive from the cases of barrel or box padlocks and lockplates.

Domestic objects

Day-to-day household equipment of medieval date is surprisingly rare within the Bon Accord assemblage but small numbers of candlesticks and iron vessel fragments are present, as are a single handle fragment and a needle.

Candlesticks: Two candlesticks were recovered from late medieval/early post-medieval deposits at Bon Accord (Surface C017 and Layer A014); both are consistent with medieval forms. One, SF392, is a straight stemmed pricket candlestick, a typical medieval form dating from the 12th to mid 14th century (Egan 2010: 140). The second example is a cupped or socketed form (SF1917, Figure 4.25), similar to an example from Rattray, Aberdeen (Goodall in Murray & Murray 1983: 182, fig 36, no 94), which saw use from the 13th century into the beginning of the post-medieval period (Goodall 2011: 300).

Needle: A single iron needle (SF2179B, Figure 4.26) came from Layer A008, associated with post-medieval ceramics and clay pipe fragments. The size is consistent with day-to-day domestic sewing equipment and is consistent in form with a post-medieval date.

Vessel fragments: Cast or sheet-iron vessels and cauldrons are rarely represented amongst medieval assemblages and are typical of a post-medieval date. In all, fragments of at least four vessels were identified within the Bon Accord assemblage, consisting of a ridge-decorated body fragment (SF1598B, Figure 4.25) from Layer B006 (Phase 6); the rim of large round bodied iron cauldron (SF709B) recovered from the fill of Well C002 (Phase 6); an unstratified rim fragment of a thin-sheet metal pale (SF741D) and a composite iron and copper alloy (and possibly cork) bucket or container (SF357) from the fill of Phase 6 Pit C081. The latter is undoubtedly 19th or 20th century in date.

Large cauldrons or round-bottomed vessels such as that represented by SF709B were used either in an open fire or suspended by a handle from a hook above it. Similar iron vessel fragments come from 18th/19th century

disturbed levels at Smailholm Tower, Roxburghshire (Good and Tabraham 1988:, 255, illus 15, no.24).

Handle: A twisted handle (SF4397), probably from a vessel such as a bucket or cauldron, came from Layer C075 associated with late medieval pottery. A similar simple twisted iron handle of 14th century date comes from Winchester, Hampshire (Goodall 2011: 324, fig 11.12, no J161).

Weights

Several cast iron weights are present, including a cache of steelyard weights (SF2424A–G) which were associated with Structure C012 (Table 4.7). These are present in a range of forms including bell-shaped, disc-shaped and cuboidal and all are consistent with a late post-medieval date. One example, SF1607, is an intact cylindrical weight which may have come from a pendulum clock mechanism (Figure 4.25). It was found in association with Late Phase 6 demolition in Area B.

Structural ironwork and miscellaneous fittings

The majority of the remaining objects (fittings, binding, hinges, strips and nails) are best viewed as structural fittings and iron components which are likely to have been associated with internal fixtures such as door, window and furniture fittings. The overwhelming majority of objects were nails, accounting for 922 possible examples (excluding horseshoe nails). This accounts for 75% of the overall iron assemblage. Forty-one fragmentary iron fittings were recovered from Phases 1 to 6 and modern deposits at Bon Accord; the majority deriving from late medieval and post-medieval contexts (Phases 5–6) or later. In addition to those summarised here, further large quantities of fittings including threaded bolts, pinned hinges and cast pipe fragments were recovered from disturbed contexts and modern levels.

Nail fragments, ubiquitous finds on archaeological sites of medieval and post-medieval periods, are the predominant type of iron fitting with 922 examples recovered. These have been classified by form following existing typologies (Ford and Walsh 1987) and are discussed in detail below by phase and possible function. As Goodall reminds us (1981: 59), iron had little place in the structures of buildings, whether timber-framed or stone-built, during the early medieval period, but its importance in fitting them out is indicated by documentary references and numerous archaeological finds.

Iron fittings are long-lived types and many internal structural iron components such as holdfasts and wall anchors continue in use today and have seen little change in form since the Roman period (Manning

1985) making comment on chronology from form alone seldom possible. The majority of iron fittings from Bon Accord were associated with late medieval, post-medieval and modern contexts and are summarised in Table 4.7. Those from earlier medieval contexts will be discussed in more detail and individual catalogue descriptions are presented.

Nails: K Paton and A Sibley A total of 820 stratified nails and ten unstratified nails were recovered from the excavations. A further 92 fine tapering bar fragments, likely to be nail shanks, were identified during examination of the iron objects. These are not included in the discussion which follows.

Through visual inspection and x-ray, the nail assemblage has been classified based on the typology developed by Ford and Walsh (1987), which classified the nails using the shape of head and the cross-section of the shank, defining eight main groups which are as follows:

A. Circular, oval, square or rectangular flat head with square or rectangular cross-sectioned shank. Ls 20–118mm; Shank W 2–9mm; Head W 4–23mm

B. Circular, oval, sub-rectangular domed head with square or rectangular cross-sectioned shank. Ls 38–132mm; Shank W 3–10mm; Head W 7–39mm

C. Circular, oval, square or rectangular flat head with circular cross-sectioned shank. Ls 39–100mm; Shank W 2–4mm; Head W 4–11mm

D. Circular, oval, sub-rectangular domed head with circular cross-sectioned shank. Only one example found. L 39mm; Shank W 4mm; Head W 13mm

E. Flat L-shaped head with square or rectangular cross-sectioned shank. Ls 44–69mm; Shank W 3–5mm; Head W 6–12mm

F. Flat T-shaped head with square or rectangular cross-sectioned shank. Ls 53–71mm; Shank W 4mm; Head W 8mm

G. Flat figure-of-eight shaped head with square or rectangular cross-sectioned shank. Ls 38–67mm; Shank W 2–5mm; Head W 9–14mm

H. Square or rectangular flat head formed by flaring rectangular or square cross-sectioned shank. Ls 39–100mm; Shank W 3–7mm; Head W 4–10mm

Classification of the Bon Accord nails has been undertaken only on intact or substantially intact examples (Table 4.8); 391 nails were excluded from classification due to their fragmentary or heavily corroded condition. A further 12 nails (not included in the total nail figures quoted above) have been identified as horseshoe nails and are discussed under *Horse equipment*.

The variety of nail size and morphology allows for an attempt to be made to ascertain functional differences between the types. The greater size and weight of Type B nails may suggest these were intended for use within load bearing timbers, although there is no evidence for their use on the structural timbers from the site (Section 4.4.1). The smaller heads of Types E–H would allow them to lie flush with timbers suggesting that these categories should be considered carpentry nails (Clark 1997b). Type H nails are the only kind observed on structural timbers from the site, in one instance being used to pin a sheet of lead to the wood (Section 4.2.1).

Table 4.8 Nail categories with dimensions

	Length			Width			Head Width			Total
	Min	Max	Mean	Min	Max	Mean	Min	Max	Mean	
A	20	118	48.5	2	9	4.7	4	23	11.9	**313**
B	38	132	51.3	3	10	5.5	7	39	15.6	**63**
C	39	100	64.1	2	4	3	4	11	6.8	**15**
D	N/A	N/A	39	N/A	N/A	4	N/A	N/A	13	**1**
E	44	69	51.1	3	5	4.4	6	12	8.3	**8**
F	53	71	65	4	4	4	8	8	8	**3**
G	38	67	49.3	2	5	4	9	14	11.3	**4**
H	39	100	47.3	3	7	4.8	4	10	6.8	**32**
Unidentified										**391**

Ring: A single ring fitting of penannular form (SF2836) was recovered from a late medieval soil layer (Phase 4, Layer C020). Such fittings could have fulfilled a range of functions such as a horse-harness fitting or chain link.

Staples: Rectangular and U-shaped staples are present within medieval contexts at Bon Accord in small numbers and further examples come from post-medieval levels (Table 4.7). Additional fractured pieces are likely to be present among the strip and bar fragments. U-shaped staples are the most common type from medieval contexts; these were driven into masonry joints or wood to hold chains and hasps on doors and gates as well as to support tethering rings and handle fixtures (Goodall 2011: 162). Two U-shaped fittings are present, deriving from Phase 2 and 4 layers (Layer C003 & A015). The damaged and distorted condition of these fittings suggests that they had been removed from their stone/timber fixtures. A single quadrangular staple (SF1735B) was recovered from the fill of a Phase 2 pit. Similar staples or fittings are present in late medieval/post-medieval contexts (SF182B & SF1702C) demonstrating their long currency of use.

Small numbers of U-shaped staples were found at Inchaffray Abbey, Perth & Kinross, one (SF34) coming from the fill of a foundation trench of the church, of probable 13th century date (Ford 1996: 503). Larger numbers are present among the iron assemblage at Perth (Franklin and Goodall 2012: 173, illus 149, nos 412-444).

Timber dogs/tenter hooks: Timber dogs are long rectangular staples with straight backs and pointed down-turned ends and were used in woodworking to secure timbers in position during working or within the structure of a building (Goodall 2011: 161). The similarity in form of timber dogs and angle hooks makes it difficult in particularly corroded examples to distinguish between these types. The small size of SF2992B, a small L-shaped narrow bar fragment, damaged at both ends, supports its interpretation as a tenter hook to stretch cloth but the similarity of form with small L-shaped structural fittings makes classification uncertain (Franklin and Goodall 2012: 139, no.135). Only three examples were sufficiently intact to enable identification; all were of wrought iron and were either medieval or post-medieval in date. Two examples (SF1982 and SF2992B) recovered from medieval contexts appear to have been removed from their timber fixtures due to the damaged condition of the arms.

Wall anchors: These fittings take the form of long tapering shanks and flattened heads which were used to attach wood to masonry and brickwork, such as for securing door and window frames in walls and securing timber panelling (Goodall 2011: 163). The example

catalogued below was recovered from Layer A002 associated with pottery of late 12th to mid 13th century date but further examples come from modern contexts (e.g. SF2353A; modern deposit, Area C) testifying to the long currency of use of structural fittings of this type.

Hasps: Hasps were used to secure gates and doors and to fasten the lids of chests. Only one example from Bon Accord was in sufficiently complete condition to enable precise identification but it is likely that further examples are present among the miscellaneous fragments. The Bon Accord hasp (SF2246) is of wrought iron and was recovered in the area of Wall C009. Although deriving from a late medieval/post-medieval context, the common use of hasps throughout the medieval period could suggest the incorporation of earlier material within the cut for this wall. The hasp conforms to Goodall's Type 1 looped hasps (2011: 168, fig 9.29, H591–626) being figure-of-eight in shape; these were in use throughout the medieval period. This example appears to have broken across the hooked end either from use or detachment. Looped hasps, some with spiral twisted shanks, were recovered from medieval contexts in Perth (Franklin and Goodall 2012: 171, 173, illus 147, no. 374–80).

Miscellaneous fittings: As with all large iron assemblages, some items cannot be readily paralleled and their exact function remains unclear. Four such objects (SF574, SF3094, SF3279, SF2637), likely to be structural fittings on account of their size and robustness, were recovered from medieval contexts at Bon Accord. Large quantities of fractured and fragmentary fittings were also present in later phases. These have been summarised in Table 4.7.

Miscellaneous objects

Four fragmentary objects from Bon Accord are frustratingly incomplete meaning that their function remains obscure. The first (SF1628A; Figure 4.25) consists of a D-sectioned fine rod which expands and flattens at one end to form a damaged square or quadrangular head, perforated off-centre with a rivet *in situ*, indicating that it was a component of a more complex object. The opposing end is damaged but appears to split into two rods, curving in opposing directions. The second, SF1850, recovered from a Phase 5 layer, is a fragment of a sheet metal object, decorated by a series of closely-spaced dome headed rivets. The original form of the object is not possible to reconstruct from such a small fragment but it may be a piece of a sheet metal riveted cauldron or even a fragment of an iron gauntlet (Willemsen 2015: 28, fig 34a & b). The third item, SF2147B is equally intriguing and frustrating in its incomplete state. It consists of two joining, perhaps pivoting, fine rectangular iron strips, each with one squared-end surviving, joined together by a small rivet or peg. This could be a distorted strap-end fragment or piece of purse frame but the production in iron rather than bronze is unusual. The final item in this category is a broken curving iron strip with adhering degraded organic material (SF2571) which was recovered from the fill of Well A001 (Phase 5).

Various bar/sheet/strip fragments

This category of artefact encompasses a wide range of fragmentary bar, strip, sheet and wire fragments which are present in large numbers at Bon Accord, particularly in the later, late medieval and post-medieval phases (Phases 5–6). These undoubtedly represent highly fractured fragments of larger objects but their broken condition precludes identification. At least one possible off-cut (SF1178 from Layer A003, Early Phase 4) is also present. A small number (ten) came from Phases 1, 2 and 4 and a further 33 fragmentary pieces come from Phases 5–6 and modern deposits and are summarised in Table 4.7.

Catalogue of illustrated
(L = length; W = width; Th = thickness; D = diameter; H = height)

SF   361 (Figure)
Phase/Feature   Early-to-mid Phase 5/Layer C034
Description: padlock key
Flat rectangular rod (W 7.5mm; Th5 mm) with asymmetric expanded shoulder (W 9mm) at one edge creating a junction between the shank and looped terminal (D 14.5mm; Th 3mm) which would have acted as a handle and for suspension. The opposite end has a simple C-shaped bit (W 12.5mm; H 12mm) set at right angles to shank. Consistent with Goodall's Type 4a padlock keys (2011: 237, 239, fig 10.3). L 123mm.

SF   1075 (Figure 4.25)
Phase/Feature   Early-to-mid Phase 5/Layer A017
Description: D-shaped buckle
Complete. Complete single-looped D-shaped buckle frame (L 26mm; W 19–24mm; Th 5.5mm). Pin survives but is no longer in original position at centre of squared edge of frame. Pin (L 27mm; D 4.5–5.5mm) consists of a narrow hipped shank which tapers to a narrow point, the opposite end has been flattened and loops around buckle frame.

SF   1394 (Figure 4.26)
Phase/Feature   Phase 1/Layer A001
Description: knife blade
Knife blade with straight back and badly corroded cutting edge and no tang. Form is consistent with late 12th century knife blades from London (Cowgill *et al.* 1987: 78, fig 54) and is most similar in form to Goodall's type C whittle-type blade (2011: 106, fig 8.2). Blade L 62mm; blade depth 17mm; blade back W 4mm.

SF   1598B (Figure 4.25)
Phase/Feature   Phase 6/Layer B006
Description: possible vessel fragment
Sub-rectangular rounded sheet of iron, the external surface divided horizontally into two zones by a clear cast ridge. Across this at right angles is a raised vertical rib (W 5.5mm) and adjacent to this is a broken square perforation, possibly a suspension or repair hole (D 13.5mm).   No original edges survive. Remaining H 55mm; W 65.5mm; Th 4–7mm.

SF   1607 (Figure 4.25)
Phase/Feature   Phase 6/Layer B006
Description: weight
Conical cast cylindrical weight with flat base and rounded top (H 150mm; D 38.5mm), from which projects a U-shaped loop (H 45mm; D 8mm) for suspension. Casting seam visible along length. L 195mm.

SF   1628A (Figure 4.25)
Phase/Feature   Phase 5/Layer A008
Description: unidentified
Incomplete, unidentified object. D-sectioned straight-sided fine rod (5.5mm x 5mm), expands and flattens at one end to form a quadrangular round cornered head (L 14mm; W 12.5mm; Th 4mm), perforated off-centre (D 5mm) with rivet *in situ*. The opposite end expands and flattens slightly to a squared tip from which bifurcate fine circular-sectioned ?symmetrical loops extend; one end lost and the surviving arm damaged. L 80mm.

SF   1917 (Figure 4.25)
Phase/Feature   Early-to-mid Phase 5/Layer A014
Description: candlestick
Cupped or socketed candlestick. Substantially complete candlestick with short conical ferrule (H 22mm; exterior D 22mm; interior D 19.5mm) with contiguous flanges. Extending from back of socket is a tapering square-sectioned shank (5.5mm x 6mm) with distinct angled bend 16mm from base of socket where shank is hipped (6mm x 7mm), tapering shank curved from use and extreme tip of shank lost. Conforms to Egan's 'cupped' and Goodall's 'socketed' candlesticks which were in use from the late 13th century onwards (Egan 2010: 142; Goodall 2011: 300). The simple design of this candlestick encouraged a long currency of use that undoubtedly stretched into the post-medieval period (Egan 2010: 142). A similar candle holder, probably 14th century in date, is known from Lochmaben Castle, Dumfriesshire (MacDonald and Laing 1975: 148, fig 11, no.20). L 71mm.

SF   2077 (Figure 4.26)
Phase/Feature   Early Phase 5/Layer A005
Description: shears
Small shears; incomplete. One arm of a set of small shears with looped bow (approx. original W 26mm) and plain curved top at junction between the tapering

wedge-profiled blade (W 10mm; Th 4.5mm) and the circular-sectioned handle (D 4.5mm). Consistent with Goodall's type 2A shears which range in length 95–328mm and typically have curved or slanted junctions between the handle and blade (2011: 111–12) with the broad date range 11th to 15th century. A very similar set of shears comes from excavations in Perth (Franklin and Goodall 2012: 137, illus 129, no 102). Minimum original L 90mm; surviving L 78.5mm.

SF	2179B (Figure 4.26)
Phase/Feature	Late Phase 5/Layer A008
Description:	needle

Needle; complete. Complete circular-sectioned tapering needle with slightly flattened head (Th 2.5mm) perforated by oval eye (L 6.5mm). Similar examples, however, are known from medieval contexts in Perth (Franklin and Goodall 2012: 139). L 83.5mm.

SF	2328 (Figure 4.25)
Phase/Feature	Phase 2/Layer A002
Description:	Clark Type 3 nail

Complete and probably unused horseshoe nail with rectangular-sectioned nail head along two opposing axes (13mm x 4mm to 6.5mm x 10mm). Shank is rectangular in section (3.5mm x 5.5mm) and is unworn.

SF	2356 (Figure 4.25)
Phase/Feature	Phase 6/Spread C071
Description:	Barbed and tanged arrowhead

Small barbed arrowhead (L 33mm; W 21.5mm; Th 4mm) with central sub-square-sectioned tang (L 15mm; D 6mm); extreme tip of point lost. L 48.5mm.

SF	2648 (Figure 4.25)
Phase/Feature	Late Phase 4/Layer A015
Description:	star rowel

Star rowel, damaged. Star rowel of six widely separated, round-sectioned points (D 4mm); traces of non-ferrous plating. The extreme tips of two points have been lost and one point is distorted, probably from use. Central sub-square hole (D 4.5mm) visible on x-ray only, slight curvature of the edges of perforation are indicative of wear from use (D 33mm). Although slightly smaller, a close parallel is known from London (Ellis 1995: 147, no. 358) which is thought to be 13th century or later in date. Layer A015.

SF	3525B (Figure 4.26)
Phase/Feature	Phase 6/Well C002
Description:	carpenter's chisel

Carpenter's chisel with gouge-shaped bit. Square-tipped chisel with dished blade (L 69mm; W 15.5mm). Square-sectioned shank (D 9mm) with expanded circular-sectioned shoulder (D 21mm) at junction between tool blade and short tapering square-sectioned tang (L 35.5mm; D 8mm). L 166.5mm.

SF	3525C (Figure 4.26)
Phase/Feature	Phase 6/Well C002
Description:	punch

Punch; damaged. Short square-sectioned bar with damaged, slightly lipped square head, shank tapering along length but damaged at tip, possibly from use. L 72mm; W 11.5mm; Th 10mm.

SF	4207A (Figure 4.26)
Phase/Feature	Early Phase 4/Layer C075
Description:	knife

Knife with straight, vertical shoulders either side of a centrally placed whittle tang, the straight back tapering from the shoulder towards the tip. Blade is straight with damage towards the shoulder that may be the result of sharpening; broken at the tip. The form is consistent with Goodall's Type F whittle tang knives which are a long-lived type with parallels known from 12th to 15th century contexts (2011: 107, fig 8.2). L 75mm; blade: L 45mm; W 14mm; Th 5mm; tang: L 33mm; W 7mm.

SF	4280 (Figure 4.26)
Phase/Feature	Phases 1–2/Gully C001 fill (A)
Description:	punch

Punch. Short square-sectioned bar, squared end is flattened and slightly burred from percussion damage; opposite end is broken across gently tapering blunt point, probably broken during use. Remaining L 72mm; D 6–9.5mm.

SF	4794 (Figure 4.27)
Phase/Feature	Phase 1/Pit C015 fill (A)
Description:	barrel padlock and bolt

Barrel padlock and bolt; incomplete. Barrel-shaped sheet metal case (L 58.5mm) with raised collars around both ends (W 8mm and 5mm) and projecting evenly spaced longitudinal straps; retains the bolt in situ. Only the rounded base of the case survives, the top has been lost making it unclear whether a separate or integral tube was present. Distorted U-shaped padlock bolt (L 76mm) with rectangular closing plate and two spines (L 38mm) each with double leaf springs; tip of square-sectioned bolt (D 6.5mm) damaged. Small loop fastening present adjacent to the end plate which would have allowed a fine chain to be fastened to the bolt. L 90mm.

Copper alloy

A total of 122 copper alloy and silver objects were recovered from Phases 1 to 6 and modern deposits (summarised, with the exception of clearly modern material, in Table 4.9). The copper alloy objects are dominated by dress accessories such as pins, brooches and buckles but also include a fine strap-end, possible vessel fragments and fittings as well as coins and

Table 4.9 Summary of major non-modern copper alloy artefacts

	Household equipment	Dress accessories	Horse equipment	Tools	Fittings	Working waste	Coins & jettons	Sheet fragment	Miscellaneous
Phase 1		SF6001 loop from buckle or brooch pin							
Phase 2		SF1397 chain mail; SF2637 19th century domed button; SF2736 annular brooch frame with thistle decoration; SF2751 brooch or buckle pin; SF2787 pin shank or wire; SF2988 Brooch pin		SF1683 Possible tool tip	SF1678 fitting for wooden object or vessel; SF3301 decorative fitting or ornament	SF1830 strip of off-cut; SF2784 casting debris; SF2874B possible casting debris; SF3021 unfinished object; SF3440 waste fragment; SF3355 possible casting debris	SF2391 cut short-armed cross penny (early 13th century)	SF2874A strip fragment	SF2418 unidentified composite object; SF2752 unidentified object; SF4160 composite object
Phase 2 or 3									
Phase 3			SF659 prick spur					SF3188 strip fragment	
Phase 3 or 4		SF3583 pin shank			SF1085 fitting; SF3589 decorative strip	SF1434 possible casting debris		SF698 strip fragment; SF1344 sheet fragment	
Phase 4				SF2222 strap-end	SF283 unidentified fitting			SF2409 sheet fragments; SF2917 sheet fragments	SF2144 unidentified composite object; SF6033 tip of decorative item
Phase 4 – 5				SF549 fish hook					
Phase 5	SF6003 zoomorphic vessel foot	SF591 wire-headed pin; SF779A pin tip; SF779B pin tip; SF779D possible lace chape fragment; SF794A pin tip; SF837A wire-headed pin; SF1133 brooch; SF1692 bar from buckle; SF1709 chain link fragment; SF1761A pin shank; SF3463 complete annular buckle & pin; SF1780 buckle fragment; SF1596 four-holed cast button; SF6004 disc-shaped button			SF1634 fine pivoting two-armed fitting or attachment; SF1761B paperclip rivet	SF794B casting debris	SF837b Black farthing (15th century); SF871 perforated Zeeland jetton ('1600'); SF1888 'ecclesiastical' farthing (15th century)	SF779C strip fragments; SF1104 sheet fragment; SF3599 strip fragment; SF6032 sheet fragments	SF1091 unidentified fragment
Phase 5 or 6				SF172 spatulae-headed tool tip, broken					
Phase 6	SF1600 decorative handle or finial; SF2122F spoon	SF269 buckle fragment; SF525 button; SF526 wire-headed pin; SF2149 composite domed button; SF6030 head of wire-headed pin; SF6031 wire-headed pin fragments (20)		SF121 spatulae-ended tool; SF1642A possible blade	SF264A rivet/tack head; SF922 chain link fragment; SF2122A perforated washer; SF2122G linear rachet or decorative mount; SF2564C chain fragment	SF1845A off-cut; SF3530 unfinished disc-shaped object	SF2122C farthing 1865; SF2122D copper penny (1806-60)	SF1642B wire fragments; SF1662 strip fragment; SF2122B sheet fragment; SF2564B sheet fragment	SF587 unidentified fragment; SF1771 unidentified fragment; SF3094 tapering bar; SF1845B unidentified fragment
Unstratified								SF583B-D sheet fragment; SF751 sheet fragment	

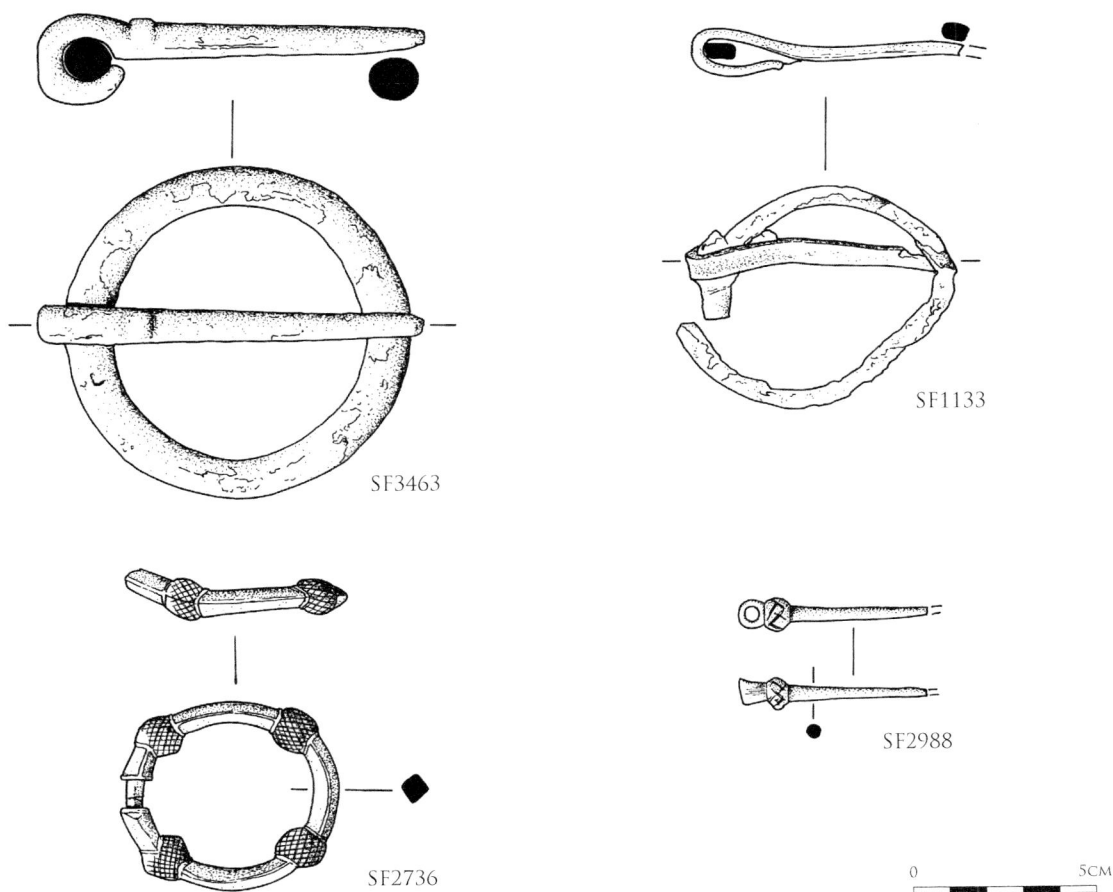

Figure 4.28 Copper alloy brooches and pins; SF3463; SF1133; SF2736; SF2988

jettons. Also present is a rare and significant late 11th/12th century highly decorated spur, a zoomorphic decorated foot from a trivet or stand and a rare early 13th century silver penny fragment from the short-lived mint at Rochester.

A small number of objects are entirely encased in organic material; these are likely to be surviving fragments of a composite organic and metal object and conservation treatment has been minimal to enable preservation of the organic components.

Dress accessories

Brooches: Two substantially intact brooch frames and fragments of three brooch or buckle pins were recovered from Phases 1, 2 and 5. The identification of the annular frames as those of brooches rather than buckles follows the criteria set out by Egan and Pritchard (1991: 50–57); both examples have a narrow contraction in the frame around which the pin would be fitted. This contraction of the frame is noted on medieval brooches but is typically absent from contemporary buckles. Both brooches are of annular form, SF1133 (Figure 4.28)

having a plain, undecorated frame while SF2736 (Figure 4.28) is decorated by four sub-circular, equidistant bosses with cross-hatched decoration imitating thistles (see Egan and Pritchard 1991: 247–49; fig 160, no 1307). A similar but plain bossed annular brooch comes from Perth (Goodall 2012a: 90, 93, illus 116, no 1). Annular brooches are known from a variety of Scottish medieval sites including Perth (Ford 1987a: 121–23, illus 59, no 2), Jedburgh Abbey (Caldwell 1995a: 85, illus 79, no 36–37) and Edinburgh Castle (Clark 1997a: 149–150, illus 128, no 5).

Three pins for brooches or buckles were also recovered (SF2751, SF2988, SF6001) from Phases 1 and 2. With the exception of SF2988 which is ornamented with a simple thistle decoration, it is uncertain whether the pin fragments are for decorative brooches or buckles and could have come from either. In contrast to SF2988 (Figure 4.28) which is cast, SF2751 and SF6001 have been produced from strips of copper alloy and tool marks from manufacture are visible on both. It is likely that SF2751 and SF6001 are replacement pins for existing brooches. Similar examples come from Perth (Ford 1987a: 121–23, illus 59, no 6).

Buckles: Three buckles (SF269, SF 1780 and SF3463) are present, all deriving from relatively late phases on site. One is a D-shaped end fragment (SF269) from a rectangular buckle frame; a variety common in the 12th to 15th centuries (Egan and Pritchard 1991: 52, fig 33). The other, intact, buckle from Bon Accord is a complete plain annular buckle and pin (SF3463, Figure 4.28). Egan and Pritchard (1991) suggest that larger framed annular or ring buckles such as these are late 14th century in date or later and were particularly common during the early 15th century, consistent with its recovery from a Mid Phase 5 charcoal-rich spread at Bon Accord (*ibid*, 62–64). An almost identical buckle has been found during previous excavations at Aberdeen (Cameron and Stones 2001: 196, no 350) and has been dated to 14th/15th centuries. A similar example comes from the medieval settlement at Springwood Park, Kelso (Ford 1998: 706–07, illus 17, no 1). The third example (SF 1780, Figure 4.29), which came from layer A007, is a cast U-shaped arm from a locking or swivel arm buckle (Ward-Perkins 1940: 279–80, pl LXXVII, nos 11–12; Egan and Prichard 1991: 97, no. 445). The locking arm is deliberately asymmetrical, abruptly narrowing in diameter mid-length along one side which would be inserted into the side of a pierced rectangular buckle frame to form the central bar and secured into position with a separate cast collar with integral pin. The opposite arm is thicker and circular in section, terminating in a globular knop. Despite it being referred to as a 'locking' arm, the arm would always have been movable, projecting out beyond the frame of the buckle itself. The use of this projecting arm is not well understood (Ward Perkins 1940: 279) but it is thought that the arm was intended to hold an item, such as a purse or knife (Egan and Pritchard 1991: 97) or even keys. Comparisons have been made in the form, and consequently date, to purse bars of 15th and 16th century date (Williams 2018: 11-12). A broad late medieval-early post-medieval date is suggested for examples recovered from Salisbury (Goodall 2012b: 100, fig 21, no 102) and London (Ward-Perkins 1940: 279; Egan and Prichard 1991: 97).

In addition to the three buckles is a facetted bar from a buckle. This bar is not closely datable on stylistic grounds but appears to be consistent with the late medieval/post-medieval, Phase 5, context of recovery.

Pins: Thirty fragments of fine copper alloy pins were identified, the majority of which derive from Phase 6 contexts (22). Only two fragmentary fine pin shanks come from well-stratified medieval contexts, SF2787 from a fill of Pit C018, of late 12th to mid 13th century date and SF3583 from Pit C048 dating from the mid 13th to 15th century. The fragmentary condition of both examples precludes identification of their original form but it is likely that they were simple wound wire headed or spherical-headed dress pins. Both types are common

on medieval sites, from the 13th century onwards and were used to fasten textile garments (Caple 1983; 1991; Egan and Pritchard 1991: 299–304).

A further 28 pins, deriving from Phase 5 and 6 contexts (see Table 4.9 for summary), are short, fine, wound wire headed pins. These pins are a well recognised type with a long currency of use from the 13th to 19th centuries, taking the form of a fine circular-sectioned tapering shank with a simple sub-spherical head produced by winding a fine wire around the squared end of the pin. Detailed studies of this pin type have enabled a typochronologial scheme to be developed which indicates that the shorter and finer the shank, the later the pin is likely to be (Caple 1991). Development in the form of the wire-wound head has also been observed: those with no or little attempt to mask the joins in the wire are typically earlier in date than those which have been crimped into a spherical or globular shape (Caple 1991: 246–50). All of the intact or substantially intact examples from Bon Accord have very fine, short shanks and well-finished crimped heads implying a late, post-medieval, rather than medieval date.

Wire-wound headed pins are known from a range of Scottish medieval and post-medieval sites, both secular and religious, including Tantallon Castle, East Lothian (Caldwell 1991: illus 3, nos 13–16); Perth (Cox 1996: 767–69, illus 19, nos 95–96; Ford 1987a: 123–24, illus 124, no 14); Elcho, Perthshire (Caldwell 1988: 71–72, fig 1), Edinburgh Castle (Clark 1997a: 151–53, illus 129, nos 36–38), Jedburgh Abbey (Caldwell 1995a: 85, illus 79, no 15) and Aberdeen (Goodall 1982a: 186–87, no 57).

A single fine nail-headed pin (SF2122E) was recovered from Phase 6 Pit C078. Pins of this type are machine made, mass produced items which have seen use from the late 19th century to the present day.

Strap-end: A fragmentary object (SF2222, Figure 4.29) is identified as an elongated strap end by the similarity of form to a more ornate but fragmentary example from Linlithgow Carmelite Friary (Stones *et al.* 1989: 157, illus 99, no 228) which came from a post 16th century context. The Linlithgow example is compared to a 14th century example from Goltho (Goodall 1975: 91, fig 43, no 4) and a slightly later example from Wharram Percy (Goodall 1979: 11, fig 55, nos 13, 14). Strap ends of this form, produced by folding copper alloy sheeting along one side is a type seen in the 14th century. Several plain but more robust examples are known from London (Egan and Pritchard 1991: 130, illus 85).

Buttons: Five buttons have been recognised amongst the assemblage. All are slightly different in form and manufacturing technique but most are 19th/early 20th century in date with the exception of SF525, a large disc-shaped button with simple looped fastening, which

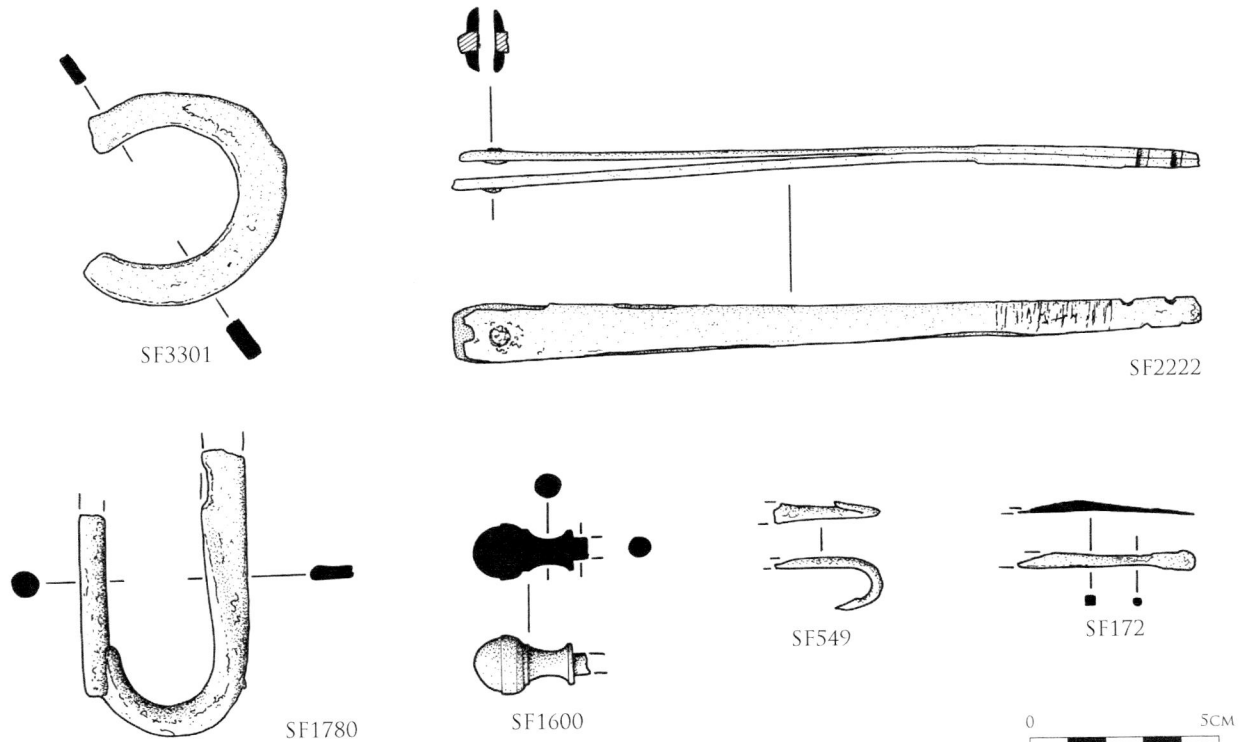

Figure 4.29 Miscellaneous copper alloy objects; SF3301; SF2222; SF1780 ('locking buckle fragment); SF1600; SF549; SF172

is likely to be 18th century in date and SF6004, a small disc-shaped example, a type common in the 18th and 19th centuries (Cuddeford 1994: 15, no.16). More recent buttons are represented on site by a four-hole machine made button (SF1596), and a composite domed button (SF2149), a type commonly used on tunics and overcoats in the early 20th century (*ibid*, 15, no. 26–29). The fifth example is a domed, cast, one-piece button with the manufacturers mark (now illegible) on the reverse face, a type common in the 18th to early 20th century (*ibid*, 15, no 23). It is an intrusive object recovered from Layer C003, dating to Phase 2.

Lace chapes: Two possible lace chape fragments were identified amongst the assemblage. One, SF2787, was recovered from the fill of Pit C018 dated to the late 12th to mid 13th century. A further fragment come from post-medieval Layer A010 but may well be late medieval in date.

These items would have been put on the end of a lace of leather or textile to prevent fraying or to aid threading. Each of the examples from Bon Accord was formed by rolling a fine sheet of copper alloy into a thin tube with a straight seam. Lace chapes are typical of mid 14th century or later date and appear to have continued into use into the 16th century (Egan and Pritchard 1991: 281–82). Similar examples are known from previous excavations in Aberdeen (Stones 2001: 198, illus 154, no 366 & 367) from 13th to 14th century contexts. Further

medieval examples are known from Jedburgh Abbey (Gabra-Sanders 1995: 88), Linlithgow Carmelite Friary (Stones *et al.* 1989: 159, illus 100, no. 214–16), Perth (Goodall 2012a: 99); Springwood Park, Kelso (Ford 1998: 707, illus 17 no. 18–20) and Dundonald Castle (Caldwell 2004: 100, fig 100 no.52).

Chain mail

A small lump of articulated chain mail (SF1397) was recovered from Phase 2 Layer A002. Each of the rings has been flattened and riveted together using a fine circular-sectioned iron peg or rivet. Although the style of the individual rings and the method of their fastening are entirely consistent with medieval chain mail armour, the material used is not. Copper alloy chain mail is unusual and is likely to have been used as decorative fringing to more functional iron or low-carbon steel chain mail. Small linked copper alloy chain links from a mail garment come from Threave Castle, Galloway (Caldwell 1981: 107, fig 10, nos 20 & 21). A further small chain link fragment (SF1709) came from Layer A (Phase 5).

Horse equipment

The most significant of the metal objects found at Bon Accord is a single, substantially intact, highly decorated prick spur (SF659, Figures 4.30 & 4.31), which was recovered from a occupation Layer C005 associated

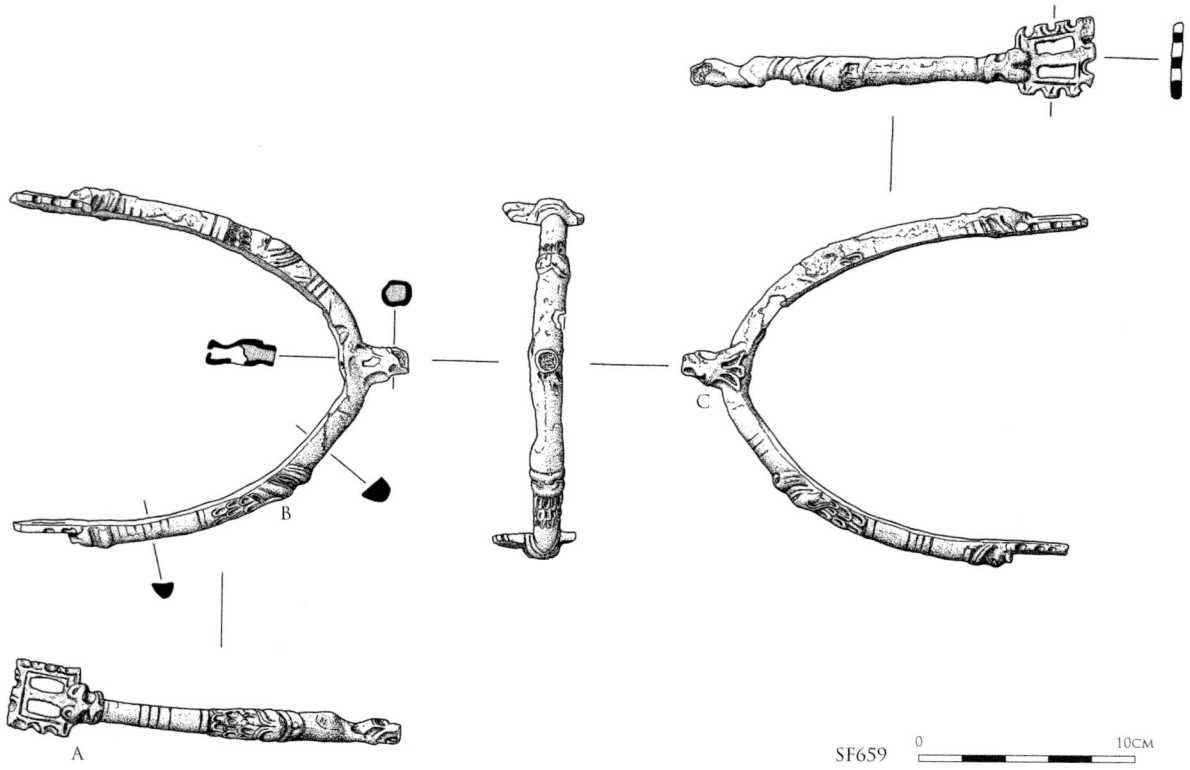

Figure 4.30 The copper alloy spur SF659. The letters A, B and C refer to detailing shown in Figure 4.32

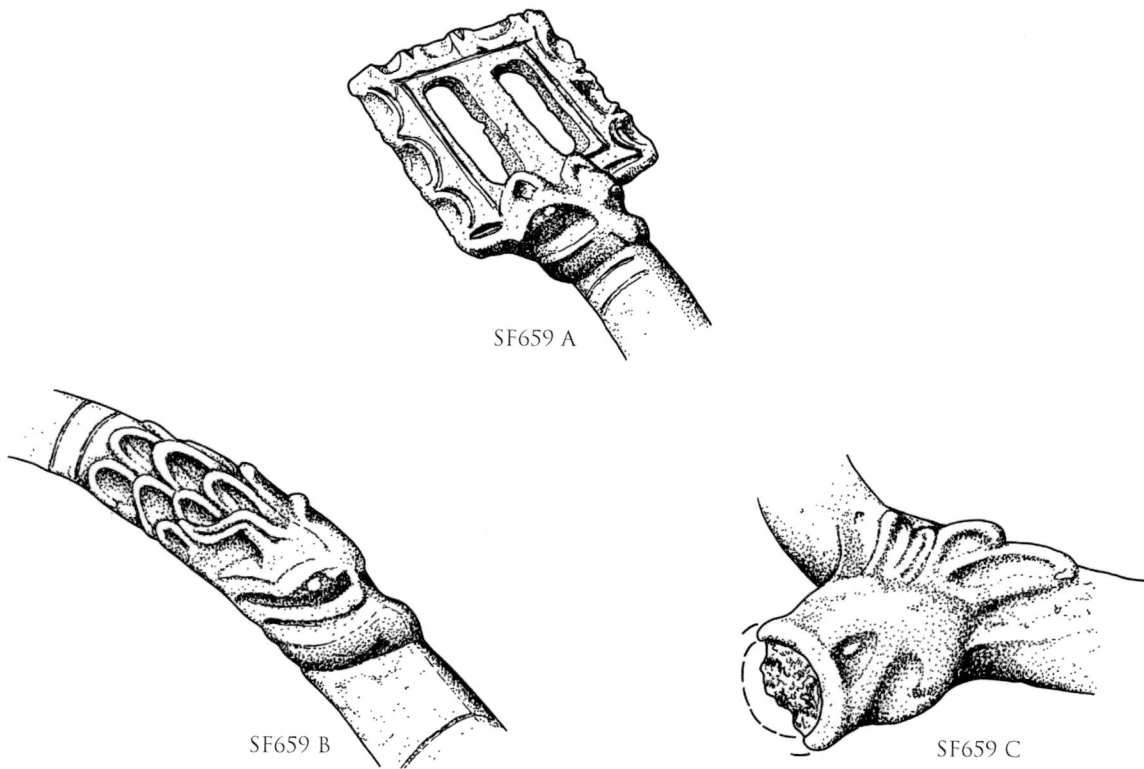

SF659

Figure 4.31 Detailing on the copper alloy spur SF659

with pottery of mid-to-late 13th century date. The spur is badly damaged on the exterior surface of one beam and the composite goad has been lost but is otherwise intact. The significance of this object lies not just in its substantially intact condition but in several aspects of its form and decoration which imply an early date for production, potentially pre-dating the associated finds within the same context by approximately a century.

The earliest spurs in Britain are Roman in date and were typically produced from wrought iron (Manning 1985: 69–70; Shortt 1959), although rare examples made of copper alloy are known, such as an example from Longstock, Hampshire (Shortt 1959: 61, fig 1). By AD 700 the use of spurs was well-established in Europe while further east the whip continued to be the preferred riding aid (Ellis 2002). As spurs developed in use and became a more common facet of the panoply of equestrian equipment their importance as a fashion accessory denoting the status of horsemen increased and they were often decorated, silvered and gilded. By the Middle Ages gilded spurs were used in the ceremonies of knighthood and had become symbolic of that rank (*ibid* 2002). No traces of gilding survive on the Bon Accord spur but the level of decoration and the high-degree of craftsmanship, skill and artistry demonstrated by the rich zoomorphic decoration implies that this was an object worn by a person of rank and importance.

Zoomorphic heads, such as those that decorate both terminals, the beams and the goad junction of the Bon Accord spur, have occasionally been used to as a decorative device on spurs and other horse-related equipment and became popular during the Anglo-Saxon period (Ellis and Bogden 2012: 194). Like the Bon Accord spur, some late Saxon spurs have a decorative boss in the form of beasts' heads about half-way along each of their sides.

Many points of similarity survive between this spur and a copper alloy pricket spur recovered from urban excavations in Perth (Ellis and Bogdan 2012: illus 154, 20; Cat No. 122/A11316): both have flat sub-rectangular double slot perforated terminals, both are well modelled and display high quality casting and, although not identical, are decorated in a similar style with stylised animal head decoration in relief. Yet, the decoration on the Bon Accord spur is more complex and ornate than the Perth example. Although elements of the design and decoration mimic 10th/11th century late Saxon spurs, the Perth example is interpreted as late 11th/12th century in date due to the shape of the arms which are designed to curve slightly under the wearer's ankle, a feature consistent with 12th century spur design (Ellis and Bogdan 2012: 194–95; Williams 2002: 117). The Bon Accord spur does not share this

feature and could be slightly earlier based on the form of the arms and the terminal shape, despite its recovery from a mid-to-late 13th century context. Comparative examples of early medieval spurs with zoomorphic decoration from Britain and the continent have been recently rehearsed and outlined by Ellis and Bogden (2012: 194–96) and require no reiteration here, suffice to say that fine spurs such as this rarely survive in the archaeological record and although examples with similar individual features are known, no exact parallels are readily found. Teasing out further individual features of the spur reinforces the interpretation of this object as an early medieval example: the form of the rectangular terminals becomes rare after the mid 12th century and the pricket fitting, decorated at the junction of the beam with a small animal head in relief, consists of an empty small cylindrical socket designed to hold a separate goad, now lost, either of iron or copper alloy, similar to an 11th century example from Soberton, Hampshire (Williams 2002: 116, fig 3b).

All these features together indicate that the Bon Accord spur is a rare early medieval example, probably dating to the late 11th or 12th century. In Scotland, the closest parallel is the example from Perth, previously discussed, but later iron spurs are known from a range of Scottish medieval sites including Tantallon Castle, East Lothian (Caldwell 1991: illus 4, nos 31), Perth (Ellis 1987; Ellis and Bogden 2012) and Inverlochy Castle, Inverness-shire (Lewis and Smith 1998: 636), *intra alia*.

The discarding of the spur may have been due to the extent of damage to the decoration on one arm which has removed the fine animal head boss. Although the goad has broken off and been lost, this appears to have been a separate component which would have been straightforward to replace. Despite this damage, the spur would still have been wearable as both terminals are intact and loss during use appears to be unlikely in this instance. Its recovery from a Phase 3 context, associated with mid-to-late 13th century activity, implies that that spur was around a century old at the time of deposition.

Commerce
Nick Holmes

Despite the volume of the metal assemblage only five coins and a single jetton were identified amongst the non-ferrous items consisting of a single cut silver halfpenny of early 13th century date and four copper alloy coins dating to between the late 15th century and late 19th century.

The silver halfpenny (SF2391), from Phase 2 Layer A002 dates from the reign of John I; it had been deliberately cut in half and only one half now survives. It is a very

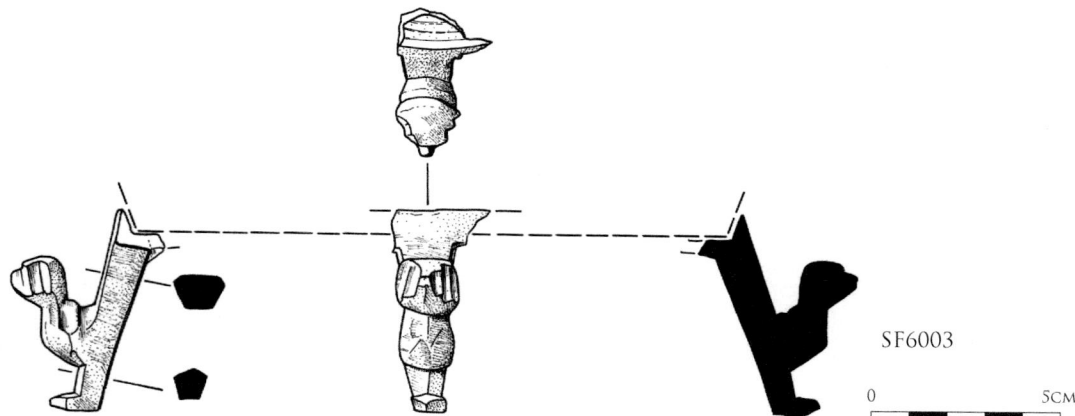

Figure 4.32 The copper alloy trivet foot, SF6003

rare example of a class Vb2 coin minted by Hunfrei at Rochester, and due to the short period in which this mint operated, can be dated quite precisely to between AD 1205 and AD 1207. Short Cross coins, both whole and cut, are found frequently in Scotland but this example is particularly significant due to the origin of the mint and moneyer. Many thousand silver pennies have been found previously in Aberdeen but almost exclusively in hoards (Evans and Thain 1989). The Rochester mint from which this coin derives was open for a short number of years, issuing coins of class Vb only. The limited distribution of coins from this mint means that the recovery of a fragment at Bon Accord is highly unusual and is a significant addition to the small number of coins of this mint and moneyer known in Scotland.

Two coins are copper farthings from the reign of James III dating to the late 15th century. One, SF1888, came from Spread A013 (Mid-to-Late Phase 5) and the other, SF837B, came from layer A007 (late Phase 5). Late 15th century copper farthings, also known as 'black money', were circulated in Scotland for a fairly restricted period, bracketed by Parliamentary Acts in AD 1466 and AD 1469 which were issued to instruct, and then subsequently repeal, the striking of copper coinage in Scotland (Holmes 1998: 23–27). Despite official attempts to cease the striking of such coinage by the repeal of the 1466 Act in the final year of the 1460s, subsequent documentary sources from the 1480s indicate that copper coins, although devalued, were still in circulation (*ibid*: 27). The recovery of two, heavily corroded, examples from Bon Accord are a useful addition to the limited number of finds already outlined by Holmes (1998: 23–24) which include a possible forgery from Linlithgow Friary (Stones *et al.* 1989: 163).

Domestic objects

Domestic objects from Bon Accord were rare amongst the non-ferrous metal assemblage and those that are present mainly derive from late medieval and post-medieval contexts. These include a cast vessel foot with zoomorphic decoration, a spoon and various fittings.

Vessel foot: The foot (SF6003, Figure 4.32), decorated with a simple, stylised, zoomorphic figure of a dog, is not readily paralleled and difficult to date as a consequence. It came from late medieval/post-medieval (Phase 5) deposits but the form and style imply an earlier date. The short height and shallow depth of the circular 'tray' which the foot supports makes it unlikely to be a fragment of a footed bowl or pot, but rather, it would seem, from a decorative shallow circular stand or trivet-like frame with a short V-shaped rim, possibly a stand for a chafing dish. Metal trivets, which would have been used to support vessels during cooking over the fire, are unusual finds from medieval contexts, not because they would necessarily have been rare during this time but due to the damage that would have been sustained over long periods of use, possibly encouraging reworking or even recycling. A substantially complete iron tripod trivet is known from London (Egan 2010: 153, fig 121) and fragments of other possible examples come from Northampton (Goodall 1981: 59–60, fig 58, 5) and Winchester (Biddle 1990: 820, 822, fig 242) dating to around the mid 14th/15th century. Although similar in form to these wrought iron trivets, the production of this item from non-ferrous metal, the degree of finish and the lack of any evidence of heat damage, makes it likely that the Bon Accord foot derives from a decorative stand rather than a functional trivet. In terms of form, it would not be out of place in a late medieval context as the iron examples testify to. The zoomorphic decoration and particularly the canine subject matter is also suggestive of a late medieval date, as for example the canine handles from 14th century hexagonal salt cellars known from excavations in London (Egan 2010: 191–93, fig 156, nos 537 and 538). It is unclear whether the dog depicted in relief on the Bon Accord foot is squatting or standing but the angle and form of the head is very similar to a hollow cast dog which forms the handle of a pewter salt cellar from a mid 14th/early 15th century context in London (*ibid*: 191, no.537).

Spoon: A single, substantially intact spoon, SF2122F, came from the fill of Pit C078, dating to Phase 6. It is of simple form with a dished oval bowl and flat expanded handle decorated with a stamped floral decorative motif. The form of the utensil and the style of decoration suggest a late 18th/early 19th century date for manufacture.

Handle/finial: A single possible copper alloy handle or finial for a composite object (SF1600, Figure 4.29) was recovered from the fill of a late Phase 6 demolition cut within Area B of the site.

Fittings and fixtures

Six possible decorative fittings or ornaments were recovered from Areas B and C across the site, the majority of which (five) come from pre-15th century contexts, including a sheet fitting, possibly for a wooden object or vessel (SF1678) which was recovered from Pit C019 (Phase 2). Additionally, a paperclip rivet (SF1761B), commonly used to fix repair patches in place on sheet metal vessels, could be medieval or post-medieval in date. A flat, cast, horse-shoe shaped object (SF3301, Figure 4.29) is likely to be a decorative mount or ornament for a casket or item of furniture although the method of fixture has now been lost through damage, perhaps from removal of the metal object from its original position.

Wire and chains

Various fittings in the form of ring fittings, chain fragments and pieces of wire were recovered from the later phases of the site (summarised in Table 4.9). None of the pieces were closely datable on stylistic grounds and could have performed a range of functions, both industrial and domestic in character. The possibility of use as components of ornate hair ornaments (Egan and Pritchard 1991: 291–96) or even as elements of stringed musical instruments should be considered but cannot be argued for with any certainty.

Sheet

Nineteen sheet and strip fragments were recovered, the majority deriving from late medieval and post-medieval contexts (summarised in Table 4.9) within Areas A, B

and C. Six fragments of copper alloy sheet and pieces of rectangular strips were associated with Phase 1 to 4 medieval contexts but due to their fragmentary condition it is not possible to determine the exact form of the object that they derive from. In many instances, very little of the original edges of the pieces survive.

Working waste

Eleven small finds have been identified as items related to non-ferrous metalworking in the form of casting debris, off-cuts (e.g. 1845a, late Phase 6 demolition deposit, Area B) and a possible unfinished object (SF3021). The majority of the casting waste comprises small amorphous globular lumps of partially vitrified copper-rich material which appear to be spills from casting. These were found in small numbers at Bon Accord from Phase 2 through to Phase 5 but the majority derive from pit fills associated with Phase 2 activity within Area C. Only one waste fragment (SF3440), possibly representing waste for recycling, came from medieval contexts in Area A, from a garden soil dating from the late 12th to mid 13th century. The quantities of casting debris from Bon Accord are so limited it is impossible to confirm whether this activity was taking place on-site or whether the waste represents secondary dumping of material which originated off-site, but the recovery of fragmentary ceramic moulds for casting metal decorative items (Section 4.3.6) demonstrates that this activity was taking place in and around Bon Accord during the 12th/13th centuries.

Tools

Possible tool fragments of non-ferrous metal were rare amongst the assemblage. A single hook, possibly a fish hook (SF549, Figure 4.29) came from occupation material of late medieval/early post-medieval date and an angled tool tip, possibly a fine chisel or gouge (SF1683), from Phase 2, have been tentatively identified. Further tool fragments, including a double edged fine blade similar to that seen on wood-working planes (SF1642A) and two spatula-headed tools, potentially used in fine metalworking, woodworking or even leatherworking (SF121 & SF172, Figure 4.29) came from post-medieval contexts and are likely to be 17th to 19th century in date.

Miscellaneous objects

One somewhat enigmatic copper alloy object is present amongst the Bon Accord assemblage. SF2122G is a fine rectangular strip with T-shaped channel formed by folding the long edges over at right angles. The back of the channel is punctuated by a series of transverse angled ribs. The identification of the function of this item, and its possible date, is not clear – it is very similar to a linear rachet fitting such as that from the

Roman fort at Elginhaugh which is believed to form part of the mechanism for a hand-held catapult or cross-bow (Allison-Jones 2007: 405, 407, fig 10.29, no.32, pl 10.5) but the delicacy of the sheet metal on the Bon Accord object places some measure of doubt over the object's potential to function as rachet fitting and may well be purely decorative. Its recovery from the fill of a post-medieval sump (Pit C078) may well suggest that the piece was part of the associated mechanism but an earlier date cannot be ruled out on stylistic grounds alone.

Several objects were unidentified due to their fractured or fragmentary state and in some cases, such as SF2144 and SF4160, the surfaces of the metal are entirely obscured by organic material, probably from composite organic/metal objects. SF2418, recovered from the fill of Pit C068, dating to the late 12th to mid 13th century, comprises fragments of a long circular-sectioned rod or wire encased in organic material that may be the remains of a wooden case or fitting. The degraded and fragmentary condition of this object precludes confident identification but it is possible that this represents a needle within an organic leather or wooden tube-like case, similar to examples known from London (Egan and Prichard 1991: 384–86, nos 1780–84; Egan 2010: 268, fig 207:889).

Catalogue of illustrated copper alloy items
(L = length; W = width; Th = thickness; D = diameter)

SF   172 (Figure 4.29)
Phase/Feature   Phase 6/Layer C011
Description: tool or decorative item
Flat, rounded, spatula-headed (L 13mm; W 5.5mm; Th 0.5mm) tool or decorative item, broken at opposing end causing damage to narrow shank which is uneven in width and thickness. L 47mm; W 1–3mm; Th 1.5–2.5mm.

SF   549 (Figure 4.29)
Phase/Feature   Phase 4 or 5/Spread C065
Description: hook
Small hook, possibly fishhook. Small circular-sectioned (D 3mm) hook, tapering toward blunt tip. Opposite end has been flattened (W 5mm; Th 1mm) but appears unperforated so the method of attachment is unknown. L 29.5mm.

SF   659 (Figures 4.30 & 4.31)
Phase/Feature   Phase 3/Layer C005
Description: prick spur
Substantially complete prick spur of slender proportions with separate goad; now lost. The tapered straight sides, triangular in section, are heavily decorated with relief animal heads and indented ridges. The terminals are quadrangular, slightly expanding towards the ankle, with deeply cusped outer edges and some incised line decoration, both pierced with two horizontal slots. At the junction between the terminals and the arms are stylised animal heads (A), better preserved on the right arm than the left where much of the surface detail has been softened by wear. These animal heads have short, rounded ears which overlap the junction with the terminal and have large almond-shaped moulded apertures representing eyes and a small rounded nose. Below the nose, the arms are decorated with two incised lines. Both arms have a decorative boss halfway along the sides in the form of a serpent-like animal head (B) in relief with elongated, curving ears which extend back upwards towards the terminal and wrap around the curving sides. Radiating from behind the ears are three rows of moulded scales or feathers. The eyes take the form of sinuous apertures set with a moulded bead-like eye and the nose is in the form of a rounded stub. Between animal heads A and B is a band of four incised parallel vertical lines, and between B and the neck a further band of parallel lines; survival restricted to the right arm only. Behind the wearer's heel the straight neck (L 17mm; W 9mm) is formed as an animal head in relief (C); the ears extending onto and overlapping the junction with the neck. The underside of the neck is damaged but appears undecorated. The mouth consists of an empty small cylindrical socket (D 6mm) to hold a separate goad, now lost, either of iron or copper alloy, similar to an 11th century example from Soberton, Hampshire (Williams 2002: 116, fig 3b). The wear and damage on the external surface of the left arm is likely to have occurred as the result of use. Surviving L 95.5mm; span 77.5mm.

SF   1133 (Figure 4.28)
Phase/Feature   Mid Phase 5/Layer C010
Description: brooch
Brooch (damaged). Plain annular brooch frame, D-shaped in section (W 3mm; Th 1.5mm), circumference distorted and broken across a constriction at one point where the pin would originally have been attached. At the point of the constriction, the ends of the circular-sectioned ring have been flattened and squared (W 3mm; Th 2mm). A plain pin (L 35mm), probably a later replacement, is present, produced from a fine tapering strip (L 35mm; W 4mm; Th 1.5mm) which loops over the frame at one end and tapers at the opposite end towards a point, the tip of which is distorted and damaged. The frame is badly corroded and much of the original surface has been lost. L 39mm; W 30.5mm; Th 1.5–2mm.

SF   1600 (Figure 4.29)
Phase/Feature   Phase 6/Layer B006
Description: handle or finial
Decorative cast knob-shaped handle or finial. Solid sub-spherical banded knob tapers to a collared rim from which a narrow short cylindrical stop (H 5mm; D 6mm) projects. L 31mm; D 6.5–15.5mm.

SF   1780 (Figure 4.29)
Phase/Feature Late Phase 5/Layer A007
Description: cylindrical padlock component
Component of cylindrical padlock. Asymmetric U-shaped copper alloy rod. One arm consists of a short, slightly off-set cylindrical rod (L 25mm; D 2mm), extreme tip lost. The opposite arm is longer (L 37.5mm) and has been flatted out towards squared, blunt, damaged end (W 5.5mm; Th 1.5mm).

SF   2222 (Figure 4.29)
Phase/Feature Phase 4/Spread A027
Description: rectangular strips
Tapering rectangular strips folded along length on one side, formerly joined together at wide squared end with small iron rivet (D 2mm). The seam between the strips is still clearly visible on the opposing edge. Both faces of the object are highly polished with a patina from wear which extends 70mm along length. 27mm from the narrow blunt point the surface texture changes and distinct transverse striations are visible from filing. On each edge, immediately above the blunt narrow damage tip are two closely spaced but off-set notches. Very similar in form to a more ornately decorated strap-end from Linlithgow Carmelite Friary (Stones *et al.* 1989: 157, illus 99, no 228). L 98mm; W 3.5–9mm; Th 1–1.5mm.

SF   2736 (Figure 4.28)
Phase/Feature Phase 2/Pit C025 fill (E)
Description: annular brooch frame
Annular brooch frame with thistle decoration. Square-sectioned annular frame constricted to facilitate pin; now lost. Four spherical knobs with cross-hatched decoration (mimicking thistles). Frame cast in a two-piece mould. Slightly distorted. Similar brooch frame but with plain, undecorated knobs comes from late 14th/early 15th century context in London (Egan and Prichard 1991: 254, fig 163, no 1330).

SF   2988 (Figure 4.28)
Phase/Feature Phase 2/Layer A002
Description: brooch pin
Brooch pin. Short tapering pin, extreme tip lost. Head (3mm x 3.5mm) perforated transversely with small circular hole (D 3mm) to allow attachment to a constriction in the now lost frame. Below head of pin is narrow collar (D 5mm) decorated with crudely incised cross cutting diagonal lines to mimic a thistle. L 26mm; D 2.5mm.

SF   3301 (Figure 4.29)
Phase/Feature Phase 2/Pit C025 fill (D)
Description: horseshoe-shaped decorative fitting
     or ornament
Flat, cast, horseshoe-shaped decorative fitting or ornament; one arm is damaged resulting in the loss of the squared tip. No obvious method of attachment survives but a small flat angular spall of iron is attached to one face; unclear if this fused through corrosion or is an original feature of the object. L 27mm; W 29mm; Th 2.5mm.

SF   3463 (Figure 4.28)
Phase/Feature Mid Phase 5/Spread C023
Description: annular buckle and pin
Complete annular buckle and pin. Intact circular-sectioned (D 5.5mm) annular ring and tapering circular-sectioned pin (L 50.5mm; D 5mm) with blunt tip. Head of pin loops around circumference of frame, joining at back, decorated below head with cast transverse ridge. A very similar buckle from late 14th–15th century deposits has been previously found during excavations at Aberdeen (Cameron and Stones 2001: 196, no.350). D 46mm.

SF   6003 (Figure 4.32)
Phase/Feature Early Phase 5/Layer A034
Description: foot with zoomorphic decoration
Well-cast short foot with zoomorphic decoration, possibly from a trivet or stand. Cast leaded brass or bronze foot, pentagonal in section, tapering towards an angled projecting blunt pointed base. Projecting from external flat face is a cast stylised head, rounded chest and foot of a small dog with pointed snout (H 41.5mm). The foot has broken off from a shallow circular stand or trivet; the height of the V-shaped rim (5.5mm) being too shallow to have functioned as a bowl. The base of the stand is at right angles to the base of the wall being horizontal or even slightly upturned in profile. The remains of two closely-spaced cast concentric grooves are present on the remaining basal surface. The entire surface of foot and dog is roughly filed with distinct striations from tooling visible. Height 55mm; W 8–13.5mm; Th 7–10.5mm.

Lead

The lead assemblage, consisting of 26 items, is dominated by lead scrap in the form of off-cuts and waste material including worked and unworked molten-looking spills of waste. Many of the scraps and off-cuts observed are damaged or cut strips and sheets probably representing patches which may have been used in the repair of objects and/or structural elements, some of which appear to have been removed from their original fitting. Most of the lead fragments are not closely datable.

The lead objects were found only in Areas A, C and D, the greatest number coming from Area C, and particularly from Phases 5 and 6. The lead assemblage is summarised in Table 4.10.

Significant and notable items are few but consist of a crudely fashioned fishing or pulley weight from Phase 1 (Area C), a fitting from a wooden object (Phase 2, Area

Table 4.10 Summary of major lead artefacts

| Area | Phase | | | | | | | | |
	1	2	3	4	5	6	Modern	Total
A	SF6014 weight	SF3098 Possible repair patch, damaged			SF1782 2fragments waste; SF6029 small tube, broken	SF2670 ingot or bar fragment		6
B								
C	SF2286 fishing/ pulley weight; SF2974 off-cut	SF3056 possible patch; SF3011 fitting for wooden object, broken	SF4328 sheet fragment, damaged	SF714 & SF762 large rolled sheets; SF1109 possible off-cut or scrap	SF896 possible off-cut or scrap; SF1010 folded sheet fragment, off-cut?; SF965A & B lead waste; SF492 decorative mount with stone inset	SF82 decorative finger ring; SF294 part-worked fragment; SF355 repair patch; SF755 lead waste; SF2618 window kame fragment	SF3133 sheet fragment	19
D	SF2165 repair patch							1
Total	4	3	1	3	8	6	1	26

C), a decorative mount with a stone inset (Phase 5/6) and an unfinished ring (Phase 6). Molten-looking spills representing waste from lead casting are confined to Phases 5 and 6. In contrast, cold-worked lead strips and off-cuts are present throughout the phases.

Weights

Two lead weights were recovered from Phase 1 deposits within Area C. They are of differing form indicating distinct functions. One (SF6014) is a small plain domed disc, likely to have been a pan weight for use with a scale-pan balance such as those recovered from the Foundry and Coppergate excavations in York (Ottaway and Rogers 2002: 2952). Although only weighing 3.7g, the form is consistent with those recovered in York and London (Ottaway and Rogers 2002: 2954–56). The plain form of SF6014 makes it difficult to assign a date with any level of certainty but it is consistent with a late 12th or 13th century date as implied by associated ceramics. The second weight (SF2286, Figure 4.33) is different in form: tapering cylindrical weight, perforated at either end with short expanding grooves which extend from both perforations across the flat ends. The surfaces of this weight are facetted with distinct vertical knife blade cuts, indicating the shape of the item was arrived at by paring away slivers of lead with a blade using the same technique one would expect in wood-working. The perforations and the hollow present at the centre of one flat end are similarly crudely worked.

Dress ring

A single dress accessory in the form of a very crude, cast lead alloy ring with an asymmetric sub-circular imitation bezel was recovered from Spread C030. Despite discovery in a Phase 6 deposit, it is likely to be several hundreds of years earlier in date. Two lead dress rings were recovered from excavations in Perth and have been dated, by associated material and context to the 13th or 14th centuries (Cherry 2012: 199, 201). Both examples from Perth are more elaborate than the ring from Bon Accord. A plain pewter stirrup ring with false stone, cast as one with the hoop, was recovered from a mid 13th century context in London (Egan and Pritchard 1991: 326). The example from Bon Accord lacks the distinctive pointed bezel typical of medieval stirrup-shaped rings but is consistent in style with other simple cabochon-inset dress rings of 13th and 14th century date (ibid: 327).

Mount or bezel

One of the most intriguing items amongst the metal finds from the site is a very small, delicate, lead or lead alloy (possibly pewter) decorative mount or bezel with semi-precious stone inset (terminology used here follows Egan and Pritchard 1991: 325; Rees 2002: 1230). The mount (SF492, Figure 4.33) takes the shape of a small stud with a sub-oval cup-shaped socket shaped around an amethyst cabochon and held in place – to what, is

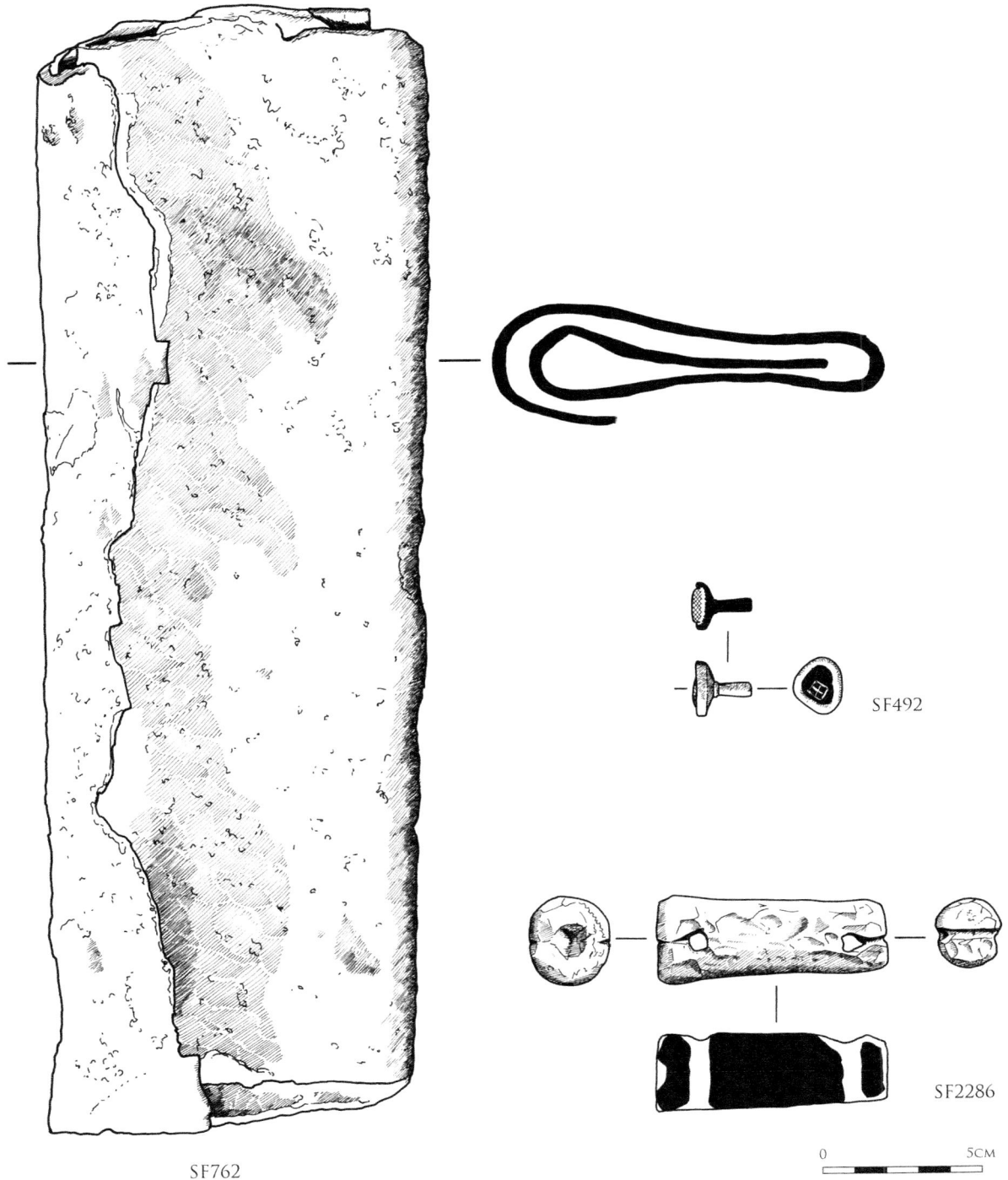

Figure 4.33 Lead objects; SF762, SF492, SF2286

unclear – by a short rod on the reverse. The metal mount has been made to fit around this particular stone, in the same way that bezels or collets for stone or glass insets on medieval dress rings were individually made rather than the stone being shaped to fit the mount. This form of mount is suggestive of a medieval rather than post-medieval date and this is borne out by the form of the

amethyst. The stone itself is a single convex cabochon, representing one of the earliest and simplest ways of shaping a gemstone. The stone was likely chipped to shape using a bone or stone hammer and then polished with an abrasive to smooth and finish (Rees 2002: 1230). The similarity in the technique of mounting to that seen on medieval stirrup rings, common from the late

12th century to as late as the 15th century (Egan and Pritchard:1991, 326) is suggestive of a similar date but this cannot be argued with any certainty in light of the mount's late and secondary context in association with Wall C006.

Amethysts such as SF492 have been used in jewellery since before the Roman period and continued to be one of the most valued gemstones until the late 18th century when a source was discovered in South America (Rees 2002: 1230).

Sheet fragments and possible off-cuts

Two distinct groups of sheets/off-cuts are present at Bon Accord, which consist of large rolled sheets, possibly surplus stock for lining or repairing roofs or other lead-lined structural features, and small sheet fragments cut from larger pieces. The size and weight of two rolls of lead (SF714 and SF762, Figure 4.33) recovered from occupation Layer C008 are substantial: both are similar in dimensions, have been rolled or folded in a similar manner and are identical in weight. The discard of almost 6.5kg of lead sheet is surprising as this would have been a valuable commodity in the late medieval period. The smaller sheet fragments, many of which appear to be off-cuts from larger sheets could well be scrap.

Simple sheet fragments are known from medieval contexts at Springwood Park, Roxburghshire (Ford 1998: 707). Lead off-cuts are also found from Castle Park, Dunbar (Cox 2000: 126), particularly in phases 20–22 of post-medieval date.

Repair patches and fittings

A range of patches and strip fittings have been identified, concentrated in Phases 1 and 2 of the site. Two, SF2165 and SF3098, are flat perforated rectangular strip or sheet fragments and are likely to have been roof fittings or repair patches to external structural elements. The damaged condition of both indicates that they had been removed from their fittings prior to disposal. Similar sheet fittings with nail holes are known from period II to IV contexts at Jedburgh Abbey (Caldwell 1995c: 89).

Patches and fittings for portable wooden objects are represented by SF3011 and SF3056. The former, a flat oval perforated sheet with scalloped edges found attached to a piece of wood, is likely to be a decorative mount or repair patch to a vessel or casket. Flat oval or diamond-shaped iron escutcheons are typical fittings for wooden stave buckets (such as those from the 17th century backfill of a well in the churchyard of St Paul-in-the-Bail, Lincoln (Morris 2008: 43–46, fig 29–31), where they were used to strengthen the

handle fitting. Although SF3011 is similar in form to these escutcheons, the softness of the lead sheet argues against this function and implies that it may have seen use as a repair patch combining a decorative element is more likely (Figure 4.13).

Catalogue of illustrated lead items
(L = length; W = width; Th = thickness; D = diameter)

SF 2286 (Figure 4.13)
Phase/Feature   Phase 1/Pit C002 fill (B)
Description: cylindrical weight
Cylindrical weight, slightly expanding in width along length. Tool marks are present across all surfaces of the object from shaping suggesting the shape was prepared by paring with a knife. Both ends flattened, one with an irregular cut groove which extends onto both faces to edge of sub-circular hole (D 7.5mm) positioned 10mm from narrow end of weight which perforates the thickness of the object. The opposite end has slightly off-centre, sub-circular hollow (D 9.5mm) and short expanding linear grooves on opposing edges which extend onto the rounded faces of the weight to the edge of a second facetted perforation (D 7.5mm) 10mm from the widest end. L 72mm; W 23–29mm; Th 21–23.5mm.

SF 492 (Figure 4.33)
Phase/Feature   Mid-to-Late Phase 5/Wall C009
Description: decorative mount
Decorative mount with semi-precious stone inset. Small sub-oval cup-shaped mount of lead alloy (9mm x 7.5mm) surrounding a roughly triangular-shaped cabochon of dark purple/blue amethyst (5.5mm x 4mm); a short circular-sectioned rod (L 4.5mm; D 2mm) projects from rounded base, presumably for insertion into socket or fitting. Stone has been filed to shape with faint scratch marks from abrasion, two edges chipped and rounded face polished prior to being set within the mount using molten lead. L 9.5mm.

SF 762 (Figure 4.33)
Phase/Feature   Late Phase 4/Layer C008
Description: rolled lead sheet
Flattened large roll of thick lead sheet (4mm), folded over on itself twice with no attempt to seal, join or conceal the ragged, unshaped long edge. The ends of the sheet have been roughly cut prior to folding. L 372mm; W 112.5–122mm; Th 21.5–37.5mm. 3217g.

Conclusions

As might be expected in an assemblage of this broad chronological span, the quantity of metal objects recovered at Bon Accord is significant and is dominated by objects of iron. Subtle differences in the composition of the iron assemblage, as opposed to the suite of copper alloy and lead alloy finds from the site, are noted, such as the not unsurprising abundance of fittings and tools amongst the iron objects and a profusion of dress accessories and other decorative items amongst the copper alloy assemblage. A distinct pattern can be seen in the distribution of objects of different materials across the site: iron objects are fairly evenly distributed across Areas A and C (with a small number from the heavily disturbed Area B) whereas the copper alloy and lead finds are concentrated in Area C, in relatively close proximity to the Gallowgate. This difference in distribution may be related to differences in activity on the Gallowgate frontage, and further back, with copper alloy and lead objects perhaps more commonly associated with domestic activities rather than small-scale industry. It may also be that casting activity was concentrated in the area just behind the Gallowgate (further indicated by the retrieval of crucible fragments from Pits C018 and C019 (Section 4.3.5).

Detailed examination of the metal finds has allowed classification of individual finds in line with established typological schemes, where possible. This has enabled the identification of diagnostic medieval objects in later, secondary contexts and the recognition of intrusive post-medieval and modern items within potentially early phase features. This distribution of medieval and post-medieval objects confirms the extent of mixing of material and disturbance of contexts as recognised during excavation.

Yet, assessing the significance of the metal objects within the later levels at Bon Accord remains problematic as many tool types and structural fittings have seen little modification in form since the Roman period and cannot be closely dated on style alone.

Despite the large quantity of metal finds recovered during the excavations at Bon Accord, Aberdeen, only a small number can be confidently identified as being medieval in date on the basis of their form, function and context of recovery. Like other urban excavations of medieval and post-medieval sites, the majority of objects are common everyday items associated with day-to-day life and include large numbers of structural and household fittings, items associated with dress and personal appearance as well as tools, vessel fragments, horse equipment and items relating to commerce and trade. Almost all of the finds are readily paralleled on other Scottish medieval sites, such as Aberdeen (Murray 1982), Rattray, Aberdeen (Murray & Murray 1993), Perth (Ford 1987a & 1987b; Franklin & Goodall 2012), Edinburgh Castle (Driscoll and Yeoman 1997) and Whithorn (Hill 1997). Although household items are present amongst the medieval finds in the form of candlesticks and cooking vessel fragments, domestic equipment makes up a very small proportion of the assemblage, reflecting the site's industrial function in the early to late medieval period.

4.3.2 Worked stone
Rob Engl with a contribution by George R. Haggarty

Introduction

A total of 43 finds of coarse and worked stone were recovered, six of which are part of a Purbeck limestone mortar. A catalogue of the illustrated material is included but a full report and catalogue of the coarse stone artefacts can be found in the site archive.

Raw material

The majority of the objects described below were formed from local granites. There were also smaller quantities of sandstone, mica schist, limestone, pumice and chalk cobbles.

Artefact categories by type

Whetstones

The nine whetstones were all made of locally-obtained fine grained micaceous siltstones. Eight were hand-held and narrow with a rectangular cross-section. Four of the artefacts were fragmentary. Artefact SF3584 had a small ground hole, 9mm in diameter, at one end, probably for carrying cordage (Figure 4.34). A similar item, SF963, is well worn and has the remains of a heavily corroded iron chain for suspension surviving within a biconical perforation, bored at the widest end of the stone (Figure 4.34). Fragment SF1926 was probably originally part of a larger tabular object, though the rounded edges indicate it had continued to be used as a fragment. Artefact SF3396 was flat and tabular.

Whetstones or hones were used throughout the medieval period for the sharpening or edging of metal objects such as knives and razors (Ford 1987: 147).
Styluses

The assemblage contained four styluses, three of which were made of slate. The fourth, SF206, was made from mica schist. All of the artefacts are thin and cylindrical, ranging from 39mm to 67mm in length and from 2mm to 6mm in diameter. SF208 and SF3133 had single ends fashioned into a rough point while SF2700 and SF537 both had smooth flattened ends. Slate styluses, termed 'pencils', were found on both the St Nicholas and 45–75 Gallowgate sites, Aberdeen (Cameron *et al*, 2001: 207).

Spindle whorls

Three abraded spindle whorls were retrieved, all made of sedimentary rock. Two of these, SF2845 and SF3640, were bun-shaped while SF3849 was melon-shaped (Figure 4.35). SF2845 displayed a simple engraved line

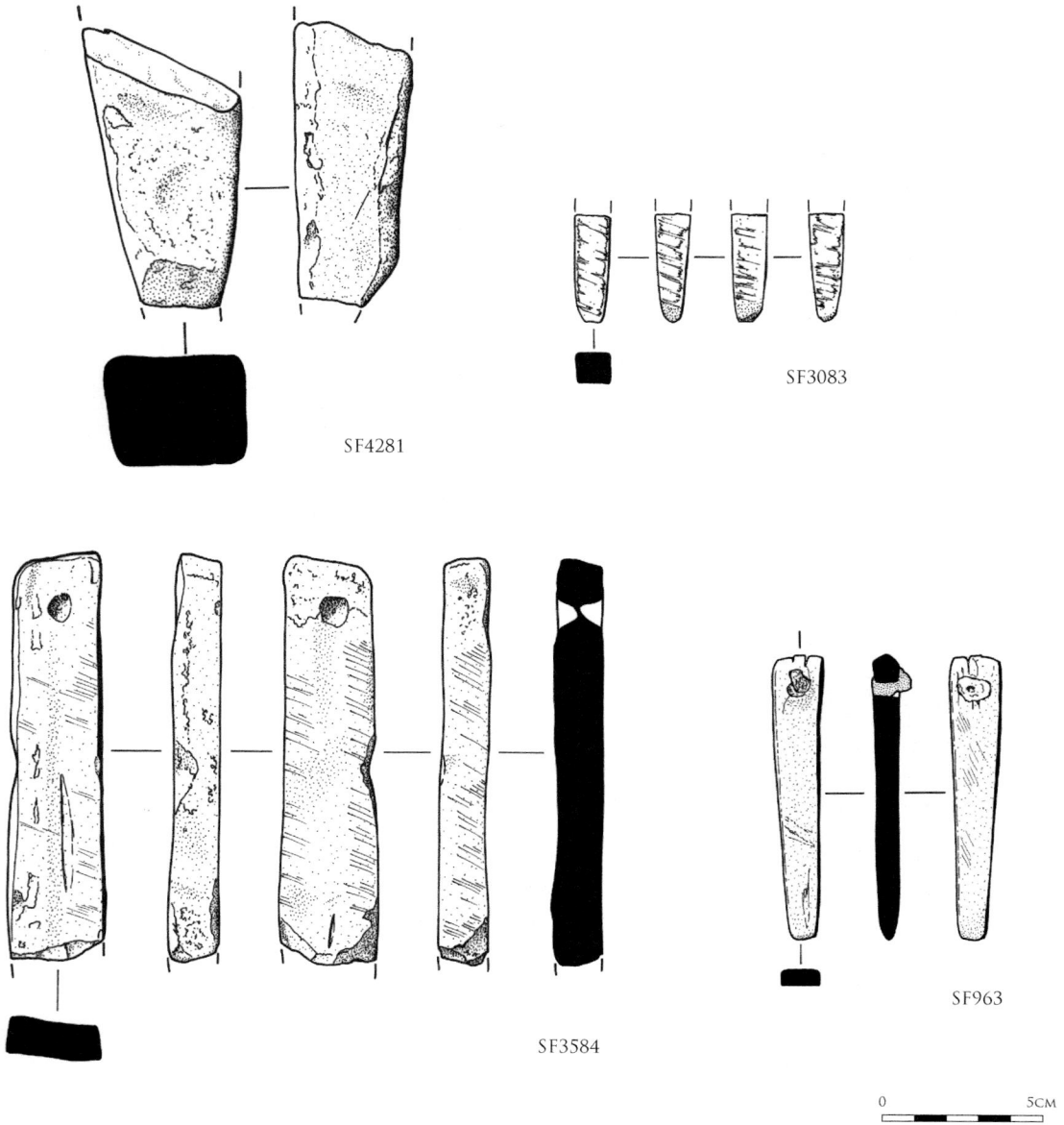

Figure 4.34 Whetstones; SF4281; SF3083; SF3584; SF963

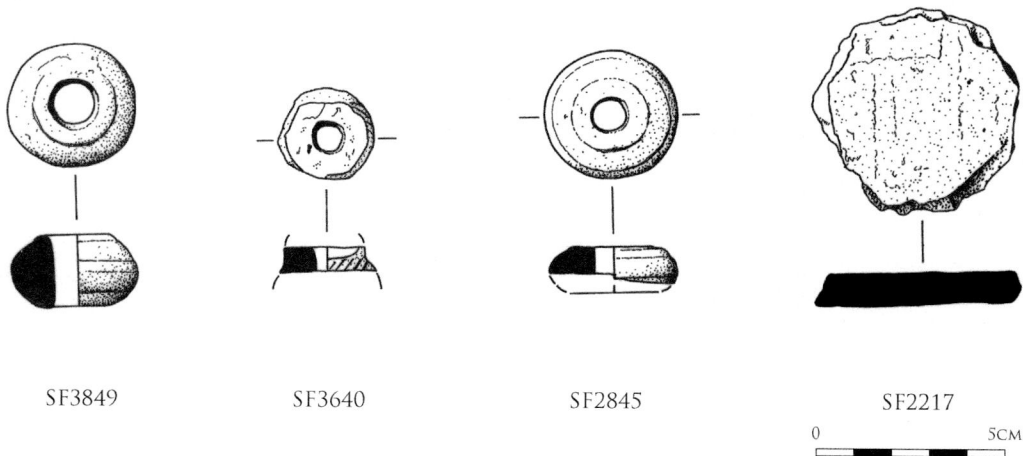

Figure 4.35 Spindle whorls; SF3849; SF3640; SF2845; SF2217

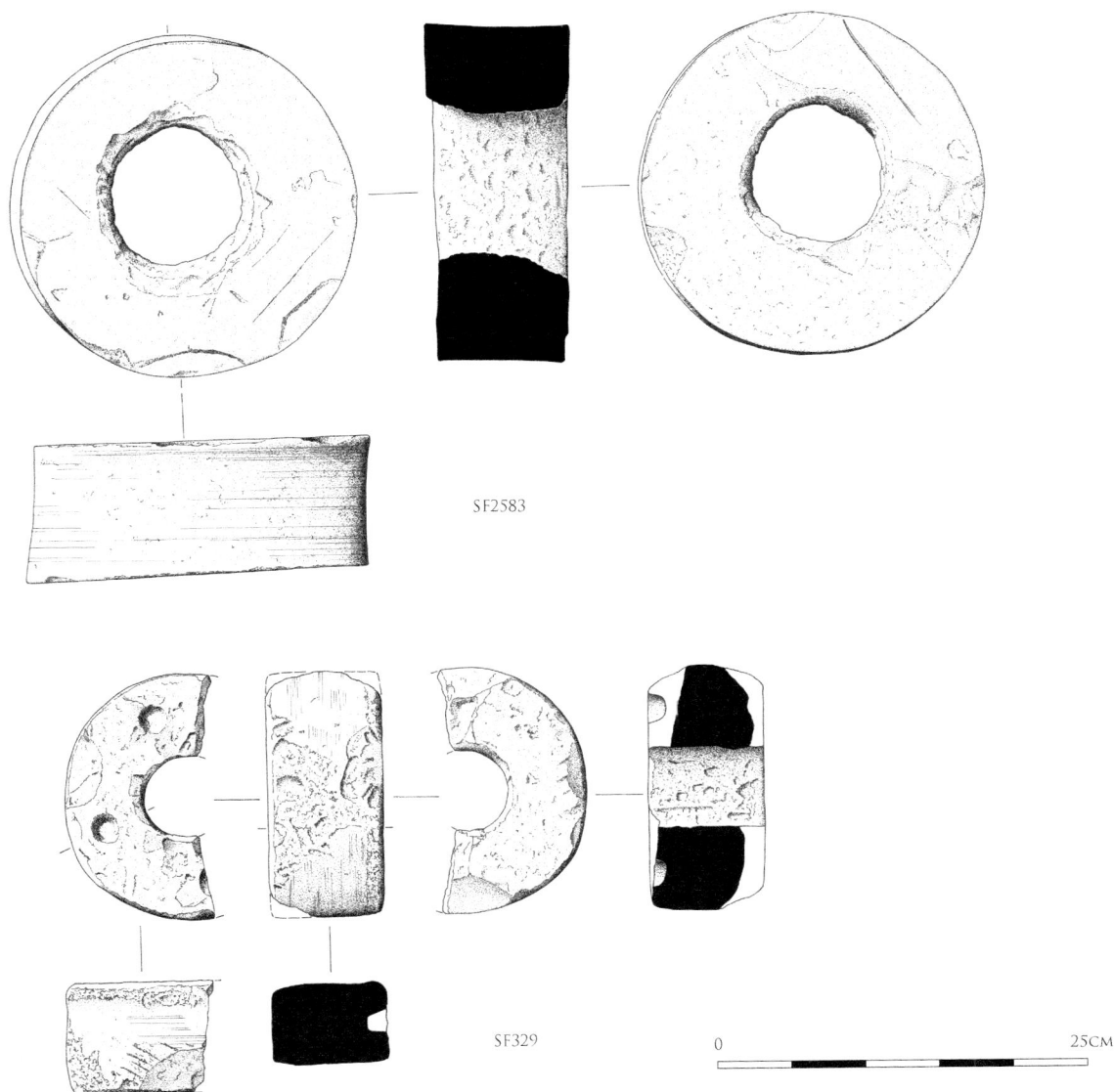

Figure 4.36 Grinding stones; SF2583; SF329

Figure 4.37 SF2583 as found, with handles and wedges *in situ*

decoration around the circumference while SF3640 appears to have cordage marks around its perimeter.

Grinding lathes

Two large circular stone artefacts are the grinding stones from composite grinding lathes. SF2583 survived virtually intact with the alder shaft *in situ* and secured tightly within the central hole of the grindstone by the use of oak wedges (Figure 4.36). Single wedges had been inserted down three faces of the shaft on either side of the grindstone and in two instances double wedges had been inserted (Figure 4.37 and see Section 4.2.1). Heavily decayed wood was also found within the central pecked hole of SF329 suggesting that it was also part of a similar composite mechanism (Figure 4.36). This artefact has three, equally spaced, small depressions set

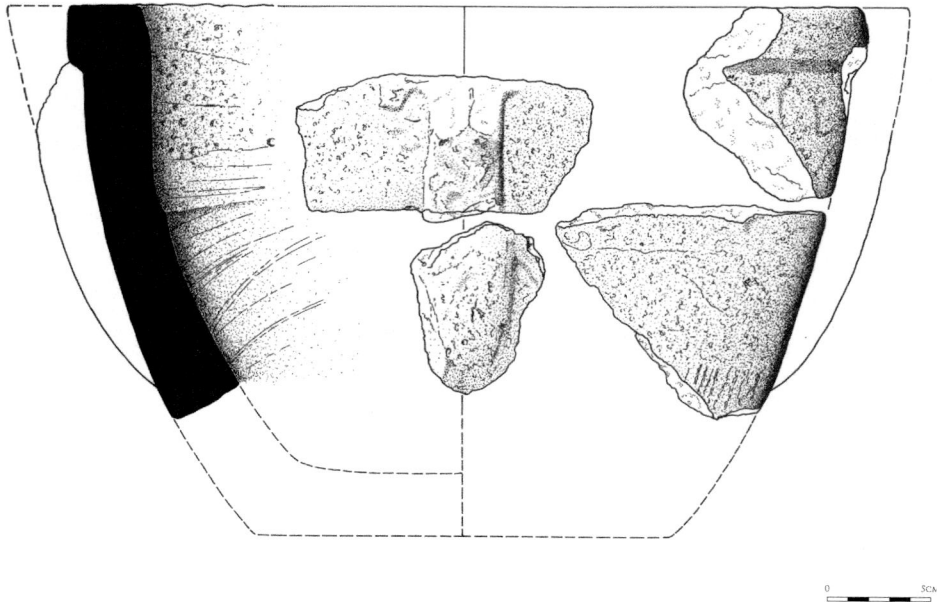

Figure 4.38 Purbeck Limestone mortar

around a larger centrally placed hole. The outer faces of both stones show smoothed patches of wear with obvious striations.

It is likely that these artefacts represent the remains of foot-operated pole lathes for the edging or working of small metal objects such as knives, chisels etc.

The use of rotary grindstones in Scotland is evidenced from the Early Historic period – a rotary quern was recovered from 8th to 9th century contexts at Scatness, Shetland (Dockrill *et al.* 2010: 64), in a structure utilised as a storeroom or workshop. The example from Scatness was 224mm in diameter and 58mm wide (Bashford 2010: 242) and unlike the grindstones recovered from Aberdeen had a central square hole (50mm square) rather than a round one, having been manufactured from an old quernstone. An assemblage of 29 Anglo-Scandinavian cylindrical rotary grindstones, from 16–22 Coppergate, York, ranged in size from between 50 to 440mm in external diameter, but were mainly under 100mm (Mainman and Rogers 2000: 2479). Two of the rotary grindstone fragments from York had external diameters of 240mm and 224mm, roughly comparable with the Bon Accord examples. Both had regular cone-shaped holes ground into one flat surface, similar to those on SF329, which may have been utilised in securing or rotating the stones (*ibid*: 2481).

Miscellaneous stone artefacts

Miscellaneous artefacts include a small bun-shaped granite rubbing stone, SF2195, and a possible potlid, SF2217. A carved fragment of pumice, SF1604, has a 'U'-shaped groove running along its length and may have

been used as an abrading tool in the smoothing of small wooden dowel rods.

Stone mortars
George R. Haggarty
(written 2015)

Recovered from the excavations were six badly abraded Purbeck limestone fragments (Figure 4.38), which almost certainly derive from a single large mortar with a 300mm interior diameter and 385mm exterior diameter. Two pieces were unstratified (SF6022 & SF6023) and one each was recovered from fill (F) of Pit C019 (SF6024), fill (E) of Pit C069 (SF6025), Layer C010 (SF1656) and Layer C075 (SF6026), ranging from Phase 2 to Phase 5. A fragment of another mortar made of local sandstone was recovered from fill (E) of Pit C069, from Phase 3 or 4 (SF2393) while another small fragment from the rim of another sandstone vessel, perhaps a mortar, was recovered from fill (F) of the same feature (SF2207).

Purbeck marble is a hard, blueish-grey limestone composed predominantly of dark, fossilised shells from a small freshwater gastropod (*viviparus cariniferus*), set within a fine-grained matrix. Extensively exploited from the 12th century onwards as building material, the main period of mortar production appears to have occurred at quarries in the Isle of Purbeck, Dorset during the 13th and 14th centuries (Dunning 1977: 324). A seaborne distribution has been noted (*ibid*), which explains their presence in a port such as Aberdeen.

There has been no general survey of medieval and later mortars in Scotland. However, it is probable, judging

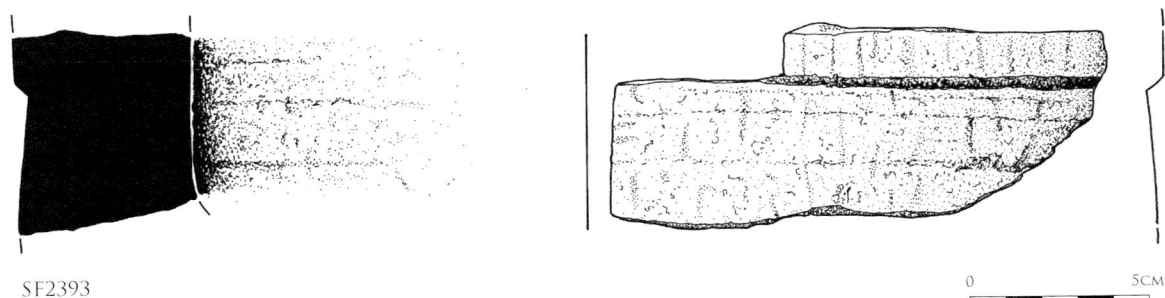

SF2393

Figure 4.39 A Scottish mortar fragment; SF2393

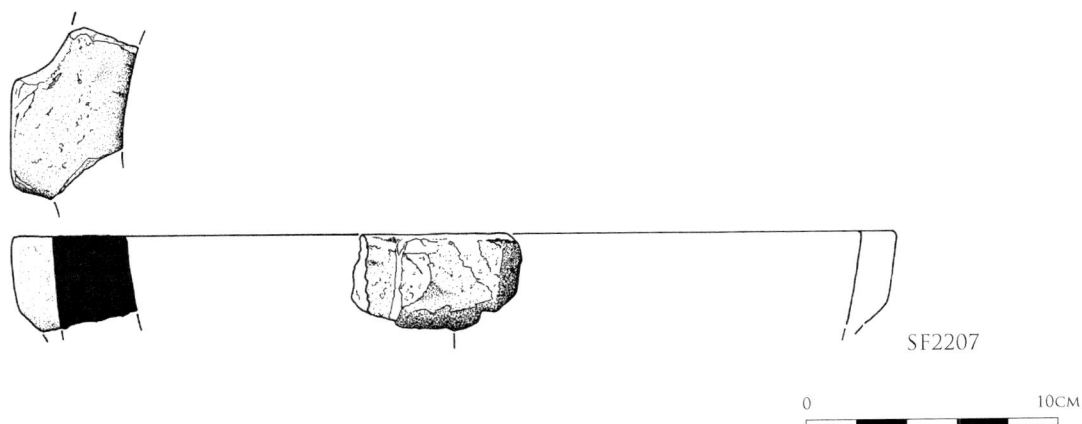

SF2207

Figure 4.40 Possible mortar fragment; SF2207

from the substantial wear pattern on a large complete marble example recovered from a mid 20th century context in Portobello, that some may have had a long lifespan (Haggarty 2011: word file 25).

Previous excavation carried out at 45–75 Gallowgate, Aberdeen recovered a heavily abraded fragment from a small mortar, which was 160mm in diameter, thought most likely to be limestone and a product of Purbeck, from a layer of daub on the base of an oven dated to between 1375 and 1400 (Cameron and Stones 2001: 91, 207–08 illus 164 fig 495, 298–90). From the same excavation, a rim fragment from a stone vessel without a band, c. 210mm in diameter, was also recovered (ibid: illus 25, fig 66), formed from a pure limestone (Trewin 1984: fiche 4: A4). Excavations carried out at 75 High Street, Perth recovered a heavy stone rim fragment, possibly a mortar, with an external rim diameter of 250mm, in what is thought to be Purbeck marble (A8450: C2476-3; Smith et al. 2011, 138). The authors also suggest that two other pieces of Purbeck marble were recovered from the site (A8221 & A5678).

Fragments of medieval Purbeck limestone mortars have also been recorded from a large number of sites in England ranging from Southampton (Platt and Coleman-Smith 1975: 307–11) to York (Ottaway and Rogers 2002: 2799–802), but predominately in the south and East Anglia (Dunning 1977: 325).

Mortars made of Purbeck limestone seldom exceed 330mm in rim diameter, although a few larger examples have been recorded, with rim diameters of 391, 440 and 460mm. The largest, at 520mm, was found in the region of Hailsham (Parfitt 1976: 183). In the main they share certain features, including a broad rim band, four exterior nibs/lugs above four vertical projections/ribs. These provided strength and enabled the mortar to be set into a wooden base. Surviving examples from the 18th century suggest this may have been a waist high log stood upright; this would have allowed the use of both hands in the grinding process. Mortars were used with a pestle for grinding various materials, including foodstuffs, and appear to have superseded rotary querns for grinding during the 13th century. Evidence from King's Lynn suggests that they were in use from the 12th century, but only entered general use during the 13th and 14th centuries (Dunning, 1977: 327–29). This is in keeping with findings at Winchester which produced no mortars earlier than the mid 12th to mid 13th centuries, suggesting that mortars were introduced in the 13th century (Biddle and Smith 1990: 891). Recent work on the Southampton evidence shows that all the mortars were discarded within high medieval or later contexts. This and the high numbers of querns being discarded during the same phases and their absence from later phases suggests that querns were being replaced by mortars (Shaffrey internet report).

SF2393 was a thick stepped, concavo-convex stone mortar body sherd, broken on all its four edges and distinctively along a horizontal bedding plane on its upper side (Figure 4.39). It shows evidence of vertical cutting on its exterior below its rim band, and a smoothed dark grey stained interior, almost certainly due to grinding. It has an internal diameter of 220mm probably just below its rim and an exterior diameter of 330mm. The banding of the coarse-grained, light grey, sub rounded, quartz rich coarse sandstone is classed as a Sub arkose Quartz arenite, which has been well lithified possibly due to slight metamorphism (Simon Howard, *pers comm*). The grain size varies from 2mm to 18mm. There is an abundance of this material in the north-east of Scotland, so local manufacture seems a reasonable hypothesis. No Scottish parallels for this mortar are known. SF2207, a single sandstone rim sherd from a stone vessel, likely also represents a mortar (Figure 4.40).

Discussion

The worked stone assemblage represents both industrial and domestic activity from the prehistoric through to the post-medieval period. The working of textiles, perhaps in a domestic context, is represented by the recovery of spindle whorls, which are a common find on medieval sites. More developed industrial activity, including metalworking, was also evidenced. The presence at Bon Accord of rotary grinding stones is likely representative of ferrous metalworking; these would have been utilised in finishing products and in sharpening tools. Similarly, the numerous hand-held whetstones could have been used in the finishing of edged tools. While the presence of the grinding stone, SF329, in a Phase 5 context accords with the evidence for ferrous metalworking in the late medieval/ early post-medieval period, the composite grinding mechanism SF2583 was recovered from the base of a Phase 1 pit, and indicates that metal tools were being used and perhaps produced on or near the site as early as the late 12th or early 13th century.

Other craft activities are represented by the presence of a pumice abrader, the fragments of a large Purbeck limestone mortar, and what are likely to be a locally produced sandstone mortars. The pumice was possibly associated with the processing of hides. The relatively large size of the Bon Accord mortar indicates that it was likely utilised in an industrial rather than a domestic

context. It may have been used in the grinding of material to be used as a tanning or dyeing agent. This use has been suggested for the fragmentary limestone mortar recovered from 45–75 Gallowgate. Pollen analysis on the interior of the Gallowgate mortar indicated the presence of oak, Scots pine, birch, alder, willow, hazel and elder, along with residues of tormentil and dock, both of which were utilised in the tanning and dyeing processes (Moffat and Penny 2001: 298–99). The provenance of this mortar, from the south-west of England, illuminates the extent of trade between Aberdeen and distant parts of the British Isles.

Catalogue of illustrated worked stone items
(L = length; W = width; Th = thickness; D = diameter)

SF 963 (Figure 4.34)
Phase/Feature Phase 2/Layer C014
Description: whetstone with metal attachment
Tapering rectangular micaceous siltstone whetstone with squared ends, perforated at widest end with small circular hole (D *c.* 6mm) to facilitate suspension, probably from a belt. Two links from a fine figure-of-eight link chain are threaded through perforation, visible on x-ray. Corrosion from iron chain has caused cracks to form at one corner of the stone. L 92.5mm; W 5.5–17mm; Th 5–8mm

SF 3584 (Figure 4.34)
Phase/Feature Phase 3 or 4/Pit C048
Description: whetstone
Siltstone. L 127mm; W 28mm; Th 15mm. Narrow rectangular whetstone. Very worn with one face having a small depression. Small ground hole (9mm x 9mm) for carrying cordage placed at one end.

SF 4281 (Figure 4.34)
Phase/Feature Phase 1/Gully C001
Description: whetstone
Siltstone. L 81mm; W 50mm; Th 35mm. Roughly triangular fragment of whetstone. Rectangular in section. Worn depressions on two larger faces. End missing.

SF 3083 (Figure 4.34)
Phase/Feature Phase 2/Pit C022 fill (A)
Description: whetstone
Siltstone. L 35mm; W 9.5mm; Th 9.5mm. Fragment, 'door wedge' shape and rectangular in cross-section.

SF 2845 (Figure 4.35)
Phase/Feature Phase 2/Pit C022
Description: spindle whorl
Sedimentary rock. L 34mm; W 34mm; Th 10mm. Circular, flat, bun-shaped loom weight with centrally ground hole 10mm in diameter and depth. Simple engraved line decoration around circumference.

SF   3640 (Figure 4.35)
Phase/Feature   Phase 5/Layer C009
Description: spindle whorl
Spindle whorl. Sedimentary rock. L 24mm; W 23mm; Th 7mm. Abraded, bun-shaped spindle whorl with cordage marks around the perimeter.

SF   3849 (Figure 4.35)
Phase/Feature   Phase 6/Spread A043, between Layers A008 and A009
Description: spindle whorl
Sedimentary rock. L 33mm; W 20mm. Abraded, melon-shaped spindle whorl.

SF   2217 (Figure 4.35)
Phase/Feature   Late Phase 4/Layer A004
Description: worked stone disc/potlid
Granite. L 55mm; W 51mm; Th 9mm. Roughly fashioned tabular disc of granite with flaked edges. Possible potlid.

SF   329 (Figure 4.36)
Phase/Feature   Phase 5/Pit C080
Description: grinding stone
Granite. Circular stone, 170mm in diameter and 75mm thick, of which roughly half survives. A large central pecked hole, 52mm in diameter pierces the stone. One face has three equally spaced ground circular depressions, one of which has been partially removed by damage. These depressions are 22mm x 12mm (depth). The outer edge of the artefact appears intentionally pitted with large patches of very smooth wear >30%.

SF   2583 (Figures 4.36 & 4.37)
Phase/Feature   Phase 1/Pit C001
Description: grinding stone
This is an element of a composite wood and stone grinding mechanism, the wooden component of which is described in Section 4.2.1 (SF2583). The grindstone is made of a mica-rich, fine-grained sandstone. It is 230mm in diameter and 93mm thick. The shaft hole, which is roughly 90mm in diameter, is positioned slightly off centre and has been crudely fashioned through pecking. The outer surface of the grindstone has been worn down and is now concave in profile. Numerous faint yet distinct striations are also present over the entire working face of the grindstone.

SF   1656, 6022, 6023, 6024, 6025 & 6026 (Figure 4.38)
Phase/Feature   Phases 2 to 5/Pit C019, Pit C069, Layer C010, Layer C075 and unstratified
Description: mortar
Purbeck limestone. Internal D 300mm; external D 385mm; surviving H 205mm. Large mortar.

SF   2207 (Figure 4.40)
Phase/Feature   Phase 3 or 4/Pit C069
Description: mortar

Sandstone. Internal D 255mm; external D 350mm; surviving H 40mm. Rim of possible mortar.

SF   2393 (Figure 4.39)
Phase/Feature   Phase 3 or 4/Pit C069
Description: mortar
Sandstone. Internal D 220mm; external D 330mm; surviving H 60mm. Rim of possible mortar.

4.3.3 Lithics
Rob Engl

Introduction

A total of 247 pieces of chipped stone were recovered from Bon Accord. A catalogue of the secondarily modified artefacts (including illustrated material) is provided but the complete report can be found in the site archive.

Raw material

The assemblage appears to be of mixed origin. Flint accounts for 238 of the 247 pieces recovered with the remainder consisting of chert (n.4), quartz (n.2), agate (n.2) and a single flake of fossilised wood.

The flint has a broad colour range with colours typical of assemblages from Aberdeenshire dominating. Honey coloured flint (n.118) is most common followed by pale grey (n.71) and red (n.16), colours typical of material derived from local Buchan gravel deposits. Other more widespread sources of flint are also represented in the assemblage. Nine pieces showed a dark blue/black colour occasionally combined with a chalky cortex. This may indicate primary source chalk flint imported from the south-east of England as 'ballast' flint in post-medieval and modern times. However, such material may also have been washed ashore from submerged deposits in the North Sea. A further 11 pieces are a mottled dark grey or brown (including a sidescraper SF4263B and platform core SF3706). This may represent material imported from the Yorkshire Wolds during the Neolithic and Early Bronze Age. The variety of raw material derivations present within Aberdonian assemblages has been previously alluded to by Saville (2001: 259) in his discussions of the lithic assemblages recovered from Castle Street and 16–18 Netherkirkgate.

The assemblage is relatively fresh in appearance with 69% of the flint showing little or no signs of patination or burning. Burnt or heat-treated material accounts for only 10% and patinated material 19%.With the exception of the chalky material mentioned above, the cortex has a largely rolled and water-worn appearance suggesting that it was obtained from the nearby shoreline or rivers. The other supplementary materials were also probably derived from these sources.

Primary technology

Debitage dominated the assemblage and most major classes were represented. Flakes (n. 117) were most numerous, with the majority being regular and often bladelike in character. True blades (W > 8mm – n.23) and bladelets (W < 8mm – n.1) were fewer in number but were again very regular and parallel sided. Only two of the blades were fragmentary and this was probably caused by post-depositional factors given that this area has undergone extensive activity.

The presence of simple, crushed and facetted striking platforms suggest that both hard and soft hammer reduction techniques were being practised.

The presence of 30 cores within the assemblage alongside tested and intact nodules, waste debris such as chips, fragments and chunks and modified tool types suggests that material was being directly worked on-site.

Of the 30 cores recovered during the excavation, all but three were made on flint. Bipolar (n.13) and platform cores (n.12) are the most common and there are also four amorphous examples and a core fragment. The platform cores are relatively small examples with a mix of narrow blade and blade-like flake removals. Eight of the examples were single platform types worked up to 50% of the striking platform surface. Two have opposed platforms and two have multiple examples. The presence of these cores would suggest a Late Mesolithic occupation of the site. However, no other strongly diagnostic tool types of this period have been found within the assemblage. It is likely that these platform cores relate to an early Neolithic occupation with their form being dictated by the relatively limited size of the parent material.

The presence of bipolar and amorphous cores indicates that an expedient lithic technology was practised on-site alongside the more formal platform struck technique. Many of the bipolar cores had been worked down to a fairly small size. This technique is often associated with the working of small, intractable pebble material (Engl 2008: 231). However, at Bon Accord only two flakes showed recognisably bipolar characteristics such as crushed platforms and associated opposing flake scars. This mirrors the findings at Kintore (*ibid:* 231) where a similar assemblage composition suggested that the bipolar technique had been introduced either to extend the flake producing life of the platform cores or to work very small or intractable material.

Secondary technology

Ten secondarily modified artefacts were present, all made on flint (Figure 4.41). These consisted of five

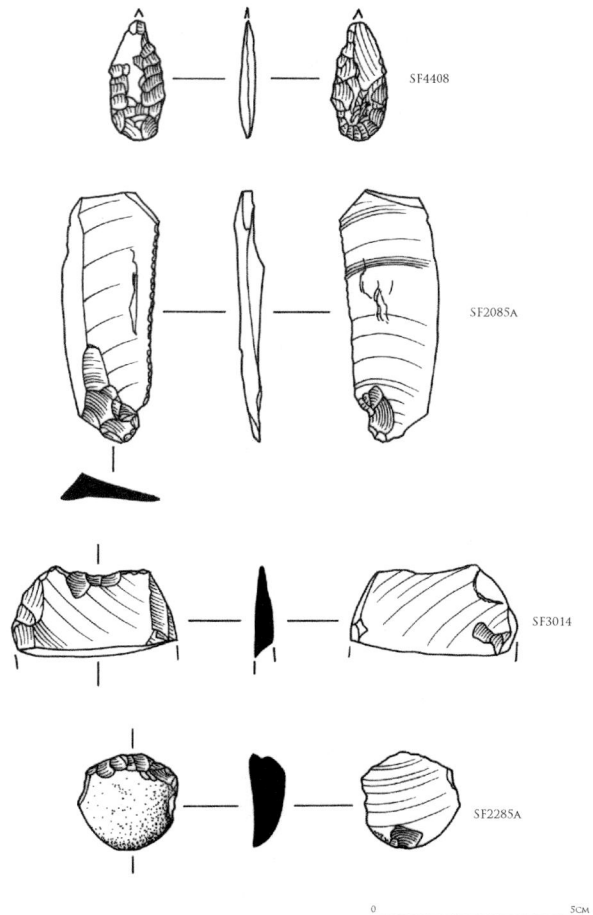

Figure 4.41 Lithics; SF4408; SF2085A; SF3014; SF2285A

scrapers, a notched blade and flake, a retouched blade, a leaf shaped arrowhead and an abrading tool. A catalogue of the material is given below.

Catalogue of lithics
(L = length; W = width; Th = thickness; D = diameter)

SF   4320 (not illustrated)
Phase/Feature   Phase 1/Gully C001
Description: abrading tool
Honey flint. L 44.8mm; W 13mm; Th 7.5mm. Blade-like flake with heavy utilisation scars along left lateral edge. The right lateral edge has very fine retouch along its length probably to aid handling during use.

SF   4263B (not illustrated)
Phase/Feature   Phase 5/Layer C009
Description: sidescraper
Honey flint L 31.6mm; W 17.3mm; Th 4.4mm. Sidescraper made on primary flake. Abrupt fine regular retouch along left lateral edge.

SF   4408 (Figure 4.41)
Phase/Feature   Phase 2/Spread C014

Description: leaf shaped arrowhead
Honey flint. L 29.4mm; W 13.2mm; Th 3.3mm. Invasively flaked arrowhead with impact fracture on tip.

SF   2085A (Figure 4.41)
Phase/Feature   Phase 2/ Layer C014
Description: retouched blade
Brown flint. L 61mm; W 22.3mm; Th 7mm. Fine regular retouch along right hand lateral edge of large blade.

SF   3014 (Figure 4.41)
Phase/Feature   Phase 2/Well C001
Description: concave sidescraper
Heat affected grey flint. L 39.2mm; W 22mm; Th 5.7mm. Semi-abrupt retouch on left lateral edge.

SF   2285A (Figure 4.41)
Phase/Feature   Phase 1/Pit C002
Description: endscraper
Honey flint. L 23.5mm; W 23.7mm; Th 7.5mm. Simple endscraper on primary flake. Abrupt regular retouch along distal end.

SF   1414 (not illustrated)
Phase/Feature   Phase 2/Layer C003
Description: notched blade
Honey flint. L18.5mm; W 19.5mm; Th 6mm. Notch on left lateral edge of medial blade fragment. Slight abrupt retouch on opposing lateral edge.

SF   37 (not illustrated)
Phase/Feature   Phase 6/Layer C021
Description: end/sidescraper
Honey flint. L 28.7mm; W 20.7mm; Th 9.2mm. Scraper made on tertiary flake. Abrupt retouch along right lateral edge and distal end.

SF   75 (not illustrated)
Phase/Feature   Phase 6/ Layer C011
Description: notched flake
Honey flint. L36.5mm; W 29.4mm; Th 5.6mm. Made on tertiary flake. Notch on right lateral edge.

SF   2402 (not illustrated)
Phase/Feature   Late Phase 4 or Early Phase 5/Wall C007
Description: concave scraper
Honey flint. Scraper made on secondary flake. Mixed abrupt and semi-abrupt retouch along left lateral edge.

Conclusions

The presence of a mixed Mesolithic and later prehistoric assemblage at Bon Accord suggests that the material represents disparate prehistoric activity within a favourable location close to both coastal and riverine resources such as food and raw materials. This fits the pattern of 'background noise' established within many previous excavation assemblages within the city (Saville 2001: 261). Though it is possible that some of the assemblage was recovered from *in situ* deposits within the primary levels of Areas A and C, it is likely that the majority represents residual material recovered from secondary contexts.

The Mesolithic component of the assemblage was identified largely on the basis of core types and there is little evidence of other typologically definitive tools generally found within Mesolithic assemblages, such as microliths. Similarly, the lack of platform rejuvenation flakes and the presence of bipolar cores suggest that platform cores were not curated but were worked by the application of the bipolar technique once the core had been reduced to a size where blades and regular flakes had become difficult to obtain.

The presence of Mesolithic core types without other associated tool-types together with later Neolithic/ Early Bronze Age material is well represented within Aberdeenshire, at Forest Road, Kintore (Engl 2008) and Hatton of Fintray (Engl, *forthcoming*). This combination probably represents small scale and intermittent Mesolithic occupation based on the procurement and reduction of lithic raw materials. These sites became a possible focus for later settlement in the later Neolithic and Early Bronze Age.

The Bon Accord also assemblage appears to contain amounts of 'ballast' flint. This is a designation used to cover a variety of potential uses of the material such as the production of gun flints, milling, strike-a-lights and the aforementioned ships ballast. This is present within many city of Aberdeen assemblages, such as 16–18 Netherkirkgate and Castle Street (*ibid*: 261).

4.3.4 *Vessel glass*
Hugh Willmott

Introduction

A small assemblage of glass was recovered that merits full reporting. It ranges in date from late medieval to early 19th century and, given the small numbers of fragments, the glass in this report is arranged typologically. Further 19th century material is discussed in the site archive.

Discussion

Fragments from nine vessels were recovered, of which four clearly pre-date the 19th century. The earliest is a small section of rim, SF338, from a pedestal goblet (Figure 4.42). Made in a clear soda-rich glass this is decorated with fine horizontal applied trails in an opaque white glass. Pedestal beakers decorated in this way are typically found in early to mid 16th century contexts, and usually on sites of a higher status. This vessel is not a type produced in Britain but was probably imported from northern France. A second vessel is of

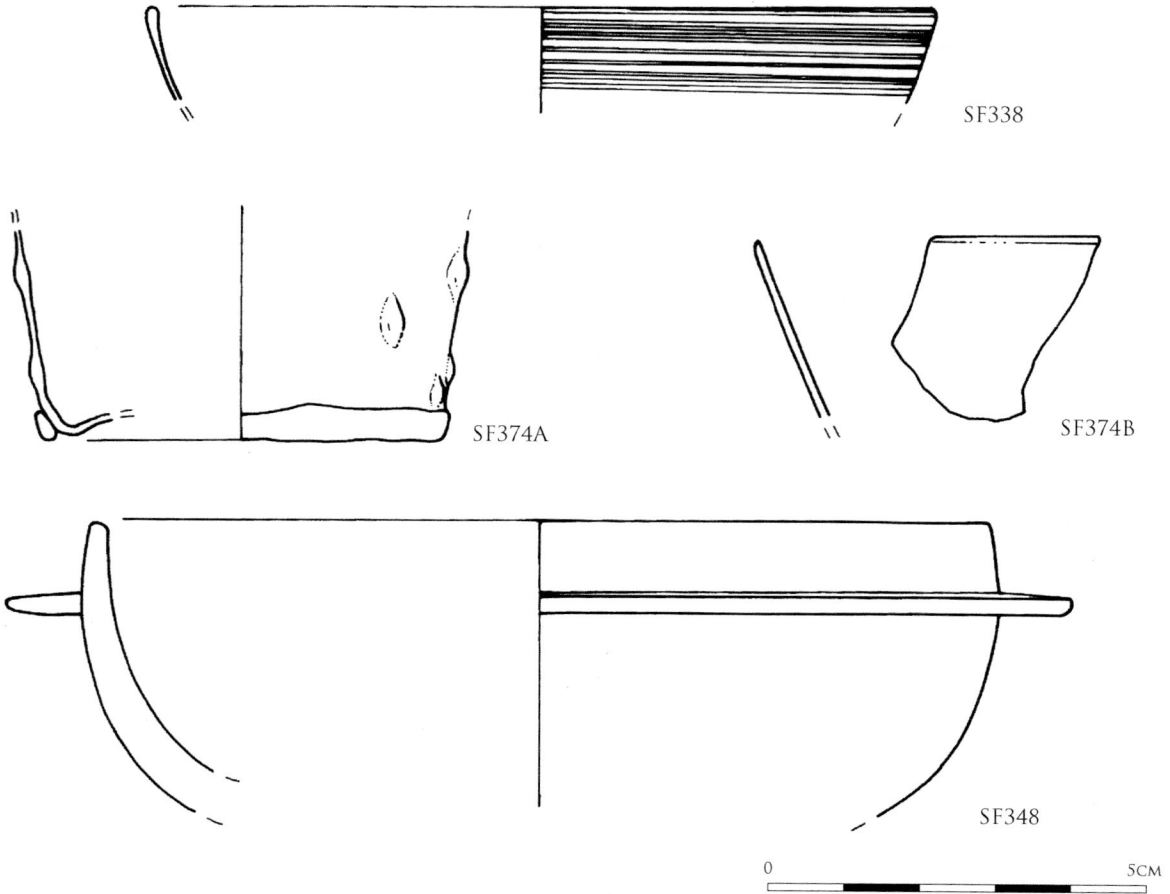

Figure 4.42 Vessel glass; SF338; SF374A; SF374B; SF348-

broadly similar date, SF374A (Figure 4.42), although this is made in a poorer quality potash-rich glass. It is a cylindrical beaker that is decorated with a moulded tear-drop design. Such beakers were made in England in large numbers in the late 16th and early 17th centuries, although at this date there was no domestic production in Scotland.

The third drinking vessel recovered is a small section of plain wine glass rim, SF374B (Figure 4.42), made in a high quality lead glass. Given its small size it is relatively undiagnostic but comes from a vessel produced in the 18th century. A more unusual vessel is represented by the rim and flanged body from a small bowl, SF348 (Figure 4.42). This is also made in a good quality lead glass typical of the 18th century, and the flange indicates that it originally had a domed lid. Although relatively rare such bowls are normally thought to have been used to contain butter at the table, although many other functions are also likely.

Catalogue of illustrated vessel glass items
(L = length; W = width; Th = thickness; D = diameter)

SF   338 (Figure 4.42)
Phase/Feature   Phase 6/Surface C018
Description: pedestal goblet rim fragment
One fragment of fine slightly everted rim from a pedestal goblet. Decorated with fine opaque white thread trailing. Clear soda-rich glass with very light weathering. Rim D 104mm. First half of the 16th century.

SF   374A (Figure 4.42)
Phase/Feature   Phase 6/Pit C081
Description: cylindrical beaker base fragment
One fragment of pushed-in base from a cylindrical beaker. Decorated with a solid applied base-ring, and optic-blown tear drops. Yellow/green mixed alkali glass with quite heavy surface weathering. Base D 58mm. Late 16th–early 17th century.

SF   374B (Figure 4.42)
Phase/Feature   Phase 6/Pit C081
Description: wine glass rim fragment
One fragment of everted rim from a wine glass. Clear lead glass with light surface weathering. Rim D uncertain. 18th century?

Table 4.11 Crucible fragments identified during pottery assessment

Find No.	Feature	Cat. No.	Phase	Description
–	Pit C018	3	2	Base from a small crucible: attached slag (melted crucible + quartz?) and traces of what looks like an internal residue
SF2782	Pit C018	2	2	Rim sherd from a small crucible with what may be an internal residue and an external red slag?
SF3076	Pit C018	1	2	Complete profile of a small, well-used crucible with attached slag and a plum coloured surface
SF1515	Pit C019	4	2	Base from a small crucible with an external plum coloured surface
SF1168	Layer C019	6	3 to 4	Rim sherd from a small crucible with an external plum coloured surface
SF4191	Pit C053	5	4	Rim sherd from a small crucible with an external plum coloured surface

Figure 4.43 Two crucible sherds; left – SF1515, a base with plum coloured zinc enriched surface; right – SF3076.1, an almost complete profile showing its quartz rich fabric and interior surface

SF   348 (Figure 4.42)
Phase/Feature   Phase 6/Pit C081
Description: wide-flanged bowl fragments
Two fragments of vertical rim and side from a wide-flanged bowl. Clear lead glass with very light weathering. Rim D 118mm. Mid-late 18th century.

4.3.5 Crucibles

George R. Haggarty

Fragments from six vitrified medieval crucibles with a total weight of 168.68g were recovered from Area C, from contexts of late 12th to 14th century date (Table 4.11).

Small and almost barrel-like in shape, they have been formed from refractory clay, heavily tempered with large quartz grains to improve thermal performance and almost certainly indicative of vessels using heat transfer through the fabric. When new they are unlikely to have been more than *c.* 70mm in height and two of the surviving sherds suggest somewhat flattish bases with diameters of between 22mm and 25mm (Figure 4.43), and rim diameters of *c.* 32mm. The sherds vary in thickness suggesting crucibles *c.* 10mm at their bases and *c.* 5mm at their rims. Two of the fragments, SF3076.1 (Figure 4.43) and SF3076.3, from Pit C018, have metal slag attached. SF3076.1 also has patches of a smooth external plum coloured surface coating, as do SF1515 (Figure 4.43) and SF4191, from Pits C019 and C053 respectively. XRF analysis of this identified a high reading of zinc which suggests they were being used in the casting of the copper alloy, brass (Richard Jones, *pers comm*). With its relatively low melting point, 900 to 940°C, depending on composition, along with its flow characteristics, brass is a relatively easy material to cast.

If filled, these small crucibles could have held a metal volume of something in the order of 20cc, but it is more likely to have been about half that. In all probability they would have been employed in the casting of small non-ferrous items, such as jewellery, buckles, pins, etc (Section 4.3.1).

In form the small Bon Accord crucibles are somewhat similar to published 10th century Viking, (Bayley & Rehren 2007: fig 4a), or Middle and Late Saxon thumb-made pots which have been recovered from Thetford, Southampton, York, Lincoln and other sites (Bayley 1991; Bayley 1992: 4 fig 1). They are different from the bag shaped or hemispherical crucibles of high medieval and later date, which have been recovered from sites in London, Chester, York, Lincoln and Winchester and of which a number of the former have been identified as products of the Stamford pottery industry (Bayley 1992: 4–5 figs 3 & 4).

They are also unlike the distinctive triangular, extensively imported, 14th–18th century examples produced in Bavaria, Hess and its surrounding regions (Martinón-torres and Rehren 2009). A large number of these small triangular examples have recently been recorded from an archaeological excavation carried out on the site of a late 18th century chemistry store at Old College University of Edinburgh (National Record of the Historic Environment Reference: NT27SE 357). The only other medieval crucibles published from Scottish sites would seem to be the two conjoining fragments from a vessel with a much larger rim diameter *c.* 105mm, recovered at Stirling Castle (Franklin 2008: 50), and the small, triangular fragment, probably hessian, although no fabric description was given, used to melt tin-bronze, recovered from Edinburgh Castle (Spearman 1997a: 165). The larger Stirling example is flat rimmed, 10mm thick, straight walled, coarsely gritted, in an off-white paste and which had white and grey industrial residues on its interior. It is said to parallel the larger English straight walled examples known from some late medieval and post-medieval contexts; for which examples recovered in London, at both the Tower and Cripplegate, have been published (Bayley 1992: 5; Bayley 2003: 4).

A further two sherds, which conjoin to form the base of a crucible were identified amongst another pottery assemblage from Stirling Castle. In size this crucible seems to be more in keeping with the Bon Accord examples, but with a slightly larger flattish base, *c.* 27mm in diameter. It also seems to be thinner, better made and visually in a somewhat smoother fabric. ICP chemical analysis was carried out on two of the Bon Accord sherds and the two Stirling Castle sherds but it was not possible to use this data (full report in site archive).

Given how common and widespread non-ferrous metalworking must have been in medieval Scotland and the increasing amount of urban excavations, one can only be surprised at the lack of evidence in the form of crucibles recovered to date.

4.3.6 Clay mould fragments
Dawn McLaren

Introduction

Fragments representing a minimum of five heat-affected clay moulds for casting non-ferrous metal decorative objects (Figure 4.44) were recovered along with a hollowed disc-like object produced from a re-worked tile, whose function remains elusive. All of the mould fragments derive from Area C, a distribution which is consistent with the recovery of a small number of crucibles from the site (Section 4.3.5). In contrast to the crucibles however, which were concentrated in a small number of pits, the mould fragments were more scattered across the excavated area, deriving from layers and pits from Phase 2 to early Phase 5.

Despite the restricted survival of non-ferrous metalworking evidence on site the mould fragments, in conjunction with the crucibles, provide important evidence of medieval non-ferrous metal casting; a craft activity which, on the balance of the commonplace use and survival of non-ferrous metal dress ornaments and accessory objects, must have been fairly typical but is so rarely attested on medieval urban sites.

Description

The Bon Accord moulds are very friable and their lightly fired condition is not conducive to survival. The implication of their fragile condition is that they were incorporated within features and layers fairly rapidly after discard. It also implies that a workshop was located in the vicinity but the focus of this activity was not identified within the excavated area. Discolouration of the casting surfaces demonstrates that at least four of the fragments were discarded after use but it has not been possible to confirm by visual analysis alone the composition of the metals being cast; a copper- or lead-based alloy is supposed. The quantity of mould fragments recovered is not suggestive of large scale production but such items survive so rarely that

SF1221

SF3089

SF1168B

POSITIVE VIEW
NOT TO SCALE

SF1168A

0   5CM

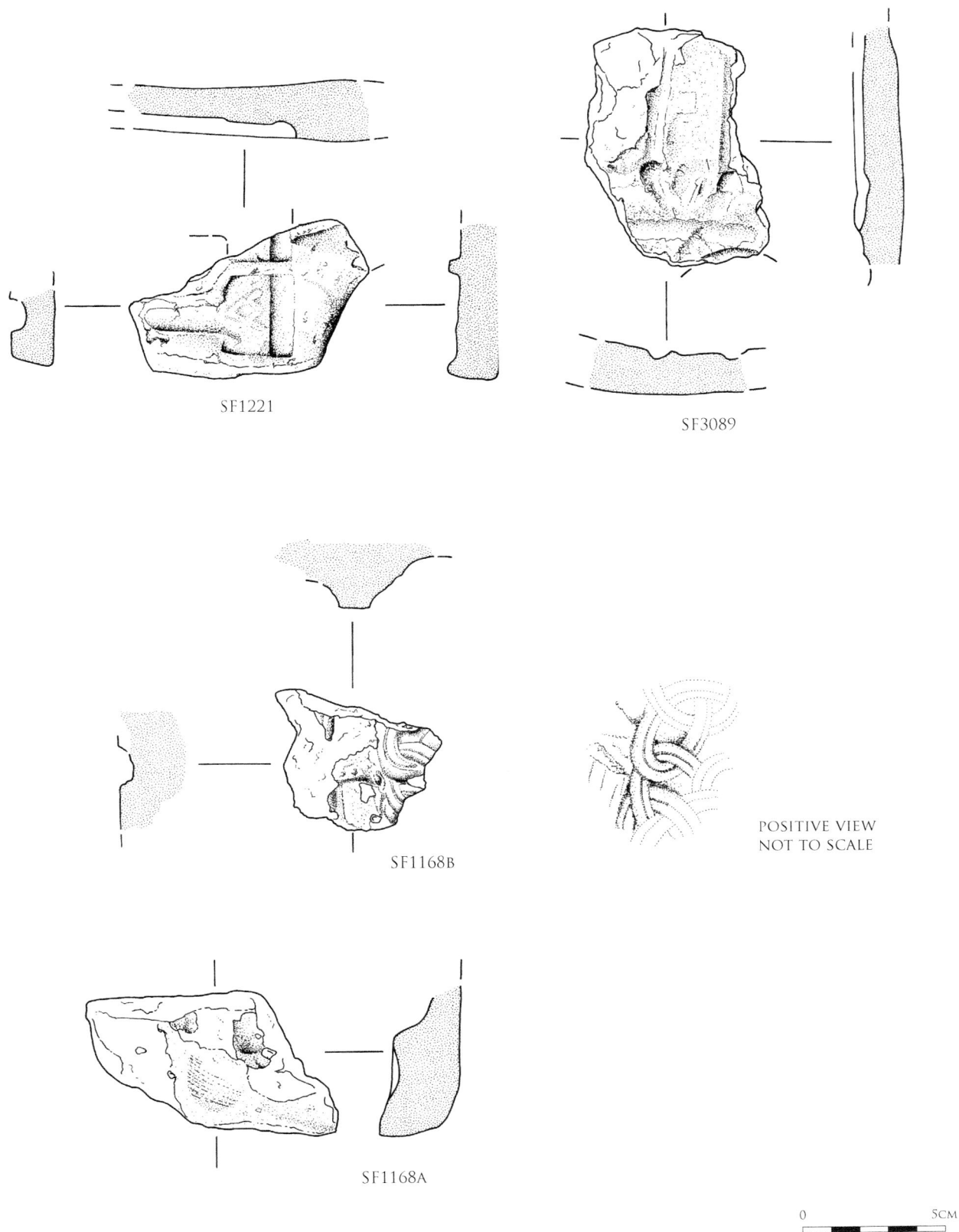

Figure 4.44 Clay mould fragments; SF1221, SF3089, SF1168B and SF1168A, with positive view of design on SF1168B

assessing the scale of production from such fragmentary evidence is difficult to quantify with confidence.

The Bon Accord clay moulds demonstrate that a variety of decorative, ornamental items, including possible pin heads, badges and/or possibly mirror cases, were being produced in this area between the late 12th century and the late 15th century. SF1221 is particularly intriguing as an almost identical mould, also apparently designed to produce several similar items in a single casting, was found previously during excavations in Aberdeen (Stones 1982: 191, illus 109, no 96). There the object was identified as a possible decorated rectangular-headed pin. Dress or hair pins with large decorated heads continued to be produced during the medieval period but they are far less common than in previous centuries and tend to be a lot finer due to increased availability and use of drawn wire as opposed to cast objects (Egan and Pritchard 1991: 297). It is likely that the square- and rectangular-headed ornaments represented by the moulds at Bon Accord and Broad Street are for the production of pins but alternative interpretations as moulds for decorative strap-end or buckle-plate components, hooked mounts (ibid: 124–246) or strap-distributors, such as the undecorated examples from Sandal Castle, Wakefield (Goodall 1983: 232, fig 1, no 37), are also possible. A similarity in form to shovel-headed tweezers, thought to be toilet instruments or page holders for books (e.g. an example from Perth; Cox 1996: 770, illus 20, no. 201) is noted but these two-armed objects are typically produced from sheet rather than cast metal, making such an interpretation here unlikely. The other objects being cast at Bon Accord are more ambiguous in form. Both SF1168B and SF3089 appear to represent heavily decorated openwork or relief decorated ornaments, possibly brooches, badges or even mirror cases (e.g. Egan and Pritchard 1991: 358–63; Hall and Spencer 2012: 208–10). The function of a further item (SF3802) produced from a re-worked fragment of tile remains elusive and an interpretation here as a possible mould is tentative.

Discussion

Small quantities of clay mould fragments attesting to medieval non-ferrous metalworking have previously been found in Aberdeen. A single mould fragment, possibly for casting decorated square- or rectangular-headed pins, was recovered from excavations at Broad Street and bears a remarkable similarity in form to that from Phase 4 Layer C041 (SF1221) at Bon Accord (Stones 1982: 191, illus 109, no 96). The Broad Street mould did not derive from a secure context but, like that from Bon Accord, is likely to be medieval in date. Earlier evidence for non-ferrous metalworking in Aberdeen comes from the excavations at 45–47 Gallowgate which recovered a small number of mould fragments attesting to the manufacture of copper-based alloy vessels, such as ewers, platters and dress pins during the 13th century (Murray 1984: 308; Spearman 1984: fiche 3: G7–12). Contemporary 13th century evidence from Elgin in the form of composite and two-piece clay moulds for the casting of copper-based alloy dress pins and decorative fittings (Hall *et al.* 1998: 809, 819, 822) is also known. Both mould and crucible fragments from casting small, possibly decorative, fittings or base metal jewellery come from period II and III layers at Perth dating to between the 13th and 14th centuries (Spearman 1987: 158). Spearman noted a difference in the character of non-ferrous metalworking in the 15th century levels at Perth with evidence of production shifting from decorative ornaments to the casting of much larger objects, such as vessels (*ibid*: 158). As well as the clay mould fragments there are also a small number of stone moulds from Perth for casting strap-ends or buckle plates, brooches and rings (Goodall 2012a: 118, illus 58–62).

Although evidence for non-ferrous metalworking on urban Scottish sites is often scant, the recovery of mould and crucible fragments from previous excavations at Aberdeen (Murray 1984: 308; Spearman 1984: fiche 3: G11; Stone 1982: 191, ill 109, no 96), Edinburgh (Spearman 1997: 165), Elgin (Hall *et al.* 1998: 809, 819, 822) and Perth (Goodall 2012a: 118, illus 58–62; Spearman 1987), *inter alia*, demonstrate the centrality of this flourishing craft within the medieval townscape. The range of decorative mounts, accessories and fittings being produced during the medieval period is staggering and provides a rich impression of changing fashions as well as highlighting the importance and variety of personal adornment as a reflection of individual identity (Egan and Pritchard 1991; Willemsen and Ernst 2012). What is clear from the mould fragments from Bon Accord is that the suite of copper-based ornaments which have survived in the archaeological record from this period is just a small percentage of the great range of objects which were once produced, worn and discarded. The form of the objects being produced at Bon Accord cannot be matched exactly to surviving decorative ornaments, either to those in the site assemblage or within other Scottish urban assemblages, but they fit broadly with the suite of non-ferrous, often base-metal decorative items in use during the 12th to 15th centuries in Scotland and beyond. This inability to match the objects being cast to the known suite of decorative items in contemporary use is a situation familiar to prehistorians and medievalists alike.

Catalogue of illustrated clay mould items
(L = length; W = width; Th = thickness; D = diameter)

SF   1168A (Figure 4.44)
Phase/Feature Phase 3 or 4/Layer C019

Description: fragment of a two-piece mould
Rounded corner fragment of a two-piece mould for casting a non-ferrous metal object, edges heavily abraded and little of original casting surface survives. An off-set row of lobate depressions are present adjacent to the fractured edge but are so heavily abraded it is impossible to confirm the design or form of the object being cast. No obvious in-gate or keying features survive. The fabric is fine clay, soft fired with frequent mica-flecks and small rounded quartz pebble inclusions. Occasional fine linear impressions imply an organic component, possibly grass or hair was added to the clay as temper (Fabric A). May be a fragment of 1168B.

SF   1168B (Figure 4.44)
Phase/Feature   Phase 3 or 4/Layer C019
Description: fragmentary valve of a mould for a decorative object
Very fragmentary, freshly broken valve for casting a decorative non-ferrous metal object. No original edges survive and the basal surface has been lost; all that survives is a patch of discoloured casting surface. The form and size of the object being cast is unclear but appears to be a symmetrical double disc design connected by a short rectangular bar. The surviving patch of decorated surface has a complex interwoven design reminiscent of Celtic interlace but so little of this survives that more precise identification is impossible. Fabric A. May be a further fragment of 1168A but no joins survive. L 30mm; W 21.5mm; Th 12mm.

SF   1221 (Figure 4.44)
Phase/Feature   Phase 4/Layer C041
Description: fragment of a two-piece mould
Heavily damaged fragment of a two-piece mould for casting a non-ferrous metal object, broken across casting surface and conical ingate or negative keying feature. One end and edge lost making identification of form of cast object ambiguous. Cast surface has at least one flat square decorated head (L 13.5mm; W 11mm; 3mm deep) expanding from a straight shank (W 5.5mm) and may be a pin, strap-end or decorated strap distributor. Traces of a second square-headed item can be seen directly adjacent to the fractured edge. Dark grey discolouration of the casting surfaces demonstrates use. The fabric is fine clay, fired medium hard with frequent mica flecks and occasional voids which may suggest an organic component to the clay (Fabric B). Very similar mould fragment has come from previous excavations at Aberdeen (Stone 1982: 191, illus 109, no 96).

SF   1572A (not illustrated)
Phase/Feature   Phase 4/Layer C020
Description: fragment of heat-affected clay
Very fragmentary piece of heat-affected clay, no original edges survive and both faces severely damaged. A squared depression (L 7mm; W 6.5mm; 4.5mm deep) is present on one face towards fractured edge which may be surviving casting surface for an unidentified object. The fabric (Fabric C) is fine clay with frequent mica flecks and occasional small rounded quartz pebbles. Rush/grass stem impressions are visible on the fractured faces demonstrating addition of organic temper in clay. L 27.5mm; W 22.5mm; Th 8mm.

SF   1572B (not illustrated)
Phase/Feature   Phase 4/Layer C020
Description: fragment of heat-affected clay
Very fragmentary angular piece of coarse heat-affected clay; no original edges or surfaces remain but a sub-square depression (L 7.5mm; W 7mm; 5mm deep) is present on one damaged face towards fractured edge. Similar in form to SF1572A but fabric is slightly different due to visible manganese or iron-rich inclusions and staining (Fabric D). L 23mm; W 19mm; Th 12.5mm.

SF   3089 (Figure 4.44)
Phase/Feature   Phase 2/Layer C003
Description: valve fragment from a two-piece mould
Fragmentary but fairly well-preserved valve fragment from a two-piece mould used to cast an unidentified decorative object. No original edges survive and the design is incomplete making precise identification of the item being cast impossible but it appears to be a flat ornamental piece with decoration in relief. The orientation of the decoration is also unclear but consists of two parallel linear shafts which bifurcate at the terminals (stylised shoes?). Above this is a curving band (W 3mm) which appears to enclose further fragmentary decorative motifs. It is possible the object being cast is an openwork or relief decorated secular badge, mirror case or similar decorative ornament. The fabric is similar to Fabric B; fine clay with frequent mica flecks but also has fine linear voids on external surfaces which suggest grass or hair inclusions. L 43mm; W 29.5mm; Th 9mm.

SF   3802 (not illustrated)
Phase/Feature   Mid Phase 5/Pit C077 fill (C)
Description: possible mould fragment
Thick, flat, sub-circular fired ceramic object, tentatively identified as a mould, broken off-centre across a perforated (D 9mm) suspension loop which projects from one rounded edge and across a flat based, steep sided, off-centre circular hollow (max D 31mm; min D 21mm; H 9mm). A row of three small circular depressions (D 2.5mm) are present on the flat edge that surrounds the hollow. The function of these hollows is unclear; they may be keying features but appear very fine for this purpose. The object has been fashioned

from a reworked red-brown tile fragment. Surviving L 62.5mm; W 37mm; Th 13mm.

4.3.7 Industrial residues
Mike Roy and Andy Heald

Introduction

A total of 49.1kg of material was visually examined, which allows it to be broadly categorised according to morphology, density, colour and vesicularity. In general, industrial residue assemblages can be divided into two categories. The first group comprises diagnostic material that can clearly be attributed to metalworking. Ironworking produces only a few types of slag which are truly diagnostic of metalworking processes. Hammerscale is diagnostic of smithing activity, while the presence of run slag and blooms can indicate smelting. A second group of non-diagnostic slags can be produced by a number of different processes and are therefore not clearly indicative of particular processes. This group of material often contains significant quantities of material that is unclassifiable, with individual pieces that are difficult to type and attribute to processes (Crew and Rehren 2002: 84). However, it is often possible for the nature of such material (e.g. hearth/furnace lining) to be elucidated through understanding of its archaeological context. The slag has been described using common terminology (e.g. McDonnell 1994; Spearman 1997; Starley 2000). A full catalogue is contained within the archive report.

There are seven diagnostic ferrous slags and residues present:

1. Plano-convex slag cakes (PCSC): a broadly plano-convex accumulation of slag formed in a pit, which can be present in a range of sizes. They may be produced during either smithing or smelting, though their dimensions and weight compare closer to slag cakes associated with smithing (e.g. McDonnell 1994: 230; McDonnell 2000: 219).
2. Slag amalgams (SA): randomly shaped pieces of slag including plano-convex slag cakes and hearth lining that have fused to form larger masses.
3. Billets (B): Iron stock derived from primary refining of the bloom from smelting furnace.
4. Run slag (R): Slag runs, commonly derived from the smelting process.
5. Unclassified slag (US): randomly shaped pieces of iron silicate slag generated by the smelting or smithing process.
6. Hammerscale (HS): small flakes of iron produced by the impact of hammers on hot iron during either the refining of blooms or the working of wrought iron. When found in sufficient

quantities, this is normally indicative of *in situ* metalworking.

7. Slag spheres (SS): spheres ejected as spherical globules of molten slag during ironworking. When found in sufficient quantities, this is normally indicative of *in situ* metalworking.

In addition, there are further, non-diagnostic slags and industrial residues:

1. Fuel ash slag (FAS): slag formed when material such as sand, earth, clay stones or ceramics are subjected to high temperatures, for example in a hearth. During heating these materials react, melt or fuse with alkali in ash, producing vitreous and porous materials. These slags can be formed during any high temperature pyrotechnic process and are not necessarily indicative of deliberate industrial activity.
2. Fuel residues: residues of coal, charcoal and coke.
3. Vitrified clay (?lining)

Material

The total quantity of material recovered is shown in Table 4.12. Small quantities of industrial residues were recovered from features and deposits throughout the excavation area. Larger quantities of ferrous metallurgical waste were identified in deposits dating between Phases 4 and 6, in particular in Areas A and C. A full catalogue is contained within the site archive. The most significant groups of material, i.e. those features and deposits containing greater than 200g of residues, or particularly informative material, are recorded in Chapter 3.

The assemblage is made up predominantly of unclassified slag, plano-convex slag cakes and slag amalgams. There are 31 plano-convex slag cakes and 70 slag amalgams. The slag amalgams should be treated alongside this material, as they are composed of plano-convex slag cake fragments (Tables 4.13 & 4.14). There is a clear preponderance of both materials in Phases 5 and 6 i.e. 45% of the plano-convex slag cakes (by weight) occur in Phase 5 and 32% in Phase 6, while 65% of the slag amalgams (by weight) derive from Phase 5 and 25% from Phase 6.

Significant quantities of slag amalgams were recovered from several Phase 5 features including a spread of ironworking debris (Spread C021/C022), which contained 12 amalgams with a weight of 3924.7g. Other features included Well A001 (seven amalgams, weighing 672.8g) and a badly truncated feature, Gully C012 (seven amalgams, weighing 1059.5g). Layer C011, a widespread, likely Phase 6 garden soil, contained 14 slag amalgams (1720.4g).

Table 4.12 Total quantities of ferrous slag and other residues (weight g)

Short description	Abbreviation	Weight (g)
Diagnostic slags		
Plano-convex slag cakes	PCSC	4810
Slag amalgams	SA	13,870
Billets	B	808
Run slag	R	126
Unclassified slag (likely Fe)	US	21,879
Microresidues (hammerscale and slag spheres)	HS; SS	1149
Undiagnostic slags and residues		
Fuel ash slag	FAS	5481
Fuel residues	FR	755
Vitrified clay (?lining)	VC	236

Table 4.13 Total quantities of slag amalgams (weight g)

Phase	Weight slag amalgams (g)	Quantity slag amalgams
1	742.28	4
2	214.25	1
3	0	0
4	411.66	2
5	9085.52	44
6	3416.06	19
Total	13,870	70

Table 4.14 Total quantities of plano-convex slag cakes (weight g)

Phase	Weight plano-convex slag cakes (g)	Quantity plano-convex slag cakes
1	172.13	1
2	366.69	4
3	0	0
4	535.72	3
5	2214.04	13
6	1522.26	10
Total	4810	31

Table 4.15: Total quantities of unclassified slag (weight g)

Phase	Weight of unclassified slag (g)
1	281.5
2	140.3
3	40.7
4	1454.9
5	14,984.6
6	4315.1
Modern	387.2
Uncertain	247.4
Unstratified	27.3
Total	21,879

Table 4.16 Mean dimensions of plano-convex slag cakes (weight g)

Dimensions	Mean	Standard Deviation
Weight (g)	160	153
Major diameter (mm)	82	21
Minor diameter (mm)	61	29
Depth (mm)	29	9

Table 4.17 Total quantities of slag microresidues (weight g)

Phase	Weight of Microresidues (g)
1	0.8
2	0.6
3	0
4	22.1
5	1103.0
6	20.6
Modern	0.1
Uncertain	2.0
Total	**1149**

Four plano-convex slag cakes, weighing a total of 923.5g, were recovered from ironworking debris Spread C021/C022. Again, Layer C011 produced significant quantities of material, with eight plano-convex slag cakes (687.7g). Well A001 produced two plano-convex slag cakes, weighing 71.3g) while Gully C012 contained one plano-convex slag cake, weighing 38.8g).

Together with the unclassified slag (Table 4.15), which was again concentrated in Phase 5 and 6 features and deposits, this assemblage likely derived from ironworking. Phase 5 features containing a significant quantity of unclassified slag included Well A001 (957.4g); Gully C012 (1111.9g); Pit C071 (497.4g) and Spread C021/C022 (8673.4g). A total of 2199.4g of unclassified slag was recovered from Phase 6 Layer C011.

As noted earlier, it is difficult to differentiate between smithing and smelting activity, but the plano-convex slag cakes are closer in size (see Table 4.16) to those associated with smithing (McDonnell 1994: 230; McDonnell 2000).

The presence of hammerscale and slag spheres (spheroidal hammerslag), particularly in Phase 5 contexts, may also be indicative of smithing rather than smelting processes (Table 4.17). Slag spheres are commonly produced during the primary smithing process, though they can also be produced during smelting and secondary smithing by welding processes (English Heritage 2001: 14). Slag spheres were recovered from Gully C012 and formed a small fraction of the 1053.5g of microresidues from Spread C021/C022, though this material was predominantly hammerscale.

A single iron billet, the iron stock produced by initial refining of the bloom (English Heritage 2001: 13), was recovered from Layer C008, a late Phase 4 deposit. Small quantities of run slag were recovered from Phase 5 Layers A008, A010, A011 and A014, and Pit C028 and Phase 6 Spread C030. The presence of both the billet and the slag spheres points to the possibility of primary smithing activity. The presence of run slag and the billet demonstrate potential for smelting activity having been undertaken in the vicinity in the late medieval/early post-medieval period. Vitrified clay, possibly a fragment of kiln lining, was recovered from Layer C008, which was of Phase 4 date.

The fuel ash slag (5481g) and fuel residues (755g) were mainly derived from Phases 5 and 6, which together produced at least 61% of the fuel ash slag and 65% of the fuel residues. This material was widely distributed, in particular within post-medieval deposits such as Phase 6 Layer C011. It may have derived in part from the ironworking activities evidenced by other materials.

A small number of ceramic crucible fragments (Table 4.11) have also been recovered, generally from Phases 2–4, and in particular from Phase 2 Pit C018 (Section 4.3.5). These are generally small, handmade objects and may indicate the production of metal artefacts from non-ferrous metallurgy, perhaps the casting of artefacts in copper alloy. This is further supported by the presence of clay moulds for decorative, ornamental items, including possible pin heads, badges and/or possibly mirror cases in later 12th to 15th century contexts (Section 4.3.6).

Discussion

While small quantities of industrial residues were recovered from Phases 1 to 4, representing the mid-to-late 12th to early 15th centuries, this material was limited in quantity and appears unlikely to represent on-site ironworking activity. However, the presence of several small crucible fragments from Phase 2 to 4 contexts (with a concentration in Phase 2 Pit C018) suggests that limited metallurgical activity, perhaps casting of brass, may have occurred in the area during this early period (Section 4.3.5). The recovery of fragments of clay moulds also suggest non-ferrous casting activity (Section 4.3.6). A limestone vessel fragment identified at the nearby excavation of 45–47 Gallowgate provides evidence for potential 13th century metal casting. The same site produced fragments of clay moulds suggested to represent the casting of metal items such as ewers and plates (Murray 1984: 306–09).

Possible primary smithing of iron as early as Phase 4 (around the 14th century) is indicated by the presence of an iron billet in Layer C008; further tentative evidence for primary smithing is the presence of slag spheres in several Phase 5 deposits, though this material comprised a very small proportion of the ferrous microresidues recovered from the excavation.

During Phase 5, and to a lesser extent Phase 6, the presence of plano-convex slag cakes and slag amalgams, together with unclassified slags and ferrous microresidues, provides evidence for smithing activity, if not on the site itself, within the immediate area. One feature in particular, Spread C021/C022, would appear to represent a discrete dump of smithing material. It is possible, given the presence of heavily corroded iron artefacts within this deposit alongside metalworking debris, that this deposit represents the reworking of iron objects.

Apart from the evidence for casting at 45–47 Gallowgate, noted above, there appears to be relatively little archaeological evidence for metalworking in medieval and early post-medieval Aberdeen. However, a building was identified in Phase 4b (1645–1720) of the 45–75 Gallowgate excavations where over 5kg of hearth lining and smithing slag were recovered (Cameron *et al.* 2001: 203).

It is possible that the metalworking and combustion residues identified within the late post-medieval Phase 6 deposits can be related to metal tradesmen identified in 19th century trades directories. The Post Office Directory of 1863–64 indicates that Hugh Gordon & Co., listed at No. 1 Gallowgate, to the south-east of the excavation area, undertook coppersmithing and tinsmithing (Aberdeen Directory 1863–64: 240, 263). At the same time, Ironmonger's Court, to the south-west, was the location of J. Rowell, ironmonger (Aberdeen Directory 1863–64: 320). By 1868, No. 14 Upperkirkgate (Ironmonger's Court) was occupied by Knox & Webster, ironmongers, who also occupied Nos. 14–16 St. Paul's Street (Aberdeen Directory 1868–69: 333, 344–45).

The industrial residues from Bon Accord provide evidence for metalworking from the late medieval period onwards, if not within the site area itself, then in close proximity. It adds to the evidence for medieval metal casting at 45–47 Gallowgate, and indicates the presence of possible primary smithing activity as early as the 14th century. In addition, smithing activity appears to have produced a considerable quantity of waste material, in particular within Spread C021/C022, which may at least in part be related to the reworking of existing iron stock.

4.3.8 Miscellaneous finds
Michael Roy

Introduction

A small number of miscellaneous finds were retrieved from the retents of processed bulk samples. The material included a small assemblage of glass beads but there was also a fragment of amber and a bone die. A group of ceramic objects and worked bone are also described in this section (Table 4.18). The material described belongs to Phases 1 to 5; Phase 6 and modern material is recorded in the site archive.

Bone die

A bone die (SF6018) was recovered from Phase 5 garden soils. It was slightly abraded but in otherwise good condition. It was formed of a 5mm x 5mm x 5mm cube of bone, with incised rings with inner dots acting as the spots of the die.

Similar bone dice have been encountered during previous excavations in the city and shire. Two solid bone dice were recovered from deposits containing late 13th and 14th century pottery at the Queen Street Midden Area excavations in Aberdeen in 1973 (Greig 1982: 23). These appear to have been somewhat larger in size (9mm x 8mm x 8mm and 8mm x 8mm x 8mm), but have a similar, incised ring and dot pattern (MacGregor 1982: 181–82). As with the Queen Street dice, the Bon Accord die follows the medieval pattern with 1 opposite 2; 3 opposite 4 and 5 opposite 6. This medieval pattern contrasts with a hollow bone die, with the pre-Norman and modern pattern of 1 opposite 6; 2 opposite 5 and 3 opposite 4, which was recovered during excavations at the former burgh of Rattray in north Aberdeenshire. Also recovered at Rattray was a solid bone die described as of 'common 13th- and 14th-century type' (Murray and Murray 1993: 197).

Beads

A small assemblage of beads was recovered, predominantly small asymmetrical glass objects (Figure 4.45). Two glass beads were recovered from Phase 2 or 3 contexts (SF6002 & SF6016), while a clear red bead fragment (SF6019) was recovered from Phase 4, and both a ceramic (SF6017) and a glass bead (SF1861) were recovered from the late medieval/early post-medieval Phase 5 (Figure 4.45). The beads were predominantly globular rather than annular in form, i.e. their height to diameter ratio was greater than 1:2 (Mainman and Rogers 2000: 2592). The translucent yellow colour of the bead from Layer A008 is typical of high-lead glass, which came into use in Britain from the 10th century AD (Mainman and Rogers 2000: 2519). It is possible that the weathered 'black' bead from Well A002 may also be a high-lead glass item.

Amber

The presence of a piece of unworked amber SF3383, from Phase 2 Pit C025, is tentative evidence for the working of amber in the 13th century. Although amber is commonly associated with trade with the Baltic, there are localised deposits on the east coast of Britain, including the Aberdeen area (Huggett 1988: 64). The

Table 4.18 Summary of miscellaneous finds

SF No.	Feature	Phase	Material	Description
SF1163	Gully C002	1	Glass	Opaque creamy yellow glass fragment, forming possible part of bottle stopper
SF2889X	Pit A026	1	Ceramic	Spindle whorl fragment of reused ceramic
SF2977	Pit C004	1	Bone and leather	Atlas of an adult cow with a small piece of leather attached; unknown function
SF4543X	Pit C015	1	Ceramic	Gaming counter of reused ceramic
SF1407	Spread A003	1	Ceramic	Gaming counter of reused ceramic
SF6027	Spread A003	1	Ceramic	Gaming counter of reused ceramic
SF2954	Layer C003	3	Bone	Ovicaprid metatarsal with a circular hole
SF3362	Layer C051	2	Bone	Cattle metatarsal, shaped at the distal end to provide a smooth, bevelled edge – possible tool for shaping of hide or finishing of leather
SF2781	Pit C018	2	Bone	Tibia from dog? Worked ends – possibly a peg or line separator
SF3288	Pit C025	2	Ceramic	Spindle whorl of reused ceramic
SF3383	Pit C025	2	Amber	Honey brown weathered fragment of translucent amber
SF6002	Layer A028	2–3	Glass	Opaque white glass bead
SF2362	Well A002	2–3	Ceramic	Gaming counter of reused ceramic
SF6016	Well A002	2–3	Glass	Weathered opaque grey/black glass bead fragment
SF6028	Pit C016	3	Ceramic	Possible pot lid of reused ceramic
SF4798	Pit C042	3	Bone	Tibia of a sheep or goat, with a circular hole, c. 8mm in diameter, drilled at the distal end
SF3223X	Layer C008	4	Ceramic	Gaming counter of reused ceramic
SF1311X	Layer C020	4	Ceramic	Spindle whorl fragment of reused ceramic
SF6019	Layer A029	4	Glass	Translucent red glass bead fragment
SF4144	Posthole C003	4	Bone	Pig metatarsal with a sub-square hole crudely drilled through the shaft: possible 'buzzbones' or a toggle used as a clothes fastener or for winding wool
SF1861	Layer A008	5	Glass	Translucent yellow glass bead with white streak
SF6017	Spread A020	5	Ceramic	Opaque brown ceramic bead
SF6018	Area A garden soils	5	Bone	Bone die

amber may have been intended for the production of amber artefacts such as beads or pendants.

Worked animal bone

A small number of the animal bones recovered from Bon Accord displayed evidence for intentional working. Two pieces of bone, SF3362 and SF2781 (Figure 4.46), have been shaped and facetted and may have been intended as tools. SF2954 and SF4798 are both bones with circular holes along the length, possibly for threading, while SF4144 (Figure 4.46) is potentially part of a toy.

SF 2977 (Figure 4.47) is an atlas from a cow, which although not worked, formed part of a composite bone and leather artefact of unknown function.

Reused ceramics; spindle whorls, counters and potlid

Nine objects produced from reused medieval ceramic vessels were recovered from Bon Accord. These have been interpreted as spindle whorls and counters, with one possible potlid. Identification of ceramic type has been carried out by George R. Haggarty.

Figure 4.45 Glass beads; top row from left – SF1861, SF6002, SF6016. Bottom row from left – SF6017 and SF6019

Figure 4.46 Upper; SF2781 – peg from possible dog tibia (Pit C018)
Lower; SF4144 – possible toy made from pig fourth metatarsal (Ph C003)

Figure 4.47 SF2977 – composite animal bone and leather artefact (Pit C004)

197

Figure 4.48 Ceramic spindle whorls; from left – SF2889X, SF3288 and SF1311X

Figure 4.49 Ceramic counters; top row from left – SF6028, SF4543X and SF3223X; bottom row
from left – SF1407, SF2362 and SF6027

Three pieces of reused ceramic were formed into spindle whorls (Figure 4.48). A possible spindle whorl (SF1546B), formed from an oak disc, was recovered from a fill of Phase 1 Pit C006 at Bon Accord, though Crone (Section 4.2.1) notes that this artefact could also be a float for a fishing net. A bone float or spindle whorl was recovered from a 15th century context at 30–46 Upperkirkgate (Cameron *et al.* 2001: 210). The reuse of ceramics for spindle whorls is not unknown. For example, three whorls from Roman potsherds were recovered from medieval layers at the Coppergate, York, though these appear to have been redeposited (Walton Rogers 2002: 2736).

Five artefacts have been identified as likely gaming counters fashioned from reused ceramic (Figure 4.49). Hurst (2001: 206) has noted that 'irregularly rounded sherds of ceramic, sometimes pierced' are not uncommon finds from medieval Aberdeen sites, including an example of a gaming counter, produced from a fragment of 15th century Valencian lustreware, recovered from 43–57 Upperkirkgate. A bone counter has also been recorded at 16–18 Netherkirkgate (Cameron *et al.* 2001: 210), while a wooden gaming counter was also recovered from 16–18 Netherkirkgate (Crone *et al.* 2001: 219). Further afield, various sites in York have produced gaming counters made from

Roman and medieval pottery sherds (Ottaway and Rogers 2002: 2951).

One further unperforated reused ceramic artefact SF6028 (Figure 4.49) is of a noticeably greater size than the material identified as gaming counters and may represent a potlid. In York, Ottaway and Rogers describe the recovery of a small number of ceramic and stone discs of greater than 70mm diameter that 'appear too large to be tablemen', but also 'probably too small to have acted as lids for any medieval pots' (Ottaway and Rogers 2002: 2951). It is likely that SF6028 falls into this category, where the size of the disc is consistent with neither a gaming counter nor a functional potlid.

Catalogue of miscellaneous finds
(L = length; W = width; Th = thickness; D = diameter)

SF 3362 (not illustrated)
Phase/Feature Phase 2/Layer C051
Description: shaped cattle metatarsal/tool?
This element of cattle metatarsal measures c. 115mm in length and has been shaped at the distal end to provide a smooth, bevelled edge. This could possibly have been used in the shaping of hide or the finishing of leather.

SF 2781 (Figure 4.46)
Phase/Feature Phase 2/Pit C018 fill (E)
Description: possible peg or line separator
This appears to be a tibia from an unidentified animal, perhaps dog. It measures 85mm in length and both the proximal and distal ends of the shaft have been worked, with faceting at the proximal end and along the shaft, and a v-shaped notch and fine facets at the distal end. It is possible that this artefact has been shaped to form a peg or line separator.

SF 2954 (not illustrated)
Phase/Feature Phase 2/Layer C003
Description: worked ovicaprid metatarsal
This is the metatarsal of an ovicaprid, which has a circular hole, c. 10mm in diameter, drilled through its proximal end.

SF 4798 (not illustrated)
Phase/Feature Phase 3/Pit C042 fill (A)
Description: worked sheep or goat tibia
This is the tibia of a sheep or goat, which has a circular hole, c. 8mm in diameter, drilled at the distal end. A similar object has been recovered from 16–18 Nethergate, Aberdeen, where an ovicaprid metatarsal was recovered from a 13th to 14th century context, which had a circular hole bored along the length of the shaft (Cameron et al. 2001: 210).

SF 4144 (Figure 4.46)
Phase/Feature Phase 4/Ph C003 fill (B)
Description: possible buzzbones toy

The fourth metatarsal of a pig, with a length of 65mm, has a sub-square hole, roughly 6mm in diameter, crudely drilled centrally through the shaft. This would have facilitated the insertion of animal sinew or cord. Such objects have been recovered from previous medieval excavations in Aberdeen, both at 45–47 Gallowgate and 45–75 Gallowgate (Cameron et al. 2001: 209) and have been interpreted as 'buzzbones', a form of toy or musical instrument where a small bone is spun with sinew or cord that has been threaded and twisted through it. In Shetland such toys are called 'snorie banes' due to the sound like snoring that they can produce. Alternatively, this may have been a toggle used as a clothes fastener or for winding wool (MacGregor 1985: 102–03).

SF 2977 (Figure 4.47)
Phase/Feature Phase 1/Fill (C) of Pit C004
Description: composite artefact of bone and leather
This item is a composite artefact of animal bone and leather. The atlas of an adult cow has had a small piece of leather tied through the left transverse foramen. The atlas is much damaged, having lost large elements of its wings. The function of this unusual composite object is unknown.

SF 2889X (Figure 4.48)
Phase/Feature Phase 1/Pit A026
Description: spindle whorl fragment
A fragment of a circular spindle whorl, representing c. 40% of the original. In the centre of the whorl is the remnant of a circular abraded hole. The whorl has been crudely shaped from a ceramic vessel, identified as a glazed jug of a sandy Local Redware fabric. D 49mm; D of central hole 8mm; Th 8.5mm.

SF 3288 (Figure 4.48)
Phase/Feature Phase 2/Pit C025
Description: spindle whorl
A circular spindle whorl with a finely drilled circular hole. The whorl has been crudely shaped from a ceramic vessel, identified as a likely unglazed vessel of an extremely gritty Local Redware fabric. D 44mm; D of central hole 8.5mm; Th 14mm.

SF 1311X (Figure 4.48)
Phase/Feature Phase 4/Layer C020
Description: spindle whorl fragment
A fragment of a circular spindle whorl, representing c. 20% of the original. In the centre of the whorl there has been a circular abraded hole. The whorl has been crudely shaped from a ceramic vessel, identified as a glazed jug of a sandy Local Redware fabric. D 50mm; D of central hole 9.5mm; Th 8mm.

SF 4543X (Figure 4.49)
Phase/Feature Phase 1/Pit C015

Table 4.19 Dates for clay tobacco pipe fragments

Feature	Phase	Bowl	Mouth piece	Stem	Bowl mark	Stem mark	Maker	Total	Date
Layer C008	4			1				1	19th century
Layer A007	5	1	0	1	basal stamp		Dutch	1	c.1660–80
Layer A008	5	0	0	1				1	17th century
Layer C009	5	0	0	1				1	17th century
Layer C052	5			3				3	17th century?
Pit B001	5	1	0	0		moulded rose	Dutch	1	mid 17th century
Layer C011	5 or 6	2	0	7		roller stamp		9	c.1640–60; c.1680–1720 & 19th century?
Layer B006	6	1	0	3				4	mid 17th century
Layer C028/ Spread C034	6	1	0	5				6	19th century
Pit C078	6	3	2	22	marked spur; rear stamp	1	Swinyard; Rattray	27	early 17th– 19th century
Pit C081	6	7	0	15	Jenny Lind; rear stamp		Swinyard	22	19th century
Spread C045	6	0	0	1				1	19th century
Structure C012	6	0	0	2				2	17th century?
Surface C018	6	0	0	1				1	17th century
Wall A001	6	0	0	1				1	17th century?
Well C002	6	3	0	8				11	19th century
Layer A009	Mod.	0	0	2				2	19th century
Pit C086	Mod.	1	0	4	B	roller stamp		5	c.1650–1720
Unstratified		4	1	13		roller stamp x 2		18	17th century; late 17th–19th century

Description: gaming counter
A suboval gaming counter. The counter has been crudely shaped from a ceramic vessel, identified as a glazed jug of a gritty Local Redware fabric. L 63mm; breadth 53mm; Th 11.5mm.

SF   1407 (Figure 4.49)
Phase/Feature   Phase 1/Spread A003
Description: gaming counter
A subcircular gaming counter. The counter has been very roughly shaped from a ceramic vessel, identified as a glazed jug of Scarborough Ware Fabric 1. D 36mm; Th 9.5mm.

SF   6027 (Figure 4.49)
Phase/Feature   Phase 1/Spread A003
Description: gaming counter
A subcircular gaming counter. The counter has been very roughly shaped from a ceramic vessel, identified as a glazed jug of sandy Local Redware fabric. D 42mm; Th 10mm.

SF   2362 (Figure 4.49)
Phase/Feature   Phase 2 or 3/Well A002
Description: gaming counter
A subcircular gaming counter. The counter has been crudely shaped from a ceramic vessel, identified as a

glazed jug of Scarborough Ware Fabric 2. D 35mm; Th 6.5mm.

SF   3223X (Figure 4.49)
Phase/Feature   Phase 4/Layer C008
Description: gaming counter
A subcircular gaming counter. The counter has been crudely shaped from a ceramic vessel, identified as a glazed jug of Scarborough Ware Fabric 1. D 57.5mm; Th 8.5mm.

SF   6028 (Figure 4.49)
Phase/Feature   Phase 3/Pit C016
Description: potlid?
A subcircular disc, possibly representing a potlid. The potlid has been crudely shaped from the base of a ceramic vessel, identified as a cooking pot of a gritty Local Redware fabric. One face of the disc, representing the interior of the base of the original vessel, is extensively sooted. D 74mm; Th 9mm.

4.3.9 Clay tobacco pipes
Dennis Gallagher

(written 2009)

Table 4.19 provides general dates for the datable pipe fragments. They range in date from the 17th century to the 19th century. There are quite a few decorated stems and the Jenny Lind pipe ('the Swedish nightingale') has not been found in Scotland before. Table 4.19 indicates only assemblages that provide marks and/or dating evidence.

4.4 Structural materials

4.4.1 Structural timber
Anne Crone

Introduction

Vast quantities of waterlogged wood were recovered from Bon Accord, registered variously as small finds (SF) or as special samples (SS); nearly 700 small finds of wood and 119 special samples of wood were registered. The small finds varied from single large planks, the largest of which was 2.33m in length, to bags containing large amounts of woody detritus. Stakes and withies from fence lines and hurdle screens were usually treated as special samples and could include numerous lengths of withies, or multiple stakes under one SS number.

All finds were sorted and only those objects which displayed evidence of manufacture were retained. The bulk of the material recovered consisted of woody detritus, twigs and branches, none of which displayed any evidence of woodworking, other than the occasional chopmark. This material was therefore set aside and not included in any further study. Small fragments of bark were ubiquitous but there were occasionally large sheets which cannot have peeled off the small roundwood found in the same context and must have been deliberately gathered. They were particularly numerous in Pits C001, C022 and C025 where they might have been used as lining in the pits (Section 4.5.1).

A total of 134 small finds, which together contained 156 objects, were identified as either structural timbers or woodworking debris; this material is described

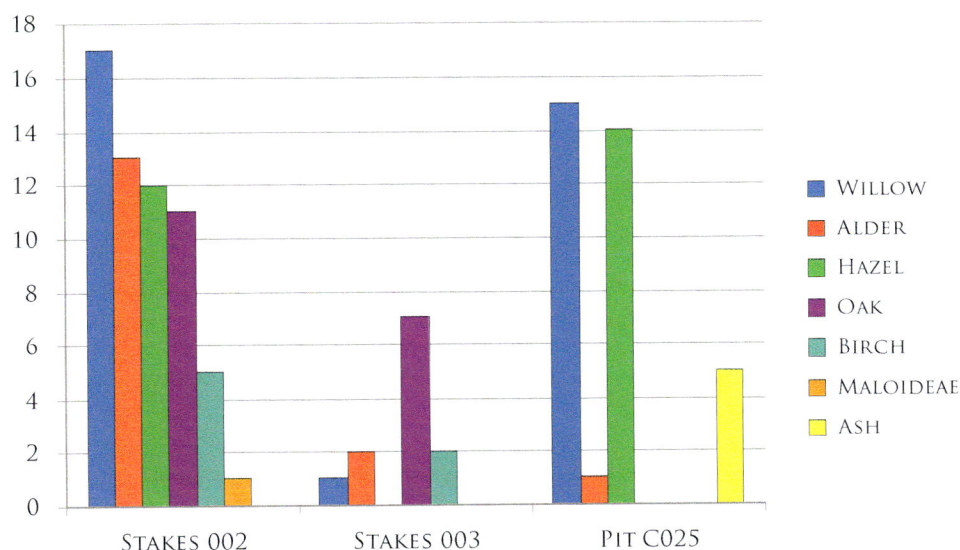

Figure 4.50 Species represented in the *in situ* structural timber assemblages

in the archive catalogue. The 119 special samples contained 155 components. The study of the fences and hurdle screens focused on species composition and a representative proportion of each component was identified; between 20% and 50% of both stakes and withies in each structure was identified, depending on the variety of species present (Figure 4.50). The full catalogue is contained in the site archive.

Woodworking debris and structural timbers were recovered from features across the site but the majority was *ex situ*, dumped as backfill in the pits. The only major example of surviving *in situ* woodwork is the lining of Well A002, although some of the large assemblage from Pit C025 may also have come from the covering over the pit. *In situ* posts were also found in some of the postholes, and there were numerous fence lines, from which the tips of stakes and associated withies were recovered.

This report focuses on the wooden material that was either *in situ* or is of interest in terms of contemporary woodworking techniques and the types of wooden constructions that they represent.

Species use

Oak (*Quercus* sp.) dominated the assemblage, comprising 59% of the identified pieces. The other main species present were hazel (*Corylus avellana* – 14%), alder (*Alnus glutinosa* – 12%), birch (*Betula* sp. – 8%) and willow (*Salix* sp. – 6%). An ash (*Fraxinus excelsior*) post (SF3634) and a small fragment of a larch (*Larix decidua*) lath (SF2614) were the only unusual species present. Although ash would have been available in the hinterland around Aberdeen, its use seems to have been restricted to the manufacture of large platters (Section 4.2.1). Larch is a native of central Europe and would have been an exotic in medieval Scotland. The lath is pierced by two nails and is part of a larger object, perhaps a chest. It is also possible that the timber arrived in Aberdeen in a different form and was subsequently recycled.

The non-oak species were invariably present as undressed roundwood stems and used either as stakes, posts or withies. The only unusual non-oak conversion was that of SF3622, a plank fashioned from a hazel log by cleaving large chords off opposing sides. The greatest mixture of species was present in the hurdle screens and fencelines (Figure 4.50). Hazel, oak, alder, willow, and birch were used for stakes but willow and hazel were more favoured for use as withies.

A small amount of undressed oak roundwood stems were also used for stakes but the majority of the oak came from much larger trunks which had been more heavily converted, either by splitting radially for planking, or by squaring logs, half-logs and quarter-logs into baulks.

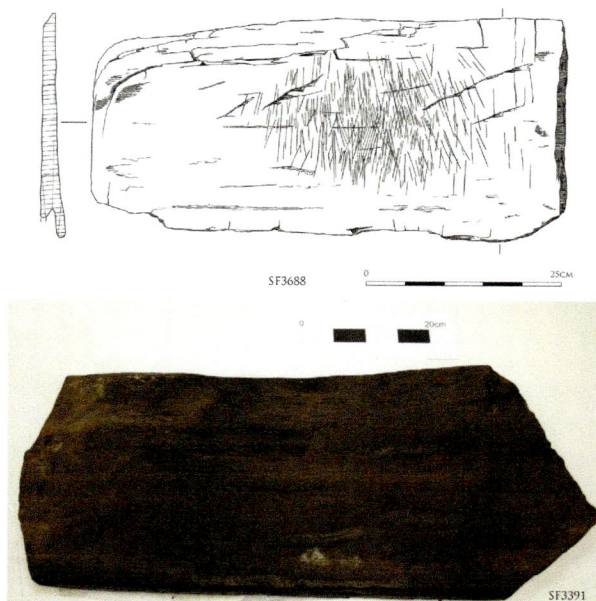

Figure 4.51 Re-used planking; SF3688 – plank with groove down one side and cutmarks on one face (Pit C025 fill C025D); SF3391 – plank shaped to tip at one end (Pit C025 fill C025D)

Oak was favoured for all major structural elements; for instance the lining of Well A002 was built entirely of oak planks and baulks.

Reuse

It is probable that much of the oak found on the site was reused. For instance, many of the planks used in Well A002 displayed peg and nail holes which appeared to be redundant in the context of the pit lining. Perhaps the clearest evidence that timber was being recycled is the group of oak planks that display grooves down their thickest edge. These include SF3566, SF3655, SF3688 (Figure 4.51) and SF3694, all found in Pit C025; SF3602 from Gully C001, and SF3719 from Pit C033. The grooves are 5–7mm wide and up to 25mm deep, and are tapered in cross-section. The longest example is 0.88m but most are no longer than 0.34m and have probably been cut down from larger lengths of panelling (see below).

Almost half of the oak were planks or fragments of planks, all radially-split. Apart from the planks lining Well A002 they were no longer *in situ* but the similarities in size and design among the assemblage suggests that many of the planks had also been used as pit linings. They were either roughly squared at both ends or squared at one end while the other was shaped to a point, probably to ease insertion into the ground (i.e. SF3391 – Figure 4.51). Some of the planks also displayed compression and buckling at one end which could only have resulted from being hammered into hard ground. The complete examples varied in length from 0.31m to

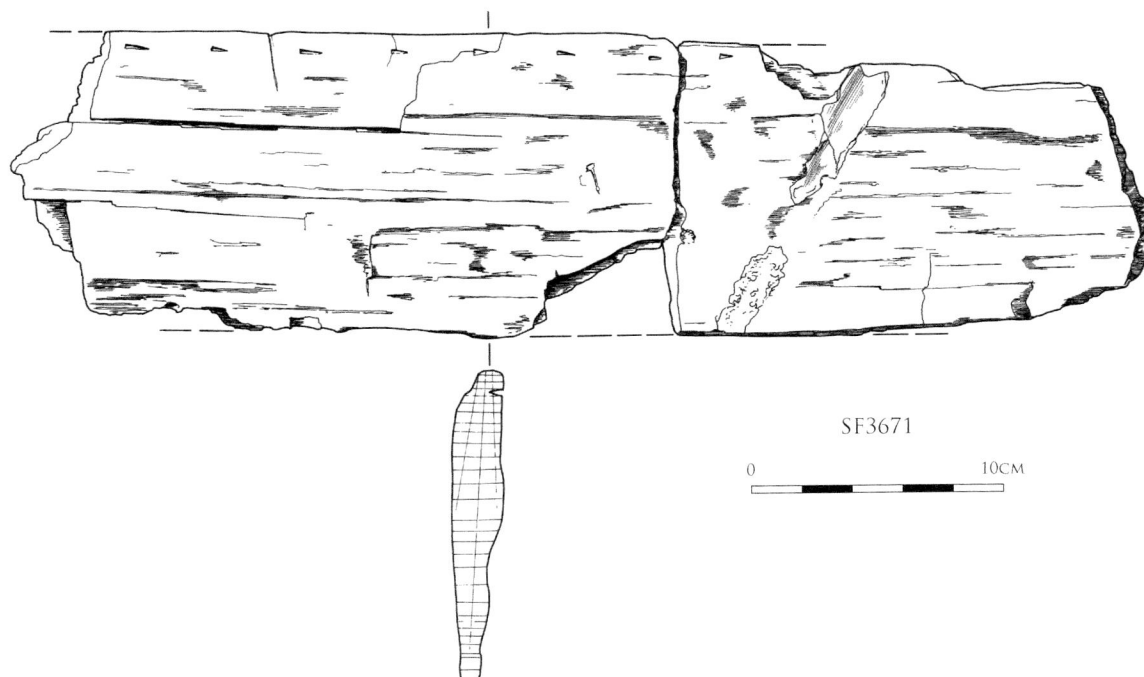

SF3671

0   10cm

Figure 4.52 SF3671– plank with pinned holes down both sides (Pit C025 fill C025D)

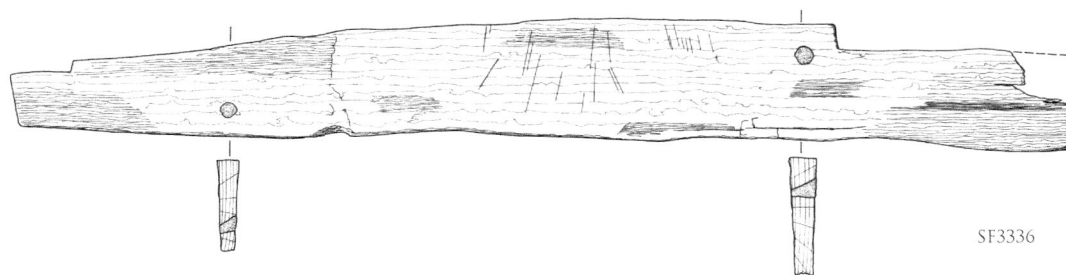

SF3336

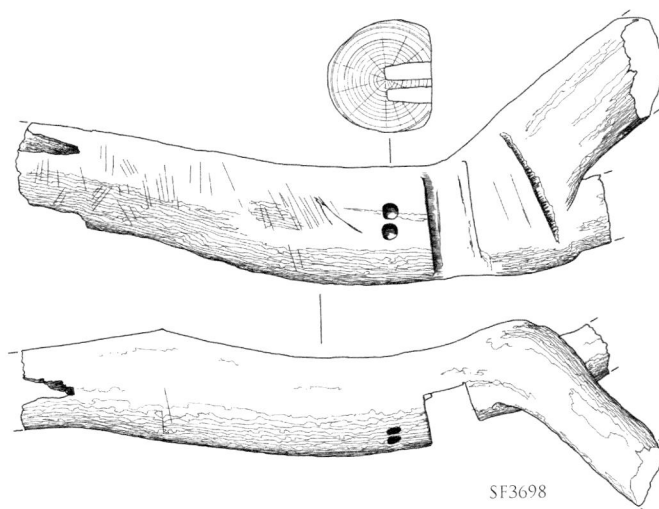

SF3698

0   20cm

Figure 4.53 Carpentry; plank SF3336 (Pit C037 fill C025D); timber SF3698 (Pit C025 fill C025D)

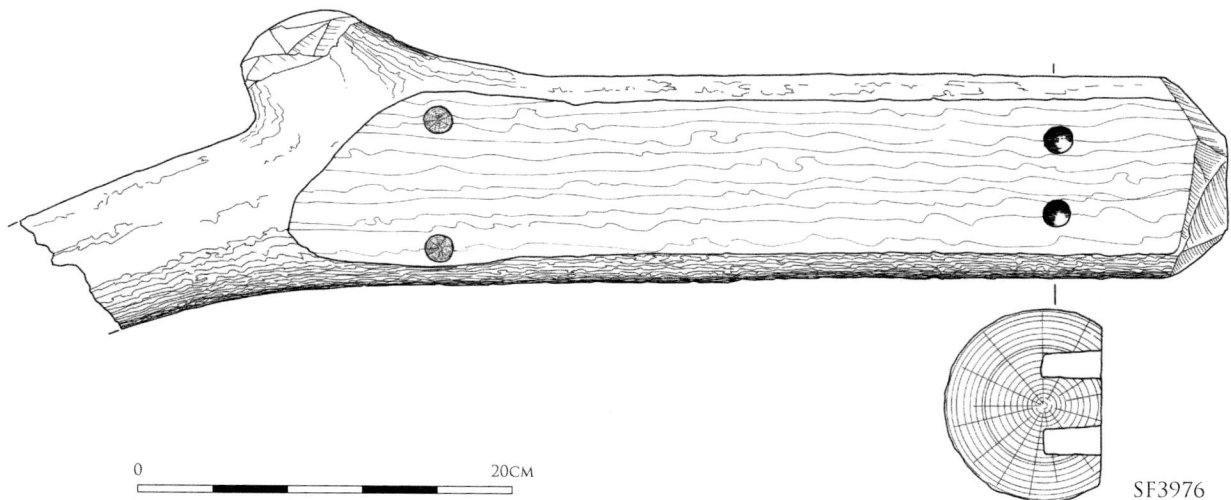

Figure 4.54 Carpentry; timber SF3976 (Pit C025 fill C025D)

0.93 mand this probably reflects the depth of the pit that they lined; some of the pits may have been very shallow.

Some of the planks were also pierced by pegholes and/or nailholes, occasionally with pegs and nails in situ and often in positions where they would have had no function, very close to the pointed tips for example. As with the fragments of grooved panelling described above, this suggests that the planks had been cut down from larger pieces. Most of the offcuts found in the assemblage were radially-split pieces of oak, and it seems likely that came from the reshaping of the planks. One of the most intriguing plank fragments is SF3671 from Pit C025. Along one edge is a series of small triangular incisions in which the tips of tiny oak pins can be seen (Figure 4.52). The most obvious explanation is that fabric or leather was pinned to the plank; it may have been a component of an internal screen or a chest.

Carpentry

The clearest evidence for the type of jointing in use is that from Well A002, where the horizontal timbers and corner posts were fixed together by means of halved lap joints, cut at the very end of the timber or just in from the end. Few of the *ex situ* timbers displayed jointing. A plank, SF3336, displayed shallow notches at each end (Figure 4.53), while SF3698, a long timber fashioned from a quarter-trunk, had a shallow ledge 130mm wide and 50mm deep cut out along one edge (Figure 4.53).

The *in situ* joints were invariably pegged together by means of radially-split oak pegs, or trenails. All of the pegholes used in the lining of Well A002 were 25mm in diameter but on other timbers pegholes of 20mm and 30mm in diameter were recorded. Nails with rectangular heads, 5 x 3mm across, were observed

on a dozen timbers, mainly planks, where they often occurred in clusters. These are Type H nails (Section 4.3.1) and were probably used to secure thin materials to the surface of the planks, such as the lead sheet attached to one of the artefacts, SF3010 (Section 4.2.1). There is no evidence from Bon Accord to suggest that nails were used to secure carpentered joints.

SF3976 is one of the more curious timbers recovered from the site (Figure 4.54). It has been fashioned from a large oak log which is forked at one end while the other end has been tapered to a flat base. One side of the log has been trimmed flat and at either end of the flattened area are pairs of holes, 30mm in diameter and 60mm deep; the pegs are still *in situ* in one pair. It was clearly fashioned for a specific purpose. The flattened end and the trimmed fork suggest that it was intended to be upright, perhaps with boards pegged to the flattened area. Although of smaller dimensions, SF3054 was also shaped to a stake tip at one end with forked tips at the other. It is possible that these timbers were erected upright around the edges of the pits and relate in some way to the use of the pits.

In summary, there was little complex carpentry applied on the site. The carpenters used whatever was to hand and there is abundant evidence for the recycling of large oak timbers. Despite this evidence, it would be difficult to reconstruct the design of the surrounding buildings on the basis of the timberwork found at Bon Accord. The grooved planks are of interest because they indicate that a primitive version of tongue-and-groove panelling, in which the tapered edge of one panel is set into the groove of the next, was in use somewhere in the vicinity. A group of grooved planks was found at Perth High Street (Curteis *et al.* 2012: 295–98), all but two of them found near Building 18, an aisled hall of mid/late 13th century date (Murray 2010: 131). One of

Figure 4.55
(A) Impressions of straw and rushes which were used to strengthen the daub
(B) Bundles of plant stems incorporated into the daub
(C) Heat-affected daub, to which extra layers of clay have been added after the heating event
(D) The impression left by a roughly rectangular timber enclosed within the daub

the walls of the building was constructed of vertical planks set into a sillbeam and it is argued that the *ex situ* plank fragments came from this construction. They are similar in thickness to the Bon Accord planks, although the illustrated examples are smaller in width and have a squared rather than tapered edge. An alternative possibility is that the Bon Accord grooved planks were set horizontally to form an external or internal wall. Very few such walls have survived but vertical slots in the posts of a 13th century aisled hall at Temple Balsall, Warwickshire, one of which contained the remains of a plank (Alcock 1982: 157), indicate that such walls were known. Set either vertically or horizontally the planks could also have formed part of a structure such as a non-load bearing internal partition or screen set in a moveable sillbeam.

4.4.2 Ceramic building material
Jackaline Robertson

Introduction

Daub material (Appendix 2, Table A.2.1) was collected from eight features either by hand or during bulk

sample processing. The daub was found in a hearth, large pits, layers and walls.

The following attributes were recorded: surface description, maximum thickness, inorganic inclusions, organic inclusions, wood impressions, burning and quantity. Thickness was only recorded for those fragments where both opposing surfaces had survived. A description of the analytical methodology and a catalogue of all recovered daub are contained within the site archive.

Fabric and condition

The fabric of the daub is composed of coarse, sandy clay with inclusions of naturally occurring fine silver mica and quartz fragments. The majority of the fragments also contained additional inorganic and organic inclusions which were deliberately added to the clay to strengthen the fabric (Figures 4.55A & B). The overall condition of the assemblage is good; however, many of the fragments including those that had been fully fired are still quite friable and easily break. The external surfaces, particularly when flattened, are prone to cracking, which has contributed to further post-depositional damage. The daub fragments range in colour from a dull to bright orange-red to a dull grey-brown. Detailed description of the material is provided by feature in Chapter 3.

Discussion

The daub does not appear to represent *in situ* material. However, enough evidence survives to determine that this fabric originated from hearth-type structures which were subjected to relatively low temperatures. These features were clearly employed for more than a single use as there is evidence that daub used to line the walls and cover the timber superstructures was subjected to numerous repairs. Many daub fragments have had extra layers of clay added to them once the original clay became heat affected and weakened as a consequence (Figure 4.55C).

Although some of the daub bears wood impressions (Figure 4.55D) there was no evidence that it had clad the types of lattice frameworks that would have been necessary for a roofing structure. The hearth structures at Bon Accord, including Hearth C002 were thus probably of a similar design to those posited at 45–75 Gallowgate (Cameron *et al.* 2001, 206). At Gallowgate the daub was interpreted as components of superstructures for hearths that were not fully enclosed by a dome, but instead were surrounded by clay walls only (Cameron *et al.* 2001: 206). A small number of curved daub fragments were recovered but these are more likely to have formed the supporting clay walls of the hearth features.

Overall, the daub from Bon Accord appears to be fairly homogeneous in nature, with the exception of the material from Pit C064. The daub from this pit contained a mixed assemblage, including fragments of thick unprocessed clay that had no evidence of burning or of strengthening by inclusions. It would have made an unsuitable wall lining or roof structure and was therefore probably used as a floor lining.

In summary, the daub assemblage points to the use of low temperature hearths throughout Phases 3 to 6. There is no evidence that any of the features from which the daub was recovered were exposed to high temperatures for prolonged periods of time, suggesting that activities requiring constant high temperatures were not undertaken within these features.

4.4.3 Window glass
Hugh Willmott
(written 2009)

A not insignificant quantity of window glass was recovered from the excavation, but the majority of this was modern and of little archaeological interest.

However, some pieces are earlier in date and merit a brief description. This latter group of window glass is all plain, and this makes precise dating difficult. Nonetheless, the colour, thickness and in particular its state of preservation do provide a good indication of age.

Four examples – SF1063/1076, SF1930, SF237 and SF3490 – are certainly late medieval in date. All are heavily devitrified due to the poor composition of the glass, and all but one, SF3490, have at least one grozed edge. Grozing was the technique by which the glazier shaped the quarry of glass by chipping its edges, in much the same way prehistoric stone tools were pressure flaked. The individual quarries were then held together with lead strips, or cames, and in the case of SF237 a distinct mark has been left on the glass due to its contact with the lead.

Three further fragments of early window glass were recovered, although these were in a better state of preservation suggesting they might be of later date. Although heavily surface weathered, SF402 and SF1090 retain green glass cores, perhaps indicating they are late 15th to early17th century in date. The final fragment, SF1475, has a smooth edge and is most likely to be 16th–17th century in date.

Catalogue of window glass fragments

SF 1063 & 1076 (not illustrated)
Phase/Feature Early-to-mid Phase 5/Layer A014
Description: plain window glass fragments
Two joining fragments of plain window glass, with one straight grozed edge. Green glass with very heavy weathering to its surfaces. Late medieval.

SF 1930 (not illustrated)
Phase/Feature Late Phase 4/Layer A015
Description: plain window glass fragment
One fragment of plain window glass, with one straight grozed edge. Nearly completely devitrified. Late medieval.

SF 237 (not illustrated)
Phase/Feature Late Phase 5 or Phase 6/Surface C012
Description: plain window glass fragment
One fragment of plain window glass, with two straight grozed edges. Nearly completely devitrified. Came marks clearly visible along the two edges. Late medieval.

SF 3490 (not illustrated)
Phase/Feature Phase 2/Pit C036
Description: plain window glass fragment
One fragment of plain window glass. Thick (up to 6mm) with no surviving edges. Nearly completely devitrified. Late medieval.

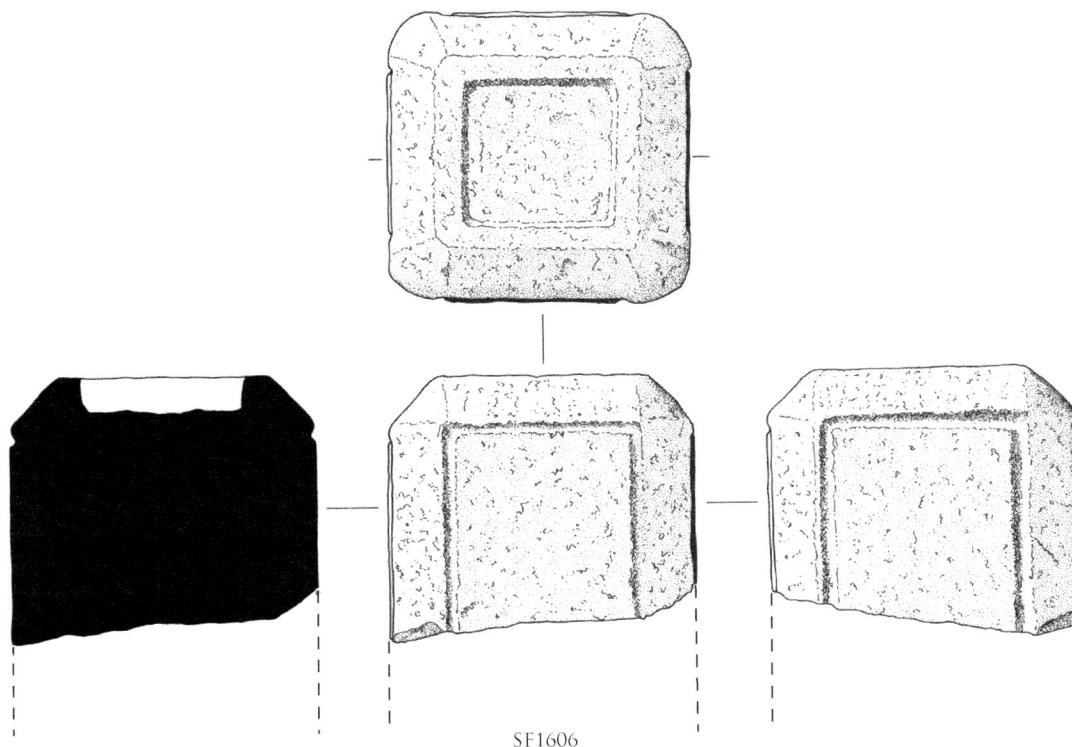

Figure 4.56 SF1606; only the upper part of the stone which was recovered is illustrated here

SF   402 (not illustrated)
Phase/Feature   Late Phase 5/Pit C080
Description: plain window glass fragment
One fragment of fine thin window glass, with two straight grozed edges. Green glass with quite heavy surface weathering. Came marks clearly visible along the two edges. 15th–early 17th century.

SF   1090 (not illustrated)
Phase/Feature   Mid Phase 5/Spread C022
Description: window glass fragment
One fragment of fine thin window glass. Green glass with quite heavy surface weathering. 15th–early 17th century.

SF   1475 (not illustrated)
Phase/Feature   Phase 6/Layer B006
Description: plain window glass fragment
One fragment of plain window glass, with one surviving straight edge indicating it was manufactured by the cylinder method. Light green tinted with medium weathering. 16th–17th century?

4.4.4 Socketed stone
Michael Roy

A dressed granite masonry block, SF1606, interpreted as a pillar base, was recovered from within a late post-medieval wall (Structure C007, Phase 6). The pillar base

was encountered set on its side, mortared within the wall, representing the reuse of dressed masonry within a later structure. When first revealed, the pillar was complete, though cracked at the point where it would break into two parts on recovery (Figure 4.56).

Its original height was 850mm, and it had a flat base and was square in section, with each side measuring 250mm. The faces of each side of the pillar base were flat and undecorated, for a height of 480mm. From this height, each of the four sides of the pillar was incised with a 4mm deep and c. 10mm wide band, running 40mm in from the edges and the top of the pillar. While the basal 450mm of the pillar was square in section, with sharp corners, the topmost 400mm had rounded corners. The upper 40mm of the pillar was chamfered at the sides and corners, the top of the pillar forming a rectangular surface, measuring 170mm x 165mm. Into this surface a square socket, 30mm in depth and 120mm square at its base, had been incised.

Its form suggests that this artefact formed the base of an architectural feature, perhaps a pillar, with the square socket on its upper surface representing the mortise for the insertion of a stone or timber pillar or post. Such a pillar might have been utilised as an element of a post-medieval house, or in jettying over the street frontage. A stone recovered during the Perth High Street excavation, with a circular socket cut in its upper surface, was similarly interpreted as having held a timber post, representing either a single interior support, or one of several such supports, perhaps for an overhanging storey or balcony (Markus 2010: 220). The use of socketed stones for uprights in a 19th century context has been seen relatively close to the present site, in Brechin, Angus (Murray and Murray 2011: 44). Stone bases supporting timber posts are utilised in farm buildings in southern Britain (cf. Harvey 1987: 17; Peters 1981: fig. 21). Alternatively, this could represent the base of a less substantial feature such as a small cross or a sundial.

The presence of a dressed piece of architecture, reused in the 19th century, indicates the likely presence of a high status building in the area, either domestic or ecclesiastical, at an earlier date. It is possible that it formed part of the structure of one of the high status residences of the post-medieval town worthies, such as Provost Robertson, who resided on the Upperkirkgate in the 18th century, or perhaps an element of a decorative feature, such as a sundial or sculpture, that might have adorned the garden of such a residence.

Catalogue of socket stone

SF   1606 (Figure 4.56)
Phase/Feature   Phase 6/Structure C007
Description: socket stone
Socket stone (likely pillar base). Height (incomplete) 850mm; width and breadth 250mm.

4.5 Ecofact analyses

4.5.1 Macroplant remains
Jackaline Robertson

Introduction

This report presents the analysis of the macroplant assemblage, which was mainly preserved through anaerobic 'waterlogging' conditions although there was a smaller quantity, mostly cereal caryopses along with some weed taxa, which were carbonised. The features analysed were a series of pits, gullies, layers, spreads, wells, hearths and hollows, most of which were found to contain mixed material originating from varied sources such as midden, cess, craft workshops and stable waste.

The results are summarised by both phase and feature. The discussion focuses on specific questions such as diet; economic importance of useful species; the local environment; exploitation of surrounding landscapes such as heath, moor and woodland, and how this assemblage can contribute to a greater understanding of the nature of this site. A comparison is made with other sites of a similar date.

Methodology

Processing was undertaken according to the method described by Kenward et al. (1980). Identifications were confirmed using modern reference material and seed atlases (Cappers et al. 2006; Jacomet 2006, Tomlinson 1985a). Four features from Phases 1 to 3 were selected for moss identifications. The macroplant assemblage was quantified using a four point semi-abundance system. The results are summarised in a series of charts (Figures 4.57 & 4.58) and short tables (Appendix 3, Tables A3.1–A3.6) A description of the methodology and full results can be found in the site archive.

The assemblage

The assemblage contained a range of plant species originating from both urban and rural landscapes. The assemblage was mainly well preserved through anaerobic 'waterlogging' conditions, with a smaller quantity of charred remains. No mineralised finds were recovered. While it is possible that such material was overlooked during processing, the identification of mineralised matter from other Aberdeen sites is limited and it is unlikely that it was missed. Of the 100 features and deposits analysed, the assemblages from 45 were of little analytical value as they contained only small quantities of plant taxa that could not be interpreted with any degree of reliability. In the remaining features it was possible to identify specific usage, e.g. features being used or reused to dispose of mixed rubbish, human cess, stable and craft workshop waste. The plant remains contribute to understanding of the utilisation of features, evidencing for example periods of temporary disuse or abandonment of their original purpose, and the taphonomic processes that formed deposits.

Cereals

A large assemblage of food remains was recovered from Phases 1 to 5, in particular cereals, which formed an important part of the diet for both humans and livestock in the medieval and post-medieval periods. Oat caryopses and to a lesser degree barley were the dominant cereal species recovered. The economic predominance of oats and barley is not unexpected given the northerly location and cold climate of Aberdeen. Wheat/rye bran was recovered from several cess pits, although not in the same quantities as the other cereal remains. The successful cultivation of bread wheat requires specific environmental conditions which would have made large-scale commercial cultivation in the Aberdeen locality difficult. It is more likely that bread wheat was either grown on a small scale or imported; it would therefore be an expensive food item in comparison with the more easily available oats and barley.

THE CEREAL CROPS

FRUITS & NUTS

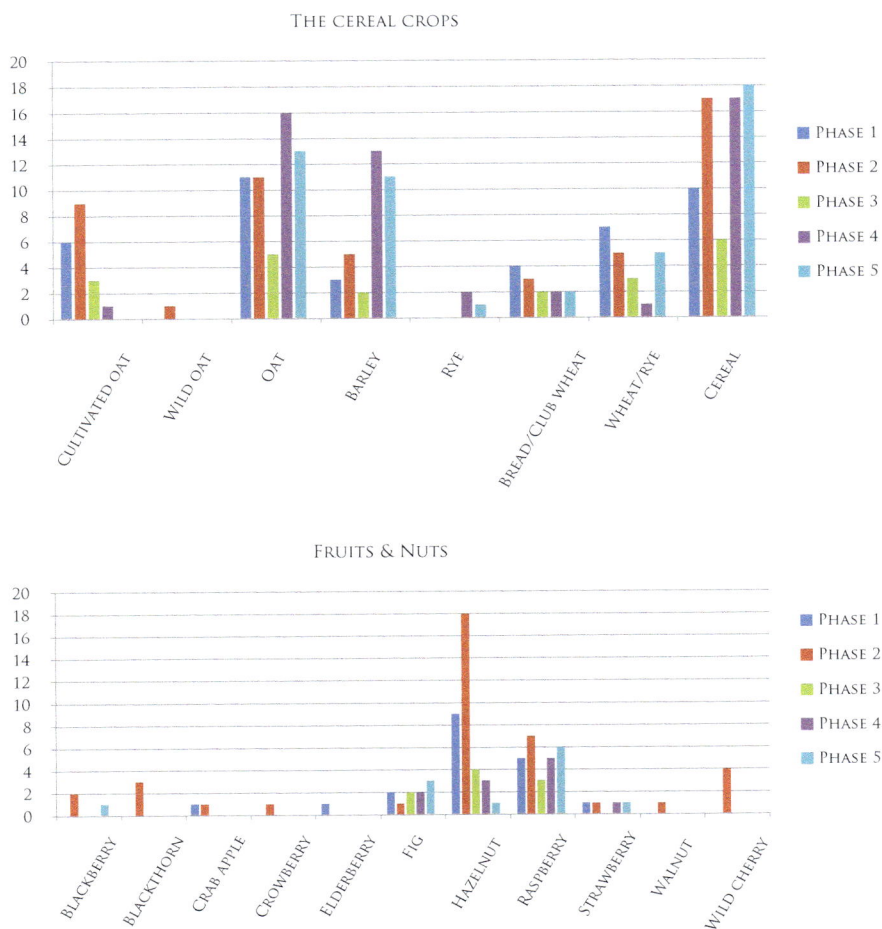

Figure 4.57 Upper; cereals recovered from Phases 1–5 by feature
Lower; fruits and nuts recovered from Phases 1–5 by feature (the numbers on the x/y
axis represent the number of contexts in which the species were found)

Large quantities of compacted cereal straw recovered from features in Phases 1 to 3, coupled with the presence of cereal chaff and embedded animal dung, indicates that these remains originated from stable floors. Much of the material identified as waste from stable floors had on visual inspection endured sustained trampling, creating distinct compact deposits that contained built up layers of straw, chaff, cereal fragments and suspected animal dung. The compilation of all these materials created distinctive indicator groups typically representative of stable floor litter (Kenward and Kenward 1997). It is unlikely that this material originated from cereal processing, roofing or other building material. Given the industrial nature of this area during Phases 1 to 3, it is unlikely that food stuffs destined for human consumption would be stored in any great quantity and then processed *in situ*.

The production of alcohol, in particular beer, was a common practice throughout the medieval period. There is, however, no substantive archaeobotanical evidence of large-scale beer production being practised

on the site. A small quantity of sprouted barley recovered from a single context in Phase 4 is not representative of large or even small-scale brewing – grain will sprout if improperly stored in damp conditions or left on urine-soaked stable floors. Nor was there any significant evidence of the use of plants for flavouring alcoholic drinks. Germinated barley caryopses recovered from Phase 4 were probably stored in a damp environment and are most likely to be domestic refuse.

Vegetables, fruits and nuts

The vegetable remains identified were onion/leek, turnip, cabbage and parsnip. The recovery of parsnip from two features in Phases 2 and 3 is unusual as this has not previously been identified at any other site in Aberdeen, and additionally is absent from excavations in medieval Perth. The parsnip is the cultivated rather than the wild variety; this suggests that this plant was deliberately introduced as a food rather than accidentally as an intrusive weed. It is unclear if this species was deliberately cultivated in Aberdeen

THE VEGETABLES

ECONOMICALLY USEFUL PLANTS

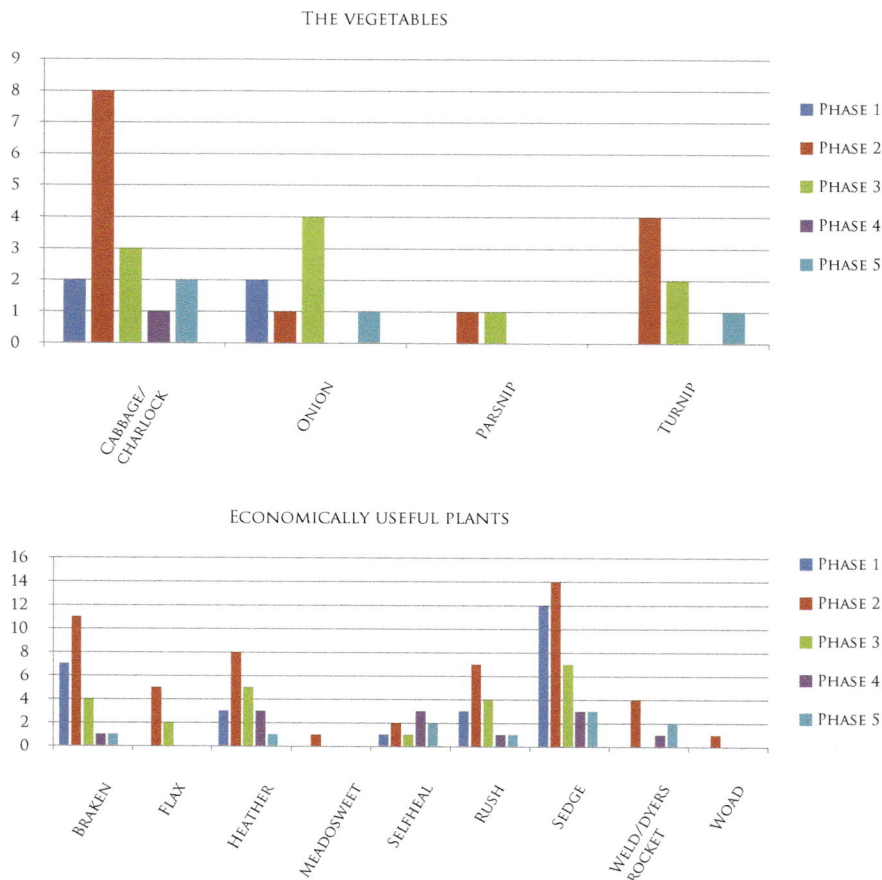

Figure 4.58 Upper; vegetable remains recovered from Phases 1–5 by feature
Lower; potentially useful plants recovered from Phases 1–5 by feature (the numbers on
the x/y axis represent the number of contexts in which the species were found)

during this period – parsnip is more likely to have been successfully grown in a warmer southerly climate. It is possible that this was an imported good. The other vegetables such as the onion/leek, turnips and cabbage were staples of the medieval diet and were cultivated on both a large scale and in family gardens and allotments. It is possible that these vegetables were grown on site to supplement the diet of the inhabitants, particularly during Phases 4 and 5 when the setting became more domestic and the land was utilised as gardens for growing food rather than housing stables and workshops.

The fruit remains were more varied – the population had access to a wide range of locally grown produce, wild resources and imported goods. Among the most readily available local products were raspberry, strawberry, apple, blackberry, wild cherry and blackthorn. The availability of these locally grown fruits would have been dependent on the season and whether the fruits had been preserved. These fruits could either be harvested from nearby wild resources or cultivated deliberately in garden plots and allotments. Unlike the other fruit remains, cherry and blackthorn stones were

only recovered from Phase 2 cess pits. It is unlikely that these fruits were unavailable during the other phases and therefore their absence from the archaeological record is likely due to other factors. A single cherry stone still had part of the badly decayed fruit attached. Several cherry stones retrieved from a cess pit also appeared to have been partly digested.

Fig seeds were recovered from Phases 1 to 5. They were almost certainly imported, and probably in a dried condition, and their presence in every phase shows that figs were readily available throughout the medieval period. Another imported food is walnut, which was recovered from a single context in Phase 2. Walnut has previously been recovered from one other site in Aberdeen and from Perth (Hall *et al.* 2004; Fraser and Smith 2011).

Hazelnut shells, in particular half shells and fragments, were recovered in abundant quantities from Phases 1 to 5. A small quantity of whole hazelnut shells was retrieved from a single pit in Phase 2, although these had suffered some damage attributable to rodents. Whether these pest attacks occurred prior to the hazelnut being disposed of is unknown. Hazelnut shells tend to be among the more abundant finds from the medieval period, due to their easy availability. It is, however, debatable whether hazelnuts were in fact economically important during the medieval period, or if they are simply relatively overrepresented within the archaeobotanical assemblage, as they tend to survive in a range of environmental conditions that prove detrimental to other, more fragile, plant taxa. However, given the abundant and varied macroplant remains present within this assemblage, it appears that hazelnuts are not overrepresented and did indeed have an important role within the medieval economy around Bon Accord. This is supported by the equally large quantities of shell fragments that have been recovered from earlier excavations in Aberdeen (Fraser and Dickson 1982; Hall *et al.* 2004), Perth (Fraser and Smith 2011) and St Andrews (Hastie and Holden 2001.

The vegetable and fruit taxa were mostly recovered from those features identified as containing cess waste, specifically suspected human faecal matter. This is probably a result of the cess pit deposits offering the most suitable environment for the preservation of fragile plant material. The vegetable and fruit remains were concentrated in Phase 2. This may be because in Phase 2 there was a greater degree of activity, with particular emphasis on craft workshops and stabling, than any other phase.

Woodland

Woodland remains were noted in all five phases but were concentrated in much larger quantities within the first three. These consisted primarily as wood chips, some of which were worked, bark, buds and leaf fragments; these were identified as a mix of birch, oak and willow. The wood fragments have derived from larger pieces of wood deliberately brought to site which were worked in this location to provide material for construction. The wood chips were either disposed of within the features or were deliberately recycled to provide floor surfaces. In Phases 1 to 3 the bark appears to have been stripped off in large sections probably to provide lining for tanning pits. The leaf fragments and buds are accidental inclusions of the wood.

Economically useful plants

Plants from the assemblage that could potentially be used to produce dyes included woad, which would have produced a blue dye, and weld/dyers rocket which produced a yellow dye. The evidence for the processing of weld/dyers rocket to produce dye is, however, difficult to substantiate.

Evidence for the production of woad dye occurred in Phase 2 in Pit C018, where small fragments of woad

(*Isatis tinctoria* silicula) and an abundance of matted spiral thickenings were recovered, along with some decayed wool fragments. No other part of the woad plant was recovered, although this is not unusual as part of the dyeing process involves leaving the sample to decompose. Similar evidence of woad dyeing has previously been recorded from a waterlogged 9th to 10th century deposit at Coppergate, York (Tomlinson 1985b). Pit C018 offered the most conclusive evidence for the presence of either a dye bath or dye waste disposal on site.

Phase 2 contained the largest concentration of weld/dyers rocket seeds; these were concentrated in specific pits within Phase 2, with only background traces recovered from Phases 4 and 5 and were completely absent from Phases 1 and 3. No other part of the plant was recovered and the absence of any other remains means that these seeds in themselves are inconclusive evidence for dyeing, as they may have been introduced as an intrusive weed. However, unlike other plants used for producing dyes, it is not unusual to recover just the seeds of dyers rocket, which are typically found in the location used for dyeing.

The presence of both woad and weld/dyers rocket within Pit C018 is strong evidence for the production of blue and yellow dyes in this area, though probably on a small scale. Flax seeds were recovered from Phases 2 and 3, although no capsules were identified. The flax seeds were concentrated in Phase 2 with no obvious evidence of selective disposal. Flax can be utilised in several ways, most obviously as a food, in the production of textiles or as a companion crop for grasses. As noted above, Phase 2 has produced evidence for small-scale dyeing and it is possible that these flax remains may be indicative of textile production. However, the small quantity of flax recovered is clearly not representative of a large-scale textile industry. Pit C018, which was found to have evidence of woad dyeing, produced no flax or finished textile remains. This supports the interpretation that the flax seeds represent food residue. Furthermore, several were identified in pits believed to have contained cess.

The only evidence for medicinal plants was selfheal, which has antiseptic properties and was believed to cure a number of ailments. This plant was also a common weed and there is no obvious concentration of remains in any phase to suggest that it had been deliberately collected rather than being an intrusive weed. Meadowsweet was used as flavouring, particularly in alcoholic drinks. As only a single achene was recovered, its importance and economic role is unclear.

Heather and bracken were present in each of Phases 1 to 5; Phase 2 contained the largest concentration. Heather may have been introduced to the site accidentally with peat that was utilised as a fuel and building material. Both burnt peat and heather were recovered; the peat at least was used as a fuel source. Heather and bracken may also have been collected deliberately as a fuel, building or bedding material. Decayed turf blocks of peat, heather and other heath and moorland vegetation were recovered from several features from Phases 1 to 3. Some turf fragments had evidence of charring, indicating that they were probably used as a fuel source. The remainder could have been utilised as a building material or pit lining.

Rush and sedge were noted in all five phases but were concentrated within the first three. These plants tend to favour damp soils so it is possible they grew naturally on the site and represent accidental accumulations of weed taxa within the assemblage. However, given the industrial nature of the site and the presence of animals during the early phases, it is equally possible that rush and sedge were deliberately collected for use as thatching, flooring and bedding within workshops and stables.

The moss species recovered are unlikely to have grown on the site and instead were imported either accidentally or deliberately. Among the species identified *Sphagnum* sp (p), while having some economic uses, was probably transferred as inclusions within peat. Mosses were found in nearly all the samples and were particularly abundant in those features found to contain cess. The moss species recovered from the cess pits have previously been identified on other medieval sites throughout Britain as being used for hygiene purposes, specifically as an alternative to toilet paper. Species including *Hylocomium splendens* (glittering woodmoss), *Hypnum Cupressiforme* (cypress-leaved plaitmoss), *Pleurozium schreberi* (red-stemmed feathermoss), *Rhytidiadelphus triquetrus* (big shaggy-moss), *Rhytidiadelphus squarrosus* (springy turf-moss), *Aulacomnium palustre* (bog groove-moss) and *Dicranum scoparium* (broom forkmoss) had specific uses analogous to modern toilet paper, antiseptic wraps, bandages and packing material. The moss recovered from those pits found to contain cess were typically those species used for hygiene purposes.

Weed taxa

The weed remains reflected a range of environments, including agricultural, waste ground, heathland, moorland, woodland and damp habitats. The most important agricultural weed, in terms of its impact on both human and animal health, was corn cockle. This was a particularly prevalent toxic weed during the medieval period and is commonly found on most archaeological sites where anaerobic conditions have aided preservation. The corn cockle fragments recovered from Bon Accord were concentrated in cess

pit deposits where bran was also present. This indicates that it was consumed with the bran; this would have had a debilitating effect on the consumer's health. Corn spurrey was found in one pit; in the past it has been used to supplement animal feed but it is also a host plant along with corn cockle which grows alongside cultivated crops.

The waste ground weed taxa were dominated by plants such as dock, nettle, fat hen, pale persicaria, nipplewort, wild radish and chickweed that were probably growing either as contaminants of the cereal crops or on disturbed ground surrounding the site. Evidence for the deliberate collection of many of these species to supplement both human diet and animal feed during periods of famine and hardship has been found on other Scottish sites (Robinson 1987). However, there is no evidence that any of these plants were deliberately harvested on a large scale. The heath, moor and woodland weeds were probably imported accidentally to the site alongside resources such as peat and wood. Those plant taxa which favour wet soils probably grew nearby and reflect the continuing damp nature of the site during its occupation. This accidentally imported but unwanted plant material was either disposed of within these features or was able to colonise available ground and create an ecological niche on site.

Site development

The plant material from Phases 1 to 5 provides an insight into how Bon Accord developed over time. From Phases 1 to 3 this area appears to have been located on the outer perimeter of the urban settlement of Aberdeen. This is reflected in the macroplant assemblage. One explanation for the peripheral nature of the site at this time is the type of unpleasant craft activities undertaken there; in the medieval period these tended to be deliberately situated on the outskirts of settlement away from more domestic neighbourhoods.

From Phases 1 to 3 there is strong artefactual evidence, alongside some environmental evidence, of tanning and leatherworking having occurred on site. Several features in Phases 1 and 2 contained large quantities of bark which had been deliberately stripped off in large sections; this could potentially have been used in tanning either as a pit lining or in some other part of the process. The recovery of the bark is not conclusive proof in itself of tanning as it could have been intended for some other process. Unfortunately, surviving bark 'sclereids', a good indicator of tanning, were not detected in any of these contexts.

The macroplant evidence for Phases 1 to 3 reflected an industrial site with particular evidence for craft activities such as tanning and dyeing. Throughout Phases 1 to 3 there is strong evidence that waste from workshops and stable floors was being disposed of on site. From Phases 4 and 5 there is no evidence of any surviving waste from industrial workshops; most of the remains appear to have originated from human cess and other domestic sources as opposed to craft and stable waste. This indicates a change in the use of the area, probably as a result of the expansion of Aberdeen. As the area around Bon Accord developed into a more domestic area of Aberdeen rather than a peripheral industrial zone on the outskirts of settlement, features such as animal stabling and workshops may have relocated. By Phases 4 to 5 there is a noticeable decrease in the quantity of heather, bracken and rural plant taxa being recovered. There is no evidence from any of these later phases that ornamental gardening was ever practised; instead the assemblage recovered included a mix of food remains, useful plants and weed taxa.

Taphonomy

Although there was some lack of precision in the phasing of some features, this is inevitable on such a heavily developed urban site where continual rebuilding has resulted in disturbance to deposits and subsequent truncation of features. However, overall the archaeological security and taphonomic development of these deposits is relatively secure. There was a noticeable difference in preservation between the different phases and levels. Phases 1 to 3 contained significantly more waterlogged remains, suggesting that the anaerobic conditions in the lower levels was more stable. It is possible that the samples from Phases 4 to 5 have undergone some degradation prior to excavation but after their original deposition. Post-medieval and modern development on the site including piling and cellar construction may have contributed to the degradation of these deposits. Similar problems with preservation that could be ascribed to changes in groundwater levels have been noted in both Aberdeen and York with regards to late medieval and post-medieval deposits (Allan Hall, *pers comm*).

Comparative assemblages

The macroplant assemblage from Bon Accord is similar to those reported from previous excavations in Aberdeen including 16–18 Netherkirkgate, 30–46 Upperkirkgate, Gallowgate Middle School, 45–75 Gallowgate, 42 St Paul Street and Queen Street Midden Area (Fraser and Dickson 1982; Hall *et al.* 2004). The Bon Accord assemblage has corroborated many of the previous findings concerning diet, utilisation of plants and the local environment of Aberdeen. Where Bon Accord differs from previous environmental studies is in the greater number of contexts analysed.

Several of the plant remains previously identified in Aberdeen were not recovered from this site, including

coriander, opium poppy, cannabis and flax capsule fragments. However, cultivated parsnip, which has not been recorded on any other site in Aberdeen, was recovered from Bon Accord. The site has also offered strong evidence for the production of woad dye. As at other Aberdeen sites, there is evidence for the regular exploitation of peat, heath and moorland resources, particularly during Phases 1 to 3. Exploitation of such resources is not evidenced in Perth on the same scale (Fraser and Smith 2011). In summary, the plant assemblage recovered from Bon Accord is not markedly dissimilar to those already identified at earlier excavations undertaken in Aberdeen (Fraser and Dickson 1982; Hall *et al.* 2004), Perth (Fraser and Smith 2011), St Andrews (Hastie and Holden 2001) and York and Doncaster (Tomlinson 1985b.

Conclusions

The varied plant assemblage contained a large quantity of generally well preserved food remains, useful plants and weed taxa. From this assemblage it was possible to analyse evidence for the chronological development of the site; the specific activities undertaken on site; the processes of utilisation and abandonment of features; the local environment and the diet of the inhabitants.

The archaeobotanical evidence gathered from Phases 1 to 3 indicates that during the late 12th century and the 13th century the site was located on the periphery of Aberdeen and was used to house animals and craft workshops. The assemblage was concentrated in Phase 2, either because preservation was particularly good at this level or alternatively, and more probably, due to a peak in activity. The best evidence of tanning and dyeing derives from Phase 2, when the site was experiencing intensive use. Phase 3 witnessed a decline in the volume of stable waste recovered and this may represent the beginning of the transition from an industrial site which housed animal pens, stables and craft workshops to a more domestic setting.

The noticeable decrease in the heath and moorland taxa recovered from Phases 4 and 5 could be due to several factors. The most likely explanation is that the heath and moorland were no longer as easily accessible as they once had been and as the area had become less peripheral and more domestic in nature reliance on these heath/moor resources may have decreased accordingly. If these materials were not brought to site in the same concentrations as previously, this would also have reduced the opportunity for wild weed taxa to be introduced.

The foods consumed by the inhabitants are all typical of the medieval period. There is a clear dependence on cereals, particularly oats, barley and to a lesser degree wheat/rye. The bran was clearly contaminated with corn cockle which, if consumed along with the grain, would have had a detrimental effect on human health. The other food staples included a variety of locally grown vegetables and fruits which would have been readily available depending on seasonality. There was also evidence of imported goods, such as figs, which were consumed throughout Phases 1 to 5.

The plant assemblage recovered from Bon Accord is similar to those previously identified from other Scottish medieval excavations. As such the conclusions reached within this report are not dissimilar to those already observed in previously excavated Aberdeen and Perth sites. Where Bon Accord differs from other studies is in the larger number of samples analysed, leading to a good representation of how the site developed between the 12th and the 17th centuries. The macroplant analysis of Bon Accord has proved valuable in contributing to furthering our understanding of the environmental archaeology of medieval Aberdeen.

4.5.2 Mammal bone
Jennifer Thoms and Jackaline Robertson

Introduction

A sub-sample of 3331 mammal bone fragments was submitted for analysis from the excavation at Bon Accord. The bulk of the mammal bone assemblage came from a range of waterlogged pits, ditches, gullies and postholes dated to the medieval to post-medieval period. Preservation of the bone was mostly described as good due to the anaerobic conditions and this has presented an excellent opportunity to understand how this location in Aberdeen developed from the medieval period onwards. The bone has accumulated through three main identifiable sources of activity: the disposal of primary butchery waste; commercial debris from tanning, horn and antler working, and a smaller concentration of domestic food refuse.

Aims

The stratified nature of the deposits at Bon Accord has created the opportunity to analyse the industrial practices and diet of Aberdeen and how the site changed from an industrial to a domestic setting within an archaeologically secure time period. This has made it possible to establish how the commercial industries including butchery, horn working and tanning were later displaced by a more domestic landscape. The aim of this study was to establish the animal species present, their role and economic significance to the people living in Bon Accord.

Methods

To ensure sufficient evidence was obtained from this large animal bone assemblage a sub-sample was selected from the six archaeological phases and modern disturbance. Particular attention was focused on features identified by artefactual and stratigraphic evidence as belonging to the 12th and 13th centuries, a period marked by abundant cut features with rich waterlogged deposits, with a much smaller number analysed from the later periods. An important aim has been the presentation of the data collected in a comprehensive and comprehensible format for storage in the archives in order that future workers can interrogate it should the need arise. There remains a large body of material, in particular from medieval contexts, which it is hoped will in the future provide the basis of a more comprehensive study of the economy of this area of medieval Aberdeen.

The bones were identified by comparison with modern reference material, keys and texts stored at AOC archaeology (Cohen and Serjeantson 1996; Hillson 1986; Schmid 1972; Boessneck 1969). Bones which could not be identified to species where described as large mammal (L/M), medium mammal (M/M) or small mammal (S/M) where appropriate. Any bone which could not be confidently identified as either sheep or goat was instead grouped together as sheep/goat. No attempt was made to identify ribs and vertebrae and they were instead categorised by size, where appropriate.

The assemblage was analysed for evidence of age at death by recording epiphyseal fusion, tooth eruption and wear (Grant 1982; Payne 1973 & 1987; Silver 1969). Evidence of butchery, pathology, burning, animal gnawing, fragmentation and staining were also catalogued (Dobney and Reilly 1988). Staining was recorded using a five point system: no staining was described as 0; staining of less than 25% of the bone surface was 1; 25–50 % surface staining was 2; 50–75% was rated 3, and more than 75% rated 4. A similar method was used for assessing the preservation of the bone fragment, the categories a, b, c and d representing bones in excellent, good, fair and poor condition respectively. Only those bones found to be intact were measured (von den Driesch 1976).

The assemblage was quantified using number of identifiable specimens (NISP). While this method has its drawbacks, it is the most reliable method to use for a site such as this. No corrections have been made to compensate for the fact that some elements (toes and teeth for example) are more abundant within the mammalian skeleton than others. Such differences will be consistent over the whole site and can be taken into consideration when interpreting the results.

Table 4.20 Number of identifiable specimens (NISP) count for mammals by phase

Species	Phase 1/3	Phase 1	Phase 2	Phase 3	Phase 3/4	Phase 4	Phase 4/5	Phase 5	Phase 5/6	Phase 6	Phase 7/Modern	Total
Cattle	20	459	567	96	68	184	3	129	20	3	1	1550
Horse		35	5	2	7	10		10				69
Red deer		18	27	5	2	4						56
Roe deer		2	3			1		1				7
Sheep	1	25	90	14	5	7		12	1			155
Goat	2	46	58	7	2	6		1				122
Sheep/goat	4	168	289	69	43	65	2	64	8			712
Pig	1	50	87	15	11	19		14	1			198
Dog		12	20	16	1	30		3				82
Dog/fox		2										2
Cat	1	22	17	2	1	7		19	1	1		71
Rodent			1									1
L/M	4	54	54	12	7	12		20	1			164
M/M		26	63	14	5	10		16		1		135
S/M			5		1			1				7
Total	33	919	1286	252	153	355	5	290	32	5	1	3331

MNI (minimum number of individuals) has not been calculated as it is believed to be a flawed method, particularly unsuited to urban assemblages (O'Connor 2003:, 133–35) as it is probable that most animals would have been bred, reared and, possibly, butchered away from the site, and it is likely that prepared joints of the larger animals especially, would have been imported onto site.

A total of 218 bones were measured and when compared to other sites in Aberdeen and Edinburgh the animals were found to be of a similar stature. This was true for both the large and small domestic species.

The assemblage

The species and number of fragments recovered by phase are listed in Table 4.20. The assemblage was dominated by domestic species, in particular cattle. While all skeletal elements were represented, the most common finds were skull fragments and foot bones, with smaller quantities of long bones, scapula and pelvises. The deposition of animal bones at this site clearly peaked during Phases 1 to 2, particularly in Phase 2. The number of bones noticeably decreased in Phase 3 before marginally increasing in Phases 4 to 5. The bone fragments from the late post-medieval Phase 6 and modern disturbance are recorded in the table but are not included within the discussion below. The differing quantities of bone recovered from Bon Accord reflect how the site itself changed over time in developing from a primarily industrial area to a domestic setting; this had consequences for how animals were utilised and ultimately disposed of within the confines of the site.

Species dominance and diet

The assemblage is dominated by domestic mammals – analysis of NISP revealed that cattle (1550) were the most economically important species in all phases. Important species also included sheep (155); goat (122); sheep/goat (712), and pig (198). The presence of sheep and pig is relatively constant throughout the history of the site but the numbers of identifiable goat remains noticeably decreases from Phase 3 onwards. The other domestic species were horse (69), dog (84) and cat (71), which were present only in small numbers. Wild species were represented by red deer (56) and roe deer (7), but only in small numbers, and these were generally concentrated in the earlier phases.

Cattle

Cattle was the most economically important species at Bon Accord, and this remained true throughout the existence of the site, but the role of these animals appears to have altered over time. The reliance on beef as the most economically important meat was constant from the medieval period onwards. The cattle present appeared to be of the short horned variety, similar to those previously analysed at Aberdeen (Smith and McCormick 2001: 273).

The animals may have been corralled at or near the site during Phases 1 and 2 – the presence of neonates likely confirms such penning. It is likely that cattle herds arrived at the site on the hoof from the nearby hinterlands and were corralled prior to slaughter which either occurred directly on site or very close to it. The animals were then butchered by professionals who disposed of the waste, generally within the pit features.

Domestic cooking waste and primary cuts of meat are largely missing from Phases 1 to 3. This is not surprising as the animals butchered at Bon Accord were destined to have their meat exported from site for sale, consumption and ultimate disposal outwith the confines of this immediate area. The bone waste during Phases 1 to 2 is largely dominated by primary butchery waste; there is also evidence to suggest that some, if not all, of the cattle were skinned for use in the tanning and dyeing workshops on site. This is supported by the presence of horn core, animal hair (Section 4.2.4) and evidence of dyeing plants (Section 4.5.1), which indicates the presence of other industries and craft shops working alongside the butchers and using the same refuse pits for disposal. In particular, relatively large amounts of animal fibre were recovered between Phase 2 and early Phase 4, including goatskin, cattle hide, calfskin and sheepskins, suggesting that some of the pits on site were used for the de-hairing of skin (Section 4.2.4).

The cattle remains deposited in Phase 3 experienced a sharp decline with only a marginal increase in Phases 4 and 5. The cattle remains from Phase 3 were still representative of butchery waste with perhaps some horn working debris but it appears that these industries were on the decline and probably relocating to the outskirts of Aberdeen. By Phases 4 to 5 the cattle remains were more representative of domestic food waste with a much smaller quantity of butchery

debris. All evidence of horn working and tanning had completely disappeared from the later phases. The quality of the cuts of beef is also relatively high in terms of meat value and this suggests that the community now living in this area were economically secure, if not members of the elite.

Sheep

Sheep were present in Phases 1 to 5 but were concentrated in the earliest two phases, especially Phase 2. The sheep remains in Phases 1 to 3 were dominated by mandibles and foot bones with a smaller number of long bones and horn cores. These remains derived from butchery waste. The elements from Phase 4 to 5 are composed mostly of long bones with a much smaller number of skull fragments and foot bones. The sheep bone recovered from the later phases appears to represent cooking and food refuse rather than primary butchery waste. There was also evidence of a small number of polled sheep skull fragments but species with horns were more numerous. The small number of sheep bones suggests that lamb and mutton was not an important source of meat but had only a secondary role in the medieval diet onwards. The quality of the cuts of meat in the later phases is relatively high and this confirms the relatively affluent status of the people living in the area of the site.

Goat

The skeletal similarities between goat and sheep can make separating the two species difficult but it was possible to confidently identify 122 fragments as goat. This was partly due to the presence of horn core, which are unique to each species. Of the 122 goat bones, 88 were horn cores with a much smaller number of skull, mandible, foot and long bone fragments. The goat remains were concentrated in Phases 1 to 2 – there appeared to be deliberate and large scale disposal of horn core within the medieval pits. These remains are representative of horn working debris and it is likely that the goat skins were also removed for tanning. Goat meat was relatively popular in the medieval period; these animals were easier to feed than the other main domesticates as they could survive on scrub land (Hodgson et al. 2011: 44). The small number of these cuts of meat indicates that they were transported off site and consumed and disposed of elsewhere during the earlier phases.

From Phase 3 onwards the number of identifiable goat bones decreases dramatically, indicating that the industrial nature of this site was changing to a domestic landscape. As the horn working, tanning and dying workshops relocated, the demand for goat at Bon Accord decreased accordingly. It is possible that some of the bone described as sheep/goat is in fact goat but even with this consideration it is obvious that by Phase 3 the economic importance of goat was limited and that this animal was not sought after for its meat in the later phases. The exploitation of goat for meat does not appear to have been a major consideration for the people living around the site in the post-medieval period.

Pig

Pig bones were recovered from Phases 1 to 5, concentrated in Phases 1 and 2. These remains were composed of mandibles, loose teeth, long bones and foot bones which comprised a mixture of both high value and low quality cuts of meat. The bones, particularly in Phases 1 to 3, were all derived from butchery waste. The small number of pig bones in all phases demonstrates that pork only ever had a minor role in the diet of the people living here.

Horse

A small number of horse remains were present in Phases 1 to 5, again concentrated in the earlier medieval phases, particularly Phase 1. These included intact skulls, vertebrae, long bones and foot bones. There was evidence that at least one individual was deposited in a semi-articulated condition, demonstrated by the recovery of at least one skull still attached to the vertebral column (Pit C015). The deposition of semi-articulated animals indicates that horse carcasses were only partially dismembered for reuse in the surrounding workshops. During life, these horses would have had value as trained working animals while after death, and when dismembered, their value resided in their flesh and skin.

Dog

While remains of dogs were found in Phases 1 to 5, on initial analysis it appeared that these were concentrated in Phase 4. Closer analysis identified that the majority of the bones derived from dogs in this phase were recovered from Layer C075, and belonged to a single individual. The next highest quantities of dog bones were within Phases 1 and 2, and pertained to multiple individuals. Two bones in Phases 1 and 3 had been butchered; this was the only evidence to indicate that this species was potentially skinned for its fur or meat. The dog material recovered from Phases 1 to 3 probably represents a mixture of craft shop waste, scavengers, working animals and pets. It is clear that the dog remains in the later phases derived solely from the disposal of pets and feral animals and not from industrial waste.

Cat

The cat remains were concentrated in Phases 1 to 2 and represented several animals. Smaller numbers of cat bones were present in Phases 3 and 4. In phase 5 a semi-articulated cat skeleton was recovered from Well A001. The cat remains from Phases 1 to 2 comprised a mixture of both adult and juvenile individuals. Three of the adult cat bones from Phase 1 had skinning marks; the butchered cat bones are a strong indicator that these animals were deliberately skinned for their fur. These animals may also have been semi-feral scavengers that were deliberately culled in an effort to control numbers of a species viewed as vermin, particularly in times of disease outbreak. The deposition of the semi-articulated animal in Well A001 in Phase 5 could have occurred through several processes, the most obvious being that the animal became accidently trapped; was buried after death, or was deliberately culled. How this cat came to be deposited in the well is therefore unclear but it is apparent that by Phase 5 this species was no longer being skinned for its fur – by the post-medieval period cats were typically house pets, working animals or opportunistic semi-feral scavengers.

Deer

Remains of two wild species, red deer and roe deer, were concentrated in Phases 1 and 2, with smaller numbers in the later phases. The red deer remains were dominated by antler fragments, which were most numerous in Phases 1 and 2. A large number of the antlers had been butchered by either being sawn off at the base where they attached to the skull, or chopped off. The remaining red deer fragments were made up of skull, mandible and foot bones with a smaller number of long bones. The red deer antler appears to have been deliberately disposed of at site during the early phases as a waste by-product of antler working. The rest of the bones were probably butchery waste.

The roe deer remains were composed of long bones and foot bones. The absence of any antler indicates that the roe deer disposed of at Bon Accord were exploited solely for meat.

Mortality profile and sex

Age at death was calculated using epiphyseal fusion, tooth eruption and wear. Where possible, the sex of the animals was determined by examination of antler and teeth.

Cattle

The age at which the cattle were culled varied between phases and was dictated by what role the animal was required to fulfil. Examination of fusion, tooth eruption and wear highlighted three specific peaks at which death occurred for these animals.

In Phases 1 and 2 there was a minimum of three neonatal calves. Two of these were located in Phase 1 Pit C015. The presence of neonates suggests that either herds were brought to site from the surrounding countryside, with their young, or that pregnant cattle gave birth on site, and the calves were quickly slaughtered. The reason for culling such young animals during the early phases at Bon Accord would have been to provide supple skin for leather working and tanning. The meat value of young animals compared to a fully mature adult is obviously smaller, so the role of the neonates was likely to provide leather rather than to provide meat. The second peak at which death occurred was between the ages of 6 months and two years – there is also evidence that one individual, at least, died between the ages of 5 and 6 months. This could be the culling of excess animals, perhaps males not required for breeding or as draught animals that had obtained a satisfactory meat value and could also be exploited for their skins for leather working. The next period of slaughter occurred after the animals were older than four years. These individuals were probably older breeding stock and dairy herds which were no longer required for these activities.

In the later phases at Bon Accord there do not appear to be any young individuals, the youngest was found to be between 3 and 4 years, while the rest were older than 4 years. In Bon Accord in Phases 1 and 2 animals appear to have been slaughtered for both their meat and skin, whereas in Phases 3, 4 and 5 this was primarily a meat economy.

Sheep

The sheep appear to have been culled at four peak ages and these peaks varied according to phase. In Phases 1 to 3 the economy was mixed, with both young and mature sheep being slaughtered for meat and skin. This changed in Phases 4 and 5 where only mature and older animals were being killed to satisfy a meat economy.

Examination of fusion and tooth wear revealed the presence of neonates in Phases 1 to 2. There was evidence that some individuals possibly died in utero or shortly after birth. Certainly, a relatively large proportion of these animals did not appear to have survived beyond the age of six weeks. It is unusual to recover such young animals on an urban site as typically the weaker young would die and be disposed of in the countryside. The most obvious explanation is that the flocks were imported to the site from the nearby countryside with their young, or that at least some of the sheep gave birth on site. The next age at which the

animals were culled, in Phases 1 to 3, was between the ages of 18 and 36 months. At this age the sheep reached their optimum size and were culled primarily for their meat. It was probably also an opportunity to cull excess males or free up fodder for the winter season.

The next peak at which animals were slaughtered was identified in Phase 4 to 5 remains and was generally around the age of 3 to 4 years. The oldest animals were found in the later phases – some were approximately six years or perhaps older at the time of death. These older animals were in all likelihood females, used first for their wool, milk and breeding before being slaughtered. From Phase 4 onwards there was no evidence of young animals, just those in their prime or older; this likely indicates that the nature of the economy had changed from a commercial/industrial one, which required young animals, to a domestic setting which was satisfied with the provision of meat from older animals.

Goat

One fragment of horn core could be identified as being from an adult goat, while a fragment of goat humerus was from an animal older than 10 months.

Pig

The analysis of fusion and tooth wear for the pigs revealed that only one individual died before the age of seven weeks. The remaining animals all appeared to be fully mature and with most over one year old. There also appeared to be more females than males – females probably generally survived longer, kept for breeding, as pigs have no secondary products to exploit during their lifetime. During Phases 1 and 2 the pigs were probably butchered for both their meat and skins whereas by the later periods their remains accumulated through the disposal of domestic food waste.

Horse

The horse remains, based on both fusion and tooth wear, demonstrated that all individuals were fully mature and adult. It was also possible to establish the presence of two males. One individual was approximately 12 years at the time of death and the other was older than 15 years.

Dog

The dog remains from Phases 1 and 2 comprised both juveniles and adults. The two youngest animals appeared to have died before the age of six months. The remaining dogs from the later phases appeared to be fully mature.

Cat

The cat remains from Phases 1 to 4 comprised a mixture of both juveniles and adults. The cat from Phase 5 was an adult.

Deer

The red deer bones were all found to belong to adult males. The roe deer were identified as a mixture of juveniles and adults.

Butchery

The term 'butchered' refers to any bone displaying marks made by a knife, saw, cleaver or any other implement. The butchery techniques employed at Bon Accord were typical of most Scottish medieval and post-medieval sites in that the carcasses were dismembered using a range of implements such as saws, cleavers, axes and knives to remove antler, horn, skin and cuts of meat.

Cattle

Butchery marks were observed on 138 cattle bones, which were concentrated in Phases 1 and 2. The analysed butchered bones from Phases 3 to 5 accounted for only 27 fragments. These were mostly foot bones followed by a smaller number of mandibles and long bones. There were combinations of marks made by chopping with a cleaver, and skinning and de-fleshing marks made by a knife. Several horn cores had also been chopped or sawn off at the base of the skull.

Sheep

A total of 28 sheep bones had been butchered, again concentrated in Phases 1 and 2 with only five noted in the later phases. The butchered bones were mostly composed of metapodials, with a smaller number of long bones. These shallow marks were interpreted as the result of de-fleshing and skinning made by a knife.

Goat

A large quantity of the goat horn had evidence of long, thin dismembering marks near where the horn joined the skull. This process was undertaken to remove the chitinous sheath of the horn, which was intended for use in bone working to make artefacts such as bowls and cutlery.

Pig

Butchery marks were noted on 29 pig bones, concentrated in Phases 1 and 2, with only three in later periods. Most of the butchered bones were long bones subjected to chopping and filleting with cleavers and knives.

Horse

There is evidence that one horse skull from Phase 1 Pit C015 had been pole-axed but it is likely that this did not kill the individual outright as a second blow was required below the right eye before the animal was felled. A second horse skull from the same feature had signs of multiple shallow skinning marks associated with the bone surrounding the left eye. A further two long bones and a metacarpal also had evidence of skinning marks. Horse meat could have been intended for consumption either by humans or animals such as working dogs. Opinion is currently divided as to whether medieval Scottish populations regularly consumed horse flesh and certainly the Christian church had opposed its use as a food source as early as the 8th century (Hodgson et al. 2011: 41–43). The evidence from Bon Accord is similar to that already reported at other Scottish sites in Inverkeithing, Inverness and Aberdeen where horses were certainly butchered, but it remains unclear whether humans or dogs were the intended recipients (ibid, 43). The skin and skeletal elements were probably used in the industrial workshops present on site, for example in leatherworking and glue making.

Dog

A single dog ulna from Phase 1 had had one shallow skinning mark. A femur from Phase 3 had ten small knife marks on its shaft. Cut marks on a dog pelvis found in a pit at 45–75 Gallowgate were interpreted by Smith and McCormick (2001) as having been made during the removal of the pelt. The femur butchered at Bon Accord had evidence of knife marks around the proximal head (where it joins the pelvis), presumably resulting from the same skinning process noted by Smith and McCormick (2001). Dog flesh has at times been eaten but normally only in times of hardship and famine. There is no evidence to suggest these animals were consumed at this site in this period.

Cat

Three cat bones had been subjected to skinning, all from Phase 1, and all belonging to an adult individual. The skinning marks were all small and shallow, probably undertaken in an effort to remove the fur with the minimum of damage. Cat as with dog has been eaten in times of hardship but again there is no evidence to support this.

Deer

A small total of 14 butchered deer bones is not surprising for a site like Bon Accord. This is because during the medieval period there were strict controls on hunting and typically venison was reserved for the upper classes such as the nobility and clergy (Hodgson *et al.* 2011: 34–35).

Bone working

Goat

Horn cores were a major component of this assemblage, particularly those of goats, and to a much smaller extent cattle and sheep. The horn core was concentrated in the pits in the medieval Phases 1 to 2 with smaller numbers present in the later periods. Goat horn cores have been noted at other sites in Scotland: Gallowgate Middle School (Cameron 2001) and 45–75 Gallowgate (Evans 2001) as well as further afield, e.g. Dordrecht, Dorestad and 's-Hertogenbosch (Prummel 1978; 1982 & 1983) in the Netherlands. Interpretation of this evidence has associated it with the presence of tanning industries. The decrease in goat horn after Phase 2, after the apparent peak of the tanning and leatherworking activity on site, may therefore similarly reflect the association of horn working and these other activities.

Some of the goat horn core had either been sawn or chopped off from the base of the skull. This would have been done to allow the horn cores to be soaked for weeks to loosen their chitinous sheaths, which would then be split lengthwise and boiled in cauldrons on hearths (Evans 2001: 113). The abundance of horns and the small bones of the lower leg on the site would also have attracted other, related industries, such as horn working and the production of neats-foot oil.

Deer

Most of the red deer antler had either been sawn or chopped in an effort to work it. The antler recovered from Phases 1 and 2 is probably bone working waste deposited by the surrounding craft workshops.

Discussion

The role of animals at Bon Accord was subject to change as the site developed from a commercial to a domestic landscape. The diet of the people living in Aberdeen remained fairly constant with beef the primary source of meat, and lamb, mutton and pork of secondary importance. This is in direct contrast to sites in the south-east of Scotland such as Advocates Close (Robertson, *forthcoming*), Jeffrey Street, Giles Street, Water Street (Tourunen 2014: 44), and the Holyrood Parliament site (Smith 2010) – all located in Edinburgh – and Bridgegate in Peebles (Smith and Henderson 2002). In this area of Scotland, lamb and mutton were typically the most important source of meat throughout the medieval period. This difference in diet is probably due

to animal husbandry techniques and environmental conditions that favoured the rearing of cattle in the north-east, in contrast to the south-east, which encouraged the exploitation of sheep as an affordable way to supply their populations with a steady source of meat. As the site at Bon Accord developed, demand for goat meat decreased and accessibility to venison was curtailed, probably as a result of stringent hunting legislation but also perhaps reflecting the economic prosperity of the later population living at Bon Accord. The quality of the cuts of meat consumed in these later phases is demonstrative of a prosperous community but perhaps not evidence of an overly affluent one.

In the early phases of Bon Accord the animals not only provided meat but also skins. This is reflected by the unusual presence of neonates in this urban setting. The meat obtained from the young animals would have been minimal and of little economic value so their presence suggests another use for them. The presence of both calves and lambs strongly indicates that animals were kept long enough for them to give birth before being slaughtered. The skins of young animals were regarded as superior due to their softness and flexibility when being worked – calfskins were highly valued for vellum production. Fully grown animals were preferred for shoe and boot soles and for making heavy harness for horses (Evans 2001). Goat, sheep and calf skins were also used for making parchment (Serjeantson 1989). This suggests that in the early phases at this site at the junction of Upperkirkgate and Gallowgate there was a mixed economy where butchery took place alongside tanning and bone working.

The presence of horses throughout Phases 1 to 5 probably derived from the disposal of carcasses and waste from industrial processes. The horses could also have been skinned for use in the leatherworking industries, while other elements from this species could have been used to make materials such as glues. The role of dogs and cats changed over the medieval to late medieval and post-medieval periods. In the 12th and 13th century phases, dogs and cats were deliberately butchered and were probably used in the fur industries to make clothing items. Dog skins were valued for making fishing floats and gloves; furs played an important part in defining social status, and the wearing of sheep or goat skin was considered unbefitting for a person of higher rank (Veale 2003). In the later phases the presence of dogs and cats was likely due to the disposal of working animals, pets and scavengers rather than having accumulated from industrial waste.

Table 4.21 Number of identifiable specimens (NISP) for bird bones by phase

Species	Phase 1	Phase 2	Phase 3	Phase 3/4	Phase 4	Phase 5	Phase 5/6	Phase 6	Total
Goose	10	17	2		10	1	1		41
Domestic fowl	10	18	4		3	1		2	38
Bantam	12	81	1	1	11	10	1		117
Duck		3			1				4
Red grouse	1								1
Indet		1							1
Total	33	120	7	1	25	12	2	2	202

Conclusion

The animal bone assemblage from Bon Accord derived from three main sources: butchery waste, industrial debris and domestic food refuse. As the site developed from a medieval workshop to an urbanised domestic landscape the nature of the refuse deposited changed accordingly. Industries such as butchery, tanning, bone working and dyeing, which were largely regarded as incompatible with domestic living, were largely relocated to the outskirts as councils began to regulate and impose health and cleaning measures. This same pattern of relocation of industry was previously observed at other sites in Aberdeen (Evans 2001: 113).

The bones disposed of in Phases 1 and 2 derived from butchery waste, bone working and tanning. The animals used in these industries ranged from the very young to the old. The cattle and pigs were mostly slaughtered in their prime whereas a larger proportion of the sheep/goat survived for longer, probably to be exploited for secondary products. While activities in Phase 3 appear still mostly commercial in nature, it is in this period that the site began to change from an industrial to a domestic setting – in the later periods neonates and young animals disappeared, to be replaced with animals in their prime or slightly older.

One constant is the main domesticated species exploited – in all phases beef was the most important source of meat, followed by lamb, mutton and pork. Venison almost disappeared from the diet, likely in part due to regulations on hunting. The role of dogs and cats evolved from animals used in commercial industries in the earlier phases to pets, working animals and probably semi-feral scavengers. For the people who lived and worked in and around the site from the medieval to the post-medieval period animals played an important role in the provision of both raw materials for industry and food.

4.5.3 Bird bone
Jennifer Thoms
(written 2009)

Introduction

A sub-sample of 202 bird bones was recovered from the excavation undertaken at Bon Accord. These were collected from a series of pits, ditches, postholes and gullies dated from the medieval and post-medieval periods. The features were archaeologically secure and offered an excellent opportunity to study how bird species were utilised over a specific time period.

The bird bone assemblage was identified to element and species with the aid of skeletal atlases (Cohen and Serjeantson 1996) and the reference collection stored at AOC Archaeology Group (Edinburgh). Where an element could not be identified to species, it was instead described as bird or small bird where appropriate. Only those bones found to be intact were measured (von den Driesch 1976).

The species and number of fragments recovered by phase are listed in Table 4.21. The dominant species was bantam (117) followed by goose (40), domestic fowl (38), mallard-sized duck (4), and red grouse (1). The remaining bone could have derived from domestic fowl, pheasant or grouse, though domestic fowl is the most likely.

Discussion

Bantams and domestic fowl

Both these species were recovered from Phases 1 to 5, with bantams the most numerous species in all phases. It is possible that the number of bantams may be overrepresented as female domestic fowl are generally on a par with male bantams in terms of size. The separation of domestic fowl and bantams is further complicated by the presence of capons. A spur was observed on a single domestic fowl tarso-metatarsal but this was the only evidence of a male. The majority of these bones were adult but six long bones, all belonging to bantams, were adolescent. Four of the bones had marks of skinning that appeared to have been undertaken in a domestic setting rather than by a professional butcher. The bantams and domestic fowl were probably exploited for their eggs and later slaughtered for their meat and feathers.

Goose

Small numbers of goose remains were present, but it was not possible to determine if the geese from Bon Accord were domesticated or a wild species. The majority of the remains belonged to adults – two were identified as immature. If this was a domesticated species then the value in keeping them until they were fully grown was to have access to eggs and the higher meat yield of the birds when fully fattened. Once slaughtered, the feathers and grease could be used; three bones had evidence of skinning marks. A single ulna had suffered a spiral fracture but there was evidence of healing. A single goose bone appeared to have been polished and worked in such a way as to resemble a whistle.

Duck

Three duck bones in Phase 2 and one in Phase 4 may have belonged to either the wild or domestic species. It has previously been argued that domestic ducks were a late arrival to Scotland, and it is therefore logical to assume that the duck species recovered from the medieval deposits are of the wild variety (Smith and Clarke 2011: 50–51). This indicates opportunistic hunting of this species to supplement the diet. One bone displayed evidence of skinning marks.

Red grouse

A single red grouse bone was recovered from Phase 1, representative of food debris and hunting of wild species to supplement the diet.

Comparison with other sites

The bird bone assemblage recovered from Bon Accord is similar to those already reported in Aberdeen and Perth (Hamilton-Dyer *et al.* 2001; Smith and Clarke 2011). The bird remains from the north-east of Scotland are similar to those recovered from the south-east of the country, for example at Advocates Close (Robertson, *forthcoming*) and Jeffrey Street (Tourunen 2014). While the bird bone assemblage from Perth High Street was much larger than the remains analysed at Bon Accord, the findings remain comparable, in that domestic birds,

in particular domestic fowl and to a lesser extent goose, were most in demand throughout the medieval period and into the post-medieval period.

Conclusion

The bird species recovered from Bon Accord are typical of a medieval and post-medieval site where domestic birds are a larger element of the diet than wild species, the latter supplementing the diet through hunting. The domestic bird species were undoubtedly exploited for egg production and only later slaughtered for their meat, feathers and fat.

4.5.4 *Fish bone*
Jennifer Harland
(written 2015)

Introduction

This report details the analysis of 7755 fish bones and otoliths from hand collected and sieved features at Bon Accord, Aberdeen. A total of 4383 fragments were identified to species or broader taxonomic group, many of them cod and cod family. Much of the identified material dated from the late 12th century to the early 15th century. This is a large and well dated urban assemblage that fills a gap in our understanding of the archaeology and history of Scottish medieval fisheries.

There follows a broad discussion related to the site as a whole, including issues of chronology, element patterning, butchery, pathologies, and the medieval fish trade. The site is then placed in context by a comparison with other published sites from Aberdeen, as well as a brief discussion of the historical sources relating to fishing, fish markets and the fish trade in medieval Aberdeen. Various tables and graphs referred to in the following text can be found in Appendix 4.

Methods

A full description of the methodology for recording the assemblage is included within the archive report. In brief, it was recorded using the York System, which entails the detailed recording of the 18 most commonly occurring and easily identified elements, termed quantification code (QC) 1 (Harland *et al.* 2003). For each of these, the element, species, approximate size, side, fragmentation, texture, weight and any modifications are recorded in detail. Fish vertebrae (QC2) are recorded in more limited fashion, with counts, element and species recorded, and for this site, fish sizes were also recorded in order to investigate questions relating to fish trade. Some elements are unusual and particularly diagnostic, like otoliths, and are fully recorded (QC4). The final category of material, (QC0), includes elements not routinely identified as well as unidentifiable

Table 4.22 Fish bone; summary of bone counts per phase

Phase	Hand collection			>2mm sieving			Grand total
	Identified	Total	% identified	Identified	Total	% identified	
1	1424	1841	77%	55	360	15%	2201
2	1585	2512	63%	98	473	21%	2985
3	198	232	85%	83	499	17%	731
4	202	320	63%	14	48	29%	368
5	37	47	79%	31	38	82%	85
6	17	27	63%	82	550	15%	577
1 or 2	1	1	100%	4	16	25%	17
2 or 3	3	3	100%	8	22	36%	25
2 to 4				5	13	38%	13
3 or 4	213	340	63%	8	22	36%	362
4 or 5				1	2	50%	2
5 or 6	12	12	100%	28	48	58%	60
Other	261	295	88%	13	34	38%	329
Total	3953	5630	70%	430	2125	20%	7755

material. Elements that are from very unusual species, or that are butchered, are recorded in detail even if not from the QC1 category.

Taphonomy

The fish assemblage from Bon Accord was well preserved, with few alterations. Basic taphonomic information was recorded for all QC1 and QC4 elements, while any fragments with other, more unusual taphonomic alterations were noted. This information is tabulated in Appendix 4 (Table A4.3 for hand collected fish; Table A4.4 for sieved). Overall, almost three quarters of the assemblage scored a 'good' texture, with much of the remainder scored as 'fair'. Fragmentation was more variable; many incomplete fragments were recovered, with only about a third of the assemblage being 80-100% complete. Some variation reflected changing taphonomic patterning through time. In Phase 1, hand collected fragments tended to be slightly better preserved and more complete than in later phases. Phase 4 was quite small in quantity but tended to contain elements that were more complete than earlier phases. This could indicate better taphonomic conditions and less disturbance in these layers. However, when viewed overall, these differences are only minor and are likely to have had minimal impact on the analysis of the assemblage.

Other taphonomic alterations were recorded when observed. Burnt fish bones were the most common of these, with 74 examples found. Over half of the burnt fragments could not be identified, but those that were tended to be the minor species, including haddock, whiting, flatfish and herring – rather than the cod or ling that formed the majority of the fish consumed at Bon Accord. This could suggest different cooking practices for the smaller, infrequently consumed species. Burnt fragments were both calcined (burnt white) and charred.

Carnivore gnawing was present throughout most phases, but at a very low level. A few crushed fish bones were also noted; these may have been chewed by either humans or animals. This low incidence suggests little scavenger activity around the material. The numerous articulating elements and the two complete and partial ling crania confirm that this material was not badly disturbed after deposition. This material is also unlikely to have been from cess pits. The large size of the fish bones makes them highly unlikely to have passed through digestive systems of humans or animals, and this can be confirmed by the low incidence of chewed bones.

A few examples of coloured staining were observed, including blue-green and red-brown colours, probably

Table 4.23 Fish bone; summary for major phases by taxa, hand collected and >2mm sieved

Recovery	Hand collected						Sieved					
Date range (century)	Mid to late 12th	Late 12th to mid 13th	Mid to late 13th	Late 13th to early 15th	Probably 15th–18th	Mid to late 18th to 20th	Mid to late 12th	Late 12th to mid 13th	Mid to late 13th	Late 13th to early 15th	Probably 15th–18th	Mid to late 18th to 20th
Taxa	Phase 1	Phase 2	Phase 3	Phase 4	Phase 5	Phase 6	Phase 1	Phase 2	Phase 3	Phase 4	Phase 5	Phase 6
Dogfish families												1
Ray family		1 0%			1			1		1		
Atlantic herring							1					3
Herring family								7				1
Carp family											1	
Salmon & trout family	2 0%							1				2
Cod	1172 82%	951 59%	127 64%	100 49%	25	13	25	42	4	7	1	4
Haddock	27 2%	43 3%		2 1%	1	2	7	17	74	2		
Ling	216 15%	579 36%	65 33%	98 48%	10	2	10	24	1		11	55
Pollack		1 0%										
Poor-cod												
Saithe	8 1%	4 0%	5 3%	1 0%			1					
Saithe/pollack	2 0%	2 0%		1 0%								
Torsk										1		3
Whiting								1	1		8	4
Cod family	1 0%	7 0%					4	1	3	1	4	7
Gurnard family								2		1		1
Sand eel family							2				4	
Turbot family		1 0%										
Turbot	1 0%											
Halibut		1 0%										
Plaice		7 0%					2					
Flounder							1					
Flounder/plaice		2 0%	1 1%									
Halibut family		12 1%		1 0%			2			1	2	
Sole family							1					1
Total identified	1429 100%	1611 100%	198 100%	203 100%	37	17	55	96	83	14	31	82
Unidentified	412	901	34	117	10	10	305	377	416	34	7	468
Grand total	1841	2512	232	320	47	27	360	473	499	48	38	550

reflecting close proximity to metal objects. Concretions were also noted on a few fish bones in several of the phases.

Results

The discussion that follows draws upon the six main phases, with features whose interpretation spans multiple phases only discussed if relevant. Only two groups of features associated with multiple phases contained significant quantities of identified bone: features identified as Phase 3 to 4 produced 221 identified bone fragments, while the group of modern, disturbed and 'other' features produced 274 identified fragments (Table 4.22).

Taxonomic diversity

The assemblage from Bon Accord was taxonomically diverse, with 27 different species or species groups recorded. However, the vast majority of the remains were from the cod family, including cod, ling and haddock, with trace quantities of a variety of other fish, including flatfishes, dogfish and rays, herring, salmon and trout family fish and gurnards.

The hand collected assemblage comprised almost 4000 identified bones, and was dominated by cod (69%), ling (26%), haddock (2%) and saithe (1%) (Appendix 4, Table A4.5). A range of other taxa was present, but each accounted for less than 1% of the identified fragments. These included, in rank order and including fragments that could only be identified to broad taxonomic grouping: the halibut family, cod/saithe/pollack, cod family, saithe/pollack, plaice, flounder/plaice, ray family, salmon and trout family, pollack, gurnard family, turbot family, turbot and halibut.

The sieved fraction produced a total of 428 bones that could be identified (Appendix 4, Table A4.6). Again, much of these were from the cod family, but with more of an emphasis on the smaller fish. Haddock was the most common species (48%), followed by cod (20%), ling (8%), whiting (6%) and cod family (6%). Other taxa accounted for less than 15% of the sieved fraction. These included, in rank order: Atlantic herring, halibut family, gurnard family, sand eel family, ray family, salmon and trout family, torsk, cod/saithe/pollack, plaice, dogfish families, herring family, carp family, saithe, pollack, poor-cod, sea scorpion family, flounder, flounder/plaice and sole family.

Variation between the phases, excluding material that could not be associated with a distinct phase, is tabulated in Table 4.23 (minor phases summarised in Appendix 4, Table A4.7). Looking only at hand collection, there is a shift from a primary focus on cod in Phase 1, towards increasing numbers of ling in Phases 2, 3 and 4. During this time cod decreased from 82% of the identified assemblage in Phase 1, to 59–64% in Phases 2 and 3, to 49% in Phase 4. Ling increased from only 15% in Phase 1, to 33–36% in Phases 2 and 3, to 48% in Phase 4. Quantities were much smaller in the final two phases but appeared to follow the general trends indicating cod and ling predominating in the diet.

Turning to the sieved fraction, quantities are smaller so conclusions must be more generalised. However, it is apparent that cod decreased in importance through time, from about half of all identified fish in Phases 1 and 2, to less than 10% in Phase 3. At the same time, haddock increased from about a tenth in Phase 1, to about a fifth in Phase 2, then increasing again to represent almost all of the fish found in Phase 3. Ling was present in moderate quantities in Phases 1 and 2, but only a single identification was made in Phase 3, and none was found in later phases. Whiting was found at low levels throughout the sieved fraction, increasing in the two early modern Phases 5 and 6. Herring represented about a tenth of the identified fish in Phase 2, with a few isolated finds in Phases 1 and 6, but this species was clearly not a major component of the diet.

A range of flatfishes was found by both hand collection and sieving. These tended to be more common in Phases 1 and 2, but overall, few were found. The majority were halibut family, probably flounder or plaice.

Many of the fish that could only be identified as cod family were small, mostly from fish of less than 30cm total length, and many from fish of less than 15cm total length. These have little value as food, but instead can be common stomach contents of the larger fish, including cod and ling. The sand eels and herrings may also fall into this category. However, although occasional stomach contents may be represented in this assemblage, there is not enough material to suggest fish were routinely being gutted and the guts discarded at Bon Accord.

While most of the fish found at Bon Accord were fished from the sea, a few finds point towards the possibility of freshwater fishing. A few salmon or trout were found in Phases 1, 2 and 6. These may indicate fishing on the Dee or Don rivers, both of which flow into the sea at Aberdeen. However, salmon and trout are anadromous species, and thus could have been caught at sea. The single carp family identification in Phase 5 is difficult to explain, but roach was likely present in southern Scotland before the present day and this example could represent a northern outlier (Froese and Pauly 2015; Wheeler 1977;). Alternatively, given the relatively recent date for this phase, this fish could have originated in a managed fish pond or stocked water course. Estuaries may have been fished, as they can be a source of some flatfish (including flounder and dab) as well as trout, but these species can also be caught in saltwater (*ibid*).

Fish sizes

All QC1 cranial elements were sized during recording, using reference comparanda to record broad ordinal categories. These results are tabulated in Appendix 4, Table A4.8 for the hand collected fraction, and Table A4.9 for the smaller sieved fraction. These broad size categories capture general trends through time and space. Metrical analysis of certain taxa and elements allows a more detailed examination of statistically reconstructed total lengths, but these are based on much smaller datasets and thus provide less of an overall picture.

The Bon Accord assemblage is dominated by very large fish, predominantly cod and ling of at least 80cm in length. Overall, almost half of the hand collected cod recovered were sized 80–100cm total length, and half were over 100cm total length. Even considering that this assemblage is slightly biased by the large quantity of hand collected material, a similar pattern can be observed in the sieved fraction: there, almost 60% of all cod were 80–100cm total length, and a third of all cod were larger than 100cm total length.

Over time, the proportion of very large cod of over 100cm total length increased between Phase 1 to Phase 3, rising from 45% in Phase 1 to 59% in Phase 2 and 57% in Phase 3 (in the hand collected material). The final three phases were smaller in quantity, but Phase 4 appeared to continue the trend towards capture of very large cod of over 100cm total length. However, by Phase 5, the majority of cod were 80–100cm total length, with only a few larger or smaller individuals fished. The smaller sieved fraction mirrored the hand collected size categories, but with a few smaller cod present in most phases; these smaller individuals ranged from 15–30cm to 50–80cm total lengths, and probably represented occasional use of different fishing grounds.

Modern reference collections seldom contain very large fish of known length, because they are so rare today – making it difficult to fully appreciate the large sizes of the Bon Accord cod and ling. Some of the cod bones were estimated as representing individuals about 150cm long. Most of the Bon Accord ling were substantially larger than any found in reference collections, despite examining several modern individuals of *c.* 80–100cm total length. Using regression equations determined by measuring modern fish of known length, it is possible to explore the cod sizes in detail. Using the two most frequently measured elements, the dentary (M1) and the premaxilla (M3), size histograms were generated (see Appendix 4, Figure A.4.1). Using this method, it is apparent most cod were between 80 and 140cm total

length, with a peak between 100 and 120cm total length. The small quantities measured make it difficult to explore temporal changes, but there does appear to be a slight increase in size through the first three phases.

The ling found at Bon Accord were exceptionally large. Almost all were at least 100cm total length, regardless of recovery method. These probably ranged up to 150cm total length, and occasionally longer, but reference comparanda were insufficient to investigate size variation in any greater detail. Today ling are known to reach 200cm total length, though more commonly they reach sizes of about 100cm total length (Froese and Pauly 2015).

Fish lengths can be determined relatively easily, but it can be more useful to get an estimate of weight in order to assess food value – though there is only a loose correlation between fish lengths and weights. A modern cod of about 90cm total length would have a gutted weight of about 7kg (Yoneda and Wright 2004: 239, 241). Extrapolating from the same study, a cod of about 100cm could have a gutted weight of about 10kg, a cod of 110cm about 13kg gutted weight, and a cod of 120cm about 17kg gutted weight. The large ling found at Bon Accord would likely have been even heavier still. Ling can sometimes reach lengths of 200cm, with an ungutted weight in the region of 45kg (Froese and Pauly 2015). These substantial weights indicate that cod and ling provided the vast majority of fish eaten in Phases 1, 2, 3 and 4, with other taxa only contributing a small amount of variety in the diet.

Haddock are naturally smaller than cod or ling, and the sizes found at Bon Accord were accordingly smaller, with just under half of the hand recovered haddock of 30–50cm total length and the other half of about 50–80cm total length (Appendix 4, Table A4.8). The sieved fraction presents a different picture (Appendix 4, Table A4.9). About a third of the sieved haddock were 15–30cm total length and two thirds 30–50cm total length, with few haddock of larger size recovered by sieving. These differences are difficult to reconcile: hand collection is obviously biased towards recovery of larger fish, but equally, the sieved samples contain none of the larger fish that would be expected. Closer investigation indicates Phase 3 Layer C005 is responsible for much of this difference. Sieved deposits from this layer account for almost all the Phase 3 haddock, almost all from fish of 30–50cm total length. Leaving aside this unusual deposit, the differences between recovery methods are less noticeable: to summarise, a range of haddock sizes were exploited, including quantities of smaller fish of less than 50cm total length, suggesting a different fishing strategies and consumption patterns than observed for cod and ling.

Some size ranges were available for the minor species.

Saithe of 50–80cm total length and 80–100cm total length were found in moderate quantities in the hand collected assemblage, along with a few larger individuals. Sizes tended to be larger in the earlier phases. Only a single saithe could be sized from the sieved fraction, suggesting there was no emphasis on catching smaller saithe; the plentiful inshore Scottish fishery for small saithe was therefore unlikely to have been a target for the Bon Accord markets.

A few whiting were found and sized in the sieved fraction; all were less than 50cm total length. Whiting are naturally smaller than cod, ling or haddock (Froese and Pauly 2015), and may have been missed during hand collection. The smaller ones of less than 30cm total length were found in Phases 3, 5 and 6, and were likely caught in shallow, inshore waters (*ibid*).

Two pollack from the hand collected fraction could be sized, indicating one individual was 50–80cm total length, and the other 80–100cm total length. These are compatible with cod sizes and may have been bycatch (incidental catch when targeting a specific species).

Sizes were recorded for a few other specimens. Most identified as cod family were small, tending to be less than 30cm total length, and thus could be stomach contents from the much larger cod family fish. A single flounder bone from Phase 1 was from a fish of 15–30cm total length, while a flounder or plaice from the same phase was sized at 30–50cm total length. Three later flounder or plaice identifications from Phases 2 and 3 were sized at 30–50cm and 50–80cm total length. There were nine plaice identifications that could be sized. Two were found in Phase 1, one from a fish of 15–30cm and one from a fish of 30–50cm total length. The remaining identifications were from Phase 2 and included five fish of 30–50cm total length and two fish of 50–80cm total length. A single halibut from Phase 2 was considerable in size, between 80 and 100cm total length. Eight further fish were sized but only identified as halibut family. Seven of these were fish of 30–50cm total length, from Phases 2, 3 or 4 and 4, and a final fish from Phase 2 was of 50–80cm total length. The two turbot or turbot family identifications that could be sized were from fish of 50–80cm total length, from Phases 1 and 2. Two gurnard family specimens were both sized at 15–30cm total length (a typical length for gurnards (Froese and Pauly 2015)), one each from Phase 2 and Phase 6, while two other specimens from Phases 1 and 3 or 4 were somewhat larger at between 30 and 50cm total length. The three torsk fragments from Phase 6 were from a fish of 50–80cm total length, and all were most likely from the same individual.

Element representation and fish preservation

A select subset of elements was identified in full, comprising 18 elements from the cranial and appendicular (shoulder) region (QC1 elements), all

vertebrae (QC2 elements), and unusual elements like otoliths and dermal denticles (termed QC4). Counts for cod, ling and haddock for the major phases are tabulated in Appendix 4, Table A4.10, and counts for the minor taxa are tabulated in Table A4.11, but the latter are not discussed further as few conclusions could be drawn from the small quantities identified.

The hand collected assemblages for cod and ling are dominated by vertebrae. This is to be expected because the vertebrae are plentiful, large, robust and easily identifiable elements. One cod contains between 46 and 56 vertebrae, while a single ling contains between 60 and 66 vertebrae (Barrett 1997), accounting for their frequency of identification compared to cranial and appendicular elements. Hand collection will miss the smaller and more fragile elements, including the last few small caudal vertebrae and the scapula and infrapharyngeal. Otoliths can often be missing, because of their small size, their calcium carbonate composition, and because they are sometimes misidentified as shell. Despite these biases, it is possible to detect some general trends through time.

Phase 1 contains a high proportion of cod vertebrae, compared with cranial and appendicular elements. Cod vertebrae represent 87% of all hand collected cod in Phase 1, compared to an average of 69%. This is to simply reflect a recovery bias, because cod vertebrae represent about three quarters of the small sieved cod assemblage in Phase 1 as well. Nor is this a reflection of poor recovery compared to later phases, because Phase 1 cranial and appendicular elements tended to be better preserved than in later phases. In Phase 2, cod vertebrae no longer appear over-represented. However, cleithra do appear in greater than expected quantities, with 101 found by hand collection. The cleithrum is a very large appendicular element found at the back of the head, at the 'shoulder' of the fish. Despite its size, it is fragile and fragments easily, and thus would not be expected in high quantities compared to robust elements like the articular, dentary or premaxilla. The ling in Phase 2 may also contain slightly elevated numbers of cleithra.

Although many of the fish taxa found at Bon Accord were likely deposited in their entirety, as seen by the wide variety of head and body elements, it appears that some cod and ling body parts may be over- or under-represented. When cod and related species, including ling and haddock, are preserved by air drying or by a combination of salting and drying, the head and some of the anterior vertebrae are removed and discarded at the production site. The remaining elements are exported with the preserved flesh and end up discarded during cooking or consumption. These include the cleithra and associated elements from the appendicular region, as well as the more posterior vertebrae (Barrett

1997; Harland 2006). When no other head elements are found, aside from the appendicular region, and the remains are from large fish, it is most likely these remains were once preserved, imported fish. This can be confirmed by distinctive butchery patterning, as discussed in more detail below.

In order to investigate element proportions in greater detail, it is necessary to take into account the number of each element in the body. Graphs representing the minimum number of elements (MNE) statistic, calculated for each element, for Phases 1 and 2 are contained within Appendix 4 (Figure A.4.2). Phase 1 is dominated by cod vertebrae. At a rough estimate, for every one cod head present, there are the remains of at least six cod bodies. This holds true for both cod of >100cm total length and cod of 80–100cm total length. Ling heads and bodies were found in more equal proportions. If this phase contained the bodies of fish that had been imported as a prepared product, then a correspondingly high proportion of appendicular elements would be expected, but is *not* observed. These cod are therefore unlikely to represent imported, prepared fish. However, butchery patterning will explore this option in greater detail below.

Detailed investigation of features within Phase 1 indicates Pit C015 is responsible for the unusual proportions of cod. The small proportion of sieved bones from this feature shared the element patterning, indicating this is a real depositional pattern, not one determined by selective hand collection. This accumulation of vertebrae could be the result of cooking processes removing the vertebrae from fresh or prepared fish and disposing of them differently.

Phase 2 cod and ling appear to have approximately equal proportions of heads and bodies. Cleithra counts were high for this phase, but once fragmentation has been taken into account, we can see that appendicular elements are found in proportion with cranial elements. These remains likely represent fish eaten when fresh and disposed of in their entirety at Bon Accord.

The MNE figures provide some indication of the quantities of cod and ling found at Bon Accord. In Phase 1, there were at least *c.* 30 cod of over 100cm total length, another *c.* 30 of 80–100cm total length, plus at least *c.* nine ling. In Phase 2, there were at least *c.* 22 cod of over 100cm total length, *c.* 15 of 80–100cm total length, and *c.* 20 ling. These quantities represent a minimum and must be used cautiously. Using the rough weight estimates as a very conservative guide to the potential minimum food value, Phase 1 includes at least 600kg of gutted cod and at least 135kg of gutted ling. In Phase 2, at least 390kg of gutted cod and at least 300kg of gutted ling were present. These calculations represent the minimum weight present in these two phases, and it is highly likely the weight of fish was actually much higher.

Butchery

A total of 185 fish bones were butchered, mostly cod and ling, and mostly from the early phases. Fish can be butchered to aid long-term preservation and storage, and/or they can be butchered during food preparation and consumption. The large size of most of the Bon Accord fish makes them very unlikely to have been cooked whole – butchery must have been necessary to divide the fish into manageable portions, regardless of whether they were preserved or freshly caught. Each process can leave a different type of butchery signature. Descriptions refer to the various anatomical planes: 'sagittal' divides the body of the fish into left and right portions, 'transverse' divides the body into front and back portions, and 'frontal' divides the body into upper and lower portions. 'Anterior' refers to the front of the fish, 'posterior' the tail, 'ventral' the belly and 'dorsal' the back. 'Chop' marks are coarse, deep and broad, often dividing the bone in two, while in contrast, 'knife' and 'cut' marks are narrow and shallow.

A total of 130 cod bones were butchered, including cranial, appendicular and vertebral elements, representing 5% of all cod bones (Table 4.24). Phase 4 has the highest proportion of butchery, with 9% of all cod bones containing some type of butchery mark. Three distinctive groups of butchered elements can be observed. Firstly, the vertebrae were the most commonly targeted elements, which is perhaps unsurprising as they are plentiful and are surrounded by the most edible parts of the fish. However, the elements around the mouth were often butchered at the medial articulation, including the dentary (lower jaw) and the premaxilla and maxilla (both found in the region of the upper jaw). Finally, a third group of butchered elements can be distinguished. These comprise the appendicular elements, particularly the commonly occurring cleithra, which is typically associated with fish processed for long-term preservation.

Vertebral butchery was the most common type of butchery mark for both cod and ling, representing just under half of all butchered cod and about 65% of butchered ling. These can be categorised into two broad types: chops or cuts to divide the bone into left and right sides along the sagittal plane, and chops or cuts that divide the bone into front and back in the transverse plane. There were a total of 58 examples of sagittal butchery, 30 of transverse, with some other examples in the frontal plane, in several planes, or that could not easily be classified. These tended to be found on abdominal vertebrae or occasionally the anterior caudal

Table 4.24 Fish bone; butchery summary by taxa and element

Taxa	Element	Phase 1	Phase 2	Phase 3	Phase 4	Phase 6	Total all major and minor phases
Cod	Articular				1		1
	Basioccipital		1				1
	Dentary	3	15	1	2		22
	Maxilla		1				3
	Premaxilla	1	5	1	1		8
	Quadrate		1				1
	Cleithrum	1	14		2		17
	Posttemporal		1				1
	Supracleithrum		4				4
	First Vertebra	1					1
	Abdominal Vert. Group 1	8	6	1	1		18
	Abdominal Vert. Group 2	8	3				12
	Abdominal Vert. Group 3	8	11		2		26
	Caudal Vert. Group 1	8	2		1		15
	Total	38	64	3	10		130
	% of identified cod	3.2%	6.4%	2.3%	9.3%		4.6%
Cod Family	Branchiostegal		1				1
Haddock	Cleithrum		1				1
	Caudal Vert. Group 2					1	1
	Total		1			1	2
Ling	Supraoccipital				1		1
	Basioccipital	1					2
	Dentary		3				3
	Parasphenoid		1				1
	Premaxilla		1				1
	Cleithrum	2	5				8
	Supracleithrum	1	1				2
	First Vertebra	2	2		1		5
	Abdominal Vert. Group 1	2	2				4
	Abdominal Vert. Group 2		8				8
	Abdominal Vert. Group 3		15				15
	Caudal Vert. Group 1		2				2
	Total	8	40		2		52
	% of identified ling	3.5%	6.6%		2.0%		4.8%

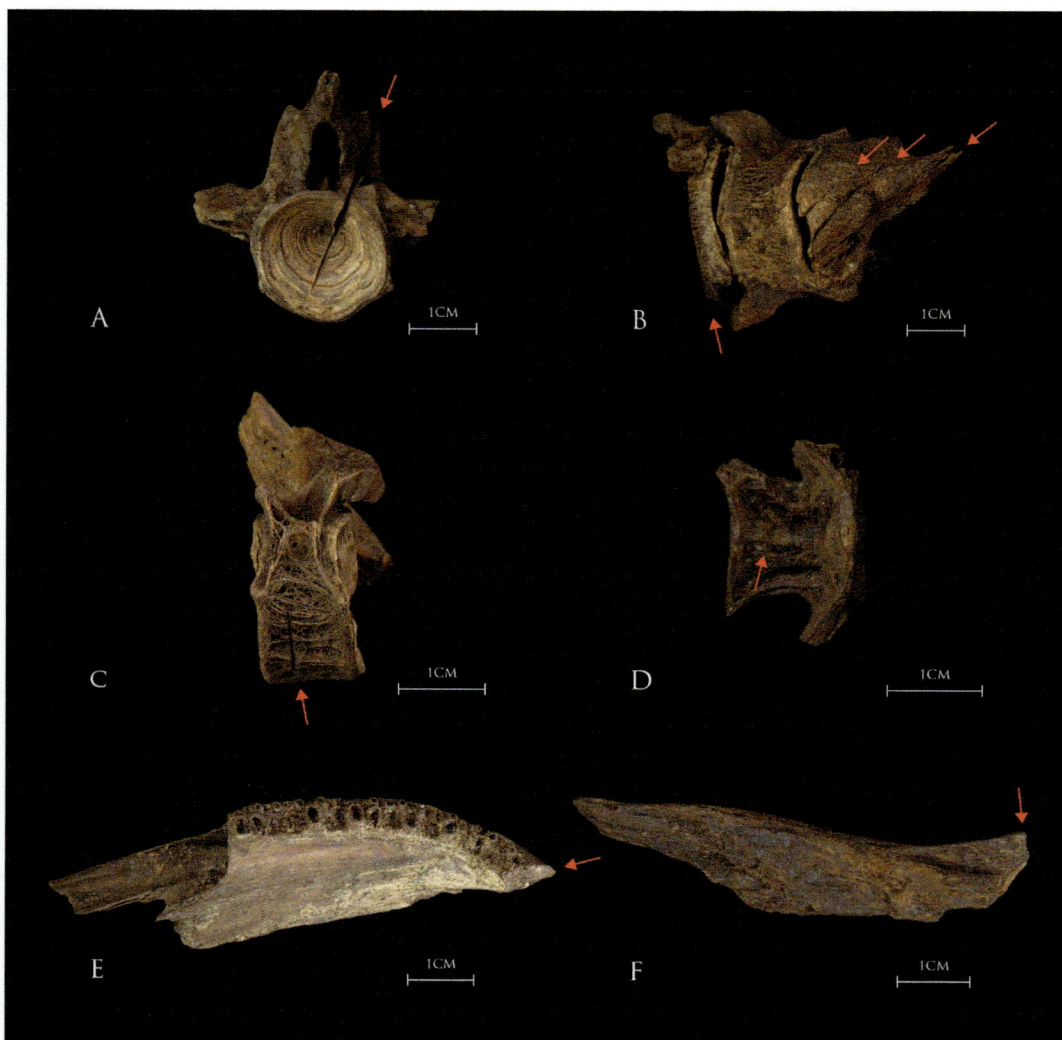

Figure 4.59 Fishbone butchery marks (scale 1cm)
(A) Butchered cod abdominal vertebra photographed from posterior, displaying sagittal chop from posterior towards anterior that did not fully split the vertebral centrum, Spread C043
(B) Sequence of ling basioccipital, first vertebra and abdominal vertebra, with multiple butchery in the frontal and transverse planes, Gully C001
(C) Cod abdominal vertebra, showing transverse cut to the ventral aspect, right side view, Ph C003
(D) Butchered cod caudal vertebra, showing small transverse knife mark on right side, unstratified
(E) Butchered cod dentary chopped in the sagittal plane at the medial articulation, Pit C018
(F) Butchered cod cleithrum, chopped in the frontal plane leaving the dorsal tip, Pit C024

vertebrae, which simply reflects the predominance of these elements at Bon Accord; the smaller posterior caudal vertebrae were underrepresented because of hand collection. Phase 1 contained 23 examples of sagittal butchery and seven of transverse, but in Phase 2, quantities were more equal with 20 and 18 examples respectively. Remaining phases contained numbers insufficient to fully explore patterning.

Sagittal chop marks found on vertebrae were often angled towards the posterior of the fish. In most cases the chop split the vertebral centrum, removing a wedge shape of the left, posterior part of the centrum.

Similar examples were found in most phases, although occasionally an anterior part of the vertebra was removed. An example from Phase 2, Spread C043 (Figure 4.59A) shows an unsuccessful chop that did not fully extend through the bone. In all cases where some degree of directionality can be observed, these butchery marks appeared to be coming from the posterior towards the anterior. Sometimes these chops removed the left processes but did not cut into the vertebral centra. Sometimes it was possible to reconstruct small sequences of vertebrae where a chop had cut into two or more adjacent centra. In Phase 1, these sagittal chops were only found on cod of 80–100cm total length (and none on any ling), but in Phase 2 and later, they were almost entirely found on larger cod and ling of at least 100cm total length. Both abdominal and caudal vertebrae displayed this butchery pattern.

Sagittal knife marks were also found on cod and ling vertebrae throughout all phases. These tended to be found on the left and right processes that extend away from the vertebral centra or on the neural spines. These were more likely to be found on both the left and right side of the fish, and in cases where directionality could be established, knife marks originated on both dorsal and ventral aspects of the fish. This type of mark was observed primarily on cod and ling abdominal vertebrae of over 100cm total length.

Transverse chop marks were found on cod and ling in Phases 1 and 2, with two further examples noted in Phase 4. These chops sometimes removed the anterior or posterior articular facets (Figure 4.59B) or were found on the ventral surface. When directionality could be established, these chops always originated on the ventral aspect. Examples from Phases 2 and 4 indicate some were butchered on the left side as well. These were found on both abdominal and caudal vertebrae, but almost all were from fish of greater than 100cm total length.

Transverse knife marks were not as common and were only observed in Phases 1 and 2. These small knife marks were found on either left or right side, or on the ventral aspect of the vertebra (Figure 4.59C). They were found on a variety of sizes and elements. The 'classic' indicator of preserved cod, ling or haddock is a small transverse knife mark on the side of the vertebral centrum, caused when removing the anterior vertebrae and the head prior to air drying (Barrett 1997; Harland 2006). A few poorly executed examples were noted on cod and ling abdominal vertebrae, but the only good example of this practice was found in an unstratified phase (Figure 4.59D).

Butchery in the frontal plane was found throughout all phases, on cod and ling of a variety of sizes. They were found on both left and right sides, and most were very small knife marks not extending far into the bone. Most were found on the neural arch or processes, rather than on the vertebral centrum. An exception is illustrated in Figure 4.59B, where a sequence of articulating ling basioccipital, first vertebra, and anterior abdominal vertebra were subject to multiple butchery marks. These were probably caused during head removal.

In addition to the articulating sequence illustrated in Figure 4.59B, a sequence of eight ling vertebrae were found with butchery extending across several elements. These eight comprised abdominal and caudal vertebrae from a ling of over 100cm total length. The

final caudal vertebra was chopped in the transverse plane, removing a wedge of posterior, dorsal centrum. All eight vertebrae have a series of knife marks running along the right side in the frontal plane, on both dorsal and ventral aspects. These cut into the neural arches and anterior processes but were mostly very shallow.

Vertebral butchery marks probably represent different stages of food preparation. At Bon Accord, the prevalence of large chop marks that cut through the bone probably indicates these very large cod and ling were reduced into manageable sections. Throughout all phases, cut and chop marks were about twice as likely to be on the left side of the fish, rather than the right. This could be related to handedness of the butchers, and/or a consistent method of butchery. The repetitive nature of many of the coarser butchery marks probably reflects standard, set methods of butchery. There are some changes through time: sagittal chops were initially restricted to cod of 80–100cm total length in Phase 1, but from Phase 2 onwards, this method tended to be used for bigger cod and ling of over 100cm total length. This method would have divided the fish into left and right halves. Transverse butchery was used throughout and would have created segments like 'steaks' of cod and ling. The fine knife marks in various anatomical planes could result from removing the flesh from the bones either just prior to cooking, or during eating. These fine marks do not follow the set patterns of other butchery marks, which could imply they were done in the home setting, by people who were not butchers. Taken in conjunction with the element patterning, there is little evidence to suggest fish had been preserved using the typical methods seen in the Northern Isles or Scandinavia. That said, there is nothing to rule out occasional consumption of prepared, dried fish but this was not a routine occurrence.

Head removal left a distinctive pattern on the bones. Examples were found throughout most phases, but numbers were insufficient to determine any methods. Several ling and cod basioccipitals, first vertebrae, successive anterior abdominal vertebrae and parasphenoids were chopped in transverse, sagittal or diagonal planes. Some displayed multiple cuts – but as the bone is very thick at the junction with the head, this is not unexpected. Other cranial elements were generally not found butchered, suggesting that if heads were used, they were used whole (perhaps boiled) or discarded whole. Elements from the mouth were commonly butchered in all phases, for both cod and ling. Cod dentaries were almost exclusively butchered in approximately the sagittal plane to remove the medial, central articulation, a trend found throughout Phases 1 to 4 (Figure 4.59E). Several of these cuts remove only a slight sliver of the central area, while others removed more of the bone.

Sagittal butchery around the midline of the mouth region is not unknown in other medieval sites with large cod and ling remains. However, they are not fully understood and are rarely discussed in print. It is possible that it is associated with hook removal, or removal of the tongue. However, these explanations are somewhat unlikely: hooks are caught in a variety of places around the mouth and face, and the tongue can be extracted through the soft flesh of the underside of the chin. There is some flesh around the mouth, cheeks and tongue that would be edible, and perhaps this was being targeted. If the heads were being split along the sagittal plane, then further cranial elements should have displayed butchery. As this was not the case, it appears that only the mouth region was of interest.

The final major area of butchery was the appendicular region, including the cleithra, supracleithra and posttemporals. Cleithra are the large pair of elements at the back of the head, and they survive well and are easily found during hand collection; in contrast, the small supracleithra is likely to be slightly under-represented at Bon Accord. These elements commonly stay in preserved fish and are deposited at consumer sites, rather than remaining with the crania at producer sites. In such contexts, the cleithra are often butchered with knife or chop marks, either from production of the preserved product, from long-distance storage and shipping, or during soaking and butchery immediately prior to consumption. At Bon Accord, there is no immediate evidence that preserved cod or ling were consumed in any quantity – given the relatively balanced element representation, but the prevalence of butchery marks to the cleithra needs exploring further.

Butchered cleithra were found in Phases 1, 2 and 3, and represented 12% of all cod cleithra and 14% of all ling cleithra. Only two examples were found in Phase 1. Both were ling, and both were butchered in the sagittal plane with small knife marks or removing small slivers of bone. In Phase 2, an entirely different type of butchery was observed: cleithra were most frequently butchered using a chop in the frontal plane to separate dorsal from ventral (Figure 4.59F). In some cases, the butchery did not fully extend through the bone, or was at a diagonal angle. A single example from Phase 1 comprised a cod cleithrum, butchered in the frontal plane leaving only the dorsal tip. Smaller knife marks were also found in Phase 2, on the medial and lateral sides or on the anterior edge. These were again commonly in the frontal plane, but otherwise displayed little obvious patterning. Similar frontal butchery was observed on a few examples from Phase 4, while a single ling cleithra in Phase 3 was butchered in the sagittal plane. Both left and right cleithra were found butchered. A few cod and ling supracleithra and a single post-temporal were also found butchered, all from Phase 2. These commonly displayed small knife marks.

Interpretation of the cleithra butchery is difficult. Small cuts to the dorsal tip may have been made when filleting the fish, and the one example from Phase 1 confirms that this was probably done when fresh. Small knife marks to other regions are more difficult to interpret but could relate to skinning or removing the cleithra from the fillet. Chops in the frontal plane are more difficult still. If the cleithra were left with the flesh, as they naturally form the leading edge of fillets, the large size may mean that they needed to be chopped to facilitate cooking, or, they were simply butchered along with the vertebrae to reduce these substantial fish into portions suitable for individual or household use. It is possible that a few of these cleithra may have arrived as prepared, preserved fish (although overall, most fish were consumed fresh and deposited whole). Contemporary material from York indicates that a greater variety of butchery was observed on cleithra that were definitely associated with a long-distance trade in preserved fish (Harland *et al.* 2016).

Two haddock bones were butchered. One was a caudal vertebra from Phase 6 which was repeatedly chopped in the sagittal plane. This was from a small fish of 15–30cm total length, so it was probably butchered to remove the tail prior to cooking. The second butchered bone was a cleithra from Phase 2, which displayed three knife marks in the frontal plane on the anterior edge. This was a fish of 30–50cm total length, so although much smaller than the cod and ling from this phase, it was still butchered using a similar method.

Finally, one butchered bone could only be identified as cod family – a branchiostegal ray with two small knife marks. There is no obvious reason for this area to be butchered as there is little flesh associated with the lower sides of the throat region.

In summary, the very large cod and ling from Bon Accord were commonly butchered, probably to reduce these large fish into manageable portions for cooking. Chop marks indicate that the coarser butchery followed a systematic, repeatable method with some changes through time, which would suggest this primary butchery was undertaken by professionals. Finer knife marks did not follow routine patterns, implying that they represent food preparation or consumption at the domestic level. There was little evidence to indicate cod and ling had been preserved and imported (or exported) on a large scale, a conclusion that matches the element patterning evidence.

Pathologies

The Bon Accord assemblage produced a surprising number of pathological specimens (summarised in Table 4.25). The study of fish diseases and injuries from archaeological assemblages is not as advanced

Table 4.25 Fish pathology summary by phase and feature

Phase and feature	Species	Element and size	Description
Phase 1			
Pit C001	Cod	Caudal vertebra group 2, 80–100cm TL	Slight flattening and splaying of anterior articular surface
	Cod	Caudal vertebrae group 2, 80–100cm TL	Two vertebrae with slightly flattened articular facets
Pit C007	Ling	Dentary, >100cm TL	Bone growth and remodelling on and ventral to the tooth row near the medial articulation; possible deep tooth abscess (also gnawed)
Pit C015	Cod	Premaxilla, 80–100cm TL	New bone growth on tooth surface at medial articulation; possible tooth abscess
	Cod	Abdominal vertebrae group 3, 80–100cm TL	Two separate vertebrae, both with a flared articular surface and a shortened and twisted vertebral body
	Cod	Abdominal vertebrae group 3, >100cm TL	Two instances of paired fused vertebrae, bodies shortened and slightly flared
	Cod	Abdominal vertebra group 1, >100cm TL	Slightly shortened and thickened vertebral body
	Cod	Abdominal vertebra group 1, >100cm TL	Shortened vertebral body, worn articular facet
	Cod	Abdominal vertebrae group 2 and 3, 80–100cm TL	? Six articulating vertebrae, all skewed, twisted and shortened, with splayed articular facets
Phase 2			
Hollow C002	Cod	Articular, >100cm TL	Large bone growth on lateral side, consisting of dense, smooth spheres of new bone
Layer C003	Ling	Maxilla, >100cm TL	'Peeling' of original bone surface, exposing inner layers of bone with some new bone growth on new inner surface
	Cod	Quadrate, >100cm TL, probably c. 150cm TL	Articular facet shows signs of polishing, grooving and eburnation
	Cod	Abdominal vertebra group 3, >100cm TL	Slight extra bone growth around ventral edges of articular facets
	Cod family	Caudal vertebra group 2, >80cm TL	Vertebral body of squashed and shortened appearance, with large, splayed articular facets; identification to species difficult because of changed morphology
	Cod	Dentary, >100cm TL	Extra indentation adjacent to the lateral foramen
Pit C022	Ling	Dentary, >100cm TL	Distortion and new bone growth around medial articulation
Pit C032	Cod	Dentary, >100cm TL	Distortion, pitting and new bone growth to medial articulation
	Cod	Ceratohyal, >100cm TL	Distortion and new bone growth to proximal articulation
Pit C033	Cod family	Abdominal vertebra group 1, 80–100cm TL	Squashed vertebral body with splayed articular facets; changes to morphology make identification to species difficult
Pit C034	Ling	Articulated cranium, mostly complete, >100cm TL	Several instances of extra bone growth, twisted or skewed morphology and lesions to the neurocranium; these are possibly cancerous growths
	Cod	Maxilla, 80–100cm TL	Wear and eburnation to medial articulation
	Cod	Maxilla, >100cm TL	Squashed appearance with bone loss and reshaping to medial articulation

Phase and feature	Species	Element and size	Description
	Ling	Dentary, >100cm TL	Bone loss around tooth sockets with new growth and layering on lateral edge, possible tooth abscess
	Cod	Dentary, >100cm TL	New bone growth and layering on medial aspect, near medial articulation
	Ling	Ceratohyal, >100cm TL	Large lump of new bone growth with mammal-like texture and appearance
Stakes C002	Cod	Dentary, 80–100cm TL	Shallow, elongated indentation just ventral to tooth row, and just posterior to the usual foramen
Phase 3			
Pit C042	Cod	Abdominal vertebra group 3, 80–100cm TL	Distorted vertebral centrum with new bone growth around edges of articular facets
Pit C047	Cod	Abdominal group 3 vertebrae, >100cm TL	Four fused vertebrae, vertebral bodies shortened and flared
Phase 4			
Layer C075	Cod	Abdominal vertebrae group 1, 80–100cm TL	Two fused vertebrae with slight remodelling to articular facets
Posthole C003	Cod	Dentary, >100cm TL	Extra bone growth in layers near medial articulation, ventral to tooth row and on inside of mouth

as that of domestic mammals, making description and interpretation difficult. A total of 42 fish pathologies were identified at Bon Accord, as well as an almost entire articulated ling cranium with multiple instances of pathologies; counting the articulated cranium as one, these represent 0.5% of the entire fish assemblage, or 1% of all identified fragments. These included both joint diseases caused by age-related wear and tear, and neoplasias (tumours) displaying new, extra bone growth. The Bon Accord assemblage comprised an unusually high proportion of very big, very old fish, and these may naturally have been more prone to diseases and illnesses manifesting in bone modifications.

Discussion

The fish remains from Bon Accord were dominated by the cod family, including cod, ling and haddock. Temporal changes in the composition of the fish assemblage can be seen, and probably reveal changes in fishing grounds and demand for taxa. In Phase 1, cod was the dominant choice. Cod decreased in prominence over the next three phases, with ling becoming more common – by Phase 4, ling had become as frequent as cod. A change occurred in the early modern period as by Phase 6, cod and haddock were preferred, while ling were no longer of much importance.

The cod and ling found at Bon Accord were exceptionally large. Cod sizes increased sequentially through time, with more and more very large cod of over 100cm found in Phases 2, 3 and 4. However, by the 15th–18th century

Phase 5, most cod were smaller, 80–100cm total length. This change would suggest different fishing grounds were being exploited, perhaps in waters that were not as deep as those exploited in Phases 1 to 4. The large size of the cod and ling suggest a consistent method of targeting specific fish at specific fishing grounds, particularly during Phases 1 to 4. Ling prefer deeper water, particularly when older and bigger, so depths of at least 100m, up to 1000m, would be expected (Froese and Pauly 2015). Fishing grounds were likely some distance from Aberdeen, in the northern portions of the North Sea or in the North Atlantic. Other fish may have been caught when targeting cod and ling and kept for consumption; the large saithe and pollack, the dogfish and the flatfish could come into this category. The smallest fish found could have been stomach contents, but overall there was little evidence that fish were routinely gutted at Bon Accord.

The smaller fish like haddock and whiting, and some of the medium sized saithe, were probably caught in different ecosystems (*ibid*). These were probably caught in shallower, inshore waters closer to Aberdeen, and tended to be more common in Phase 5 and 6, providing more evidence of a change to fishing grounds. These fish were also found to a lesser degree in Phase 3, suggesting that some shallow or inshore waters were exploited on a small scale in this phase.

The large cod and ling found at Bon Accord and elsewhere in Aberdeen were most likely caught by long-lining, a method of marine fishing using a long line with multiple hooks held over the side of a boat (Fenton 1978). The actual evidence for fishing in medieval and early post-medieval Aberdeen is slight: excavations at Castle Street produced a single hook of 13th to 14th century date that closely resembles contemporary fish hooks (Steane and Foreman 1988). A second hook in poor condition from 43–57 Upperkirkgate is of 16th–18th century date (Cameron *et al.* 2001: 200). Historical sources mention fishing for cod using lines in association with medieval Aberdeen (Jackson 2002: 162). Fishing weights to hold down nets or lines are sometimes recovered from archaeological sites, but none are known from Aberdeen.

The small quantities of salmon family fish suggest some fishing of local river systems, most likely with hook and line or with nets. Historical evidence describes 'stells' being used to catch salmon in the Dee and around the natural harbour area at the coast; this was a method of net fishing using wooden stakes or boats to support the nets (Jackson 2002: 161). This was probably the case throughout all phases.

The medieval fish trade is a well recognised and documented phenomenon around the North Sea region (Barrett *et al.* 2008). Preserved, dried fish can be traced from producer site to consumer using zooarchaeology and isotopic signatures. The large cod and ling from Bon Accord were analysed using element proportions, taphonomy, fish sizes and butchery to assess whether or not they had been preserved and traded. It is most likely that they arrived in Aberdeen as fresh fish, which were then consumed and deposited in their entirety. A few examples may have been preserved, but not in a quantity sufficient to alter the overall balanced deposition of element parts.

Individual features generally conformed to the overall pattern of each major phase, but a few are exceptional. Phase 1 was dominated by cod, with some ling. Although a few other taxa were recovered, much of these originated from a single feature that appeared quite different from others in this phase: Spread C002. The fish remains indicated that herring, four types of flatfish, haddock and cod of small, medium and large size were consumed and deposited in this single feature, which could represent the remains of high status dining, as a variety of more unusual fresh fish appears to have been consumed.

The high proportion of vertebrae found in Phase 1 Pit C015 is unusual. This could represent the remains of one particular stage of food preparation. Another unusual feature was Phase 2 Hollow C002, which contained 23 cod cleithra fragments from a total of 116 cod remains. Phase 2 Layer C003 also showed higher than expected numbers of cleithra. Overall, there is no indication that cleithra were over- or under-represented in the assemblage, meaning that fish were generally consumed fresh and deposited whole. However, these two features may indicate that occasionally, some imported, preserved and headless cod might have been consumed. Or, like Pit C015, these may represent kitchen waste from particular stages of food preparation.

Analysis of the butchery patterning indicates the large cod and ling were routinely chopped into segments in the mid-to-late 12th to early 15th century. The repetitive nature of the chops, and the occasional preference of one side of the fish, suggests this was done by professional butchers. In contrast, the many fine knife marks found on vertebrae and cleithra were more varied, and probably resulted from cooking and consumption at the domestic level. Butchery to the central, midline articulation of mouth elements was occasionally undertaken following a set pattern but the purpose of this is not known. It is, however, known from multiple contemporary sites around the North Sea.

Cooking differences are also apparent in the types and quantities of burnt bone. The charred and calcined fish tended to be minor species, including haddock, whiting, flatfish and herring. Most of these were much smaller than the more popular cod and ling. It is likely these smaller taxa were cooked near open fires, whereas cod and ling were prepared and cooked in a way that made burning less likely.

Historical evidence for markets and trade in Aberdeen

Historical sources describe Aberdeen's role in the fish trade in some detail, noting Aberdeen's importance in the trade and exchange networks of the North Sea from as early as the 12th century, when a royal charter was granted to the city. At that time, Aberdeen was known to export cloth, wool, animal skins, leather and fish, while timber, iron, manufactured goods, quality cloth and wine were imported (Jackson 2002: 159–60). Aberdeen probably traded widely with continental cities like Bruges, as well as English ports, from the 13th century to the mid 15th century, with Edinburgh gradually gaining predominance in the 16th century (*ibid*, 160). However, Aberdeen remained an important centre for fishing (*ibid*).

Aberdeen's medieval fish trade centred around salmon and herring, as well as 'whitefish', most likely cod and ling. Salmon were caught using nets in the Dee or its estuary and were preserved by salting or barrelling in brine or dry; this preserved product was exported as far as London from at least the mid 14th century (Jackson 2002: 161). Between the second half of the 15th century and the end of the 16th century Aberdeen's salmon probably represented at least 40% of the salmon exported from Scotland, reaching markets around the North Sea, the Baltic and Iberia (*ibid*, 162). Very few of the products of this trade were eaten and deposited at Bon Accord, either through dietary preference or because salmon was too valuable as an export product.

The Aberdeen cod trade was small compared to its salmon trade, but still important historically. Cod were 'also popular because their size allowed the split fish to be lightly salted at sea and then dried and barrelled on land. There are signs that this was once a lucrative trade: in 13th century Flanders cod was known as *aberdaan*' (Jackson 2002: 162). This trade probably declined from the 15th century, when Newfoundland cod became more widely available (Barrett *et al.* 2011). Fish that were gutted and 'split' at sea, as implied here, could have been landed at Aberdeen and then barrelled for export, with few fish actually consumed in Aberdeen itself. Aberdeen's proximity to fishing grounds would mean fresh fish could have been caught and landed regularly, and these may have been preferable to inhabitants.

The herring trade was extensive and involved many ports around the North Sea (Starkey *et al.* 2000). However, by the late 15th century, there were complaints that much of the herring stocks in Scottish waters were being fished by other countries. It is likely that Aberdeen's role in the herring trade became fairly minimal, if indeed it was ever extensive, with only small quantities of fresh fish being landed (Jackson 2002: 163). The complete lack of herring bones suggests there was little demand or availability of herring at Bon Accord.

Aberdeen's large population was fairly wealthy (Jackson 2002: 162), and thus provided a demand for fresh fish. Although tending to be more expensive than preserved fish, fresh fish were much in demand in medieval urban centres. From the 15th century onwards, small fishing towns like Findhorn, Banff and Peterhead supplied Aberdeen with fresh fish from inshore and deeper waters (Jackson 2002: 162). Aberdeen itself had a small fishing village called Futty (Dennison *et al.* 2002: 16); from at least the early 16th century fishermen from this village fished for salmon in the local waters, as well as local inshore fisheries along the coastal regions (Jackson 2002: 162). The rise of the small fishing towns can probably be traced through the zooarchaeological record: from the 15th century, smaller, more inshore fish became more common. Some of these small inshore fisheries could be 'owned' and were subject to controls. Although its extent is not known, this system became problematic by the mid 15th century, when the city was forced to decree that no person from outside of Aberdeen should be allowed to control the inshore fisheries (Boardman 2002: 216); this corresponds to inshore fish becoming more common at Bon Accord. A century later, there were still problems over control of the inshore fisheries, when 'John, sixth Lord Forbes, was involved in a long-running, occasionally violent dispute with the burgh, ostensibly over fishing rights'

(White 2002: 224). Records from 1522 show half the profits from fisheries around the mouth of the Dee were paid to a particular post at King's College (Lynch and Dingwall 2002: 198), suggesting ownership and control could be lucrative.

Legislation and grievances relating to medieval markets often feature fishmongers, and Aberdeen is no exception. A weekly market was held from the 13th century onwards (Blanchard *et al.* 2002: 137), probably involving sales of fresh or preserved fish. Regulations were in place to ensure locally caught fish were not sold at Futty or other nearby villages, but were brought to the market, with dues payable to the city (*ibid*, 145). From the mid 15th century there are records of 'fleshers' charging set rates for cleaning and butchering larger varieties of fish, and other records described 'keling' or cod, being cleaned and butchered in the market (*ibid*, 139, 142). A record of 1482 describes fines charged for selling fish too early and making too much profit on 'breaking' fish (*ibid*, 139). This matches the butchery evidence from Bon Accord: the large cod and ling show evidence of being chopped into manageable segments using set, routine methods of chopping from the mid-to-late 12th to the early 15th century.

Comparative assemblages

Immediately adjacent to Bon Accord is the excavation site of 45–75 Gallowgate, while 30–46 and 43–57 Upperkirkgate and Gallowgate Middle School are within 200m of Bon Accord. The sites of Kirk of St Nicholas, St Nicholas Triangle and 16–18 Netherkirkgate/1–15 Guestrow and Castle Street are all less than 500m away. Fish remains have been found at some of these sites and form useful comparanda. Fish were also found during recent excavations at St Nicholas Kirk, including large cod and ling of medieval date (Aberdeen City Council 2008), but this site has yet to be fully published.

The publication of excavations in the immediate vicinity of Bon Accord in the 1970s and early 1980s (Murray 1982) included an analysis of late 12th to 14th century animal bone from 42 St Paul Street and Queen St Midden Area, and 'significantly, the Queen Street site was rich in fish bones' (Hodgson and Jones 1982: 232). A paper considering the zooarchaeology from medieval sites in eastern Scotland similarly ignored the fish remains (Hodgson 1983: 6).

Recent excavations provide more useful comparanda. The 45–75 Gallowgate site produced fish remains in some quantity, some of which 'hinted' towards fish processing evidence (Evans 2001: 83). Archaeological material from the Gallowgate area dates from the 12th to 14th centuries and includes a variety of industrial processing. In the 13th and 14th centuries, middens accumulated around the edge of the loch, probably

Table 4.26 Fish bone; summary of comparative material from Castle Street, 16-18 Netherkirkgate, 30-46 Upperkirkgate, Gallowgate Middle School and 45-75 Gallowgate (Cameron and Stones 2001)

Taxa	12–13th century		13–14th century[1,2]		14–15th century[1]		15–18th century[2]		18–20th century[2]	
Cod	119	56%	282	41%	69	54%	91	50%	43	37%
Ling	42	20%	230	33%	45	35%	37	20%	28	24%
Haddock	7	3%	23	3%	3	2%	7	4%	10	9%
Gadid	40	19%	153	22%	11	9%	46	25%	31	27%
Salmon									1	1%
Flatfish									1	1%
Saithe/pollack	5	2%	3	0%					1	1%
Turbot	1	0%								
Total identified	214	100%	691	100%	128	100%	181	100%	115	100%
Not identified	99		263		34		8		25	

[1] Includes 'some' sieved material from 16-18 Netherkirkgate, quantity unknown
[2] Includes 'some' sieved material from 45-75 Gallowgate, quantity unknown

associated with the nearby buildings (Evans 2001: 105). Fish assemblages were recorded from five sites in the area (Cameron and Stones 2001, particularly Hamilton-Dyer *et al.* 2001). Individual bone counts from each of these sites are of moderate size, but when combined, a total of 1329 bones were identified. These include: 45-75 Gallowgate (483 fish remains in total, mid 13th century to *c.* 1770/80), Castle Street (184 fish remains in total, 13th-20th century), 16–18 Netherkirkgate (672 fish remains in total, 13th–15th century), 30–46 Upperkirkgate (86 fish remains in total, 12th–18th century), and Gallowgate Middle School (333 fish remains in total, late 12th–20th century).

The fish taxa recovered from these sites were similar to those from Bon Accord: cod, ling and haddock were the most commonly recovered taxa, with a few examples of salmon, flatfish, saithe/pollack and turbot also recorded (comparative sites are summarised by period in Table 4.26). Cod and ling dominated the assemblages from the 12th–13th century to the 15th–18th century, with cod found in the greatest quantities. Haddock was found at low levels throughout, which appears similar to Bon Accord. This is understandable as haddock is likely under-represented by hand collection. A few saithe/pollack and a single flatfish were identified in the 12th–13th century, and a few more saithe/pollack in the 13th–14th century.

Fish sizes were described, but not quantified. Cod tended to be fish of 100–120cm total length, while some of the ling recovered were of 120cm total length and others were substantially bigger – very similar to the size ranges found at Bon Accord. The haddock remains represented fish of 35 to 70cm total length, again typical of Bon Accord.

The tentative evidence for fish processing in the Gallowgate area dates from the mid 13th century, and included cod, haddock and ling. Large quantities of cranial remains were found, as were several butchered bones, which were interpreted as evidence for filleting, gutting and cleaning on site. Furthermore, the authors believed that Aberdeen was 'receiving cod from the Norwegian fishing grounds which were then controlled by Bergen' in the mid 13th century or earlier (Evans 2001: 107).

Detailed investigation of the data suggests that these claims are indeed very tentative. The quantities of fish bone recovered are very small, once each phase of each site is considered. Fish elements and skeletal representation were both discussed qualitatively, making it difficult to reconstruct the arguments for fish processing. At most sites, the vertebrae and cleithra were said to be under-represented compared to cranial elements, which was interpreted as evidence for fish processing in Aberdeen: the vertebrae and cleithra were thought to be removed with the prepared flesh, leaving the waste cranial elements here. It seems very unlikely that fish were being prepared for preservation in an urban centre, given that air drying or drying and salting typically took place in cold areas with plenty of space for hanging or laying out the fish e.g. the Northern Isles, Norway (Perdikaris 1999). The quantities of recorded bones for any one phase of these comparative sites is very small – the maximum recorded is 158 cod bones from a 13th–14th century phase at 16–18 Netherkirkgate, followed by 108 ling bones from a phase dating to *c.* 1250–1375 from 45–75 Gallowgate. In neither example were quantities sufficient to fully explore the interplay of taphonomy, fragmentation and element representation – the latter being of particular relevance given that a single cod can contain up to 56 vertebrae and dozens of large, robust cranial bones. Had Norwegian cod been imported to Aberdeen as a dried, preserved product, then an abundance of appendicular and vertebral elements would have been expected but this was not observed.

Butchery evidence from the comparative sites was recorded, although not quantified. Butchery was most common on the appendicular elements, including the cleithra, supracleithra and posttemporals, and was interpreted as filleting evidence. Other evidence included butchery to remove the gills, to remove deeply swallowed hooks, and to remove the tongue. A few cranial bones were 'axially' chopped. Perforated opercular bones were thought to indicate fish were threaded together and hung up on lines, which is certainly possible although no examples were found at Bon Accord. This butchery evidence appears similar overall, particularly regarding the butchered cleithra and mouth elements, but it is curious that butchered vertebrae do not appear as common at the comparative sites as at Bon Accord.

While assessing samples from a number of sites for plant remains, some fish remains were noted (Hall 2003). Although not investigated in any detail, they are unusual in that they include some small fish bones. These included four samples from a Carmelite friary, one of which was of 16th–17th century date. Two were thought to contain cess material, including crushed fish bones; this perhaps suggests that small fish were being consumed, as cess material tends to include smaller fish like herring or eel. A sample from 43–57 Upperkirkgate, dating to the 15th–16th century contained fish bones, some burnt, while Gallowgate Middle School produced a sample of late 12th to 13th century date that contained very large fish bones. However, the most remarkable evidence to emerge from sampling is the consistent lack of small fish from the early material; large cod and ling appear to have been the food of choice throughout the 12th, 13th, 14th and 15th centuries.

Conclusions

According to historical sources medieval Aberdeen was an important hub in trade and exchange networks around the North Sea exporting preserved salmon, herring and cod and ling. However, the zooarchaeological evidence from Bon Accord and comparative sites suggests that while Aberdeen may have been an important centre for the fish trade, very little of these traded products were consumed in Aberdeen itself. Salmon and herring were present, but only a few specimens. This may have been a dietary choice, or because these goods were too valuable for local consumption.

Cod and ling were the dominant fish consumed throughout the late 12th to early 15th century. There was no indication that fish preservation was undertaken at Aberdeen (contrary to earlier zooarchaeological studies), and nor was there evidence that only the preserved product was being consumed, although the odd preserved fish may have been eaten occasionally. These large fish were routinely butchered, probably by professionals to reduce them to smaller, manageable portions which were then consumed in the domestic setting.

Throughout, fishing by long line seems to have been particularly important, though nets may have been used in shallower waters closer to Aberdeen itself. Trends in consumption over time, with shifts in fish sizes and availability of species, most probably relate to a move towards exploitation of inshore or shallower fishing grounds around the 15th century. Prior to this, the deep and open waters of the northern North Sea or North Atlantic were the preferred fishing grounds.

A few features display elements or species that differ from the norm and that may hint at specific patterns of consumption linked to status.

4.5.5 Insects
Harry Kenward

Flots from 16 bulk soil samples were examined for insect and other macro-invertebrate remains using a low-power binocular microscope. A full report is contained within the site archive.

Almost all of the flots contained some insects, but the total numbers were never great and often small. Only fly puparia and mites were sometimes abundant. Preservation varied considerably, some assemblages containing fresh-looking remains, often with entire sclerites, but others including numerous highly fragmented remains which would not be reliably identified.

In terms of estimated minimum numbers of individuals, all of the assemblages would be regarded as 'small' or borderline for interpretative purposes, with at most a few tens of individuals, so that statistics derived from them would only be used with caution. In no case was any beetle species represented by more than three individuals.

Ecologically, the assemblages were broadly similar, with a mix of habitats represented, including open water and waterside mud and litter, decomposing matter from fairly dry to foul, ruderal plants and, very rarely, dead wood. Synanthropes (species favoured by artificial habitats) were generally present, but in small numbers. None of the assemblages could be regarded as ecologically distinctive, lacking species-rich or dominant components, and thus they cannot be argued to have any great archaeological significance.

4.5.6 Soil micromorphology

Lynne Roy

Introduction

Micromorphological analysis was undertaken on 12 samples from three stratigraphic sequences (164, 165 and 167).

The samples were prepared for analysis using the methods of Murphy (1986) and analysed using the descriptive terminology of Bullock *et al.* (1985). The samples were prepared at the University of Stirling in the Department of Environmental Sciences. Samples are discussed in stratigraphic sequence (from the base up) and with reference to archaeological features. A full report, including detailed methodology and soil unit descriptions, is included within the site archive.

Marked changes in local depositional processes were evidenced in each sequence by changes in the density of the packing structure, colour and texture of deposits, orientation of inclusions and frequency of organic inclusions. The majority of the samples analysed were relatively undisturbed; this was reflected in the finely stratified nature of the deposits. Many samples displayed evidence of artificial additions to the soil in the form of charred wood, plant material and rare possible metal and bone fragments.

The 12 samples were taken from a series of occupation deposits to the west of the Gallowgate frontage (Figures 2.56 & 2.57, Chapter 2). This area contained possible hearths and associated stone structures. Towards the bottom of the three sampled sequences were dark silty clays, with common large pits for refuse and industrial activities, probably including tanning (Phases 1 to 4). Bedrock beneath the site comprises granite, described as foliated muscovite biotite granite, being a medium to coarse-grained crystalline granite and the mineral composition of most samples reflects this igneous origin.

Interpretation

Sequence 164 (Samples 164.1–164.7, Figure 2.57, Chapter 2)

The hypothesis that Layer C003 represented the remains of an occupation layer was supported by micromorphological evidence which included common anthropogenic indicators in the form of fuel residues, polyconcave voids and dusty coatings on voids which could provide further evidence of deliberate deposition followed by trampling (Courty *et al.* 1989).

An hypothesised dump Spread C159 overlying Layer C003 was rich in organic material including probable mixed midden material including ash, sand, silt, charcoal, very rare pottery fragments and very rare shell indicating that this deposit represents the dumping of waste material. The presence of vivianite in Spread C159 could tentatively be interpreted as a response to an input of cess (Macphail 1998: 550), further adding weight to the hypothesis that this was a midden/waste deposit.

The horizontal orientation of voids and cracks and laminated nature of the upper part of the deposits of Oven C001 (Sample 164.6) was indicative that this was a waterlain deposit and perhaps represented a period of flooding or deliberate dumping of alluvial or lacustrine clay possibly to seal/cover the underlying midden deposit. The boundary between this unit and those it overlay and underlay was sharp and may indicate that this layer was rapidly and possibly deliberately deposited.

Spread C157, an upper element of Oven C001 was hypothesised as a levelling layer. This deposit contained frequent organic material consistent with the dumping of midden material as discussed above, although post-depositional pedoturbation had blurred boundaries and removed evidence for sediment formation processes.

Unit 2 of 164.4, Spread C166, was comprised almost entirely of burnt organic matter. It was hypothesised that this represented *in situ* burning. However, the surrounding soil/mineral material was not burnt. Intermixed with the charred organic matter was biogenic silica including phytoliths and it is probable that this material was the 'washed' remnants of grass rich ash. It may therefore be hypothesised that this unit was derived from burnt matter rich in grasses – possibly fuel, fodder or bedding. Furthermore, the dipping angle of the organic fragments would be unusual for an *in situ* deposit and it is thus likely that the burnt organic material is derived from burning elsewhere – possibly ash from a hearth deposited in a waste pit. Indeed, given the diversity of material identified in Spread C166 and also in Oven C001 it is expected that midden piles comprising domestic and/or industrial wastes were periodically spread across the site.

Spread C027 (164.4-3) has been interpreted as another dumped deposit. Micromorphological analysis of Spread C027 revealed it to be an organic-rich layer with parallel referred distribution and a banded basic distribution of organic material indicating a gradual infilling/build up of material rather than a single dump. The majority of organic material was reddish-yellow/orange amorphous but fragments of cellular charcoal and fuel residues provided evidence for anthropogenic input. Several patches of darker organic fabric have been interpreted as possible coprolites. The presence of very few woody plant fragments (bark?) are consistent with the suggestion made elsewhere on the site (Roy 2008) for material derived from the tanning process.

Spread C019 (164.2) may represent a dumped or sealing deposit. In thin section the deposit was observed to be mixed and bioturbated, consisting of a mix of mineral and organomineral material ranging from light to dark brown to grey, with lighter areas showing a slightly higher incidence of degraded plant fragments. Textural pedofeatures consistent with physical movement and disturbance were also present, with fine silt material infilling several larger voids and some small clay infills present. The coarse mineral nature of Spread C027 and limited anthropogenic evidence is indicative that this perhaps represented a levelling or cleaning layer between occupation horizons.

Whilst evidence for depositional alterations by biological agencies was absent in the majority of samples some post-depositional alteration was evident in the thin sections from Sample 164.1, Spread C146, and included bioturbation from root activity, indications of organic diagenesis, decay associated with amorphous organic staining and pseudomorphic voids, particularly of plant remains. The presence of rootlets near the top of Spread C146 is indicative of post-depositional pedoturbation. The diffuse boundary between Units 1 and 2 of 164.6 and apparent transportation of organic matter from the upper to the lower layer suggested a degree of biological reworking of these layers following deposition. Bioturbation is also evident in the form of faecal pellets, the by-product of small arthropods (Dawod and Fitzpatrick 1992).

Sequence 165 (Samples 165.4 &165.5, Figure 2.57, Chapter 2)

It was hypothesised that the sequence represented by Samples 165.4 and 165.5 includes a possible hearth. Micromorphological indicators of fuel ash residues include colour, indicative of iron immobilisation when heated; charcoal material; calcitic pseudomorph crystals; and silica phytoliths and diatoms and can

sometimes allow distinctions to be made between wood sources, grass, sedge and animal manure sources (see Simpson *et al.* 2003). Experimental observations of Umbanhower and McGrath (1998) have highlighted distinctions between wood, leaf and grass charcoals. The presence of black isotropic organic material with rough-serrate edges in Sample 165.4 is possibly burnt animal dung. However, micromorphological analysis has revealed that in addition to fuel residue and charred organic remains this deposit also contains frequent unburnt organic material including partially decomposed cellular plant fragments and possible coprolites indicating that this is a midden/waste dump where fuel ash (along with other waste) was spread rather than burnt.

Unit 2 of Sample 165.5 and Unit 1 of Sample 165.4 comprise Spread C157 overlying Oven C001. Both could be derived from a surface associated with a hearth. The high occurrence of ash and other fuel residues in the general matrix of Samples 165.4 and 165.5 as well as the presence of ash coatings on voids are indicative of deposition of fuel waste. The surrounding soil constituent was not burnt and as such it is likely that this deposit represented the fuel rakings from a hearth as opposed to the actual hearth itself. Unburnt inclusions indicative of human activity, including bone and plant fragments, were also present. Furthermore, the condition of the mineral grains was such that if the sediment as been subjected to periodic heating the temperature cannot have reached above 800°C (Courty *et al.* 1989: 117).

The base unit of Sample 165.5, an element of Oven C001, was a poorly sorted silty clay compact deposit with low porosity, sub-angular banded mineral component and a banded organic component associated with a cobble surface. The existence of varied fabrics within each unit and presence of numerous pedofeatures were indicative of a relative lack of disturbance following deposition. The banded nature of this deposit was indicative that it was formed periodically perhaps in a series of dumps or spreads. It was in marked contrast to overlying and underlying layers and organic matter appears to have derived from units above. The compaction of sediment in this deposit suggested intentional tamping or ramming of earth. The polyconcave nature of voids and hypocoatings of silt on some voids were also consistent with a deposit that had been trampled. It is possible that this may represent preparation for the construction of a building, hearth or floor.

The deposits represented within Sequence 165 thus represent the accumulation of occupation debris including organic waste, hearth rakings and animal debris. The dipping and aligned nature of some of the components within this sequence was indicative that this area was periodically levelled or subject to spreading of material and lenses of clay mineral material applied possibly as floor surfaces.

Sequence 167 (Samples 167.1–167.3, Figure 2.56, Chapter 2)

Layers C003 and C005, medieval dump or occupation build-ups of very dark grey silty clay, covered the area behind the Gallowgate. The discontinuous sequence represented by samples 167.1–3 includes a series of hypothesised occupation layers overlain with clay and silt deposits which have been interpreted as possible levelling layers.

The base of Sample 167.3 (Units 1&2) comprised an element of Layer C005. The high organic content and diversity of material present, including evidence for anthropogenic input in the form of burnt bone and charred cereal grains, was indicative that this was an occupation surface or possible midden. The presence of banded horizontally aligned plant fragments (possibly reed or sedge?) may be indicative of the intentional deposition of plants material over the occupation surface, possibly as a floor covering.

Layer C005 was overlain by Layers C026A and C026. The boundary between Layer C026A and Layer C005 was sharp and the dipping nature of the minerals in this deposit indicate that it was dumped possibly to seal the rich organic layer below and to allow reuse of this area for occupation and/or industry.

Sample 167.2 contained Layers C026A and C026, the differences in microstructure and organic content indicated that this was a different deposit to Layer C005. The deposit comprised two fabrics, the first of which included frequent organic matter and fuel residues which are indicative that this was an occupation horizon, whilst the second fabric was predominantly comprised of banded mineral silt and sand. The two distinct fabrics within this deposit are intriguing and numerous processes could be responsible for

this sediment structure including periodic natural deposition of sand and silt interspersed with periodic dumping of occupation waste, or indeed intentional infilling of an uneven floor surface with sand and silt deposits.

Sample 167.1 contained two units comprising a possible occupation deposit, Spread C015, overlain by a less organic banded deposit, Spread C146, which may have accumulated (at least in part) during a less intense phase of occupation/use of this area.

The discontinuous sequence represented by 167.1–167.3 thus appears to represent a series of occupation horizons including possible trampled floor deposits which were periodically 'cleaned' or levelled by the dumping of a silt/sand layer.

Conclusion

In summary the deposits represented by Sequences 164, 165 and 167 provide evidence for a range of sediment formation processes across the site. The presence of organic-rich anthropogenic layers in all sequences is indicative of intensive human use and occupation of the site over an extensive period and indicates that the intensity and nature of use changed over space and time.

The coarse nature, the irregular and vertical orientation of the rock fragments and generally compacted nature visible in several of the samples (e.g. 167.3, 164.2, 164.3) indicate that some of the deposits may have been deliberately laid and compacted and is indicative that some of the deposits may have been intentionally dumped, upcast perhaps following the excavation of pits. The combination of trampled floor deposits and intervening dumped sandy deposits raises the following question regarding local use of space: was material periodically dumped on the occupation surface as a means of levelling or cleaning or did structures undergo cycles of changing function?

5 Discussion:
The Site in Its Context

This study is indebted to previous authors and fieldworkers for their efforts in illuminating the archaeology of medieval and early post-medieval Aberdeen. In particular the author is indebted to the writers of the *Burgh Survey* undertaken by Dennison and Stones (1997), which provides a thorough account of the recorded history of Aberdeen, much of which is repeated here to provide context for the excavations at Bon Accord. Additionally, much background information on the recorded archaeology and history of the Gallowgate and Upperkirkgate areas has been obtained from the Society of Antiquaries monograph, *Aberdeen: an In-Depth View of the City's Past* (2001), edited by Cameron and Stones.

5.1 The origins of Upperkirkgate and Gallowgate (phases 1 to 3)

Archaeological evidence indicates that there was settlement in Aberdeen by the mid-to-late 12th century. Aberdeen may be identifiable with *Apardion*, a medieval township attacked by the Norwegian King Eystein around AD 1153, mentioned in the *Heimskringla Saga* (Dennison and Stones 1997: 11). Documentary evidence indicates that the medieval township was well established by the late 12th century. King David I (1124–53) issued a charter from Aberdeen while from AD 1174 Aberdeen was one of the locations at which William the Lion held court after losing control of Roxburgh, Berwick and Edinburgh (*ibid*, 11).

Several theories exist regarding the location of the earliest medieval settlement in Aberdeen; one possible early focus was the low-lying waterside area at the west of the burgh, known as the Green. This theory is based on the location of the early ecclesiastical site, St Nicholas Church, near the Green and outwith the city ports, and the belief that a former royal palace existed in the Green. The Green was, however, a marshy and waterlogged area, prone to flooding, and far from being the best defensible location in the area (*ibid*, 14). Dennison and Stones suggest an initial nucleus at the drier, east end of the Green at the foot of St Katherine's Hill, perhaps utilising the hill as a defensive position.

A lack of space for town expansion is postulated as a reason for movement of the town centre to higher, drier land in the Broadgate/Castlegate area at a later date (*ibid*, 15), which would have led to the Bon Accord site occupying a more central, and thus arguably more significant, location. Medieval Aberdeen was divided into four quarters, and the excavation site lay in the Even Quarter, which included the west side of the Gallowgate above what is now Broadgate (in the medieval period the southern end of the Gallowgate). It also included the area to the north of Upperkirkgate (Dennison *et al.* 2002: 31; Tyson 2002: 126).

Entrance to the medieval and early post-medieval town was controlled at the town's ports. Gallowgate Port (also called the Calsie or Causey Port), to the north of Bon Accord, controlled the route between New Aberdeen and the settlement of Old Aberdeen to the north, and was already considered ancient by AD 1518. It is possible that by the early 16th century the Gallowgate Port was located further north than the earlier medieval port, as it may have been moved further out from the centre of settlement as the town expanded (Dennison and Stones 1997: 13). In the mid-17th century it likely stood near 'the Wynde Mill' depicted on Gordon's map (Figure 5.1). In AD 1518, there were works on the Gallowgate Port as two individuals, Johnne Brabner and Alexander Gray, are identified as providing lime (11 October) for these works (Stuart 1844: 95). On 18 November 1519, 'Johne Alex. Rudirfurd, Willeam Holland, and Patrik Leslie, baizes [baillies] of this burgh…grantit, and assignit the aschatis [escheats], vnlayis [unlaws], and amerciament for this instant yeir to the biging and completing of thar port of the Gallowget, for wile [weal] and honour of the gud toune' (*ibid*, 96).

A major topographical feature of medieval Aberdeen was the Loch, to the west of the ridge of the Gallowgate. Properties on the Gallowgate and Upperkirkgate backed onto the Loch, which was fed by the Spital Burn and West Burn (Dennison and Stones 1997: 6). It has been postulated that water may have been diverted from entering the Loch as early as the 12th century towards the Guest Row/Broadgate area i.e. the foot of the Gallowgate, though Dennison and Stones note that this theory lacks archaeological proof (Dennison and Stones 1997: 16; Smith 1985: 5). Upperkirkgate Port, to the west of Bon Accord, was located at Schoolhill, within the mill burn that ran south from the Loch; it was demolished by the end of the 18th century (Dennison and Stones 1997: 13).

Bon Accord lay at a location significant from at least the later medieval period, on the junction of the two major medieval thoroughfares: Upperkirkgate to the south and Gallowgate to the east, both of which would eventually develop into important areas of domestic

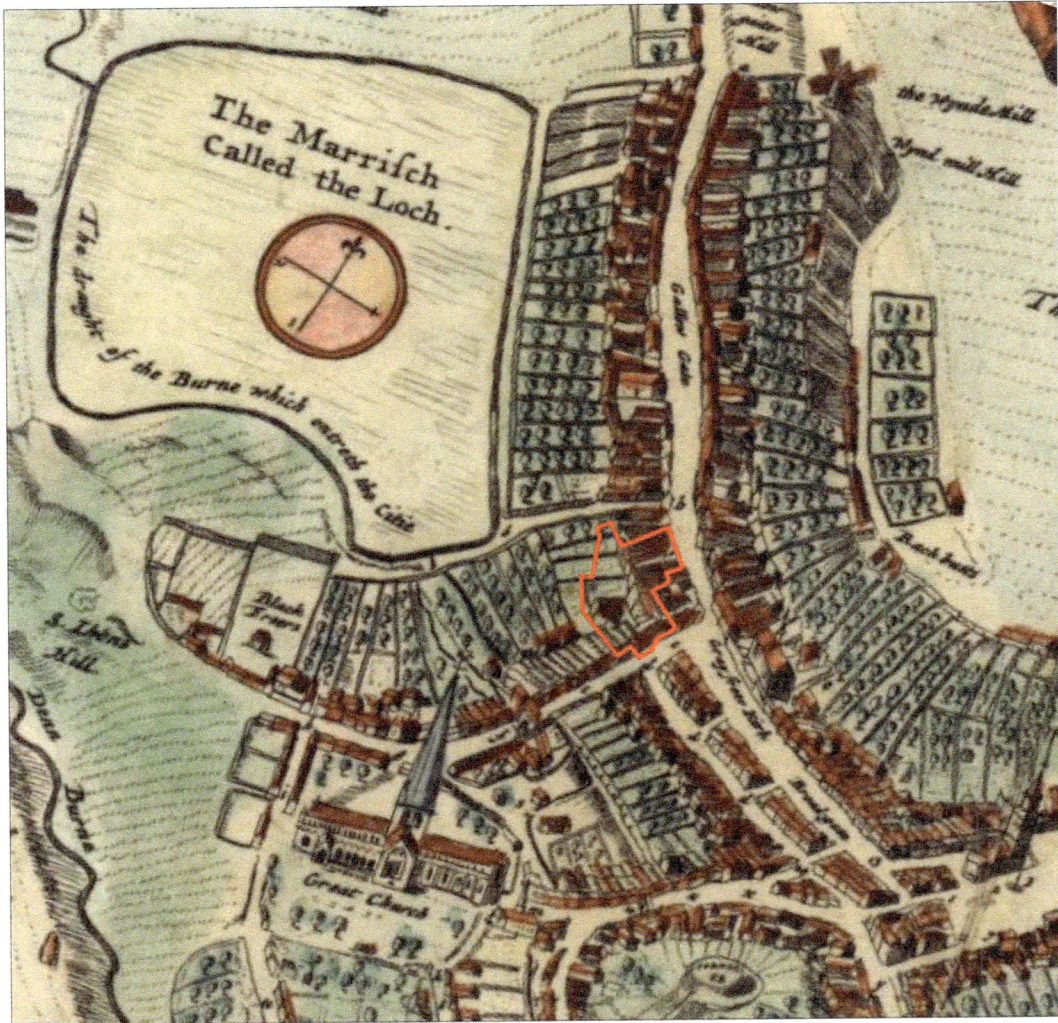

Figure 5.1 Extract from Gordon of Rothiemay's map of Aberdeen, 1661 (Reproduced with the permission of the National Library of Scotland and under Creative Commons (CC BY 4.0) https://creativecommons.org/licenses/by/4.0/)

settlement. The excavation at Bon Accord did not identify domestic buildings within the medieval phases on the frontage of the Gallowgate, perhaps indicating that the Gallowgate was not developed north of the Upperkirkgate until the later medieval period. However, the degree of truncation in the east of the site, the area that might have provided information regarding the first development of this thoroughfare, limits what can be said about the nature of the frontage prior to the late post-medieval period. A series of cut features, mostly large pits, were cut through surviving Phase 1 and Phase 2 deposits in this area, and there was a lack of structural evidence (apart from an unusual group of stakeholes (Stakes C001) recorded over a Phase 2 pit fill), suggesting that the Gallowgate frontage may not have been developed during Phases 1 and 2, before the mid 13th century. However, limited work was done near the frontages and it is possible that remains of earlier buildings may lie under the present Gallowgate. Also, the presence of human waste in features such as Pits C018, C019 and C023, and of stable waste in numerous pit features, including Phase 1 Pits C004 and C005 near the Gallowgate, alongside the substantial ceramic assemblages from these phases indicates that domestic activity may have been present nearby, perhaps with the craftsfolk occupying properties on the Gallowgate as well as the Upperkirkgate frontages.

The Bon Accord excavation did not extend to the Upperkirkgate frontage, and the south-west part of the site (Areas B and D) that approached the Upperkirkgate most closely was also heavily truncated, with only a few deep pits and the slight remains of a putative drystone wall (Wall B001; Figure 2.3, Chapter 2) surviving. Indeed, although this wall (and the cut features in this area), which given its alignment may represent an early boundary running off the Upperkirkgate, has been tentatively defined as belonging to Phase 1, the level of truncation means that it may realistically have originated at any point during Phases 1 to 3. Thus, as near the Gallowgate, no substantive evidence for features associated with potential domestic structures on the frontage was identified.

It has been noted elsewhere that it is likely that the Gallowgate and eastern Broad Street were largely undeveloped until the 13th century (Blanchard *et al.* 2002: 134), in line with the lack of development visible in Phases 1 and 2 of the Bon Accord site. A property on the Gallowgate or Broad Street was rented around AD 1281 by Colin Sellar, identified as a probable saddler (Innes 1845: 278–79; Ewan 1998: 167). The land lay between that of Ralph Foddoc to the south and Andrew of Culter to the north on the *vicus* or *via furcarum*, the way of forks, a former name of the Gallowgate (Keith 1843: 124). However, this term was also used at this time to refer to Broad Street, while perplexingly 'Gallowgate' (in various spellings) could also refer to the Broad Street area (Johnstone and Speirs 2001: 146). Gallowgate and Broad Street appear to have become separated during the late 15th century and 16th century: in the early 16th century Broad Street was the 'Broadgutter of the Gallowgate' which then became 'Broadgate'.

The presence of a building, unusually for this period stone-built, in the Gallowgate is mentioned in a court case of AD 1317 (Dickinson, 1957: 14; Stell 2002: 108). The Gallowgate is also mentioned in AD 1338 in a '*Charter by Hugh de Dunbarr, granting to John de Black Dunbarr his son two particates of land in the Gallowgate*' (Anderson 1909: 15).

Although references to the Kirkgate appear earlier, for example in a charter of between AD 1311 and AD 1327, the '*Carta Bernardi abbatis facta Patricio de Abirden super terra de Aberden in vico de Kirkgat*' (Innes and Chalmers 1848: 203, No. 269), these may refer to the Netherkirkgate, to the south. The first clear reference to the 'Upperkirkgate' appears much later, in AD 1382, in a '*Charter by John Crab, burgess, granting to the White Carmelites annuals amounting to ten merks sterling, from his crofts and lands and houses in Rubislaw, Upperkirkgate, Gallowgate, Netherkirkgate, Castlegate, Shiprow, and the Green. Dated on the Feast of Saint Bartholomew*' [24 August 1382] (Anderson 1909: 19; Johnstone and Speirs 2001: 142). However, there is clear archaeological support for the earlier development of this thoroughfare, as previous excavations have identified evidence for the laying out of burgage plot boundaries from at least the early 13th century, if not the 12th century, onwards on the Upperkirkgate (Murray 1982; Stones and Cameron 2001: 62 & 71). To the west of the Bon Accord site in backlands off the Upperkirkgate at 42 St Paul Street

(Murray 1982: 77) properties were laid out at right angles to the Upperkirkgate from around AD 1200.

The excavation at Bon Accord has identified a series of linear boundaries in Phases 1 and 2, running across the site approximately perpendicular to the Upperkirkgate. These include Gully C001 (likely linked to Gully C002 to its south), which originated in Phase 1 and appeared to be renewed during Phase 2, and numerous stakelines on the same alignment in Phase 2, which were found to divide part of the site near the Gallowgate frontage into apparent burgage plots running back from the Upperkirkgate, perhaps as early as the late 12th century (Figure 1.3, Chapter 1). The clearest example at the Bon Accord site was the area defined by Stakes C002 and C003 (Figure 2.14, Chapter 2), which was *c.* 5m wide, perhaps indicating a single plot width. Dennison (2008: 61), describing the site now covered by the new Scottish Parliament, comments on the large variation in the width of medieval burgage plots in Scotland and notes that the standard might be one burgh perch (3m) or twice this (6m).

Also in this area was a more substantial boundary, Wall C001. While it is possible that the wall and stakelines were contemporary, the roughly 1m-wide strip between Stakes C002 and Wall C001 possibly functioning as an access off the Upperkirkgate to the backlands of burgage plots, it is postulated that this wall represents a late Phase 2 feature, delimiting a boundary for property off the Gallowgate and superseding the parallel Upperkirkgate plot boundary lines to its east. In support of this, much of Wall C001 also underlies a post-medieval wall line. It is possible that Wall C001 marks the earliest version of this back limit to property off the Gallowgate, long before the insertion of the post-medieval wall. Alternatively, it may be related to a process noted by Murray, discussing the 42 St Paul Street site to the west of Bon Accord, where it is noted that although in the 13th century plot widths off the Upperkirkgate were irregular, around AD 1300 a regular pattern of wider plots, between 5.5 and 6.0m in width, was created (H.K. Murray 1982: 77–79; J.C. Murray 1982, 247); it could be that the insertion of Wall C001 was part of this process, as it would have produced a plot of this width.

If this area behind the Gallowgate was indeed delimited by the end of Phase 2, it may be that the frontage was occupied for domestic purposes from this time. Unfortunately, as noted above, the truncation of the area prevents the testing of this hypothesis. The presence of several pits in the south of this area in Phases 3 to 4 (Pits C047, C048 and C051) could either represent domestic refuse disposal or more industrial features (or a mixture of both). Pits C047 and C048 contained fragments of textile and leather assemblages, in the case of Pit C048 a substantial assemblage (Chapters 3 and 4.2.2). This pit was of substantial depth, suggesting that it may have originally had an industrial function, perhaps being a 'layaway' pit.

It is notable that there were significant occupation deposits near the Gallowgate frontage at Bon Accord from Phases 1 to 4, suggesting that the activities undertaken throughout the medieval period led to the rapid build up of ground level in close proximity to the Gallowgate. Further west, it appeared that the rise in ground level in Phases 1 to 4 was less rapid; indeed in this area it was not always possible to identify Phases 1 to 3 as distinct periods. While these were characterised as occupation deposits, they bore some resemblance to the homogeneous 'garden soils' identified elsewhere. Carter (2001) has noted, however, that it is possible that the deep homogeneous deposits identified in Scottish burghs such as St Andrews as imported medieval 'garden soils' may in actuality be derived from intensive occupation of backlands, the product of processes including weathering, decay and building replacement, with decomposition of turf and timber material from structures. The relative lack of features in the west of the Bon Accord site in Phases 1 to 3 need not necessarily reflect a lack of use in comparison with the area closer to the Gallowgate. Indeed, it is possible that a small structure (Posthole Cluster A001), measuring roughly 4m or more east/west by 5m north/south, was present in this area between Phases 1 and 3. A width of 4m, assuming this was a building within a plot off the Upperkirkgate, would accord well both with the width of rigs in Aberdeen, discussed above, and with the width of buildings excavated at Perth High Street, commonly between 3.5 and 4m or between 5 and 6m (Murray 2010: 128).

Certainly, the presence in the 13th century of substantial deep wells to the west of the Gallowgate frontage, beyond but in close proximity to the concentration of refuse and industrial pit features, indicates the utilisation of this area of backlands behind the Upperkirkgate. Both the timber-lined Phase 2 Well C001 and the large barrel-lined Phase 3 Well A002, though very different in form, must have required some effort to construct. The use of barrels or casks (Chapter 4.2.1) represents the simplest form of lining for wells, a form identified in excavations in several Scottish medieval burghs including Elgin, Aberdeen and Perth, while timber-lined wells have been recorded in Elgin, Aberdeen, Perth, Glasgow and perhaps St Andrews (cf. Murray *et al.* 2009: 224–25).

5.2 Industrial activity in the medieval gallowgate (phases 1 to 4)

According to rentals, Gallowgate appears by the 14th century to have been an area of relatively valuable

properties, one of the places where wealthier Aberdonians would have lived; by that time the focus of the burgh was the market area in the Castlegate (Dennison and Stones 1997: 19). However, archaeological evidence supports the interpretation of the Gallowgate area as a relatively marginal zone until around the 14th century. Prior to this, north of its junction with Upperkirkgate, the Gallowgate appears to have been 'a form of industrial complex', with evidence for metalworking, leatherworking and horn working (Stones 2001: 307). Excavations at the adjacent site of 45–47 Gallowgate to the north demonstrated 'no evidence of late 12th century use of the site' and though in the 13th and early 14th century there was some building on the Gallowgate frontage, the presence of yards and cess pits indicated that this was not a highly developed area (Murray 1984: 311). This is largely in line with the results of the excavation at Bon Accord, where the remains recorded from the medieval phases reveal a more industrial rather than a domestic area, with evidence suggesting a similar range of activities to the neighbouring 45–47 Gallowgate (Murray 1984). It is possible, however, that the frontage properties in this area housed the craftspeople who worked in the backlands but later development has obscured the nature of frontage occupation. The extent of this industrial quarter can be seen by the recovery during excavations at the Gallowgate Middle School Site, on the opposite side of the Gallowgate (Figure 1.1, Chapter 1), of evidence for a range of activities including shoemaking, cobbling and textile working (including leatherworking waste and a scutching knife associated with the processing of flax) within late 12th/13th century contexts (Cameron 2001: 73, 80–81).

Crafts would have employed a large proportion of the roughly 1000 individuals estimated to make up the population of Aberdeen during the 13th century (Ewan 1998: 157–58). By the late 13th century Aberdeen Castle would have acted as a major stimulus to production, as would the presence of the Episcopal See of Aberdeen, which was established to the north, at Old Aberdeen, in the 12th century (Ewan 1998: 159). The textile assemblage from Bon Accord comprised mainly cheap rural fabrics, perhaps indicative of a relatively impoverished (and marginal) population (Chapter 4.2.3), rather than the soft-finished products found elsewhere in Aberdeen.

Such activities as tanning and skinning were foul-smelling and were generally undertaken at a distance from town centres (Spearman 1988: 139). The relatively undeveloped nature of the area behind the Upperkirkgate and the Gallowgate prior to the 14th century would have been one reason for the possible concentration of relatively noxious industrial activities in this area. Another reason would have been the proximity of the Loch, a major source of water. Evidence for the eastern edge of the Loch was encountered during archaeological works at 45–75 Gallowgate (Dennison and Stones 1997: 43; Evans 2001: 85) to the north-west of Bon Accord (Figure 1.1, Chapter 1). This was an industrial area in the 13th and 14th century, including in the later 14th century a short-lived tannery or skin yard, evidenced by a complex of pits and a yard surface with ovens (Evans 2001: 83, 90–94).

Trades such as the skinners, dyers and saddlers needed to be close to a water source, and additionally trades utilising the same resources (such as fleshers and skinners) might be expected to concentrate together (Ewan 1998: 166). The economic success of medieval towns was much aided by the ability of different craft specialists, utilising the same raw materials, to work in close proximity (Spearman 1988: 136). The recently published excavations at Perth High Street, for example, provided evidence for the coexistence of butchery, hide preparation, horn working and leatherworking in adjacent areas (Thomas and Bogdan 2012: 297). A huge range of animal products were utilised by the various medieval crafts. As well as the production of meat, milk and hides, hooves were used to produce neat's foot oil (a product used in the preparation of skins) and gelatine; and both horn and bone were carved into objects (Ewan 1998: 168). The Loch would have provided a common resource, and a focus for the carrying out of such trades. Its location on the edge of the burgh may also have facilitated the supply of raw materials. A wide range of domestic animals, including cattle, horses and sheep, were kept in medieval Scottish towns (Spearman 1988: 136), with livestock probably being penned in the backlands of properties at night (Ewan 1998: 163). While evidence for the maintenance of animals and for the large scale slaughtering of animals on site was not clearly identified at Bon Accord, several pits contained quantities of material that may have been stable waste, and there was evidence for calves and lambs dying as neonates in Phases 1 and 2, suggesting penning in close proximity (Chapter 4.5.1 and 4.5.2). Ewan (1998: 161–62) identifies the north end of the Gallowgate, an area in close proximity to the Loch, as a major area of crofts in 13th century Aberdeen. These crofts were an area of arable crop cultivation – including oats, barley and wheat – and functioned as the immediate grazing land of the burgh. The moorland beyond these crofts was not suitable for crops and would have been used for grazing (Ewan 1998: 161–62; Smith 1985: 6). At Bon Accord, there was some evidence for the receipt of hides in a state ready for their preparation, some of which may have been butchered nearby. The medieval animal bone assemblage at Bon Accord contained significant quantities of horns and metapodials, elements of the skulls and the lower legs which it is believed were left on the hides to ease handling of the skins, for example

to facilitate hanging weights for stretching and drying the hides (Schmid 1972: 10).

5.2.1 Leatherworking and associated processes

Previous excavations have demonstrated that much leatherworking activity took place in the medieval Gallowgate, where 'substantial deposits of worn shoes and leather offcuts have been found at all sites, in contexts ranging from the late 12th century to the 14th century' (Stones 2001: 307). Stones contrasts this material with the worn domestic leather recovered elsewhere, including 30–46 Upperkirkgate (Figure 1.1, Chapter 1).

It is of little surprise then, that the most striking of these activities at Bon Accord is probably the turning of hides into leather, with perhaps subsequent cobbling. The leather assemblage (Chapter 4.2.2), though large with over 12,000 separate items, is broadly similar in the range of objects to several other Aberdeen excavations. The vast majority consisted of offcuts and scraps, but also included nearly 1000 shoe components, including turnshoes, largely of 12th to 13th century date. The shoe construction methods and styles represented at Bon Accord are paralleled elsewhere in Scotland (notably the excavations undertaken on the High Street of Perth in the 1970s (Thomas and Bogdan 2012).

The concentration of waste material is clear evidence for leatherworking on or near the site. Indeed, the predominance of waste offcut material indicates that this is material of industrial, not domestic, origin. Most of the activity appears to have been the production of new items (most significantly shoes) from new leather.

Tanning and leatherworking are present from Phase 1 at Bon Accord, evidenced in both the leather assemblage and in the form of several pits from this period. Two distinctive types of pit were commonly used in the tanning process in the medieval period. In the early stage of tanning, the hide is immersed in a weak tanning liquor and moved until the hides have a uniform colour; these pits are called 'handlers' (it is possible that the paddle-like wooden tools recovered at Bon Accord were used in this process – Chapter 4.2.1). Following this, the hides are set aside in 'layaways', deep pits with layers of vegetable tanning material such as oak bark interspersed with hides, until the pit is full then filled with water and left for a long period, perhaps 12 months plus. After this, the hides would need a place to dry, such as a shed (Cherry 1991a: 297).

In this earliest phase, leather appears in the fills of several pits, including Pits C001 and C015 (Chapter 3). The presence of bark and other rich organic material, commonly in basal, possible lining fills, suggests that tanning of hides was also undertaken at this early period (Chapter 4.5.1). It is possible that a grinding mechanism recovered from Phase 1 Pit C001 might have been utilised in the crushing of bark for use in tanning solutions (Córdoba and Müller 2011: 281). While many of these pits would have at least latterly served a refuse disposal function, it is unlikely that this was the primary purpose of them all. For example, the great depth of Pit C015 suggests that it may originally have served as a 'layaway' feature in the tanning of leather, while Pit C001 may have been a 'handler' pit. In the west of the site is a concentration of pits interpreted as being associated with the tanning process: 'layaway' pits A026 and A027, and possible 'handler' features Pits A028 and A029. There is a paucity of evidence for land division in this early phase, and it is likely that the west of the site was very peripheral, both to the Gallowgate and the more developed Upperkirkgate. However, there is limited evidence, in the form of a scatter of postholes (interrupted by later features), for a possible structure (Ph Cluster A001) in close proximity to the west of the concentration of leatherworking remains (Figure 2.3, Chapter 2). These also could be the remains of a structure associated with the preparation of hides, or a workshop. To the east, Pits C005 and C007 contained evidence in the form of animal skull and feet bones, for the preparation of hides; Pit C005 also containing both lambskin and goat hair.

It was notable that several of the pits identified as related to the tanning industry, such as potential layaway Pit A026, had evidence in the form of twigs and hazel branches which could represent lining material. The possible use of willow or hazel binding material as a pit lining is noted by Shaw (1996: 118) at The Green, Northampton. Shaw also notes the potential use of half barrels or casks, and timbers to line circular and rectangular pits respectively in the tanning process.

An assemblage of wooden tools (Chapter 4.2.1) was retrieved from the Phase 2 pits. These implements included shovels, scrapers, and paddle and bat-like tools suitable for beating, pounding and stirring, which could have been employed in the preparation of hides and tanning. Scrapers and the bat-like tools could have been used for pounding and scouring hides to remove hair and flesh. Shovels could have been utilised in the shifting of ash, dung and oak bark in the tanning process, while paddle-like tools could have been used for moving and lifting the leather in the tanning pits. Also recovered were fragments of a Purbeck limestone mortar (Chapter 4.3.2) that may have been utilised in the production of tanning or dyeing agents – a fragment of a smaller mortar recovered from 45–75 Gallowgate contained residues of tormentil and dock, both of which were utilised in the tanning and dyeing processes (Moffat and Penny 2001: 298–99).

The greater part of the leather assemblage (Chapter 4.2.2), and also the greatest concentration of features identified with the tanning industry, belong to Phase 2, when a series of such pits can be identified within what appears to be a single burgage plot defined by stakelines (Stakes C002 and C003) off the Upperkirkgate. The edges of several of these features were defined by lining materials. The features within this plot included potential 'layaway' Pits C021, C025 and C032, 'handler' Pits C022, C023 and C024, and Pit C034, a feature possibly associated with hide preparation, as well as Pit C018, which contained macroplant evidence for dyeing, and animal fibres (goatskin). To the immediate west of this plot was a likely 'layaway' feature, Pit C027. The boundary formed by Stakes C002 included several postholes and appeared similar in form to a structural feature formed by post pits and, possibly, stakes adjacent to 14th century tannery pits at Castlecliffe, St Andrews (Lewis 1996: 616–17). Lewis (1996: 679) postulates that, if not just a simple boundary feature, Structure 4 at Castlecliffe may have represented the wall of a long building that would have covered tanning pits, noting that the layaway pits in particular would have required covering to prevent dilution of the fluids within the tanning pits by rainwater. While there were relatively few identifiable postholes in Phase 2 of the Bon Accord site, it is not impossible that the plot defined by Stakes C002 and C003 could have been covered. Alternatively, this may represent a simple use of a fence as a safety screen to avoid accidents involving deep pits filled with extremely foul-smelling material. A wattle hurdle screen over timbers was recovered from near the top of Phase 2 Pit C025; this could represent the disposal of such a fence, or perhaps the intentional sealing of the feature after its usefulness had ended. A number of similar pit covers were encountered at Perth High Street (Perry 2010: 112).

By Phase 3 the leather assemblage has reduced in size but is still substantial. Pit C048, located within the same burgage plot as the majority of the Phase 2 pits identified with leatherworking, contained animal fibres identified as goatskin, and given its size may have been a 'layaway' feature. A further potential 'layaway', Pit C053, belongs to the early part of Phase 4 (i.e. late 13th to 14th century). It is clear, however, given the great reduction in the leather assemblage in this and subsequent phases that by this stage tanning would have been a minor activity.

As noted above, there is evidence for the early preparation of hides, in the form of animal fibres, indicative of the removal of hairs during fellmongering, as well as for tanning and subsequent working of leather into shoes and other articles, such as scabbards and other pieces of clothing. The coexistence of several trades associated with leatherworking by the later medieval period is clear from documentary evidence. Bain notes that the cordiners did more than produce shoes. They were commonly practising curriers, producing their own leather, and they controlled trade in hides and bark. 'Any person detected bringing rough hides into the city without having made the deacon acquainted with the fact rendered himself liable to a substantial fine (Bain 1887: 272–73)'. By AD 1484 the shoemakers, or cordiners, had already associated under a deacon (*ibid*, 265). Bain quotes the Council Register for 27th May 1484: '*The same day the alderman, baillies, and counsall, because thai have fundin grete faute in the craft of the cordinaris, at this tyme thai have put down the deacons of the said craft, annulland all powaris that thai gif to thaim of befor, and will fra hynce furth tak the correction of thaim all in tyme to cum, and to puniss thaim after thair demerits that sal be committit in tyme command*' (Bain 1887: 265).

5.2.2 Other industrial processes

While the leatherworking and related industries provided evidence for a notable concentration of such activity, in particular with an apparent specialisation in one rig on tanning and associated activities in Phase 2, it was clear that numerous trades were being undertaken in close proximity. At Perth High Street it was noted that there was a lack of specialisation within rigs, with multiple industries in the same rigs 'even in each phase'. It appeared that 'each merchant, who owned a rig, in addition to his own house and shop on the frontage and foreland, employed (housed?) several different types of craftsmen (and their families?) to work at the back of his rig, producing different products for him to sell' (Perry 2010: 115). However, at Bon Accord, while there was considerable evidence for the presence of different craft activities, there was little sign of associated shelters or workshops. This may be because the frontages had been removed or obscured by later development and it is very possible that the Upperkirkgate frontage and perhaps the Gallowgate frontage were occupied by those undertaking the many activities in the backlands.

High temperature processes

Evidence for high temperature processes, possibly industrial in nature, was recorded in the form of two hearths, perhaps small-scale industrial ovens, Hearths C001 and C002, in Phase 3, and a pair of larger features, perhaps with an industrial function, Ovens C001 and C002. Ovens C001 and C002 probably represented a rebuilt single structure in the early part of Phase 4 (late 13th to 14th century).

Evidence for a 13th century oven was found during excavations at the 42 St Paul Street site (Figure 1.1, Chapter 1). According to Murray this feature was situated in the open air away from frontage buildings to reduce the risk of fire. Murray interprets the feature as belonging to a burgess family living on the frontage, rather than that of a baker (Murray 1982: 53, 81). Given the backland situations of the Bon Accord features it is likely that these also were located away from frontage structures to limit the danger of fire. Ovens were also discovered during excavations at the nearby 45–75 Gallowgate, in phases dating to the later 14th century, where Evans discussed the possibility of their use in horn working, tanning or currying crafts (Evans 2001: 112–13).

Hearth C002 contained a daub assemblage, which may represent a hearth lining (Chapters 3 and 4.4.2). Timber lath impressions indicate that this clay daub covered a network of wooden structures to form part of the wall lining. Small fragments of curved daub appear, on comparison with material recovered at 45–75 Gallowgate to derive from an unroofed hearth (Cameron *et al.* 2001: 206). If the hearth was not enclosed, this could have lowered the temperature to which the daub lining would have been exposed, suggesting that the feature was not used in a very high temperature process, though the nature of this process is unknown. Similarly, the nature of the likely industrial function of Ovens C001 and C002 is unclear. Like Hearth C002, it is unlikely the ovens were used for such a high temperature process as the non-ferrous metalworking (likely the casting of brass) evidenced by the recovery of crucible fragments from Phases 2 to 4 (Chapter 4.3.5). A study of sediments with ash and other fuel residues overlying Oven C001 indicates that if the material associated with that feature was subjected to periodic heating the temperature could not have reached above 800°C (Chapter 4.5.6). The casting of brass, with a melting point of between *c.* 900 and 940°C, or other copper alloys, was therefore not likely associated with this feature – for example, yellow brass (65% copper; 35% zinc) has a melting point of 1660°F (904°C) while the melting point of bronze varies between 1550°F (843°C) and 1900°F (1037°C) (Untracht 1969: 18). It is tempting, however, to link these features (and/or the smaller Phase 3 hearths) to a process that produced fire damage on elements of the ceramic assemblage, including vessels such as cooking pots and jugs from Phase 2 Layer C003, and Phase 3 or 4 Pit C069. At 45–47 Gallowgate, Evans records the recovery of a late medieval transitional jug with sooting marks indicating that it had been 'laid lengthways in a charcoal bed', interpreting it as potential evidence for the production of 'a grease or oil solution, to be used in leather dressing'. Evans notes the need for curriers, involved in the dressing, finishing and colouring of leather, to have a source of heat 'to prepare solutions – both for the initial soaking of the leather to remove the bloom left by drying tanning liquors, and for making up warm dubbins of substances such as tallow and fish oils' (Evans 2001: 113).

Evans also notes the need for heat to prepare dyes used to decorate leather, though noting that such activity might not have occurred in close proximity to the more noxious trade of tanning (Evans 2001: 113). It is not impossible that the hearths or ovens at Bon Accord were therefore used in the preparation of dyes, in particular as tanning activity appears to be diminishing by Phase 3. There is some evidence for the presence of the woad plant (*Isatis tinctoria*) in Phase 2 Pit C018, as well as a small quantity of textile fibres, which suggests that this feature was used as either a dye bath or for the disposal of dye residue. It is possible that the fragmentary Purbeck limestone mortar (Chapter 4.3.2) recovered in the excavations was used in the processing of dyeing agents.

Evans notes that the sort of activities likely to have been undertaken in close proximity to tanning areas would have not been those requiring a source of clean water or a healthy atmosphere, and that horn working and other crafts related to leatherworking would have been likely candidates (Evans 2001: 112–23). Thoms and Robertson (Chapter 4.5.2) suggest that the animal bone assemblage, which included a large number of horn cores may indicate such activities at Bon Accord as horn working and the production of neats-foot oil (processes that would have accompanied the preparation of hides). The presence of butchery marks around the bases of horn cores from Bon Accord indicates that at least a proportion of the horn derived from the preparation of hides was being worked. Horn cores would have been soaked for weeks to loosen their chitinous sheaths, which would then be split lengthwise and boiled in cauldrons on hearths (Evans 2001: 113). While horn working is likely to have been concentrated in Phases 1 and 2, it is possible that the hearths and ovens at Bon Accord were connected to the provision of hot water for horn working in Phases 3 and early in Phase 4. However, Shaw, in discussing the tannery at The Green, Northampton, notes that deposits of horn cores are evidence primarily of tanning and need not indicate horn working (Shaw 1996: 117).

Fish processing

The presence of a large quantity of cod and ling vertebrae within a single feature (Phase 1 Pit C015) certainly points to some form of fish processing, most likely an element of food preparation. Indeed, the repetitive nature of butchery chop marks seen on this material suggests that the fish were prepared by professional fishmongers, probably off-site, perhaps in the nearby market area, and that this material largely represents waste from consumption.

However, the large quantity of fishbone remains from medieval phases at Bon Accord might be evidence for its use in the production of glue or oils. Fish oil, including oil derived from the cod so commonly found at Bon Accord, has historically been used for leather currying (Waterer 1946: 145).

There is evidence that the radiocarbon dates from carbon residues on pottery and leather may have been affected by the marine reservoir effect (Appendix 1). This raises the possibility that at least some of the pottery with evidence for burning residues was used for cooking fish or the heating of fish oils. Such fish oils could have been applied to leather, again leading to the potential for the marine reservoir effect to be apparent within radiocarbon dated samples of leather.

Non-ferrous metalworking

Small-scale non-ferrous metalworking, likely the casting of copper alloy, is evidenced by the small number of ceramic crucible fragments recovered from Phase 2 and 4 contexts (Chapter 4.3.5). These are generally small, handmade objects and appear to indicate the production of copper alloy artefacts. Clay casting mould fragments for non-ferrous metal decorative objects were recovered from several medieval contexts at Bon Accord, ranging from Phase 2 to Phase 5 (Chapter 4.3.6), while casting waste from non-ferrous metalworking was also recovered from Phase 2 deposits, including fills of Phase 2 Pits C018 and C019 (Chapter 4.3.1). While the location of the casting was not ascertained during the excavation, it is likely to have been in relatively close proximity. The moulds from Bon Accord indicate that decorative, ornamental items, including possible pin heads, badges and possibly mirror cases, were being produced between the late 12th century and the late 15th century. Non-ferrous metalworking on urban Scottish sites has been evidenced by the recovery of mould and crucible fragments from previous excavations at Aberdeen, Edinburgh, Elgin and Perth (Chapter 4.3.6), indicating the importance of this craft in Scotland's medieval burghs. Artefacts, including fragments of clay casting moulds recovered from 13th century contexts at 45–47 Gallowgate, suggest the presence of a metal casting workshop at that site (Murray 1984: 307–08); it is possible that such activity extended into Bon Accord. However, as noted above, at least one of the hearths at Bon Accord was unroofed, while Ovens C001 and C002 were likely not used in processes producing a temperature greater than 800°C. Thus there is no evidence that the hearths and oven-like features at Bon Accord were used in this industry.

Other crafts

There was also evidence of woodworking at Bon Accord, in the form of wood chips, commonly present in pits, primarily in Phases 1 and 2, which were either disposed of as refuse or used in the tanning process. Similar evidence was encountered in the Perth High Street excavations, where it was believed to largely derive from the construction of structures including buildings and fences (Perry 2010: 114). The presence of whetstones and grinding stones, in particular the composite grinding apparatus from Phase 1 Pit C001, and a whetstone from Phase 2 Pit C022 is further evidence for craft activities (Chapter 4.2.1 and 4.3.2).

5.3 Late medieval and early post-medieval properties (phase 4 to mid phase 5)

Excavations at 45–75 Gallowgate (Figure 1.1, Chapter 1) produced evidence of a variety of processes involved in the manufacture of leather goods, including 'fell-mongering, tanning and possibly currying' (Stones 2001: 307) in the later 14th century, suggesting that the Gallowgate continued as an industrial area long into the late medieval period. However, it also appears that the frontages of Gallowgate and its southern extension, Broad Street, were more densely occupied by domestic buildings by the same time. At 45–47 Gallowgate, occupation of the frontage was, until the early 14th century, at a relatively low density (in comparison with the Upperkirkgate), but by the mid 14th century the Gallowgate was more popular, with buildings on the frontage and an apparent paved street at the front of the area. However, following the Black Death it appears that the area was again perhaps less densely occupied (Murray 1984: 311). As noted above, the presence of significant oven features in early Phase 4 indicates that the Bon Accord backlands were likely utilised in the late 13th to 14th century for relatively high temperature industrial processes. Moreover, it is possible that primary smithing of iron was undertaken in the vicinity during late Phase 4 as an iron billet was recovered from an occupation deposit, Layer C008 (Chapter 4.3.7). Unfortunately, it is unclear whether the lack of evidence for domestic structures at Bon Accord in the 14th century is due largely to truncation, or whether this reflects the undeveloped character of the area. The Black Death of the mid 14th century, which was followed by repeated visitations of the plague, led to a diminution of the population of Aberdeen and slow growth in the succeeding centuries. By 1400 the population was *c.* 3000; in 1570 it was *c.* 5500 and even by the 1640s it was only 8300 (Dennison *et al.* 2002: xxvi).

It is unfortunate that there is limited evidence at Bon Accord for later medieval property boundaries: no property boundaries were identifiable in Phase 3,

and only tentative evidence for boundaries off the Upperkirkgate were recorded around the 14th century (Gully A003 early in Phase 4, and Wall C007 later in this phase), while even the boundary walls (Walls A004 and C019) recorded in the early and middle parts of Phase 5 are fragmentary. This is in large part due to the truncation caused by such structures as the Aberdeen University Press and the late post-medieval frontage structures on the Gallowgate.

The truncation of 14th century to 17th century deposits was total on the Gallowgate frontage. Further west, dumped anthropogenic occupation deposits continued through much of Phase 4 (late 13th to early 15th century), indicating relatively intense use of the area. However, from around the end of Phase 4 and in particular through Phase 5 the west of the site was built up with deposits, characterised on site as 'garden soils' that generally appeared to be fairly homogeneous, less organic-rich than earlier deposits, and showing fewer signs of an anthropogenic nature. The existence of gardens and orchards behind the 17th century Gallowgate and Upperkirkgate is clear on Gordon's map of 1661 (Figure 5.1), but it is not certain that these areas were utilised in this way in the 15th and 16th centuries as it is possible that such 'garden soils' might also derive from intensive occupation (Carter 2001).

Evidence for the 15th/16th century occupation of the area can be found in the presence of a barrel-lined water butt or well (Well A001) apparently a renewal of a 14th century feature. Its location between Walls A004 and C019 suggests that this was an undeveloped open area, and it is interesting that this area appears as a courtyard in mapping of the 18th and 19th century. This barrel-lined well is located in close proximity to the earlier (Phase 3) Well A002, and it is tempting to see it as a replacement. Several late medieval and early post-medieval wells have been encountered nearby, including the late 14th/early 15th century barrel-lined well or water-butt at Gallowgate Middle School (Cameron 2001: 77), and the 17th century well at 45–75 Gallowgate (Evans 2001: 95).

As noted above, truncation limited the survival of structural remains, in particular between the beginning of Phase 4 and the middle of Phase 5. Apart from boundary features, several small segments of putative structures were recorded, but none survived to the extent that their form or nature could be confidently identified. In Phase 4 Wall C002 may represent the remains of a stone wall, or demolition debris, north of and perhaps associated with Oven C001. In late Phase 4/early Phase 5 a possible stone wall base, Wall C010, associated with cobble Surface C013 to its north, might also represent a structure. In early Phase 5, clay-bonded rubble Walls C003 and C004 appeared to form the north-east corner of a building. Similarly, in mid-to-late Phase 5 Wall C009, associated with the remains of a clay and cobble surface, Surface C009, may represent elements of another possible structure.

Documentary sources such as the *Cartularium Ecclesiae Sancti Nicholai Aberdonensis* (Cooper 1892) and the *Registrum Episcopatus Aberdonensis* (Innes 1845) contain references to the ownership of rigs or 'lands' or 'tenements' in the Upperkirkgate and Gallowgate/Broad Street areas in the late medieval period. Johnstone and Speirs (2001: 143–45) have identified several possible owners of lands on the Upperkirkgate. In spite of the difficulties in identifying individual properties from such documents, some of the owners of properties on the north side of the eastern Upperkirkgate can tentatively be identified. Some work was undertaken by Murray on identifying late medieval ownership at the neighbouring site of 42 St Paul Street, where four property plots (rigs) were identified, numbered 1 to 4 from east to west. Murray's Plot 1 lies immediately west of the Bon Accord site (Murray 1982: 77–81). Murray, in discussing these adjacent properties, noted that the yards and gardens appeared to pertain to the frontage properties on the Upperkirkgate until the late 16th/early 17th century, and that the plots were not subdivided until after this date (*ibid*, 81); it is likely that this was also true of the Bon Accord properties off the Upperkirkgate. It is likely that there were also properties off the Gallowgate at Bon Accord in the later medieval period, though remains of those within the site were removed by later post-medieval structures.

In the mid 15th century, documentary records appear to describe a series of at least five Upperkirkgate properties lying adjacent to each other in a north/south alignment, rather than east/west, as would be expected given the alignment of the street. It is tempting to see this as an indication of the occupation of south/north rigs at the east end of the Upperkirkgate, behind the Gallowgate. This accords with Gordon's map of 1661 (Figure 5.1) where there is a concentration of buildings in this area. Occasional examples of the infilling of burgage plots by development had begun in Aberdeen by the medieval period (Dennison *et al.* 2002: 33). A series of proprietors can be tentatively identified, running from south to north: John Crag; Thomas Club, Thomas Traill; Thomas Litsteir and Adam Liststeir. The same sequence of landowners is repeated in a Charter by William Scherar, formerly Provost of Aberdeen, endowing the altar of St Duthac in 1464 (Cooper 1892: II, 17–18, No. X), i.e. '*the land of Thomas Litster lying in the Upperkirkgate between the land of Adam Litster on the north, and the land of Thomas Trayl on the south*' and '*the land of the said Thomas Traal lying in the same street, between the land of the said Thomas Litster on the north, and the land of Thomas Club on the south*' and '*the land of the said Thomas*

Club lying in the said street, between the land of Thomas Tralle on the north, and the land of John Crag on the south'.

However, it is possible that the coincidence of names is fortuitous and does not represent a sequence of five north/south properties, but rather three examples of a tripartite division: foreland, inland and yard. From around the mid 15th century, separate subdivisions of the long rigs of burgage plots in Aberdeen are commonly described as foreland (frontage), inland and backland. While the practice of subdividing properties thus may have already been extant, it is not recorded before 1400 (Johnstone and Speirs 2001: 125). In discussing the medieval occupation of the site of 30–46 Upperkirkgate Johnstone and Speirs (2001: 145) note that the Traills 'owned several tenements within the burgh and in the mid 15th century owned adjacent tenements in... the Upperkirkgate'. In the 30–46 Upperkirkgate area, rigs were divided into just two divisions as late as the early 16th century, with division into foreland, inland and yard commonplace by the mid 16th century (ibid), while Cripps (1982: 77) notes that the rigs to the west of the Bon Accord site were sparsely occupied in the 15th century, stretching from Upperkirkgate to the Loch.

To the west of Bon Accord, a rental of the altar of Saint Peter (Cooper 1892, II: 43–44, No. XXVII) notes that a portion of land was formerly owned by John Cadiow, '*lying on the north side of the Upperkirkgate between the land of Adam de Craufurd on the east*'. Cripps (1982: 77) identifies John Cadiow as John Cadiou, MP for the burgh in 1449 and a possible town clerk. She identifies this land with that of Rigs 2/3 on the 42 Loch Street site, according to a 15th century grant of annual rent to St Peter's altar (Innes 1845: I, 262–63), likely to date to between 1449 and 1459. This document identifies '*a land of Johannis Cadzow lying on the north side of the Upperkirgate, between the land of Ade de Crafurde on the east and a land of Johannis de Scrogis, son, on the west*'. Adam Crauford's property would thus be equivalent to Rig 1, immediately west of the Bon Accord site, i.e. No. 18 Upperkirkgate.

A Charter by Stephen Balrony of 1454 (Cooper 1892: II, 107–08, No. LXV), and therefore of comparable date to the aforementioned rental documents, indicates that '*the land of Adam Crafurde lying within the said burgh on the north side of the Upperkirkgate*' lay '*between the land of Mr. John Cadiou on the west and the land of John Litstar, the son of Edward, on the east*'. Thus John Litstar was in the mid 15th century the occupier of the property to the east of 42 St Paul Street Rig 1, and therefore on the west side of the Bon Accord site. His surname might indicate that he was a dyer by trade. The surname, Litstar (or variants), appears in Aberdeen during the late medieval period and indicates the trade of the 'litster', a dyer of cloth. It is unfortunate that the western part of the Bon Accord site had suffered from heavy late post-medieval truncation, but dyeing activity on the site is certainly attested earlier in the medieval period.

In 1526, a charter of Janet Crauford (Cooper 1892: II, 133–34, No. LXXXI), described as the relict of the late Gavin Murray, notes that her front and backland (i.e. an entire rig) lay on the north side of the Upperkirkgate, 'between the land of the heirs of the late Robert Crag on the east and the land of John Murray on the west'. John Murray is described in a note on the rental of the altar of St Peter (Cooper 1892: II, 43–44, No. XXVII) as owning the land formerly owned by John Cadiow (i.e. Rig 2/3 of the 42 St Paul Street site). Thus Janet Crauford was the owner of Rig 1 in 1526, and Robert Crag was the owner of the westernmost plot of the Bon Accord site, an area almost entirely truncated by later activity. The charter of David Anderson of 1536 (Cooper 1892: II, 148–50, No. XCII), identifies a tenement of John Crag to the north of the Upperkirkgate and 'between the land of John Arthour on the east, and the land of Thomas Crafurd on the west, the king's highway on the south [Upperkirkgate], and the common vennel [the Vennel] of the said burgh on the north'. Given the coincidence of surnames, it would seem reasonable to identify Thomas Crauford's property with that of Janet, and John Crag's property with that of Robert. The description of John Crag's property lying to the south of the Vennel (later St Paul Street), as logically must that of his neighbour to the east, John Arthour, supports the identification of the Crag's property as lying on the west side of the Bon Accord site. Arthour would therefore have occupied the property to the immediate east of this, likely lying between the 19th century Ironmonger's and Ross's Courts (Figure 1.3, Chapter 1).

It is likely that properties on the west side of the Gallowgate had back gates giving access to the Loch. To the immediate north of the Bon Accord site, a lane called 'The Vennel', subsequently replaced by Gordon's Wynd and later St Paul Street, also gave access to the Loch from the Gallowgate. The Vennel was formerly accessed from the Gallowgate via 'a pend under a house' (Milne 1911: 273). Cripps (1982: 77) encountered a reference in the Sasine Register (SR V¹/176) describing 'the vennel leading to the loch' as early as 1526. Around this time, in the middle of Phase 5, an east/west aligned stone boundary feature, incorporating a drain, Structure C006, which apparently continued as Structure A018 to the west, crossed a large area of the site, and might represent a boundary off the Gallowgate, or perhaps more likely a boundary behind the Vennel. The presence of two small patches of yellow clay (Surfaces C010 and C022) located to the north and south of this boundary respectively suggest that floor surfaces may have existed against parts of this wall line. However, the presence of smithing waste in Spread C021/C022 (see below) in the corner formed by Wall C019 and Structure C006 indicates that this may have

been a peripheral area on the edge of a property, where industrial residue could be disposed of.

5.4 Later post-medieval occupation: the gardens of aberdeen (mid-to-late phase 5)

The area behind the Gallowgate, occupied by the Loch, was improved by drainage works over the course of the late medieval/early post-medieval period. On 7 April 1507, the Council dictated that when necessary, householders were to provide labour for works on the Loch, 'that evere fyrhouse within this burghe sale furnis and sende ane sufficient work seruand, with spaide, schwile, or barrowe, to help to rede the common loche, quhen euere thai be warnit thairto be the officiaris or the hande bele, vnder the pane of 8 shillings. Vnforgevin' (Stuart 1844: 76). By the early 17th century works were put in place to dry out the area, under the oversight of the town's master of works, David Andersone. The Council on 20 April 1603 ordered 'that the said locht salbe maid dry, be the sicht and advyse of Dauid Andersoun, elder, the townis maister of wark, and that the haill trinck of the water salbe drawn doun the south syd of the Lochfeild croft, and to rin at the west syd of the Gallowgett, and eist syd of the said loch, in the auld trinck, to be cassin deper and wyder, and that the water trinck on the south-vest syd of the said locht, nixt the Womanhill, salbe stoppit and condamnit, and that this wark of the drying of the said locht, and casting of the same, salbe done in all convenient diligence, be the labouris and travellis of the haill inhabitantis of this burght' (Stuart 1848: 239–40).

While this early exercise in land reclamation and environmental improvements would have had the potential to improve the ground conditions behind the Gallowgate, no doubt facilitating the expansion of domestic settlement, perhaps it also served to reduce the ready availability of water from the Loch for industrial purposes (Dennison et al. 2002: 36). In any case, the area around the burgh was becoming more urban in nature. As Crone suggests (Chapter 4.1.1), while woodlands including the royal Forest of Aberdeen formerly stood adjacent to the burgh, it appears that the demands of the burgh during the 13th century may have reduced this to smaller, discrete pockets of woodland by the 14th century. This may have impacted the environment of the Bon Accord site. As Robertson notes (Chapter 4.5.1), a noticeable decrease in the heath and moorland plant taxa recovered from Phases 4 and 5 may indicate that heath and moorland were no longer as easily accessible as they once had been given the less peripheral nature of the site. There appears to have been some effort made in the late medieval/early post-medieval period to ameliorate the environment of the Gallowgate. The Council Records note that on 11 April 1538 it was ordained that 'na maner of nychtbour [neighbour] within this toun duelland [dwelling] suld [should] lay ony fulze [dirt] or filtht in the maist oppin *place of the Gallowgat, quhilk* [which] *is afor Johnn Mairis zet* [gate], *and umquhill* [the former/late] *Johnn Cullanuis hous...and gif it sell hapin ony maner of persoun to lay ony maner of fulze thair in tymmis cumming* [times coming], *thai sell pay the baizes* [baillies] *vnlaw* [a fine] *of viij s.* [8 shillings] *vnforgewin* [without remission], *and it selbe lesum* [shall be permitted] *to quhatsumeuer* [whichever] *nychtbour that reprehendis* [apprehends] *the layaris of the said fulze in the place forsayd, to tak the veschell* [vessel] *that it sell happin to be brocht in, to be keipit quhill* [until] *thai be punyst* [punished] *for the braking of this statut'* (Stuart 1844: 156).

By the time of James Gordon's plan of 1661 (Figure 5.1), the Loch appears to have become relatively dry and is referred to as '*The Marrisch called the Loch*'. Gordon notes that it is '*a fenne or pudle rather*' (Innes 1842: 10). His map also shows the productive use of the backlands of the Gallowgate and Upperkirkgate, towards the Loch, for kitchen gardens and orchards (Smith 1985: 6). Gordon states that, '*Many houses have ther gardings and orcheyards adjoyning; every garding has its posterne, and thes are planted with all sorts of trees which the climat will suffer to grow*' (Innes 1842: 9). Writing in the early 18th century, Samuel Forbes of Foveran noted that most of Aberdeen's houses '*have the conveniency, or beauty, of a garden belonging to them; and all the gardens of one street* [the Gallowgate], *have a small rivulet* [the Loch], *running in a straight line with their walls, upon one hand, and beautified, on the opposite side, by a thick plantation of the profitable willow*'. The rivulet '*entering the town, vaulted and built above, waters some gardens*' (Forbes of Foveran 1843: 44).

It would appear from the excavation evidence that by around the turn of the 17th century the Bon Accord site, with the exception of the Gallowgate frontage, was largely occupied by gardens of the properties fronting on Upperkirkgate and Gallowgate, as evidenced by the extensive 'garden soils' in the west of the area. The gardens of post-medieval Aberdeen appear to have been relatively productive, both in fruit and vegetables and in trees. The Old Statistical Account (OSA) lists cabbages, carrots, spinach, cucumbers, gooseberries, currants and raspberries among the products of Aberdeen's gardens at the end of the 18th century. It also notes that while ash, elm, beech, maple, birch, lime, willow and holly were planted in hedgerows, gardens were used as nurseries for such trees as oak, elm, pine, larch and laburnum for sale to both the Scottish and English markets (OSA 1791–1799: 156).

A succession of cobble yard surfaces, Surfaces C009A, C011 and C012 in turn may represent the remains of an access route from the Upperkirkgate during this period. Many of the features of the later, 15th/16th to 18th century late Phase 5 appeared to be related

to drainage, perhaps indicating the persistence of the control of water as an issue, e.g. possible soakaway Pit C104 and Gullies C008 and C012, and most clearly the extensive linear stone-lined drainage Structure A019. Gordon's map of 1661 shows the nature of land division in the Upperkirkgate/Gallowgate area in the early post-medieval period (and likely the late medieval period). It clearly shows the Gallowgate and Upperkirkgate area with buildings along the frontages and long narrow rigs running at right angles to the roads behind these frontages. It is noticeable that while the rigs off the west end of the Upperkirkgate run a significant distance towards the Vennel, the rigs off the Gallowgate appear to have been relatively short, as were the rigs off the eastern end of the Upperkirkgate, which were cut off by Gallowgate properties. Even at this relatively early date there are numerous buildings depicted behind the Gallowgate frontage, indicating that the inlands of the Gallowgate and eastern Upperkirkgate burgage plots had been overbuilt. Evans (2001: 96, 114) suggests that the rise in Aberdeen's population between 1400 and 1700 led to encroachment of buildings, associated with yards, cess pits and wells, in backlands, such as an early-to-mid 17th century timber or cob building identified at 45–75 Gallowgate. Nearby, at 45–47 Gallowgate, a large stone building was present in the backlands by the 17th century (Murray 1984: 311). Unfortunately, however, the survival of significant structural and boundary features was rare at Bon Accord even in this late period, with the remains of a single possible structure, represented by Walls C011 and C012, and clay floor surface C014, being heavily truncated, so that neither its form or function could be ascertained. A single major north/south boundary off the Upperkirkgate, Wall C014, the rebuild of Wall C019, also survived later truncation. However, it is likely that the wall lines of later industrial features in the west of the site may follow pre-existing boundaries.

The Council Records for 3 August 1641 note that one resident of the Gallowgate was Patrick Jack, younger, litster (Stuart 1871: 267), circumstantial evidence for the presence of the dyer's trade in the area. However, Dennison and Stones indicate that, at least by the early post-medieval period, the main areas of operation for the dyers were the Netherkirkgate, Putacheside and the east side of the Green (Dennison and Stones 1997: 16). No indication of dyeing was encountered at Bon Accord at this late date but although tanning and other former industries were not in evidence by the 15th and 16th centuries, industrial processes were still undertaken in the area in the post-medieval period. During Phase 5, and to a lesser extent Phase 6, the residues of iron smithing activity were recovered; for example Spread C021/C022 represented a substantial dump of smithing material (Chapter 4.3.7). The recovery of a rotary grinding stone is further evidence for ferrous metalworking at this time (Chapter 4.3.2); this could

Figure 5.2 Extract from Alexander Milne's map, 1789 (Reproduced with the permission of the National Library of Scotland and under Creative Commons (CC BY 4.0) https://creativecommons. org/licenses/by/4.0/)

have been utilised either in the finishing of products or in the sharpening of tools. The presence of post-medieval smithing was similarly identified at the 45–75 Gallowgate excavations to the north, where a building dated to between 1645 and 1720 contained a significant quantity of hearth lining and smithing slag (Cameron *et al.* 2001: 203).

5.5 Later post-medieval occupation: houses of the gentry (late phase 5)

The presence of the MP John Cadiou and John de Scroggs the younger, provost, on the Upperkirkgate in the mid 15th century is indicative that it enjoyed a relatively high status even at that early date (Cripps 1982: 77). Certainly, between the 17th and early 19th centuries the north side of the Upperkirkgate (and the west side of the Gallowgate) was a fashionable part of Aberdeen, where town houses were built by the wealthy. Later, the area would become less exclusive, and a pattern developed where shop premises were to be found on the ground floor, with flats above (Morgan 2004: 122).

An idea of the occupations of the residents of the Even Quarter of Aberdeen, within which the Bon Accord site is located, in the mid 17th century can be gained from the *'Generall Band of Relieff for the yeir of God 1639'*, drawn up in 1640, which lists those Aberdonians willing, and unwilling, to pay a tenth of their yearly rents to the covenanting cause (Aberdeen City Council 1639). The occupations of individuals within the Even Quarter include many crafts: flesher, skinner, saddler, shoemaker, candlemaker, weaver, tailor, smith, wright, cooper, glazier and slater. It also includes individuals involved in food, alcohol and pharmaceutical provision: maltman, fisher, baker, vintner and apothecary, and many white collar professionals: advocate, notary, doctor, surgeon and writer. Numerous merchants, of unspecified goods, were recorded. Several town bailies lived in the area, as did *'Robert Johnstonne, old Provost'* and *'Mr James Sandilands, Commissary of Aberdeen'*. Given the horticultural use of many backland areas at this time, it is not unusual that a professional gardener should be present; a stabler was also listed.

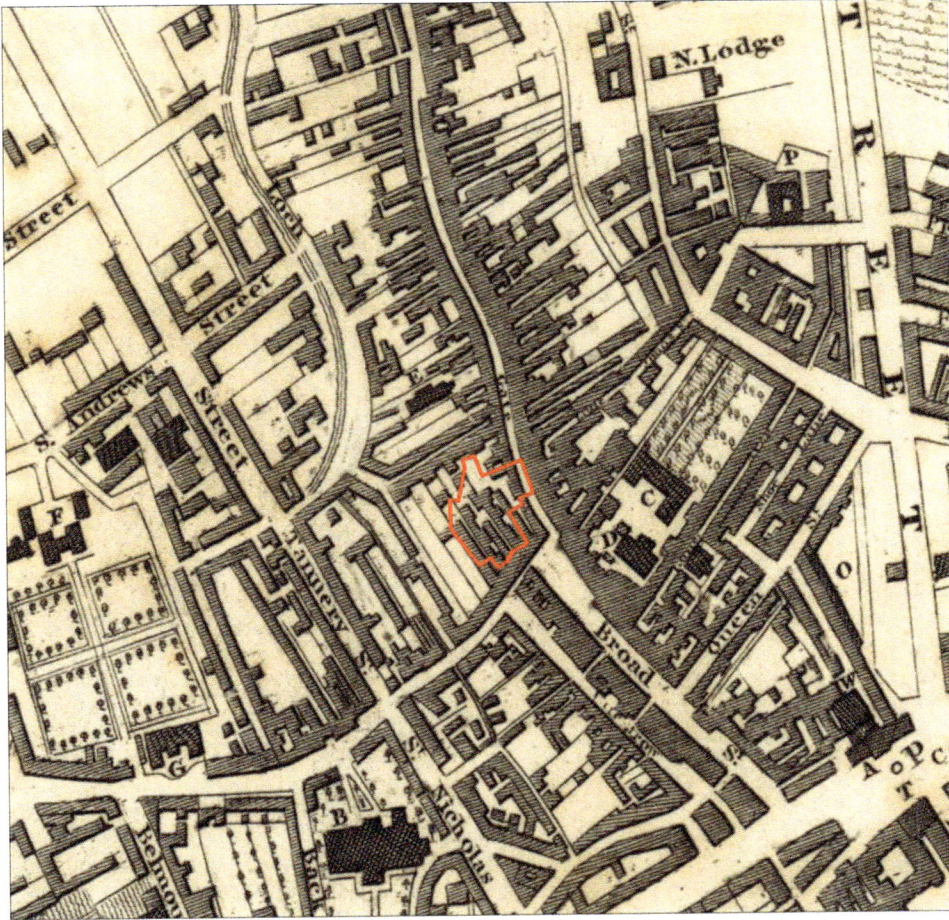

Figure 5.3 Extract from John Wood's map, 1828 (Reproduced with the permission of the National Library of Scotland and under Creative Commons (CC BY 4.0) https://creativecommons.org/licenses/by/4.0/)

While timber was commonly used for buildings into the 18th century, both slate and locally-produced brick were also utilised. Granite also became more commonly used from the first half of the 18th century (Dennison *et al.* 2002: 39). It is therefore likely that the buildings fronting on both the Upperkirkgate and the Gallowgate were of more substantial nature from the 18th century, and that it was at this point that the Gallowgate frontage suffered considerable truncation.

While the excavation at Bon Accord did not extend as far as the Upperkirkgate frontage, it is likely that the gardens in the west of the site pertained to these properties. To the immediate south of the Bon Accord site, at Nos. 6–8 Upperkirkgate, stands Provost Robertson's House, which contains elements dating to the 17th century. A house was constructed here *c.* 1680 by George Leslie, who was provost of Aberdeen between 1685 and 1687. The house was modified and enlarged in the 18th century by Alexander Robertson, who was three times provost between 1740 and 1757 (Morgan 2004: 125). The present property contains fabric from

the earlier buildings, including a 16th century moulded doorway with an armorial panel, dated 1730, which is described as a survival from Provost Robertson's house, bearing both his name and that of his wife 'Jean Strachan' (Morgan 2004: 125). According to Meldrum, George Leslie's son, James, an advocate, sold the property to James Robertson, the father of the 18th century provost Alexander Robertson. Alexander Robertson's improvements included the addition of a wing along the west side of Ross's Court, which formed a pend under the 17th century house (Meldrum 1986: 151). It was the construction of the Aberdeen University Press buildings around 1899 that led to the demolition of Provost Leslie's forehouse and the back wing of Provost Robertson's back-house. Ross's Court formerly gave access to the gardens of Leslie and Robertson's house (Morgan 2004: 125), which lay within the Bon Accord site, and would have contained the drainage Structure A019 and been defined by walls including Wall C014 to the west. These gardens are clearly visible on 18th and 19th century historic maps (Figures 5.2–5.5); by the time of the First Edition Ordnance Survey map of 1871,

255

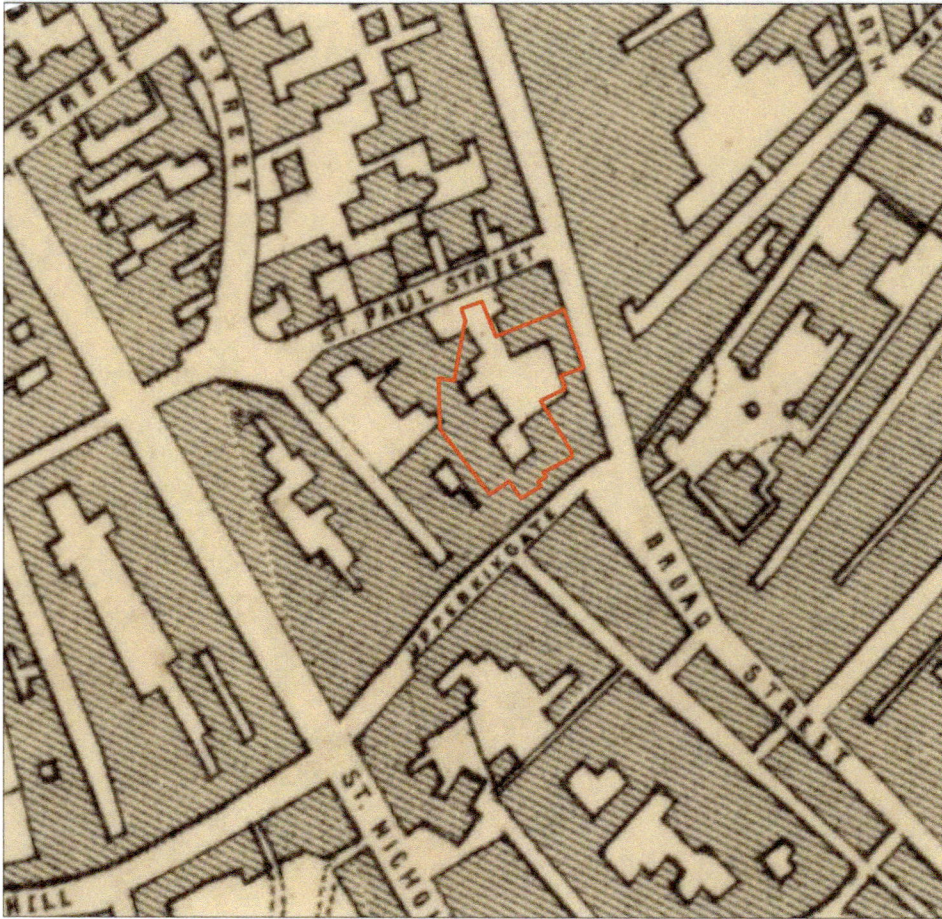

Figure 5.4 Extract from Keith & Gibb's map, 1862 (Reproduced with the permission of the National Library of Scotland and under Creative Commons (CC BY 4.0) https://creativecommons. org/licenses/by/4.0/)

the gardens stretched to the St Paul Street frontage. It is largely due to the existence of these gardens and further gardens to the east, depicted on historic maps, that such deep stratigraphy survived within parts of the excavated area.

To the south-west of the Bon Accord site, 24–26 Upperkirkgate is also said to have been a provost's residence, dating to 1694 (Morgan 2004: 124). Nearby, and just to the west of the excavated area, Patrick Anderson of Bourtie built a house in 1741 at the end of what was later known as Boy's Hospital Court. Anderson's ancestor, 'Skipper John Anderson of Torry' held title to land in this area by 1659, and the family gained much of the surrounding property (Morgan 2004: 127). This land acquisition continued until 1828, when Alexander Anderson sold the Anderson properties to David Gill and John Farquhar, who had set up a paint manufacturer and brassfounders and used this land to expand their business. The Alexander town house became the Boy's Hospital, and the paint works would eventually cover a huge area between

the western limit of the Bon Accord site, marked by the former Farquhar's Court, and Drums Lane (Morgan 2004: 127), an early demonstration of the evolution of the area from town gardens to an industrial zone.

5.6 The late 18th century onwards: expansion of commerce and industry (phase 6)

By the end of the 18th century, the population of Aberdeen had increased hugely. The OSA states that in July 1795, the first rent roll recorded 5052 inhabitants within the Even Quarter alone, while a population of 24,493 is given for the city and parishes of Aberdeen as a whole (OSA 1791–99: 170, 180). With population growth came a building boom around the 1760s. Many of the gardens in Aberdeen were lost to courts, backland buildings and tenements (Pittock 2002: 371). Maps and plans from the late 18th century onwards show that the backland areas visible as undeveloped spaces, with gardens and trees on Gordon's map, were being overbuilt. Alexander Milne's map of 1789 (Figure 5.2) demonstrates that very little had changed in terms of

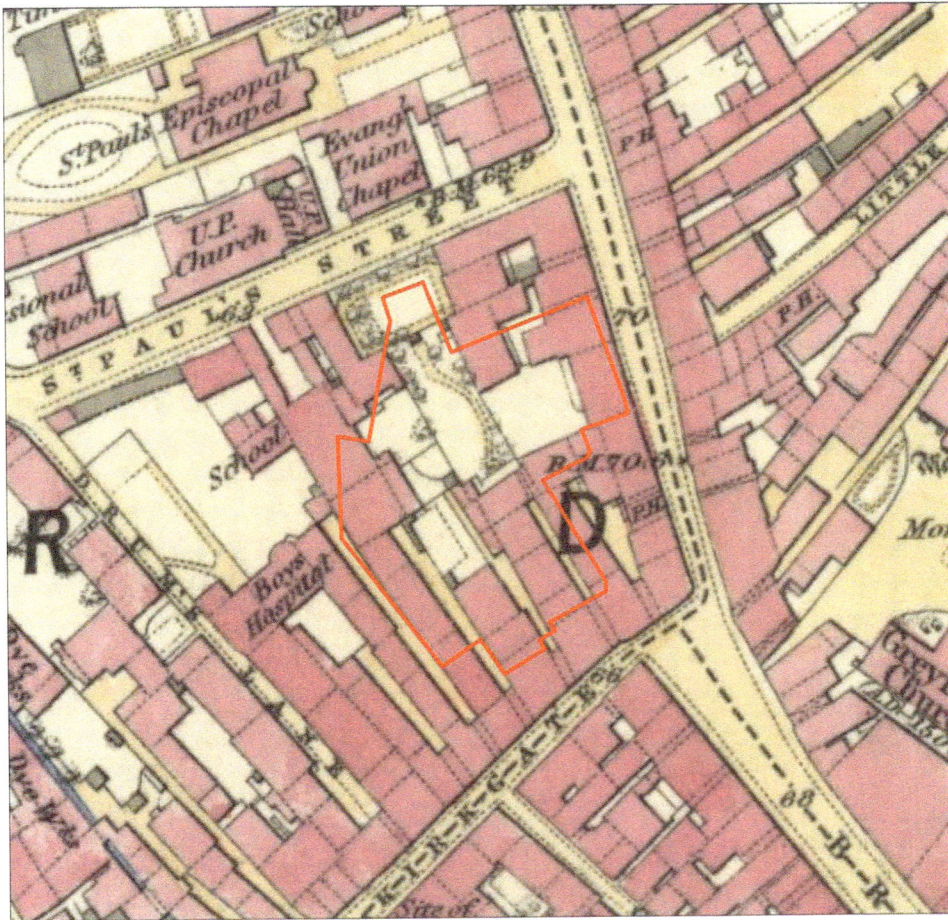

Figure 5.5 Extract from Ordnance Survey map, 1871 (Reproduced with the permission of the National Library of Scotland and under Creative Commons (CC BY 4.0) https://creativecommons. org/licenses/by/4.0/)

the division of land, with linear property plots clearly visible off the Upperkirkgate. However, there is far less open space than previously, though open courtyards remain to the west of the Gallowgate and south of 'the Vennel', and there are several closes for accessing properties in the former inlands and backlands. Boundary walls of one of the courtyards were identified during excavation: Wall A001 formed the north-east corner of a yard encompassing garden soils.

Wood's map of 1828 (Figure 5.3) is less detailed than Milne's map and depicts the area behind the Gallowgate frontage buildings as a single large irregular courtyard area, but this is likely due to the lack of detail on the map. However, the linear boundaries off the Upperkirkgate are still clearly present and the majority of the building outlines visible on Milne's map are also visible.

Given the schematic nature of these early maps, it is difficult to identify with certainty the remains of walls identified during the excavation with boundaries shown on the maps. It is possible that at least some of the lime-

bonded walls excavated on site may be 18th century in origin. In particular, Structure C008 clearly predates Structure C007 (Figure 2.78, Chapter 2) and may be identifiable with a wall line on Milne's plan. Properties around the Upperkirkgate/Gallowgate corner were busy with commercial activities throughout the 19th century, with shops, printwork, workshops and offices being present, and it is possible that the cellar structures identified during the excavation pertained to such commercial premises.

5.7 Late 19th and 20th century development

Keith and Gibb's map of 1862 (Figure 5.4) names St Paul Street to the north of the Bon Accord site. A clear difference from Wood's map of 1828 is an undeveloped area on the south side of St Paul's Street, later visible as a garden on the Ordnance Survey town plan of Aberdeen of 1871 (surveyed between 1866 and 1867) (Figure 5.5). The south wall of this garden was identified during the excavation (Wall A001); it also formed the north wall of an open space also visible on Milne's map. Within

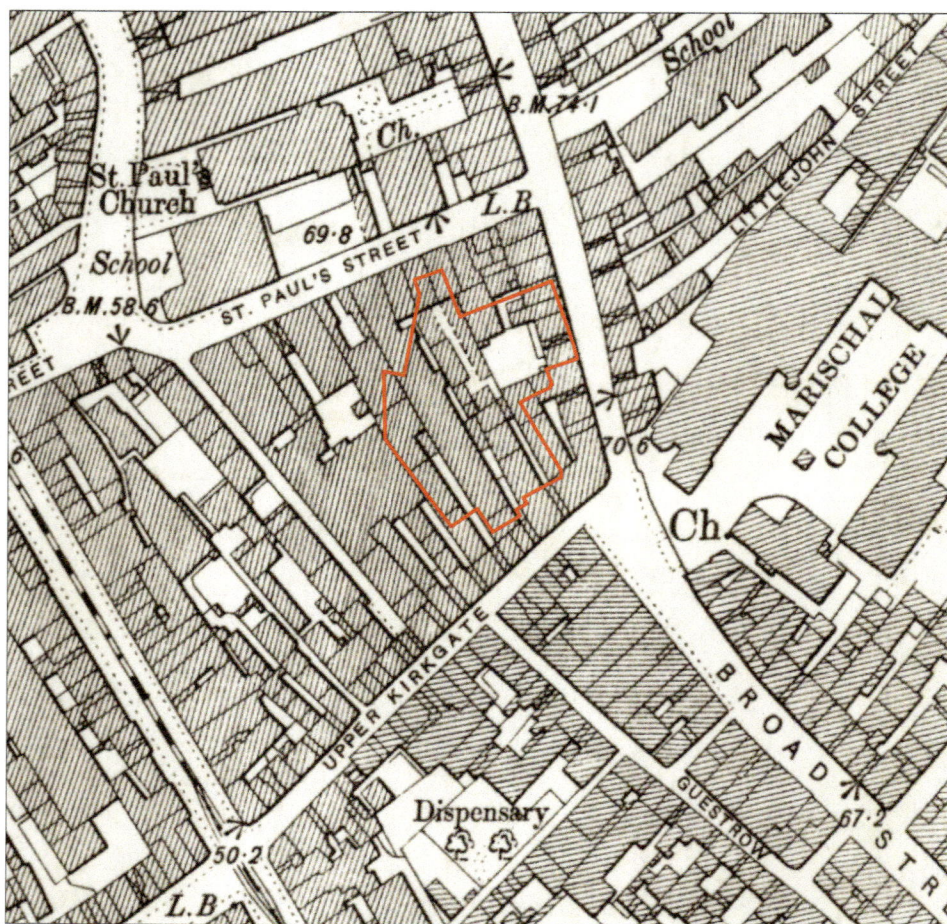

Figure 5.6 Extract from Ordnance Survey map, 1902 (Reproduced with the permission of the National Library of Scotland and under Creative Commons (CC BY 4.0) https://creativecommons. org/licenses/by/4.0/)

the Bon Accord site, at least two large buildings are marked on Keith and Gibb's map behind the Gallowgate frontage (likely those evidenced by cellar walls during the excavation). Ordnance Survey mapping shows several small courts behind the Upperkirkgate and Gallowgate with larger open yards or gardens. Behind Gallowgate, the surface of Concert Court was identified during the excavation, along with cellar walls behind the Gallowgate street frontage (Structure C007a). In 1977 two underground circular chambers were recorded off St Paul Street, east of Farquhar & Gill's warehouse. A brick-covered duct ran southwards from the larger chamber (Judith Stones, *pers comm*). The purpose of these structures is unknown, though a well is marked around this location on the 1871 map, near '*Sick Wards*'. The brick Conduit A/B001 that skirted the western edge of the Bon Accord site might be related to these structures, though it was more obviously connected to the industrial buildings that housed the printworks of the Aberdeen University Press. Significant structural remains that covered the west of the Bon Accord site were associated with this late 19th century and

20th century printworks. By the late 1880s, A. King & Company, already termed the Aberdeen University Press, was listed at '6 and 14 Upperkirkgate' (Aberdeen Directory 1888–89: 371; 1889–90: 85, 485). On 31 May 1886 the Upperkirkgate coin hoard was discovered '*at a depth of 4 feet by workmen of Messrs. King & Co., printer's, Ross's Court, Upper Kirkgate*' (The Scotsman 1886), just south of the Bon Accord site. The main offices and printing works of the press were on Upperkirkgate until 1963 (The Scottish Printing Archival Trust 2000: 12–13). The introduction of Linotype machines may have been one of the reasons for the expansion of premises occupied by the company, which by the time of the Ordnance Survey map of 1902 (Figure 5.6) stretched across the west of the Bon Accord site to St Paul's Street. New printworks were constructed, which were occupied from 1899 (Beavan 2006: 21–22), when the present form of the frontage building at 6–8 Upperkirkgate was constructed by Robert Gordon Wilson, reusing earlier elements, for the Aberdeen University Press (Brogdan 2012: 33).

By 1902, Ordnance Survey mapping indicates that the south side of St Paul's Street was entirely built up, covering the former area of gardens. South and east of the Bon Accord site, the property on the junction of Gallowgate and Upperkirkgate was through much of the later 19th and early 20th century occupied by Henry Gray's emporium, 'Greyfriars House' (Morgan 2004: 87). This large corner property was replaced in the 1930s by the Aberdeen University student's union building (Morgan 2004: 87), which closed in 2004 (University of Aberdeen Media Release 2004).

6 Conclusions

The excavation at the Bon Accord site at the junction of Upperkirkgate and Gallowgate has revealed aspects of the settlement and economy of the area from the 12th century through to the present day, through a sequence of occupation deposits and some significant artefact assemblages. As with many of the earlier archaeological investigations in the medieval core of Aberdeen, the Bon Accord excavation has produced evidence of the backlands of medieval and post-medieval properties, including industrial, agricultural/horticultural, and domestic activity. In particular, the remarkable survival of organic materials, including a vast assemblage of leather and significant assemblages of mammal bone, fish bone and wooden artefacts, has illuminated a late medieval industrial area. A range of activities associated with the use of animal hides, from hide processing to tanning to shoemaking, were evidenced along with less extensive evidence for the dyeing of textiles and for high temperature processes including metal working.

The Bon Accord site lies near the core of New Aberdeen, a major market and trading centre in the medieval period, both in terms of Scotland and the wider European continent through which the city was linked by the North Sea.

Aberdeen's trade across the North Sea to Europe was established by the later 13th century, and this was consolidated during the Anglo-Scottish war of 1296–1328 as the port remained under Scottish control. Scotland had major trading interests in the medieval period with Flanders and Artois, and Aberdeen's principal exports of wool, leather, and fish were marketed mainly to the Low Countries, which dominated the city's trading links until the 17th century (Ditchburn and Harper 2002:, 386–87; Schofield and Vince 2003: 28). At Bon Accord evidence was found, in particular in 12th and 13th century contexts, of goods with the potential for export (such as leather, textiles and fish), though much of the recovered material was actually likely consumed on or near the site. Such goods included wool twills likely to have been worn by the poorer social strata (Chapter 4.2.3), and cod and ling butchered for consumption locally (rather than the important export product of salmon) (Chapter 4.5.4). However, there is evidence, in particular within the later medieval and early post-medieval periods, for the import of relatively high status goods, such as ceramics from England and the continent (Appendix 5), indicative of a change in status of the inhabitants of the area around Bon Accord.

Work undertaken in 1979 to the north at 45–47 Gallowgate, suggests that this part of the Gallowgate may have been relatively undeveloped prior to the 14th century (Murray 1984: 311). Bon Accord may thus have been in a relatively peripheral area, though an area well-suited to the undertaking of industrial activities such as tanning, leatherworking and dyeing, ancillary to the developing market. Throughout western Europe, especially from the 12th century onwards, industries marked by the need for extensive facilities (such as tanning and dyeing) and high levels of competence tended to be focused within towns, with at least 50 different trades known in the town of Winchester around 1148, for instance (Schofield 2013: 127). A relatively marginal urban location was preferred for certain industries, such as tanning, due to the nature of the activities undertaken. 'The fringes of a town will always be attractive to those industries which require large areas for storage or preparation, for example timber yards, tanneries and foundries' (Schofield and Vince 2003: 144).

Unlike other large fieldwork projects in medieval burghs of Scotland, in particular the recently published Perth High Street excavations (Perry *et al.* 2010), there was relatively little evidence in the 12th and 13th century phases at Bon Accord for buildings. The most significant remains related to craft activities in yards throughout the medieval period. However, from the later 13th century (Phase 3) and in particular from the 14th century (Phase 4) onwards structural remains, though often heavily truncated, were identified, as well as garden soils, boundaries and evidence for proximate industrial activities, including metalworking.

The absence of evidence for buildings fronting on the Gallowgate prior to the late post-medieval period may be due in part to truncation; little can therefore be said with certainty of the development of the Gallowgate frontage until the 18th century, apart from the indication from those remains encountered from the earliest (12th to 13th century) phases that at that time the area lacked structural remains, with the exception of boundaries (stake lines, gullies and a wall) that represented plots running back from the Upperkirkgate frontage to the south. Apart from a limited watching brief the excavation works did not extend to the Upperkirkgate frontage which has been densely overbuilt, resulting in a lack of survival of archaeological features and deposits in this area. However, it is likely that frontage properties would have been present, especially on the Upperkirkgate, occupied by the craftspeople that worked in the associated backlands.

The earliest phases of the site, dating from the later 12th through the 13th century, provided the vast majority of large assemblages of both artefactual and ecofactual remains. Commonly these were derived from the waterlogged fills of the many pits, both large and small, typical of the site during this period. These attested to a plethora of craft activities, not just in the 12th to 13th centuries, but extending into the post-medieval period. The survival of an impressive array of organic artefacts and ecofacts at Bon Accord (and at several other medieval sites excavated in Aberdeen), is in part due to its lying within the 'organic crescent', an area of northern Europe extending between Finland and Ireland that is recognised for 'outstanding preservation of wood, leather, textiles and other organic materials' (Carver 2011: 24). The survival of significant organic assemblages at Bon Accord demonstrates that Aberdeen can join such excavated urban areas as Bergen, Dublin and York as being capable of providing a wealth of insights into medieval life. While much of the material recovered indicates that this was an industrial area, on the edge of the urban centre of New Aberdeen, the copious faunal remains recovered, predominantly from 12th and 13th century contexts, are a reminder that even in a period of significant urban growth in medieval Europe, 'connections with the countryside and experiences of the natural world were extensive, even for the town-dweller' (Pluskowski 2011: 80–82).

During the 12th and 13th century period the site was clearly more industrial in nature than domestic. The presence of bark and other organic material, commonly in basal fills, can be related to the tanning of hides. These appear to be 'layaway' pits, where hides would have been left for months as part of the tanning process. Possible 'handler' pits were also identified, where hides were immersed in a tanning liquor and moved until attaining a uniform colour.

Many of the medieval pit features were rapidly backfilled with both human and animal waste and cess. The dominant cereal in the macroplant was cultivated oats, unsurprising given the northerly location and climate of Aberdeen. This was mostly recovered from features containing possible stable waste and it is likely that it was being used as animal feed along with hay and other fodder. Other food remains identified included flax, vegetables (including turnip, cabbage, leek, onion and parsnip), fruits such as fig, grape, cherry, apple and berries and both hazelnut and walnut. The macroplant material provided some indication that dyeing was being carried out in the area with the presence of woad in Pit C018, of late 12th/early 13th century date

suggesting that this feature was likely used as either a dye bath or for the disposal of dye residue.

The remarkable assemblage of ceramics recovered included both local and more exotic wares and contains important evidence for the development of local wares of Aberdeen and the east coast of Scotland and for trade with England and further afield. Imported English ceramics such as Scarborough-type ware and Developed Stamford ware appear in features and deposits as early as Phase 1 indicating trade across the British Isles. Later, in the late medieval/early post-medieval period, the significance of imports from England and the continent is clear, indicating that this was an area of high status dwellings at that time. Very unusually, a number of the medieval pits contained large ceramic assemblages. Some of this material was so badly burnt that it was difficult to identify, but a large proportion is Scarborough ware, with highly decorated but fragmentary sherds. It is possible that the fire damage is the result of the use of pottery in an unidentified, relatively high temperature industrial process, perhaps the production of dyes, glue or substances involved in the finishing of leather. Internal residues and damage on external surfaces from high temperature on several pottery vessels also point to an unidentified high temperature process.

Large pieces of daub-like material were also present, often in later medieval contexts, likely indicating a relatively high temperature industrial process. Several hearths and remains of larger kilns or ovens in Phases 3 and 4 also evidenced high temperature processes, which can perhaps be associated with the ovens identified at 45–75 Gallowgate to the north (Evans 2001: 90–93) or at 42 St Paul Street (Murray 1982: 53, illus 24). Fragments of small crucibles, associated with working of metal, were recovered – including two fragments each from two late 12th/early 13th century pits; analysis of these indicates that they were used in the working of brass. Later, substantial quantities of metallurgical residues certainly indicate iron smithing, and perhaps limited smelting, in the post-medieval period. Fragments of Purbeck limestone, derived from a single large mortar of perhaps late medieval or early post-medieval date, attest to the extent of trade between Aberdeen and other parts of the British Isles to which it was linked by the sea, such as Dorset where the mortar's raw material was quarried. Given its size, it may have been utilised in an industrial process. A fragment of a smaller Purbeck limestone mortar recovered from 45–75 Gallowgate contained impressed residues of tormentil and dock, both of which were utilised in the tanning and dyeing processes (Moffat and Penny 2001: 298–99).

As well as the remains of this mortar, elements of several rotary grinding stones were recovered at Bon Accord.

These may be representative of ferrous metalworking and could have been utilised either in the finishing of products or in the sharpening of tools. While the presence of the grinding stones in late medieval and post-medieval contexts accords with the evidence from industrial residues for ferrous metalworking at that time, a composite grinding mechanism was recovered from the base of a Phase 1 pit, indicating that metalworking may have been undertaken as early as the late 12th century. However, it has been noted that grindstones were also used to crush bark for use in tanning solutions (Córdoba and Müller 2011: 281).

Wooden artefacts from Bon Accord reflect both the domestic and industrial activities of the population, in particular in the 12th and 13th centuries – numerous tools attest to the industrial aspect of the site at this time, while some of the more simple bowls may represent the personal possessions of labourers. However, several more high status items such as a boxwood handle and a maple bowl, both made from woods exotic to Aberdeen (Chapter 4.2.1), provide evidence for the possible presence of wealthy households nearby and significant trading links. As noted in Chapter 4.2.1 stands of box in a band across southern Europe and into Asia Minor (Smirnova 2007: 299) provided the main sources of boxwood as a raw material used in the manufacture of combs and handles throughout the medieval and post-medieval periods in Europe. The field maple used in the bowl is found throughout southern England and much of Europe (Perring and Walters 1990: 173), but is not native to Scotland, and so again attests to trade in raw materials or finished goods.

Wooden artefacts also included one complete and one partial wooden barrel, which functioned as the linings for cisterns or wells. A similar feature was previously found nearby in a late 14th/early 15th century phase at the Middle School site on the eastern side of the Gallowgate (Cameron 2001: 77). While the Middle School barrel came from the Baltic, one of the Bon Accord barrels, of similar date, came from north France or Belgium, and provides further evidence for trade with the continent, likely in the form of the wine trade, another signifier of the consumption of high status goods in this part of Aberdeen.

The small finds of wood included tools such as knife handles, scrapers, paddle-like tools and fragments of composite spades. These could have been used in the tanning and hide-processing for the movement of materials in and out of the pits. The recovery of a number of wooden vessels evidences high status consumption in the later medieval period, particularly those which may have been imported from the Continent.

There was also much discarded or reused structural timber. The analysis of these large timbers has provided a significant dendrochronological dataset, the largest from any urban medieval site in Scotland, covering the 415 years between AD 867 and AD 1281, which can be correlated with chronologies as far afield as northern England, Denmark and Sweden.

The leather assemblage comprised over 12,000 separate items and was broadly similar in the range of objects found on other Aberdeen excavations, and excavations elsewhere in Scotland, such as Perth High Street (Thomas and Bogdan 2012). The vast majority consisted of offcuts and scraps, but also included nearly 1000 shoe components. The survival of abundant evidence for leatherworking at Bon Accord is due to the presence of waterlogged anaerobic conditions, in particular within 12th and 13th century pit features. This is fortuitous, as on many urban excavations in the British Isles (and further afield), such conditions are not present, and therefore an industry producing organic debris (offcuts) is commonly rendered invisible archaeologically (Schofield and Vince 2003: 143–44). The concentration of waste material at Bon Accord represents clear evidence for leatherworking on or near the site, and is indicative of industrial, rather than domestic, waste. Most of the activity appears to have been the production of new items (most significantly shoes) from new leather. The shoes are primarily 12th to 13th century in date, and display construction methods and styles paralleled at medieval sites elsewhere in Scotland, England and the continent.

Approximately 20,000 fragments of animal bone were retrieved, primarily from 12th to 13th century contexts. The presence of a wide variety of animals in an assemblage not entirely dominated by food-producing animals, as well as the relatively poverty of material displaying butchery marks, indicates that this assemblage does not represent typical food-related waste. The apparent bias towards bones of the head and feet is to be expected in an assemblage associated with the early preparation of hides and subsequent processes. Skulls, antler and horn cores were relatively abundant within the assemblage, the latter often displaying knife marks relating to the removal of the horn, perhaps evidencing horn-working. It is possible that the presence of large quantities of horn core and fish bone reflects production of substances such as glue and neats-foot oil on the site.

The largely 12th and 13th century fish bone assemblage included over 4000 fragments identifiable to species or broader taxonomic group. Fish of the cod family were most common, some of the fish exceptionally large in size. The repetitive nature of butchery chop marks seen on this material suggests that the fish were prepared by professional fishmongers, probably off-site, perhaps in the nearby market area; few features produced evidence of possible on-site preparation of fish. Aberdeen was an important medieval centre for the export of fish, with this trade focused on salmon and herring, as well as 'whitefish' – salmon being exported as far as London from at least the mid 14th century (Jackson 2002: 161). In the later medieval period salmon reached markets around the North Sea, the Baltic and Iberia (Jackson 2002: 162). As Harland (Chapter 4.5.4) notes, however, very few of the products of this trade were eaten and deposited at Bon Accord perhaps because salmon was too valuable a product. At Bon Accord, trends in fish consumption over time probably relate to a move towards exploitation of inshore or shallower fishing grounds around the 15th century rather than the deep open waters of the northern North Sea or North Atlantic previously favoured.

In the late 12th and 13th century the Bon Accord area was the location of many backland industrial activities, perhaps related to the development of New Aberdeen as a market centre. The large quantity of pits, with their evidence for hide preparation, leatherworking and perhaps dyeing, indicate that at this time Bon Accord was likely an industrial area behind the Upperkirkgate frontage. It is likely that craftspeople occupied the Upperkirkgate frontage (and perhaps the Gallowgate frontage) at this time though there was a paucity of evidence from the present works for occupation of the frontages due largely to truncation by later development. It was not until much later that the backland area was built up with domestic housing, as can be seen in post-medieval mapping. It would have been an unhealthy, smelly area, part of an industrial quarter behind the Upperkirkgate frontage where noxious activities such as tanning, leatherworking, dyeing and perhaps glue making were undertaken. It lay in the vicinity of the Loch, a major source of open water that would have proved invaluable in both the tanning and dyeing industries.

During Phase 1, dated to around the mid-to-late 12th century, there was tentative evidence that medieval plot boundaries ran off the Upperkirkgate to the south. It is during this period that the pits possibly associated with hide preparation and tanning are first recorded. Approximately 1500 of the 10,000 leather offcuts belong to this phase. The existence of plot boundaries off the Upperkirkgate is confirmed in Phase 2 (late 12th to mid 13th century), marked by stake and wattle lines. During Phase 2 evidence for leatherworking activities was strongest – around 6000 of the 10,000 offcuts date to this phase, often associated with deep, sometimes organic-lined, pits; both 'handler' and 'layaway' pits

have been identified. Leatherworking, and in particular shoemaking, had by the turn of the 13th century developed into a small-scale industry. One property plot defined by stakelines may have been a particular focus of this activity. By Phase 3 (the later 13th century) the quantity of leatherworking material had reduced, although with almost 3000 offcuts recovered, the area was still clearly in use as an industrial area. Córdoba and Müller (2011: 281), in discussing the development of the leather industries of Europe around the 12th and 13th centuries note the 'fine dividing line between manufacture, recycling and repair' – this diversity of activity is paralleled at Bon Accord, where although the main emphasis in the assemblage appeared to be on the production of new items, the shoe assemblage indicates that repair and reuse was also undertaken.

From the 14th century onwards the quantities of animal bone, fishbone, leather and other organic materials diminished greatly, partly perhaps because there were fewer waterlogged contexts, but also because there appears to have been a change in the function of the area. There were fewer deep industrial pits and more structural features, and much of the site was covered in garden soils that contained exotic, high status pottery, likely indicating that the area had undergone a change in its status, from a primarily industrial to a more domestic role. Murray postulates that the Gallowgate became more popular with wealthy Aberdonians by the 14th century, as the centre of the town around Broad Street/Castle Street and the routes towards the shore and harbour became built up (Murray 1984: 311). No doubt this would have been associated with the end of the leatherworking trade at 45–75 Gallowgate around the late 14th century (Evans 2001: 113), and with the changes in activity seen at Bon Accord around the 14th century, with a clear diminution in the evidence for tanning and related activities. There is clear evidence, however, in particular in the form of large oven or kiln structures and of metalworking waste, that the late medieval and early post-medieval period saw some, albeit rather different, industrial activity.

By the later post-medieval period, Bon Accord would have largely been covered by properties on the Gallowgate/Upperkirkgate corner and their gardens, evidenced by garden soils and the remains of rubble walls. The buildings on the frontages, however, continued into the 19th century and beyond as areas associated with the commercial and industrial life of the city.

References

Bibliographic References

Aberdeen City Council 1639 'General Band of Relief', viewed February 2011, <http://www.aberdeencity.gov.uk/LocalHistory/archives/loc_CatalogueInformation.asp?text=large>.

Aberdeen City Council 2008. Excavation at East Kirk of St Nicholas, viewed May 2008, <http://www.aberdeencity.gov.uk/LocalHistory/loc/loc_ArchKirkNicholas.asp.>.

Aberdeen Directory 1863–64. *Post Office Aberdeen Directory 1863-64*. Aberdeen: Arthur King and Co.

Aberdeen Directory 1868–69. *Post Office Aberdeen Directory 1868-69*. Aberdeen: Arthur King and Co.

Aberdeen Directory 1888–89. *Post Office Aberdeen Directory 1888-89* Aberdeen: A. King and Company.

Aberdeen Directory 1889–90. *Post Office Aberdeen Directory 1889-90*. Aberdeen: A. King and Company.

Alcock, N. 1982. The hall of the Knights Templar at Temple Balsall, W. Midlands. *Medieval Archaeology* 26: 155–158.

Allan, J. and C.A. Morris 1984. The wood, in Medieval and Post-Medieval Finds from Exeter 1971–1980. *Exeter Archaeology Report* No. 3: 305–315.

Allen, S.J. 1995. Medieval Coopered Vessels. *Finds Research Group 700-1700*, Datasheet 19.

Allison-Jones, L. 2007. The small objects, in W.S. Hanson *Elginhaugh: A Flavian fort and its Annex*. Britannia Monograph Series No. 23: 396–442. London Society for the Promotion of Roman Studies.

Anderson, M.L. 1967. *A History of Scottish Forestry* Vol. 1. London: Nelson and Sons Ltd.

Anderson, P.J. (ed.) 1909. *Aberdeen Friars, Red Black, White, Grey: Preliminary Calendar of Illustrative Documents*. Aberdeen.

Appleyard, H.M. 1978. *Guide to the Identification of Animal Fibres*. Leeds: Wool Industries Research Association.

Baillie, M.G.L. 1995. *A Slice Through Time. Dendrochronology and Precision Dating*. London: Batsford.

Bain, E. 1887. *Merchant and Craft Guilds: A History of the Aberdeen Incorporated Trades*. Aberdeen.

Barber, J. 1981. Wooden objects, in G.L. Good and C.J. Tabraham, Excavations at Threave Castle, Galloway, 1974–8. *Medieval Archaeology* 25: 90–140.

Barker, P.A. 1961. Excavation on the Town Moor, Roushill, Shrewbury *Medieval Archaeology* 5: 181–211.

Barney, S.A., W.J. Lewis, J.A. Beach and O. Berghof 2006. *The Etymologies of Isidore of Seville*. Cambridge: Cambridge University Press.

Barrett, J.H. 1997. Fish trade in Norse Orkney and Caithness: A zooarchaeological approach. *Antiquity* 71: 616–638.

Barrett, J., C. Johnstone, J.F. Harland, W. Van Neer, A. Ervynck, D. Makowiecki, D. Heinrich, A.K. Hufthammer, I. Enghoff, C. Amundsen, J. Christiansen, A.K.G. Jones, A. Locker, S. Hamilton-Dyer, L. Jonsson, L. Lougas, C. Roberts and M. Richards 2008. Detecting the medieval cod trade: a new method and first results. *Journal of Archaeological Science* 35: 850–861.

Barrett, J.H., D. Orton, C. Johnstone, J. Harland, W. Van Neer, A. Ervynck, C. Roberts, A. Locker, C. Amundsen, I.B. Enghoff, S. Hamilton-Dyer, D. Heinrich, A.K. Hufthammer, A.K.G. Jones, L. Jonsson, D. Makowiecki, P. Pope, T.C. O'Connell, T. de Roo and M. Richards 2011. Interpreting the expansion of sea fishing in medieval Europe using stable isotope analysis of archaeological cod bones. *Journal of Archaeological Science* 38: 1516–1524.

Bashford, D.J. 2010. Coarse stone, in S.J. Dockrill, J.M. Bond, V.E. Turner, L.D. Brown, D.J. Bashford, J.E. Cussans and R.A. Nicholson (eds) *Excavations at Old Scatness, Shetland Vol.1: The Pictish village and Viking settlement*: 231–258. Lerwick: Shetland Heritage Publications.

Baxter, R. 1998. *Bestiaries and their Users in the Middle Ages*. Stroud and London: Sutton Publishing and Courtauld Institute.

Bayley, J. 1991. Anglo-Saxon non-ferrous metalworking; a survey. *World Archaeology* 23 (1): 115–130.

Bayley, J. 1992. Metalworking ceramics. *Medieval Ceramics* 16: 3–10.

Bayley, J. 2003. Metalworking debris from Cripplegate buildings (WFG 18) City of London. *English Heritage Centre for Archaeology Report 80/2003*, viewed on 15/10/2020 https://research.historicengland.org.uk/ Report.aspx?i=8867&ru= %2fResults.aspx%3fp%3d1%26n%3d10 %26ry% 3d2003 % 26t%3dcripplegate%26ns%3d1

Bayley, J. and T. Rehren 2007. Towards a functional and typological classification of crucibles, in S. La Niece, D. Hook and P. Craddock (eds) *Metals and Mines, Studies in Archaeometallurgy*: 46–55. London: Archetype Books.

Beavan, I. 2006. Printing for the British publishing industry: the rise and fall of Aberdeen University Press. *Journal of the Edinburgh Bibliographical Society* No.1: 20–40.

Bedini, S.A. 1997. *The Pope's Elephant*. Manchester: Carcanet Press Ltd.

Bennett, H. 1987. The textiles, in P. Holdsworth (ed.) *Excavations in the Medieval Burgh of Perth, 1979-1981*. Society of Antiquaries of Scotland Monograph Series No. 1: 159–166. Edinburgh.

Biddle, M. (ed.) 1990. *Winchester Studies. Artefacts from Medieval Winchester. Part I. Object and Economy in Medieval Winchester*. Oxford: Clarendon Press.

Biddle, M. and D. Smith 1990. The mortars, in M. Biddle (ed.) *Object and Economy in Medieval Winchester*. Oxford: Clarendon Press.

Blanchard, I., E. Gemmill, N. Mayhew and I.D Whyte 2002. The economy: town and country, in E.P. Dennison, D. Ditchburn and M. Lynch (eds) *Aberdeen Before 1800: a new history*: 129–158. East Linton: Tuckwell Press Ltd.

Boardman, S. 2002. The burgh and the realm: medieval politics, *c.*1100–1500, in E.P. Dennison, D. Ditchburn and M. Lynch (eds) *Aberdeen Before 1800: A new history*: 203–223. East Linton: Tuckwell Press Ltd.

Boessneck, J. 1969. Osteological differences between sheep (*Ovis aries Linne*) and goats (*Capra hircus Linne*), in D. Brothwell and E. Higgs (eds) *Science in Archaeology* 2: 331–358. London: Thames and Hudson.

Bolton, E.M. 1991 (revised 2nd edition). *Lichens for Vegetable Dyeing*. McMinnville, Oregon: Robin and Russ.

Brogdan, W.A. 2012. *A City's Architecture: Aberdeen as a Designed City*. Farnham: Ashgate Publishing Ltd.

Brøgger, A.W. and H. Shetelig 1971. *The Viking Ships; their Ancestry and Evolution*. Oslo: Dreyers Forlag.

Bullock, P., N. Fedoroff, A. Jongerius, G. Stoops, T. Tursina and U. Babel 1985. *Handbook for Soil Thin Section Description*. Wolverhampton: Waine Research Publications.

Caldwell, D. 1981. Metalwork, in G. Good, and C. Tabraham, Excavations at Threave Castle, Galloway, 1974–78. *Medieval Archaeology* 25: 106–116.

Caldwell, D. 1988. Metalwork, in D.R. Perry, A.G. Reid and D.M. Lye (eds) *Pitmiddle Village and Elcho Nunnery: Research and Excavation on Tayside*: 70–75. Perth: Perthshire Society of Natural Science.

Caldwell, D. 1991. Tantallon Castle, East Lothian: a catalogue of the finds. *Proceedings of the Society of Antiquaries of Scotland* 121: 335–357.

Caldwell, D. 1995a. Copper alloy, in J. Lewis and G. Ewart (eds) *Jedburgh Abbey. The Archaeology and Architecture of a Border Abbey*. Society of Antiquaries of Scotland Monograph Series No. 10: 84–88. Edinburgh.

Caldwell, D. 1995b. Iron, in J. Lewis and G. Ewart (eds) *Jedburgh Abbey. The Archaeology and Architecture of a Border Abbey*. Society of Antiquaries of Scotland Monograph Series No. 10: 91–93. Edinburgh.

Caldwell, D 1995c. Lead objects, in J. Lewis and G. Ewart (eds) *Jedburgh Abbey. The Archaeology and Architecture of a Border Abbey*. Society of Antiquaries of Scotland Monograph Series No. 10: 89–90. Edinburgh.

Caldwell, D. 2004. The metalwork, in G. Ewart and D. Pringle (eds) Dundonald Castle Excavations 1986–93. *Scottish Archaeological Journal* 26: 100–103 (1–166).

Caldwell, D. and N. Bogden, 2012. The weapons, in *Perth High Street, Archaeological Excavations, 1975-1977. Fascicule 2, The ceramics, the metalwork and the wood*: 189–194. Perth: Tayside and Fife Archaeological Committee.

Cameron, A.S. 2001. Gallowgate Middle School: 12th century and later leatherworking, in A.S. Cameron and J.A. Stones (eds) *Aberdeen: An In-depth View of the City's Past*. Society of Antiquaries of Scotland Monograph Series No. 19: 73–82. Edinburgh.

Cameron A.S., D.H. Evans and J.A Stones. 2001. Small finds of metal, glass, stone, clay, bone and other organics, in A.S. Cameron and J.A. Stones (eds) *Aberdeen: An In-depth View of the City's Past*. Society of Antiquaries of Scotland Monograph Series No. 19: 193–210. Edinburgh.

Cameron, A.S. and J.A. Stones (eds) 2001 *Aberdeen: An In-depth View of the City's Past*. Society of Antiquaries of Scotland Monograph Series No. 19. Edinburgh.

Caple, C. 1983. Pins and wires, in P. Mayes and L.A.S. Butler (eds) *Sandal Castle Excavations 1964-73*: 269–278. Wakefield.

Caple, C. 1991. The detection and definition of an industry: the English medieval and post-medieval pin industry. *Archaeological Journal* 148: 241–255.

Cappers, R.T.J., R.M. Bekker and J.E.A. Jans 2006. *Digital Seed Atlas of the Netherlands*. Groningen: Barkhuis Publishing and Groningen University Library.

Carter, S. 2001. A reassessment of the origins of the St. Andrews "Garden Soil". *Tayside and Fife Archaeological Journal* 7: 87–92.

Carver, M. 2011. Chapter 1: aims and methods: part 1 scope and agenda, in M. Carver and J. Klápště (eds) *The Archaeology of Medieval Europe, Vol.2 Twelfth to Sixteenth Centuries*: 15–47. Aarhus: Aarhus University Press.

Casselman, K.D. 1996. *Lichen Dyes: a Source Book*. Privately published, Nova Scotia: Studio Vista Cheverie.

Cherry, J. 1991a. Leather, in W. J. Blair and N.L. Ramsay (eds) *English Medieval Industries: Craftsmen, Techniques, Products*: 295–318. London: Hambledon.

Cherry, J. 1991b. *Medieval Decorative Art*. London: British Museum.

Cherry, J. 2012. Dress rings of metal, in *Perth High Street, Archaeological Excavations, 1975-1977. Fascicule 2, The ceramics, the metalwork and the wood*: 199. Perth: Tayside and Fife Archaeological Committee.

Clark, J. (ed.) 1995. *The Medieval Horse and its Equipment c1150-1450*. Museum of London Medieval Finds from Excavations in London 1. London: Her Majesty's Stationery Office.

Clark, J. 1997a. Medieval copper-alloy artefacts, in S.T. Driscoll and P.A. Yeoman *Excavations within Edinburgh*

Castle in 1988-91. Society of Antiquaries of Scotland Monograph Series No. 12: 149–153. Edinburgh.

Clark, J. 1997b. Medieval ironwork, in S.T. Driscoll and P.A. Yeoman, *Excavations within Edinburgh Castle in 1988-91*. Society of Antiquaries of Scotland Monograph Series No. 12: 154–162. Edinburgh.

Cohen, A. and D. Serjeantson 1996. *A Manual for the Identification of Bird Bones from Archaeological Sites*. London: Archetype Publications.

Comey, M.G. 2007. Stave-built vessels, in M. Brisbane and J. Hather (eds) *Wood Use in Medieval Novgorod*: 165–188. Oxford: Bournemouth University and Oxbow Books.

Comey, M.G. 2010. *Coopers and Coopering in Viking Age Dublin*. Dublin: National Museum of Ireland.

Cook, J.M. 2004. *Early Anglo-Saxon Buckets: A Corpus of Alloy and Iron-bound, Stave-built Vessels*. Oxford: Oxford University School Archaeology Monograph 60.

Cooper, J. 1892. *Cartularium Ecclesiae Sancti Nicholai Aberdonensis*. Aberdeen: Spalding Club.

Córdoba, R. and U. Müller 2011. Chapter 7: Manufacture and production: part 1 craft into industry, in M. Carver and J. Klápště (eds) *The Archaeology of Medieval Europe, Vol.2 Twelfth to Sixteenth Centuries*: 277–287. Aarhus: Aarhus University Press.

Courty, M.A., P. Goldberg and R.I. Macphail 1989. *Soils and Micromorphology in Archaeology*. Cambridge: Cambridge University Press.

Cowgill, J., M. de Neergaard and N. Griffiths 1987. *Medieval Finds from Excavations in London: 1 Knives and Scabbards*. London: Her Majesty's Stationery Office.

Cox, A. 1996. Backland activities in medieval Perth: excavations at Meal Vennel and Scott Street. *Proceedings of the Society of Antiquaries Scotland* 126: 733–821.

Cox, A. 2000. The artefacts, in D.R. Perry (ed.) *Castle Park, Dunbar*. Society of Antiquaries of Scotland Monograph Series No. 16: 113–178. Edinburgh.

Crew, P. and T. Rehren 2002. High temperature workshop residues from Tara: iron, bronze and glass, in H. Roche (ed.) *Excavations at Ráith na Ríg, Tara, County Meath, 1997*. Discovery Programme Reports 6: Royal Irish Academy.

Cripps, J.A. 1982. The documentary evidence, in H.K. Murray '2:5 42 St Paul Street 1977-8, in J.C. Murray (ed.) *Excavations in the Medieval Burgh of Aberdeen 1973-81*, Society of Antiquaries of Scotland Monograph Series No. 2: 76–77 (46–84). Edinburgh.

Crone, B.A. 2000a. *The History of a Scottish Lowland Crannog: Excavations at Buiston, Ayrshire 1989-90*. Scottish Trust for Archaeological Research Monograph Series 4. Edinburgh.

Crone, B.A. 2000b. Native tree-ring chronologies from some Scottish medieval burghs. *Medieval Archaeology* 44: 201–216.

Crone, B.A. 2000c. The cordage, in B.A. Crone *The History of a Scottish Lowland Crannog: Excavations at Buiston, Ayrshire 1989-90*. Scottish Trust for Archaeological Research Monograph Series 4:133-134. Edinburgh.

Crone, B.A. 2001. Wooden objects, in C. Moloney and L.M. Baker (eds) Evidence for the form and nature of a medieval burgage plot in St Andrews: an archaeological excavation of the site of the Byre Theatre, Abbey Street, St Andrews. *Tayside and Fife Archaeology Journal* 7: 70–71 (48–86).

Crone, B. A. 2005. A tale of three tuns: a 12th century French barrel from the High Street, Perth. *Tayside and Fife Archaeology Journal* 11: 70–73.

Crone, B A. 2006. A 10th century tree-ring event in Scotland – proxy evidence for social and economic change? in A. Woolf, (ed.) *Landscape and Environment in Dark Age Scotland*: 49–56, St Andrews: St John's House Papers No. 11.

Crone, B.A. 2008a. Carbonised wood assemblage, in M. Cook and L. Dunbar (eds) *Rituals, Roundhouses and Romans: Excavation at Kintore, Aberdeenshire 2000-2006, Volume 1: Forest Road*: 272–289.

Crone, B.A. 2008b. The Coopered Vessel from St Patrick's Church, Cowgate, Edinburgh, Unpublished report for Headland Archaeology.

Crone, B.A. forthcoming. The waterlogged wooden objects, in A. Beckett, G. MacGregor, D. Maguire and D. Sneddon (eds) *Living and Dying on the Bonnie Banks: Ten Thousand Years at the Carrick, Midross, Loch Lomond*. Scottish Archaeology Internet Reports.

Crone, B.A. and M. Baillie 2010. Appendix 5; Perth High Street dendrochronological studies, in Perth High Street Archaeological Excavation 1975-1977. Fascicule 1, The excavations at 75–95 High Street and 5–10 Mill Street, Perth: 221–225. Perth: Tayside and Fife Archaeological Committee.

Crone, B.A., D.H. Evans, and C. Tracy 2001. Wood including dendrochronological analysis of the barrel staves, in A.S. Cameron and J.A. Stones (eds) *Aberdeen: An In-Depth View of the City's Past*: 2. Society of Antiquaries of Scotland Monograph Series No. 19: 211–222. Edinburgh.

Crone, B.A. and C.M. Mills 2012. Timber in Scottish buildings, 1450–1800; a dendrochronological perspective. *Proceedings of the Society of Antiquaries of Scotland* 142: 329–369.

Crowfoot, E. 1975. The textiles, in C. Platt and R. Coleman-Smith *Excavations in Medieval Southampton, 1953-1969*: 334–340. Leicester: Leicester University Press.

Crowfoot, E., F. Pritchard and K. Staniland 1992. *Textiles and Clothing c.1150-c.1450* Medieval Finds from Excavations in London 4. London: Her Majesty's Stationery Office.

Cuddeford, M. J. 1994. *Identifying Metallic Small Finds*. Ipswich: Greenlight Publishing.

Curle, A.O. 1911. *A Roman Frontier Post and its People: The Fort of Newstead in the Parish of Melrose.* Glasgow: Glasgow University Press.

Curteis, A., C. A. Morris, C. Martin, D. Wright and the late N.Q. Bogdan 2012. The wood, in *Perth High Street, Archaeological Excavations, 1975-1977. Fascicule 2, The ceramics, the metalwork and the wood*: 223–374. Perth: Tayside and Fife Archaeological Committee.

Dawod, V. and E.A. Fitzpatrick 1992. Some population sizes and effects of the enchytraeidae (oligochaeta) on soil structure in a selection of Scottish soils. *Geoderma* 56: 173–178.

Dennison, E. P., D. Ditchburn and M. Lynch (eds) 2002. *Aberdeen Before 1800: a new history.* East Linton: Tuckwell Press Ltd.

Dennison, E. P. and J. Stones 1997. *Historic Aberdeen: the archaeological implications of development.* Scottish Burgh Survey.

Dennison, E. P., A.T. Simpson and G.G. Simpson 2002. The growth of two towns, in E.P. Dennison, D. Ditchburn and M. Lynch (eds) *Aberdeen Before 1800: a new history*: 13–43. East Linton: Tuckwell Press Ltd.

Dennison, E.P. 2008. The medieval burgh of Canongate, in Holyrood Archaeology Project Team, *Scotland's Parliament Site and the Canongate: archaeology and history*, 59–68.

Dent, J. 1982. 12–26 Broad Street 1973, in C.J. Murray (ed.) *Excavations in the Medieval Burgh of Aberdeen 1973-81.* Society of Antiquaries of Scotland Monograph Series No. 2:3: 26–34. Edinburgh.

Dickinson, W.C. (ed.) 1957. *Early Records of the Burgh of Aberdeen 1317, 1398-1407*, Aberdeen: Scottish History Society.

Dickson, J.H. 1973. *Bryophytes of the Pleistocene.* Cambridge: Cambridge University Press.

Ditchburn, D. and M. Harper 2002. Aberdeen and the outside world, in E.P. Dennison, D. Ditchburn and M. Lynch (eds) *Aberdeen Before 1800: a new history*: 377–407. Linton: Tuckwell Press Ltd.

Driscoll, S.T. and P.A. Yeoman 1997. *Excavations within Edinburgh Castle in 1988-91.* Society of Antiquaries of Scotland Monograph Series No. 12. Edinburgh.

Dobney, K. and K. Reilly 1988. A method for recording archaeological animal bones: the use of diagnostic zones, *Circaea* 5: 79–96.

Dockrill, S.J., J.M. Bond, V.E. Turner, L.D. Brown, D.J. Bashford, J.E. Cussans and R.A. Nicholson 2010. *Excavations at Old Scatness, Shetland* Vol. 1, The Pictish village and Viking settlement. Lerwick: Shetland Heritage Publications.

Dreisch, von den, A. 1976. *A Guide to the Measurements of Animal Bones from Archaeological Sites.* Harvard: Peabody Museum.

Dunning, G.C. 1939. A thirteenth-century midden at Windcliff, near Niton. *Proceedings of the Isle of Wight Natural History and Archaeology Society* 3.2: 128–137.

Dunning, G.C. 1977. Mortars, in H. Clarke and A. Carter *Excavations in King's Lynn 1963-1970.* Society for Medieval Archaeology Monograph 7: 327–329.

Egan, G. 1995. Spur straps, in J. Clark (ed.) *The Medieval Horse and its Equipment, c1150-1450*: 150–156. Museum of London Medieval Finds from Excavations in London 1. London: Her Majesty's Stationery Office.

Egan, G. 2010. *The Medieval Household. Daily Living c1150-1450.* Museum of London Medieval Finds from Excavations in London 6. London: Her Majesty's Stationery Office.

Egan, G. and F. Pritchard 1991 *Dress Accessories, c1150-1450.* Museum of London Medieval Finds from Excavations in London 3. London: Her Majesty's Stationery Office.

Ellis, B.M.A. 1987. Spur, in P. Holdsworth (ed.) *Excavations in the Medieval Burgh of Perth 1979-1981.* Society of Antiquaries of Scotland Monograph Series 5: 137. Edinburgh.

Ellis, B. M. A. 1995. Spurs and spur fittings, in J Clark *The Medieval Horse and its Equipment c.1150-c.140. Medieval Finds from Excavations in London 5*: 124-56. London: HMSO.

Ellis, B.M.A. 2002. *Prick Spurs 700-1700.* Finds Research Group, Datasheet 30.

Ellis, B.M.A. and N. Bogden 2012. The spurs, in *Perth High Street, Archaeological Excavations, 1975-1977. Fascicule 2, The ceramics, the metalwork and the wood*: 194–198. Perth: Tayside and Fife Archaeological Committee.

Engl, R. 2008. Chipped stone, in M. Cook and L. Dunbar *Rituals, Roundhouses and Romans: Excavations at Kintore, Aberdeenshire 2000-2006*, Vol.1 Forest Road: 226–238.

Engl, R. forthcoming. Chipped stone, in L. Dunbar *Excavations at Kintore, Aberdeenshire* Vol.2.

English Heritage 2001. *Centre for Archaeology Guidelines: Archaeometallurgy.*

Evans, D.H and S. Thain 1989. New light on old coin hoards from the Aberdeen area. *Proceedings of the Society of Antiquaries of Scotland* 119: 327–244.

Evans, D.H. 2001. 45–75 Gallowgate: Medieval and post-medieval occupation beside the Town Loch, in A.S. Cameron and J.A. Stones (eds) *Aberdeen: An In-depth View of the City's Past.* Society of Antiquaries of Scotland Monograph Series No. 19: 83–115. Edinburgh.

Ewan, E. 1998. An urban community: the crafts in thirteenth century Aberdeen, in A. Alexander Grant, and K.J. Springer (eds) *Medieval Scotland: Crown, Lordship and Community*: 156–173. Edinburgh: Edinburgh University Press.

Ewart, G. 1996. Inchaffray Abbey, Perth and Kinross: excavation and research, 1987. *Proceedings of the Society of Antiquaries of Scotland* 126: 469–516.

Fenton, A. 1978. *The Northern Isles: Orkney and Shetland.* Phantassie (East Linton): Tuckwell Press.

Forbes of Foveran, S. 1843 (originally published 1716–17). Description of Aberdeenshire, in J. Robertson (ed.) *Collections for the History of the Shires of Aberdeen and Banff*: 31–66. Aberdeen: The Spalding Club.

Ford, B. 1987. Stone objects, in P. Holdsworth (ed.) *Excavations in the Medieval Burgh of Perth 1979-1981*. Society of Antiquaries of Scotland Monograph Series No. 5. Edinburgh.

Ford, B. 1987a. Copper alloy objects, in P. Holdsworth (ed.) *Excavations in the Medieval Burgh of Perth 1979-1981*. Society of Antiquaries of Scotland Monograph Series No. 5: 121–30. Edinburgh.

Ford, B. 1987b. Iron objects, in P. Holdsworth (ed.). *Excavations in the Medieval Burgh of Perth 1979-1981*. Society of Antiquaries of Scotland Monograph Series No. 5: 130–141. Edinburgh.

Ford, B. 1996. The small finds, in G. Ewart. Inchaffray Abbey, Perth and Kinross: excavation and research, 1987. *Proceedings of the Society of Antiquaries of Scotland* 126: 498–505 (469–516).

Ford, B.A. 1998. The metal objects, in P. Dixon A rural medieval settlement in Roxburghshire: excavations at Springwood Park, Kelso, 1985–6. *Proceedings of the Society of Antiquaries of Scotland* 128: 706–19 (671–751).

Ford, B. and D. Robinson 1987. Moss, in P. Holdsworth (ed.) *Excavations in the Medieval Burgh of Perth 1979-1981*. Society of Antiquaries of Scotland Monograph Series No. 5: 153–154. Edinburgh.

Ford, B. and A. Walsh 1987. Iron nails, in P. Holdsworth (ed.) *Excavations in the Medieval Burgh of Perth 1979-1981*. Society of Antiquaries of Scotland Monograph Series No. 5: 139. Edinburgh.

Franklin, J. 2008. Stirling Castle Palace Archaeology and Historical Research Finds Report 2006–2008, Viewed on 15/10/2020 https://webarchive.nrscotland.gov.uk/20180403094120/http://sparc.scran.ac.uk/publications/pdfs/L2%20finds%20report.pdf

Franklin, J. and I. Goodall 2012. The iron, in *Perth High Street, Archaeological Excavations, 1975-1977. Fascicule 2, The ceramics, the metalwork and the wood*: 123–187. Perth: Tayside and Fife Archaeological Committee.

Fraser, M. and J. H. Dickson 1982. Plant remains, in J.C. Murray (ed.) *Excavations in the Medieval Burgh of Aberdeen 1973-81*. Society of Antiquaries of Scotland Monograph Series No. 2: 239–243. Edinburgh.

Fraser, M. and C. Smith 2011. The botanical remains, in *Perth High Street Archaeological Excavation 1975-1977 Fascicule 4 Living and Working in a Medieval Scottish Burgh. Environmental Remains and Miscellaneous Finds*: 67–79. Perth: Tayside and Fife Archaeological Committee.

Froese, R. and D. Pauly 2015. FishBase. World wide web electronic publication, viewed April 2015, <http:www.fishbase.org>.

Gabra-Sanders, T. 1995. Lace tag, in J. Lewis and G. Ewart *Jedburgh Abbey. The Archaeology and Architecture of a Border Abbey*. Society of Antiquaries of Scotland Monograph Series No. 10: 88. Edinburgh.

Gabra-Sanders, T. 2001. Textiles, textile fibres and animal hairs, dyes and ropes, in A.S. Cameron and J.A. Stones (eds) *Aberdeen: An In-depth View of the City's Past*. Society of Antiquaries of Scotland Monograph Series No. 19: 222–241. Edinburgh.

Good, G.L. and C.J. Tabraham 1988. Excavations at Smailholm Tower, Roxburghshire. *Proceedings of the Society of Antiquaries of Scotland* 118: 231–266.

Goodall, A.R. 1979. Copper alloy objects, in D.D. Andrews and G. Milne (eds), Domestic Settlement 1: Areas 10 and 6, Vol 1 of J.G. Hurst (ed.) *Wharram: A Study of Settlement on the Yorkshire Wolds*. Society for Medieval Archaeology Monograph Series No.8: 108–114. London.

Goodall, A.R. 1982a. Copper alloy objects, in J.C. Murray (ed.) *Excavations in the Medieval Burgh of Aberdeen 1973-81*. Society of Antiquaries of Scotland Monograph Series No. 2: 186–187. Edinburgh.

Goodall, A.R. 1982b. Iron objects, in C.J. Murray (ed.) *Excavations in the Medieval Burgh of Aberdeen 1973-81*. Society of Antiquaries of Scotland Monograph Series No. 2: 188–190. Edinburgh.

Goodall, A.R. 1983. Non-ferrous metal objects [except military finds, spurs and pins], in P. Mayes & L.A.S Butler *Sandal Castle Excavations 1964-73*: 231-39. Wakefield: Wakefield Historical Publications.

Goodall, A. 2012a. The non-ferrous metalwork, in *Perth High Street, Archaeological Excavations, 1975-1977. Fascicule 2, The ceramics, the metalwork and the wood*: 89–118. Perth: Tayside and Fife Archaeological Committee.

Goodall, A. 2012b. Objects of copper alloy, in P. Saunders (eds) *Salisbury Museum Medieval Catalogue. Part 4*, 90-142. Salisbury: Salisbury and South Wiltshire Museum.

Goodall, I.H. 1975. Metalwork from Goltho, in G. Beresford *The Medieval Clay-land Village: Excavations at Goltho and Barton Blount*. Society for Medieval Archaeology Monograph Series No. 6: 79–98. London.

Goodall, I.H. 1981. The Medieval blacksmith and his products, in D.W. Crossly (ed.) *Medieval Industry*. Council for British Archaeology Research Report No. 40: 63–71. London.

Goodall, I.H. 2011 *Ironwork in Medieval Britain: an Archaeological Study*. Society for Medieval Archaeology Monograph No. 31. London.

Goodman, W.L. 1964. *The History of Woodworking Tools*. London: G Bell.

Gordon, J. 1661. *Abredoniæ novæ et veteris descriptio*.

Goudge, C.E. 1979. The leather, in C.M. Heighway, A.P. Garrod, and A.C. Vince, Excavations at 1 Westgate Street, Gloucester. *Medieval Archaeology* 23: 193–196 (159–223).

Grant, A. 1982. The use of toothwear as a guide to the age of domestic ungulates, in C. Grigson, R. Wilson and S. Payne (eds) *Ageing and Sexing Animal Bones*: 91–108. Oxford: BAR British Series 109.

Grant, I.F. 1961. *Highland Folk Ways*. London: Routledge.

Greig, C. 1982. 2:2 Queen Street midden area 1973, in J.C. Murray (ed.) *Excavations in the Medieval Burgh of Aberdeen 1973-81*. Society of Antiquaries of Scotland Monograph Series No. 2: 20–25. Edinburgh.

Grew, F. and M. de Neergaard 1988. *Shoes and Pattens*, London: Museum of London.

Grierson, S. 1986. *The Colour Cauldron: The History and Use of Natural Dyes in Scotland*. Perth: privately published.

Haggarty, G.R. 2011. Ceramic Resource Disc: Thistle Pottery Portobello Buchan's hand painted stoneware. National Museums Scotland, Viewed online 7 December 2011,
<http://repository.nms.ac.uk/291/>.

Haggarty, G. forthcoming *The Ceramics from Bon Accord, Aberdeen*.

Hahn, D. 2003. *The Tower Menagerie Being the Amazing True Story of the Royal Collection of Wild and Ferocious Beasts*. London: Simon and Schuster.

Hall, A. 1989. ...a contribution on hair-moss, in P. Walton (ed.) *Textiles, Cordage and Raw Fibre from 16-22 Coppergate*. The Archaeology of York Fascicule 17/5: 395–397. London: Council for British Archaeology.

Hall, A. 2003. Assessment of samples from medieval deposits from ten excavations in Aberdeen: plant remains and the nature of the deposits. Unpublished reports from the Centre for Human Palaeoecology 2003/05, University of York.

Hall, A.R., H.K. Kenward, and J. Carrot 2004. Technical Report: plant and invertebrate remains from medieval deposits at various sites in Aberdeen. Unpublished reports from the Centre for Human Palaeoecology, University of York.

Hall, D.W., A.D.S. MacDonald, D.R. Perry, and , J. Terry 1998. The archaeology of Elgin: excavations on Ladyhill and in the High Street, with an overview of the archaeology of the burgh. *Proceedings of the Society of Antiquaries of Scotland* 128: 753–829. Edinburgh.

Hall, M.A. 2001. An ivory knife handle from the High Street, Perth, Scotland: consuming ritual in a medieval burgh. *Medieval Archaeology* XLV: 169–88.

Hall, M.A. 2007. Crossing the pilgrimage landscape: some thoughts on a Holy Rood reliquary from the River Tay at Carpow, Perth and Kinross, Scotland, in S. Blick (ed.) *Beyond Pilgrim Souvenirs and Secular Badges: Essays in Honour of Brian Spencer*: 75–91. Oxford: Oxbow Books.

Hall, M. and B. Spencer 2012. Devotion and belief on Perth High Street, in *Perth High Street, Archaeological Excavations, 1975-1977. Fascicule 2, The ceramics, the metalwork and the wood*: 203–219. Perth: Tayside and Fife Archaeological Committee.

Hamilton-Dyer, S., C. Smith, A.E. Bullock, and A.K.G. Jones 2001. The fish and bird bones, in A.S. Cameron and J.A. Stones (eds) *Aberdeen: An In-depth View of the City's Past*. Society of Antiquaries of Scotland Monograph Series No. 19: 276–80. Edinburgh.

Harland, J.F. 2006 Zooarchaeology in the Viking Age to Medieval Northern Isles, Scotland: an investigation of spatial and temporal patterning. Unpublished PhD thesis, University of York.

Harland, J.F., J. Barrett, J. Carrott, K. Dobney and D. Jaques 2003. The York System: an integrated zooarchaeological database for research and teaching. *Internet Archaeology* 13.

Harland, J.F., A.K.G. Jones, D.C. Orton and J.H. Barrett 2016. Fishing and fish trade in Medieval York: The zooarchaeological evidence, in J.H. Barrett and D.C. Orton (eds) *Cod and Herring: the Archaeology and History of Medieval Sea Fishing*. Oxford: Oxbow Books.

Harvey, N. 1987. *Old Farm Buildings*, Shire Album 10. Shire Publications Ltd.

Hastie, M. and T. Holden 2001. The plant remains, in C. Moloney and L. Baker, Evidence for the form and nature of a medieval burgage plot in St Andrews: an archaeological excavation of the site of the Byre Theatre, St Andrews. *Tayside Fife Archaeology Journal* 7: 77–79.

Henshall, A.S. 1950. Textiles and weaving appliances in Prehistoric Britain. *Proceedings of the Prehistoric Society* 16: 130–162.

Hill, P. 1997. *Whithorn and St Ninian. The Excavation of a Monastic Town 1984-91*. Stroud.

Hillson, S. 1986. *Teeth*. Cambridge: Cambridge University Press.

Hodgson, G.W.I. 1983. The animal remains from mediaeval sites within three burghs on the eastern Scottish seaboard, in B. Proudfoot (ed.) *Site, Environment and Economy, Symposia of the Association for Environmental Archaeology No. 3*. British Archaeological Reports International Series 173: 3–32. Oxford.

Hodgson, G.W.I. and A. Jones 1982. The animal bone, in J.C. Murray (ed.) *Excavations in the Medieval Burgh of Aberdeen 1973-81*. Society of Antiquaries of Scotland Monograph Series No. 2: 229–238. Edinburgh.

Hodgson, G.W.I., C. Smith, and A. Jones 2011. The mammal bone, in *Perth High Street Archaeological Excavation 1975-1977. Fascicule 4, Living and working in a medieval Scottish burgh. Environmental remains and miscellaneous finds*, Perth: Tayside and Fife Archaeological Committee: 5–44.

Holmes, N. 1998. *Scottish Coins. A history of small change in Scotland*. Edinburgh: National Museums Scotland Publishing.

Holtzapffel, C. 1864. *Turning and Mechanical Manipulation* Vol. III, London.

Huggett, J.W. 1988. Imported grave goods and the early Anglo-Saxon economy. *Medieval Archaeology* 32: 63–96.

Hurley, M.F. 1997. *Late Viking Age and Medieval Waterford: excavations 1986-1992.* Waterford.

Hurley, M.F. and S.W.J. McCutcheon 1997. Wooden artefacts, in M.F. Hurley *Late Viking Age and Medieval Waterford: excavations 1986-1992*: 553–634. Waterford: Waterford Corporation.

Hurst, J. 2001. Counters, in A.S. Cameron, D.H. Evans and J.A. Stones, Small finds of metal, glass, stone, clay, bone and other organics, in A.S. Cameron and J.A. Stones (eds) *Aberdeen: An In-depth View of the City's Past.* Society of Antiquaries of Scotland Monograph Series No. 19: 206. Edinburgh.

Innes, C. (ed.) 1842. *Aberdoniae Utriusque Descriptio. A Description of Both Touns of Aberdeen. By James Gordon, parson of Rothemay.* Edinburgh: Spalding Club Publications No. 5.

Innes, C. 1845. *Registrum Episcopatus Aberdonensis,* Edinburgh: Spalding Club Publications No. 14, Vol. II.

Innes, C. and P. Chalmers, (eds) 1848. *Liber S Thome de Aberbrothoc,* Edinburgh: Bannatyne Club.

Jackson, G. 2002. The economy: Aberdeen and the sea, in E.P. Dennison, D. Ditchburn and M. Lynch (eds) *Aberdeen Before 1800: a new history*: 159–180. East Linton: Tuckwell Press Ltd.

Jacomet, S. 2006. *Identification of Cereal Remains from Archaeological Sites* (2nd edition). Basel: Archaeobotany Lab IPAS, Basel University.

Jessop, O. 1996. A new artefact typology for the study of medieval arrowheads. *Medieval Archaeology* 40: 192–205.

Johnstone, A. and D. Speirs, 2001. The documentary research, in A.S. Cameron and J.A. Stones (eds) *Aberdeen: an In-depth View of the City's Past.* Society of Antiquaries of Scotland Monograph Series No. 19: 116–152. Edinburgh.

Keith, A. 1843 (originally published 1732). A view of the diocese of Aberdeen, in J. Robertson (ed.) *Collections for the History of the Shires of Aberdeen and Banff*: 67–658. Aberdeen: The Spalding Club.

Keith and Gibb 1862. *Keith and Gibb's Map of the Cities of Aberdeen, 1:7,200.*

Kenward, H.K., A.R. Hall, and A.K.G. Jones 1980. A tested set of techniques for the extraction of plant and animal macrofossils from waterlogged archaeological deposits. *Science and Archaeology* 22: 3–15.

Kenward, H.K. and Kenward H. 1997. Enhancing bioarchaeological interpretation using indicator groups: stable manure as a paradigm. *Journal of Archaeological Science* 24: 663–673.

Kolchin, B.A. 1989. *Wooden Artefacts from Medieval Novgorod.* British Archaeological Reports International Series 495. Oxford.

Kublo, E.K. 2007. Spinning and weaving, in M. Brisbane and J. Hather (eds) *Wood Use in Medieval Novgorod*: 136–137. Oxford: Bournemouth University and Oxbow Books.

Lewis, J. 1996. Excavations at St Andrews, Castlecliffe, 1988–90. *Proceedings of the Society of Antiquaries of Scotland* 126: 605–688.

Lewis, J. and H. Smith 1998. Excavations at Inverlochy Castle, Inverness-shire, 1983–95. *Proceedings of the Society of Antiquaries of Scotland* 128: 619–644.

LMMC 1940. *London Museum Medieval Catalogue,* London.

Lynch, M. and H.M. Dingwall 2002. Elite society in town and country, in E.P. Dennison, D. Ditchburn and M. Lynch (eds) *Aberdeen Before 1800: a new history*: 181–200. East Linton: Tuckwell Press Ltd.

MacDonald, A.D.S. and L. Laing 1975. Excavations at Lochmaben Castle, Dumfriesshire. *Proceedings of the Society of Antiquaries of Scotland* 160: 124–157.

MacGregor, A. 1982. Bone, antler and ivory objects, in J.C. Murray (ed.) *Excavations in the Medieval Burgh of Aberdeen 1973-81.* Society of Antiquaries of Scotland Monograph Series No. 2: 180–184. Edinburgh.

MacGregor, A. 1985. *Bone, Antler, Ivory and Horn: The Technology of Skeletal Materials Since the Roman Period.* London: Barnes and Noble.

MacIvor, I. and D. Gallagher 1999. Excavations at Caerlaverock Castle, 1955–66. *Archaeology Journal* 156: 143–245.

Macphail, R.I. 1998. A reply to Carter and Davidson's, An evaluation of the contribution of soil micromorphology to the study of ancient arable agriculture. *Geoarchaeology* 13: 549–564.

Mainman, A.J. and N.S.H. Rogers 2000. *Craft, Industry and Everyday Life: Finds from Anglo-Scandinavian York.* The Archaeology of York: The Small finds Fascicule AY 17/14. York: Council for British Archaeology.

Manning, W.H. 1985. *Catalogue of the Romano-British Iron Tools, Fittings and Weapons in the British Museum.* London: British Museum Publications Ltd.

Markus, M. 2010. Appendix 4; The architectural stone, in *Perth High Street Archaeological Excavation 1975-1977, Fascicule 1, The excavations at 75-95 High Street and 5-10 Mill Street, Perth*: 218–220. Perth: Tayside and Fife Archaeological Committee.

Martinón-torres, M. and T. Rehren 2009. Post-medieval crucible production and distribution: a study of materials and materialities. *Archaeometry* 51.1: 49–74.

McCormick, F. 1994. Excavations at Pluscarden Priory, Moray. *Proceedings of the Society of Antiquaries of Scotland* 124: 391–432.

McDonnell, G. 1994. Slag report, in B. Ballin-Smith (ed.) *Howe: Four Millennia of Orkney Prehistory. Excavations 1978-82.* Society of Antiquaries of Scotland Monograph Series No. 9: 228–234. Edinburgh.

McDonnell, G. 2000. Ironworking and other residues, in A. Lane and E. Campbell *Dunadd: an Early Dalriadic Capital*: 218–220. Oxford.

The Medieval Bestiary online, viewed 30 November 2011. <http://bestiary.ca/beasts/beast140.htm> and viewed 30 November 2011 <http://bestiary.ca/beasts/beast165.htm>

Meldrum, E.A. 1986. *Aberdeen of Old*. Inverness: Aberdeen and North East Scotland History Society.

Miller, A.G. 1947. Bronze Age graves at Ferniegair, Hamilton. *Transactions of Glasgow Archaeology Society* 11: 17–21.

Milne, A. 1789. *A Plan of the city of Aberdeen with all the enclosures surrounding the town to the adjacent country from a survey taken 1789*, W. and A.K. Johnston Ltd (1902).

Milne, J. 1911. *Aberdeen: Topographical, Antiquarian and Historical Papers on the City of Aberdeen*. Aberdeen.

Moffat B. and M. Penny 2001. Residues from a ceramic vessel and stone mortar, in A.S. Cameron and J.A. (eds) *Aberdeen: An In-depth View of the City's Past*. Society of Antiquaries of Scotland Monograph Series No. 19: 297–299. Edinburgh.

Morgan, D. 2004. *Lost Aberdeen: Aberdeen's Lost Architectural Heritage*. Edinburgh: Birlinn.

Morris, C. 1980. A group of Early Medieval spades. *Medieval Archaeology* 24: 205-10.

Morris, C.A. 1999. Late Norse and medieval woodworking, wooden artefacts and products, in B.A. Crawford and B. Ballin Smith (eds) *The Biggings, Papa Stour, Shetland: the History and Archaeology of a Royal Norwegian Farm*. Society of Antiquaries of Scotland Monograph Series No. 15: 182–193. Edinburgh.

Morris, C.A. 2000. *Craft, Industry and Everyday Life. Wood and Woodworking in Anglo-Scandinavian and Medieval York*. The Archaeology of York Fascicule 17/13. York: The Council for British Archaeology.

Morris, C. 2008. Wooden vessels, in J. Mann (ed.) *Finds from the Well at St Paul-in-the-Bail, Lincoln*: Lincoln Archaeology Studies No. 9: 40–51. Oxford: Oxbow.

Mould, Q., I. Carlisle and E. Cameron 2003. *Craft, Industry and Everyday Life. Leather and leatherworking in Anglo-Scandinavian and Medieval York*. The Archaeology of York: The Small Finds, Fascicule 17/16. York: Council for British Archaeology.

Munro, R. 1882. *Ancient Scottish Lake-Dwellings or Crannogs*. Edinburgh: David Douglas.

Murphy, C.P. 1986. *Thin Section Preparation of Soils and Sediments*. Berkhamsted: AB Academic Press.

Murray, H.K. 1982. 42 St Paul Street 1977-8, in J.C. Murray (ed.) *Excavations in the Medieval Burgh of Aberdeen 1973-81*. Society of Antiquaries of Scotland Monograph Series No. 2: 46–84. Edinburgh.

Murray, H. 1984. Excavation at 45–47 Gallowgate, Aberdeen. *Proceedings of the Society of Antiquaries Scotland* 114: 303–313.

Murray, H.K. 1984a. Wood (Fiche 3.G6), in H. Murray, Excavations at 45–47, Gallowgate, Aberdeen. *Proceedings of the Society of Antiquaries of Scotland* 114: 303–313.

Murray, H. 2010. The buildings, in Perth High Street Archaeological Excavation 1975–1977. Fascicule 1, The excavations at 75–95 High Street and 5–10 Mill Street, Perth: 127–128. Perth: Tayside and Fife Archaeological Committee.

Murray, H.K. and J.C. Murray 1993. Excavations at Rattray, Aberdeenshire: a Scottish deserted burgh. *Medieval Archaeology* 37: 109–119.

Murray, H.K. and J.C. Murray 2011. Excavations at the Bishop's Palace, Brechin. *Tayside and Fife Archaeological Journal* 17: 36–67.

Murray, H.K., J.C. Murray and W.J. Lindsay 2009. Medieval timber lined wells in Elgin. *Proceedings of the Society of Antiquaries of Scotland* 139: 213–227.

Murray, J.C. (ed.) 1982. *Excavations in the Medieval Burgh of Aberdeen 1973-81*. Society of Antiquaries of Scotland Monograph Series No. 2. Edinburgh.

O'Connor, T.P. 1984. Selected groups of bones from Skeldergate and Walmgate, in P.V. Addyman (ed.) *The Archaeology of York: The Animal Bones*. The Archaeology of York: The Animal Bones Fascicule AY15/1: 1–60. London: Council for British Archaeology.

O'Connor, T.P. 2003. The analysis of urban animal bone assemblages: a handbook for archaeologists, in P.V. Addyman (ed.) *The Archaeology of York: Principles and Methods*. The Archaeology of York Fascicule AY 19/20. York: York Archaeological Trust/Council for British Archaeology.

Ordnance Survey 1871 *Aberdeenshire sheet LXXV.11.8*, 1:500

Ordnance Survey 1871 *Aberdeenshire sheet LXXV.11.13*, 1:500

Ordnance Survey 1902 *Aberdeenshire sheet LXXV.11* (revised 1899–1900), 1:2500

Ordnance Survey 1926 *Aberdeenshire sheet LXXV.11* (revised 1924), 1:2500

Ordnance Survey 1955 *Plan NJ 9406 SW*, 1:1250

Ordnance Survey 1955 *Plan NJ 9406 NW*, 1:1250

OSA 1791–1799. Sir John Sinclair (ed.) *The Statistical Account of Scotland, 1791-99* Vol. XIX: 140–233. Aberdeen. County of Aberdeen.

Ottaway, P.J. and N.S.H. Rogers 2002. *Craft, Industry and Everyday Life: Finds from Medieval York*. The Archaeology of York: The Small Finds Fascicule AY 17/15. York: Council for British Archaeology.

Parfitt, J.H. 1976. A Moated Site at Moat Farm, Leigh, Kent *Archaeologia Cantiana* 92: 173–201.

Payne, S. 1973. Kill-off patterns in sheep and goats. *Anatolian Studies* 23: 281–303.

Payne, S. 1987. Reference codes for wear states in the mandibular cheek teeth of sheep and goats. *Journal of Archaeological Science* 14: 609–614.

Perdikaris, S. 1999. From chiefly provisioning to commercial fishery: long-term economic change in Arctic Norway. *World Archaeology* 30 (3): 388–402.

Perring, F.H. and S.M. Walters 1990. *Atlas of the British Flora*. London: Nelson and Sons Ltd.

Perry, D. 2010. The excavation: discussions, in D. Perry, H. Murray, T. Beaumont James and the late N.Q. Bogdan *Perth High Street Archaeological Excavation 1975-1977. Fascicule 1, The excavations at 75-95 High Street and 5-10 Mill Street, Perth*: 103–125. Perth: Tayside and Fife Archaeological Committee.

Perry, D., H. Murray, T. Beaumont James and the late N.Q. Bogdan 2010. *Perth High Street Archaeological Excavation 1975-1977. Fascicule 1, The excavations at 75-95 High Street and 5-10 Mill Street, Perth*. Perth: Tayside and Fife Archaeological Committee.

Peters, J.E.C. 1981. *Discovering Traditional Farm Buildings*. Shire Publications Ltd.

Pittock, M.G.H. 2002. Contrasting cultures: town and country, in E.P. Dennison, D. Ditchburn and M. Lynch (eds) *Aberdeen Before 1800: a new history*: 347–373. East Linton: Tuckwell Press Ltd.

Platt, C. and R. Coleman-Smith 1975. *Excavations in Medieval Southampton 1953-1969, Vol. 2 The Finds*. Leicester: Leicester University Press.

Pluskowski, A. 2011. Chapter 2: the medieval landscape: part 3 the tame and the wild, in M. Carver and J. Klápště, (eds) *The Archaeology of Medieval Europe, Vol.2 Twelfth to Sixteenth Centuries*: 80–96. Aarhus: Aarhus University Press.

Polzer, M.E. 2008. Toggles and sails in the ancient world: rigging elements recovered from the Tantura B shipwreck, Israel. *International Journal of Nautical Archaeology* 37.2: 225–252.

Prummel, W. 1978. Animal bones from tannery pits at 's-Hertogensbosch', *Berichten van de Rijkdienst voor het Oudheidkundig Bodermonderzoek* 28: 399–422.

Prummel, W. 1982. The archaeozoological study of urban Medieval sites in the Netherlands, in A. Hall and H.K. Kenward *Environmental Archaeology in the Urban Context*. London: Council for British Archaeology Research Report 43: 117–122.

Prummel, W. 1983. *Excavations at Dorestad 2. Early Medieval Dorestad: an archaeozoological study*, NederlandseOudheden 11, Amerfoort: Rijksdienst voor het Oudheidkundig Bodemonderzoik.

Pukiene, R. and D. Baubaite 2011. Identification of wood species of waterlogged archaeological artefacts and its role in choosing the conservation method, in *Synthesis of Art and Science in Conservation: Trends and Achievements*: 151–161. Vilnius: Lithuanian Art Museum.

Rees, S. 2002. The gemstones, in P.J. Ottaway and M.S.H. Rogers *Craft, Industry and Everyday Life: Finds from Medieval York*. The Archaeology of York: The Small Finds Fascicule AY 17/15: 2928-2931. York: Council for British Archaeology.

Rhodes, M. (ed.) 1982. The finds, in G. Milne and C. Milne *Medieval Waterfront Development at Trig Lane, London*. Middlesex Archaeology Society Special Paper 5: 84–108. London.

Richardson, K.M. 1959. Excavations in Hungate, York. *Archaeological Journal*, 116: 51–114.

Robinson, D. 1987. Spice and famine food? The botanical analysis of two post-reformation pits from Elgin, Scotland. *Circaea* 5: 21–27.

Robinson, J 2008. *Masterpieces: Medieval Art*. London: British Museum.

Robertson, J. forthcoming. Animal bone report. Advocates Close. Edinburgh.

Roy, M. 2008. Bon Accord Centre, Aberdeen: Archaeological Evaluation, Excavation and Watching Brief. Unpublished archive report.

Russell, F. (ed.) 1999. *A Sense of Heaven: 16th Century Boxwood Carvings for Private Devotion*. Leeds: The Henry Moore Institute.

Russell, N., G.T. Cook, P.L. Ascough and A.J. Dugmore 2010. Spatial variation in the marine radiocarbon reservoir effect throughout the Scottish post-Roman to late medieval period: North Sea values (500–1350 BP). *Radiocarbon* 52: 1166–1181.

Russell, N., G.T. Cook, P.L. Ascough and E.M. Scott 2015. A period of calm in Scottish seas: a comprehensive study of ΔR values for the northern British Isles coast and the consequent implications for archaeology and oceanography. *Quaternary Geochronology* 30: 34–41.

Rybina, E.A. 2007. Fishing and hunting, in M. Brisbane and J. Hather (eds) *Wood Use in Medieval Novgorod*: 124–135 Oxford: Bournemouth University and Oxbow Books.

Ryder, M.L. 1987. *Cashmere, Mohair and other Luxury Animal Fibres for the Breeder and Spinner*. Southampton: White Rose II.

Samson, R. 1982. Finds from Urquhart Castle in the National Museum, Edinburgh. *Proceedings of the Society of Antiquaries of Scotland* 112: 465–476.

Saville, A. 2001. Flint artefacts, in A.S. Cameron and J.A. Stones (eds) *Aberdeen: an In-depth View of the City's Past*. Society of Antiquaries of Scotland Monograph Series No. 19: 259–261. Edinburgh.

Schmid, E. 1972. *Atlas of Animal Bones - for prehistorians, archaeologists and Quaternary Geologists*. Amsterdam: Elsevier.

Schnack, C. 1992. *Die mittelalterlichen Schuhe aus Schleswig, Ausgrabung Schild 1971-1975*. Ausgrabungen in Schleswig, Berichte und Studien, 10, Neumunster.

Schofield, J. 2013. Chapter 4: urban development: part 1 western Europe, in J. Graham-Campbell and M. Valor (eds) *The Archaeology of Medieval Europe, Vol.1 Eighth to Twelfth Centuries*: 111–129. Aarhus: Aarhus University Press.

Schofield, J. and A. Vince 2003. *Medieval Towns*. London: Continuum.

The Scotsman 1886. *The Scotsman* newspaper report, quoted in National Record of the Historic Environment of Scotland ref. NJ90NW 65, viewed 15 October 2020, < https://canmore.org.uk/site/20189/aberdeen-upperkirkgate>.

The Scottish Printing Archival Trust 2000. *A Reputation for Excellence: a History of the Aberdeen and Northern Counties Printing Industries*. Edinburgh.

Serjeantson, D. 1989. Animal remains and the tanning trade, in D. Serjeantson and T. Waldron 1989. *Diet and Craft in Towns: the Evidence of Animal Remains from the Roman to the Post-Medieval Periods*. Oxford: BAR British Series 119.

Shaffrey, R. Worked Stone Overview: Southampton French Quarter SOU1382, viewed 7 December 2011, <http://library.thehumanjourney.net/53/1/SOU_1382_Specialist_report_download_F11.pdf>.

Shaw, M. 1996. The excavation of a late 15th- to 17th-century tanning complex at The Green, Northampton. *Post-Medieval Archaeology* 30: 63–127.

Shortt, H. de S. 1959. A provincial Roman spur from Longstock, Hants, and other spurs from Roman Britain, *Antiquaries Journal* 39: 61–76.

Silver, I. 1969. The ageing of domestic animals, in D. Brothwell and E. Higgs (eds). *Science in Archaeology 2*: 283–302. London: Thames and Hudson.

Simpson, I.A., I.W. Vesteinsson, P. Adderley and H. McGovern 2003. Fuel resource utilisation in landscapes of settlement. *Journal of Archaeological Science* 30, 11: 1401–1420.

Smirnova, L.I. 2007. Wooden combs in the light of the history of comb-making in Novgorod, in M. Brisbane and J. Hather (eds) *Wood Use in Medieval Novgorod*: 298-334. Oxford: Bournemouth University and Oxbow Books.

Smith, C. 2010. Mammalian, bird and molluscan remains, in G.G. Barclay and A. Ritchie (eds) *Artefactual, Environmental and Archaeological Evidence from the Holyrood Parliament Site Excavations*. Scottish Archaeology Internet Report 40.

Smith, C. and A.S. Clarke 2011. The bird bone, in *Perth High Street Archaeological Excavations 1975-1977. Fascicule 4, Living and working in a medieval Scottish burgh, Environmental remains and miscellaneous finds*: 45–52. Perth: Tayside and Fife Archaeological Committee.

Smith, C. and D. Henderson 2002. The animal bone, in P.J. Dixon, J.R. Mackenzie, D.R. Perry and P. Sharman *The Origins of the Settlements at Kelso and Peebles, Scottish Borders*. Scottish Archaeological Internet Report 2.

Smith, C., J. Lawson Brown and M. Hall 2011. The stone objects, in *Perth High Street, Archaeological Excavations, 1975-1977, Fascicule 4, Living and working in a medieval Scottish burgh, Environmental remains and miscellaneous finds*: 127–138. Perth: Tayside and Fife Archaeological Committee.

Smith, C. and F. McCormick 2001. The animal bones, in A.S. Cameron and J.A. Stones (eds) *Aberdeen: An In-depth View of the City's Past*. Society of Antiquaries of Scotland Monograph Series No. 19: 271–275. Edinburgh.

Smith, J.S. 1985. The physical site of historical Aberdeen, in J.S. Smith (ed.) *New Light on Medieval Aberdeen*. Aberdeen: Aberdeen University Press.

Spearman, R.M. 1984. The clay moulds, in J.C. Murray (ed.) 1982 *Excavations in the Medieval Burgh of Aberdeen 1973-81*. Society of Antiquaries of Scotland Monograph Series No. 2: fiche 3, G11. Edinburgh.

Spearman, R.M. 1987. Mould and crucible fragments, in P. Holdsworth (ed.) *Excavations in the Medieval Burgh of Perth 1979-1981*. Society of Antiquaries of Scotland Monograph Series No. 5: 157–158.

Spearman, R.M. 1988. Workshops, materials and debris – Evidence of Early Industries, in M. Lynch, M. Spearman and G. Stell (eds) *The Scottish Medieval Town*: 134–147. Edinburgh.

Spearman, R.M. 1997. The smithy and metalworking debris from Mills Mount, in S.T. Driscoll and P.A. Yeoman. *Excavations within Edinburgh Castle in 1988-91*. Society of Antiquaries of Scotland Monograph Series No. 12: 164–168. Edinburgh.

Spearman, R.M. 1997a. Crucible fragment, in S.T. Driscoll and P.A. Yeoman. *Excavations within Edinburgh Castle in 1988-91*. Society of Antiquaries of Scotland Monograph Series No. 12: 165. Edinburgh.

Spencer, B. 1998. *Medieval Finds from Medieval Excavations in London: 7 Pilgrim Souvenirs and Secular Badges*. London: Museum of London.

Starkey, D., C. Reid and N. Ashcroft (eds) 2000. *England's Sea Fisheries: The Commercial Sea Fisheries of England and Wales since 1300*. London: Chatham Publishing.

Starley, D. 2000. Metalworking debris, in K. Buxton and C. Howard-Davis (eds) *Bremetenacum: Excavations at Roman Ribchester 1980, 1989-1990*. Lancaster Imprints Series No. 9: 337–347. Lancaster.

Steane, J.M. and M. Foreman 1988. Medieval fishing tackle, in M. Aston (ed.) *Medieval Fish, Fisheries and Fishponds in England*. British Archaeological Reports British Series 182: 137–186. Oxford.

Stell, G. 2002. Housing in the two towns, in E.P. Dennison, D. Ditchburn and M. Lynch (eds) *Aberdeen Before 1800: a new history*: 97–108. East Linton: Tuckwell Press Ltd.

Stell, G. and M. Baillie 1993. The Great Hall and roof of Darnaway Castle, Moray, in W.D.H. Sellar (ed.) *Moray: Province and People*: 162–186. Edinburgh.

Stones, J.A. 1982. The small finds, in J.C. Murray (ed.) *Excavations in the Medieval Burgh of Aberdeen 1973-81*. Society of Antiquaries of Scotland Monograph Series No. 2: 177–223. Edinburgh.

Stones, J.A. 1982a. Leather objects, in J.C. Murray (ed.) *Excavations in the Medieval Burgh of Aberdeen 1973-81*. Society of Antiquaries of Scotland Monograph Series No. 2: 191–197. Edinburgh.

Stones, J.A. 1982b. The wooden objects, in J.C. Murray (ed.) *Excavations in the Medieval Burgh of Aberdeen 1973-81*. Society of Antiquaries of Scotland Monograph Series No. 2: 177–180. Edinburgh.

Stones, J.A. 2001. In conclusion: presenting medieval Aberdeen in context, in A.S. Cameron and J.A. Stones (eds) *Aberdeen: An In-depth View of the City's Past*. Society of Antiquaries of Scotland Monograph Series No. 19: 300–312. Edinburgh.

Stones, J. A., D. Bateson, J. Cherry, B. Ford, , A.R. Goodall, , I.H. Goodall, D.W. Hall, J. Higgitt, N. Holmes, H. Howard, D. Lehane, W.J. Lindsay, R. Oddy, I.A.G. Shepherd and G. Stell 1989. The small finds, in J.A. Stones (ed.) *Three Scottish Carmelite Friaries. Excavations at Aberdeen, Linlithgow and Perth, 1980-1986*. Society of Antiquaries of Scotland Monograph Series No. 6: 147–163. Edinburgh.

Stones, J. and A. Cameron 2001. 30-46 Upperkirkgate: medieval backland activities from the 12th century, in A.S. Cameron and J.A. Stones (eds) *Aberdeen: an In-depth View of the City's Past*. Society of Antiquaries of Scotland Monograph Series No. 19: 60–72. Edinburgh.

Strutt, J. 1796 (reprinted in facsimile of the updated 1842 edition in 1970). *The Dress and Habits of the People of England* (2 vols.). London: Tabard.

Stuart, John (ed.) 1844. *Extracts from the Records of the Burgh of Aberdeen 1398-1570*. Aberdeen: printed for the Spalding Club.

Stuart, John (ed.) 1848. *Extracts from the Records of the Burgh of Aberdeen 1570-1625*. Aberdeen: printed for the Spalding Club.

Stuart, John (ed.) 1871. *Extracts from the Records of the Burgh of Aberdeen 1625-1642*. Edinburgh: printed for the Scottish Burgh Records Society.

Swallow, A.W. 1973. Interpretation of wear marks seen in footwear. *Transactions of the Museum Assistants Group* 12: 28–32.

Thomas, C. 1981. Leatherwork, in G.L. Good and C.J. Tabraham, Excavations at Threave Castle, Galloway, 1974-78. *Medieval Archaeology* 25:123–126.

Thomas, C. 1988. The leather, in P. Holdsworth (ed.) *Excavations in the Medieval Burgh of Perth 1979-1981*. Society of Antiquaries of Scotland Monograph Series No. 5. Edinburgh.

Thomas, C. 1991. The leather shoes and leggings, in M.A. Hodder Excavations at Sandwell Priory and Hall, 1982-88. *South Staffordshire Archaeological Society Transactions* 31: 102–111.

Thomas, C. 2001. The leather, in A.S. Cameron and J.A. Stones (eds) *Aberdeen: An In-depth View of the City's Past*. Society of Antiquaries of Scotland Monograph Series No. 19: 241–258. Edinburgh.

Thomas, C. The leather, in B. Williams *Bristol Bridge*. Unpublished archive report.

Thomas, C. and N. Bogdan 2012. The leather, in *Perth High Street, Archaeological Excavations, 1975-1977, Fascicule 3, The Textiles and the Leather*: 147–346. Perth: Tayside and Fife Archaeological Committee.

Tomlinson, P. 1985a. An aid to the identification of fossil buds, bud-scales and catkin-bracts of British trees and shrubs. *Circaea* 3, No. 2: 45–130.

Tomlinson, P. 1985b. Use of vegetative remains in the identification of dye plants from waterlogged 9th–10th century AD deposits at York. *Journal of Archaeological Science* 12: 269–283.

Tourunen, A. 2014. Faunal remains, in P. Masser, M. Kimber, J. Franklin, M. Cross and A. Tourunen *Excavations at Jeffrey Street, Edinburgh; the development of closes and tenements north of the Royal Mile during the 16th-18th centuries*. Scottish Archaeological Internet Report 58.

Trewin, N. 1984. Stone, in H. Murray, Excavation at 45–47 Gallowgate, Aberdeen. *Proceedings of the Society of Antiquaries of Scotland* 114: fiche 4: A4.

Tyson, R.F. 2002. People in the two towns, in E.P. Dennison, D. Ditchburn and M. Lynch (eds) *Aberdeen Before 1800: a new history*: 111–128. East Linton: Tuckwell Press Ltd.

Umbanhower, C.E. and M. McGrath 1998. Experimental production and analysis of microscopic charcoal from wood, leaves and grasses. *The Holocene* 8: 341–346.

University of Aberdeen Media Release 2004, viewed 21 January 2014, <http://www.abdn.ac.uk/mediareleases/archive/2004/pr1340.hti.>.

Untracht, O. 1969. *Metal Techniques for Craftsmen*. London: Robert Hale Ltd.

Van Beuningen, H.J.E. and A.M. Koldeweij (eds) 1993. *Heilig en Profaan: 1000 Laatmiddeleeuwse Insignes uit de Collectie H.J.E. Van Beuningen*, Cothen: Rotterdam Papers 8.

Van Beuningen, H.J.E., A M. Koldeweij, and D. Kicken (eds) 2001. *Heilig en Profaan 2: 1200 Laatmiddeleeuwse Insignes uit Openbare en Particuliere Collectives*, Cothen: Rotterdam Papers 12.

Veale, E.M. 1966. *The English Fur Trade in the Later Middle Ages*. Oxford: Clarendon.

Veale, E.M. 2003. *The English Fur Trade in the Later Middle Ages* (2nd edition). London: London Record Society Volume 38.

Vince, A.C. 1991. *Aspects of Saxon and Medieval London II: Finds and Environmental Evidence*. London.

Walton, P. 1988. Caulking, cordage and textiles, in C. O'Brien, L. Bown, S. Dixon and R. Nicholson *The Origins of the Newcastle Quayside: Excavations at Queen Street and Dog Bank*. Society of Antiquaries of Newcastle upon Tyne Monograph Series No. 3: 78–92. Newcastle upon Tyne.

Walton, P. 1989a. *Textiles, Cordage and Raw Fibre from 16-22 Coppergate.* The Archaeology of York: The Small Finds Fascicule AY 17/15. London: Council for British Archaeology.

Walton, P. 1989b. Caulking, textiles and cordage, in C. O'Brien *et al.* Excavations at Newcastle Quayside: the Crown Court site. *Archaeologia Aeliana,* 5th series 17: 167–176.

Walton, P. *Coventry.* Unpublished.

Walton, P. and G.W. Taylor 1991. The characterisation of dyes in textiles from archaeological excavations. *Chromatography and Analysis* 17: 5–7.

Walton Rogers, P. 1999. Textile, yarn and fibre from The Biggings, in B.E.Crawford and B. Ballin Smith *The Biggings, Papa Stour, Shetland: the History and Archaeology of a Royal Norwegian Farm.* Society of Antiquaries of Scotland Monograph Series No. 15: 194–202. Edinburgh.

Walton Rogers, P. 2002. Textile production, in P.J. Ottaway and N.S.H. Rogers *Craft, Industry and Everyday Life: Finds from Medieval York.* The Archaeology of York: The Small finds Fascicule AY 17/15: 2732-2745. York: Council for British Archaeology.

Walton Rogers, P. and A. Hall 2001. Ropes, in A.S. Cameron and J.A. Stones (eds) *Aberdeen: An In-depth View of the City's Past.* Society of Antiquaries of Scotland Monograph Series No. 19: 240–241. Edinburgh.

Ward-Perkins, J. B. 1940. *London Museum Medieval Catalogue.* London.

Waterer, J.W. 1946. *Leather in Life, Art and Industry.* London: Faber.

Wheeler, A. 1977. The origin and distribution of the freshwater fishes of the British Isles. *Journal of Biogeography* 4 (1): 1–24.

Williams, D. 2018. Copper alloy purse components: a new classification using finds from England and Wales recorded by the Portable Antiquities Scheme. Finds Research Group. London.

White, L. 1962. *Medieval Technology and Social Change,* Oxford: Oxford University Press.

White, A. 2002. The Menzies era: sixteenth-century politics, in E.P. Dennison, D. Ditchburn and M. Lynch (eds) *Aberdeen Before 1800: a new history*: 224–237. East Linton: Tuckwell Press Ltd.

Wild, J.P. 1994. A hair moss cap from Vindolanda, in *Archaeological Textiles in Northern Europe: 5th NESAT Symposium*: 61–68. Neumunster: Textilmuseum.

Wildman, A.B. 1954. *The Microscopy of Animal Textile Fibres.* Leeds: Wool Industries Research Association.

Willemsen, A. 2015. The Geoff Egan Memorial Lecture 2013. Taking up the glove: finds, uses and meanings of gloves, mittens and gauntlets in Western Europe, cAD 1300–1700. *Post medieval Archaeology* 49.1: 1–36.

Willemsen, A. and M. Ernst 2012. *Hundreds of.... Medieval chic in metal. Decorative mounts on belts and purses from the Low Countries, 1300-1600.* Zwolle: Rijksmuseum van Oudhen (Stichting Promotie Archeologie).

Williams, D. 2002. Two Late Saxon spur fragments from Sussex and Hampshire. *Medieval Archaeology* 46: 115–118.

Wood, J. 1828 *Plan of the Cities of Aberdeen,* Edinburgh.

Wright, E.V. and D.M. Churchill 1965. The boats from North Ferriby, Yorkshire, England, and a review of the origin of the sewn boats of the Bronze Age. *Proceedings of the Prehistoric Society* 31: 1–24.

Yoneda, M. and P.J. Wright 2004. Temporal and spatial variation in reproductive investment of Atlantic cod *Gadus morhua* in the northern North Sea and Scottish west coast. *Marine Ecology Progress Series* 276: 237–248.

Appendices

1 Radiocarbon dating programme

Michael Roy with contribution by Gordon Cook

Samples from carbon residues on pottery vessels were submitted for radiocarbon dating (Table A.1.1 & Figure A.1.1) to aid understanding of the pottery sequence, i.e. to address questions of early local ceramic manufacture and longevity of use. Organic materials, primarily leather offcuts from the same contexts as the pottery residues, were submitted as a control, the logic being that the age of the leather offcuts at the point of deposition was more likely to be coterminous with the date of deposition, while the use of the ceramics could have been earlier.

Commonly, the ages recovered from the carbon residues were found to be significantly older than that anticipated through study of the ceramic evidence from stratigraphically associated deposits. In an extreme example, residues from one medieval ceramic vessel in particular, from Phase 2 Pit C027 (SUERC-26955), produced a remarkably early date of cal AD 240–400, a variance of almost 1000 years between the medieval date of the sherd and the radiocarbon date.

However, this variation between the radiocarbon dates from residues and the anticipated date of the sherds based on their typology, the stratigraphic sequence and other dating evidence was not uniform. The carbon residue from a vessel from Pit C069 (Phase 3 or 4) (SUERC-26675) produced a date of cal AD 1215–1300 that correlated relatively well with the expected date from associated artefacts. Furthermore, dendrochronological analysis provided a felling date for a structural timber within the fill of this pit of AD 1281. However, the presence of radiocarbon dates that are somewhat at odds with the associated artefactual assemblages is difficult to comprehend apart from the action of a process such as the marine reservoir effect. The presence of significant quantities of fish bone, representing the utilisation of marine resources, indicates a potential mechanism for the contamination of terrestrial samples with marine material.

The sampled residues could potentially derive from the use of pots for cooking fish, in particular in the clearly anomalous sample from Pit C027; radiocarbon dates from such residues would have a marine reservoir age associated with them and potentially appear too old. Deviations caused by the marine reservoir effect, which affects radiocarbon dates dependent on oceanic water composition, have been studied for post-Roman to late medieval Scotland (Russell *et al.* 2010); this study has provided deviations from the global average marine radiocarbon reservoir effect for the Gallowgate Middle School site (-57) and 16–18 Netherkirkgate (-95) in Aberdeen. These studies have shown that an alternative to determining the context ages would be to analyse the fish bone collagen as there is good evidence for the extent of the marine reservoir effect for this location and period in time (Russell *et al.* 2010, 2015).

The dates from leather artefacts from two Phase 2 features, Layer C003 and Pit C032, provided dates of cal AD 990–1160 (SUERC-26673) and cal AD 1020–1210 (SUERC-26664) respectively, which were in reasonable accord with the 12th to mid 13th century date indicated for this phase by the artefactual and dendrochronological evidence. However, a sample of leather from the fill of Pit C048 (Phase 3 or 4) provided a date of cal AD 890–1150, somewhat earlier than the 13th or 14th century date indicated by artefacts and dendrochronological data from these phases.

Table A1.1: Radiocarbon dating

Lab code	Feature	Stratigraphic phase	Material	Radiocarbon age BP	Δ13C (‰)	Calibrated date 68.2% probability	Calibrated date 95.4% probability
SUERC-26671 (GU-20302)	Gully C001	Phase 1 and 2 (mid 12th to mid 13th century AD)	Carbon residue (external surface of pottery vessel below rim)	1100 ± 35	27.8‰	AD 895–925, AD 935–990	AD 880–1020
SUERC-26672 (GU-20303)	Layer C003	Phase 2 (late 12th to mid 13th century AD)	Carbon residue (internal surface of pottery vessel)	1220 ± 35	-28.1‰	AD 720–740, AD 770–880	AD 680–890
SUERC-26673 (GU-20304)	Layer C003	Phase 2 (late 12th to mid 13th century AD)	Leather (offcut)	975 ± 35	-27.5‰	AD 1010–1050, AD 1080–1150	AD 990–1160
SUERC-26674 (GU-20305)	Layer C003	Phase 2 (late 12th to mid 13th century AD)	Carbon residue (external surface of pottery vessel below rim)	1080 ± 35	-27.9‰	AD 890–920, AD 940–1020	AD 890–1020
SUERC-26955 (GU-20301)	Pit C027	Phase 2 (late 12th to mid 13th century AD)	Carbon residue (external surface of pottery vessel below rim)	1730 ± 30	-26.9‰	AD 250–350, AD 370–380	AD 240–400
SUERC-26663 (GU-20296)	Pit C032	Phase 2 (late 12th to mid 13th century AD)	Carbon residue (external surface of pottery vessel above base)	1160 ± 35	-26.7‰	AD 780–790, AD 800–900, AD 920–950	AD 770–980
SUERC-26664 (GU-20297)	Pit C032	Phase 2 (late 12th to mid 13th century AD)	Leather (sample from shoe)	915 ± 35	-27.1‰	AD 1040–1170	AD 1020–1210
SUERC-26665 (GU-20298)	Pit C048	Phase 3 or 4 (mid 13th to 14th century AD)	Carbon residue (surface of pottery vessel above base)	1140 ± 35	-25.8‰	AD 870–980	AD 780–990
SUERC-26669 (GU-20299)	Pit C048	Phase 3 or 4 (mid 13th to 14th century AD)	Leather (offcut)	1025 ± 35	-27.5‰	AD 980–1030	AD 890–920, AD 940–1050, AD 1080–1150
SUERC-26670 (GU-20300)	Pit C048	Phase 3 or 4 (mid 13th to 14th century AD)	Carbon residue (external surface of pottery vessel below rim)	1075 ± 35	-24.8‰	AD 890–920, AD 960–1020	AD 890–1020
SUERC-26675 (GU-20306)	Pit C069	Phase 3 or 4 (mid 13th to 14th century AD)	Carbon residue (internal surface of pottery vessel)	740 ± 35	-23.4‰	AD 1250–1290	AD 1215–1300

OxCal v4.2.4 Bronk Ramsey (2013); r:5 IntCal13 atmospheric curve (Reimer et al 2013)

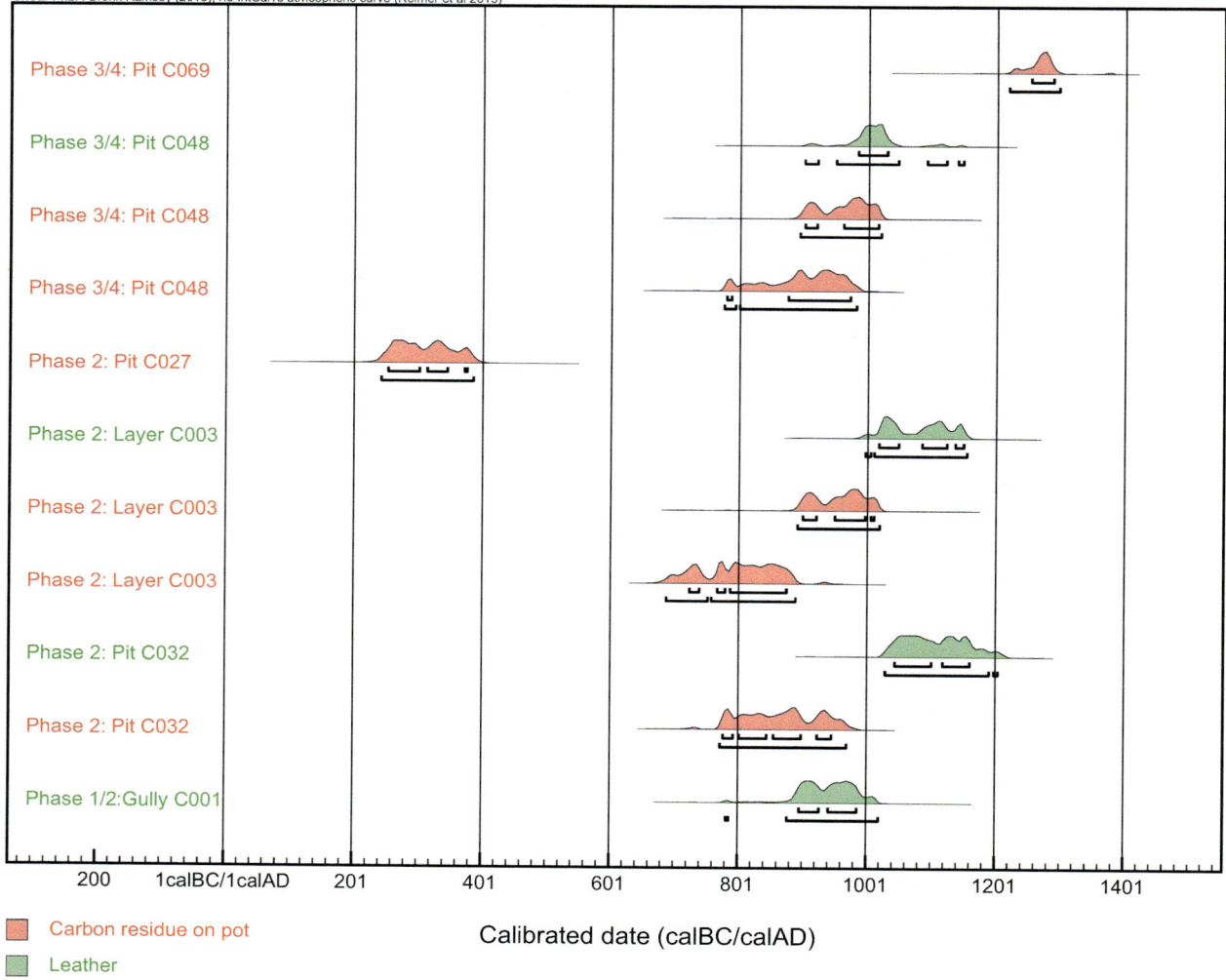

Phase 3/4: Pit C069

Phase 3/4: Pit C048

Phase 3/4: Pit C048

Phase 3/4: Pit C048

Phase 2: Pit C027

Phase 2: Layer C003

Phase 2: Layer C003

Phase 2: Layer C003

Phase 2: Pit C032

Phase 2: Pit C032

Phase 1/2:Gully C001

| 200 | 1calBC/1calAD | 201 | 401 | 601 | 801 | 1001 | 1201 | 1401 |

Calibrated date (calBC/calAD)

■ Carbon residue on pot

■ Leather

Figure A.1.1 Oxcal graph showing distribution of radiocarbon dates from Bon Accord

2 Ceramic building materials

Table A.2.1 Daub assemblage

Key: (I)= Infrequent, (O)=Occasional, (F)=Frequent, (A)=Abundant, RT=Retent

Feature	Fill of feature	Phase	Find No.	Surface description	Thickness (cm)	Inorganic	Organic	Wood (width mm)	Burnt	Total No.
Hearth C002	B	3	RT	Top/bottom/ edge curved	4	(O) small stone/ pebble/grit	(I) straw	No	Yes	1
Hearth C002	B	3	RT	Top/bottom surface flat	3	(O) small stone/ pebble/grit	(I) straw	Yes	Yes	1
Hearth C002	B	3	RT	Top/bottom surface flat	3	(O) small stone/ pebble/grit	(I) straw	Yes	No	1
Hearth C002	B	3	RT	Top/bottom/ edge curved	3	(O) small stone/ pebble/grit	(I) straw	Yes	No	1
Hearth C002	B	3	RT	Top/bottom surface flat	4	(O) small stone/ pebble/grit	(I) straw	Yes	Yes	1
Hearth C002	B	3	RT	Top/bottom surface flat	3	(O) small stone/ pebble/grit	(I) straw	No	No	6
Hearth C002	B	3	RT	One surface flat		(O) small stone/ pebble/grit	(O) straw	Yes	Yes	3
Hearth C002	B	3	RT	Irregular		(O) small stone/ pebble/grit	(I) straw	No	Yes	6
Hearth C002	B	3	RT	Irregular		(O) small stone/ pebble/grit	(I) straw	No	No	37
Pit C069	A	3 or 4	4448	Irregular		(I) grit	(I) straw	No	No	2
Pit C069	A	3 or 4	4448	One surface flat	>8	(O) small stone/ pebble/grit	(I) straw	No	Yes	1
Pit C069	A	3 or 4	4448	One surface flat		(I) medium/small stone grit	(I) charcoal	No	Yes	1
Pit C069	A	3 or 4	4448	One flat surface, straight edge, curved edge		(I) grit	No	No	No	1
Pit C069	A	3 or 4	4448	Irregular		(I) grit	No	No	Yes	19
Pit C069	A	3 or 4	4391	Irregular		(F) small stone/grit	(I) straw	Yes (20mm)	No	1
Pit C069	A	3 or 4	4391	One surface flat		(F) medium/small stone, grit	(F) straw/ charcoal	No	Yes	5
Pit C069	A	3 or 4	4391	Irregular		(O) small stones/grit	(O) straw	No	No	5
Pit C069	B	3 or 4	2363	Top/bottom surface flat	2.5	(F) small stone/grit	(F) straw and charcoal	No	Yes	1
Pit C069	B	3 or 4	2363	Top/bottom surface flat	2	(F)small stone/grit	(F) straw and charcoal	No	Yes	1
Pit C069	B	3 or 4	2363	Top/bottom flat	2.5	(A) medium-small stone/pebble/grit	(F) straw, (I) charcoal	No	No	1

Feature	Fill of feature	Phase	Find No.	Surface description	Thickness (cm)	Inorganic	Organic	Wood (width mm)	Burnt	Total No.
Pit C069	B	3 or 4	2363	Top/bottom surface flat	2	(A) small stone/ pebble/grit	(O) straw/ (I) charcoal	No	No	1
Pit C069	B	3 or 4	2363	One surface flat		(O) small stone/ pebble/grit	(O) straw/ (I) charcoal	Yes	Yes	1
Pit C069	B	3 or 4	2363	One surface flat		(O) small stone/ pebble/grit	(I) charcoal	No	No	1
Pit C069	B	3 or 4	2363	Irregular	2	(F) medium-small stone/grit	(O) straw/ (I) charcoal	No	No	5
Pit C069	F	3 or 4	2207	Top/bottom surface flat, one edge straight	4	(F) small stones/grit	(I) straw	No	Yes	1
Pit C069	F	3 or 4	2207	One surface flat		(A) small stone/ pebble/grit	(A) straw/ (F) charcoal	No	Yes	1
Pit C069	F	3 or 4	2207	One surface flat		(A) small stone/ pebble/grit	(F) straw and charcoal	Yes (1cm)	Yes	1
Pit C069	F	3 or 4	2207	Irregular		(F) small stones/grit	(F) straw	No	yes	4
Pit C069	F	3 or 4	2207	Irregular		(F) medium/small stones/grit	(F) straw/ (O) charcoal	No	Yes	17
Pit C069	F	3 or 4	2207	One surface flat		(F) small stones/grit	(F) straw	No	Yes	1
Layer A004		4	2214	One surface flat		(F) small stone/ grit		Yes	No	3
Layer A004		4	2214	Irregular		(F) small stone grit		No	No	20
Pit C064	D	4		Top flat, side curves towards base	13	(F) large stones, grit/ pebbles	(F) Straw/ (O)charcoal	Yes (40mm)	Yes	1
Pit C064	D	4		Top/bottom flat, edge curved, one edge straight with a wood impression	5.5	(F) inclusions of large stones, grit/pebbles	(F) Straw/ (O) charcoal	Yes (15mm)	Yes	1
Pit C064	D	4		Top/bottom flat	5	(O) small stone/ pebble/grit	(I) charcoal	No	No	1
Pit C064	D	4		One flat side	>7	(O) small stone/ pebble/grit	(I) charcoal	Yes	Yes	1
Pit C064	D	4		All sides are flat/ rounded as if it was used to cover wood	5.5	(I) small stone/ pebble/grit	(O) straw	Yes	No	1
Pit C064	D	4		One surface is flat, one curved	3	(O) small stone/ pebble/grit	(I) straw	Yes (30mm)	No	1
Pit C064	D	4		One surface is flat, one curved	4	(O) small stone/ pebble/grit	(I) straw	Yes (30mm)	No	1
Pit C064	D	4		Two flat surfaces with two straight edges	5.5	(O) small stone/ pebble/grit	(I) straw	No	No	1

Feature	Fill of feature	Phase	Find No.	Surface description	Thickness (cm)	Inorganic	Organic	Wood (width mm)	Burnt	Total No.
Pit C064	D	4		One side is flat and the edge is curving upwards	5.5	(O) small stone/pebble/grit	(I) charcoal	No	No	1
Pit C064	D	4		One surface is flat and the edge is straight	4.5	(O) small stone/pebble/grit	(I) charcoal	No	No	1
Pit C064	D	4		Irregular		(F) large stones, grit/pebbles	(F) straw	No	Yes	1
Pit C064	D	4		Top/bottom flat	2	(O) grit	No	No	No	1
Pit C064	D	4		One surface flat		(O) small stone/pebble/grit	(I) straw	No	Yes	1
Pit C064	D	4		One surface flat		(O) small stone/pebble/grit	No	No	No	1
Pit C064	D	4		Irregular		(O) small stone/pebble/grit	No	No	Yes	1
Pit C064	D	4		Irregular		(O) small stone/pebble/grit	No	No	No	27
Pit C064	D	4		One flat surface		(O) small stone/pebble/grit	No	No	No	4
Pit C064	D	4		Irregular		(O) small stone/pebble/grit	(O) straw	No	No	12
Pit C064	D	4	33	Top/bottom flat	10.5	(O) small stone/pebble/grit	(I) charcoal	Yes (45mm) oak	No	1
Pit C064	D	4	33	Bottom flat/one side curved upwards as part of the side	8	(O) small stone/pebble/grit	(I) charcoal	Yes	Yes	1
Pit C064	D	4	33	Top/bottom flat	11	(O) small stone/pebble/grit	(O) charcoal	No	Yes	1
Pit C064	D	4	33	One surface flat/ sides curve upwards	11	(O) small stone/pebble/grit	(I) charcoal	No	No	1
Pit C064	D	4	33	One side flat	8	(O) small stone/pebble/grit	(O) straw/(I) charcoal	Yes	No	1
Pit C064	D	4	33	One side flat	7	(O) small stone/pebble/grit	(O) straw/(I) charcoal	Yes	No	1
Pit C064	D	4	33	Top/bottom surface flat	7	(O) small stone/pebble/grit	(F) charcoal/straw	No	Yes	1
Pit C064	D	4	33	Top/bottom surface flat	6	(O) small stone/pebble/grit	(O) straw	No	Yes	1
Pit C064	D	4	33	Top/bottom surface flat	6	(O) small stone/pebble/grit	(I) straw/charcoal	No	No	1
Pit C064	D	4	33	Top/bottom surface flat, one side curving at angle	8	(O) small stone/pebble/grit	(I) charcoal	No	Yes	1

Feature	Fill of feature	Phase	Find No.	Surface description	Thickness (cm)	Inorganic	Organic	Wood (width mm)	Burnt	Total No.
Pit C064	D	4	33	One surface flat		(F) small grit/stone	(F) charcoal/straw	No	No	13
Pit C064	D	4	33	Flat on one surface and curving slightly upwards		(O) small stone/pebble/grit	(O) straw/(I) charcoal	No	Yes	1
Pit C064	D	4	33	Irregular		(O) small stone/pebble/grit	(O) straw/charcoal	No	Yes	5
Pit C064	D	4	33	Irregular		(O) small stone/pebble/grit	(I)charcoal	No	Yes	2
Pit C064	D	4	33	Irregular		(O) small stone/pebble/grit	(F) charcoal/straw	No	No	25
Pit C064	D	4	33	Irregular		(O) small stone/pebble/grit	(F) charcoal/straw	No	Yes	20
Pit C064	D	4	33	Top/bottom surface flat	2.5	(F) small grit/stone	(I) charcoal	No	No	1
Pit C064	D	4	33	One surface is flat, the other surface and one side curve	5	(O) small stone/pebble/grit	(O) straw	No	Yes	1
Pit C064	D	4	33	One surface is curved		(O) small stone/pebble/grit	(A) straw/(I) charcoal	No	No	1
Pit C064	D	4	33	One surface is flat the edge curves down towards the base	8	(O) small stone/pebble/grit	(I) charcoal/straw	No	Yes	1
Pit C064	E	4	RT	Irregular		(F) small stones/grit	(F) straw	Yes	Yes	1
Pit C064	E	4	RT	One flat surface		(O) small stone/pebble/grit	(F) straw	No	Yes	1
Pit C064	E	4	RT	One flat surface		(O) small stone/pebble/grit	(I) straw	No	Yes	1
Pit C064	E	4	RT	One flat surface		(O) small stone/pebble/grit	(O) straw	No	No	2
Pit C064	E	4	RT	Irregular		(F) small stones/grit	(O) straw/(I) charcoal	No	No	24
Pit C064	E	4	RT	Irregular		(F) small stones/grit	(O) straw	No	Yes	7
Pit C064	F	4		Irregular		(F) small stones/grit	(F) straw/(O) charcoal	No	No	26
Pit C064	F	4		Irregular		(F) small stones/grit	(F) straw	No	Yes	3
Pit C064	F	4		Top/bottom flat	5	(O) small stone/pebble/grit	(O) straw	No	No	1
Pit C064	F	4		One flat surface		(O) small stone/pebble/grit	(O) straw/charcoal	No	Yes	1

Feature	Fill of feature	Phase	Find No.	Surface description	Thickness (cm)	Inorganic	Organic	Wood (width mm)	Burnt	Total No.
Pit C064	F	4		Top/bottom flat, one side is smooth and angled at 90°	3.5	(O) small stone/ pebble/grit	No	No	yes	1
Pit C064	F	4		Top/bottom flat with slight depressions	2.5	(O) medium stone	No	No	yes	1
Pit C064	F	4		Top/bottom flat with slight depressions	2	(F) small stones/grit	(F) straw	No	No	1
Pit C064	F	4		One flat surface, one edge smoothed and flat		(F) small stones/grit	(F) straw	Yes	Yes	1
Pit C064	F	4		One flat surface		(F) small stones/grit	(F) straw	No	Yes	2
Pit C064	F	4		One flat surface		(A) small stone/grit	(F) straw	No	No	1
Pit C064	F	4		Curving on one side		(A) small stone/grit	(A) straw	Yes	No	1
Pit C064	F	4		One flat surface		(F) medium stones/ grit	(F) straw	No	Yes	1
Layer C009		5	3650	Irregular		(I) grit	(F) heather/ grass	No	No	1
Layer C010		5	1863	Top/bottom flat	4	(A) small stone/grit	(I) straw	No	Yes	1
Layer C010		5	1863	Irregular		(O) small stone/grit	(I) straw/(I) charcoal	No	No	4
Layer C010		5	1863	One flat surface		(F) small stones/grit	(F) straw	No	No	1
Layer C010		5	1863	One flat surface		(F) small stones/grit	(O) straw	No	Yes	1
Layer C010		5	1863	One flat surface		(F) medium small stones/grit	(O) straw	Yes (>25mm) oak	Yes	1
Layer C010		5	1863	One flat surface	8	(A) small/medium stones/pebble/grit	(O) straw	Yes (>25mm)	Yes	1
Structure C007		6	721	Top/bottom flat	1.5	(O) medium stone/ pebble/grit	(F) straw/ grass	No	No	1
Structure C007		6	721	Irregular		(I) grit	(A) straw/ grass	No	No	1
Structure C007		6	721	Irregular		(I) grit	(A) straw/ grass	No	No	3
Structure C007		6	721	Irregular		(I) grit	(F) straw	No	No	7
Structure C007		6	721	One surface flat		(O) small stone/grit	(F) straw	No	No	1

Feature	Fill of feature	Phase	Find No.	Surface description	Thickness (cm)	Inorganic	Organic	Wood (width mm)	Burnt	Total No.
Wall C009		5	421	Top/bottom surface flat, one edge is angled towards base	2	(O) small stone/grit	(I) charcoal	No	No	1
Wall C009		5	421	Top/bottom surface flat	2	(O) small stone/grit	(I) straw/ charcoal	No	No	1
Wall C009		5	421	One surface flat		(O) small stone/grit	(O) straw	No	No	1
Wall C009		5	421	One surface flat		(O) small stone/grit	(O) straw	No	Yes	1
Wall C009		5	421	Irregular		(O) small stone/grit	(A) straw/ (O) charcoal	No	No	23
Wall C009		5	421	One surface flat		(O) small stone/grit	(F) straw/ (O) charcoal	Yes	Yes	1
Wall C009		5	421	One surface flat		(O) small stone/grit	(F) straw/ (I) charcoal	No	No	2

3 Macroplant remains

Table A3.1 Phase 1 macroplant remains

Key: *=<10, **=10-29, ***=30-100, ****=>100. All plant remains preserved through waterlogging unless highlighted with a (C) which represents carbonised material

Feature	Common name	Plant part	Gully C001	Gully C002	Pit A019	Pit A026	Pit A027	Pit A030	Pit B002	Pit C001	Pit C002	Pit C003	Pit C004	Pit C005	Pit C007	Pit C008	Pit C012	Pit C015	Pit C017	Spread A003	Spread A048
Sample vol (kg)			2	1	1	3	1	3	1	2	3	3	2	3	12	1	3	50	2	1	1
% Analysed			100	100	100	100	100	100	100	100	100	100	100	100	100	100	100	100	100	100	100
Vernacular name																					
Crops and stable waste																					
Avena sativa L.	Cultivated oat	Spikelet(s)						**													
Avena sativa L.	Cultivated oat	Caryopsis/es											***	***		*			*		
Avena sativa L.	Cultivated oat	Floret bases											****	***		*			***		
Avena sp.	Oat	Spikelet(s)													*						
Avena sp.	Oat	Caryopsis/es											*		*						
Avena sp.	Oat	Caryopsis/es (C)		*	*			*			*	*	*		**					*	*
Avena sp.	Oat	Bran frag(s)						*	*			*									
Hordeum sp.	Barley	Caryopsis/es (C)																		*	
Triticum aestivum/compactum L.	Bread/club wheat	Caryopsis/es													**						
Triticum aestivum/compactum L.	Bread/club wheat	Caryopsis/es (C)		*	*						*				*	*					
Triticum/Secale sp.	Wheat/rye	Caryopsis/es (C)																		*	
Triticum/Secale sp.	Wheat/rye	Bran frag(s)	*					*		*				**	*			**			
Cerealia sp.	Cereal	Caryopsis/es								*	*		**	*					***		
Cerealia sp.	Cereal	Caryopsis/es (C)			*			**		*	*	*			*						

285

Feature			Gully C001	Gully C002	Pit A019	Pit A026	Pit A027	Pit A030	Pit B002	Pit C001	Pit C002	Pit C003	Pit C004	Pit C005	Pit C007	Pit C008	Pit C012	Pit C015	Pit C017	Spread A003	Spread A048
Cerealia sp.	Cereal	Chaff frag(s)											**	*		**					
Cerealia/Gramineae sp.	Cereals/grass	Chaff frag(s)								*			*	*							
Cerealia/Gramineae sp.	Cereals/grass	Culm node(s)	*							***			***	****	*	*					
Cerealia/Gramineae sp.	Cereals/grass	Stem frag(s)						*		***			***	***							
Vegetables, fruits & nuts																					
Allium sp.	Onions/leeks	Leaf epidermis frag(s)	*											*							
Brassica sp.	Cabbages	Seed(s)						***								*					
Brassica/Sinapis sp.	Cabbage/mustard	Seed(s)						*													
Corylus avellana L.	Hazel	Nut(s) and/or nutshell frag(s)	*					*		*		***		**	****	****		***	*		
Corylus avellana L.	Hazel	Nut(s) and/or nutshell frag(s) (C)										*			**	*					
Ficus carica L.	Fig	Seed(s)						**								***					
Fragaria ananassa L.	Strawberry	Seed(s)											*								
Malus sylvestris (L.) Mill	Crab apple	Seed(s)	*																		
Rubus idaeus L.	Raspberry	Seed(s)				*		*	*	*					*						
Sambucus nigra L...	Elderberry	Seed(s)																*			
Woodland																					
Bark	Indeterminate	Frag(s)	*	*		***	**	****		****	**	**	****	***	**			****	*		

Feature			Gully C001	Gully C002	Pit A019	Pit A026	Pit A027	Pit A030	Pit B002	Pit C001	Pit C002	Pit C003	Pit C004	Pit C005	Pit C007	Pit C008	Pit C012	Pit C015	Pit C017	Spread A003	Spread A048
Betula sp.	Birch	Fruit(s)	*								*		*	*		*		*			
Betula sp.	Birch	Bud(s) and/or bud-scale(s)					*			*			*		*						
Bud	Indeterminate	Bud(s) and/or bud-scale(s)	*							*				*	*						
Leaf	Indeterminate	Frag(s)	*							*			*	*					*		
Salix sp.	Willow	Leaf frag(s)													*						
Wood	Indeterminate	Frag(s)	***			****	***	****	**	****	***	***	****	****	****			****	****		
Economically useful taxa (mixed habitats)																					
Calluna vulgaris L.	Heather	Bud(s)												*							
Calluna vulgaris L.	Heather	Leaf/leaves											*	*	*	*					
Carex sp.	Sedges	Nutlet(s)							*		*		**	*	****	**	**		**		
Carex sp.	Sedges	Nutlet(s) (C)			*																
Erica cinerea L.	Bell heather	Seed(s)												*							
Erica cinerea L.	Bell heather	Leaf/leaves												*	*	*					
cf. Juncus articulatus L.	Jointed rush	Seed(s)	*									*			*						
Juncus bufonius L.	Toad rush	Seed(s)													*						
Juncus inflexus/effusus/conglomeratus sp.	Hard/soft/compact rush	Seed(s)	*											*	*						
Juncus sp.	Rush	Seed(s)	*												*						
Prunella vulgaris L.	Selfheal	Nutlet(s)						*													
Pteridium aquilinum L.	Bracken	Pinnule frag(s)	*					*		***			***	**	****	*					

287

Feature			Gully C001	Gully C002	Pit A019	Pit A026	Pit A027	Pit A030	Pit B002	Pit C001	Pit C002	Pit C003	Pit C004	Pit C005	Pit C007	Pit C008	Pit C012	Pit C015	Pit C017	Spread A003	Spread A048
Pteridium aquilinum L.	Bracken	Stalk frag(s)								**			*		*	*					
Weed taxa																					
Arable & wasteground habitat																					
Achillea sp.	Sneezewort/yarrow	Achene(s)									*										
Agrostemma githago L.	Corncockle	Seed frag(s)	*												*			**			
Atriplex sp.	Oraches	Seed(s)				*								**							
Bupleurum rotundifolium L.	Thorow-wax	Fruit(s)																*			
Cerastium sp.	Mouse-ear chickweeds	Seed(s)																***	*		
Chenopodium album L.	Fat hen	Seed(s)						****	***	**	*	**	**	*	**			**			
Chenopodiaceae sp.	Goosefoot	Seed(s)	*			*		*	*			*	*	*	*		*	***	*		
Chrysanthemum segetum L.	Corn marigold	Achene(s)							**												
Fallopia convolvulus L.	Black bindweed	Fruit(s)																*			
cf. *Festuca* sp.	Fescues	Caryopsis/es														*					
Galeopsis Subgenus Galeopsis	Hemp nettle	Nutlet(s)	*					*					*		**	*	*	***			
Lapsana communis L.	Nipplewort	Achene(s)				***						*			***			****	*		
Persicaria lapathifolium L.	Pale persicaria	Fruit(s)		*		***		****	*	*	*		**	*	*	*		*	*		

Feature			Gully C001	Gully C002	Pit A019	Pit A026	Pit A027	Pit A030	Pit B002	Pit C001	Pit C002	Pit C003	Pit C004	Pit C005	Pit C007	Pit C008	Pit C012	Pit C015	Pit C017	Spread A003	Spread A048
Persicaria maculosa L.	Redshank	Fruit(s)	*							*						*		**			
Polygonum aviculare L.	Knotgrass	Fruit(s)						***			*	*				*		****			
Raphanus raphanistrum L.	Wild radish	Seed(s)						****		**		*			**	**		*	*		
Raphanus raphanistrum L.	Wild radish	Pod frag(s)						**		*		*			*	*		*	*		
Rumex acetosella L.	Sheep's sorrel	Fruit(s)				*		*		***			*	**	**			**			
Rumex sp.	Docks	Fruit(s)												**				***	**		
Rumex sp.	Docks	Fruit(s) (C)													**						
Senecio sp.	Groundsels/ragworts	Achene(s)																*			
Sonchus. arvensis L.	Corn sow-thistle	Achene(s)						*		*					*						
Sonchus asper L.	Prickly sow-thistle	Achene(s)																			
Stellaria media L.	Common chickweed	Seed(s)	*					***					**					****	***		
Stellaria sp.	Chickweed	Seed(s)	*			*		*			*							**			
Urtica diocia L.	Stinging nettle	Achene(s)						**					*		**			*			
Urtica urens L.	Annual nettle	Achene(s)	*					****	*				*		*	*		****			
Heathland habitat																					
Potentilla erecta L.	Tormentil	Achene(s)						*													
Viola sp.	Violet	Seeds(s)							**										*		
Damp & wet habitat																					

289

Feature			Gully C001	Gully C002	Pit A019	Pit A026	Pit A027	Pit A030	Pit B002	Pit C001	Pit C002	Pit C003	Pit C004	Pit C005	Pit C007	Pit C008	Pit C012	Pit C015	Pit C017	Spread A003	Spread A048
Eriophorum vaginatum L.	Cotton-grass	Rhizome and/or stem frg(s)											*		*						
Hydrocotle vulgaris L.	Marsh pennywort	Fruit(s)																*			
Lychnis flos-cuculi L.	Ragged robin	Seed(s)						*							*				*		
Potentilla sp.	Cinquefoils	Achene(s)														*					
Ranunculus sp.	Meadow/ creeping/ bulbous buttercup	Achene(s)								*	*										

290

Table A3.2 Phase 2 macroplant remains

Key: * =<10, ** =10–29, *** =30–100, **** =>100. All plant remains preserved through waterlogging unless highlighted with a (C) which represents carbonised material

			Layer	Layer	Gully	Gully	Pit	Pit	Pit	Pit	Pit	Pit	Pit	Pit	Pit	Pit	Pit	Pit	Pit	Pit	Pit	Pit	Pit	Pit	Pit	Spread	Spread	Spread	Well
Feature			C003	C071	A003	C004	C018	C019	C020	C021	C022	C023	C024	C025	C026	C027	C029	C031	C032	C033	C034	C036	C037	C099	A019	A024	C010	C001
Sample vol (kg)			6	1	2	3	3	4	2	1	5	3	1	5	4	1	1	3	2	3	1	4	4	1	1	1	1	6
% Analysed			100	100	100	100	100	100	100	100	100	100	100	100	100	100	100	100	100	100	100	100	100	100	100	100	100	100
	Common name	Plant part																										
Crops and stable waste																												
Avena sativa L.	Cultivated oat	Spikelet(s)	*															*	*				*					
Avena sativa L.	Cultivated oat	Caryopsis/es																*	*		*							
Avena sativa L.	Cultivated oat	Floret bases	***													*	*	***	**	***			*	*				
Avena sativa L.	Cultivated oat	Floret bases (C)																	*					*				
Avena strigosa L.	Wild oat	Floret base													*													
Avena sp.	Oat	Spikelet(s)									*							*										
Avena sp.	Oat	Caryopsis/es									*								*									
Avena sp.	Oat	Caryopsis/es (C)	*																			*	*	*				
Avena sp.	Oat	Floret bases									*								**									
Avena sp.	Oat	Bran frag(s)	*				*	*			*		*					*										
Hordeum sp.	Barley	Caryopsis/es (C)	*			*	*				*				*													
Triticum aestivum/compactum L.	Bread/club wheat	Caryopsis/es (C)	**								*	**		**	*			**	*			*	*					
Triticum aestivum/compactum L.	Bread/club wheat	Glume(s)	*			*						*																
Triticum/Secale sp.	Wheat/rye	Bran frag(s)					*							**			*	**				**			*	*		*
Cerealia sp.	Cereals	Caryopsis/es	**				*	*			*	**		*	*			**	*			*	*		*	*		
Cerealia sp.	Cereals	Caryopsis/es (C)	*			*	*				*	**			*							*	*	*	*			
Cerealia sp.	Cereals	Chaff frag(s)		*							*		*	**	*													

291

Feature			Layer C003	Layer C071	Gully A003	Gully C004	Pit C018	Pit C019	Pit C020	Pit C021	Pit C022	Pit C023	Pit C024	Pit C025	Pit C026	Pit C027	Pit C029	Pit C031	Pit C032	Pit C033	Pit C034	Pit C036	Pit C037	Pit C099	Spread A019	Spread A024	Spread C010	Well C001
Cerealia sp.	Cereals	Chaff frag(s) (C)									**	**																
Cerealia/Gramineae sp.	Grasses/cereals	Chaff frag(s)		*							*							**							*			*
Cerealia/Gramineae sp.	Grasses/cereals	Culm node(s)	*	**	*	*				**	****			***					**			*					*	**
Cerealia/Gramineae sp.	Grasses/cereals	Stem frag(s)	***	***			***	**			****	****		***	*	*		***	****	***			**					***
Linum usitatissimum L.	Cultivated flax	Seed(s)	*										*				*	*				*						
	Vegetables, fruits & nuts																										
Allium sp.	Onions/leeks	Leaf epidermis frag(s)											*															
Brassica rapa L.	Turnip	Seed(s)						*				*	*									***						
Brassica sp.	Cabbages	Seed(s)	*					*				*	*			*					*	**	*					
Brassica/Sinapis sp.	Cabbage/mustard	Seed(s)										*										**	*					
Corylus avellana L.	Hazel	Nut(s) and/or nutshell frag(s)	**			*	**	**	*	*	***	**	*	****	*	*		**	**			***	*					**
Corylus avellana L.	Hazel	Nut(s) and/or nutshell frag(s) (C)															*											
Empetrum sp.	Crowberry	Seed(s)																										**
Ficus carica L.	Fig	Seed(s)															***											
Fragaria ananassa L.	Strawberry	Seed(s)												*														
Juglans regia sp.	Walnut	Shell frag(s)												*														
Malus sylvestris (L.) Mill	Crab apple	Seed(s)																				*						
Pastinaca sativa L.	Parsnip	Fruit(s)										*																
Prunus avium L.	Wild cherry	Fruitstone(s)									**			**				**				*						
Prunus spinosa L.	Blackthorn	Fruitstone(s)						*						***								*						

Feature			Layer C003	Layer C071	Gully A003	Gully C004	Pit C018	Pit C019	Pit C020	Pit C021	Pit C022	Pit C023	Pit C024	Pit C025	Pit C026	Pit C027	Pit C029	Pit C031	Pit C032	Pit C033	Pit C034	Pit C036	Pit C037	Pit C099	Spread A019	Spread A024	Spread C010	Well C001
Rubus fruticosus L. agg	Blackberry/bramble	Seed(s)					*	*																				
Rubus idaeus L.	Raspberry	Seed(s)	*			**		*	*								*						*					*
Woodland																												
Bark	Indeterminate	Frag(s)	***			*	****	*	*	*	****	**	**	*****	*****	*	*	*	**	**	*	**	**				*	***
Betula sp.	Birch	Fruit(s)													*			*		*			*					
Betula sp.	Birch	Bud(s) and/or bud-scale(s)	*																									*
Buds	Indeterminate	Bud(s) and/or bud-scale(s)	*											**	*			*		*			**				*	*
Leaf	Indeterminate	Frag(s)	*								*			*									*				*	*
Quercus sp.	Oak	Bud(s) and/or bud-scale(s)																	*						*			
Salix sp.	Willow	Leaf frag(s)									*																	
Wood	Indeterminate	Frag(s)	*****			**	*****	**	**	*	*****	***	***	*****	*****	****	**	**	**	***	**	*****	*****	*				****
Economically useful taxa (mixed habitats)																												
Calluna vulgaris L.	Heather	Bud(s)	**								*				*			**	**				***			*		
Calluna vulgaris L.	Heather	Flower(s)																**	**				**					
Calluna vulgaris L.	Heather	Seed(s)																										
Calluna vulgaris L.	Heather	Leaf/leaves	***															**	**				*****				**	
Calluna vulgaris L.	Heather	Leaf/leaves (C)	***								*				**													
Carex sp.	Sedges	Nutlet(s)	*			*	**	**						**			*	*	**	*		**	*	*				*
Filipendula ulmaria L.	Meadowsweet	Achene(s)					*																					
Isatis tinctoria L.	Woad	Silicula fruit					*															*						
cf. *Juncus articulatus* L.	Jointed rush	Seed(s)																										

293

Taxon	Common name	Part	Layer C003	Layer C071	Gully A003	Gully C004	Pit C018	Pit C019	Pit C020	Pit C021	Pit C022	Pit C023	Pit C024	Pit C025	Pit C026	Pit C027	Pit C029	Pit C031	Pit C032	Pit C033	Pit C034	Pit C036	Pit C037	Pit C099	Spread A019	Spread A024	Spread C010	Well C001
Juncus inflexus/effusus/ conglomeratus sp.	Hard/soft/compact rush	Seed(s)	*																									
Juncus sp.	Rush	Seed(s)	*				*				*							*		*		*	**					
Prunella vulgaris L.	Selfheal	Nutlet(s)																**					**					
Pteridium aquilinum L.	Bracken	Pinnule frag(s)	*								****	**	*	*			*	*	***	*			*	*			**	**
Pteridium aquilinum L.	Bracken	Stalk frag(s)									***	*							**	*			*				*	
Reseda luteola L.	Weld/dyers rocket	Seed(s)					**	*												*		**						
Weed taxa																												
Arable & wasteground habitat																												
Agrostemma githago L.	Corncockle	Seed frag(s)					***	*									**	*				*						
Aphanes sp.	Parsley-pierts	Achene(s)																										
Atriplex sp.	Oraches	Seed(s)																					*					*
Cerastium sp.	Mouse-ear chickweeds	Seed(s)					*	*	*						*							**						
Chenopodium album L.	Fat hen	Seed(s)	**				***	**		*	*	**	*	**	****		*	*		*	**	***	***	*				*
Chenopodiaceae sp.	Goosefoot	Seed(s)	**				*				*	*	*	*	**	**	*	**		**	*	**	**					**
Chrysanthemum segetum L.	Corn marigold	Achene(s)																										
cf. *Festuca* sp.	Fescues	Caryopsis/es									*								*									
Galeopsis Subgenus *Galeopsis*	Hemp nettle	Nutlet(s)									*						*					**	*					***
Lapsana communis L.	Nipplewort	Achene(s)						**									**		*		****	****	**				*	**

294

Feature			Layer C003	Layer C071	Gully A003	Gully C004	Pit C018	Pit C019	Pit C020	Pit C021	Pit C022	Pit C023	Pit C024	Pit C025	Pit C026	Pit C027	Pit C029	Pit C031	Pit C032	Pit C033	Pit C034	Pit C036	Pit C037	Pit C099	Spread A019	Spread A024	Spread C010	Well C001
Myosotis sp.	Forget me nots	Nutlet(s)																				*						
Persicaria lapathifolium L.	Pale persicaria	Fruit(s)	***			*	****	*	*	*	**		*	****	*****	**	**	*	*	*	*	***	***				*	***
Persicaria maculosa L.	Redshank	Fruit(s)	*					*							**							*						
cf Poa annua L.	Annual meadow-grass	Caryopsis/es									*	*																
Polygonum aviculare L.	Knotgrass	Fruit(s)	**				*	*	*		*			*			**			**		*	**					*
Raphanus raphanistrum L	Wild radish	Seed(s)						*				*		**	**				**			**						
Raphanus raphanistrum L	Wild radish	Pod frag(s)						*				*		**	**				*			*						**
Raphanus raphanistrum L	Wild radish	Pod frag(s) (C)															*											
Rhinanthus sp.	Yellow rattles	Seed(s)									*																	
Rumex acetosella L	Sheep's sorrel	Fruit(s)	*	*			*					*	*	*			**		***				**					**
Rumex sp.	Docks	Fruit(s)					*	*														*						
Rumex sp.	Docks	Fruit(s) (C)														*												
Senecio sp.	Groundsels/ragworts	Achene(s)		**																			*					
Silene vulgaris L.	Bladder campion	Seed(s)																			*		*					
Sonchus asper L.	Prickly sow-thistle	Achene(s)								*										*	*							
Spergula arvensis L.	Corn spurrey	Seed(s)													*				*									
Stellaria media L.	Common chickweed	Seed(s)	*			*	**				*			***	*		**	*	*	***		***	**				*	***
Stellaria sp.	Chickweed	Seed(s)	*			*	*							*		*				*	*	*						
Urtica diocia L.	Stinging nettle	Achene(s)	*				*												*									
Urtica urens L.	Annual nettle	Achene(s)	*			*	***	**			*	*		**	**	**	***		*	****		***	****					****

Feature			Layer C003	Layer C071	Gully A003	Gully C004	Pit C018	Pit C019	Pit C020	Pit C021	Pit C022	Pit C023	Pit C024	Pit C025	Pit C026	Pit C027	Pit C029	Pit C031	Pit C032	Pit C033	Pit C034	Pit C036	Pit C037	Pit C099	Spread A019	Spread A024	Spread C010	Well C001
Heathland habitat																												
Potentilla erecta L.	Tormentil	Achene(s)							*			*			*													
Viola sp.	Violet/pansies	Seed(s)				**				*					*		*	*	*				**				*	*
Damp & wet habitat																												
Eriophorum vaginatum L.	Cotton-grass	Rhizome and/or stem frag(s)										*										*						
Lychnis flos-cuculi L.	Ragged robin	Seed(s)					*							*								***	*					
Potamogeton sp.	Pondweeds	Fruit(s)					*				*																	
Potentilla reptans L.	Creeping cinquefoil	Achene(s)																*				*						
Potentilla sp.	Cinquefoils	Achene(s)						*			*	*		*			*					*	**					*
Ranunculus acris L.	Meadow buttercup	Achene(s)																*										
Ranunculus sp.	Meadow/creeping/bulbous buttercup	Achene(s)												*	**			*					*					*

Table A3.3 Phase 3 macroplant remains

Key: *=<10, **=10-29, ***=30-100, ****=>100. All plant remains preserved through waterlogging unless highlighted with a (C) which represents carbonised material

Feature	Common name	Plant part	Layer C005	Layer C073	Hearth C001	Hearth C002	Pit A002	Pit C016	Pit C035	Pit C042	Pit C044	Pit C047	Pit C048	Pit C051	Pit C069	PhC 011	Spread C110
Sample vol (kg)			1	1	4	4	1	1	1	1	1	3.5	2	1	5	1	1
% Analysed			100	100	100	100	100	100	100	100	100	100	100	100	100	100	100
Vernacular name	Common name	Plant part															
Crops and stable waste																	
Avena sativa L.	Cultivated oat	Spikelet(s)			*					*							
Avena sativa L.	Cultivated oat	Floret bases			****								*				
Avena sp.	Oat	Caryopsis/es (C)	*			*		*						*	**		
Avena sp.	Oat	Floret bases			***												
Avena sp.	Oat	Bran frag(s)												*			
Hordeum sp.	Barley	Caryopsis/es (C)				*									*		
Triticum aestivum/compactum L.	Bread/club wheat	Caryopsis/es (C)															*
Triticum aestivum/compactum L.	Bread/club wheat	Glume(s) (C)													*		
Triticum/Secale sp.	Wheat/rye	Bran frag(s)					*					*		*			
Cerealia sp.	Cereals	Caryopsis/es			**							**	*		**		
Cerealia sp.	Cereals	Caryopsis/es (C)		*	*	**						*			*		
Cerealia sp.	Cereals	Chaff frag(s)											*		**		
Cerealia sp.	Cereals	Chaff frag(s) (C)													*		

Feature			Layer C005	Layer C073	Hearth C001	Hearth C002	Pit A002	Pit C016	Pit C035	Pit C042	Pit C044	Pit C047	Pit C048	Pit C051	Pit C069	PhC 011	Spread C110
Cerealia/Gramineae sp.	Cereals/grass	Culm node(s)	*		***							*	**				
Cerealia/Gramineae sp.	Cereals/grass	Stem frag(s)	*		**								**		**		
Linum usitatissimum L.	Cultivated flax	Seed(s)			*				*								
Vegetables, fruits & nuts																	
Allium sp.	Onions/leeks	Leaf epidermis frag(s)					*					*		*	*		
Brassica rapa L.	Turnip	Seed(s)					*					*					
Brassica sp.	Cabbage	Seed(s)										*		*	*		
Corylus avellana L.	Hazel	Nut(s) and/or nutshell frag(s)	*		*								***		**		
Corylus avellana L.	Hazel	Nut(s) and/or nutshell frag(s) (C)											*				
Ficus carica L.	Fig	Seed(s)					**								****		
Pastinaca sativa L	Parsnip	Fruit(s)					*										
Rubus idaeus L.	Raspberry	Seed(s)				*		*						*			
Woodland																	
Bark	Indeterminate	Frag(s)	*		***					**		*	**				
Betula sp.	Birch	Fruit(s)	*			*	*					*			*		
Betula sp.	Birch	Bud(s) and/or bud-scale(s)										*			*		

Feature			Layer C005	Layer C073	Hearth C001	Hearth C002	Pit A002	Pit C016	Pit C035	Pit C042	Pit C044	Pit C047	Pit C048	Pit C051	Pit C069	PhC 011	Spread C110
Bud	Indeterminate	Bud(s) and/or bud-scale(s)			*								*			*	
Leaf	Indeterminate	Frag(s)			*											*	
Wood	Indeterminate	Frag(s)	**		****					***	**	**	****				
Economically useful taxa (mixed habitats)																	
Calluna vulgaris L.	Heather	Bud(s)	*									*	*	*	*		
Calluna vulgaris L.	Heather	Leaf/leaves											**	*			
Carex sp.	Sedges	Nutlet(s)			****		**		*	*		***	*		*		
Carex sp.	Sedges	Nutlet(s) (C)			*												
cf. Juncus articulatus L.	Jointed rush	Seed(s)			**		*										
Juncus sp.	Rush	Seed(s)			**			*					*				
Prunella vulgaris L.	Selfheal	Nutlet(s)					**										
Pteridium aquilinum L.	Bracken	Pinnule frag(s)			**					**		**	*		*		
Pteridium aquilinum L.	Bracken	Stalk frag(s)										*			*		
Weed taxa																	
Arable & wasteground habitat																	
Agrostemma githago L.	Corncockle	Seed frag(s)										**			***		
Anthriscus caucils L.	Bur chervil	Fruit(s)					*										
Atriplex sp.	Oraches	Seed(s)			**		**			**			*				
Carduus/Cirsium sp.	Thistles	Achene(s)															

299

Feature			Layer C005	Layer C073	Hearth C001	Hearth C002	Pit A002	Pit C016	Pit C035	Pit C042	Pit C044	Pit C047	Pit C048	Pit C051	Pit C069	PhC 011	Spread C110
Chenopodium album L.	Fat hen	Seed(s)	*		*	*	****	**	**			**	**		*		
Chenopodiaceae sp.	Goosefoot	Seed(s)	*		****	*	**	***	*	*		*	***	*	**	*	
Chrysanthemum segetum L.	Corn marigold	Achene(s)						*									
Fallopia convolvulus L.	Black bindweed	Fruit(s)										*					
cf. Festuca sp.	Fescues	Caryopsis/es								*							
Galeopsis Subgenus Galeopsis	Hemp nettle	Nutlet(s)			**		*			*			*		*		
Lapsana communis L.	Nipplewort	Achene(s)			****				*			*	*		****		
Leontodon sp.	Hawkbits	Achene(s)			*					***			*				
Persicaria lapathifolium L.	Pale persicaria	Fruit(s)	*		****		**	*		*	*	*	*		***	*	
Persicaria maculosa L.	Redshank	Fruit(s)					*		*								
Polygonum aviculare L.	Knotgrass	Fruit(s)	*		*	*	***	*			*						
Raphanus raphanistrum L.	Wild radish	Seed(s)			*					*							
Raphanus raphanistrum L.	Wild radish	Pod frag(s)			*					*							
Rumex acetosella L	Sheep's sorrel	Fruit(s)			**	*	*					**	*		**		
Rumex sp.	Docks	Fruit(s)	*		*								*	*	*		
cf. Sinapis arvensis L.	Charlock	Seed(s)										*					
Sonchus asper L.	Prickly sow-thistle	Achene(s)				*	*						*		**		
Spergula arvensis L.	Corn spurrey	Seed(s)			**												

Feature			Layer C005	Layer C073	Hearth C001	Hearth C002	Pit A002	Pit C016	Pit C035	Pit C042	Pit C044	Pit C047	Pit C048	Pit C051	Pit C069	PhC 011	Spread C110
Stellaria media L.	Common chickweed	Seed(s)			***		****	**		*	**	*			***	*	
Stellaria sp.	Chickweed	Seed(s)	*		*		**	*		*				*	***	*	
Urtica diocia L.	Stinging nettle	Achene(s)	*					*									
Urtica urens L.	Annual nettle	Achene(s)			**		****	***		****	****	*	*	*	**		
Heathland habitat																	
Potentilla erecta L.	Tormentil	Achene(s)	*						*					*			
Viola sp.	Violet	Seed(s)					*					**	**	*	*		
Damp & wet habitat																	
Eriophorum vaginatum L.	Cotton-grass	Rhizome and/or stem frag(s)													*		
Lychnis flos-cuculi L.	Ragged robin	Seed(s)			*												
Montia fontana sp.	Blinks	Seed(s)					*										
Potentilla sp.	Cinquefoils	Achene(s)			*			*		*				*			
Ranunculus acris L.	Meadow buttercup	Achene(s)													*		
Ranunculus flammula L.	Lesser spearwort	Achene(s)											**		*		
Ranunculus sp.	Meadow/creeping/bulbous buttercup	Achene(s)			**		*								*		

301

Table A3.4 Phase 4 macroplant remains

Key: *=<10, **=10-29, ***=30-100, ****=>100, All plant remains preserved through waterlogging unless highlighted with a (C) which represents carbonised material

Feature	Common name	Plant part	Layer A003	Layer A004	Layer C008	Layer C067	GullyA 008	Gully C006	Hollow A002	Hollow C007	Pit A011	Pit C053	Pit C054	Pit C056	Pit C064	PH C003	Spread A009	Spread A031	Spread A041	Spread C123	Spread C153	Surface C005	Surface C008
Sample vol (kg)			2	1	1	1	2	1	1	1	1	1	1	1	3	1	1	1	1	1	1	1	1
% Analysed			100	100	100	100	100	100	100	100	100	100	100	100	100	100	100	100	100	100	100	100	100
Crops and stable waste																							
Avena sativa L.	Cultivated oat	Floret bases (C)					*																
Avena sp.	Oat	Caryopsis/es (C)	*	*	**	*	**	*	*		*		*	*	*	*	*	*		*	*		
Hordeum sp.	Barley	Caryopsis/es (C)	*	*	*	*	**	*		*	*				*			*	*			*	*
Secale cereale L.	Rye	Charred caryopsis/es						*							*								
Triticum aestivum/compactum L.	Bread/club wheat	Caryopsis/es (C)					*						*										
Triticum/Secale sp.	Wheat/rye	Caryopsis/es (C)																	*				
Cerealia sp.	Cereal	Caryopsis/es (C)	*		*	*	**	*	*		*		*	*	*	*	*	*	*	*	*		
Cerealia/Gramineae sp.	Cereals/grass	Stem frag(s)														*							
Vegetables, Fruits & Nuts																							
Brassica sp.	Cabbages	Seed(s)													*								
Brassica/Sinapis sp.	Cabbage/mustard	Seed(s)													*								

Feature			Layer A003	Layer A004	Layer C008	Layer C067	GullyA 008	Gully C006	Hollow A002	Hollow C007	Pit A011	Pit C053	Pit C054	Pit C056	Pit C064	PH C003	Spread A009	Spread A031	Spread A041	Spread C123	Spread C153	Surface C005	Surface C008
Corylus avellana L.	Hazel	Nut(s) and/or nutshell frag(s)										*			**	**							
Ficus carica L.	Fig	Seed(s)			**										**								
Fragaria ananassa L.	Strawberry	Seed(s)													*								
Rubus idaeus L.	Raspberry	Seed(s)			*						*	**						*			*		
Woodland																							
Bark	Indeterminate	Frag(s)										*			*	**							
Betula sp.	Birch	Fruit(s)															*						
Betula sp.	Birch	Bud(s) and/or bud-scale(s)										*											
Bud	Indeterminate	Bud(s) and/or bud-scale(s)										*			*								
Leaf	Indeterminate	Frag(s)										*											
Salix sp.	Willow	Bud(s)										*											
Wood	Indeterminate	Frag(s)				*						*			**	***							
Economically useful taxa (mixed habitats)																							
Calluna vulgaris L.	Heather	Bud(s)										*											
Calluna vulgaris L.	Heather	Leaf/leaves										**											
Calluna vulgaris L.	Heather	Leaf/leaves (C)																				*	
Carex sp.	Sedges	Nutlet(s)																*					
Carex sp.	Sedges	Nutlet(s) (C)															*						*

303

Feature			Layer A003	Layer A004	Layer C008	Layer C067	GullyA 008	Gully C006	Hollow A002	Hollow C007	Pit A011	Pit C053	Pit C054	Pit C056	Pit C064	PH C003	Spread A009	Spread A031	Spread A041	Spread C123	Spread C153	Surface C005	Surface C008
Juncus sp.	Rush	Seed(s)																					
Prunella vulgaris L.	Selfheal	Nutlet(s)			**						*				*			*					
Pteridium aquilinum (L.)	Bracken	Pinnule frag(s)													**								
Reseda luteola L.	Weld/dyers rocket	Seed(s)													*								
Weed taxa																							
Arable & wasteground Habitat																							
Achillea sp(p).	Sneezewort/yarrow	Achene(s)										*											
Cerastium sp.	Mouse-ear chickweeds	Seed(s)													*								
Chenopodium album L.	Fat hen	Seed(s)			*							**			*								*
Chenopodiaceae sp.	Goosefoot	Seed(s)										**				*							
cf. Festuca sp.	Fescues	Caryopsis/es										*											
Persicaria lapathifolium L.	Pale persicaria	Fruit(s)										*			*								
Polygonum aviculare L.	Knotgrass	Fruit(s)			*										*								
Raphanus raphanistrum L.	Wild radish	Pod frag(s) (C)										*											
Rumex sp.	Docks	Fruit(s)										*			*								
Rumex acetosella L.	Sheep's sorrel	Fruit(s)										*			*								
Stellaria sp.	Chickweed	Seed(s)										*				*							
Stellaria media L.	Common chickweed	Seed(s)										*			*	*							
Urtica urens L.	Annual nettle	Achene(s)										***			***								

304

Feature			Layer A003	Layer A004	Layer C008	Layer C067	GullyA 008	Gully C006	Hollow A002	Hollow C007	Pit A011	Pit C053	Pit C054	Pit C056	Pit C064	PH C003	Spread A009	Spread A031	Spread A041	Spread C123	Spread C153	Surface C005	Surface C008
Heathland habitat																							
Viola sp.	Violet/pansies	Seeds(s)										**			*								
Damp & wet habitat																							
Lychnis flos-cuculi L.	Ragged robin	Seed(s)													*								
Potentilla sp.	Cinquefoils	Achene(s)										*											
Ranunculus sp.	Meadow/ creeping/ bulbous buttercup	Achene(s)										*											

Table A3.5 Phase 5 macroplant remains

Key: *=<10, **=10-29, ***=30-100, ****=>100, All plant remains preserved through waterlogging unless highlighted with a (C) which represents carbonised material

Feature	Common name	Plant part	Layer A005	Layer A006	Layer A007	Layer A025	Layer A033	Layer A034	Layer C010	Layer C015	Layer C017	Gully A001	Pit AC001	Pit C071	Pit C101	Ph A001	Spread A020	Spread C017	Spread C059	Spread C084	Well A001
Sample vol (kg)			1	1	2	1	1	1	2	1	1	1	1	1	1	2	1	1	1	1	25
% Analysed			100	100	100	100	100	100	100	100	100	100	100	100	100	100	100	100	100	100	100
Crops and stable waste																					
Avena sp.	Oat	Caryopsis/es (C)	*	*	*			*	*		*	*	*			*		**	*	*	*
Hordeum sp.	Barley	Caryopsis/es (C)	*	*	*			*		*		*	*				*	**	*		**
Secale cereale L.	Rye	Caryopsis/es (C)																*			
Triticum aestivum/ compactum L.	Bread/club wheat	Caryopsis/es (C)																			
Triticum/Secale sp.	Wheat/rye	Caryopsis/es (C)		*				*										*	*	*	*
Triticum/Secale sp.	Wheat/rye	Bran frag(s)																			**
Cerealia sp.	Cereal	Caryopsis/es																			*
Cerealia sp.	Cereal	Caryopsis/es (C)	*	*	**	*	*		*	*		*	*	*	*	*	*	***	*	*	**
Cerealia sp.	Cereal	Chaff frag(s) (C)						*										*			
Cerealia/Gramineae sp.	Grasses/ cereals	Culm node(s)																			**
Cerealia/Gramineae sp.	Cereals/grass	Stem frag(s)																			**
Vegetables, fruits & nuts																					
Allium sp.	Onions/leeks	Leaf epidermis frag(s)																			**
Brassica rapa L.	Turnip	Seed(s)																			*

Feature			Layer A005	Layer A006	Layer A007	Layer A025	Layer A033	Layer A034	Layer C010	Layer C015	Layer C017	Gully A001	Pit AC001	Pit C071	Pit C101	Ph A001	Spread A020	Spread C017	Spread C059	Spread C084	Well A001
Brassica sp.	Cabbages	Seed(s)																			*
Brassica/Sinapis sp.	Cabbage/mustard	Seed(s)																			**
Corylus avellana L.	Hazel	Nut(s) and/or nutshell frag(s)																			***
Corylus avellana L.	Hazel	Nut(s) and/or nutshell frag(s) (C)																			*
Ficus carica L.	Fig	Seed(s)												***					**		**
Fragaria ananassa L.	Strawberry	Seed(s)																	*		
Rubus fruticosus L. agg	Blackberry/bramble	Seed(s)																			*
Rubus idaeus L.	Raspberry	Seed(s)						*	*					*				*	**		**
Woodland																					
Bark	Indeterminate	Frag(s)																			****
Betula sp.	Birch	Bud(s) and/or bud-scale(s)																			*
Wood	Indeterminate	Frag(s)																			****
Economically useful taxa (mixed habitats)																					
Calluna vulgaris L.	Heather	Bud(s)																			***
Calluna vulgaris L.	Heather	Seed(s)																			*
Calluna vulgaris L.	Heather	Leaf/leaves																			***
Carex sp.	Sedges	Nutlet(s)									*										*
Carex sp.	Sedges	Nutlet(s) (C)																	*		
cf. Juncus articulatus L.	Jointed rush	Seed(s)																			*
Juncus bufonius L.	Toad rush	Seed(s)																			*

Feature			Layer A005	Layer A006	Layer A007	Layer A025	Layer A033	Layer A034	Layer C010	Layer C015	Layer C017	Gully A001	Pit AC001	Pit C071	Pit C101	Ph A001	Spread A020	Spread C017	Spread C059	Spread C084	Well A001
Juncus sp.	Rush	Seed(s)																			**
Prunella vulgaris L.	Selfheal	Nutlet(s)																	***		**
Pteridium aquilinum L.	Bracken	Pinnule frag(s)																			**
Pteridium aquilinum L.	Bracken	Stalk frag(s)																			*
Reseda luteola L.	Weld/dyers rocket	Seed(s)																*			*
Weed Taxa																					
Arable & wasteground Habitat																					
Agrostemma githago L.	Corncockle	Seed frag(s)																			***
Aphanes sp.	Parsley-pierts	Achene(s)			*													*			
Atriplex sp.	Oraches	Seed(s)												*							****
Cerastium sp.	Mouse-ear chickweeds	Seed(s)																			*
Chenopodium album L.	Fat hen	Seed(s)						*	*					*					**		***
Chenopodiaceae sp.	Goosefoot	Seed(s)							**					*	*			*	**		***
Chrysanthemum segetum L.	Corn marigold	Achene(s)										*									*
Fallopia convolvulus L.	Black bindweed	Fruit(s)	*																		*
Galeopsis Subgenus Galeopsis	Hemp nettle	Nutlet(s)												*							**
Lapsana communis L.	Nipplewort	Achene(s)																			*
Persicaria lapathifolium L.	Pale persicaria	Fruit(s)												**							***
Polygonum aviculare L.	Knotgrass	Fruit(s)																*			**

308

Feature			Layer A005	Layer A006	Layer A007	Layer A025	Layer A033	Layer A034	Layer C010	Layer C015	Layer C017	Gully A001	Pit AC001	Pit C071	Pit C101	Ph A001	Spread A020	Spread C017	Spread C059	Spread C084	Well A001
Raphanus raphanistrum L.	Wild radish	Pod frag(s)											*								
Raphanus raphanistrum L.	Wild radish	Pod frag(s) (C)																			*
Rumex acetosella L.	Sheep's sorrel	Fruit(s)																*			
Rumex sp.	Docks	Fruit(s)																*			
Senecio sp.	Groundsels/ragworts	Achene(s)																			*
Sonchus arvensis L.	Corn sow-thistle	Achene(s)																			*
Sonchus asper L.	Prickly sow-thistle	Achene(s)																			*
Stellaria media L.	Common chickweed	Seed(s)																			****
Stellaria sp.	Chickweed	Seed(s)																*			***
Urtica diocia L.	Stinging nettle	Achene(s)																			**
Urtica urens L.	Annual nettle	Achene(s)							*					*							****
Heathland habitat																					
Potentilla erecta L.	Tormentil	Achene(s)							*												
Viola sp.	Violet/pansies	Seed(s)												*							**
Damp & wet habitat																					
Potentilla sp.	Cinquefoils	Achene(s)																			*
Ranunculus sp.	Meadow/creeping/bulbous buttercup	Achene(s)																			*

Table A3.6: Moss species.

Context		Pit C008	Pit C018	Pit C033	Pit C047
Phase		1	2	2	3
Sphagnum imbrication s.l.	Leaf/leaves and/or stem frag(s)	P			
Sphagnum sp.	Leaf/leaves and/or stem frag(s)		P	P	
Dicranum scoparium	Leaf/leaves and/or stem frag(s)	P	P	P	
Campylopus sp.	Leaf/leaves and/or stem frag(s)		P	P	
Aulacomnium palustre (Hedw.) Schwaegr	Leaf/leaves and/or stem frag(s)	P	P	P	
Antitrichia curtipendula (Hedw.) Brid.	Leaf/leaves and/or stem frag(s)	P			
Thuidium tamariscinum (Hedw.) Brid.	Leaf/leaves and/or stem frag(s)				P
Hypnum. Cupressiforme Hedw.	Leaf/leaves and/or stem frag(s)		P		
Hypnum. cf. Cupressiforme Hedw.	Leaf/leaves and/or stem frag(s)	P	P		
Rhytidiadelphus triquetrus (Hedw.) Warnst.	Leaf/leaves and/or stem frag(s)	P	P		P
Rhytidiadelphus squarrosus (Hedw.) Warnst.	Leaf/leaves and/or stem frag(s)		P		
R. cf. squarrosus (Hedw.) Warnst.	Leaf/leaves and/or stem frag(s)	P		P	
Rhytidiadelphus loreus (Hedw.) Warnst	Leaf/leaves and/or stem frag(s)		P		
Pleurozium schreberi (Brid.) Mitt	Leaf/leaves and/or stem frag(s)		P	P	P
Hylocomium splendens (Hedw.) Br. Eur	Leaf/leaves and/or stem frag(s)	P	P	P	P

4 Fish bone

DENTARY FIRST MEASUREMENT

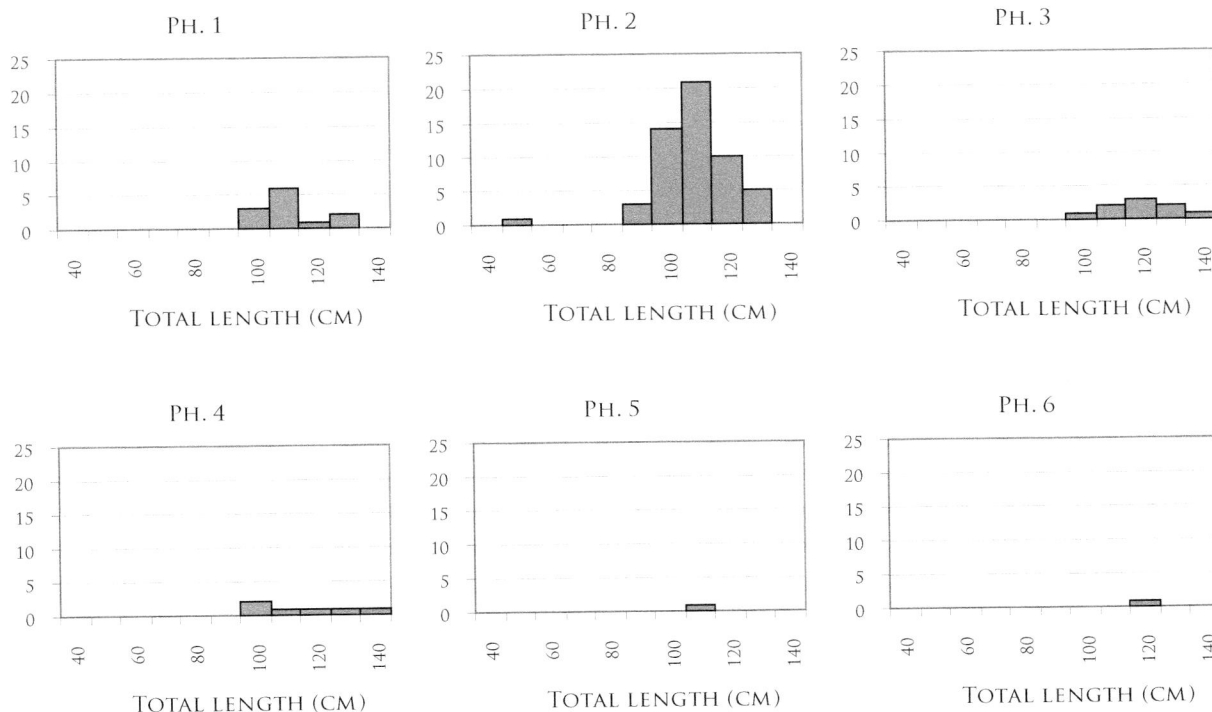

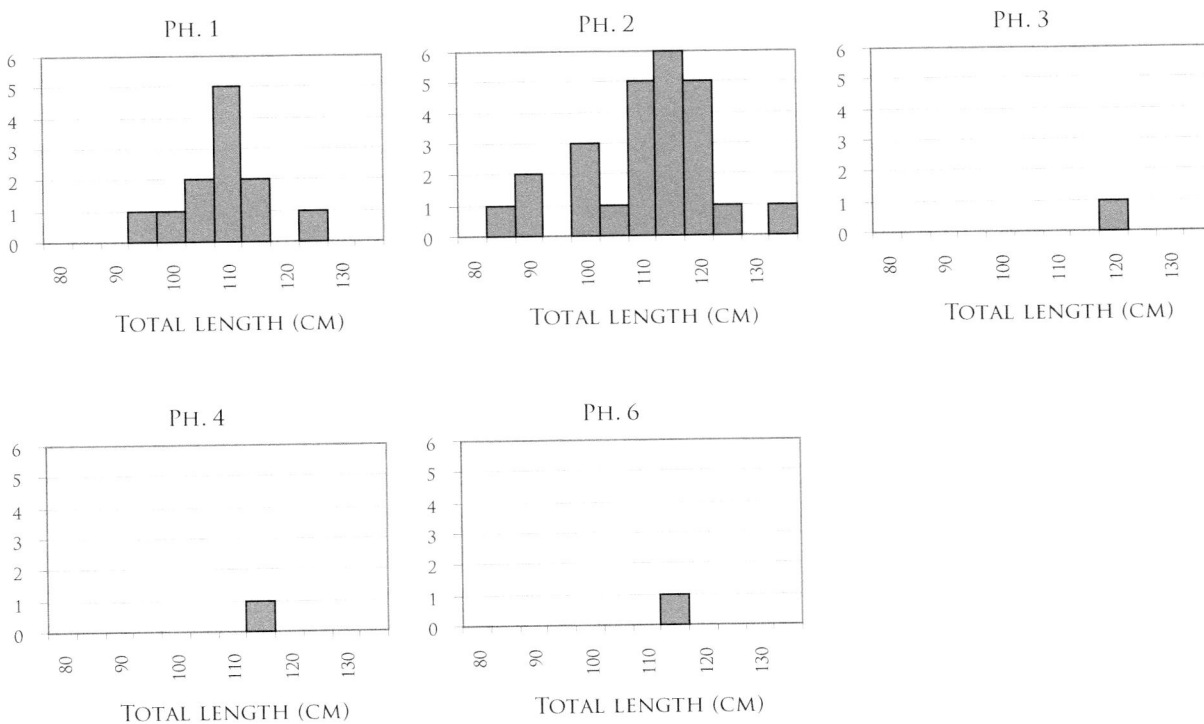

Figure A.4.1 Cod size histograms, based on regression formulas applied to selected measurements

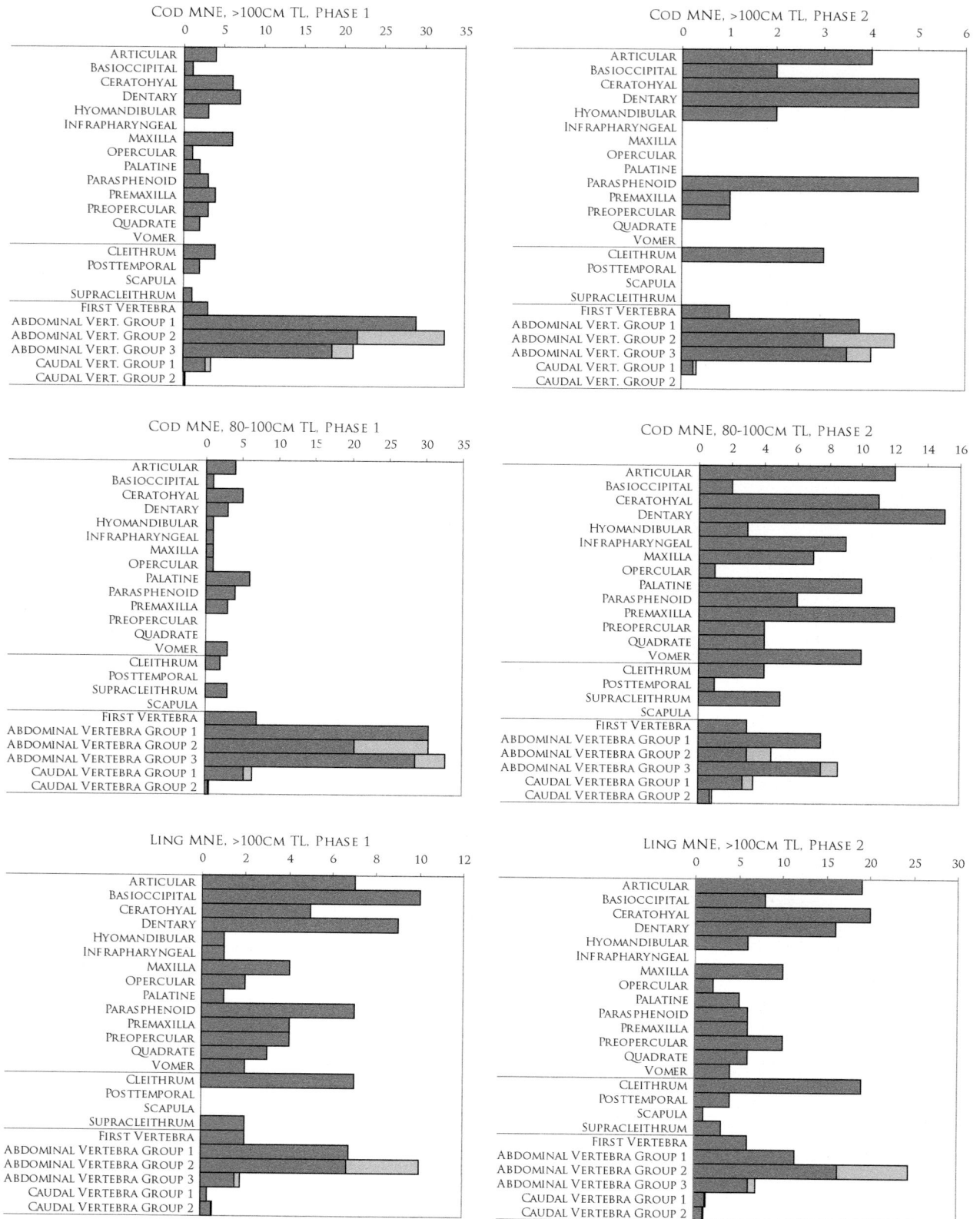

Figure A.4.2 Cod and ling minimum number of elements (MNE) for Phases 1 and 2, hand collected data only, taking into account fragmentation and number of elements in the body (lighter bars indicate the range of MNE for vertebrae, because there is natural variation in the numbers of vertebrae in cod and ling)

Table A.4.1 Summary of fish bone assemblage Phase 1, Pit C015

Taxa	Element	30–50cm	50–80cm	80–100cm	>100cm	Total	Notes
Hand collected							
Cod	Articular			1	2	3	
	Basioccipital			1		1	
	Ceratohyal		1	2	3	6	1 fragment with signs of recent breakage
	Dentary				1	1	
	Hyomandibular			1	1	2	
	Maxilla		1			1	
	Palatine			1	1	2	
	Parasphenoid			3		3	
	Posttemporal			1		1	
	Premaxilla			2	1	3	1 80–100cm TL with pathology
	Preopercular			1	3	4	
	Quadrate				1	1	
	First Vertebra			7	1	8	1 80–100cm TL butchered
	Abdominal Vertebra Group 1			110	105	215	1 80--00cm TL and 1 >100cm TL vertebra with light blue-green staining, 5 >100cm TL vertebrae with pathologies, 5 80–100cm TL butchered, 3 >100cm TL butchered
	Abdominal Vertebra Group 2			106	123	229	1 80–100cm TL with light blue-green staining, 1 >100cm TL with concretions, 3 80–100cm TL with pathologies, 6 >100cm TL butchered
	Abdominal Vertebra Group 3		1	212	137	350	1 80–100cm TL and 1 >100cm TL with light blue-green staining; 3 80–100cm TL and 3 >100cm TL with pathologies, 3 80–100cm TL butchered, 3 >100cm TL butchered
	Caudal Vertebra Group 1			72	39	111	7 80–100cm TL butchered
	Caudal Vertebra Group 2			1		1	
Cod total			3	521	418	942	
Saithe	Abd. Vert. Group 1			1		1	
	Abd. Vert. Group 3		2		4	6	
Saithe total			2	1	4	7	
Saithe/ Pollack	Abd. Vert. Group 1			1		1	
	Cau. Vert. Group 1			1		1	
Saithe/ Pollack total				2		2	

Taxa	Element	30–50cm	50–80cm	80–100cm	>100cm	Total	Notes
Ling	Basioccipital				1	1	
	Ceratohyal				1	1	
	Cleithrum				2	2	
	Dentary			1	1	2	
	Parasphenoid				1	1	
	Preopercular				1	1	
	Abd. Vert. Group 1				6	6	1 butchered
	Abd. Vert. Group 2				16	16	
	Abd. Vert. Group 3			2	10	12	
	Cau. Vert. Group 1				2	2	
Ling total				**3**	**41**	**44**	
Gurnard family	Unidentified	1				1	Cranial element not routinely identified
Unidentified						97	
Total hand collected						**1093**	
>2mm sieving							
Cod	Articular				1	1	
	Preopercular			1		1	
	Abd. Vert. Group 1			1	1	2	
	Abd. Vert. Group 2			1		1	
	Abd. Vert. Group 3		1	6		7	1 80–100cm TL butchered
	Cau. Vert. Group 1			1		1	
Cod total			**1**	**10**	**2**	**13**	
Ling	Abd. Vert. Group 2				1	1	
	Abd. Vert. Group 3				1	1	
Ling total					**2**	**2**	
Saithe	Abd. Vert. Group 3			1		1	
Unidentified						20	
Total sieved						**36**	

Table A.4.2: Summary of fish bone assemblance Phase 2, Layers C003 and C014

Taxa	Element	30–50cm	50–80cm	80–100cm	>100cm	Total	Notes
Hand collected							
Ray family	Dermal Denticle					1	
Cod	Articular			3	4	7	
	Ceratohyal	1		4	4	9	
	Cleithrum			7	16	23	
	Dentary			6	8	14	1 >100cm TL pathological, 1 80–100cm TL butchered, 2 >100cm TL butchered
	Hyomandibular			1	2	3	
	Maxilla			4	7	11	
	Opercular			6	3	9	
	Palatine			1	1	2	
	Parasphenoid			3	2	5	
	Posttemporal			1	3	4	1 80–100cm TL butchered
	Premaxilla		1	1	6	8	2 >100cm TL butchered, 1 80–100cm TL calcined
	Preopercular			5	1	6	
	Quadrate			2	2	4	1 >100cm TL pathological
	Supracleithrum			5		5	1 butchered
	Vomer			2	4	6	
	First Vertebra			2	2	4	
	Abdominal Vertebra Group 1		2	12	16	30	1 >100cm TL gnawed by carnivore, 1 80–100cm TL butchered
	Abdominal Vertebra Group 2			8	14	22	
	Abdominal Vertebra Group 3		2	25	27	54	2 >100cm TL butchered
	Caudal Vertebra Group 1		1	16	6	23	
	Caudal Vertebra Group 2			4	6	10	1 >100cm TL gnawed by carnivore
Cod total		**1**	**6**	**118**	**134**	**259**	
Cod family	Caudal Vertebra Group 2			1	2	3	1 >100cm TL pathological and gnawed by carnivore
Haddock	Cleithrum	7	6			13	1 50–80cm TL gnawed by carnivore
	Posttemporal	1	1			2	
	Preopercular	2				2	
	Abdominal Vertebra Group 3	2	1			3	
	Caudal Vertebra Group 1	1				1	

Taxa	Element	30–50cm	50–80cm	80–100cm	>100cm	Total	Notes
Haddock total		**13**	**8**			**21**	
Ling	Articular				12	12	
	Basioccipital				1	1	
	Ceratohyal			1	12	13	
	Cleithrum				8	8	2 butchered
	Dentary				10	10	2 butchered
	Hyomandibular				8	8	
	Maxilla				9	9	1 pathological
	Palatine				4	4	
	Parasphenoid			1	3	4	
	Posttemporal				2	2	
	Premaxilla				4	4	
	Preopercular				5	5	
	Quadrate				3	3	
	Supracleithrum				2	2	
	Vomer				3	3	
	First Vertebra				4	4	2 butchered
	Abdominal Vertebra Group 1			1	14	15	
	Abdominal Vertebra Group 2				54	54	3 butchered
	Abdominal Vertebra Group 3				40	40	1 butchered
	Caudal Vertebra Group 1				13	13	
	Caudal Vertebra Group 2				8	8	
Ling total				**3**	**219**	**222**	
Pollack	Maxilla			1		1	
Plaice	Preopercular	1				1	
Halibut family	Abdominal Vertebra	1				1	
Unidentified						236	
Total hand collected						**745**	
>2mm sieving							
Atlantic Herring	Abdominal Vertebra					2	
	Caudal Vertebra					2	
Atlantic Herring total						4	

Taxa	Element	30–50cm	50–80cm	80–100cm	>100cm	Total	Notes
Cod	Ceratohyal				1	1	
	Premaxilla			1	1	2	
	Supracleithrum			1		1	
	Abdominal Vertebra Group 1			3		3	
	Abdominal Vertebra Group 2			5	1	6	
	Abdominal Vertebra Group 3				7	7	1 pathological, 1 butchered
	Caudal Vertebra Group 1			3	2	5	1 80–100cm TL butchered
	Caudal Vertebra Group 2			9		9	
Cod total				22	12	34	
Haddock	Ceratohyal	1				1	
	Cleithrum	2				2	
	Dentary	1				1	
	Opercular	1				1	
	Scapula	1				1	
Haddock total		6				6	
Ling	Cleithrum				2	2	
	Abdominal Vertebra Group 1				1	1	
	Abdominal Vertebra Group 2				3	3	2 butchered
	Abdominal Vertebra Group 3				14	14	
	Caudal Vertebra Group 1				4	4	1 butchered
Ling total					24	24	
Unidentified						295	
Total sieved						363	

Table A.4.3 Taphonomic summary for all hand collected fish bone

Phase	1		2		3	4	5	6	Total for all major and minor phases	
Percent completeness, recorded for QC1 and QC4 elements										
1–20%	8	3%	19	2%	1				32	2%
20–40%	36	13%	155	19%	3	15	5		245	18%
40–60%	41	15%	150	18%	4	14	2	4	239	17%
60–80%	82	30%	256	31%	11	15	3	2	416	30%
80–100%	109	39%	254	30%	10	49		1	447	32%
Total	**276**	**100%**	**834**	**100%**	**29**	**93**	**10**	**7**	**1379**	**100%**
Texture, recorded for QC1 and QC4 elements										
Poor	8	3%	42	5%	1	12	4	3	90	7%
Fair	41	15%	208	25%	11	11	6	1	319	23%
Good	224	81%	578	69%	17	66		3	957	69%
Excellent	3	1%	6	1%		4			13	1%
Total	**276**	**100%**	**807**	**100%**	**29**	**93**	**10**	**7**	**1379**	**100%**
Other modifications, recorded for all elements										
Carnivore gnawing	3		6			1			11	
Burnt, calcined	1		1						4	
Fresh breakage	3		3						6	
Blue-green staining	6								6	
Red-brown staining									2	
Concretions	2								4	

Table A.4.4 Taphonomic summary for all sieved fish bone

Phase	1	2	3	4	5	6	Total for all major and minor phases	
Percent completeness, recorded for QC1 and QC4 elements								
1–20%	1		1				2	2%
20–40%	2	3	4			3	16	20%
40–60%	2	1	2			3	8	10%
60–80%	3	8	6	1		7	26	32%
80–100%	6	5	5	1	1	9	30	37%
Total	14	17	18	2	1	22	82	100%
Texture, recorded for QC1 and QC4 elements								
Poor		2				2	4	5%
Fair	4					10	17	21%
Good	10	15	18	1	1	10	60	73%
Excellent				1			1	1%
Total	14	17	18	2	1	22	82	100%
Other modifications, recorded for all elements								
Crushed	2					2	4	
Burnt, calcined	2	9	20	1	9	7	51	
Burnt, charred	1	7	8		2		19	
Concretions							1	

Table A.4.5 Summary of hand collection by area, phase and taxa

Taxa	A1	A4	A5	B1	B5	C1	%	C2	%	C3	%	C4	%	C5	C6	C1 or 2	C2 or 3	C3 or 4	%	C5 or 6	Other	Grand total	%
Ray family								1	0%													2	0%
Salmon & trout family						2	0%															2	0%
Cod	24	1	5		1	1148	83%	951	59%	127	64%	99	49%	19	13	1	1	101	47%	8	249	2748	69%
Haddock		1				26	2%	43	3%			1	0%	1	2			18	8%		1	94	2%
Ling	23		5			193	14%	579	36%	65	33%	98	49%	5	2		2	58	27%	4	10	1044	26%
Pollack								1	0%									1	0%			2	0%
Saithe	1					7	1%	4	0%	5	3%	1	0%					12	6%			30	1%
Saithe/pollack						2	0%	2	0%			1	0%					5	2%			10	0%
Cod/saithe/pollack																		13	6%			13	0%
Cod family								7	0%									3	1%		1	11	0%
Gurnard family						1	0%											1	0%			2	0%
Turbot family								1	0%													1	0%
Turbot						1	0%															1	0%
Halibut								1	0%													1	0%
Plaice								7	0%													7	0%
Flounder/plaice								2	0%	1	1%											3	0%
Halibut family								12	1%			1	0%					1	0%			14	0%
Total identified	49	2	11	0	1	1380	100%	1611	100%	198	100%	201	100%	25	17	1	3	213	100%	12	261	3985	100%
Unidentified	72	2	1	1		339		901		34		117		9	10			127			34	1645	
Grand total	121	4	12	1	1	1719		2512		232		318		34	27	1	3	340		12	295	5630	

Table A.4.6 Summary >2mm sieving by area, phase and taxa

Taxa	A1	A4	A5	A6	A1 or 2	A2 or 3	A2 to 4	A4 or 5	C1	C2	C3	C4	C5	C6	C3 or 4	C5 or 6	Other	Grand total	
Dogfish families														1				1	0%
Ray family										1		1			1			3	1%
Atlantic herring									1	7				3		1		12	3%
Herring family														1				1	0%
Carp family			1															1	0%
Salmon & trout family										1				2				3	1%
Cod		1				1			25	42	4	6	1	4		1		85	20%
Haddock	6	1	3	1	2	5	4	1	1	17	74	1	8	54	3	16	9	206	48%
Ling									10	24	1							35	8%
Pollack															1			1	0%
Poor-cod												1						1	0%
Saithe									1									1	0%
Cod/saithe/pollack					1										1	1		3	1%
Torsk														3				3	1%
Whiting			8		1	1	1			1	1			4	1	5	3	26	6%
Cod family	2		3						2	1	3	1	1	7		4	1	25	6%
Gurnard family										2		1		1				4	1%
Sea scorpion family															1			1	0%
Sand eel family			4															4	1%
Plaice									2									2	0%
Flounder									1									1	0%
Flounder/plaice									1									1	0%
Halibut family						1			2			1	2	1				7	2%
Sole family									1									1	0%
Total identified	8	2	19	1	4	8	5	1	47	96	83	12	12	81	8	28	13	428	100%
Unidentified	1	3	1		12	14	8	1	304	377	416	31	6	468	14	20	21	1697	
Grand total	9	5	20	1	16	22	13	2	351	473	499	43	18	549	22	48	34	2125	

Table A.4.7 Summary by minor phase group and taxa, hand collected and >2mm sieved

Recovery	Hand collected					>2mm sieved						
Taxa	Phase 1 or 2	Phase 2 or 3	Phase 3 or 4	Phase 5 or 6	Other	Phase 1 or 2	Phase 2 or 3	Phase 2 to 4	Phase 3 or 4	Phase 4 or 5	Phase 5 or 6	Other
Ray family									1			
Atlantic herring											1	
Cod	1	1	101	8	249		1				1	
Haddock			18		1	2	5	4	3	1	16	9
Ling		2	58	4	10							
Pollack			1						1			
Saithe			12									
Saithe/pollack			5									
Cod/saithe/pollack			13			1			1		1	
Whiting						1	1	1	1		5	3
Cod family			3		1						4	1
Gurnard family			1									
Sea scorpion family									1			
Halibut family			1				1					
Total identified	1	3	213	12	261	4	8	5	8	1	28	13
Unidentified			127		34	12	14	8	14	1	20	21
Grand total	1	3	340	12	295	16	22	13	22	2	48	34

Table A.4.8 Summary of hand collected fish sizes, for major taxa and phases

Taxa	Size (TL)	Phase1		Phase 2		Phase 3		Phase 4	Phase 5	Phase 6	Total for all major and minor phases	
Cod	30–50cm			4							5	0%
	50–80cm	10	1%	12	1%	4	3%		2		33	1%
	80–100cm	631	54%	372	39%	51	40%	46	15	5	1333	49%
	>100cm	531	45%	563	59%	72	57%	54	8	8	1377	50%
Total		1172	100%	951	100%	127	100%	100	25	13	2748	100%
Haddock	15–30cm									1	1	1%
	30–50cm	13	48%	24	56%					1	43	46%
	50–80cm	14	52%	19	44%			2	1		50	53%
Total		27	100%	43	100%			2	1	2	94	100%
Ling	50–80cm			2							2	0%
	80–100cm	10	5%	9	2%	2		1		1	25	2%
	>100cm	202	95%	541	98%	63		97	9	1	985	97%
Total		212	100%	552	100%	65		98	9	2	1012	100%
Saithe	50–80cm	2	25%			3					15	50%
	80–100cm	1	13%	4	100%	2		1			10	33%
	>100cm	5	63%								5	17%
Total		8	100%	4	100%	5		1			30	100%

Table A.4.9 Summary sieved fish sizes, for major taxa and phases

Taxa	Size (TL)	Phase 1	Phase 2	Phase 3	Phase 4	Phase 5	Phase 6	Total for all major and minor phases	
Cod	15–30cm	1	1					2	3%
	30–50cm	1		1			1	3	4%
	50–80cm	1						2	3%
	80–100cm	14	27	2	2	1		47	59%
	>100cm	3	14	1	5		3	26	33%
Total		20	42	4	7	1	4	80	100%
Haddock	15–30cm	2	6	3	1	7	34	67	33%
	30–50cm	5	10	70	1	4	21	137	67%
	50–80cm		1					1	0%
Total		7	17	73	2	11	55	205	100%
Ling	>100cm	10	24	1				35	
Saithe	80–100cm	1						1	
Whiting	15–30cm			1		8	3	21	81%
	30–50cm		1				1	5	19%
Total			1	1		8	4	26	100%

Table A.4.10 Fish element counts for major taxa

| Taxa and element | Hand collected | | | | | | | >2mm sieved | | | | | | |
| | Phase | | | | | | Total all major and minor phases | Phase | | | | | | Total all major and minor phases |
	1	2	3	4	5	6		1	2	3	4	5	6	
Cod														
Articular	15	58	3	6	3	1	98	1		1				2
Basioccipital	2	8	1	1			14							
Ceratohyal	18	48	3	5	1		83		1					1
Dentary	15	74	5	9	1	1	118							
Hyomandibular	7	19	1	1			30							
Infrapharyngeal		1					1	1						1
Maxilla	12	48		5			80		1					1
Opercular	2	22		2	1		27							
Palatine	3	6					9							
Parasphenoid	9	24	1	3			44							
Premaxilla	14	30	1	1	1		52	1	2					3
Preopercular	14	38		7			61	1			1			2
Quadrate	3	13	1	2	1		21							
Vomer		14				1	15	2						2
Cleithrum	21	101	3	3	1		137							
Posttemporal	7	15		1		1	27						1	1
Scapula		1					1							
Supracleithrum	5	15				1	22		1					1
First Vertebra	10	11	1	2			24							
Abdominal Vert. Group 1	239	88	25	13	4	1	413	2	3	2	1			8
Abdominal Vert. Group 2	254	64	32	9	3	5	430	1	6		3			10
Abdominal Vert. Group 3	381	142	37	22	9	1	714	7	12				1	21
Caudal Vert. Group 1	128	79	12	7		1	278	2	5		2	1		11
Caudal Vert. Group 2	11	32	1	1			47	7	11	1			2	21
Caudal Vertebra	1						1							
Otolith	1						1							
Cod total	1172	951	127	100	25	13	2748	25	42	4	7	1	4	85
Haddock														
Articular	2						2						1	1
Basioccipital									1					2

325

Taxa and element	Hand collected							>2mm sieved						
	Phase						Total all major and minor phases	Phase						Total all major and minor phases
	1	2	3	4	5	6		1	2	3	4	5	6	
Ceratohyal	4						4	1					3	4
Dentary	1						2	1					2	4
Hyomandibular		1					1		1				1	2
Maxilla	1						1		2				1	3
Opercular	1						1		2				1	4
Palatine	1						1	1	1				1	3
Parasphenoid	2						5		1					1
Premaxilla	1						1		1				1	3
Preopercular	1	2				1	4						1	1
Quadrate													1	1
Vomer													2	2
Cleithrum	12	33		2			51		2	2			1	6
Posttemporal		2					3			2			3	5
Scapula									1	1				2
Supracleithrum								1	2	2				5
First Vertebra										1			1	3
Abdominal Vert. Group 1									1	3		1	5	14
Abdominal Vert. Group 2								1		3		1	2	11
Abdominal Vert. Group 3	1	3				1	5	3	3	22	2	6	6	55
Caudal Vert. Group 1		2			1		9	2		9		1	8	27
Caudal Vert. Group 2							4		3	19		2	14	44
Otolith										3				3
Haddock total	27	43		2	1	2	94	7	17	74	2	11	55	206
Ling														
Articular	13	35	2	6			60							
Basioccipital	10	8		2			21							
Ceratohyal	8	38	2	6	1		61	2						2
Dentary	17	30	2	3			55							
Hyomandibular	2	12		2			16							
Infrapharyngeal	1			1			2							
Maxilla	7	18		3			30							
Opercular	2	2		3			7							

Taxa and element	Hand collected						Total all major and minor phases	>2mm sieved						Total all major and minor phases
	Phase							Phase						
	1	2	3	4	5	6		1	2	3	4	5	6	
Palatine	2	7	1	4			17							
Parasphenoid	8	9	1	2			23							
Premaxilla	4	10		3			17							
Preopercular	5	15	1	4			29							
Quadrate	3	10					13							
Vomer	2	5	1	1			10							
Cleithrum	12	35		3		1	55		2					2
Posttemporal		5					6	1						1
Scapula		1					1							
Supracleithrum	4	4		1			10							
First Vertebra	2	6		2		1	12							
Abdominal Vert. Group 1	28	47	12	7	1		103		1					1
Abdominal Vert. Group 2	40	114	28	32	5		238	1	3					4
Abdominal Vert. Group 3	28	99	10	10	2		159	1	14					15
Caudal Vert. Group 1	7	31	5	2	1		49	1	4	1				6
Caudal Vert. Group 2	7	12					19	4						4
Otolith		1					1							
Ling total	212	554	65	97	10	2	1014	10	24	1				35

Table A.4.11 Fish element counts for minor taxa

Taxa	Element	Hand collection Phase 1	2	3	4	5	Total all major and minor phases	>2mm sieved Phase 1	2	3	4	5	Total all major and minor phases
Dogfish families	Vert.												1
Ray family	Dermal Denticle		1			1	2		1		1		3
Atlantic herring	Abdominal Vert.								3				7
	Caudal Vert.							1	4				5
Herring family	First Vert.												1
Carp family	Abdominal Vert.										1		1
Salmon & trout family	Abdominal Vert.								1				2
	Caudal Vert.	2					2						1
Cod/Ssithe/pollack	Abdominal Vert. Group 3												1
	Caudal Vert. Group 1												2
	Caudal Vert. Group 2						13						
Pollack	Maxilla		1				1						
	Abdominal Vert. Group 3												1
	Caudal Vert. Group 1						1						
Poor-cod	Dentary									1			1
Saithe	Cleithrum		1				1						
	Dentary						1						
	Hyomandibular						1						
	Opercular						1						
	Palatine						1						
	Parasphenoid	1					1						
	Premaxilla						1						
	Vomer		1				1						
	Abdominal Vert. Group 1	1					1						
	Abdominal Vert. Group 2			1			4						
	Abdominal Vert. Group 3	6	2	2	1		15	1					1
	Caudal Vert. Group 1			2			2						
Saithe/pollack	Abdominal Vert. Group 1	1					1						
	Abdominal Vert. Group 2						1						
	Abdominal Vert. Group 3		1		1		2						
	Caudal Vert. Group 1	1	1				2						
	Caudal Vert. Group 2						4						
Torsk	Caudal Vert.												3
Whiting	Maxilla												1
	Quadrate												1
	Abdominal Vert. Group 1										2		2
	Abdominal Vert. Group 3								1		2		9
	Caudal Vert. Group 1									1	3		12
	Caudal Vert. Group 2										1		1

Taxa	Element	Hand collection					Total all major and minor phases	>2mm sieved					Total all major and minor phases
		1	2	3	4	5		1	2	3	4	5	
Cod family	Branchiostegal		1				1						
	Articular						1						
	Dentary						1						
	Maxilla		1				1						
	Parasphenoid						1						
	Quadrate						1						2
	Scapula										1		1
	Abdominal Vert. Group 1		1				1						1
	Abdominal Vert. Group 2												2
	Abdominal Vert. Group 3		1				1	1			3		6
	Caudal Vert.							1	1	1			4
	Caudal Vert. Group 1								1	1			2
	Caudal Vert. Group 2		3				3	1					5
	Penultimate Vert.								1				1
	Ultimate Vert.							1					1
Gurnard family	Opercular												1
	Parasphenoid						1						
	Abdominal Vert.									1			1
	Caudal Vert.								1				1
Sea scorpion family	Abdominal Vert.												1
Sand eel family	Vert.										4		4
Turbot	Preopercular	1					1						
Turbot family	Caudal Vert.		1				1						
Flounder	Premaxilla							1					1
Halibut	Quadrate		1				1						
Plaice	Cleithrum		2				2						
	Premaxilla							1					1
	Preopercular		2				2						
	Quadrate							1					1
	1st Anal Pterygiophore		3				3						
Flounder/plaice	Basioccipital		1				1						
	Preopercular		1				1						
	1st Anal Pterygiophore			1			1	1					1
Halibut family	Hyomandibular		1				1						
	Abdominal Vert.		2				2	2					3
	Caudal Vert.		5				5			1	2		4
	1st Anal Pterygiophore		4		1		6						
Sole family	Abdominal Vert.							1					1

5 Ceramics

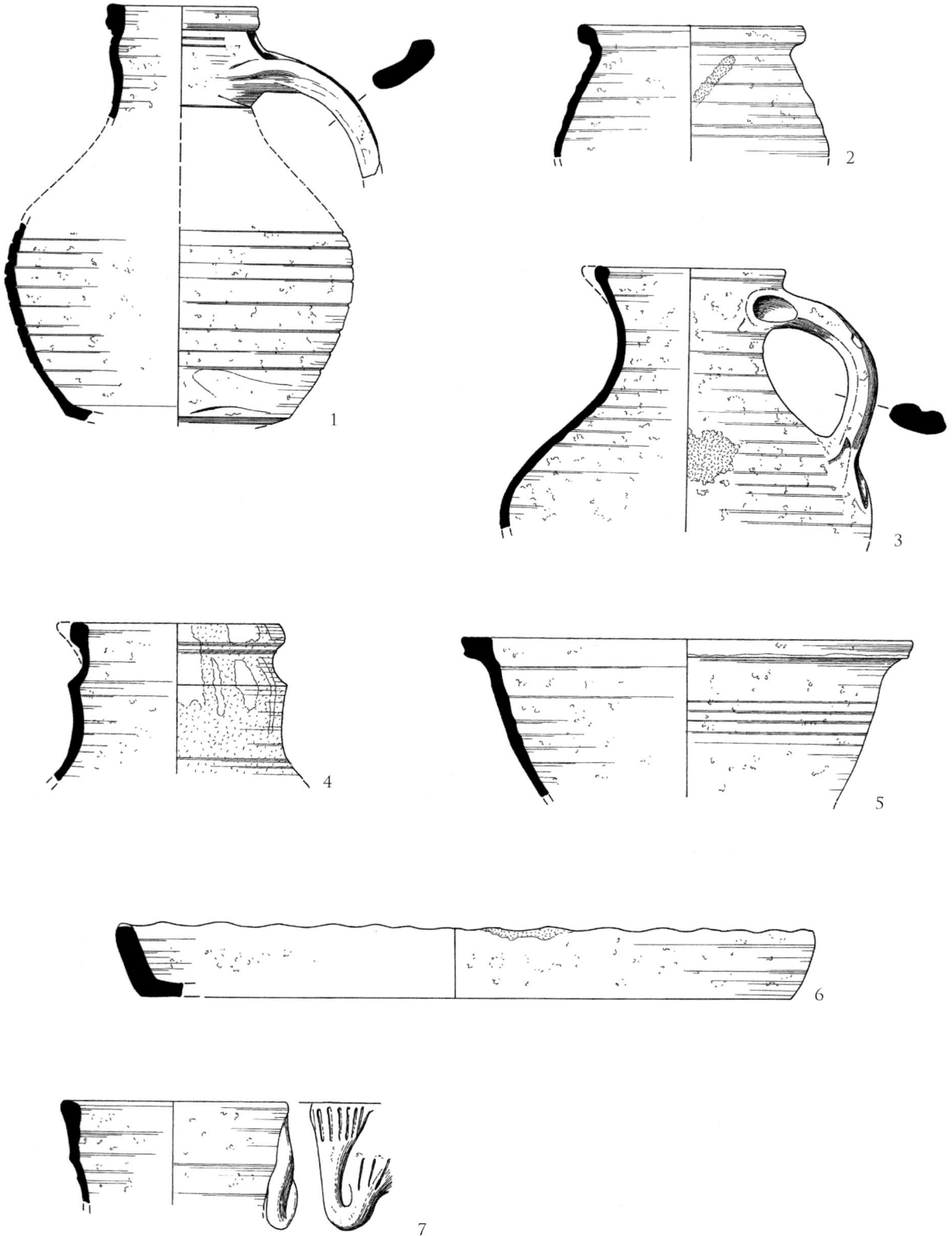

Figure A.5.1 Phase 1; 1–7 Local Redware

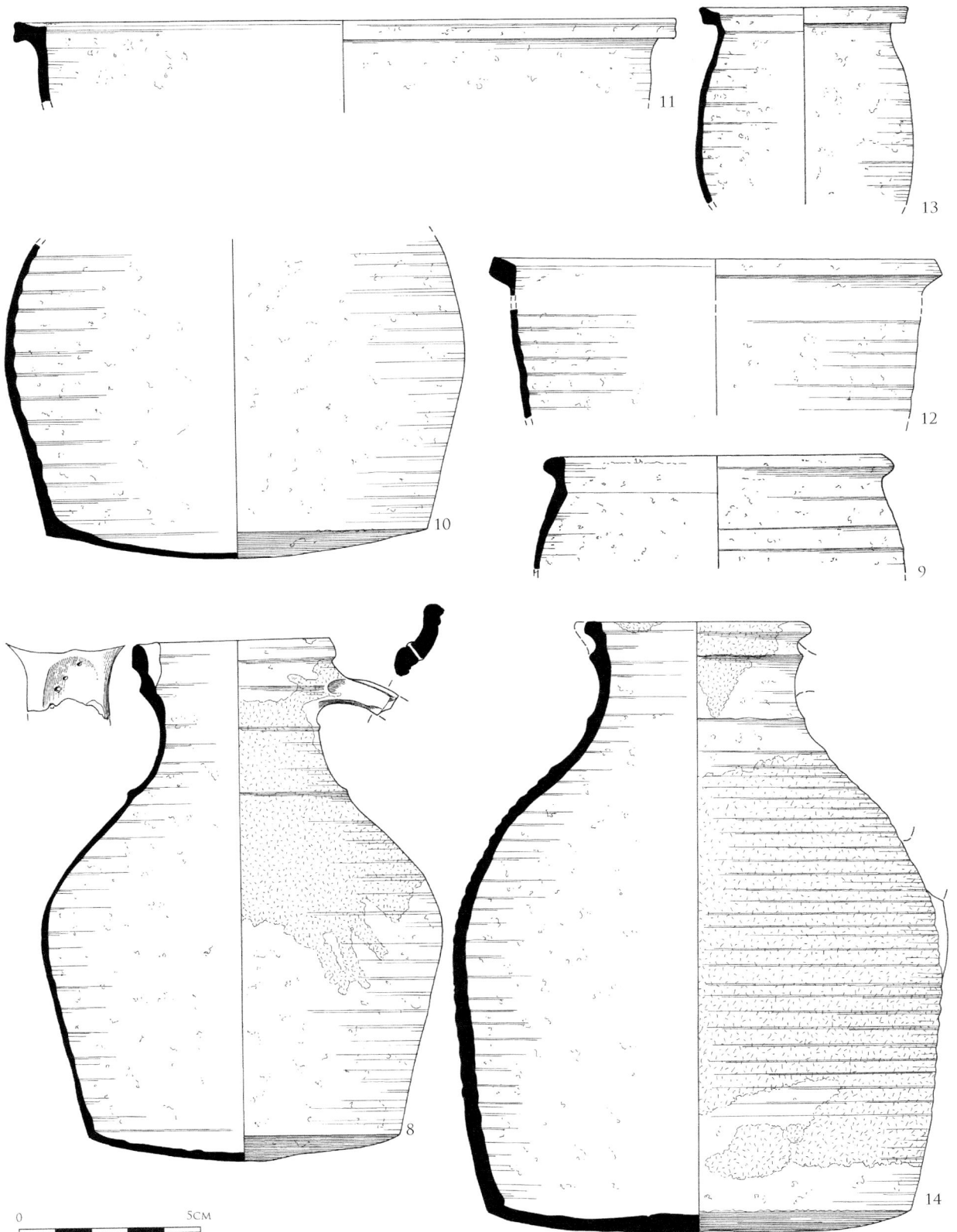

Figure A.5.2 Phase 1; 8–14 Scottish White Gritty Ware

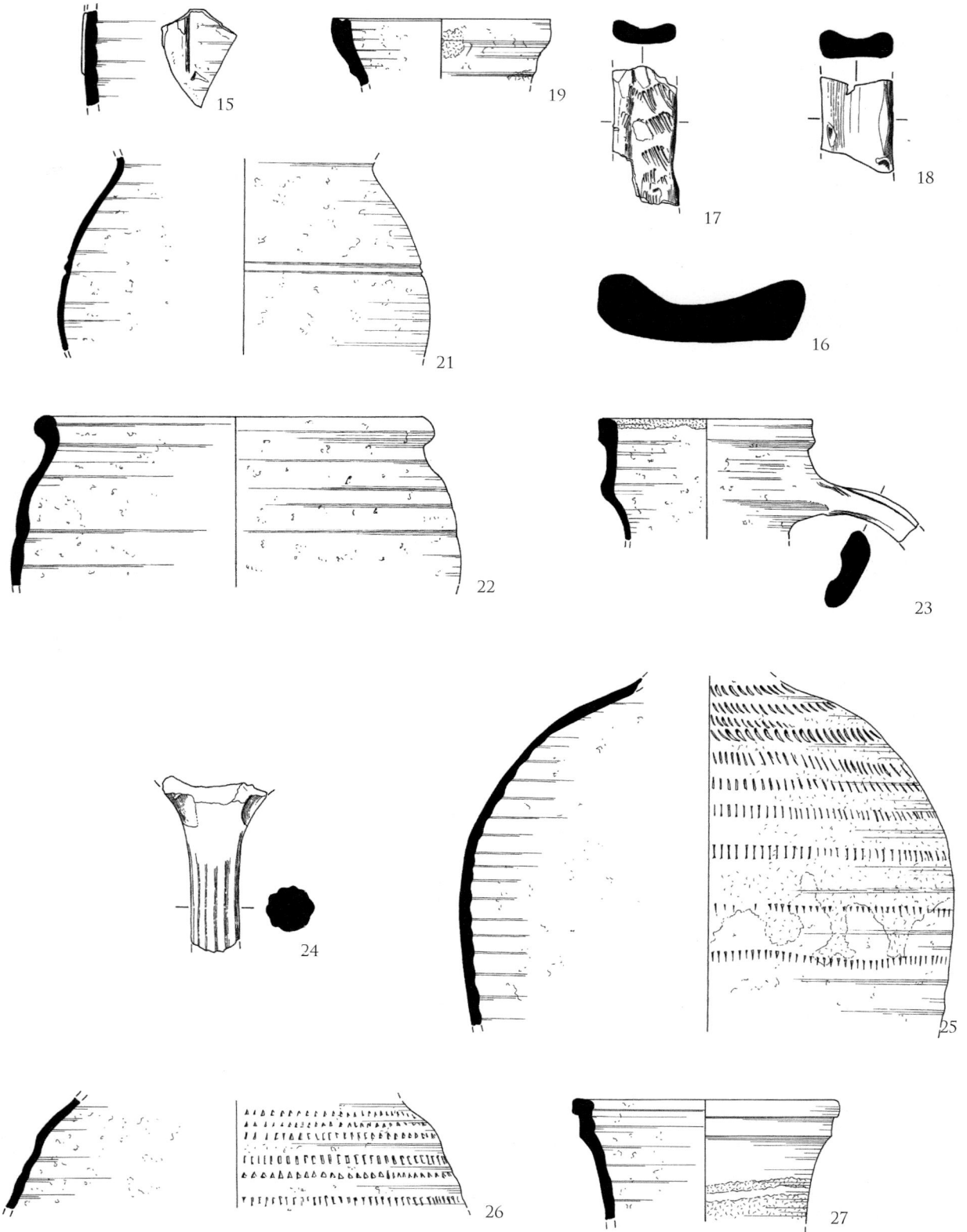

0   10CM

Figure A.5.3 Phase 1; 15-19, 21 Stamford Ware; 22–27 Yorkshire Ware

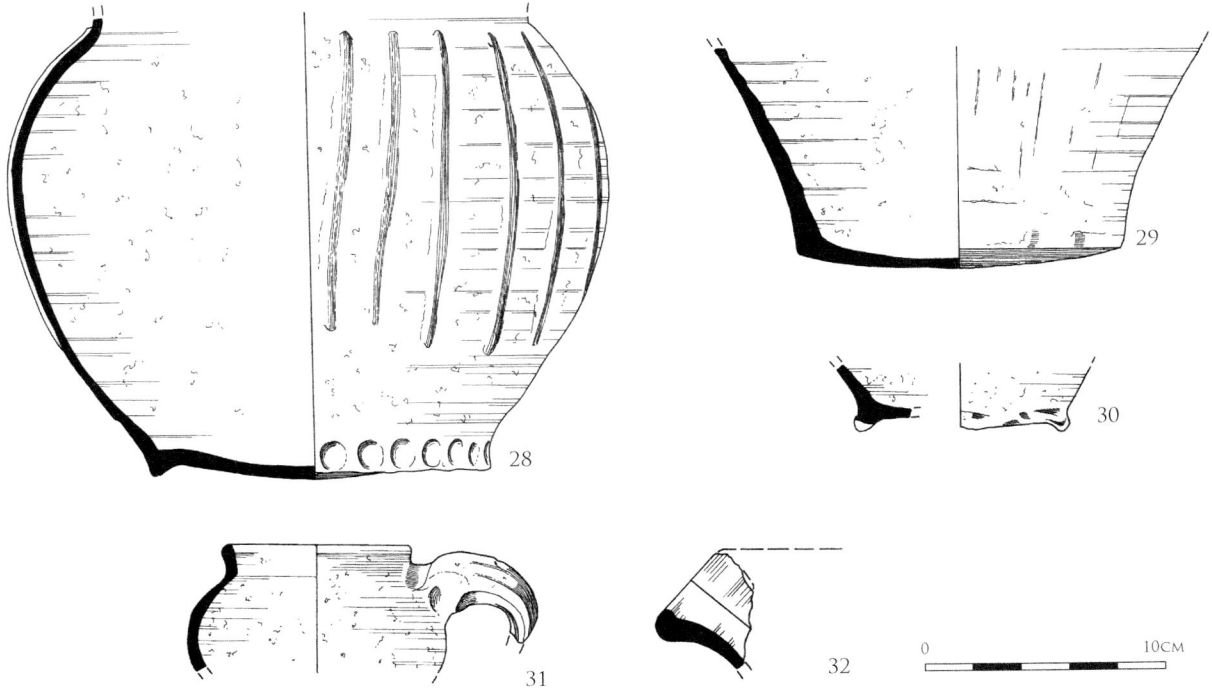

Figure A.5.4.Phase 1; 28 North French redware? 29 Normandy Gritty? 30 Pingsdorf Ware. 31 Paffrath ladle. 32 Late Saxon/early medieval socketed bowl

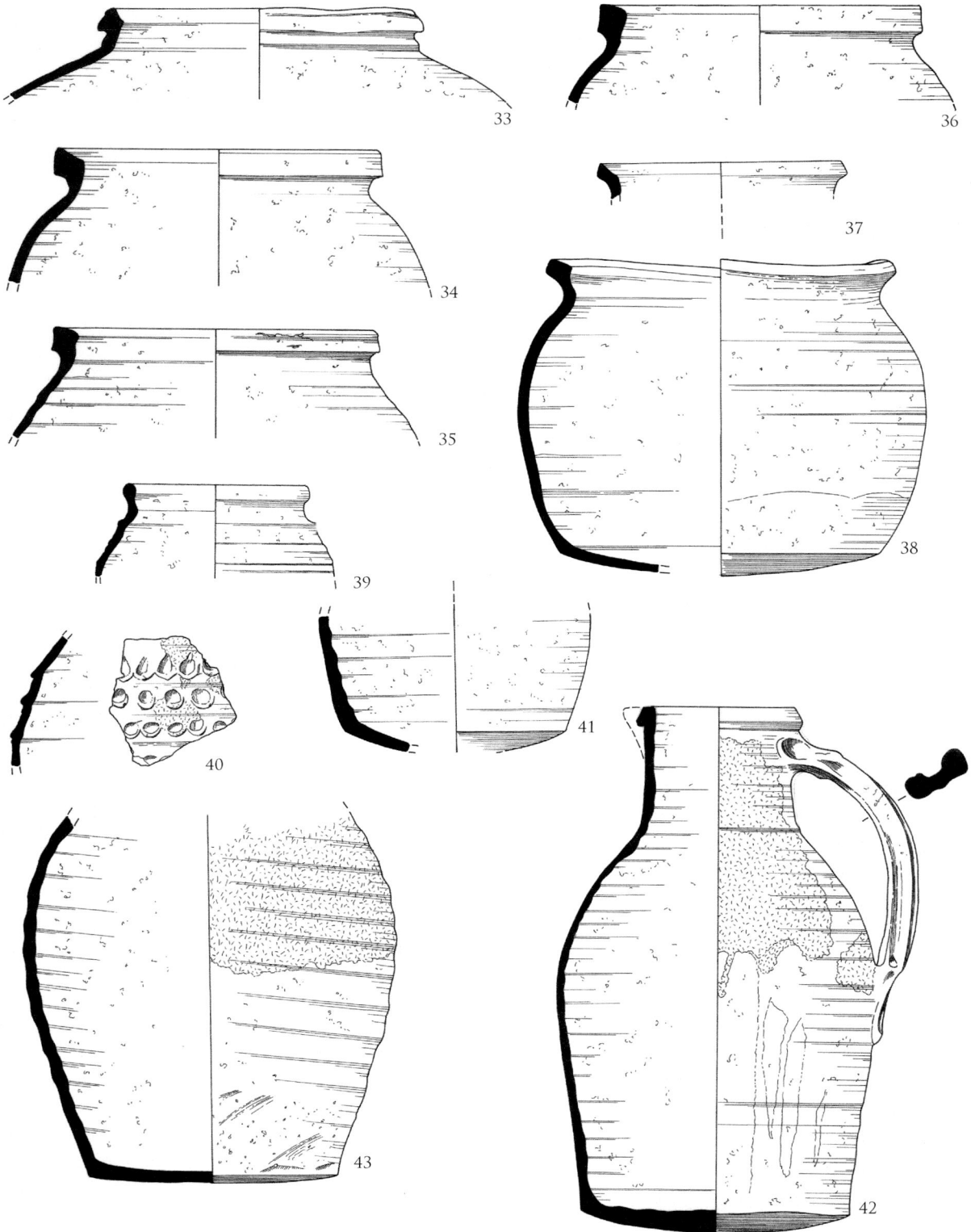

Figure A5.5 Phase 2; 33–43 Local Redware

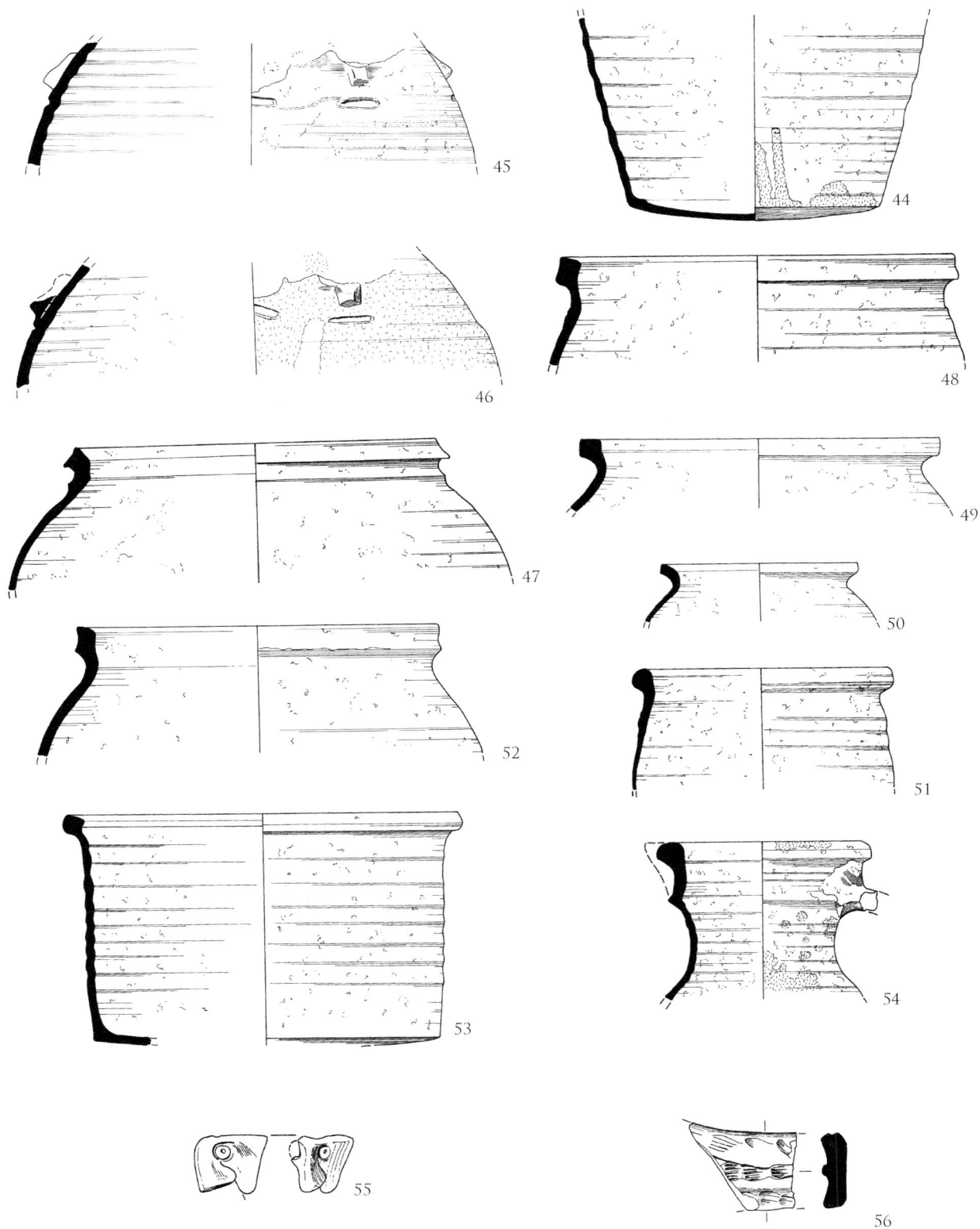

Figure A.5.6 Phase 2 & 2/3; 44–46 Local Redware. 47–55 Scottish White Gritty Ware. 56 Stamford Ware

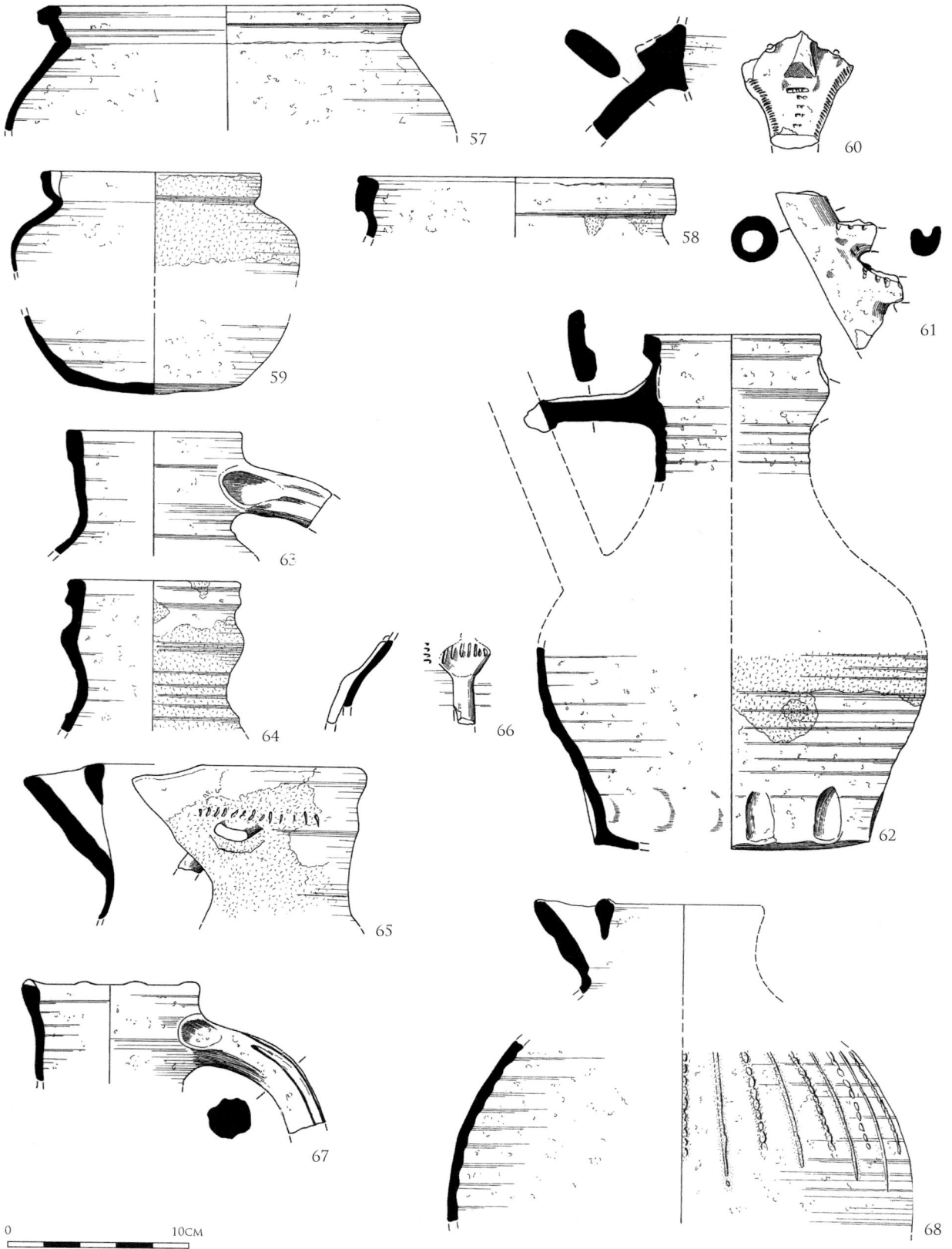

0   10CM

Figure A.5.7 Phase 2; 57–64 Yorkshire Ware. 65–68 Scarborough Ware 1

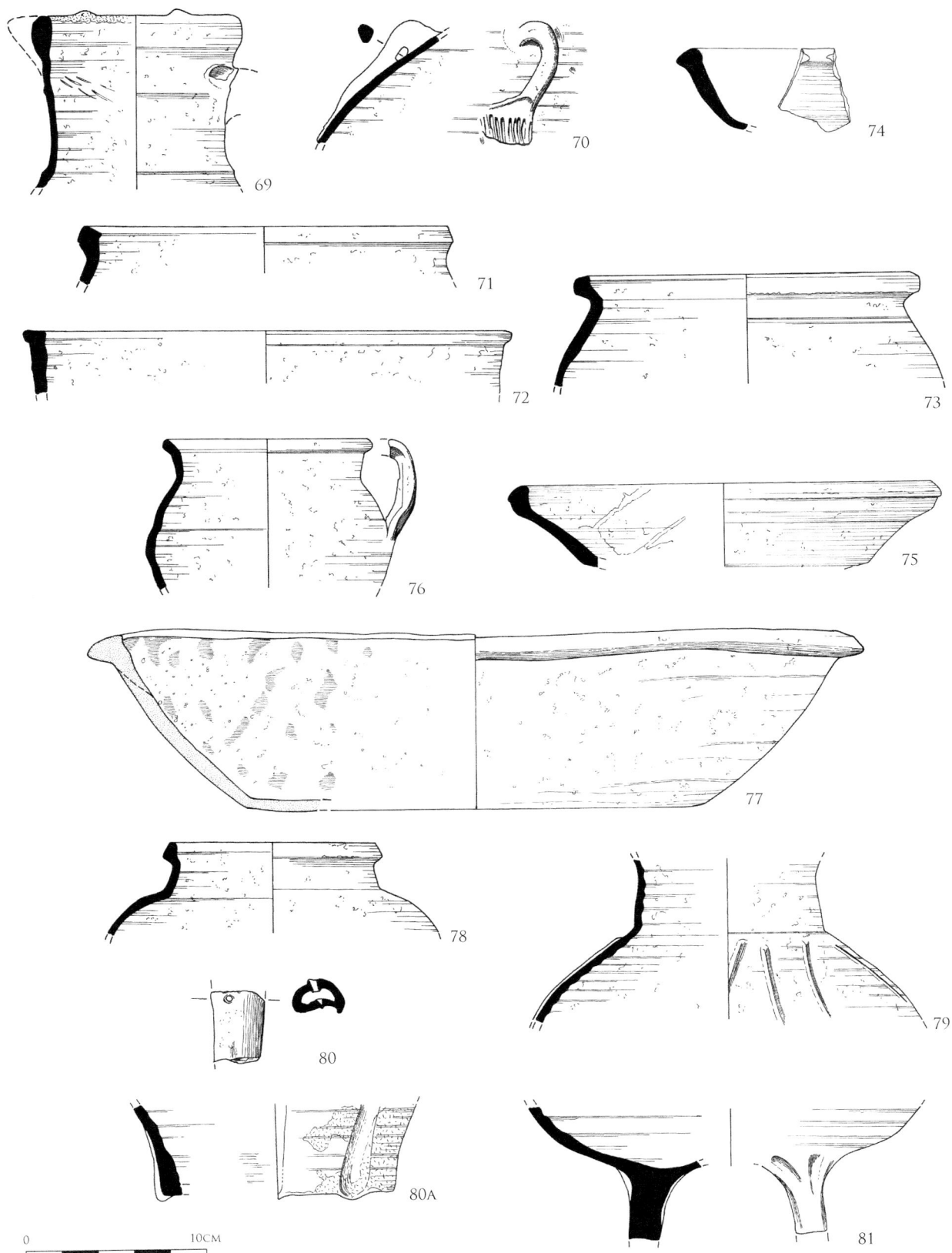

Figure A.5.8 Phase 2; 69–70 Scarborough Ware 2. 71–77 East Anglian. 78 Paffrath cooking pot. 79 North French jug. 80 French Saintonge jug. 81 skillet unknown

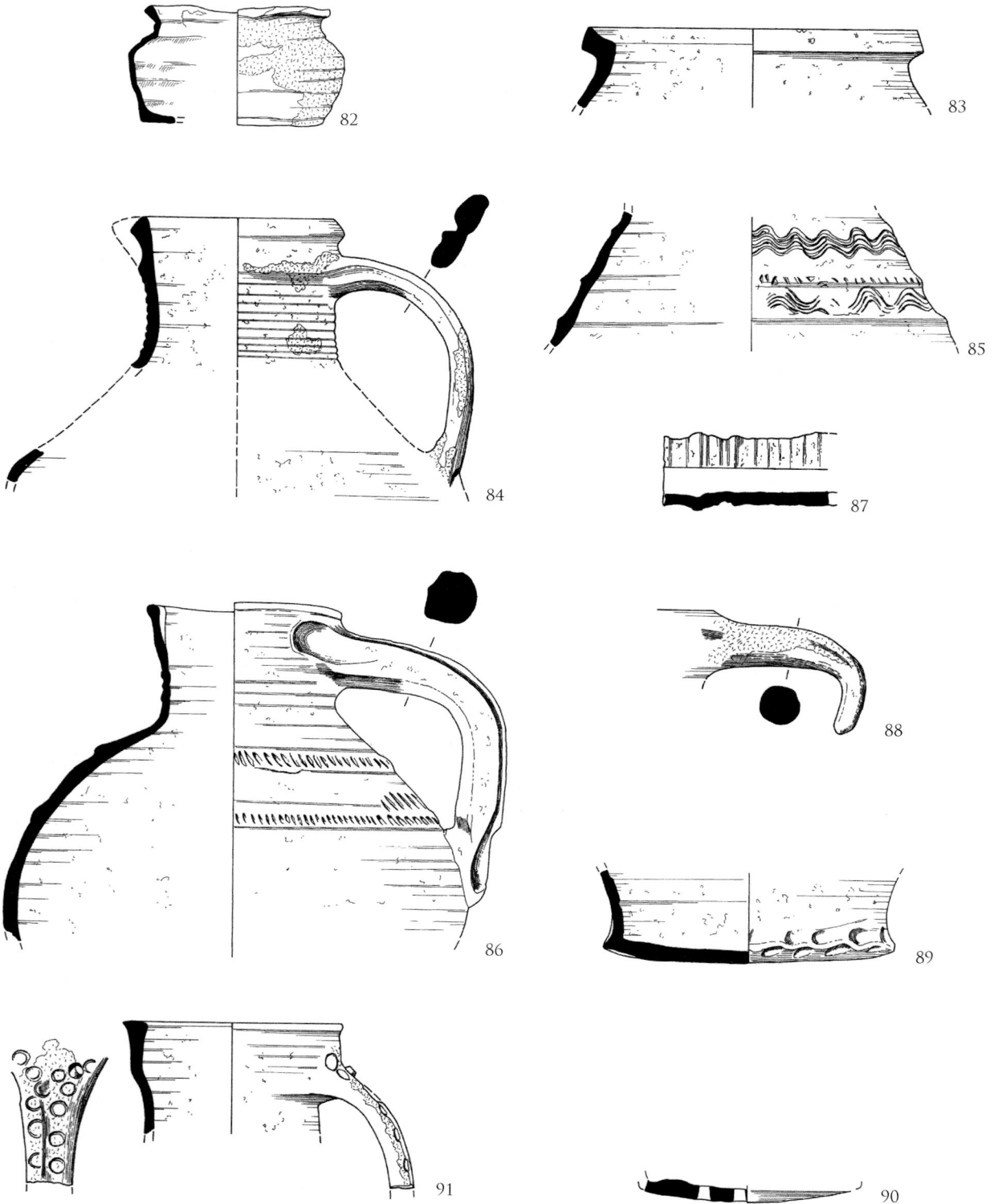

Figure A.5.9 Phase 3 & 3/4; 82–91 Local Redware

0   10CM

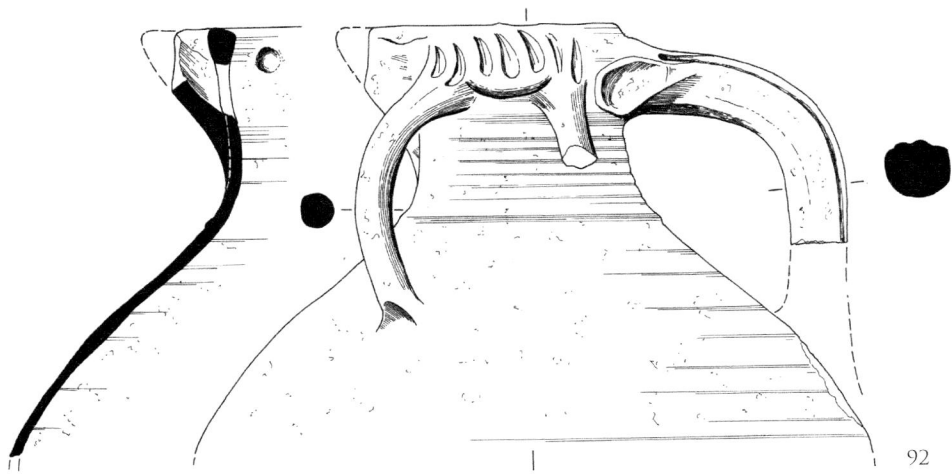

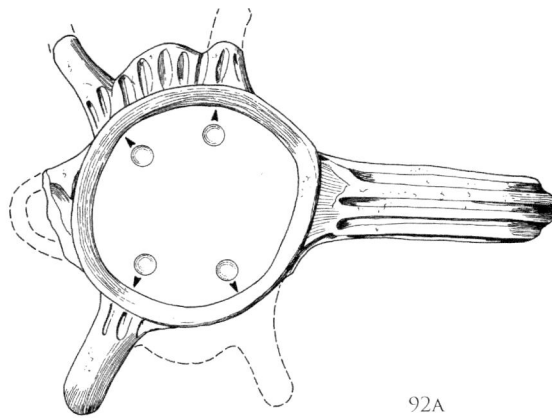

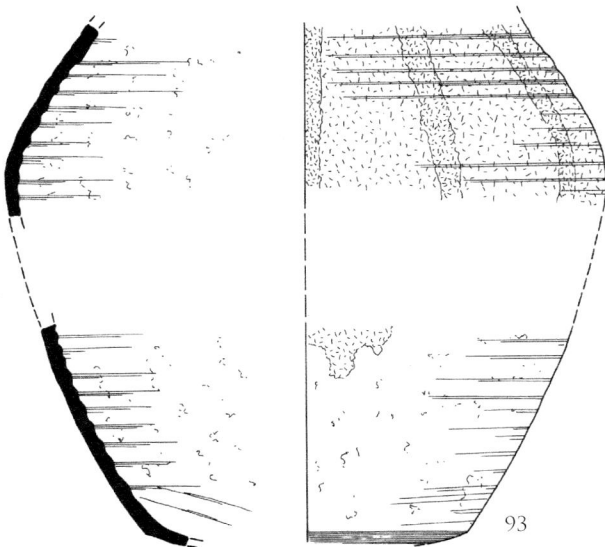

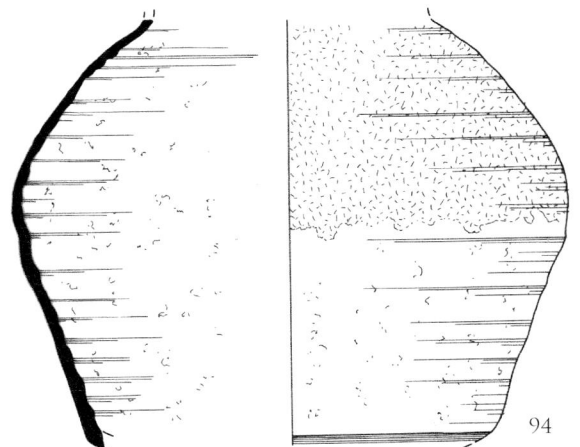

Figure A.5.10 Phase 3 & 3/4; 92–94 Local Redware

0   10CM

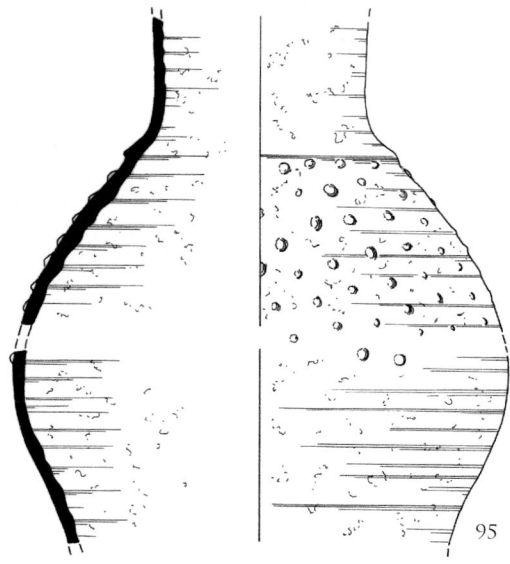

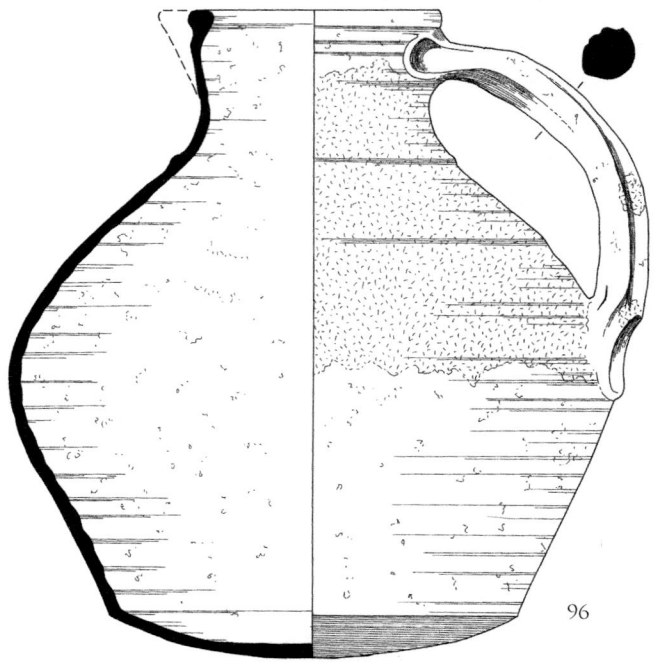

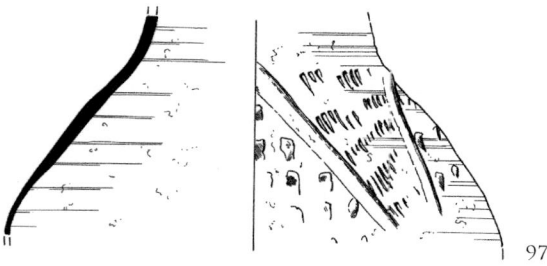

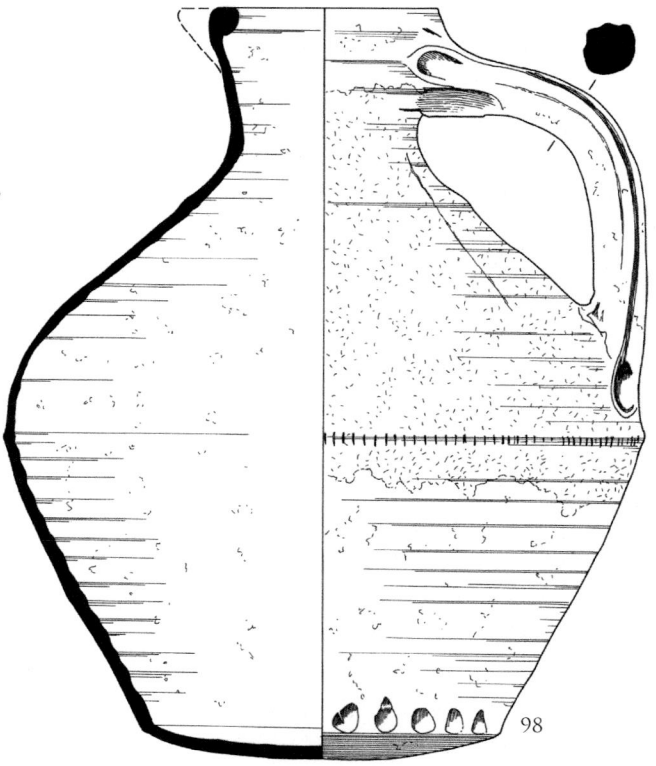

Figure A.5.11 Phase 3 & 3/4; 95–98 Local Redware

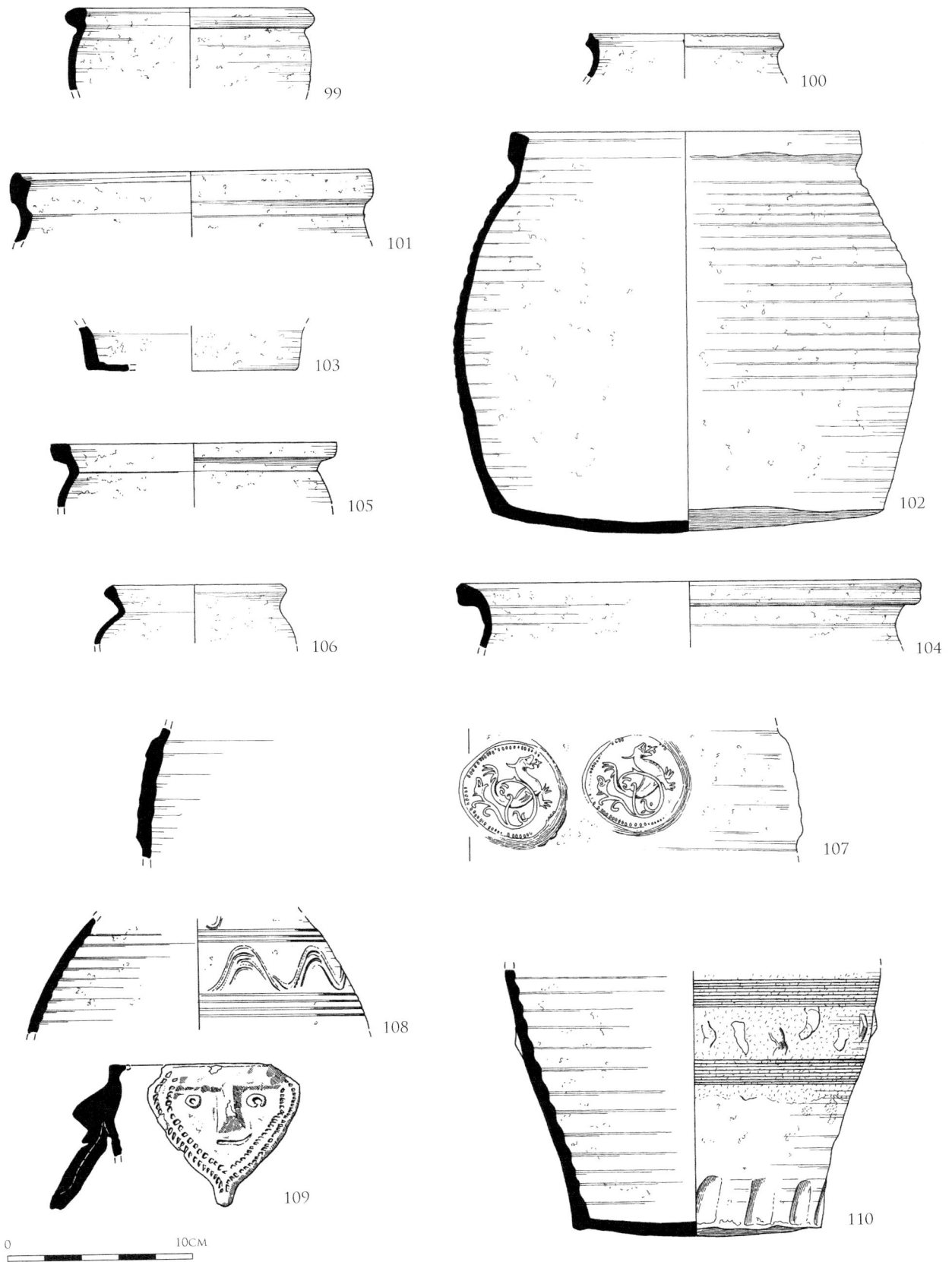

Figure A.5.12 Phase 3 & 3/4; 99–103 Scottish White Gritty Ware. 104–110 Yorkshire Ware

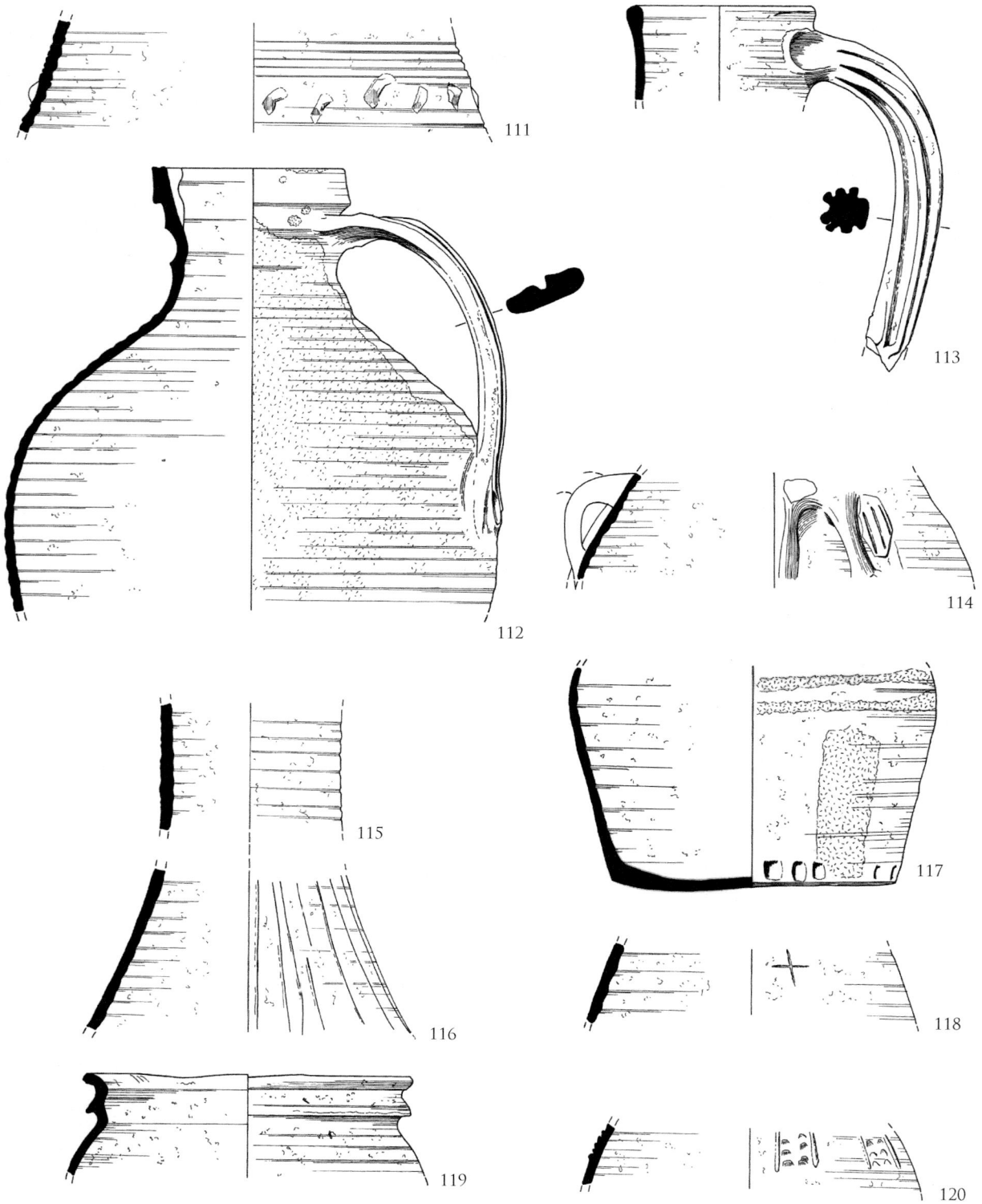

0   10CM

Figure A.5.13 Phase 3 & 3/4; 111 – 113 Yorkshire ware. 114 -117 Scarborough Wares 1 & 2. 118 Low Countries Greyware. 119 French Gritty Ware. 120 jug unknown

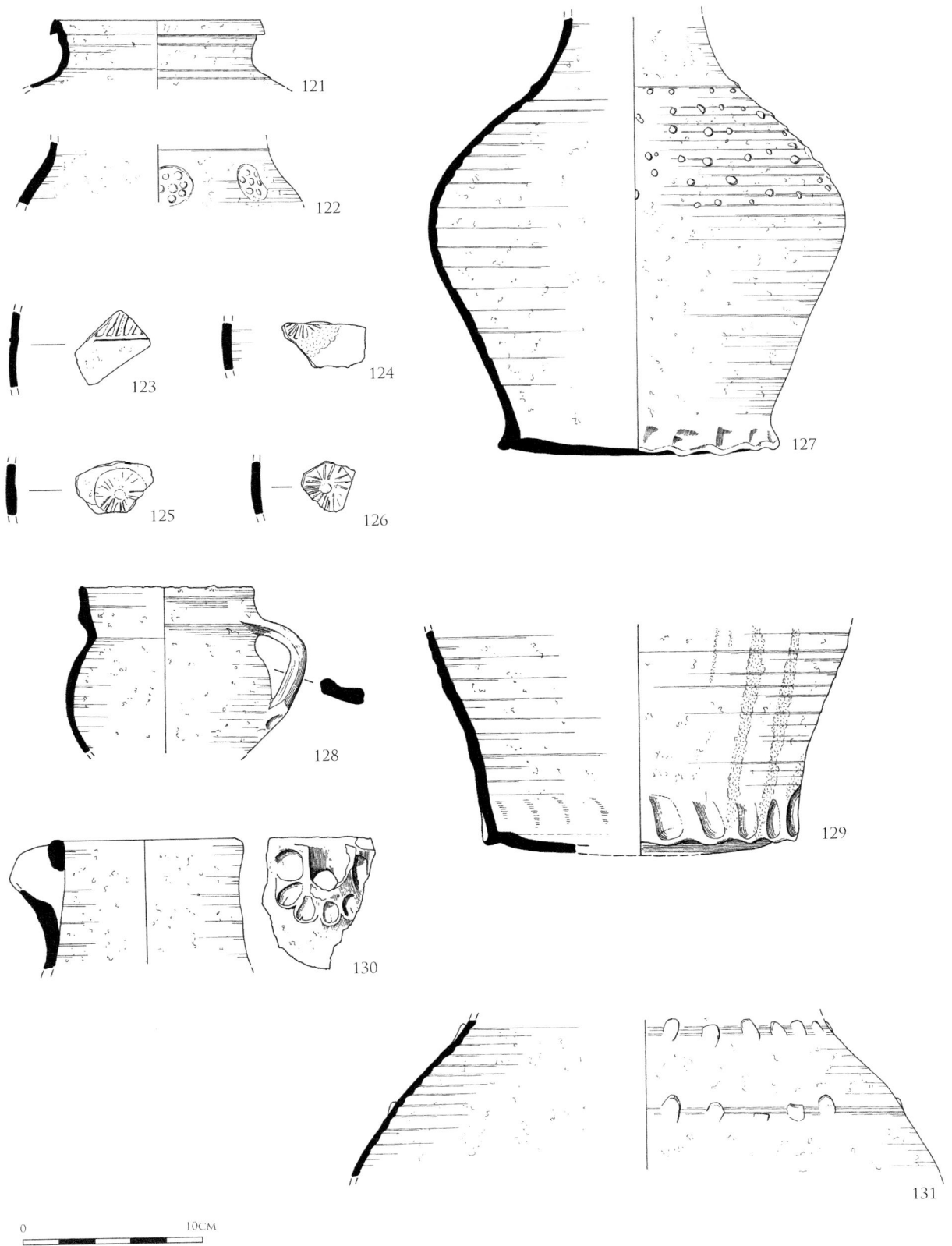

Figure A.5.14 Phase 4; 121–131 Local Redware

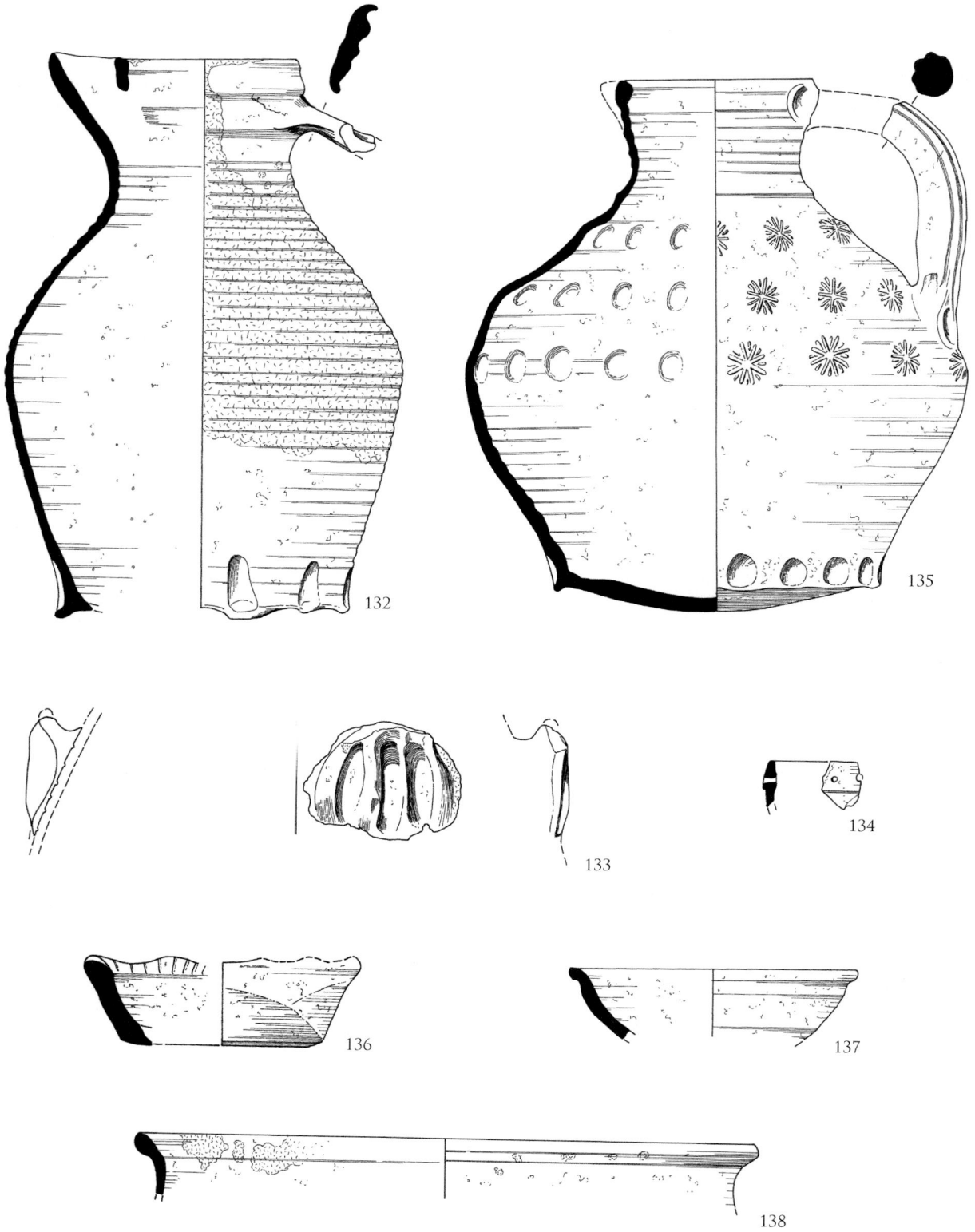

Figure A.5.15 Phase 4; 132–138 Local Redware

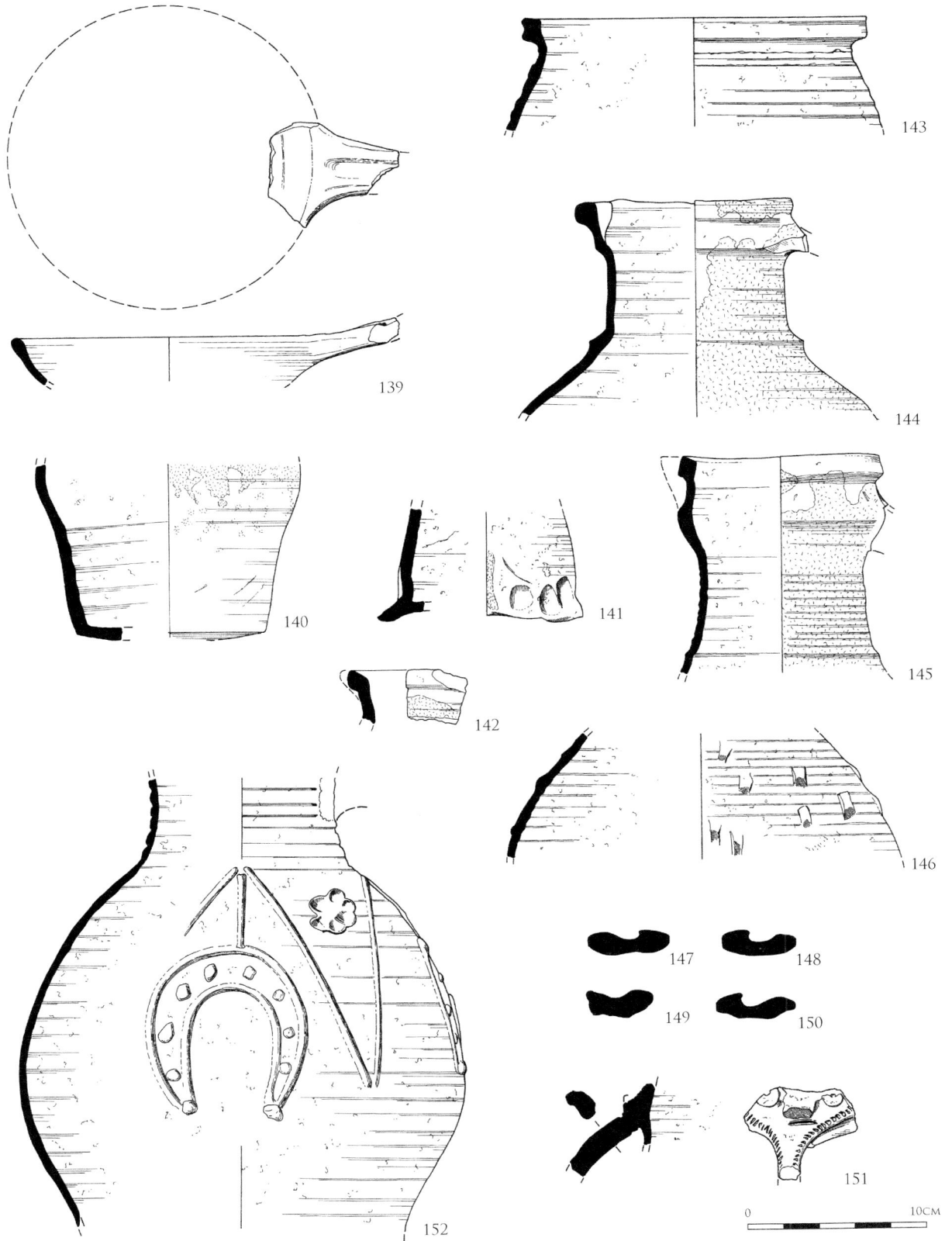

Figure A.5.16 Phase 4 & 4/5; 139–142 Local Redware. 143–144 Scottish White Gritty Ware. 145–152 Yorkshire Ware

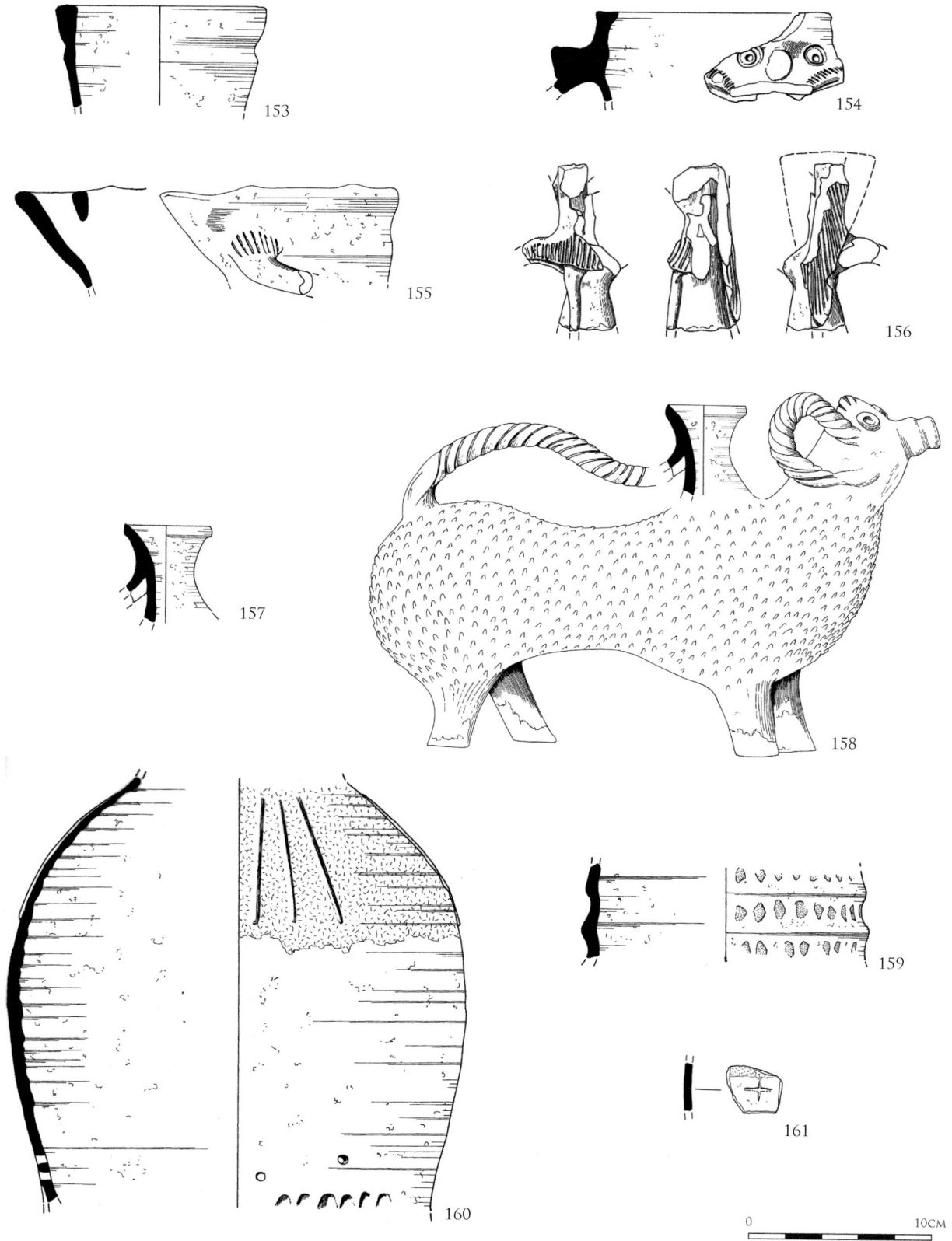

Figure A.5.17 Phase 4; 153–161 Scarborough Ware 1 & 2

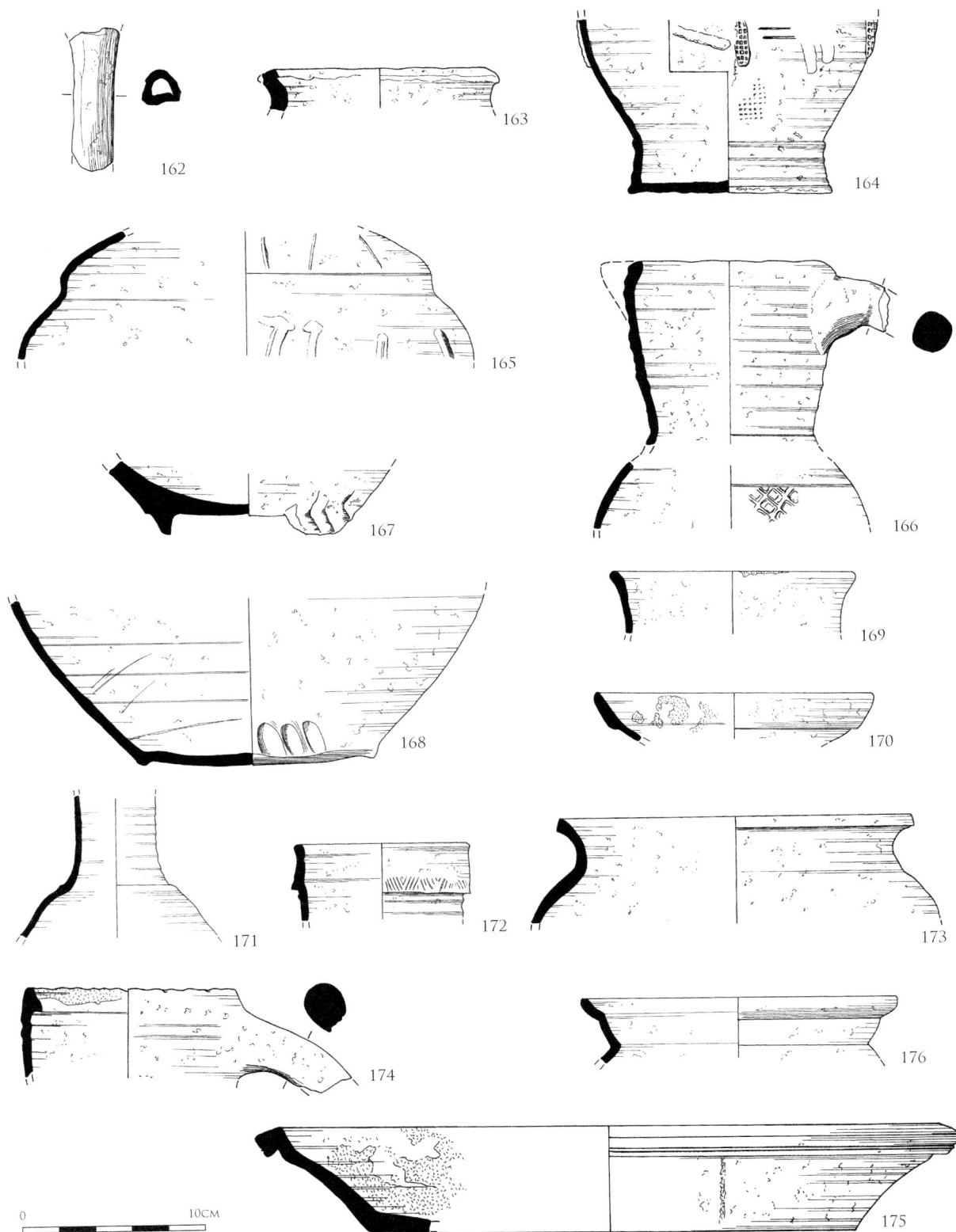

Figure A.5.18 Phase 4 & 4/5; 162–163 North French. 164 French Rouen. 165–166 Low Countries Highly Decorated Ware. 167–168 Low Countries Greyware. 169–170 Low Countries Redware. 171 Siegburg Stoneware. 172 Langerwehe Stoneware. 173 East Anglian. 174 London Sandy. 175–176 unknown

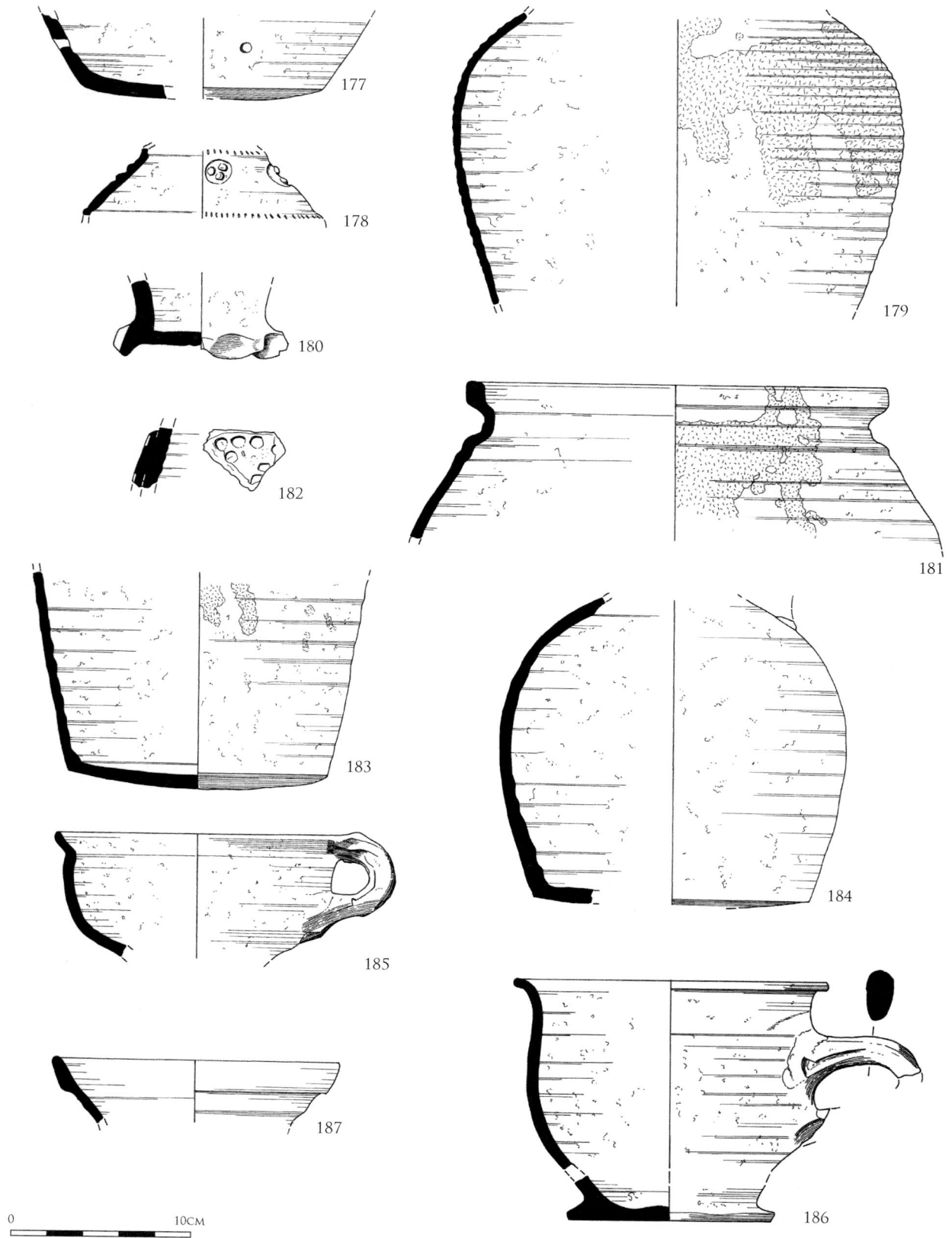

0   10CM

Figure A.5.19 Phase 5; 177–187 Local Redware

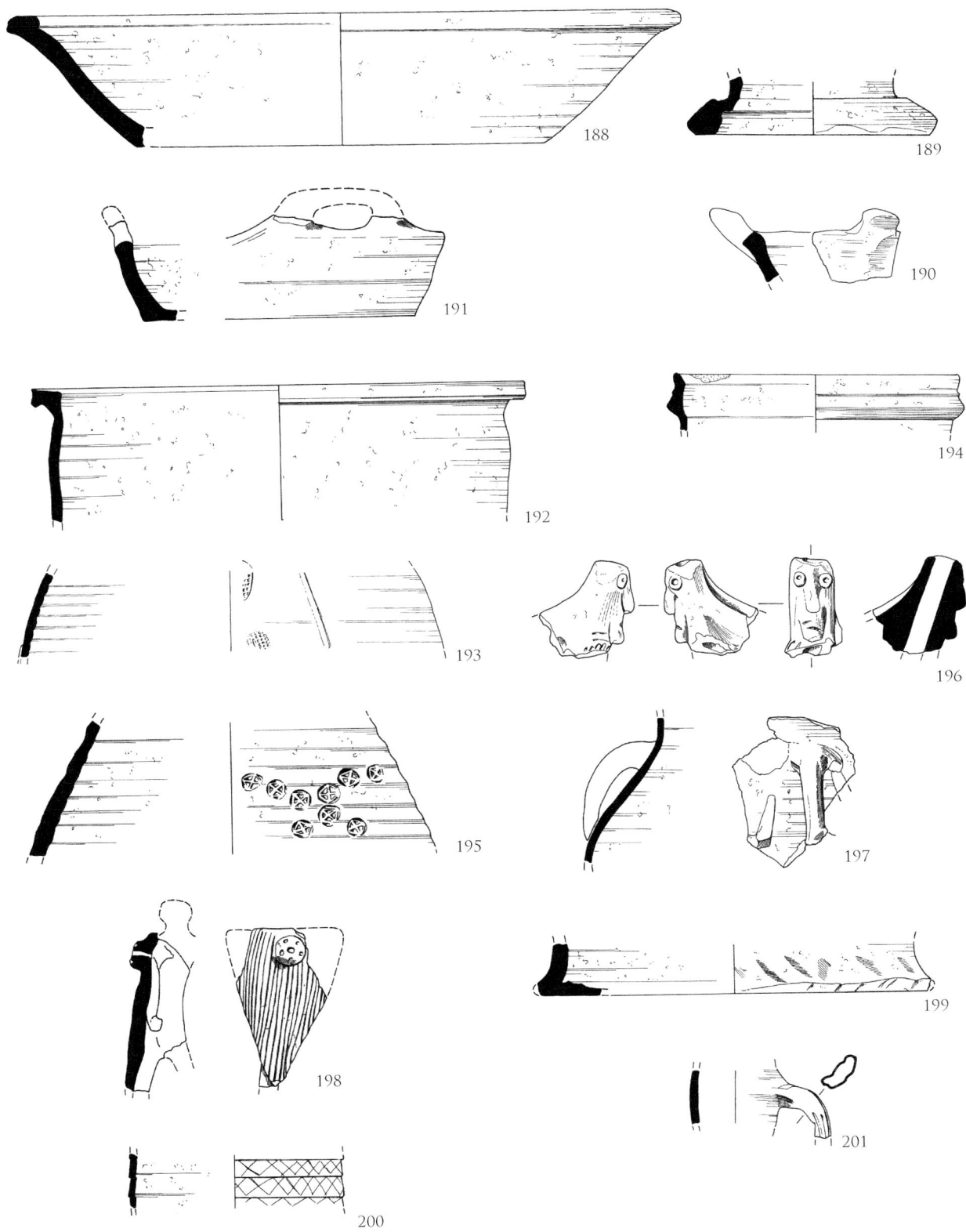

Figure A.5.20 Phase 5 & 5/6; 188–191 Local Redware. 192 Scottish White Gritty Ware. 193 Yorkshire Whiteware. 194 Yorkshire Redware. 195 Yorkshire Sandy. 196–198 Scarborough Ware 1 & 2. 199 French Gritty Normandy? 200 North French. 201 French Beauvais

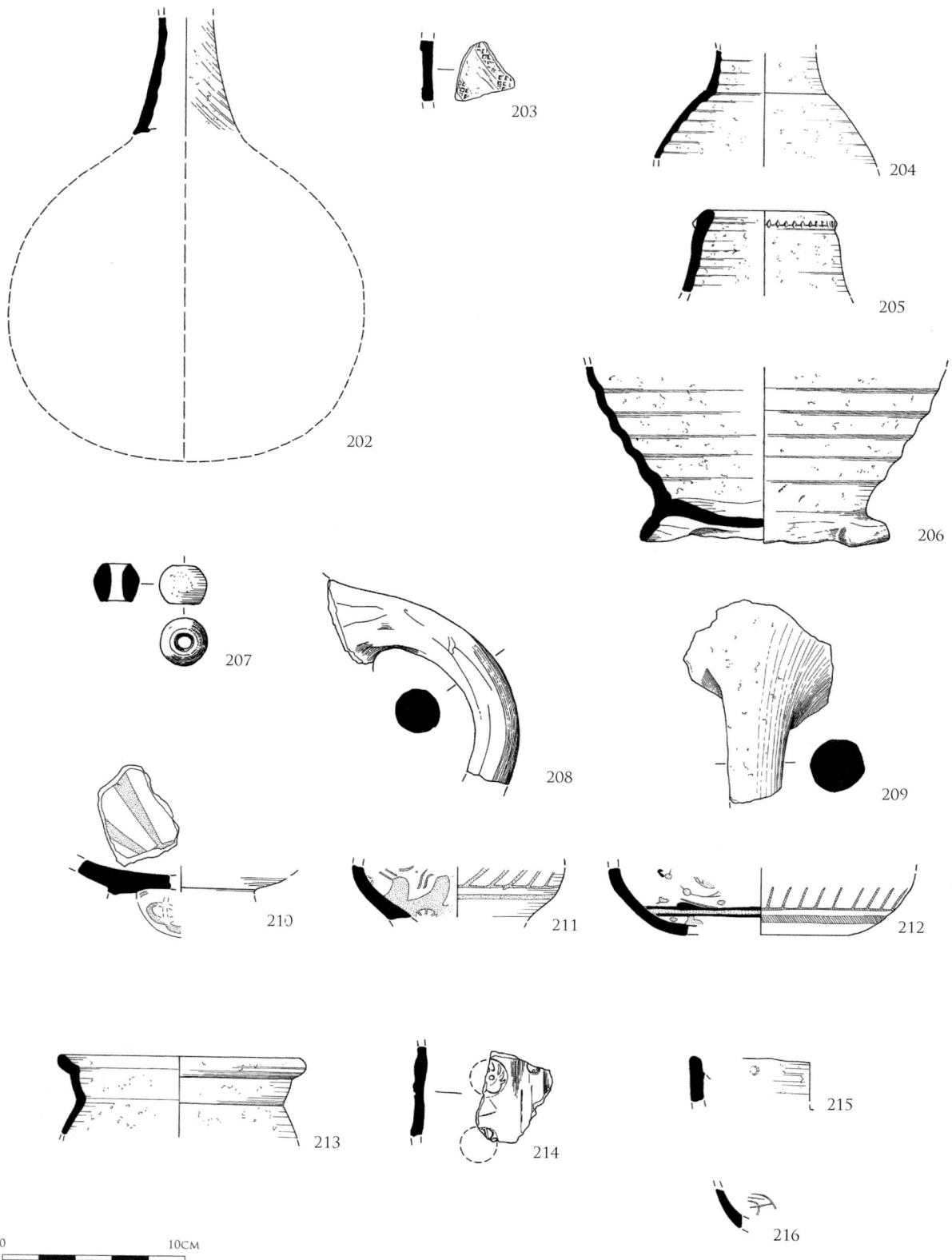

Figure A.5.21 Phase 5; 202 Martincamp. 203 French Rouen. 204 Siegburg Stoneware. 205–207 Raeren Stoneware. 208–209 Iberian Redware. 210–212 Valencian Lustreware. 213 Low Countries Greyware. 214–215 Low Countries Highly Decorated Ware. 216 Italian Scraffitto

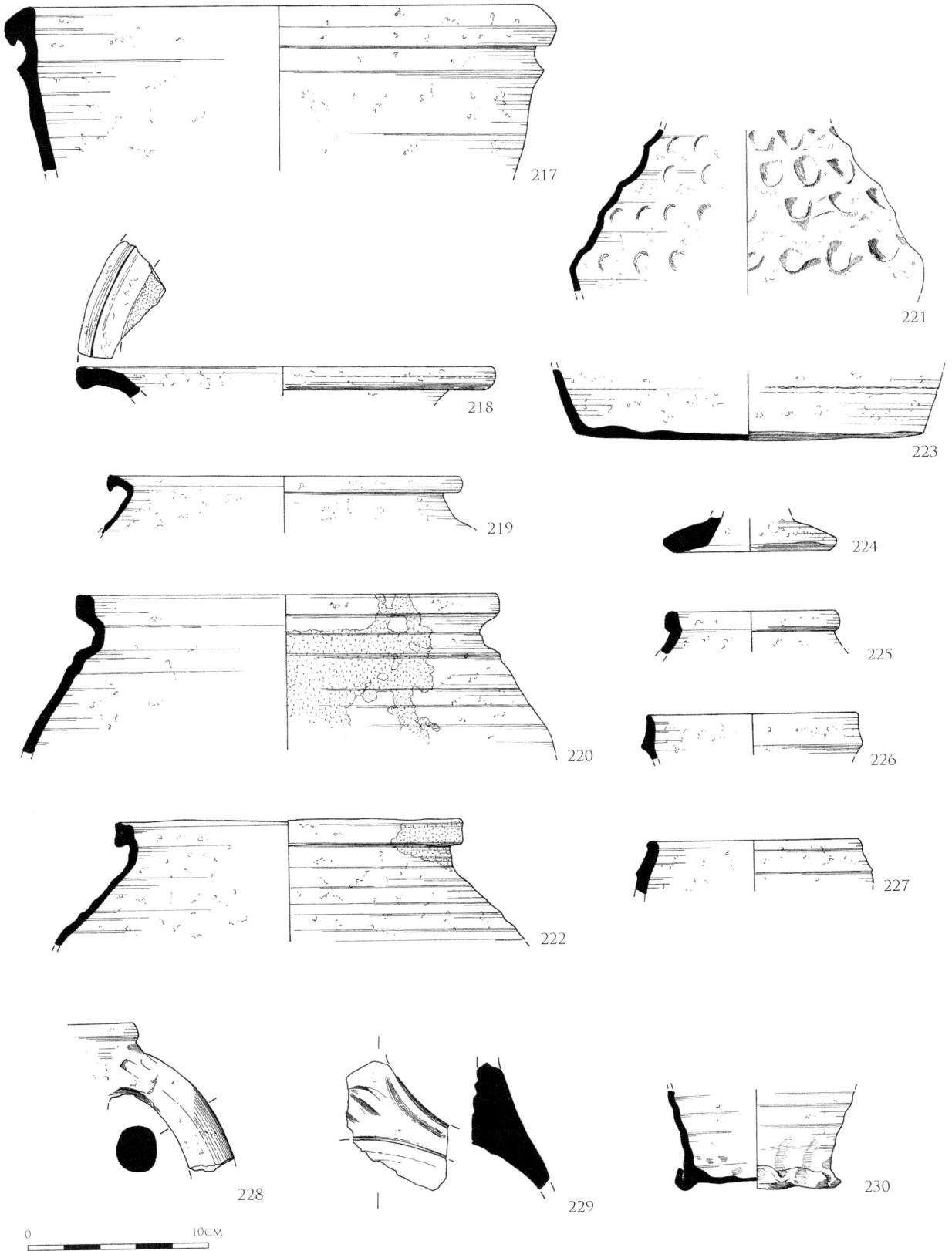

Figure A.5.22 Phases 5 & 6; 217–219 unknown. 220–221 Local Redware. 222–223 Scottish White Gritty Ware. 224 Scarborough Ware 1. 225–228 Low Countries Greyware. 229 Scottish Post-Medieval Oxidised Ware. 230 Siegburg Stoneware

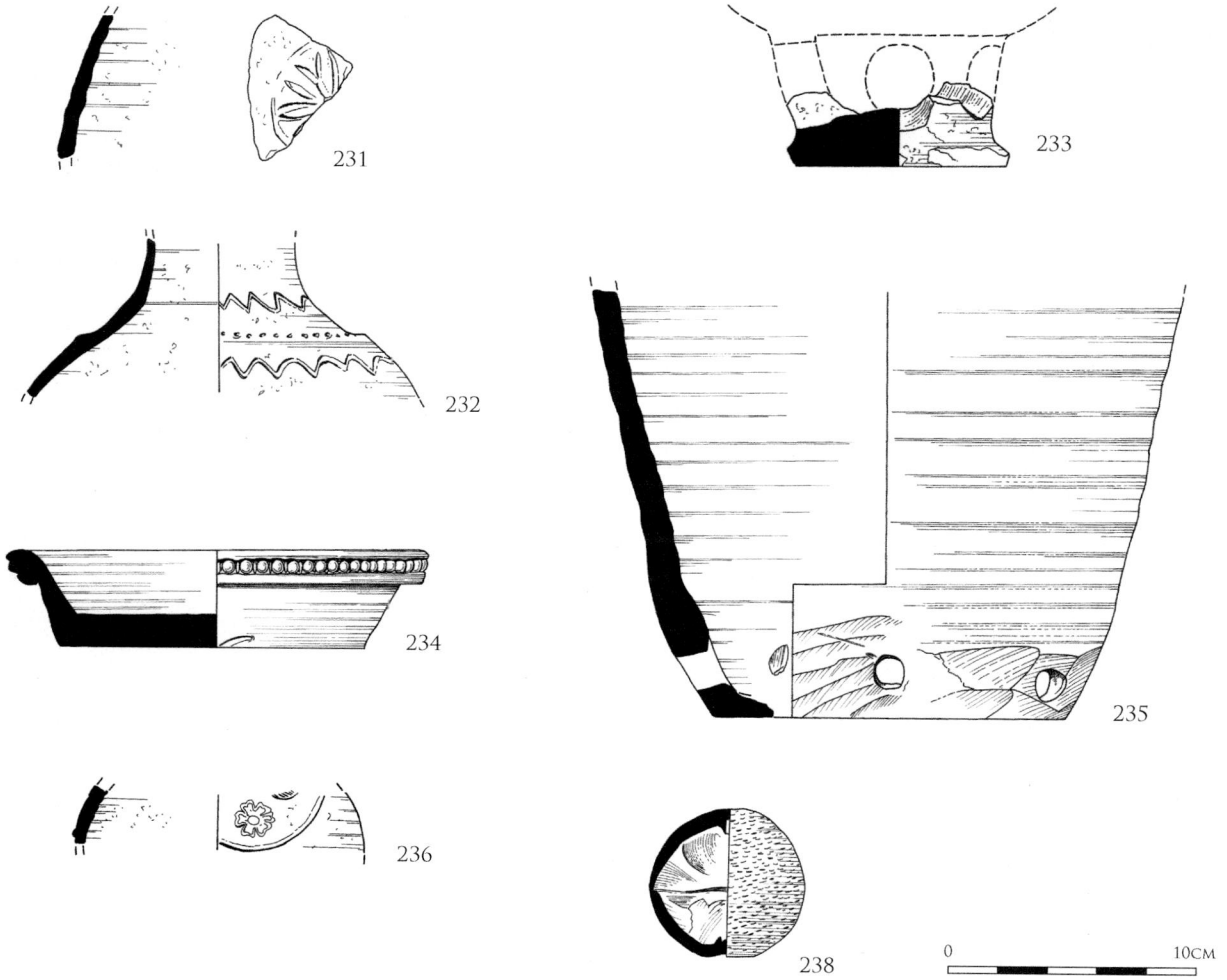

Figure A.5.23 Modern; 231 Scottish White Gritty Ware. 232-235 Local Redware. 236 Cologne Stoneware. 238 Ball – bank? Unknown.